ADMINISTRATION AND LEADERSHIP IN STUDENT AFFAIRS

ACTUALIZING STUDENT DEVELOPMENT IN HIGHER EDUCATION
Second Edition

EDITORS

Theodore K. Miller, Ed.D.

Professor of Counseling and
Human Development Services
Coordinator of Student Personnel
in Higher Education
Preparation Program
Director of Student Development
Laboratory
University of Georgia

Roger B. Winston, Jr., Ph.D.

Professor in the Student Personnel
in Higher Education Program
Head of Department of Counseling
and Human Development Services
University of Georgia

ASSOCIATES

Margaret J. Barr
Suzanne S. Brown
Richard B. Caple
Wayne Carlisle
D. Stanley Carpenter
Carmy Carranza
Robert D. Conyne
Don G. Creamer
Michael J. Cuyjet
David A. DeCoster
Dwight O. Douglas
Steven C. Ender
T. Dary Erwin
Pamela M. Frederick
Donald G. Gehring
Daniel A. Hallenbeck
Patricia A. Hollander

Barbara Jacoby
George D. Kuh
Phyllis Mable
Alfred J. Menard, Jr.
Theodore K. Miller
William S. Moore
Fred B. Newton
Robert F. Rodgers
Sue A. Saunders
John H. Schuh
Robert L. Scott
Louis C. Stamatakos
Carney Strange
Elizabeth J. Whitt
Roger B. Winston, Jr.
D. Parker Young
FOREWORD—Robert H. Shaffer

ACCELERATED DEVELOPMENT INC.

MUNCIE   INDIANA

ADMINISTRATION AND LEADERSHIP
IN STUDENT AFFAIRS

Actualizing Student Development in Higher Education
Second Edition

Technical Development: Virginia Cooper
Tanya Dalton
Delores Kellogg
Marguerite Mader
Sheila Sheward

Library of Congress Cataloging-in-Publication Data

Administration and leadership in student affairs : actualizing student development in higher education / editors, Theodore K. Miller, Roger B. Winston, Jr. ; contributors, Margaret J. Barr . . . [et al.]. -- 2nd ed.
    p. cm.
Includes bibliographical references and index.
ISBN 1-55959-022-X
1. Personnel service in higher education--United States--Administration.   2. College student personnel administrators--United States.   3. College student development programs--United States.   I. Miller, Theodore K.   II. Winston, Roger B.   III. Barr, Margaret J.
LB2343.A36   1991   90-81438
378.73--dc20   CIP

LCN: 90-81438

ACCELERATED DEVELOPMENT INC.
Publishers
3400 Kilgore Avenue
Muncie, IN 47304-4896
(317) 284-7511
Toll Free Order Number 1-800-222-1166

DEDICATION

William R. Mendenhall

This book is dedicated with respect to and in fond memory of William R.(Bill) Mendenhall. Bill shared in conceptualizing and editing the first edition of this book nearly a decade ago. He also participated in the discussions and planning for this revision until his health prevented his continuing. In May 1988 he succumbed to a long, painful illness. He was an inspiration to all around him to the end; even when his pain was severe, he always showed concern for others and how his illness was affecting them.

He received the B.S. degree in social science education and M.S. degree in sociology from Indiana State University and Ph.D. in higher education administration and sociology from Florida State University.

At the time of his death, Bill was Associate Vice President for Student Affairs and Assistant Professor in the Department of Counseling and Human Development Services and the Department of Sociology at The University of Georgia. His more than twenty years of administrative experience included working in housing at Indiana State University and Illinois State University. At the University of Florida he served in a variety of roles which included responsibility for Greek organizations, new student orientation, staff development, and budget management.

For Bill's wife, Martha, their sons Mark and Travis, and the students he led, advised, disciplined, and encouraged through the years, we offer this book in remembrance of a **true** student affairs professional *who cared.*

FOREWORD

Robert H. Shaffer
Professor Emeritus
Indiana University

To say that a new book is particularly timely is a cliche. However, the fast moving events and revolutionary changes nationally and internationally make the cliche meaningful for this revised edition of *Administration and Leadership in Student Affairs.* Sweeping changes internationally combined with the current national political and social climate are having significant impacts upon campuses across the country. Change is having a radical impact upon not only governments and society at large, but also upon campuses and their institutions. The field of student affairs is being challenged even more than in the 1960s because of the speed and breadth of events. While those in student affairs are still trying to learn to pronounce the term easily, paradigmatic shifts are affecting their work and institutions daily.

The current environment of higher education is forcing every institution to reexamine its relationships with students and other constituencies. Who would have predicted just a few years ago that some of the most prestigious colleges and universities in the United States would face antagonistic questioning about and even possible prosecution for alleged price fixing? Public and private institutions alike face microscopic examination and questioning of long-held assumptions, beliefs, and even cherished values. Traditional goals and specific purposes are being reexamined, redefined, and restated. Also the organizational structure and functions of many institutions are being reevaluated and redesigned to attain greater effectiveness which is often judged by criteria traditionally alien to higher education. These steps are often being forced or demanded by contradictory forces and values in such a manner as to create suspicion, fear, antagonism, and perplexity.

What has long been considered good and proper on a given campus may be challenged as no longer worth doing or even improper!

For critics of higher education to point out that the situtation on campuses throughout the country merely reflects the confusion surrounding the social, economic, and political problems of American life in general is not enough. Colleges and universities as social institutions mirror the society of which they are a part. However, various segments and voices in that society are becoming increasingly vocal and strident. No longer do they simply debate with each other. Proponents of various causes are demanding that colleges and universities align themselves with specific causes and views. These demands confront higher education with novel issues and dilemmas involving such wide ranging topics as animal research, freedom of speech and assembly, liability, and intellectual honesty.

Individual institutions and their student affairs divisions are responding in different ways. However, business as usual is not one of the options if the institution or its student affairs offices are to remain viable. Many individuals in higher education as well as in other walks of life, are asking that colleges and universities take greater leadership in studying and resolving many of society's current issues and problems. These critics want colleges and universities to prepare their students to face the problems plaguing the nation and world. The situation demands confident self examination and skilled, creative response. Withdrawing to traditional procedures and policies result in other agencies and offices being created to meet new needs, demands, and challenges being posed.

For these reasons, a book emphasizing administration and leadership in student affairs focused on actualizing student development is particularly valuable at this time. Even critics with the most academic orientations agree that individual student development is a significant aspect of higher education. Students themselves give this aspect of their college experience a very high priorty. However, how to achieve individual growth most effectively in the widely diverse settings of United States' colleges and universities is a highly debated subject. Each institution must decide for itself given its particular contexual setting. Failure on the part of student affairs administrators and their staffs to engage forcefully and competently in their institution's deliberations is an abdication of professional responsibilities. Further, it is a lost opportunity to make a significant contribution not only to the lives of the many students with whom they work but also to the quality of the institution itself.

A number of forces and trends contribute to the need for reexamination of present programs and practices. Budgets which do not even keep pace with inflation coupled with predictions of continued financial stringency in both public and private institutions force intensive scrutiny of all expenditures. Student affairs as an area is particularly vulnerable because traditional academic policies and procedures protect the faculty to a great extent, while union, civil service, or system personnel procedures protect clerical and maintenance staff members. Student affairs practitioners are often in limbo and, therefore, more vulnerable even though they enjoy popular support. These budget crunches are coming on many campuses at the very time that new and extended services are being required to meet needs of older, disabled, minority, and other non-traitional students.

Stringent finances, however, are not the only reason institutions are being required to take a closer look at themselves. Outcomes and value-added assessments are being put into place in many states. Responsibility centered budgeting is being adopted by many institutions. These and many similar trends are occurring at the same time that the great diversity of students arriving on campuses and changed relationships to constituencies are challenging some basic assumptions underlying traditional practices in the various areas of student affairs. The question is being asked, what should be the institution's role in shaping life styles, in contributing to value formation, and in challenging traditional beliefs? Faculty memberes are asking if the concern of some institutions for total individual development is undermining the emphasis upon intellectual development and rigorous scholarship. The prevalent emphasis upon a legalistic relationship with students emphasizing a mere seller-consumer posture, or at least a narrow contractual agreement, challenges the concern of student affairs professionals for a broader institutional commitment and contribution to students. Each institution must ask itself if an essentially legalistic relationship between it and its students is the best paradigm for fostering intellectual growth, scholastic achievement, and individual development.

One of the most obvious implications of current trends and forces is the inescapable realization that student affairs practitioners need to be true professionals in their work and in their relationships within the total institutional environment. They must be thoroughly knowledgeable about the theoretical foundations of their work which underlie specific practices and which support the educational efforts of the institution. Thus, when institutional practices are at variance with or even contradictory to sound theory, professionals must be forthright, confident, and sound in their opposition to them.

Part One, Theoretical Foundations, consisting of six chapters and Part two, Parameters of Professional Practice, consisting of seven chapters, present essential information which staff members in student affairs organizations need to function effectively and professionally. The professional response to problems and issues is to utilize relevant theory and sound practice in defining and resolving problems relating to the achievement of personal, professional, and organizational goals. Professionals must then be instrumental in initiating appropriate responses to policies, practices, and events within their respective settings to achieve desired and agreed-upon outcomes.

Part Three, Strategies for Administration and Leadership, addresses the complex problems associated with the day to day professional application of theory to practice. The rise of activism by committed individuals combined with institutional conservatism and adherence to traditional values is creating dilemmas that truly challenge the best theory and practice. For example, resolving dilemmas posed by racism, sexism, animal welfare, abortion, peace, non-violence and environmental issues on one hand and the values and rights of free speech and assembly on the other requires new and creative approaches. Balancing actions and speech relating to these and similar issues and yet inhibiting crude and boorish or even violent behavior in an educationally sound manner tests traditional theory and practice to the utmost. Policy making must rise to a new level of effectiveness on most campuses! Values being professed are often held so deeply that adhering to them conflicts with equally deeply held values of others. Single issue activists are extremely difficult to work with in institutional settings; yet the complex problems facing society may require the aggressive efforts of such individuals to force it to face up to crucial issues. Failure on the part of higher education to take an active role in society's resolution of these conflicts and dilemmas will further reduce its credibility and reputation for integrity. Student affairs has a significant role to play in leading their institutions in making creative, effective, and educationally productive responses.

No one book will change practices and solve all complex issues facing student affairs in postsecondary education today. However, editors Miller and Winston have made a significant contribution not only through their own chapters but also through those written by outstanding theorists and practitioners recruited by them to be authors. These authors represent different philosophical orientations and institutions and yet the book provides a holistic, in-depth view of student affairs administration and leadership.

It is a privilege to be associated with a publication dedicated to William R. Mendenhall. His professionalism, calm bearing, and friendly colleagueship enriched the profession and those who knew him. The field is stronger because of him and his contributions.

Robert H. Shaffer of Indiana University received his master's degree from Teachers College, Columbia University, and the Ph.D. from New York University. He is now professor emeritus of Education and Business Administration. Among the positions he held over a 40 year span at Indiana University were Director of Counseling, Dean of Students, and Chairman, Departments of College Student Personnel and Higher

Education. He has held major offices in a number of student affairs associations including the Presidency of the American Personnel and Guidance Association, Chairmanship of the Council of Student Personnel Associations, Editorship of the *NASPA Journal*, Associate Editorship of the *Personnel and Guidance Journal*, and service on the editorial boards of other journals. He has authored, edited, or contributed to a number of books and monographs.

PREFACE

In the view of many practitioners two rather incompatible philosophical orientations or occupational *raisons d'être* have been operating in tandem in student affairs: an administrative orientation—associated with providing services, maintaining the institutional organization, allocating resources, and managing facilities—and an educational orientation—associated with influencing the learning, growth, and development of individual students (Ambler, 1989). As evidence that this dichotomy continues to exist, Ambler argued that on the preponderance of campuses today students and academic leaders alike see student affairs professionals as "administrators" and not as "educators."

Even though such observations reflect the reality of the thinking of both students and higher education leaders on many campuses, the operational premise of this book is that the observed dichotomy between administration and education (student development) is both unjustified and a major impediment to the advancement of the field. We maintain that student affairs divisions have both administrative and educational missions and that to be judged *successful* both missions must be vigorously pursued.

Most students affairs activities can be classified into four broad somewhat overlapping categories: organizational maintenance, staffing, management, and educational.

Organizational maintenance functions are those activities that must be performed to keep the organization working, which often includes attention to a myriad of details and performance of many essential, though mundane tasks, such as assuring that equipment is available, facilities are properly cleaned and maintained, institutional procedures and policies are followed, and appropriate forms completed. These activities are crucial to the successful functioning of a student affairs division and its parent institution; failure to attend to these details cause both students and institutional administrators to question the basic competence of practitioners and will usually undermine their other efforts. If organizational maintenance responsibilities are not fulfilled, then institutional leaders will generally question the value of the student affairs division, and may well take steps to replace the leadership (Winston, 1989). As Ambler (1989, p.250) noted concerning student affairs practitioners, "Colleges and universities could not afford us or—worse yet-tolerate us if we were not related to their basic service functions."

Staffing functions generally require more of the practitioner's professional knowledge and skills than do maintenance functions. Staffing includes selecting appropriate persons (professional, allied professional, paraprofessional, and support personnel) to address the organization's mission, providing training and supervision, and evaluating performance. Understandings of theories about human behavior and how to influence that behavior in positive, productive ways require practitioners to use effective communications skills, interpersonal helping strategies, and conceptually sound personnel evaluation techniques. Success in this area is dependent on a combination of personality characteristics (of both the professional and the staff members with whom she or he works) and knowledge and skill in leadership and motivation (Winston, 1989).

Management functions include program, personnel, and fiscal planning; policy development; program and services evaluation; and creation of utilitarian organizational structures. The general principles of management from business are applicable in higher education. They are shaped, however, by the unique and often ambiguous missions of higher education, a heterogeneous clientele, general availability of resources, conflicting interests and expectations, the organizational culture, nature of existing facilities, and the administrative orientation and style of the chief executive officer and other institutional leaders.

Educational functions address student learning in both the formal academic sense and informal (outside-the-classroom, co-curricular) sense. Student affairs has often defined itself as serving a complementary function to the formal curriculum, helping students overcome impediments to academic achievement and development of essential academic skills and attitudes. We maintain that student affairs practitioners also have many primary educational roles to fulfill as well. Winston (1990, pp. 35-6) argued that student affairs professionals should be dedicated "to creating environments for students . . . that contribute to the: (1) education of their intellects; (2) development of healthy, fully functioning personalities; (3) promotion of democratic ideals and fundamental justice; (4) development of wholesome lifestyles; and (5) adoption of a set of considered moral, ethical, and/or religious values." Failure to address this area of functioning is to argue against student affairs as a professional field of endeavor. If practitioners do not make substantive contributions to students' educations, then the field could best, and less expensively, be staffed by talented amateurs who have outgoing personalities and good common sense. To be successful as educators in the student affairs arena requires (1) an appreciation of the unique environment that is American higher education, (2) a sophisticated understanding of the organizational culture in which one works, and (3) an in-depth knowledge of student development and relevant administrative/organizational theories that can be utilized to address the fundamental goals of higher education.

PURPOSE

This book was written by and for student affairs leaders and educators who espouse a commitment to the goals of student development. Its principal purpose was to address student affairs practice in the full glory of its plethora of goals, missions, and clientele. We have attempted to address both theoretical and practical issues faced by entry-level and mid-level practitioners. The first edition was created specifically to address the need for a text for use by graduate students in the student affairs preparation program at The University of Georgia. When we talked with other faculty members across the country, we found that other preparation programs had a similar need. This revision, however, is intended to be more than merely a graduate text; it also was conceptualized to be used by practitioners as a basic reference and professional resource as they move forward on their individual career ladders. In this revision we have attempted to make the content even more relevant for student affairs practitioners than was that of the first edition.

BASIC PREMISES

The ultimate success of a student affairs division must be measured by how effectively it addresses its educational mission, while also acknowledging that education is not its sole mission. The quintessential *raison d'être* for student affairs is the intentional development of students who are aided in realizing their potential in the intellectual, social, esthetic, career, moral, and physical areas of their lives through participation in the higher education experience.

If student affairs administration is to address the varied missions assigned it on most campuses, then its practitioners require a broad, integrated base of knowledge, skills, and professional values. Although management techniques are extremely important to effective administration of student affairs programs, techniques alone are not enough to accomplish the myriad of required tasks. Likewise, student development principles that can guide the design and implementation of important educational and organizational activities are not in and of themselves sufficient to carry on an effective student affairs operation. In effect, basic principles of both management and human development are essential to successful practice in student affairs, and are, when taken individually, insufficient as either a theoretical or pragmatic base. The integration of theory, technique, philosophy, and technology is essential to effective professional student affairs practice.

Student affairs practice is an unique specialty within higher education that requires more than knowledge of higher education, experience dealing with students, and good management skills. Those kinds of skills and knowledge are essential, but effective practitioners also need to exhibit quality helping skills, knowledge of student development and organizational theories, knowledge of the parameters of higher education practice (such as, professional, legal, and ethical standards), command of an array of practical skills (such as, budgeting, program development, needs assessment, and outcomes evaluation) and congenial personalities that promote cooperation and collaborative efforts. Specialized, intensive professional preparation is needed by practitioners if they are to master truly and fully the wide range of knowledge and skills required.

TERMINOLOGY

As Crookston (1976) noted almost two decades ago, and unfortunately it is still true today, the field is unsettled about how to describe itself. **Student personnel, student affairs, student services,** and **student development** are often used interchangeably. In order to introduce some order into the confusion, the editors have followed the advice of Crookston about appropriate terminology throughout this book. Following is a brief listing of the nomenclature used in this book.

- **Student personnel** is an anachronistic term that is no longer a suitable description. It appears only in quotations from earlier works.

- **Student affairs** is used to describe the organizational structure or unit on a campus responsible for the out-of-class education, and in some cases in-class education as well, of students.

- The administrative head of the principal student affairs organizational unit on a campus is referred to interchangeably as **vice president for student affairs** or **chief student affairs administrator** (CSAA).

- **Student affairs administration or practice** is viewed as a generic term for the professional field.

- **Student development** is both a theory base and a philosophy about the purposes of higher education and is the *raison d'etre* for the student affairs field. It is the application of human development principles to students in the higher education environment.

"Student development" is not used in titles for individuals or administrative units. On the other hand, **student development programs** is used to describe activities designed to stimulate self-understanding, to strengthen skills, and/or to increase knowledge. Student development programs reflect specific educational interventions.

- Nomenclature regarding organizational structure varies considerably from campus to campus. For consistency the following schema has been adopted throughout this book. The overall administrative unit is referred to as the **student affairs division.** It may be organizationally divided into **departments,** such as housing, student activities, or financial aid. Departments may be composed of smaller units called **offices** or **centers,** such as family housing office, student organizations office, Black cultural center, or career planning center.

- Professional practitioners are referred to interchangeably as **student affairs administrators, student affairs professionals, student affairs practitioners, and student affairs staff members.**

- **College** is used as a general term to refer to all types of postsecondary educational institutions.

CONTENT

This edition of *Administration and Leadership in Student Affairs* is a major revision of the 1983 edition. All chapters have been revised and updated. There are seven chapters on topics that were previously unaddressed in the first edition or that were addressed in a more abbreviated form. We are indebted to those practitioners and preparation program faculty members who provided us suggestions on ways to strengthened this edition.

This book is organized in three sections: theoretical foundations, parameters of professional practice, and strategies for administration and leadership.

In Part I, *Theoretical Foundations*, are six chapters. In Chapter 1, Miller and Winston summarize important principles of college student development theory and offer suggestions on their application in student affairs. Kuh and Whitt offer a primer on organizational theory in Chapter 2 and provide guidance in understanding student affairs within the context of higher education. In Chapter 3, Conyne summarizes many organization development strategies and comments on their use in higher education by student affairs professionals. In Chapter 4, Caple and Newton summarize the major theories of organizational leadership and give examples of their application in student affairs. Major management and administration theories are summarized by Creamer and Frederick in Chapter 5. They also offer a model of planned change in organizations that has particular relevance for those who wish to introduce student development programs in higher education. Then, in Chapter 6, Strange summarizes theories and research on higher education environments and discusses how knowledge of environments is essential to successful administrative leadership and program development.

Part II is titled *Parameters of Professional Practice* and is composed of seven chapters. This part articulates many of the issues, concerns, and restrictions that define professional practice in student affairs. Chapter 7 discusses the use of theory in practice. Rodgers presents a model that can aid practitioners in combining theories of college student development and a variety of implementation strategies to produce effective interventions with students. Carpenter, in Chapter 8, follows with a discussion of the issues related to the professional status of college student affairs administration and presents a model for interpreting professional development. In Chapter 9, Jacoby presents data about the diversity of today's college students and provides a model that practitioners can use to conceptualize interventions that will address the plethora of unique needs and concerns of this heterogeneous population. Winston and Saunders discuss professional ethics in Chapter 10 and suggest a decision-making model for addressing professional ethical questions. In Chapter 11, Mable and Miller describe the development of professional standards and outline a variety of ways that these standards can be employed in student affairs practice. Gehring (Chapter 12) summarizes the major legal issues of which student affairs administrations must be cognizant as they develop programs and administer institutional policies. Finally, in Chapter 13, Hollander and Young delineate the legal issues related to employment practices in student affairs and offer guidance in protecting employee rights and institutions' best interests.

Part III of this book is devoted to consideration of *Strategies for Administration and Leadership* of student affairs organizations. In Chapter 14, Winston and Miller discuss professional preparation and its relationship to effective practice and outline important considerations in the selection of staff members at all levels. Schuh and Carlisle (Chapter 15) address issues related to staff supervision and evaluation and offer practical guidance in implementing effective staffing practices. In Chapter 16, Ender and Carranza provide a thorough discussion of the use of student paraprofessionals and outline effective ways to select, train, and supervise paraprofessionals and evaluate programs in which they are employed. DeCoster and Brown examine the place and importance of staff development activities and programs in Chapter 17 and offer suggestions on developing programs that contribute both to the personal development of individual staff members and the accomplishment of the organization's goals. In Chapter 18, Douglas presents fundamentals of budgeting in student affairs and offers guidance in understanding the sometimes baffling process. Hallenbeck (Chapter 19) explains the importance of effectively managing facilities and offers suggestions on strategies for accomplishing these tasks while minimizing costs. In Chapter 20, Stamatakos explores the roles and responsibilities that the student affairs professional has as an institutional leader and offers suggestions for fulfilling those obligations in ways that will further the goals of student development. Chapter 21 is a primer on the establishment of effective student development programs. Barr and Cuyjet present a step-by-step process for designing programs and identify issues that should be addressed if one wishes to create interventions that will meet students' needs. In Chapter 22, Erwin, Menard, and Scott address the increasingly important topic of program evaluation and student outcomes assessment. Many predict that this is an area that will both receive increased attention in the 1990s and offer student affairs professionals new and varied opportunities to provide institutional leadership. In conclusion, in Chapter 23, Moore identifies many of the critical issues the field will face in the decade of the 1900s and offers recommended strategies for addressing them.

ACKNOWLEDGEMENTS

We wish, finally, to thank our thirty-one associates who were involved in this project and to recognize the importance of their contributions to both the format and substance of this book. Without their knowledge of and commitment to the profession of student affairs, this revision would have never become a reality.

Athens, Georgia   Theodore K. Miller
November 1990   Roger B. Winston, Jr.

REFERENCES

Ambler, D. A. (1989). Designing and managing programs: The administrator role. In U. Delworth, G. R. Hanson, & Associates, *Student services: A handbook for the profession, 2nd. ed.* (pp. 247-264). San Francisco: Jossey-Bass.

Crookston, B. B. (1976). Student personnel: All hail and farewell! *Personnel and Guidance Journal, 55,* 26-29.

Winston, R. B., Jr. (1990). Using theory and research findings in everyday practice. In D. D. Coleman, J. E. Johnson, & Associates, *The new professional: A sourcebook for new professionals and supervisors in student affairs.* Washington, DC: National Association of Student Personnel Administrators.

TABLE OF CONTENTS

LIST OF FIGURES

LIST OF TABLES

Part I

THEORETICAL
FOUNDATIONS

Theodore K. Miller, Ed.D., is Professor of Counseling and Human Development Services at the University of Georgia in Athens, Georgia in the Division of Counseling, Educational Psychology, and Educational Technology in the College of Educaton. He is currently the Director of the University of Georgia's Southern Association of Colleges and Schools (SACS) Accreditation Reaffirmation Self-Study and is Chairman of the Self-Study Steering Committee.

Roger B. Winston, Jr., Ph.D., is Professor in the Student Personnel in Higher Education Program, College of Education, at The University of Georgia. He was awarded the A.B. in history and philosophy from Auburn University and the M.A. in philosophy and Ph.D. in counseling and student personnel services from The University of Georgia. Prior to joining the faculty at The University of Georgia in 1978, he was Dean of Men and Associate Dean of Students at Georgia Southwestern College.

Chapter 1

HUMAN DEVELOPMENT AND HIGHER EDUCATION

Theodore K. Miller
Roger B. Winston, Jr.

American higher education, as all social institutions, develops neither in a vacuum nor in a fashion unrelated to those cultures which surround, nurture, and guide its progress. As Brubacher and Rudy (1976) so aptly noted, European traditions, when merged with native American conditions and augmented by the growth of American democracy, have resulted in a truly unique system of higher education. The student affairs area, an important component of that system, is the result of philosophical presuppositions about the nature of humankind; theoretical postulations about how people grow, learn, and develop; and the intuition of practitioners over the years who have sought to create environments that would nurture the growth of higher education. Both the ideas and the actions of philosophers, theorists, and practitioners have created the student affairs area. Today, human development theory has merged with the student personnel point of view to create an effective foundation for the area. Integrating the principles of developmental theory with the presuppositions of this point of view provides increased potential for the field of student affairs.

Human development theory and the basic principles underlying that theory have great utility for student affairs leaders who view their role as active participants in the education of students. This book is predicated on the belief that student affairs administrators of the future will be successful, not simply because they are good and well intentioned people, but because they are competent professionals who comprehend their roles and responsibilities as being founded upon a set of theoretical principles that guide their everyday efforts. Human developmental theory is an appropriate foundation upon which to build. The intent in this chapter is to present both an historical perspective and a rationale for development and future expansion.

HISTORICAL PERSPECTIVE

As with all dynamic entities, higher education in America has been in transition since its inception. Higher education has, in other words, been growing, changing, and developing over the past 350 years in this country. The same social, cultural, and environmental influences that have sculpted the nation have had impact on higher education. Much can be learned from observing and interpreting the passages of higher education over the years, and this knowledge can be beneficial to those responsible for guiding the institutional life cycles of higher education in the years ahead.

Just as it is possible to understand better the growth and development of an individual by observing the challenges that person faces and the responses made to those challenges, so too is it possible to obtain a better understanding of the dynamics of higher education through an examination of its historical development. Lippitt and Schmidt (1967) postulated three stages of development through which organizations typically move as they become mature. They named the stages Birth, during which creation of the new organization and survival as a viable system are critical; Youth, when gaining stability, achieving reputability, and developing pride are of the essence; and Maturity, where critical concerns are to achieve uniqueness and adaptability and to contribute to society. Examining the development of higher education in America from this three-stage perspective is enlightening especially as that development is reflected in the way institutions have related to their student clientele and their organizational responses to challenges faced over the years. This perspective also is helpful for visualizing how the field of student affairs developed.

Birth

The first three institutions of higher learning founded in America—Harvard, William and Mary, and Yale—were more closely related in both conception and government to the then contemporary academies, gymnasia, and independent grammar schools of Elizabethan England than they were to medieval universities. William and Mary, in fact, was for its first 36 years a grammar school for Indian boys and local children. Also notable is the fact that these founding institutions served colony-wide publics and were not limited to a single local community's origin or control. These institutions were funded initially by trusts from public monies and their initial government was by appointed boards of trustees (Herbst, 1974).

Because religious objectives tended to dominate the first colonial institutions, the early years of higher education in America largely reflect a picture of cohesiveness and unity concerning student life, educational goals, and institutional missions. Students themselves, however, represented more diverse socioeconomic backgrounds than often is recognized in historical literature. Students were not all of the social elite—some came from ordinary farming families, and most were relatively young (many in their early teens). The poor but ambitious youth also had the opportunity to attend college and thus elevate himself (only males were in attendance) into the professional classes (Brubacher & Rudy, 1976). Even in colonial times commonly some financial support was available for students of limited means, usually in the form of petty work positions.

The Collegiate Way of Life. Because most of the early colleges were founded outside the confines of urban communities of the day, the need for lodging students at or near the college was necessary. The decision to create "dormitories" in which students must live in order that they could be better supervised and thereby controlled reflects clearly the philosophy of paternalism that prevailed. Herein lies a major distinction between early American higher education institutions and universities of Europe. Rudolph (1962), as well as Brubacher and Rudy (1976), recognized the collegiate way of life with its emphasis upon concern for all aspects of the student's life as being a major factor in the unique development of higher education in America. What the student did before, after, and between his academic studies was viewed as important, perhaps even paramount, to the educational mission involved. This philosophical concept contributed to the formation of student affairs units.

Motives of the founding fathers of many early colleges included concern for good citizenship, prescribed moral conduct, and the capacity to meet basic vocational needs of the New World. The collegiate way of life seemed most appropriate for such aims and purposes, especially in light of the pioneer social conditions that existed. By extending their supervisory role into all areas of student life, institutions were able to replace much of what, in the Old World, would have been the responsibility of the young men's families. For instance, many rules and regulations existed to guide student conduct and the consequences for even minor infractions were often quite severe, including public floggings and confessions in the presence of the assembled faculty and students (Leonard, 1956). This student-institution "family" relationship ultimately resulted in the concept of *in loco parentis*, in the place of the parents, becoming *d'rigor* in American higher education well into the 20th Century. The institution, through its faculty and staff, functioned as a surrogate parent to the students it served.

Although the president and faculty were responsible for supervising the moral training and behavior of students, peer pressure was often more influential. At its worst, the collegiate way of life restrained intellectual potential, prolonged adolescent behavior, and promoted excessive paternalism. At its best, however, it offered a vehicle for providing susceptible young students with community support, social consciousness, better tastes, higher aims, and a mature intellectual and moral capacity

(Rudolph, 1962). Even today remnants of this style of the collegiate way of life can be found in institutions of American higher education.

Student Activities. Observing the evolution of the first 200 years of higher education in America, the increasing influence of students can be seen through their often spontaneous and sometimes systematic progress toward creation of what became known as the "extracurriculum." The first organized student activities grew out of the traditional college class structure in which upperclassmen, especially sophomores, initiated new students into the college community. As informal hazing declined, it was often replaced by an institutionalized activity called "rush" in which the sophomore class would wage organized struggles, such as wrestling matches with the freshman class to see who persevered. If the freshmen won, then they would be accorded certain privileges not otherwise awarded them (Brubacher & Rudy, 1976). Some of these traditions carried on well into the 20th century.

Soon literary societies flourished and brought with them intellectual debate and oratory, literary magazines, and even libraries. In their beginnings, literary societies commanded passionate student loyalties and even serious rivalries, for usually at least two literary societies were organized on most campuses (Brubacher & Rudy, 1976). In large part, the literary society can be viewed as one of the first instances of organized student activity—activity organized and largely controlled by students themselves, that is. As one might expect, before long institutional leaders became aware of the immense popularity and influence these societies had upon students, and sought to gain some control over them.

Other types of student clubs and organizations became evident by the late 18th and early 19th centuries. College students were obviously manifesting certain personal and social needs not readily being met by the organized college curriculum and related programs of the day. Amateur dramatics and students' singing clubs were not uncommon by the turn of the 19th century, and the Greek-letter fraternity movement, with its purpose to change the focus to present-day worldly events rather than to the "hereafter" was soon forthcoming

(Rudolph, 1962). The fraternity appeal to many college students was very powerful because it offered them an outlet not available within the formal framework of colleges in which they studied. In some ways, the advent of these secret societies within the college communities may have heralded the completion of the first stage of organizational development of student affairs in American higher education.

Just as earlier student rebellions had given evidence of the colleges' failure to provide adequate outlets for the normal exuberance of youth (Rudolph, 1962), so too does the initiation of secret societies show that students' needs were not being met. These organizations, along with the need for physical exercise and athletics, provided the foundation for movement into the next stage of development for American higher education.

Youth

As so often occurs within a life cycle, the point at which it appears that things are at last stable is very likely to be followed quickly by the unexpected and possibly most challenging new circumstances to be faced for some period of time. In other words, just when all seems well with the world, it may be the most likely time for that world to turn upside down.

As the young country developed in complexity during the 1800s, so did its educational institutions. Coeducation in its earliest form grew from the establishment of Oberlin College in Ohio in 1833. Soon thereafter colleges established for women only came into being: first in the South in 1836 with the Wesleyan Female College of Macon, Georgia, and later in the north with Rockford College in Illinois in 1849 (Brubacher & Rudy, 1976).

During the first half of the 19th century reform ran rampant throughout the land. One result was more egalitarian and utilitarian approaches to education. A primary example of the practical application emphasis of higher education during this time was the establishment of land-grant colleges. These colleges, committed to agricultural and mechanical education, were the recipients of some of the earliest federal aid to higher education upon passage of the Morrill Act of 1862.

Student Activities. As changes occurred throughout higher education, so did they take place in regard to student collegiate life as well. Secret society and Greek-letter fraternity organizations, whose seeds had been planted during the first half of the 19th century, came into full blossom during the second half of the century.

Early in the 20th century students were becoming increasingly influential in those areas of college life not directly linked to academic disciplines and rigors of the classroom. American higher education was indeed moving through a transition that demanded alterations of programs and processes involved. Somehow, for American higher education to survive as a viable force, the college student's out-of-class life needed to be reinstitutionalized as an integral part of the higher education enterprise.

By the early 1920s American higher education was facing consequences of rapid growth, extensive change, and impersonalization. In a harbinger of things to come three decades later, colleges were both expanding in size and faced with an increasingly divergent student clientele.

Maturity

The student personnel services movement blossomed during the first half of the 20th century. Student housing, always an influential feature in American higher education, shifted from an emphasis upon the small, close-knit, English residential college approach to a residence hall approach for housing larger numbers of single students as well as an increasing number of apartment-style facilities for married students (Schneider, 1977).

Student health programs were also on the increase, for World War I had pointed out the physical limitations of young Americans, and there were several epidemics that concerned both college administrators and government leaders. Another major indicator of the post World War I emphasis on individualizing the college campus was the advent of counseling bureaus. Vocational counseling, along with the testing movement, resulted in many colleges hiring counselors to help students make decisions about their educational and vocational plans. Closely related to this was the area of graduate placement. More and more students were seeking higher education as a way for advancing their careers. With the Great Depression of the 1930s came the understanding that a college degree was no assurance of employment. Colleges responded by increasingly offering students counseling in their search for post college jobs.

In the more advanced stages of organizational development, according to Lippit and Schmidt (1967), the organization seeks to achieve uniqueness and adaptability and to make a significant contribution to society as a whole.

Following World War II there was again a burst in student enrollment and an increase in diversity. The Federal Government was becoming increasingly involved in higher education, and student services functions were being increasingly organized within divisions of student affairs, which led to increased need for student affairs administrators. By 1966 the U.S. Department of Health, Education, and Welfare had identified 17 student service administrative functions common to most institutions of higher learning for which the student affairs office was primarily responsible. These included: (1) recruitment, (2) admissions, (3) nonacademic records, (4) counseling, (5) discipline, (6) testing, (7) financial aid, (8) foreign students, (9) nurse-care services, (10) medical services, (11) residence halls, (12) married student housing, (13) job placement, (14) student union, (15) student activities, (16) intramural athletics, and (17) religious affairs (Ayers, Tripp, & Russel, 1966).

Obviously, by the middle of the twentieth century the student personnel movement had matured into an emerging profession. The second quarter of the century had produced not only descriptive studies of the field (Cowley, 1936; Hopkins, 1926; Maverick, 1926), but also philosophically founded statements of student personnel work, such as *The Student Personnel Point of View* (American Council on Education, 1937, 1949). These seminal documents articulated four basic assumptions concerning college students and the responsibilities of higher education institutions in relation to those students. Miller and Prince (1976) stated these assumptions as

(1) the individual student must be considered as a whole; (2) each student is a unique person and must be treated as such; (3) the total environment of the student is educational and must be used to achieve his or her full development; (4) the major responsibility for a student's personal and social development rests with the student and his or her personal resources. (p. 4)

Implicit within these assumptions is a philosophical position that undergirds what has, in recent years, come to be viewed as the "student development movement."

The essence of intentional student development is the interaction between the student and the educational environment so that all aspects of the student's life are attended to and the environmental resources both challenge the student and give the support needed to meet these challenges so that more advanced levels of development result.

Ample evidence exists for supporting the belief that history will record that the student development movement was a critical and significant influence on American higher education during the latter part of the 20th Century. Human development theories, along with management theories, are increasingly becoming integrated into the fabric of student affairs administration. No professional preparation program worthy of its name overlooks the importance of these burgeoning theories as an integral part of its core curricula. Not only has the field of student affairs continued to emerge as a professional entity in recent years, but its practitioners have benefited from these theories immeasurably. The field has moved rapidly from simply providing students with basic support services to intentionally facilitating holistic development as an integral part of students' formal educations.

A DEVELOPMENTAL RATIONALE
FOR STUDENT AFFAIRS

Student affairs is in transition. This transition basically reflects the ways professionals view their primary missions, their primary responsibilities, and the ways they should structure organizations and implement programs.

Student affairs is currently viewed by increasing numbers of professionals in the academic community as parallel to formal instruction as an essential part of the overall educational program (Wrenn, 1968).

Developmental Theory as a Foundation

For the past three decades a strengthening trend toward the student development movement has evolved. This school of thought quickly captured the imagination of many student affairs professionals as a way of adding credibility and validity to the work of administrators and practitioners responsible for organizing, guiding, and facilitating the out-of-class education and development of college students.

The professional student affairs practitioner of the future must know and understand human development theory as it applies to the life cycles of the students served. Student affairs administrators must understand the theory that underlies the work of staff members whom they supervise because without such understanding, conflicts and even adversary relationships may develop. All professionals need not necessarily agree on what is the best theoretical view or the most effective way of implementing theory in practice. But all professionals must have a basic understanding of what is involved, or communications will become so snarled that failure likely will result. At the very least, an understanding of the basics and a general agreement on how to proceed needs to be established on the part of all concerned.

Schools of Thought. At least three major theoretical schools of thought have been identified as important to guiding student affairs. These include (1) the cognitive theories concerned with intellectual and moral development, (2) the psychosocial theories concerned with personal and life cycle development, and (3) the person-environment interaction theories that focus attention upon the ecology of student life.

The intellectual and moral development theories represented in the work of Piaget (1952), Perry (1970, 1981), and Kohlberg (1969) focused attention primarily upon process. How people learn, think, reason, make decisions, establish ethical positions, and make meaning out of available information are the key elements in most cognitive theories. Cognitive theorists are not particularly concerned with *what* people learn. Rather they are concerned with *how* people learn. Most of these theorists recognize the existence of a number of *stages* that people move into, through, and beyond to more advanced levels. Perry, however, uses the concept of *phases* instead, a way of looking at development that may have more validity. Most theorists of this school of thought view the stages as being *sequential* and *invariant* in nature. That is, not only does a *hierarchy* of stages exist in which each advanced stage incorporates what has been learned in the preceding stages, but the individual moves through stages in a relatively prescribed order. The implication is that if a person has not progressed through a particular intermediate stage, then he or she will not be able to move to a more advanced stage. Likewise, cognitive developmental theorists hold that cognitive and moral development is universal in nature and that persons from all cultures probably experience similar processes, stages, and sequences. Rather definitive *qualitative differences* exist between stages in which the new learning is not simply additive in nature, but rather reflects change in the basic characteristics or qualities of the reasoning processes from those apparent in earlier stages.

Of equal importance to student affairs practitioners is the second group of theories, the developmental theories espoused by those representing the psychosocial school of thought. Theorists with this frame of reference include Erikson (1963, 1968), Havighurst (1953, 1972), Chickering (1969, 1981), Sanford (1967), and Sanford and Axelrod (1979) as well as many of the adult life cycle theorists. Psychosocial theories focus more attention upon the *what*, or the content, involved in the developmental processes than upon the processes themselves. The concept of developmental stages is prevalent in the thinking of these theorists, and they often tend to correlate stages with chronological age. In this construct, stages are viewed as being sequential, but not necessarily invariant. One progresses from one stage to another by accomplishing a number of related developmental tasks (Havighurst, 1972) or vectors (Chickering, 1969) or by successfully resolving developmental crises (Erikson, 1963).

Most theorists agree that the content involved in development at one stage, for example, establishing mature interpersonal relationships, developing autonomy, achieving identity, resolving the child-parent relationship, can and often does reappear in a later stage of development, usually in an altered form. Psychosocial theorists are greatly concerned with life transitions and the development of life-coping skills.

The third school of thought particularly viable for student affairs professionals is person-environment interaction theory. This theoretical approach is represented in the work of Moos (1979), Holland (1973), Pace (1979), Banning (1978), and Huebner (1979, 1980) and is based upon the principle that behavior is a direct function of the relationship between the individual and the environment (Lewin, 1936; Stern, 1970)—a simple but powerful idea. Many implicit behavioral elements are involved; effects of environmental stimuli on individual responses can be seen readily. The establishment of a healthy student environment is viewed as an important consideration, and the ability to assess that environment is basic to the success of this approach. As a result, a number of environmental assessment techniques have been developed to determine the effect the institutional environment has upon both the perceptions and the behavior of its students.

Principles of Student Development. A number of basic principles derived from developmental theories can be very helpful to student affairs practitioners wishing to facilitate development in students. These principles can help professionals as they seek to implement developmental theory. First, *human development is both continuous and cumulative in nature.* That is, individuals are constantly and continuously in the process of transition. Although the direction one's life development takes is influenced by life experiences, development will continue in some form no matter what attempts are made to diminish it. Development is also cumulative in nature because what has been learned and experienced in the past influences the form future development takes. People and situations experienced, decisions made to act or not to act, attitudes and perceptions of those to whom one is exposed, the type and amount of stimulation available, and the support or lack of support experienced all have the capacity to influence the character of one's development and growth. One is, to a large extent, the result of what one has experienced in the past.

Development is also a matter of movement from the simpler to the more complex. Sanford (1967) stated that most essentially, development is defined as the organization of increasing complexity, and that it is this directional movement toward greater complexity and competence that distinguishes development from growth. Growth is defined as simply an expansion or enlargement of what already exists. For the student affairs practitioner this principle is particularly important because it suggests that one's energies and activities need to be guided by the idea that an individual student can best be served by being aided to move from where he or she is at the moment to a slightly higher level of complexity. Plus-One, a concept originating with Kohlberg (1969) that can be used by student affairs practitioners, reasons that a challenge offered to a student that is just slightly more complex in concept, reasoning, or acquired skill may result in a slightly more complex level of response on the part of the student. Challenge that does not stimulate a higher level response or that requires response at a much higher level will very likely fail to stimulate development and, in fact, may retard it. As Heath (1968) and Chickering (1969) noted, the first "law" of human development is that development results through cycles of differentiation and integration. Student affairs practitioners who intentionally wish to promote development in those with whom they work must be concerned about creating stimulating and challenging environments.

Another principle of human development is that it tends to be orderly and stage related. The stage concept, however, should not be literally or too narrowly interpreted because a great deal of variability exists in human development. Because of this variability and to avoid false assumptions often associated with stage theory approaches, some authorities strongly suggest that thinking about developmental phases, as opposed to stages, would be wiser and more descriptively accurate (Montagu, 1981; Perry, 1970). Montagu suggested that a stage implies discontinuity whereas a phase implies continuity with the developmental changes passing imperceptibly into one another as a normal process. In other words, practitioners and theorists alike have tended to set arbitrary limits to the phases of development and called them stages. Research with the Student Developmental Task and Lifestyle Inventory, for example, confirms that age alone is not a good predictor of the developmental status of traditional aged college students (Winston & Miller, 1987). For student affairs practitioners, this suggests that seeking to establish group norms or similar expectations for all students is not desirable. Rather, the more that the developmental milieu can be individualized the better; it can stimulate and support students as they progress through their own unique developmental processes.

A divergent opinion concerning some of these basic developmental principles has been forthcoming recently in the wake of a new and emerging paradigm postulated by some professional colleagues (Caple, 1987a, 1987b; Howard, 1985; Lucas, 1985; Kuh, Whitt, & Shedd, 1987); see Chapters 2 and 4 which follow. Proponents of the emergent paradigm suggest that the conventional wisdom of current developmental theory "supports the illusion that control can be exercised over what is essentially an indeterminate, unpatterned process" (Kuh, Whitt, & Shedd, 1987, p.45). This perspective, which argues that development is a result of many mutually shaping events that can result in sometimes spontaneous, "second order morphogenetic changes," raises serious questions about the validity of the aforementioned conventional developmental principles. Although it behooves practitioners to keep current with alternative viewpoints and to take the risk of openly examining contrary beliefs regarding the application of theory to practice, the emergent paradigm has yet to be fully validated and must therefore be viewed from a perspective of what may be. Without doubt our understandings of the nature of human development will change with time and new knowledge. For the time being, however, the suggestion is that practitioners keep their "minds' eyes" open to proposed new paradigms but carry forward their daily responsibilities using the knowledge and principles presently available to them. Although reasoning would support that current developmental process models will shift over time and that new ones will take their places, these models would appear to have greater utility for most practitioners in the immediate future than seeking to apply in practice the ambiguities presented by paradigm shifts that are yet somewhat fuzzy.

A Process Model for Student Development

Although a fundamental purpose of theory is the plausible explanation of observed phenomena, its primary value to student affairs professionals is as a guide to practice. In this regard, several student development models have been created that have enhanced the profession's capacity to implement programs of intentional student development. These include the Ecosystem Model (Aulepp & Delworth, 1976), Developmental Instruction (Knefelkamp, 1974), the Cube Model (Morrill & Hurst, 1980), the Grounded Formal Theory Process Model (Rodgers & Widick, 1980), the Student Development Education Model (Rippey, 1981), and the Seven-Dimensional Model of Student Development (Drum, 1980), and The Intentionally Structured Group Model (Winston, Bonney, Miller, & Dagley, 1988) among others. Such models are not intended to be initiated or copied intact, rather they have utility to be used as prototypes for creating programs, organizations, or approaches on one's own campus. Because every institution is unique, all programs of student development need to be especially created with that uniqueness in mind.

During the 1970s two parallel projects resulted in creation of a definitive model for intentional student development programming. In 1972 the Council of Student Personnel Associations (COSPA) proposed a student development model for use in student affairs programs (Cooper, 1972). In that same year the American College Personnel Association (ACPA) sponsored a monograph entitled *Student Development in Tomorrow's Higher Education: A Return to the Academy* (Brown, 1972). These two documents stimulated rapid movement toward a "student development point of view." When the book *The Future of Student Affairs* (Miller & Prince, 1976) was published as Phase II of the ACPA project, many of the basic concepts and principles reflected in both the COSPA statement and the Brown monograph were integrated into the Tomorrow's Higher Education (THE) Student Development Process Model. This model represents one viable approach for those seeking to apply informal theory in a planned, timely, and organized fashion.

The model postulates four primary functions essential to implementing an intentional student developmental approach. These are (1) goal setting, (2) assessment, (3) procedural strategies for change including instruction, consultation, and environmental resource management, and (4) program evaluation. The translation of these components into practice allows for the creation of a substantive student development program.

The Goal Setting Function. Often students have not taken the time or had the opportunity to identify carefully why they are in college and what they hope to accomplish in college and in life. Setting goals and determining specific objectives can help students find the kind of structure they need for achieving the more complex behavior essential for advancing their development. Goal setting, therefore, is viewed as one of the primary survival skills needed in life, and most students can benefit from expanding their capacity to use this strategy. Student affairs practitioners can help students acquire goal setting skills.

Goal setting, from the Process Model's perspective, involves collaboration between students and developmental facilitators and is intended to help students identify the specific behaviors and life situations toward which they wish to strive. The more tangible the desired outcomes and the more they are based upon students' felt needs, the more viable they will be. Without predetermined goals, assessing developmental progress or the effectiveness of a given strategy is all but impossible. The practitioner who regularly and systematically introduces and educates students to the use of this important skill is making a developmental difference that will benefit the recipient throughout life. Noteworthy, however, is the fact that students must learn this skill for themselves; practitioners setting goals for students will diminish the opportunities for students to accomplish this important learning. Helping students to move from vague, general goals through a clarification process to an attainable goal is an excellent method for facilitating planned development as a normal part of one's learning experience.

Similarly, those responsible for administrative and student development programs can benefit from the use of goal setting.

Nearly all developmental intervention models incorporate goals and objectives as an essential planning ingredient and as prerequisites to program implementation. Without clearly established program goals it is highly unlikely that any development intervention strategies will be truly viable.

The Assessment Function. Assessment has the capacity to help students determine their present developmental status as well as what remains to be accomplished. It represents a general sequence of interlocking relationships. These include (1) an initial profile of students' developmental needs, (2) specification of their educational and personal goals and objectives, (3) an inventory of current levels of behavior or accomplishment, (4) creation of a plan using available change strategies and resources to achieve the desired outcomes, (5) continuous assessment of performance as the plan is being implemented, and (6) evaluation of movement toward the identified goals and their final achievement. This process is cyclical in nature, for the final step of one phase can serve as the initial assessment for the next.

Procedural Strategies for Change. The THE Process Model identified three primary strategies that planners can use to good advantage. These strategies encompass intervention approaches that are both appropriate to and available within higher education to facilitate developmental growth. They include *instruction*, which is concerned with the teaching-learning function; *consultation*, which emphasizes counseling and advising functions; and *environmental resource management*, which focuses upon the establishment of climates conducive to development and learning. Although other strategies may be used, conceptionally, they would appear to be included within one of these three.

In the developmental planning phase of these processes, special competence and expertise on the part of practitioners are paramount. *Setting goals and assessing* developmental status are meaningful only to the extent that they identify human developmental needs and circumstances that require attention. Developmental action plans require both accurate information about needs and knowledge about how they may be met. Knowledge of available resources is essential, as is the ability to create innovative approaches when necessary.

The *instructional strategy* fits easily into educational settings. Collaboration between student affairs practitioners and faculty members is essential to the establishment of developmental task achievement under the instructional mode. In some instances creating instructional opportunities (courses, workshops, training sessions) not otherwise available on campus for personal development purposes may be necessary.

The *consultation strategy* calls for one person to engage with another person, group, or organization to help identify needs and capabilities, and plan, initiate, implement, and evaluate action designed to meet or develop those needs and capabilities (Lanning, 1974). As a change strategy, this approach is of particular value when practitioners establish collegial relationships with the goal of collaboratively serving the developmental needs of greater numbers of students than they could serve individually.

Environmental resource management is somewhat more complex than is either instruction or consultation. In this approach pertinent resources are organized within both the institution and the larger community to shape the environment in ways designed to maximize human development. In this instance, practitioners act as both managers of the learning environment and experts in structuring climates that will promote healthy development. The ultimate intent is to design a learning environment that is planned carefully to build systematically upon the existing competencies and accomplishments of individuals and to create an environment to which exposure increases growth in appropriate facets of development. The term "resource" refers to all human, physical, and fiscal support systems with which the student interacts. The term "management" is not synonymous with control. Rather, it recognizes that students, practitioners, faculty, and administrators are all shareholders in both the educational process and its outcomes. Students must become active and involved participants in structuring their environments because their lives and development are to be affected especially.

The Program Evaluation Function. In addition to implementing the action strategies as noted, evaluating the programs which result to assure that they are both effective and viable is essential. The evaluation process should begin with an examination of how program goals and activities relate to participants' goals and objectives and the influence the former has upon the latter. Evaluation provides the best means for clarifying both individual and program objectives and thereby provides a sound basis for modification and future planning.

Recently a concerted effort has occurred on the part of the higher education community to integrate concepts of institutional effectiveness and outcomes assessment into its main educational streams. Although these efforts have been spearheaded largely by academic faculty members, student affairs professionals, as reflected in the THE Student Development Process Model, anticipated this phenomena nearly two decades earlier. Both the establishment of desirable goals and objectives and program evaluation functions reflected highly visible concern for outcomes assessment. Without doubt high quality developmental intervention programs incorporate outcomes assessment as an essential element in their evaluation strategies.

Application of the THE Student Development Process Model does not call necessarily for reorganization of the student affairs structure, although its application may well lead to new and different associations and alliances being established. Freedom and encouragement to develop new and different linkages result usually in more viable programming with more involvement evidenced on the part of all concerned. Cooperative endeavors of an informal nature which may blossom into comprehensive programs, or which can be withdrawn if evaluated as being ineffective, represent an excellent method for using human resources.

STUDENT DEVELOPMENT AND STUDENT AFFAIRS ADMINISTRATION

The historical perspective, theoretical constructs, and the developmental process models noted are prologue to the paramount issue in student affairs administration: the education of individual students. Those in student affairs, whether parent-surrogates, teachers, or Chief Student Affairs Administrators (CSAA) have always sought to aid students in growing up and gaining a meaningful education. Student affairs practitioners must appreciate the wealth of knowledge, much of it gained through trial and error in the early years, that is their professional heritage. From a modern perspective many of their approaches, while well intended, were only partially effective because they were developed *ad hoc* without an extensive theoretical underpinning, and often required a charismatic personality to be made effective. Nevertheless, they laid a foundation that the current generation of professionals can build upon. The responsibility of the professional student affairs staff is to use all available resources to both maintain and enhance the educational environments and opportunities available to students.

Professional practitioners must consider at least four important issues when seeking to carry forward the developmental mission of student affairs: (1) the role and function of theory in practice, (2) the relationship between student development and student affairs administration, (3) the influence of the institutional context on practice, and (4) the designation of responsibility for intentionally applying theory in the educational setting.

Using Theory in Administration

One of the most misunderstood, and probably most debilitating, problems faced by the student affairs profession concerns the theoretical underpinnings that essentially guide professional practice. Too often those who espouse developmental theory as a foundation for student affairs practice are charged with being idealistic, "blue sky dreamers" who are impractical, importunate, and quixotic in the eyes of those responsible for administering student affairs programs. Many with day-to-day administrative responsibilities have a management style that views attempts to initiate new or different functions, programs, or procedures as irritations to be avoided. Practitioners who seek to administer programs primarily to avoid conflict, to overcome present crises, and to maintain the status quo cause those who espouse developmental theory to wring their hands and pull their hair because of those administrators' apparent insensitivity to students' developmental needs. Somehow, for the good of higher education, leaders, practitioners, and theoreticians must be brought together so that they can collaboratively create better and more effective growth enhancing environments.

Student development represents a theoretical foundation, not a formula, for student affairs practice. In many ways, student development reflects an informal theory upon which student affairs practice can be based. Student affairs administration, on the other hand, represents an action element, a pragmatic approach to solving problems and achieving goals and is only as good as the theory upon which it is based and for which it is intended. Appleton, Briggs and Rhatigan (1978) challenged the essential connection between theory and practice by setting them off, one against the other when they noted "one must eventually move from statements of ideals, however, to the essentials of practice" (p.22). Such statements appear to deny that practitioners should view theory and practice as coordinate parts of a larger whole so that the practice of student affairs reflects directly the theory upon which it is founded. Only as this important principle becomes better understood and integrated will the evolution of the student affairs profession move to more effective processes and procedures that will ultimately lead to more advanced cycles of professional development.

Without question colleges are responsible for influencing the personal development of students. The question then is not whether student development is an assigned mission of higher education, and logically of student affairs, but how student affairs is going to participate in accomplishing that mission. Student development theory seems to be the best available foundation for organizing this effort. As Hurst (1980b) noted, "it serves as the core construct around which goals are identified, programs developed, agencies organized, and interventions evaluated" (p. 151).

Those in student affairs prior to the emergence of student development theory as a foundation viewed their work as building and maintaining an administrative structure that could efficiently provide students with services and supports ordinarily provided by family.

> With the emergence of student and environmental resource development, the emphasis is changing toward educators operating within the administrative and academic structure to teach and provide students with the skills, attitudes, and resources necessary for them to maximally utilize the educational environment and fully develop their individual potential. (Hurst, 1980a, p. 321)

More recently, Kuh, Whitt, and Shedd (1987) have cautioned practitioners that the processes traditionally associated with student development are not as orderly or as patterned as had been previously thought. They propose a caveat for student affairs practitioners to consider when applying developmental theory in administrative settings. That warning is "to avoid the attractive alternative of oversimplifying the very complex process of human development. It is also a challenge, a call to seek new and different meanings and uses for human development theory" (p.46). Their position was that students develop as a result of a variety of mutually shaping events, and that practitioners cannot assume that direct causal influences actually exist between programs designed to provide students with developmental challenge and support and the actual outcomes resulting from such deliberate action. Because students are viewed as being open to spontaneous and unpredictable developmental change, these authors suggested that "intention is neither a necessary nor a sufficient condition for development or for encouraging students' development" (p.52). Such emerging paradigms notwithstanding, much is to be said for student affairs administrators seeking to use developmental theory as a foundation for practice.

Student Development and Student Affairs

Not unlike the difficulty the profession has had in understanding the distinction between developmental theory and practice, so too its understanding of the differences between student development and student services has been problematic. Riker (1977), for instance, viewed the term "student development" as nothing more than a new appellation assigned to the earlier term "student personnel." Others (Appleton, Briggs, & Rhatigan, 1978) took the position that both deans of men and women and "personnel workers" of the past had the development of their students in mind as a primary purpose for their work, and therefore, the idea and ideals of student development are neither new nor fundamentally different from years gone by. What these authors seem to be suggesting is that the whole concept of student development is largely a reflection of some of today's professionals trying to put old wine into new bottles, or new labels on old bottles. This thinking is at best a misconception of the developmental theories and their testing and at worse a conscious attempt to deny the theoretical breakthroughs that have occurred recently. The fact that arguments abound concerning whether or not student affairs work is a profession; that some practitioners do not understand it; that the future is tenuous; or that someone is usually working to reorganize, reevaluate, reshape, or rename the field (Appleton, Briggs, & Rhatigan, 1978) does not, in and of itself, belie the evolutionary processes involved.

Much of the controversy about "student development," as it relates to "student affairs," may be attributed to a semantic confusion. "Student development" has been and continues to be used in at least four distinct ways. First, "student development" refers to a body of knowledge, both theoretical and data-based, that describes how persons in higher education settings behave. The focus may be on the content of development (for example, career decision making, autonomy formation, interpersonal relations with peers) or on the process of development (such as cognitive processes, moral reasoning, challenge and response). This has been called "formal theory" by Rodgers (Chapter 7) and Widick, Knefelkamp, and Parker (1980). Its value is to describe the phenomena of higher education (that is the participants, the environments and the interaction between the two), but it does not dictate what one should do as a student affairs professional. Administrators who argue that "student development" is academic, not practical, are viewing formal theory as if it were applied technique.

Second, "student development" also has been used to describe a wide variety of behavioral and social science-based interventions, some relatively new such as ecosystem intervention and some quite old such as individual counseling, that have been used by student affairs practitioners with students. Disciplines of psychology, sociology, education, and management have all contributed techniques used by student affairs professionals. This bag of tools is diverse and sometimes based upon incompatible philosophical positions. No distinct set of techniques can be called "student development techniques." For this reason it has been difficult for many to distinguish those devoted to student development from those hostile to it by looking at the day-to-day practice of professionals. What makes an intervention "student development" is not the approach, but the purpose for which the approach is intended. The final test is whether the intervention enhances the quality of students' educational experiences and facilitates their accomplishment of developmental tasks.

A third use of "student development" has been to describe the purpose or outcome desired as a result of a student's attendance at college. Miller and Prince (1976, p.3) described "student development" as a goal that "everyone involved [in higher education] . . . *master increasingly complex developmental tasks, achieve self-direction, and become interdependent."* While the language is different, that goal is not dissimilar to what the 1937 Student Personnel Point of View espoused. From this perspective, it is not difficult to see why some professionals assume that "student development" is little more than a new term for old ideas. On the other hand, today we are much more concerned with identifying and assessing the developmental outcomes of college attendance. To establish a goal is one thing, to be able to determine the extent to which that goal has been achieved is entirely something else. Student development outcomes assessment will increasingly become a reference point for student affairs administrators to consider.

Finally, in some instances the term "student development" has been used to replace "student affairs" or "student services" in position titles. In many cases this change has been cosmetic at best and has influenced in any significant way neither organizational structures nor daily contact with students. This has been an inappropriate use of the term and has added greatly to the confusion of its understanding.

What the field of student affairs needs now are more divergent thinkers who can identify new and creative ways for doing better what has always been intended, namely education that will enhance the quality of students' lives. Student developmental theory continues to hold great potential for aiding student affairs professionals in conceptualizing their work.

Whether or not practitioners over the years were developmentally facilitative is not at issue; on many occasions they were! The question is one of how to do better what has been to varying degrees the purpose of the field from the beginning. That early deans and "personnel workers" were less effective than they could have been had they possessed the current body of knowledge and experience upon which to base their work is not the issue. What is at issue is how well today's administrators and practitioners can accomplish their more clearly defined developmental goals and purposes using the skills and knowledge currently available. Student development reflects theories of human growth and environmental influences as applied to student affairs practice. Student affairs administration reflects the structuring and managing of the goals of student development. The goals of student development are not new, but many of the objectives, methods, and approaches for achieving them are. Student development is not "student personnel" revisited.

The Context for Student Development

As Cyert (1980) noted when identifying the problems faced by those responsible for institutions of higher learning, management problems are in part a function of both the type and location of the institution. Funding sources (public-private), endowments (miniscule-ample), size (large-small), type (residential-commuter), sex (single sex-coed), and location (rural-urban), among others, are factors that differentially influence the nature and character of the student affairs administrative approaches used.

Institutional Size and Type. Although there are many factors that influence the nature and scope of student affairs practice, both the size and the type of the institution are extremely important variables. Institutional size, therefore, becomes an important factor in both the type and quality of experience available to students. Although larger institutions probably have more resources available, the very fact that more students are seeking to take advantage of them decreases their potential for impact. "As the number of persons outstrips the opportunities for significant participation and satisfaction, the developmental potential of available settings is attenuated for all" (Chickering, 1969, p. 148).

Growth and development are largely a result of the quality of the interaction between the individual and his or her environment, and although programs of student development may not be feasible on a campus-wide basis in larger institutions, the various components and subunits are appropriate settings. In other words, the larger the campus, the greater is the need for subdividing developmental programming efforts to smaller, more manageable organizational units. Whereas on a campus of 2,000, initiating a campus-wide program of student development may be quite feasible; on a campus of 20,000 or more, initiating many coordinated, but individualized, efforts to the same end may be necessary. The key to success is the availability and easy access to campus and community resources designed to facilitate developmental growth and change. Large institutions need concurrent programs within different units and settings throughout the campus community. In some instances academic divisions are working with student affairs leaders to create student affairs components within instructional units to enhance and augment existing campus support and service systems. Size makes a difference, but it is not, in and of itself, a deterrent to developmental programming for students. One advantage large institutions have is more staff members who possess a greater variety and depth of intervention skills.

Institutional type also influences students' developmental outcomes. The traditional resident institution where many students spend most of their time on campus has greater influence on student's total development than does the predominantly nonresident, commuter institution (Chickering, 1974). Residential students have more contact with faculty, perform better academically, and are more satisfied with their undergraduate experience than commuters. Residents are also more likely to aspire to graduate or professional degrees (Astin, 1973, 1975, 1978; Chickering, 1974).

Obviously student affairs administrators can communicate with resident students more conveniently than with students living off campus. Still much can be done with commuter students to enhance their development. The more student affairs administrators can make available opportunities for commuters to establish campus related reference groups, the more commuters will tend to identify with the campus on a personal and individual basis. The key issue is that all students have developmental life cycle needs, and the educational enterprise is more than an intellectual supermarket. Personal development is equally important, and higher education will do both students and society a disservice if it does not seek diligently to make experiences of quality equally available to all.

Student involvement may well be a keystone to achieving the goals of student development. As Astin (1985, p.157) so clearly proclaimed in his book *Achieving Educational Excellence,* "the greater the student's involvement, the greater the learning and personal development."

Responsibility for Student Development

The building of personal and organizational territory, turf, or property is evident in most institutions of higher learning. This is not surprising because in many ways American society is founded on competition and individual freedom to a much greater extent than it is upon mutuality and cooperation. In the educational enterprise, teamwork and collaboration must be encouraged and emphasized when developing the total student, for no single individual, program, or institutional subunit can do the job alone. Quality education and development result from the interaction of the individual with a comprehensive environment and not bits and pieces thereof. All involved in the education and development of students must realize this important fact and use it as a guide in their work with students. This is as true for student affairs administrators as it is for faculty members or other institutional staff members.

The intentional development of college students is not the private domain of student affairs practitioners and administrators, even though it may sometimes seem that way in the eyes of many on the college campus. If student development is indeed the application of human development principles in a college environment, then all responsible parties need to be involved. In this sense, student development theory is integrative in nature. It has the potential to bring all elements of the campus community into a goal-oriented focus designed to create growth-engendering environments. Integration implies mutuality, equality, cooperation, and collaboration among all parties concerned. Student affairs professionals must not become caught in the territorial trap, for this promotes adversary relations and divisive environments that are not conducive to healthy development. This does not mean that student affairs administrators seek to give over to others their power to make a developmental difference in the lives of students, but it does mean that collaboration as an educational doctrine should be the cornerstone of practice. Higher education is a system that is influenced by all people, structures, technologies, and tasks involved and belongs to no single individual or organizational entity. Student affairs professionals must take leadership in seeking to effect this type of educational environment for the task of those dedicated to the development of the total student goes far beyond the limited perspectives of any single group. Student development is the domain of all those involved. Just as no student should be denied access to resources and support services needed, neither should any part of the educational enterprise view itself as the ultimate authority or the sole responsible agent for the development of students everyone serves.

As Shaffer (1980) stated, an integrated approach can work only if based on a careful, systematic analysis of the specific institutional setting. "Constraints need to be identified and weakened by specific, consciously planned steps. Support strengths located in given situations need to be further strengthened by specific, consciously planned steps" (p. 311). The task of student affairs administration, then is to find ways to realize goals of student development.

REFERENCES

American Council on Education (1937). *The student personnel point of view.* American Council on Education Studies (Series 1, Vol. 1, No. 3). Washington, DC: Author.

American Council on Education (1949). *The student personnel point of view* (Rev. ed.). American Council on Education Studies (Series 6, Vol. 13, No. 13). Washington, DC: Author.

Appleton, J. R., Briggs, C. M., & Rhatigan, J. J. (1978). *Pieces of eight: The rites, roles, and styles of the dean by eight who have been there.* Portland, OR: NASPA Institute of Research and Development.

Astin, A. W.(1973). Impact of dormitory living on students. *Educational Record, 54,* 204-10.

Astin, A. W. (1975). *Preventing students from dropping out.* San Francisco: Jossey-Bass.

Astin, A. W. (1978). *Four critical years: Effects of college on beliefs, attitudes, and knowledge.* San Francisco: Jossey-Bass.

Astin, A. W. (1985). *Achieving educational excellence: A critical assessment of priorities and practices in higher education.* San Francisco: Jossey-Bass.

Aulepp, L., & Delworth, U. (1976). *Training manual for an ecosystem model.* Boulder, CO: Western Interstate Commission on Higher Education.

Ayers, A. R., Tripp, P. A., & Russel, J. H. (1966). *Student services administration in higher education* (OE-53026 Bul. 1966, No. 16). Washington, DC: U.S. Government Printing Office.

Banning, J. H. (Ed.). (1978). *Campus ecology: A perspective for student affairs.* Cincinnati: National Association of Student Personnel Administrators.

Brown, R. D. (1972). *Student development in tomorrow's higher education: A return to the academy.* Washington, DC: American College Personnel Association.

Brubacher, J. S., & Rudy, W. (1976). *Higher education in transition: A history of American colleges and universities,* 1636-1976 (rev. ed.). New York: Harper & Row, Publishers.

Caple, R.B. (1987a). The change process in developmental theory: A self-organization paradigm, Part 1. *Journal of College Student Personnel, 28,* 4-11.

Caple, R.B. (1987b). The change process in developmental theory: A self-organization paradigm, Part 2. *Journal of College Student Personnel, 28-* 100-104.

Chickering, A. W. (1969). *Education and identity*. San Francisco: Jossey-Bass.

Chickering, A. W. (1974). *Commuting versus residence students: Overcoming the educational inequities of living off campus*. San Francisco: Jossey-Bass.

Chickering, A. W., & Associates. (1981). *The modern American college: Responding to the new realities of diverse students and a changing society*. San Francisco: Jossey-Bass.

Cooper, A. C. (1972). *Student development services in higher education*. Report from Commission on Professional Development, Council of Student Personnel Associations.

Cowley, W. H. (1936). The nature of student personnel work. *Educational Record, 17*, 198-226.

Cyert, R. M. (1980). Managing universities in the 1980s. In C. Argyris & R. M. Cyert (Eds.), *Leadership in the '80s: Essays on higher education*. Cambridge, MA: Institute for Educational Management.

Drum, D. J. (1980). Understanding student development. In W. H. Morrill & J. C. Hurst (Eds.), *Dimensions of intervention for student development*. (pp. 14-38). New York: John Wiley & Sons.

Erikson, E. H. (1963). *Childhood and society (2nd ed.)*. New York: W. W. Norton & Co.

Erikson, E. H. (1968). *Identity: Youth and crisis*. New York: W. W. Norton and Co.

Havighurst, R. J. (1953). *Human development and education*. New York: Longman's.

Havighurst, R. J. (1972). *Developmental tasks and education (3rd ed.)*. New York: McKay.

Heath, D. (1968). *Growing up in college: Liberal education and maturity*. San Francisco: Jossey-Bass.

Herbst, J. (1974). The first three American colleges: Schools of the reformation. *Perspectives in American History, 8*, 7-52.

Holland, J. L. (1973). *Making vocational choices: A theory of careers*. Englewood Cliffs, NJ: Prentice-Hall.

Hopkins, L. B. (1926). Personnel procedure in education. *The Educational Record Supplement, 7*(3).

Howard, G. S. (1985). Can research in human sciences become more relevant to practice? *Journal of Counseling and Development, 63*, 539-44.

Huebner, L. A. (Ed.) (1979). *Redesigning campus environments* New directions for student services (No. 8). San Francisco: Jossey-Bass.

Huebner, L. A. (1980). Interaction of student and campus. In U. Delworth & G. R. Hanson (Eds.), *Student Services: A handbook for the profession.* (pp. 117-155). San Francisco: Jossey-Bass.

Hurst, J. C. (1980a). Challenges for the future. In W. H. Morrill & J. C. Hurst (Eds.), *Dimensions of intervention for student development.* (pp. 321-324). New York: John Wiley & Sons.

Hurst, J. C. (1980b). The emergence of student/environmental development as the conceptual foundation for student affairs and some implications for large universities. In D. G. Creamer (Ed.), *Student development in higher education: Theories, practices, and future directions.* (pp. 151-163). Washington, DC: American College Personnel Association.

Knefelkamp, L. L. (1974). *Developmental instruction: Fostering intellectual and personal growth.* Unpublished doctoral dissertation: University of Minnesota.

Kohlberg, L. (1969). Stages and sequences: The cognitive-developmental approach to socialization. In D. P. Goslin (Ed.), *Handbook of socialization theory and research.* Chicago: Rand McNally.

Kuh, G. D., Whitt, E. J., & Shedd, J. D. (1987). *Student affairs work, 2001: A paradigmatic odyssey.* ACPA Media Publication No. 42. Alexandria, VA: American College Personnel Association.

Lanning, W. (1974). An expanded view of consultation for college and university counseling centers. *Journal of College Student Personnel, 15,* 171-6.

Leonard, E. A. (1956). *Origins of personnel services in American higher education.* Minneapolis: University of Minnesota Press.

Lewin, K. (1936). *Principles of topological psychology.* New York: McGraw-Hill.

Lippitt, G. L., & Schmidt, W. H. (1967). Crises in a developing organization. *Harvard Business Review, 45,* 102-12.

Maverick, L. A. (1926). *The vocational guidance of college students.* Cambridge, MA: Harvard University Press.

Miller, T. K., & Prince, J. S.(1976). *The future of student affairs: A guide to student development for tomorrow's higher education.* San Francisco: Jossey-Bass.

Montagu, A. (1981). *Growing young.* New York: McGraw-Hill Book Co.

Moos, R. H. (1979). *Evaluating Educational Environments.* San Francisco: Jossey-Bass.

Morrill, W. H., & Hurst, J. C. (1980). (Eds.). *Dimensions of intervention for student development.* New York: John Wiley & Sons.

Pace, C. R. (1979). *Measuring outcomes of college: Fifty years of findings and recommendations for the future.* San Francisco: Jossey-Bass.

Perry, W. G., Jr. (1970). *Forms of intellectual and ethical development in the college years.* New York: Holt, Rinehart and Winston.

Perry, W. G., Jr. (1981). Cognitive and ethical growth: The making of meaning. In A. W. Chickering and Associates (Eds.), *The modern American college: Responding to the new realities of diverse students and a changing society.* (pp. 76-116). San Francisco: Jossey-Bass.

Piaget, J. (1952). *The origins of intelligence in children.* New York: International Universities Press.

Riker, H. C. (1977). Learning by doing. In G. H. Knock (Ed.), *Perspectives on the preparation of student affairs professionals.* Washington, DC: American College Personnel Association.

Rippey, D. (1981). *What is student development?* Washington, DC: American Association of Community and Junior Colleges.

Rodgers, R. F., & Widick, C. (1980). Theory to practice: Uniting concepts, logic, and creativity. In F. B. Newton & K. L. Ender (Eds.), *Student development practices: Strategies for making a difference.* (pp. 3-25). Springfield, IL: Charles C. Thomas.

Rudolph, F. (1962). *The American college and university: A history.* New York: Random House.

Sanford, N. (1967). *Where colleges fail.* San Francisco: Jossey-Bass.

Sanford, N., & Axelrod, J. (Eds.) (1979). *College and character.* Berkeley, CA: Montaigne.

Schneider, L. D. (1977). Housing. In W. T. Packwood (Ed.), *College student personnel services.* (pp. 125-152). Springfield, IL: Charles C. Thomas.

Shaffer, R. H. (1980). Analyzing institutional constraints upon student development activities. In D. G. Creamer (Ed.), *Student development in higher education: Theories, practices, and future directions.* (pp. 303-312). Washington, DC: American College Personnel Association.

Stern, G. G. (1970). *People in context: Measuring person-environment congruences in education and industry.* New York: John Wiley and Sons.

Widick, C., Knefelkamp, L., & Parker, C. A. (1980). Student development. In U. Delworth, G. R. Hanson, & Associates (Eds.), *Student services: A handbook for the profession.* (pp. 75-116). San Francisco: Jossey-Bass.

Winston, R. B., Bonney, W. C., Miller, T. K., & Dagley, J. C. (1988). *Promoting student development through intentionally structured groups.* San Francisco: Jossey-Bass.

Winston, R. B., Jr., & Miller, T. K., (1987). *Student developmental task and life style inventory manual.* Athens, GA: Student Development Associates.

Wrenn, C. G. (1968). The development of student personnel work in the United States and some guidelines for the future. In M. J. Minter (Ed.), *The student and the system.* Boulder, CO: Western Interstate Commission on Higher Education.

SUGGESTED READINGS

Brown, R. D. (1972). *Student development in tomorrow's higher education: A return to the academy.* Washington, DC: American College Personnel Association.

Brubacher, J. S., & Rudy, W. (1976). *Higher education in transition: A history of American colleges and universities, 1636-1976 (rev. ed.).* New York: Harper and Row Publishers.

Chickering, A. W., & Associates. (1981). *The modern American college: Responding to the new realities of diverse students and a changing society.* San Francisco: Jossey-Bass.

Creamer, D. G. (Ed.). (1980). *Student development in higher education: Theories, practices, and future directions.* Washington, DC: American College Personnel Association.

Delworth, U., Hanson, G. R., & Associates. (1989). *Student services: A handbook for the profession.* San Francisco: Jossey-Bass.

Drum, D. J., & Lawler, A. C. (1988). *Developmental interventions: Theories, principles, and practice.* Columbus, OH: Merrill Publishing.

Knefelkamp, L. L., Widick, C., & Parker, C. A. (Eds.). (1978). *New directions for student services: Applying new developmental findings, No. 4.* San Francisco: Jossey-Bass.

Miller, T. K., & Prince, J. S. (1976). *The future of student affairs: A guide to student development for tomorrow's higher education.* San Francisco: Jossey-Bass.

Morrill, W. H., & Hurst, J. C. (Eds.). (1980). *Dimensions of intervention for student development.* New York: John Wiley and Sons.

Newton, F. B., & Ender, K. L. (Eds.). (1980). *Student development practices: Strategies for making a difference.* Springfield, IL: Charles C. Thomas.

Winston, R. B., Bonney, W. C., Miller, T. K., & Dagley, J. C. (1988). *Promoting student development through intentionally structured groups.* San Francisco: Jossey-Bass.

George D. Kuh, Ph.D., is Professor of Higher Education in the Department of Educational Leadership and Policy Studies at Indiana University. Kuh has been the Coordinator of the College Student Personnel Administration Program, Chairperson of the Department of Educational Leadership and Policy Studies, and Associate Dean for Academic Affairs at the School of Education at Indiana. He has authored and co-authored 95 books and monographs, chapters, and articles and made more than 150 presentations at state, regional and national meetings. His current research is focused on out-of-class experiences of students and the use of organizational theory, particularly cultural perspectives, in colleges and universities. He has received awards from the American College Personnel Association and the National Association of Student Personnel Administrators for his contributions to the higher education literature. He presently serves as editor of the NASPA Monograph Series.

Elizabeth J. Whitt, Ph.D., is an Assistant Professor of Higher Education at Iowa State University. She holds degrees from Drake University (B.A.) and Michigan State University (M.A.), and received a Ph.D. in higher education administration and sociology from Indiana University. She has worked in residence life and served as Dean of Students at Doane College. Immediately prior to her present position, Dr. Whitt was an assistant professor of higher education administration at Oklahoma State University. Her current research interests include institutional cultures, faculty socialization, student involvement, and higher education and student affairs administration.

CHAPTER 2

ORGANIZATIONAL THEORY: A PRIMER

George D. Kuh
Elizabeth J. Whitt

Many students are attracted to student affairs as a career because of an abiding interest in the welfare of students. To the vast majority of student affairs graduate students, theory and research describing the growth and development of college students of all ages are interesting and edifying. The human development perspective is the *sin qua non* of student affairs work. The student development literature, however, does not describe many important activities in which student affairs professionals are engaged, such as decision making, resource allocation, planning, evaluation, programming, and external relations.

Seasoned professionals know that the institutional context has a significant effect on what one does, how one does it, and whether the contributions of student affairs organizations are considered useful by faculty and students. Most preparation programs now require one or more courses that examine collegiate organizational structures and the contributions of organizational theory to understanding the behavior of faculty, administrators, and students. Just as different theories have been formulated to describe various aspects of student development, multiple models and perspectives have been developed to understand and appreciate behavior in colleges.

The purpose of this chapter is to provide an introduction to models and perspectives on organizing that have utility for entry-level and middle-managers in student affairs organizations. Organizational theory is an eclectic field that incorporates concepts from disparate disciplines such as sociology, social psychology, anthropology, and philosophy (Morgan, 1986; Pfeffer, 1982). In recent years, derivative models from business and education also have appeared (Deal & Kennedy, 1982; Weick, 1976). The models and perspectives have been chosen that, when taken together, represent the range of interpretations of college life that organizational theory can provide.

First, four conventional views of colleges as organizations are described: (1) classical organizational perspectives, (2) the human relations approach, (3) organizational behavior models, and (4) two models developed specifically for use in higher education, the collegial and political models. In addition, some non-orthodox views of organizing have appeared in the past 15 years. To establish a context for understanding and appreciating the differences between conventional models and the non-orthodox perspectives, a brief discussion is provided of the characteristics of the paradigm shift that have unalterably changed the ways in which meaning is made in many fields of study. A sampler of non-orthodox perspectives (e.g., organized anarchy, loosely coupled systems) is provided. One of the non-orthodox views, a cultural perspective, is described in somewhat more detail. Finally, implications of different models and perspectives of organizing are discussed.

CONVENTIONAL MODELS

Conventional views of organizations are rooted in expectations for order and control, assumptions about the world that date back to the 17th century. The world view predominant at the time was of an ordered, pyramid-like universe. At the apex was God; on earth the Sovereign of England was God's own immediate deputy. Other groups of people were ordered down to peasants. This "natural" order was to be protected; chaos was to be avoided at all costs. This belief is reflected in Ulysses speech in Shakespeare's *Troilus and Cressida:*

> Take but degree away, untune that string,
> And Hard what discord follows! Each thing meets
> In mere oppugnancy. The bounded waters
> Should lift their bossoms higher than the shores.
> And make a sop of all this solid globe. (I.iii.109-113)

The belief in a natural order of things has had a pervasive influence on theory and research in virtually every field, including conventional models of organizing.

Classical Perspectives

Classical organizational theory developed within the context of the industrial revolution, a period in which work, and lives away from work, became increasingly routinized, mechanized, and specialized (Morgan, 1986). Theories of organizations were derived from experience in the successful organizations of the time, particularly the military. Thus, hierarchical control, standard regulations, task specialization, and divisions between line and staff positions received particular emphasis (Morgan, 1986; Owens, 1981). Efficiency and rational processes, such as purposeful actions and intended outcomes, were indispensible keys to exemplary, production-oriented organizations (Weick, 1979).

Scientific Management. The period from 1910 to 1935 has been labeled the era of scientific management (Filley, House, & Kerr, 1976), and its pioneer was Frederick W. Taylor, "one of the most maligned and criticized of all organizational theorists [and] also one of the most influential" (Morgan, 1986, p. 30). Taylor was committed to improving efficiency of people and organizations. In fact, he asserted that prosperity could be achieved *only* when each individual achieved his or her highest state of efficiency (Taylor, 1911). Maximum efficiency was to be attained by means of rational, scientific processes. According to Taylor (1911), "the best management is a true science resting upon clearly defined laws, rules, and principles as a foundation" (p.7).

In pursuit of efficiency, Taylor formulated five principles (Morgan, 1986).

1. Responsibility for the organization of work resides with managers, not with workers. Efficiency is reduced when workers and managers attempt to perform tasks outside their expertise and functions, although close cooperation between workers and managers is essential.

2. Scientific methods, such as time and motion studies, are used to determine the most efficient way of doing a particular job. Jobs are broken into small, serial tasks and workers have precise instructions for how to perform their tasks.

3. Each job is performed by the person best suited to the requirements of the job.

4. Proper training enables workers to perform their jobs in the most efficient manner with minimum interaction with other workers.

5. Close supervision of workers ensures that the specified procedures are followed; workers are to be paid according to the number of units they produce.

Principles of scientific management, when put into practice, had both negative and positive consequences. Productivity increased in certain kinds of organizations, particularly those involving repetitious tasks and mass production, but craftspeople responsible for producing a completed product were replaced by unskilled workers responsible for only a small part of the final outcome (Morgan, 1986). High rates of worker turnover and alienation were attributed to treating workers as interchangeable machine parts and separating decision making from implementation—separating "hand and brain" (Morgan, 1986, p. 32). Although scientific management has been criticized for depicting people as machines, Taylor's ideas provided a foundation for the organization of work for much of the 20th century (Owens, 1981).

Bureaucracy. Labor disputes and the development of Communism were manifestations of the increasing conflict between people and organizations which characterized the early 20th century (Owens, 1981). Governmental, industrial, and religious organizations were ruled by powerful individuals exercising traditional forms of authority including patriarchal (allegiance owed to a family or monarch by right of heredity or ownership) and charismatic (obedience owed to a strong personality) (Morgan, 1986; Owens, 1981; Weber, 1978).

Max Weber, a German sociologist, wrote extensively during the 1920s about sources of authority, including patriarchal, charismatic, and rational-legal. Of these three, rational-legal authority was perceived by Weber to be the most fair, predictable, rational, and efficient because it required obedience on the basis of rules and allegiance owed to persons placed in authority under those rules. Rational-legal authority systems characterized the military and the Roman Catholic church (Weber, 1978).

The characteristics of rational-legal authority and bureaucratic organizations include (1) rules for conducting business; (2) hierarchical organization of offices, with each lower position under the authority of one higher; (3) selection of office holders on the basis of technical qualifications and training in the specific requirements of the job; (4) separation of organizational and personal property; (5) administrative decisions, rules, and procedures recorded in writing; (6) promotions based on seniority and achievement; (7) division of labor among offices according to specific areas of technical competence; and (8) impersonality in interpersonal relationships (Weber, 1978). Weber asserted that these characteristics resulted in equality of treatment for all workers and predictability of organizational processes, as well as efficiency in operations. Thus, his concern was not only with efficiency, but also with fair, equitable treatment of people, the leveling of status possible only, he believed, with rational-legal authority (Weber, 1978).

Although Weber described his picture of bureaucracy as a pure type, perfect only in its ideal form, he was absolutely convinced of its appropriateness for all organizations. "However many people complain about the 'red tape', it would be sheer illusion to think for a moment that continuous administrative work can be carried out in any field except by means of officials working in offices. . . . The choice is only that between bureaucracy and dilettantism in the field of administration" (Weber, 1978, p. 223).

Bureaucratic assumptions and activities are manifested in student affairs divisions in forms of prohibitions against "end runs" and requirements that one must "go through channels" (or at least appear to go through channels) to get things done, job descriptions and standard operating procedures, separation of personal and professional concerns, and commitment to hierarchal structures (Clark, 1985). Elements of bureaucracy can be found in the organizational structure of most colleges, particularly in "its 'people processing' aspects: record keeping, registration, graduation requirements, and a multitude of other routine, day-to-day activities designed to help the modern university handle its masses of students" (Baldridge, Curtis, Echer, & Riley, 1977, p. 17). At the same time, however, the bureaucratic model focuses on formal structures rather than informal processes, thereby limiting the model's usefulness in understanding colleges.

Summary of Classical Perspectives. Classical organizational theories are characterized by several themes. They assume that organizations can and should be rational, efficient systems, and they assume that one best way to organize exists—one set of principles which, if applied properly, can result in efficient management, productive workers, and freedom from problems in all types of organizations (McKibbin, 1981).

Classical approaches to organizing seem to work best in settings in which what exist are straightforward tasks, a stable environment, and one product to be reproduced repeatedly (Morgan, 1986). When implemented in other contexts, organizations based on classical principles are difficult to change (due to over-reliance on predetermined goals and rules), dehumanize employees (by assigning decision making only to certain offices), and hinder coping with conflict (Morgan, 1986). The classical models also discount the influence of personal goals on organizational performance (Clark, 1985). Individual needs and aspirations which may compete with institutional goals, informal interactions, and work group norms were considered problems to be solved rather than inherent, certainly complicated, and perhaps healthy, aspects of life in organizations.

Human Relations Management

The importance of individual and group needs to organizational performance was strikingly evident in the results of research of environmental factors at the Western Electric plant in Hawthorne, Illinois. From 1927 until 1932, Elton Mayo and his associates studied effects on productivity of elements such as illumination, physical layout of the workplace, and the relationship of fatigue to productivity (Filley et al., 1976). Their most important finding, however, was that human factors such as worker involvement, motivation, morale, and group dynamics were significant determinants of productivity (Owens, 1981).

The Hawthorne findings precipitated the human relations management movement, which refocused attention of organizational theorists toward the people in organizations (Filley et al., 1976). Social and behavioral scientists occupied a prominent role in the development of human relations theory by studying the emotional and social nature of people, as well as their experiences and interactions within organizations. Two of the best known of the human relations theorists were Douglas McGregor (1960) and Chris Argyris (1964).

McGregor (1960) proposed the existence of alternative views of control and people. The first of these views, *Theory X*, was based on the assumption that most people do not like, and will avoid work if possible. Thus, in order to be productive, workers must be controlled, coerced, and threatened; in fact, most people prefer to be told what to do in work settings. The alternative view, *Theory Y* was based on the assumption that work is natural and that people will exercise self-control and self-direction to achieve goals to which they are committed. Commitment to organizational goals is a function of the rewards associated with achieving the goal. On the basis of these contrasting assumptions, McGregor (1960) asserted that the most effective means to direct worker effort required that members of an organization be able to achieve their own goals through achievement of the organization's goals. For example, student affairs staff who are committed to their own growth and development may work most effectively in an organization that has student development as its primary goal.

The work of Argyris (1964) emphasized integrating individual and organizational goals and focused on informal organizational structures and processes. Argyris believed that formal, intentional organizational structures, such as division of labor, impersonality, and hierarchy, were incongruent with human needs for psychological success and maturity. The informal structures and processes, such as work group norms, that people created for themselves were intended to meet personal psychological needs as well as perform assigned tasks. "The point is that the organization as a going, living system has many 'parts' that do not appear on the drawing board; that indeed may not be recognized by the top administration; that may, however, keep the total organization viable and operating" (Argyris, 1964, p. 36).

Argyris advocated treating workers as adults, sharing risks and responsibility, encouraging questioning and creativity, and providing opportunities for developing new skills (Kuh, Whitt, & Shedd, 1987). Following this argument, residence hall directors for example, should be encouraged to work with staff members and residents to help them develop and enforce their own policies and rules.

Organizational Behavior

As with the human relations movement, the organizational behavior movement (1950-1975) evolved out of frustration with the inadequacy of the classical perspectives to explain what was going on in organizations (Owens, 1981). For example, Simon (1957) used the phrase "bounded rationality" to explain the limits on rational behavior imposed by insufficiency of information and time. He developed the concept of *satisficing* to describe the tendency to implement the first generally satisfactory alternative discovered. Other elements of organizational behavior theory included the relationships between formal and informal organizations (Barnard, 1937) and organizations as social systems (Getzels & Guba, 1957).

According to Barnard (1937), informal organizations were made up of personal interactions within the organization that alter employees' attitudes and feelings toward each other and the organization. The outcomes of these contacts are social norms, customs, folklore, and ideals. In addition, informal organizations establish conditions for other aspects of the formal organization to function effectively. As informal social interactions become more purposive, permanent support structures, dues-charging clubs made up of co-workers for example, are needed to maintain the interactions and achieve their purposes.

Getzels and Guba (1957) identified two discrete, yet interactive, dimensions in organizations: (1) the nomothetic, or institutional dimension, and (2) the idiographic, or personal dimension. Any individual behavior within a college or university would, therefore, derive simultaneously from these two dimensions—from personal needs and expectations *and* organizational expectations.

Organizational behavior theory has been described by Clark (1985) as **"neo-orthodox" theory,** a phrase which underscores subtle differences from classical models. Neo-orthodox theorists acknowledged that the psychological and social environments that make up organizations shape human behavior—including productivity. Organizational performance is also affected by their social, economic, political, and technological contexts (Clark, 1985). At the same time, neo-orthodox views assumed the necessity of rational processes, such as goal setting, and hierarchical structures for effective organizing (Clark, 1985).

Collegial and Political Models

According to Millett (1962), the "ideas drawn from business and public administration have only a very limited applicability to colleges and universities" (p.4). The history, traditions, and unique purposes of colleges—the maintenance, transmission, and advancement of knowledge—affect their internal structures and processes (how business is conducted) as well as relationships with external agencies (Baldridge et al., 1977; Millett, 1962). Nevertheless, colleges are organizations, a fact that leads to constant tension between their administrative and educational roles (Ruscio, 1987). Two organizational models that are particularly well suited for explaining activities and events in colleges are the collegial model and the political model.

The **collegial model** eschews bureaucratic processes, focusing instead on coordination through consensus of members of the academic community (Millett, 1962). Authority for self-governance is based on professional expertise. The special knowledge and skills of faculty members empower them to make decisions as individuals, such as what to study and how, and as a group, such as curricular offerings and promotion and tenure decisions, free from organizational restrictions (Millett, 1962).

The extent to which the collegial model accurately describes the structures and processes of a particular college depends in part on cultural factors. For example, in institutions with an "academic temperament" (Ruscio, 1987, p. 355), decision making and governance are performed at the operational level, by faculty members within departments and disciplines. In colleges with a management orientation, decision making and constraints on actions are determined by administrators who have a broad vision for the institution across departments and disciplines (Ruscio, 1987). This arrangement may be typical of institutions in which administrators have longer service than faculty or in which faculty are not committed to active participation in institutional governance (Kuh & Whitt, 1988).

Baldridge and others (1977) have criticized the collegial model for being too simple: "Proponents of the collegial model are correct in declaring that simple bureaucratic rule making is not the essence of decision making. But in making this point, they take the equally indefensible position that major decisions are reached primarily by consensus" (Baldridge et al., 1977, p. 19). Thus, because the collegial model assumes consensus, it does not address the issue of conflict. In addition, bureaucratic structures and processes do exist in colleges (Perrow, 1972), something which the collegial model ignores.

In the **political model,** conflict, rather than consensus, in policy making is the focus. The political model emphasizes institutional policy-making processes because policies reflect and define organizational goals and, therefore, determine organizational priorities, strategies, and activities (Baldridge et al., 1977). The political model is based on the following assumptions:

1. Colleges are fragmented by internal and external interest groups representing varied goals and values.

2. In a fragmented, dynamic system in which resources are limited, conflict is a natural, positive—not negative— force for change.

3. Policy making involves a few interested people or groups rather than the whole community: "inactivity prevails" (Baldridge et al., 1977, p. 20) in the process of decision making.

4. Those who are involved in the policy-making process are involved only sporadically, moving in and out on the basis of time, energy, and commitment. As a consequence, those who persist are likely to prevail.

5. Interest groups inhibit the functioning of formal (bureaucratic) authority. Policies reflect negotiated compromises rather than rational decision-making processes.

To understand policy making as seen through the lens of the political model, consider the process of establishing a new alcohol policy for a public college in a state which has just raised the drinking age from 18 to 21. Groups who have a stake in the outcome include student affairs staff, students, local law enforcement agencies, legislators, trustees, faculty members, anti-drunk driving groups, parents of students, and local restaurant and bar owners. Typically, determining who makes the decision is a contested process; student affairs staff members may believe that they have the largest stake in the decision because of their responsibility for alcohol education, residence life, programming, and judicial processes. On the other hand, faculty believe the potential impact of a decision on the institution's academic climate makes the faculty senate the appropriate body to adjudicate the matter. Policy options are probably limited by previous events or conflicts; perhaps a student has died from an alcohol overdose; perhaps the residence halls are perceived by legislators, faculty, and parents as "zoos"; perhaps local bar owners have seen a drop in business because of alcohol use on campus; perhaps the Greek system has been criticized by faculty, but attempts to eliminate fraternities have been unsuccessful. Conflict will arise during the decision-making process as groups and individuals compete for input and to protect their interests. Timing will affect participation; this year's seniors who are committed to keeping alcohol on campus will graduate, the faculty senate will suspend meetings at the end of the academic year, the legislature is only in session in the fall. Once a decision is made, implementation may be protracted as related policy concerns arise; for example, if alcohol is to be permitted on campus for students of legal age, how can abstinence on the part of underage students be ensured? If a policy is not adopted, the issue will surely come up again in a different form, such as a proposal to serve beer in the union or a resolution to ban hazing, with different interests at stake.

Summary of Conventional Models

In essence, simplification was the aim, and consequence, of conventional approaches (Clark, 1985). Conventional models provide a normative view of organizing and assume that (1) hierarchical structures are normal and necessary for organizational effectiveness; (2) goals reflect intentions, direct the actions of workers, and are directly linked to outcomes; (3) communication channels are clearly delineated; and (4) the rationality, reliability, and predicatability of organizational processes are limited only by knowledge and technology (Clark, 1985, Kuh et al., 1987).

The collegial and political models reflect more complexity than other conventional perspectives and, as a consequence, enable greater understanding of organizational processes in colleges. At the same time, these models also are based on conventional assumptions of goal-directed behavior and direct links between intentions and outcomes.

The efforts of the neo-orthodox theorists resulted in models that were more comprehensive and more complex than the classical perspectives. Nevertheless, if one assumes that efficiency, rationality, predictability, and intentionality are the way things are supposed to work in organizations, actions, such as "end runs" or unclear, broad goals and multiple and conflicting values, that are inconsistent with these qualities are interpreted as "noise in the system"—problems to be fixed (by more precise planning or clearer policies or more careful supervision) or aberrations to be dismissed. When it is assumed that events and actions are predictable and solutions to problems can be found, the challenge to leaders is to identify the one best solution and determine how the solution can be best implemented.

Normative approaches are functional when the conditions facing a college are stable and predictable, where goals and the way to attain goals are clear, where problems appear infrequently, and when efforts to solve problems and improve performance can be evaluated. Unfortunately, these characteristics do not describe most collegiate environments. For decades, conventional models have offered the illusion of control over what is now known to be constantly changing institutional contexts buffeted by often contrary forces in the external environment.

NON-ORTHODOX PERSPECTIVES ON ORGANIZATIONS AND ORGANIZING

The dominant paradigm is the framework most people in Western culture use to understand and make meaning of events in the natural world. Theorists in many disciplines, including organizational studies, assert that a paradigm shift is underway, a shift to an emergent world view based on a new set of assumptions (Kuh et al., 1987). The concept of paradigm shift was developed and explicated by Thomas

Kuhn (1970). According to Kuhn (1970) and others (Capra, 1983; Ferguson, 1980; Gleick, 1987), a dominant paradigm begins to unravel when new findings and experiences can no longer be accommodated or adequately explained by the conventional world view, when the accumulation of inconsistencies brings the existing paradigm to the point of collapse. The inconsistencies between conventional assumptions (such as clearly delineated communication channels) and what happens (people communicate up, down, and across channels) become so numerous they seem to be the rule rather than the exception. In other words, the deviations become the norm. Instead of believing that what happens are problems to be solved (through tighter controls, better staff training, written procedures), the emergent paradigm offers a new set of assumptions that describe a different order, an alternative explanation for making sense.

Non-Orthodox Assumptions

The following assumptions about organizations and organizing are suggested by the emergent paradigm.

1. **Organizational structures are context-specific and evolve over time.**

Structure represents an attempt to respond to organizational exigencies, including the skills and needs of individuals. Structures change as the needs of people change. An organizational chart may, in fact, be necessary, but it does not accurately depict relationships between people and functions. Hierarchical structures may not make the best use of the knowledge and skills of all members of the organization. Distinctions between super- and sub-ordinates can hamper an individual's sense of efficacy as well as the capacity of the organization to learn from its experience and change over time.

2. **Useful information is available from many sources and flows in many directions.**

All individuals in the organization have the potential to influence organizational behavior in an effective, positive, creative manner. Communication is a web of valuable connections linking every individual and group in the organization; therefore, useful information is available from every participant. As information is more widely distributed, ownership and commitment to institutional purposes can be enhanced.

3. Outcomes of actions in organizations are unpredictable.

Individual and group behavior, events, and outcomes affect one another in variable ways over time, blurring distinctions between cause and effect. Thus, predicting what will happen via planning and goal-setting activities is difficult, if not impossible. For example, can an increase in student retention be attributed to new programs, or clarification of institutional mission, or recruiting students of better "fit"? The answer is, "Perhaps." Goal setting and planning activities are effective to the degree that they bring people together to talk about priorities, values, beliefs, and aspirations (Hossler, Carnaghi, Love, Schmit, & Whitt, 1988). Learning happens by doing; "chaotic action is preferable to orderly inaction" (Weick, 1979, p. 245).

4. No one best solution exists for any problem.

The future is unpredictable, change is constant, and reality (the definition of problems and solutions) is subjective. As consequence, what "works" is, at best, temporary and in the eye of the beholder. Several organizational perspectives that are compatible with non-orthodox assumptions about organizing have been developed (e.g., Argyris & Schon, 1978; Georgiou, 1973; Hedberg, Nystrom, & Starbuck, 1976; Morgan & Ramirez, 1983). Two such perspectives, organized anarchy and loose coupling, are described in the following sections.

Organized Anarchy. The oxymoronic phrase, "organized anarchy," was developed by Cohen and March (1974) to describe organizations in which non-rationality co-exists with functionality. Cohen and March (1974) asserted that colleges are "prototypical organized anarchies" (p. 3). Characteristics of organized anarchies include problematic goals, unclear technologies, and fluid participation. In many institutions, preferences tend to be "inconsistent and ill-defined" and goals tend to be "either vague or in dispute" (Cohen & March, 1974, p. 3). For example, although teaching, research, and service are usually identified as primary functions of colleges, how these functions are defined and the priority given to each are typically contested issues.

How these functions are to be accomplished is also debatable. The processes of teaching, learning, and student development, and the technologies by which they can be encouraged, are generally unclear even to the people involved in them (Cohen & March, 1974). As a consequence, operations take place by trial and error, on the basis of practical experience, and in reaction to crises (Baldridge et al., 1977).

Participation in planning, goal setting, and policy making tends to be fluid. Actors move in and out of decision contexts (Cohen & March, 1974). Students are usually around for no more than four or five years, faculty take sabbaticals, and administrative positions may be filled on the basis of rotating appointments. The time and effort given to any issue or task is variable.

Thus, an organized anarchy is characterized by non-rationality, fluidity, and ambiguity (Baldridge et al., 1977). Although messy, this perspective provides a more complex, and thus accurate, view of colleges that can be used to understand more of what happens in those settings. For example, multiple and contradictory priorities, such as maximizing selectivity or access and emphasizing undergraduate instruction or research productivity, are commonplace. Recognizing the tradeoffs allows an administrator or faculty member to focus energy on activities other than trying to develop and enforce consensual goals.

Loose Coupling. Coupling is the relationship among or between elements (for example people, offices, divisions) of an organization (Clark, Astuto, & Kuh, 1986). Conventional assumptions about organizations imply tight coupling: direct and causal links between events and outcomes, direct and unobstructed links between and among people and departments, efficient coordination of all parts of the whole, shared goals and values (Weick, 1982). In most colleges, however, variable connections are not unusual among student affairs and academic affairs or between activities and outcomes such as grading policies and student achievement. Decentralized coordination among academic departments is ordinary, not unusual (Kuh et al., 1987).

The contradiction between conventional assumptions of tight coupling and the "reality" of educational institutions was summarized by Weick (1982):

> These characteristics of schools are mistakenly treated as evidence of fallible management, indecisiveness, and the need for administrators to run a tighter ship help together by performance appraisals and management by objectives. All of these judgments result from the application to schools of the wrong model . . . the rational bureaucratic model . . . . Seldom do people step aside long enough to realize that the task of education is simply not the kind of task that can be performed in a tightly coupled system. (p. 674)

An alternative, and more useful, perspective is that of loose coupling, descriptive of a system in which only some, or weak, variables are common across an organization (Clark et al., 1986). A loosely coupled system displays the characteristics applied above to colleges: sporadic communication, intermittent linkages, decentralized coordination. Loosely coupled systems have both advantages and disadvantages. Loose coupling allows greater responsiveness to environmental change because more units have more varied interactions with the environment which bring in more information from the outside. Also, in loosely coupled systems, innovations can take place in some areas without risking failure in all. For example, the "new colleges," which were popular in the late 1960s and early 1970s, allowed experimentation with admissions, curriculum, and grading policies without committing the entire institution to radically modify its structure and mission. Finally, loose coupling enables units to take responsibility for their own decisions and actions (Weick, 1976, 1982).

On the other hand, loosely coupled systems can be disadvantageous when isolated units adopt priorities of local reference groups that conflict with the priorities of the institution as a whole (Weick, 1982). For example, the admissions office may recruit students with a quota in mind rather than predictions for academic success or social "fit," or student affairs staff may zealously develop social and educational programs while ignoring students' academic commitments.

Of course, the structural elements of any college or university are never completely unconnected. Even the most loosely coupled system may be tightly coupled around certain values, such as academic excellence or student development, or have some tightly coupled processes such as payroll and registration. Nevertheless, loose coupling offers interesting insights into organizational behavior. Looking at colleges and their components as loosely coupled systems allows different, more flexible interpretations of what is going on than does the expectation for tight coupling. In addition, "less time is wasted in reinforcing, or attempting to create, sequential linkages; more time can be spent reinforcing what seems at the moment to be working" (Kuh et al., 1987, p. 63).

The Cultural Perspective. Organized anarchy and loose coupling concepts generate provocative, useful insights into certain kinds of activities, such as decision making. One major limitation of these non-orthodox perspectives is that they do not provide a broad framework within which both routine and unusual events and actions can be interpreted. In recent years, a cultural view of organizations has been employed with increasing frequency to provide a holistic interpretation of events and actions in organizations. In the higher education context, culture is the collective, mutually shaping patterns of norms, values, practices, beliefs and assumptions which guide the behavior of individuals and groups and provides a frame of reference within which to interpret the meaning of events and actions on and off the campus (Kuh & Whitt, 1988).

The cultural view holds that to understand and appreciate behavior, assumptions and beliefs shared by a group of people must be considered. Although the most pervasive and influential assumptions are essentially tacit, many are represented by observable forms or artifacts (Schein, 1985). To analyze cultural properties, Schein divided culture into a conceptual hierarchy of three levels; (1) artifacts, (2) values, and (3) basic assumptions and beliefs.

Artifacts. Artifacts include norms, mores, formal and informal rules, routine procedures, behaviors which are rewarded or sanctioned, customs, folkways, myths, daily and periodic rituals, ceremonies, interaction patterns, signs, and a language system common to faculty, students, and student life staff (Broom & Selznick, 1973; Morgan, 1986; Schein, 1985; Tierney, 1985, 1988; Van Maanen & Barley, 1984). For illustrative purposes, three categories of artifacts—rituals, language, and stories—are briefly described.

Rituals in a college or university are essentially social constructions that serve different purposes: (1) they communicate important values, (2) they welcome and socialize new colleagues (Gardner, 1986), and (3) they celebrate accomplishments of members. Examples of familiar rituals in which students and student affairs staff often participate include new student orientation, convocations, chapel, fieldhouse registration, commencement, and elaborate social activities sponsored by fraternal groups and student government. Such activities are important because they structure social interaction and provide insight into the quality of life within the community. Rituals also serve as standards against which members of a particular group can assess the appropriateness of their behavior (Kuh & Whitt, 1988).

Language, the spoken and written word, is a powerful vehicle through which values, thoughts, perceptions, and feelings are transmitted (Bredeson, 1987, Langer, 1953). Student affairs professionals have developed a language to communicate with each other. Words such as "student development," "milieu management," and "discipline" have varied meanings for different student affairs staff and faculty members. The precise meaning and implications of these terms also are context-bound; that is, how these terms are translated into practice differs from one campus to another. Substantive products such as policy statements and standard operating procedures such as written statements of the division's philosophy, mission, and purpose, also communicate important messages to faculty, students, and others about what student affairs professionals value. Because colleges are rich in symbolism and ceremony, sensitivity to the nuances of language across groups is important for accurately interpreting events and actions (Kuh et al., 1987; Masland, 1985).

Stories are narratives—complete with plots, protagonists and antagonists, and action—and provide a good deal of information about a student affairs division or institution. As stories are passed on from one student generation to another, stories sometimes take on legendary proportions and become tightly woven into the fabric of the institutional culture. For example, stories are told at Wabash College in Indiana about the founders of the college kneeling in the snow watching the burning of South Hall, the marching off to war of the "entire" student body in the 1860s, and the bloody class fights on Washington's birthday. When the Wabash community faces adversity, the commitment and faith of the College's founders are emphasized by retelling the South Hall story. Told during orientation, the story about marching off to war introduces new students to the social consciousness that is a trademark of Wabash. Such stories, and companion anecdotes, are compelling, persuasive, and often are more influential in determining institutional priorities than so-called "hard data" generated by management information systems (Kuh & Whitt, 1988).

Other artifactual elements familiar to most student affairs staff members include buzzwords and concepts reflected in student development assessment instruments such as "vectors" and "Perry levels" or "positions" of intellectual development, written codes of student behavior such as the institution's statement of students' rights and responsibilities, and annual staff holiday gatherings and end-of-the-year celebrations.

Values. Schein's (1985) second level of culture is made up of values, widely held beliefs or sentiments about the importance of certain goals, activities, relationships, and feelings. Many values espoused by student affairs professionals are expressed as themes or guiding principles such as every student is unique (American Council on Education, 1937) and that students are ultimately responsible for their own behavior (National Association of Student Personnel Administrators, 1987). Cultural values are likely to be tightly linked to, or at least congruent with, basic beliefs and assumptions.

Values sometimes surface as exhortations about what is right or wrong, what is encouraged or discouraged—what "ought" to be. For example, statements by the chief student life officer about the debilitating consequences of the inappropriate use of alcohol can communicate the institution's values under certain circumstances; for example, when statements are repeated often and are accompanied by behavior which suggests depth of conviction.

Of course, some values are merely espoused (Argyris & Schon, 1978) and predict what people will say in certain situations but may not represent what they do. Espoused values are more like aspirations or rationalizations (Schein, 1985). Examples of espoused values abound in many student affairs divisions: public statements about the need to increase minority representation among students and staff yet few people of color are admitted or hired; the assertion that students are adults and, therefore, responsible for their lives yet each year additional rules are added to the code of student conduct; and division documents that underscore the institution's commitment to holistic development of students yet staff devote a disproportionate amount of time to student leaders and repeat disciplinary offenders.

Basic Assumptions and Beliefs. The third level, what Schein (1985) believed to be the core of culture, consists of basic, but often unstated, assumptions which undergird artifacts and values. Schein asserted that these assumptions and beliefs are learned responses to threats to institutional survival and exert a powerful influence over what people think about, what they perceive to be important, how they feel about things, and what they do. Indeed, assumptions and beliefs determine the way in which reality is perceived and, albeit unconsciously, guide behavior. These conceptions are so deeply ingrained that they are by definition "taken-for-granted. . .not confrontable or debatable" (Schein, 1985,

p. 18); thus, such assumptions are difficult to identify. One way of identifying assumptions is by asking questions: Do we trust students? What is emphasized in activities sponsored by the student affairs division—intellectual or social development?

Culture. What does the cultural perspective imply? Every institution's culture is different. Therefore, the meaning of behavior can be interpreted only in a real life situation within a specific institutional milieu (Hall, 1976). Policies and practices that seem to be effective in one institution may or may not be effective in another; what appear to be similar actions and events will mean different things in different settings (Kuh et al., 1987).

Culture connects institutional stakeholders to the institution's past, present and future and militates against, or engenders, the development of commitment, loyalty, and cohesiveness. The dominant constellation of assumptions, values and preferences that carry cultural themes introduces and socializes new members into the accepted patterns of behavior, thereby perpetuating—for all practical purposes— many of the dominant assumptions and beliefs of the culture. Culture can be a stabilizing influence, providing a sense of continuity and a consistent framework within which behavior can be interpreted during turbulent periods such as the first few months under a new president.

Culture may change over time, however. New staff members bring different attitudes and perspectives which have a reciprocal shaping influence on the culture (Van Maanen, 1984). Several new staff members committed to using student development theory in the residence halls can influence particular features of the culture, such as the language used to communicate ideas. Thus, culture is not a static entity but is continually evolving.

Culture explains differences in opinion. Some aspects of student subcultures, such as racist behavior on the part of white students toward students of color or vice versa, and faculty subcultures, such as loyalty to the discipline rather than to the institution, can thwart attainment of institutional purposes as well as denigrate the integrity of certain individuals and groups. Persons who share values and beliefs that differ somewhat from the host culture may form a subculture (Bolton & Kammeyer, 1972; Sergiovanni, 1984). Subcultures are positive forces when they engender a sense of identity, cohesiveness, and loyalty to the institution or make it possible for persons out of the mainstream to succeed in an alienating environment, such as black students on a predominately white campus. However, when the values and norms of the subculture, a fraternity for example, deviate significantly from the institution's expectations for appropriate behavior, the subculture can become divisive. Thus, culture in a student affairs division can be either a barrier to developing a sense of community or may serve as the "glue" that binds a student affairs staff.

Because much of culture exists beneath conscious thought, control over culture by the chief student affairs administrator or student activities director is more limited than some writers have suggested (Kilmann, Saxton, & Serpa, 1986). Therefore, to intentionally change culture is very difficult, perhaps impossible (Kuh & Whitt, 1988).

Culture is revealed by examining artifacts such as policies, decision-making processes, and language. Through observations and interviews, what is important to a group of people can be discovered. What are the common slogans or public statements that transmit values and goals of the student affairs division? Do the slogans depict what student affairs staff wish to communicate to others? Does jargon indigenous to the "student affairs rain forest" (Schroeder, Nicholls, & Kuh, 1983) empower members of the tribe? Are persons of color or women degraded by certain rituals, such as fraternity rush and "Little Sister" activities? Do ceremonies vividly portray (symbolize) who student affairs staff are (identity), how the student affairs division got to where it is today (history), and where the division wishes to go in the future (vision)? Are ceremonies powerful public affirmations of the importance of student affairs (Kuh, 1985)?

Additional insights into culture may be gleaned from an analysis of organizational structures (Clark & Trow, 1966). For example, the structure of a division of student affairs, as represented by an organizational chart, provides a point of reference for the way people think about and make sense of the contexts in which they work (Deal & Kennedy, 1982).

Summary of Non-conventional Views

What people attend to and how they interpret actions and events are filtered through lenses colored by past experiences, current circumstances, and personal agendas (Capra, 1983; Lincoln, 1985; Schwartz & Ogilvy, 1979; Weick, 1979). Each person constructs reality for himself or herself. Therefore: (a) multiple realities exist; (b) subjectivity is valid; (c) the illusion of a single objective reality that permeates conventional models of organizing is eschewed. This is not to say behavior cannot be understood; it can, but interpretations are context and person-specific, generated by individuals making sense of what they observe and experience.

Non-orthodox theories and assumptions encourage the use of many lenses to examine organizations and organizational processes. In this way, colleges can be understood as complex, loosely coupled, and non-rational as well as (in some cases) tightly coupled and coordinated. This presents a more accurate and fruitful perspective for administrators, faculty, and researchers than that offered by the conventional world view. More complex understandings encourage appreciation for diverse perspectives and ambiguity and discourage attempts to make colleges rational, predictable, and tightly coupled. Table 2.1 summarizes the differences between conventional and non-orthodox assumptions.

IMPLICATIONS OF ORGANIZATIONAL THEORY FOR STUDENT AFFAIRS WORK

Space does not permit a comprehensive treatment of how organizational theory can be used by student affairs professionals. Practical applications can be found elsewhere in this volume (in particular, Chapters 3, 4, 7, 14, and 19) and in related publications (e.g., Kuh, 1983, 1984, 1985; Kuh et al., 1987). The following suggestions are offered to stimulate discussion and further reading in the area.

(Continued on page 62)

TABLE 2.1
A Comparison of Conventional and Non-Orthodox
Assumptions About Organizing[1]

CONVENTIONAL ASSUMPTIONS ABOUT ORGANIZATIONS	NON-ORTHODOX ASSUMPTIONS ABOUT ORGANIZATIONS
Organizations function most effectively and efficiently with hierarchical structures.	Appropriate organizational structures are context-specific and evolve over time.
Decision making and communication follow organizational chain of command.	Useful information is available from many sources and flows in many directions.
Clear goals produce desirable organizational outcomes.	Outcomes of actions in organizations are unpredictable.
The best solution for a problem is discovered though rational processes.	There is no one best solution for a problem.

[1] The authors acknowledge and appreciate the work of John L. Matkin (Indiana University) in helping to develop this table.

1. Things may not be (probably are not) what they seem at first glance.

The organizational theory literature indicates that many different ways exist to interpret the meaning of routine events as well as unusual circumstances. Choice of perspectives, and the assumptions on which the perspectives are based, influences what one can comprehend. Extensive use of any one model or perspective will result in an unbalanced view of one's work environment. To make the best use of organizational perspectives, one should attempt to suspend judgment for a day; that is, to consciously avoid familiar patterns of interpretation. Although awkward at first, several days of practice in applying principles characteristic of different views will generate fresh, usually interesting, and often useful insights into workplace dynamics.

As Weick (1985) suggested, *expectations matter.* That is, what is expected to happen places constraints on one's capacity to generate alternative interpretations of what occurs. Therefore, one must exercise considerable caution in determining in advance what students, faculty, and colleagues will do. This is not to say that all expectations are inappropriate or debilitating; quite the contrary. Holding high performance expectations is positively related to exceptional output in many different endeavors (Walberg, Strykowski, Rovai, & Hung, 1984). However, permitting expectations to go unexamined and unchallenged may be irresponsible, or worse, unfair to one or more groups.

2. Try to imagine the bigger picture, from different points of view.

To get caught up in one's own immediate problems is easy. Indeed, student affairs staff would be irresponsible if they did not take their jobs seriously. However, student affairs functions are part of a large, more complex whole—a college. Efforts to understand the institution as a whole, using organizational models and perspectives, also must acknowledge external forces beyond the control of any one person or group of institutional agents. Colleges are increasingly influenced by external agencies such as state legislatures, corporate and philanthropic foundations, accrediting bodies, and state and regional education commissions (Education Commission of the States, 1980). The interests of these constituencies further complicate a college environment characterized by competing values and preferences of faculty, professional staff, administrators, and students (Cohen & March, 1974; Baldridge et al., 1977).

Familiarity with certain organizational perspectives, the political model for example, permits one to acknowledge, if not explain, these complex relationships. Indeed, conventional models do explain certain aspects of college life reasonably well. Student affairs staff must know enough about both conventional and non-orthodox models to talk with colleagues in an informed manner. Understanding the theory in an academic sense and knowing its limitations in a practical sense are indispensable.

3. Theory is most informative when tested against experience. When theory doesn't explain what you observe, build your own theory.

Theory is, at best, an approximation of life, an attempt to illuminate the relationships between certain features of the world which, without the theory, may be overlooked or underemphasized. Theories about human development, campus environments, group processes, and organizational behavior provide different views of what takes place on a college campus. But theories tend to focus on relatively narrow aspects of human experience. By definition, a theory generally offers a detailed picture of certain features while overlooking others. Recall the humorous example of several blind men, each touching different parts of an elephant. Not one of them was able to guess the identity of the object because each had only limited knowledge drawn from his part of the beast.

Student affairs staff members must reflect on their experiences using different frameworks to determine if theoretical propositions are useful in describing and explaining their work. Theory-building seems like a very serious, erudite activity that only advanced scholars should attempt. We suggest that every student affairs professional become a practicing theorist and create "mini-theories" or propositions that link and explain certain events and actions in student affairs organizations but do not address others.

4. The student affairs division, and the institution, can be best understood by looking under, through, and beyond the formal organizational structures.

Organizational charts, line-staff designations, job descriptions, manuals delineating standard operating procedures, and the like make important statements about control, authority, and what is valued. In many ways, the formal organizational structure, represented by artifacts such as titles and reporting lines, is symbolic of the values and assumptions of the institution. However, the meaning and significance of these symbols may not be self-evident. That is, some investigation may be necessary to more fully understand why individuals hold certain titles or are assigned responsibility for certain units.

Similarly, written rules don't direct behavior; how people feel and what they believe are more powerful influences. In general, students and faculty do what is culturally desirable; manuals and codes of conduct typically reflect what the corporate body has agreed is appropriate.

5. Think up different ways to do things. Innovate.

No one best solution exists to most problems. Standard operating procedures (SOPs) are not necessarily a product of carefully reasoned, rigorously evaluated approaches. Many SOPs were put into place as stopgap measures and have evolved over time into their current institutionalized form. Further, often little data are available to suggest which programs work better than others. If these observations reflect the situation in one's institution, probably the time has come to experiment and try some different responses to the difficulties that are commonplace in most student affairs organizations; for example, eliminate resident assistant positions which allows residents to govern themselves (Schroeder et al., 1983). Trying out different approaches will force others to think more carefully about what they are doing and may help to identify policies and practices that are antithetical to what is desired.

6. Empowering leadership is everyone's responsibility.

Conventional models of organizing, with their preference for order and hierarchical structures, designate those at or near "the top" of an organizational chart as "leaders." Non-orthodox views suggest that good ideas and problem solving are not confined to certain institutional positions. Indeed, those often in the best position to develop creative responses to organizational problems are persons closest to the action, such as a resident assistant, not the chief student affairs officer who may know little about the context in which the problem is embedded or the subtleties that surround the issue(s).

Directives or admonitions, characteristic of a top-down administrative style, don't seem to work very well in most situations. *Leadership* is best thought of as "the process of persuasion and example by which an individual (or leadership team) induces a group to take action that is in accord with the leader's purposes or the shared purposes of all" (Gardner, 1986, p. 6). The confidence staff have in their leaders is related to the amount of confidence they have in themselves (Gardner, 1986). Greenleaf's (1977) conception of leader as servant is consistent with this view—others "freely respond only to [those] who are . . . proven and trusted servants" (p. 10). To be accepted by their followers, leaders must promote independent thinking, risk taking, and sharing intellectual and emotional responses (Gardner, 1986). Flexibility, creativity, trust, and empowerment replace conventional leader functions of control, delegation of authority, and evaluation.

Thus, leaders must encourage staff to dream, to experiment without fear of failure and punishment, and to challenge institutional norms with impunity, a tactic consistent with action learning (Morgan & Ramirez, 1983). To avoid organizational stagnation, leaders must be open to testing limits, taking risks, admitting failure, and embracing error

(Michael, 1985), behaviors which reflect a healthy disdain for error detection and correction (Argyris & Schon, 1978).

CONCLUSION

College life is many things: interesting, complicated, routinized, frustrating, challenging, lively, boring, manageable, stimulating, frenetic, and contemplative among others. The organizational theory literature offers considerable variety from which to choose to interpret the cacophony of events and actions in a college that results in such a wide variety of emotional and intellectual stimuli.

No "one best organizational model" or perspective exists. Using different developmental theories in concert provide a richer understanding of students' growth and development during college. Similarly, different organizational theories generate different insights into various aspects of college administration. Theory-building in this area is not static. The popularity and utility of various perspectives depends to a large degree on the assumptions of the people who are using theory to understand their organization. For this reason, student affairs staff members must become familiar with more than one model or perspective if they are to better understand and more deeply appreciate the mysteries of organizational life in an institution of higher education. Only then will one be able to take advantage of the many opportunities available in the college environment which can be used to encourage the development of students.

REFERENCES

American Council on Education. (1937). The student personnel point of view. *American Council on Education Studies* (series 1, Vol. 1, No. 3). Washington, DC: Author.

Argyris, C. (1964). *Integrating the individual and the organization.* New York: Wiley.

Argyris, C., & Schon, D.A. (1978). *Organizational learning: A theory of action perspective.* Reading, MA: Addison-Wesley.

Baldridge, J.V., Curtis, D.V., Ecker, G.P., & Riley, G.L. (1977). Alternative models of governance in higher education. In R. Birnbaum (Ed.) (1986), *ASHE reader on organization and governance in higher education* (rev. ed.) (pp. 11-27). Lexington, MA: Ginn.

Barnard, C.I. (1937). *The functions of the executive.* Cambridge, MA: Harvard University Press.

Bolton, C.D., & Kammeyer, K.C.W. (1972). Campus cultures, role orientations, and social types. In K. Feldman (Ed.), *College and student: Selected readings in the social psychology of higher education* (pp. 377-92). New York: Pergamon.

Bredeson, P.V. (1987). *Languages of leadership: Metaphor making in educational administration.* Paper presented at the University Council for Educational Administration, Charlottesville, VA.

Broom, L., & Selznick, P. (1973). *Sociology: A text with adapted readings.* New York: Harper and Row.

Capra, F. (1983). *The turning point: Science, society, and the rising culture.* New York: Basic Books.

Clark, B.R., & Trow, M. (1966). The organizational context. In T. Newcomb and E. Wilson (Eds.), *College peer groups: Problems and prospects for research* (pp. 17-70). Chicago: Aldine.

Clark, D.L. (1985). Emerging paradigms in organizational theory and research. In Y. Lincoln (Ed.), *Organizational theory and inquiry: The paradigm revolution* (pp. 43-78). Beverly Hills, CA: Sage.

Clark, D.L., Astuto, T.A., & Kuh, G.D. (1986). Strength of coupling in the organization and operation of colleges and universities. In G. Johnston & C. Yeakey (Eds.), *Research and thought in educational administration* (pp. 69-87). Lanham, MD: University Press of America.

Cohen, M., & March, J.G. (1974). *Leadership and ambiguity: The American college presidency.* New York: McGraw-Hill.

Deal, T.E., & Kennedy, A.A. (1982). *Corporate cultures: The rites and rituals of corporate life.* Reading, MA: Addison-Wesley.

Education Commission of the States (1980). *Challenge: Coordination and governance in the '80s* (Report No. 134). Denver: Author.

Ferguson, M. (1980). *The Aquarian conspiracy: Personal and social transformation in the 1980's.* Boston: Houghton Mifflin.

Filley, A.C., House, R.J., & Kerr, S. (1976). *Managerial process and organizational behavior* (2nd ed.). Glenview, IL: Scott, Foresman.

Gardner, J.W. (1986). The heart of the matter: Leader-constituent interaction. *Leadership Papers No. 3.* Washington, DC: Independent Sector.

Georgiou, P. (1973). The goal paradigm and notes toward a counter paradigm. *Administrative Science Quarterly, 18,* 291-310.

Getzels, J.W., & Guba, E.G. (1957). Social behavior and the administrative process. *School Review. 65,* 423-41.

Gleick, J. (1987). *Chaos: Making a new science.* New York: Viking.

Greenleaf, R.K. (1977). *The servant as leader.* Peterborough, NH: Center for Applied Sciences.

Hall, H.T. (1976). *The hidden dimension.* Garden City, NY: Anchor Books.

Hedberg, B., Nystrom, P., & Starbuck, W. (1976). Camping on seesaws: Prescriptions for a self-designing organization. *Administrative Science Quarterly, 21,* 41-65.

Hossler, D., Carnaghi, J., Love, P., Schmit, J., & Whitt, E. (1988). *An investigation of the knowledge claims supporting goal-based planning and organizational culture as keys to excellence in educational organizations.* Final Report, Proffitt Research Grant, School of Education, Indiana University.

Kilmann, R.H., Saxton, M.J., Serpa, R., & Associates. (1986). *Gaining control of the corporate culture.* San Francisco: Jossey-Bass.

Kuh, G.D. (1983). Tactics for understanding and improving student affairs organizations. In G.D. Kuh (Ed.), *Understanding student affairs organizations* (pp. 67-78). New Directions for Student Services (No. 23). San Francisco: Jossey-Bass.

Kuh, G.D. (1984). Suggestions for remaining sane in institutions that don't work the way they're supposed to. *NASPA Journal, 21,* 55-61.

Kuh, G.D. (1985). What is extraordinary about ordinary student affairs organizations? *NASPA Journal, 23* (2), 31-43.

Kuh, G.D., & Whitt, E.J. (1988). *The invisible tapestry: Culture in American colleges and universities.* ASHE-ERIC Higher Education Report, No. 1. Washington, D.C.: Association for the Study of Higher Education.

Kuh, G.D., Whitt, E.J., & Shedd, J.D. (1987). *Student affairs, 2001: A paradigmatic odyssey.* Alexandria, VA.: American College Personnel Association Media.

Kuhn, T.S. (1970). *The structure of scientific revolutions (2nd ed.).* Chicago: University of Chicago Press.

Langer, S.K. (1953). *Feeling and form.* New York: Scribner and Sons.

Lincoln, Y.S. (1985). Introduction. In Y.S. Lincoln (Ed.). *Organizational theory and inquiry: The paradigm revolution* (pp. 29-40). Beverly Hills, CA: Sage.

Masland, A.T. (1985). Organizational culture in the study of higher education. *Review of Higher Education, 8,* 157-68.

McGregor, D. (1960). *The human side of enterprise.* New York: McGraw-Hill.

McKibbin, S. (1981). Traditional organizational theory in educational administration. In D.L. Clark, S. McKibbin, & Malkas, M. (Eds.), *Alternative perspectives for viewing educational organizations* (pp. 1-14). San Francisco: Far West Laboratory for Educational Research and Development.

Michael, D.N. (1985). The new competence: Management skills for the future. In R. Davis (Ed.), *Leadership and institutional renewal (pp. 91-104).* New Directions for Higher Education (No. 49). San Francisco: Jossey-Bass.

Millett, J. (1962). *The academic community.* New York: McGraw-Hill.

Morgan, G. (1986). *Images of organization.* Beverly Hills, CA: Sage.

Morgan, G., & Ramirez, R. (1983). Action learning: A holographic metaphor for guiding social change. *Human Relations, 37,* 1-28.

National Association of Student Personnel Administrators (1987). *A perspective on student affairs.* Iowa City: NASPA.

Owens, R.G. (1981). *Organizational behavior in education* (2nd ed.). Englewood Cliffs, NJ: Prentice-Hall.

Perrow, C. (1972). *Complex organizations: A critical essay.* Glenview, IL: Scott, Foresman.

Pfeffer, J. (1982). *Organizations and organizational theory.* Boston: Pitman.

Ruscio, K.P. (1987). Many sectors, many professions. In B.R. Clark (Ed.), *The academic profession* (pp. 331-68). Berkeley, CA: University of California Press.

Schein, E.H. (1985). *Organizational culture and leadership.* San Francisco: Jossey-Bass.

Schroeder, C.C., Nicholls, G.E., & Kuh, G.D. (1983). Exploring the rain forest: Testing assumptions and taking risks. In G.D. Kuh (Ed.), *Understanding student affairs organizations (pp. 51-65).* New Directions for Student Services, No. 23. San Francisco: Jossey-Bass.

Schwartz, P., & Ogilvy, J. (1979). *The emergent paradigm: Changing patterns of thought and belief.* Menlo Park, CA: SRI International Analytical Report No. 7. Values and Lifestyles Program.

Sergiovanni, T.J. (1984). Leadership as cultural expression. In T. Sergiovanni & J. Corbally (Eds.), *Leadership and organizational culture: New perspectives on administrative theory and practice* (pp. 105-14). Urbana: University of Illinois Press.

Simon, H. (1957). *Models of man.* New York: Wiley.

Taylor, F.W. (1911). *The principles of scientific management.* New York: W.W. Norton.

Tierney, W.G. (1985). *The cultural context of time management in higher education.* Boulder, CO: National Center for Higher Education Management Systems.

Tierney, W.G. (1988). *The web of leadership: The presidency in higher education.* Greenwich, CT: JAI Press, Inc.

Van Maanen, J. (1984). Doing new things in old ways: The chains of socialization. In J. Bess (Ed.), *College and university organization: Insights from the behavioral sciences* (pp. 211-47). New York: New York University Press.

Van Maanen, J., & Barley, S.R. (1984). Occupational communities: Culture and control in organizations. *Research in Organizational Behavior, 6,* 287-365.

Walberg, H.J., Strykowski, B.F., Rovai, E., & Hung, S.S. (1984). Exceptional performance. *Review of Educational Research, 54,* 87-112.

Weber, M. (1978). *Economy and society: An outline of interpretive sociology, Vol 1* (Translated). In G. Roth and C. Wittich (Eds.). Berkeley: University of California Press.

Weick, K. (1976). Educational organizations as loosely coupled systems. *Administrative Science Quarterly, 21,* 1-19.

Weick, K. (1979). *The social psychology of organizing* (2nd ed.). Reading. MA: Addison-Wesley.

Weick, K. (1982). Administering education in loosely coupled schools. *Phi Delta Kappan, 62,* 673-76.

Weick, K.E. (1985). Sources of order in underorganized systems: Themes in recent organizational theory. In Y.S. Lincoln (Ed.), *Organizational theory and inquiry: The paradigm revolution* (pp. 106-36). Beverly Hills, CA: Sage.

SUGGESTED READINGS

Bess, J. (Ed.). (1984). *College and university organization: Insights from the behavioral sciences.* New York: New York University Press.

Birnbaum, R. (Ed.). (1984). *ASHE reader on organization and governance in higher education* (rev. ed.). Lexington, MA: Ginn.

Kuh, G.D. (Ed.). (1983). *Understanding student affairs organizations*. New Directions for Student Services (No. 23). San Francisco: Jossey-Bass.

Kuh, G.D., Whitt, E.J. & Shedd, J.D. (1987). *Student affairs, 2001: A paradigmatic odyssey*. Alexandria, VA: American College Personnel Association Media.

Lincoln, Y.S. (Ed.). *Organizational theory and inquiry: The paradigm revolution*. Beverly Hills, CA: Sage.

Masland, A.T. (1985). Organizational culture in the study of higher education. *Review of Higher Education, 8,* 157-168.

Morgan, G. (1986). *Images of organization*. Beverly Hills, CA: Sage.

Weick, K.E. (1979). *The social psychology of organizing (2nd ed.)*. Reading, MA: Addison-Wesley.

Robert K. Conyne, Ph.D., is Professor and Head of the School Psychology and Counseling Department at the University of Cincinnati. He received his bachelor's degree from Syracuse University and his Master's and Doctoral Degrees from Purdue University.

Prior to assuming his present administrative responsibilities at UC, he served for six years as Associate Vice Provost for Student Life, where he was responsible for a broad range of developmental and preventive programs and services. In addition, he worked for several years previously at Illinois State University, where he held a joint appointment in the Student Counseling Center and in Counselor Education.

His research and writing emphasizes group work and primary prevention. His books include *Environmental Assessment and Design* (with Clack, 1981, Praeger), *The Group Workers' Handbook* (1985, Thomas), *Primary Preventive Counseling* (1987, Accelerated Development), and *Group Work: Developing People and Communities* (in press, Sage).

Dr. Conyne maintains a small private practice in Cincinnati and consults with a number of human service and educational organizations, including Student Affairs Divisions.

Chapter **3**

ORGANIZATION DEVELOPMENT: A BROAD NET INTERVENTION FOR STUDENT AFFAIRS

Robert K. Conyne

The purpose of this chapter is twofold: *to provide the reader with a basic framework for conceptualizing organization development (OD) and to explore potential uses of OD for student affairs administrators in higher education.* The first goal is addressed by examining important conceptual and practical dimensions in OD, such as definitions, the open-system model, and intervention typologies. Application of OD strategies by student affairs administrators is perhaps of more interest to readers of this volume. Despite recent contributions (e.g., Borland, 1980; Caple, 1987; Creamer & Creamer, 1986, 1988), the current state of the art still requires that a tentative, if not primarily heuristic, treatment be given this topic. The second section of this chapter contains general directions for applying OD within higher education.

DEFINING ORGANIZATION DEVELOPMENT

Organization development has been defined by many theorists in a variety of ways. French, Bell, and Zawacki

(1978) have organized much of the material according to author, using the following critical components to analyze the definitions: (1) nature and scope of the effort, (2) nature of activities/interventions, (3) targets of intervention/activities, (4) knowledge base, and (5) desired goals, outcomes, or end states of organization development effort. Table 3.1 presents a definitional summary that results from this scheme.

What does all this mean? Very simply, OD consists of a broad net of applied behavioral science techniques. Following careful diagnosis, any of these techniques might be used in a planned process for change to benefit both the organization and its members.

OPEN-SYSTEM:
A FRAMEWORK FOR OD

Potential uses to which organization development approaches can be put are dependent, in part, on the organizational model adopted. That is, OD needs to be implemented within an appropriate conceptual (as well as situational) context. It is important to identify what models of organizations are well suited for conducting OD.

The open-system model (Katz & Kahn, 1978) has been shown to be especially useful for conceptualizing about organizations (Huse, 1980; Seiler, 1967), and it has proven to be of heuristic value in generating appropriate organizational assessments (Kast & Rosenzweig, 1970; Weisbord, 1978), and organizational design interventions (Huse & Bowditch, 1973; Weisbord, 1978). Basically, an organization viewed from the open-system model of Katz and Kahn (1978) is comprised of five mutually influencing dimensions: (1) *input*, or the importation of energy (e.g., personnel, money, equipment, etc.), (2) *throughput*, or the transformation process (e.g., information flow, purposes, leadership, etc.) used by the organization to convert input into products, (3) *external environment*, the influence exerted on the organization from outside its boundaries (e.g., legislation, economic conditions, community demands, etc.), (4) *output*, or the products (e.g., courses by an academic department, counseling for a counseling center) produced by the organization and exported to the

(Continued on page 76)

Table 3.1

Standard Definition of Organization Development Summarized According to Authors and Elements of OD Process

Author	Focus of Effort	Elements of OD Process		
		Activities/Interventions	Targets	Desired Goals
Beckhard	Planned, organization-wide, managed from top.	"Organizational Process" planned interventions	Total organizations processes	Improved organization, effects.
Bennis	Response to change using complex educational strategy	Change-Oriented educational strategy	Beliefs, attitudes, values, and structures of organizations	Increased capacity to adapt to change, new technologies markets, and challenges.
French & Bell	A long-range effort	Change agent is used to help design a more effective, collaborative management of organizational culture	Culture of organization, formal work teams; organizational problem solving and renewal processes	Increase organize problem solving renewal processes
Lawrence & Lorsch	A series of sequential stages	Educational, structural, transactional change strategies	Organization-Environment interface	Better fit between organization and environment and organization and its members.
Schmuck & Miles	A planned and sustained effort	Reflexive, Self-analytic methods are used to apply behavioral science for system improvement.	Total Organization	System improvement

Note: Based on and modified from French, Bell, and Zawacki, 1978, p. 8.

environment, and (5) *feedback,* or information that is made available to the organization to keep it on course.

The open-system concept underscores the position that an organization and its external environment are mutually permeable (Emery & Trist, 1960). That is, they are continually interdependent and, therefore, are always subject to turbulence and change arising from the organization-environment interface, as well as from interfaces occurring within the organization itself—among groups, between the employee and the organization, and between employees (Lawrence & Lorsch, 1969). By contrast, a misplaced reliance on a closed system perspective leads, as Katz and Kahn (1978) have indicated, to a disregard for the nature of organizational interdependency with its environment and to excessive concern with internal functioning. Such imbalanced attention threatens organizational survival.

The open-system model for understanding how an organization functions also is useful for understanding OD. It provides a general, systemic framework that comfortably accommodates qualities of dynamism and interdependence that are closely associated with OD interventions. Further, the open-system framework provides such flexibility and coherence that concrete organizational models have been generated from it. One illustrative model is in Figure 3.1, "a six-box model" of Weisbord (1978).

The six boxes in Weisbord's (1978) organizational assessment model refer to six organizational processes in the throughput dimension of the open-system model. These six organizational processes are involved in transferring inputs, or imported energy and resources (such as ideas and money), into outputs (such as human relations workshops or concerts); as well, these six processes are involved in negotiating continual pushes and pulls of the external environment, such as a sudden change in a college's administrative direction, and incorporating these outcomes into the transformation process.

Weisbord (1978) labeled the six processes as follows:

Purposes: What is the organization's mission?

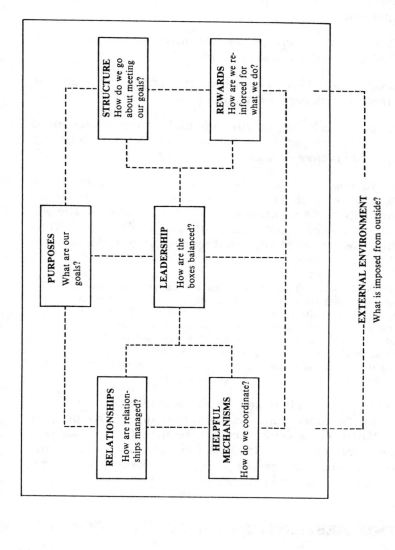

Figure 3.1. Organizational assessment Model: Six organizational processes (dimensions) of the open system model.

Note: Based on and modified from M. Weisbord, 1978.

Structure: How is the organization assembled to perform necessary tasks?

Relationships: How effectively do employees, work groups, and employees and their technologies (equipment) interrelate?

Rewards: Are there proper incentives and reinforcement for doing what needs to be done?

Leadership: How well does the leader keep all the processes balanced and maintained?

Helpful mechanisms: Are adequate technologies used (e.g., policies, agendas, planning, budgeting, socializing space) to promote work and staff needs?

Weisbord suggested that use of six boxes in organizational diagnosis can be analogous to use of a radar screen by air traffic controllers. Appearance of a blip in any of the six boxes indicates a potential organizational problem area. Thus visualizing the six interconnected boxes as a radar screen, he stated,

> "Process" issues show up as blips in one or more boxes, blocking work on important tasks. Air controllers use radar to manage relationships among aircraft—height, speed, distance apart—and to avoid heavy weather. Similarly, a blip in any one box cannot be managed independently of its relationship to the other boxes. However, six potential starting places give you several alternatives when choosing an improvement strategy. (Weisbord, 1978, p. 8)

Once blips are identified in an organization's internal and/or external functioning, inauguration of an OD program may be in order. Or, it could very well be that the organizational diagnosis itself marked the inception of such a program. Regardless, a broad net of OD intervention strategies, evolving directly from the open-system model, is available for use.

ACTION RESEARCH AS A CHANGE PROCESS

Organization development interventions, to be discussed in detail in a later section of this chapter, are undertaken within a coherent change framework. That is, while the nature of the interventions themselves may vary considerably (e.g., a physical structure change in office locations versus a consultation about staff communication patterns), they tend to be lodged within a change process wherein the internal structure is guided by a series of interlocking steps.

This last phrase, "guided by a common series of interlocking steps," suggests that change can be managed. In fact, as has been implied, OD is a long-term, planned, and sustained effort that is centered on an overall strategy. As traditionally understood, OD is a form of managed change (Huse, 1980), as compared with the incessant, inevitable, uncontrolled change that occurs in and around organizations as a natural function of life itself. However, since this seminal work, evolving conceptions of OD question the assumption of managed change. For instance, Faucheux, Amado, and Laurent (1982), in their extensive review of OD, emphasized the essential nature of organizational context in the change process. That is, they suggested that organizational change—in most instances— occurs due to alterations in the contexts and conditions that organizations create for themselves out of their own natural interaction. Beer and Walton (1987), in a more recent but equally comprehensive review of OD, reinforced and extended this notion. They concluded that organizational change occurs, not from slavishly following some grand master plan, but from the continual readjustment of direction and goals. They suggested that "external events and crises precipitate changes far more than planned events" (p.357). Therefore, the ability to capitalize on unplanned, or naturally occurring events, is being viewed increasingly as crucial to successful organization development efforts.

Nonetheless, important managed-change approaches exist for use in organization development activities. Among them are the intervention theory and method of Argyris (1970); the linkage model of Havelock (1969); the research, development, and diffusion model of Clark and Guba (1965); the utilization-focused evaluation approach of Patton (1978); and, perhaps especially, the planned-change model of Lippitt, Watson, and Westley (1958). However, the action-research model (Collier, 1945; Corey, 1953; Frohman, Sashkin, & Kavanagh, 1978;

Huse, 1980; Lewin, 1946) to managed change in organization development will be given attention. Action research is selected because assumptions underlying its use are highly compatible with those that support OD. Both sets of assumptions endorse (1) a planned, systematic approach to change arising from collaboration between change agent and client system, (2) an emphasis on solving current organization problems through specific attention to process issues, and (3) client system members gaining the working knowledge and skills necessary to use and adapt an OD innovation in the future.

Furthermore, action research offers a model that does not seek "to answer little questions precisely" (Beer & Walton, 1987, p.362). Rather, action research allows for the study of broader longitudinal issues amid the creation of usable knowledge. This emphasis on longitudinal investigation, with concomitant attention given to the long-range study of organizational contexts, is indicative of the latest trends in OD.

Beyond these direct compatibility areas between OD and action research, the action-research model offers substantially attractive evaluation and research capacities that are not shared by all other change models. Action and research occur simultaneously through a project. Thus, the managed-change process is couched within an evaluation context, with evaluative feedback used planfully to guide and modify actions. Further, and of particular note, a successful action research project generates from its research activity new knowledge that addresses broader concerns than the specific interests of the client system itself (such as intervention effects, client system amenability to OD, or general process issues). If worthwhile, these research findings can be disseminated for the scientific and professional community at large, thus adding to the reservoir of knowledge in the public domain.

Action research as a generic change process within OD has been described previously as an OD form (Frohman, Sashkin, & Kavanagh, 1978). According to them, action-research OD involves data collected together by an OD practitioner and a client. Working collaboratively, they obtain information enabling them jointly to conceive and conduct action plans in the client system, evaluate the effects of these plans, and implement further action plans.

Frohman, Sashkin, and Kavanagh (1978) discussed eight phases of action-research OD that result from the product of action research. More subtly, perhaps, these phases can be seen as extending to OD expanded variations of Lewin's (1946) three-phases social system change method (unfreezing, moving, refreezing) and of Lippitt, Watson, and Westley's (1958) planned-change approach (developing a need for a change, establishing a change relationship, working toward change, generalizing and stabilizing change, and achieving a terminal relationship).

The eight phases of action-research organization development are summarized briefly in the next eight headings along with a short, continuing example. When considering these phases, one should heed the counsel of Beer and Walton (1987) that change does not really occur in a linear, lock-step fashion, but it is cyclical and incremental. Still, these eight phases are generally useful to note.

Scouting

A research function used by the OD practitioner to decide whether to enter an organization is called scouting. For instance, Dr. Brown, the OD consultant from the Counseling Department, evaluates information made available to her about the general quality of student life at the University and the role of the Student Life Department in its creation to determine if she should seek to become involved with the Student Life Department.

Entry

Entrance into the organization is an action function used by the OD practitioner to establish a collaborative working relationship with members of the client system. Steps to be conducted include initial problem identification and determining procedures for data collection and feedback. Once Dr. Brown decides tentatively to proceed, she begins talking with the Student Life Director and staff about existing needs, how best to acquire assessment information, and if working together might be suitable.

Data Collection

A *research* function in which suitable data collection methods are selected and/or developed, followed by data collection is the next step. Dr. Brown may interview selected staff and students, examine archival sources, observe relevant groups in action, or conduct a survey.

Data Feedback

Data feedback is an *action* function in which data are shared with the client system members through any number of means, such as a group meeting. Data gathered are organized by the consultant and communicated personally to Student Life staff members for their discussion. In this case, a series of total staff group meetings was held.

Diagnosis

Diagnosis is a *research* function clearly illustrated by the collaboration between OD practitioner and client system members. The intent is to develop a mutually derived understanding of the state of the organization, its problems, and its strengths. Dr. Brown works closely with staff members, helping them to develop their own understanding of the information and to draw their own conclusions. For instance, they may identify a primary problem of low staff morale resulting from a lack of staff development activities and that this deficit negatively affects their capacity to be consistent advocates for enhanced student life on campus.

Action Planning

As the name implies, action planning is an action function in which the OD practitioner assists the client to create specific action plans, based on results obtained through the preceding phases. This includes deciding what will be done, by whom, when, and how evaluation will be accomplished. The Student Life staff may work with Dr. Brown to design a staff development program emphasizing a variety of skill training components, such as in working with groups, and how these skills could be used in student life programming.

Action Implementation

Action implementation is an *action* function that implements the conceived plan through a wide range of OD interventions that relate directly to the current situation. In this example, the detailed plan for a staff skill training program is carried out by colleagues of Dr. Brown, under her immediate supervision, with specific attention to programmatic applications.

Evaluation

Evaluation is a *research* function designed to determine the effects and effectiveness of the action implementation, resulting (1) in recycling to a previous phase and continued change efforts, or (2) in terminating the project. The staff training program in this example is evaluated by the staff at several points. Their mid-program evaluation requested greater emphasis on task, as compared with human relations groups, and the remainder of the program was restructured successfully.

Action-research OD serves to articulate the generic action research mode of change found in many organization development models. Moreover, action research represents a turning point for OD research (Beer & Walton, 1987) through its incorporation of double-loop, self-corrective learning (Argyris, Putnam, & Smith, 1987).

CLASSIFYING AND USING OD INTERVENTIONS

According to French, Bell, and Zawacki (1978), the term "OD interventions" refers to the range of planned, sequential activities in which clients and consultants alike participate during an organization development program. They observed that these are mostly diagnostic and problem-solving activities that ordinarily would occur with the assistance of an external

OD practitioner, and that the client system adopts and integrates many of the activities as a successful OD process evolves.

A substantial number of OD interventions are available for use. Important ones include: team building (Reilly & Jones, 1974), process consultation (Schein, 1969), survey feedback (Hausser, Pecorella, & Wissler, 1977), grid OD (Blake & Mouton, 1976), life planning (Kirn & Kirn, 1978), T-groups (Bradford, Gibb, & Benne, 1964), and physical setting change (Steele, 1973). Likewise, a variety of OD classification schemata have been developed to assist in bringing increased order to all of this diversity. French and Bell (1973), French, Bell, and Zawacki (1978), and Huse (1980) are among those who have offered summaries of these several schemata. Four of these classification approaches are examined briefly in this chapter.

Organization-Environment Interface

Lawrence and Lorsch (1969) based their schema on diagnosed mismatches that are revealed in the transactions of an organization with its external environment. Interventions are selected based on nature and size of the identified mismatch between actual and desired states. These interventions may include a range of structural and procedural changes, such as altering formal communication and control procedures, changing division of labor and authority system, or changing selection criteria. A variety of educational designs have been employed, also, including sensitivity and human relations training and the case study method of instruction.

As stated earlier, tremendous attention in OD today is being placed on understanding—and taking advantage of— the naturally occurring environmental contexts that surround an organization. The capacity for OD consultants, as well as organizational managers, to harness these forces in planful ways is being increasingly viewed as essential to productive OD efforts (Beer & Walton, 1987).

Caple's (1987) application of general systems theory to student development ("self-organization theory") reflects this gathering emphasis. In brief, the self-organization perspective holds that student affairs organizations need to evolve within the context of disequilibrium and that organizational planning and development must creatively seek and include the processes associated with uncertaintly and turbulence.

Depth of Intervention

Harrison (1970) differentiated OD interventions according to the depth of emotional involvement tapped. The deeper the intervention, the greater the potential positive or negative impact on individuals. He has suggested that two criteria be used for determining the appropriate depth of any OD intervention. The first consideration is that the intervention be no deeper than is needed to produce enduring solutions to the presenting problems. The second consideration is that the intervention depth should be consistent with the energy and resources that the client can commit to problem solving and change. Harrison's analysis indicated that OD interventions become successively deeper as they move from systemwide approaches such as survey feedback, to *individual/organizational interfaces* (e.g., job design), to *concern with personal work style* such as team building, to the deepest level, *intrapersonal analysis and relationships* (e.g., encounter groups).

Individual-group and Task-process

French and Bell (1973) have classified OD interventions based on how much they placed relative emphasis on individual versus group phenomena, such as learning, insight, skill building, and on task or process issues, where task represents what is being done (skills are being developed, jobs are being redesigned) and process represents how these events are occurring (through training, consultation, T-groups, education, etc.). OD interventions are classified, with natural overlap, into quadrants produced by these dimensions: *individual-task* (e.g., career planning), *group-task* (e.g., intergroup activities), *individual-process* (e.g., coaching), and *group-process* (e.g., process consultation). Indeed, attention to the mutual relationship between *tasks* and *people* ("Sociotechnical" approach) is of great importance in contemporary OD (Faucheux et al., 1982).

Target Groups

French and Bell (1973) offered a classification schema of OD interventions that is based on the size and complexity of the target group. That is, interdependencies and complexity increase as OD interventions are targeted progressively at *individuals*, through coaching, or role analysis, etc., to *dyads/ triads* (e.g., interviews, third-party peacemaking), to *teams and groups* (e.g., team building, process consultation, etc.), to *intergroup relations* (e.g., organizational mirroring, subgrouping), and to the *total organization*, through survey feedback, strategic planning, etc. As with the previously described classification schema, interventions in this system can overlap different target levels depending on the situation. Although this may be confusing, it nevertheless reflects the real life of uses to various interventions.

Consultant vs. Manager in OD

OD has been conceptualized and practiced as a specialized intervention undertaken by an internal or external organization consultant. Recent literature (Beer & Walton, 1987; Creamer & Creamer, 1986, 1988, Chapter 5 of this volume) appears to indicate that a revision is occurring. Increased emphasis is being placed on the organizational manger's role in OD. Creamer and Creamer's model for student affairs, "Probability of Adoption of Change" (1986, 1988 & Chapter 5 of this volume), attests to the important function of student affairs "leaders" (managers) and "champions" (project heads) in the creation of successful organizational change. The work of Bennis and Nanus (1985) and Kanter (1983) supported the idea that the leadership of managers is central to producing and sustaining substantial organizational change. Themes of "transformation" and "empowerment" run through these conceptions of organizational leadership.

SELECTED OD INTERVENTIONS

Four representative and frequently used OD interventions are presented here because they are particularly well suited for use by student affairs administrators. For instance, when structure, relationships, rewards, leadership, and helpful mechanisms) these four interventions could be applied to seek improvement in any of those areas.

Two implications emerge. First, OD practice may become more centrally incorporated and implemented by organizational managers as they conduct their daily work. Second, OD specialists may need to move away from pre-programmed, structured OD interventions toward adoption of the perspective of the manager if they expect to obtain contracts and to facilitate meaningful change. Among other features, this managerial perspective includes developing interventions that are fully consistent with the full, dynamic context being faced by the organization (Beer & Walton, 1987).

However, this does not mean that all interventions can be expected to be equally effective in all situations. Team building, for instance, is particularly well designed for relationship and less so for structural interventions. In fact, as Beer and Walton (1987) have observed, "Rather than cataloging the technology of organization change, we need to catalog how external forces create the opportunities for change" (p. 362). More needs to be developed about what alternative change strategies might be sensitive to an organization's particular stage of development. That is, to develop a contingency theory of organizational change may be more important than to concentrate on OD techniques that are thought to be generally applicable.

Recognizing that need, it is still vital to recognize that a variety of OD interventions are available. The objective of this section is to provide a sense of what OD interventions are like. It is meant *to describe their nature rather than to prescribe when they should be used.*

Sensing Interview

Jones (1973) has labeled a certain form of face-to-face diagnostic OD interviewing as the "sensing interview." This interview has three main purposes. (1) The interview process allows for the generation of subjective, intuitive data that is a useful expansion of objective survey data. (2) The sensing interview allows the opportunity for OD consultants to clarify objective data generated by checking consultant perceptions with those of the client group. (3) The personal, involving format of the sensing interview encourages interviewees to increase their ownership in the diagnosis, with the potential for their greater ownership of the complete OD program itself.

The sensing interview can nonthreateningly explore many content areas. Those proposed by Weisbord (1978) represent appropriate examples. Argyris (1970) has offered another list of content areas, including roles, goals, the job itself, the organization, interpersonal relations, interpersonal perceptions, the work team, necessary changes, and the here-and-now of the interviewee. The "nonthreatening exploration," sensing interview process, includes important helping techniques such as appropriate probing and leading through open-ended questions, general and follow-up leads, demonstration of interviewer understanding through restatement, paraphrasing, reflection, and summarization, and communication of interviewer support through sharing, consoling, and expressed caring. An appropriate blending of content and process in a sensing interview can lead to a collaborative effort to produce the sum of the information that is needed to produce internal change in the system.

Sensing interviews are highly compatible with human relations emphasis common to many student affairs programs. Therefore, their potential as an organizational assessment method for student affairs is high. Sensing interviews are commonly used by OD practitioners not only to gather information needed, but also to enrich the consultative relationship.

Survey Feedback

Bowers and Franklin (1974) and Hausser, Pecorella, and Wissler (1977) considered survey feedback to be a comparatively complex guidance method that uses the questionnaire survey to improve the change process in a social organization by making it more complete, rational, and sufficient. As a method, survey feedback is sometimes set in the broader paradigm of "survey-guided development." In addition to survey feedback, the more inclusive procedure includes the following steps:

- goal setting,
- survey administration to organizational members,
- diagnosis of present organizational functioning,
- feeding back survey data to work groups that generated data,
- planning and implementing action steps at the work-group level,
- feedback of survey data about the entire organization to its leaders,
- planning and implementing action steps at the organizational level, and
- re-administration of the survey.

Thus, both assessment and action phases overlap and together constitute survey-guided development (Hausser, Pecorella, & Wissler, 1977). Embedding survey feedback in this sequential and cyclical process clearly extends it far beyond "a sheet of tabulated data" (Bowers & Franklin, 1974, p. 1) to become an important element in an ongoing change process. While survey feedback has been used with some frequency by OD practitioners in student affairs, it has less often been successfully implanted within an ongoing change process. All too commonly, the OD expert gathers survey information, submits a report, and leaves. This kind of approach is contrary to the intervention discussed, which is quite closely related to OD action research. It represents a direction of choice for OD work in student affairs.

Team Building

Many organization development writers regard team-building activities as the most important single class of OD interventions. According to Reilly and Jones (1974), team building aims at improving the problem-solving ability among team (work group) members by providing means for working through task and interpersonal issues that may impede a team's functioning. Beckhard (1967) has identified four general purposes for team building, and he further suggested that one purpose should be designated as primary for a given project in order to avoid a misuse of energy. These team building purposes are to (1) establish goals and/or priorities, (2) analyze or assign the way work is conducted, (3) examine how a group works, and (4) explain relationships among workers.

Reilly and Jones (1974) identified the purposes for team building as being to: (1) promote a better understanding of each member's role in the work group, (2) develop a better understanding of the team's overall role in the total functioning of the organization, (3) increase communication among team members about issues affecting group efficiency, (4) enhance group member support, (5) increase group process understanding, (6) find effective ways of handling task and interpersonal problems that the team faces, (7) become more able to use conflict constructively, (8) promote collaborative team functioning over a competitive style, (9) increase the group's ability to work effectively with other groups in the organization, and (10) enhance interdependence among group members.

The OD consultant's role in team-building activities is that of "process facilitator." In this intervention, the consultant's responsibility is to develop the process awareness (Reilly & Jones, 1974) team members need in order to realistically assess both task accomplishments and group maintenance. Illustrations of process interventions in task accomplishment include helping a group convert an issue to a problem statement, or suggesting to the group that members evaluate their functioning during a designated work time. Examples of process interventions in group maintenance include reinforcing positive member behaviors like gatekeeping, and encouraging the giving and receiving of feedback.

Attention to process issues is given considerable importance in team building. This intervention has been used frequently in student affairs. For instance, team building activities are offered on many campuses to student organizations to develop member skills in planning tasks, leading meetings, working together, and communicating with others in the group. Rarely is team building in student affairs a part of a concerted, long-range, planned OD effort however.

Process Consultation

Schein (1969) has written the basic treatise on process consultation and its role in OD. Process consultation is "a set of activities on the part of the consultant which help the client to perceive, understand, and act upon process events which occur in the client's environment" (Schein, 1969, p. 9). As French and Bell (1973) have stressed, process consultation nearly exclusively emphasizes the diagnosis and management of personal, interpersonal, and group processes. Schein (1969) has identified the human processes that are most critical for effective organizational performance as: (1) communication (e.g., who talks to whom?); (2) member roles and functions in groups (e.g., initiator, harmonizer); (3) group problem solving and decision making; (4) group norms and growth (e.g., conflict is to be avoided at all costs); (5) leadership and authority (e.g., democratic vs. autocratic); and (6) intergroup cooperation and competition.

As in team building, process consultation is used to increase awareness of human processes, the consequences of these processes, and how they might be changed. A critical difference between the two OD interventions is found in their respective scopes. Where team building is restricted to a work team focus, process consultation takes a total organizational perspective and occurs within the stages of a general consultative model that includes (1) establish contact, (2) define work relationships, (3) select a setting and method of work, (4) gather process data, (5) intervene, (6) evaluate, and (7) disengage. Process consultation is, then, a complete consultation program that is undertaken to improve the human processes throughout an organization. Team building, for instance, could become a part of process consultation at the intervention stage, or it could stand alone.

A range of process consultation interventions is available for use. These interventions have been organized by Schein (1969) into four categories.

Agenda Setting Interventions. Procedures are used to generate agenda for potential later action, such as in process-analysis periods at the end of every work meeting.

Feedback of Data Generated. Feedback can be given by consultants during process analysis, regular work time, and/ or to individuals following such events. Guidelines for providing feedback include being descriptive rather than evaluative, and specific as opposed to general. The intent of the consultant in giving feedback is to promote acceptance and understanding of the data so that corrective action can effectively result.

Coaching or Counseling Individuals or Groups. The consultant often needs to work with individuals or groups following feedback. The purpose of this activity is to assist, concretely and supportively, the client in effectively processing and attributing his/her own meaning to the feedback, hopefully leading to problem solving.

Structural Suggestions. Such areas as work allocation, authority lines, and committee organization are used far less frequently in process consultation than the above interventions, because these kinds of suggestions are more in line with an "expert model" of consulting than with a process model. However, Schein (1969) observed that structural suggestions such as these may be occasionally offered, if appropriate.

A student affairs example of process consultation may be interesting. A counseling center contracted the services of an outside consultant in order to improve the functioning of the agency. The consultant, after working with the staff for a while, suggested that one reason the agency was floundering may be because of the way meetings were conducted—they were unstructured, fun but vague, and were usually left without closure. The consultant's suggestion that all future meetings include ten minutes of process observation at their end, in order to analyze what had worked and what had not, was accepted and used later to good advantage.

OD IN HIGHER EDUCATION

Institutions of higher learning typify organizational environments that present distinct barriers for successful organization development efforts. Borland (1980) has identified several of them, including resistance to change, improper analysis of the problem, and improper strategy choice, among others. As Bennis (1973) has observed, OD has been successful in organizations, primarily business and industrial, that are

> self-contained, large, rich, and where the product is easily identifiable and measurable . . . . In the university, . . . [one is] not dealing with a family group face-to-face; . . . [one is] dealing with a large, heterogeneous, pluralistic, professional, and political set of constituencies. (p. 390)

Likewise, Boyer and Crockett (1973) suggested that colleges, when compared to industry, (1) have more diverse goal structures, (2) are pluralistic subsystems, (3) present difficulty in measuring the quality of their products, and (4) are more dependent on their external environment, such as state legislatures, federal agencies, foundations, parents, alumni, or community groups. Moreover, teaching and research tend to promote norms of individualism and autonomy in higher education that counter the cooperative norms encouraged by OD practice. These authorities conclude that problems of power and conflict abound in higher education institutions.

These analyses of college organizational life imply that unique challenges face the effective conduct of OD. Any one college organization (such as an academic department or a student affairs unit) is confronted with an internal institutional environment that is characterized by autonomy and low interdependence, and an external environment that is highly changeable. Taken together, these two general conditions mean that college organizations are often isolated entities, cut off from one another and at the behest of outside forces. To use a metaphor drawn from the field of primary prevention, they are organizations *at risk* for not only their future growth and development but for their very survival.

The larger institutions of which these organizations are a part are themselves in trouble. Many smaller schools have been forced to close and many more are threatened, to varying degree, by that prospect. During the 1980s, lowered enrollment, decreased funding levels appropriated for higher education by state legislatures and reductions in federal funds for education, and rampant inflation all illustrate forces in the external environment that combine synergistically to produce not only at-risk organizations within institutions but, even more critically, at-risk institutions themselves.

During the 1980's and certainly applicable to the 1990's as well: most higher education institutions during the coming decade are going to be stressed by these (and other) very harsh, inhospitable external environmental factors. These stressors will strain colleges and their internal organizations. Decreased resources will force the direct confrontation of uncomfortable issues. For instance, which institutional programs will be retained and which limited or dropped? Which target populations get served and which do not? Can current staffing patterns be continued or will a decrease in staff positions be necessary? How is staff morale maintained in times of uncertainty and adversity? Can other more effective and efficient organizational patterns be adopted? This pattern of stress and strain promises to be both naggingly pervasive and difficult to address satisfactorily. For some institutions it may be cataclysmic, while for others it may prove to yield adaptive and useful innovations.

New ways are needed for educational institutions to tackle this crisis head-on or, better yet, before it reaches crisis proportions. Methods must be found to prevent the failure of sound institutions and their organizational entities. OD is one potential means to use in protecting and in some cases promoting the continued development of higher education.

A Future for OD in Higher Education

Organization development as an intact intervention area has been in existence for only about 25 years, used mostly in business and industry. However, OD has found its way into other settings, including higher education (Alderfer, 1977). What appears to be happening is that OD has been garnering increasing attention in higher education (Astin, Comstock, Epperson, Greeley, Katz, & Kauffman, 1974; Bolton & Boyer, 1973; Borland, 1980; Boyer & Crockett, 1973; Caple, 1987; Creamer & Creamer, 1986, 1988; Martorana & Kuhns, 1975; Miller & Prince, 1976). Its use in higher education will grow in direct proportion to two interrelated factors: the forecasted retrenchment that faces postsecondary education and the emergence of college staff members who are committed to finding ways to cope creatively with the strains that are inevitably produced.

By all signs it seems clear that hard times will increase in the immediate future. That reality implies many potential strategies for staff and faculty including, of course, leaving the field of higher education. From another perspective, one may view this crisis as a challenge to be struggled and experimented with so as to produce innovative and adaptive mechanisms that serve to more ably secure and advance higher education. There is utility in the belief that OD as a broad net of interventions has something significant to offer higher education. However, in order for OD to be used effectively and maintained over time, a sanctioned campus group may need to assume responsibility for offering a campus organization development program. Student affairs divisions could provide such a home base.

STUDENT AFFAIRS AS AN
OD NUCLEUS IN
HIGHER EDUCATION

Adoption of a system view to college life easily allows one to see that issues related to student welfare and development are involved closely with issues related to a host of other populations and conditions, both internal and external to the campus. Everything seems interconnected. A policy enacted by a governing body in July regarding tuition costs and payments has certain effects on students the entire next year; faculty members undergoing severe psychological problems may be unable to prevent their debilitating effect on classroom teaching; civil service employees who feel underpaid and overworked may make life uncomfortable for faculty and students alike; and so on. Student affairs divisions that recognize the high degree of interdependence present in higher education (and the baffling reluctance of this phenomenon to be directly addressed) could begin to interpret themselves as a group whose mission, at least in part, becomes one of promoting greater integrity of the components in the system.

OD provides a conceptual model and a broad net of interventions that could be used in this effort. Three basic strategy levels are available for use by student affairs divisions that would adopt this approach: (1) internal OD work within individual student affairs departments, (2) network generator of division-wide OD work, and (3) OD to the college or university community.

Level 1: Internal OD Work

"Charity begins at home." This homily suggests that perhaps the most realistic point to initiate an OD project in the student affairs division is within the individual departments themselves. Thus, a housing department might inaugurate its own OD project, the counseling center might do the same, and so on. The OD consultant could be a skilled within-agency-staff member, be drawn from the division central office, or be imported from outside the college or university. The critical questions faced by these student affairs departments are how to review and evaluate, and whether and how to change? Failure to effectively resolve these and other important issues at the agency level can expose the organizations to risk factors that begin consistently to outstrip available resources; one outcome of such a process is organizational death.

OD can be instituted within hospitable agencies in order to avoid stagnation, and perhaps death, and to promote organizational health (Fordyce & Weil, 1971). In a healthy organization the following are present:

1. Objectives are shared widely by members and energy is devoted to executing them properly.

2. Members point out difficulties with the expectation that they will be solved effectively.

3. Problem solving is very pragmatic, unconfined by status, territoriality, or fearing what the boss might think. Ample nonconforming behavior is accepted.

4. Who makes what decisions is not rigidly predetermined. It is flexibly determined, a function of information

availability, skills, sense of responsibility, work load, and so on.

5. Members mobilize their resources to respond to crisis situations.

6. Conflicts are viewed as useful for organizational growth and they are encountered openly.

7. Risk is accepted as a consolation of growth and change.

Miller and Prince (1976) have attempted to convert notions associated with a healthy organization into organization principles of an ideal "student development organization." They suggested that goals set and decisions made should be consistent with the collegiate mission. Because all system parts are interdependent, planners must be certain that all members understand and are committed to the purposes of the proposed change. Following goal support, attention can be given to the means for change. All available physical, financial, and human resources should be integrated so that the student affairs staff can respond effectively to present demands as well as to anticipate future needs. Throughout the change effort, decision makers must maintain an open communication system so that each participant can give and receive timely and accurate information and so that continuous evaluation procedures can be implemented. Finally, Miller and Prince (1976) emphasized that the healthy student affairs organization should have a climate that encourages and rewards personal and professional development by all its members.

Quality circle programs have emerged in the last few years in higher education and, to a lesser extent, in student affairs. A quality circle program is an OD strategy used to increase organizational productivity and quality through enhanced employee participation in decision-making and problem-solving processes. Steele, Rue, Clement, and Zamostny (1987) reported on three quality circle projects undertaken in an Office of Admissions, with varying results. In Circle 1, which realized positive change, a group of six clerical recorders met for nine months after receiving quality circle training. They succeeded in identifying a group problem, which was the storage of materials, and in obtaining organizational approval to implement several suggested organizational changes, including a new system of inventory for critical publications and office supplies.

In a grand design, OD programs might begin at the individual student affairs department level and then be generalized across the entire division. The notion here is that once the individual parts are strengthened, attention can then be given more fully to strengthening the whole body.

Level 2: Division-wide OD Work

Sarason and colleagues (Sarason, Carroll, Maton, Cohen, & Lorentz, 1977) have provided a model called "resource exchange" that holds promise for division-wide OD work in student affairs.

The concepts of "resource exchange" and "networking" build from the conviction that people and organizations can sometimes do together what each is unable to do individually. This collaborative stance conflicts with dominant interorganization behaviors of competitiveness, standoffishness, and narrow self-interest and self-reliance; productive mutuality may be an espoused value, but it is rarely enacted, especially in the rugged individualist world of the academy.

Student affairs departments function within a formally constructed organizational system. Most typically, these separate agencies exist in parallel form, reporting directly and independently to the division's central office administrator. Although the capacity for an interorganizational network (Turk, 1970) is present, seldom is it activated; agencies function autonomously from each other. A Level 2 OD strategy represents the infusion of an OD program throughout the student affairs division. It is toward this end that the concepts of resource exchange and of interorganizational networking can be useful.

Collaboration, the give-and-get exchange of resources, and the sense of psychological connection can emerge from these processes. A critical variable is that these activities are conducted around a *real life* set of tasks or demands that requires the combined participation of all agencies to obtain satisfaction. When the tasks are accepted as important and agencies begin to collaborate on their accomplishment through joint action, conditions can be created that support implementation of a division-wide OD project. The proximal goal for Level 2 OD in student affairs should be to design ways to put departments in contact with each other in order to solve important problems. It is here that resource exchange, for instance, can contribute directly. Once connections begin to solidify among agencies around important tasks or goals, then they can be capitalized on by implanting an appropriately shaped OD program that would continue to strengthen the collaborative activities clearly underway while attributing meaning to them from a divisional perspective.

Three illustrations of this level are presented. In one, a resource-exchange network at a midwestern college (Conyne, 1980) was formed. The program emerged from a four-year campus environmental assessment project (Conyne, 1975, 1978) that had developed a considerably large body of student-environment fit data. A "project team," comprised of student affairs staff and administrators (plus some individuals from outside student affairs), was formed to develop a collaboratively based change program derived from selected aspects of these data. A benignly neglected group was targeted, students who were new to the university (freshmen and transfers who lived off campus). The interdependence that was demanded in creating joint interventions that spoke to this group led to the mutual pooling of resources, to a developed sense of community among project team members, and to setting the climate for subsequent OD activities.

Cochran (1982) reported an OD project conducted by a university counseling center staff with a student affairs financial aid organization. The project sought to improve aspects of the organization's social climate. The OD consultants made heavy use of a representative planning group to guide the change process. This planning group followed a 10-step action research model as it functioned over eight months. Some of the project results included work schedule changes, clarified promotion policies, and a commitment to continue work on restructuring staff responsibilities.

In a third example of division-wide OD work, Conyne (1983) has developed and implemented a student organization development approach that puts trained student helpers into consultative contact with campus student organizations. Student organization development refers to the intentional facilitation of student organizations by trained interveners in order to help the organizations, and their members, develop in desired directions. A model, called "CORE" ("Cohesion, Organization, Resourcefulness, and Energy") has been created to guide organizational assessment and intervention, as well as the training of the student interveners. In one recent case, trained graduate students have followed the CORE model as they assisted a Student Marketing Association to assess its social climate and overall functioning and take steps to assure improved leadership transition from old to new officers.

Level 3: OD to the Institutional Community

The general procedure of a resource-exchange network can be applied, also, to a total institutional focus, although OD at Level 3 becomes a very complex process. OD becomes increasingly intricate at this level because of the size and diversity of the institution itself. One aspect of the diversity dimension, values, provides an example of this complexity. Consider the question, "What values are espoused by the institution?" If one thinks about it for a moment, one soon realizes that, phrased in this manner, the question is largely unanswerable. While a college of liberal arts, for instance, purports to value the generation and dissemination of artistic, scientific, and cultural knowledge, a college of agriculture is said to value applied, technical knowledge and practice; within the two colleges diversity can be easily found in terms of values. For instance, the physics and English departments in liberal arts differentially support mathematics and literature as avenues to knowledge. The combination of diversity and size suggests that conceptualizing the entire institution as an organization amenable to OD may be, not only overly ambitious, but also unrealistic.

Rather, targeting organizations within the institution and external to student affairs seems to be a more manageable Level 3 approach. Offering OD consultation to academic departments, central administration, and civil service, represents a means by which student affairs can put itself in the position of having a significant impact on the institution. As Miller and Prince (1976) have indicated in regard to student development, *collaboration* among student affairs staff, faculty members, and students is essential to success. Becoming known on campus as a credible nucleus for conducting OD interventions available to other campus organizations would provide the student affairs division with an important function, especially in times of constricted resources.

Several examples of OD exist in the campus community that could constitute models for student affairs to consider.

The first illustration of OD in the college community is a project conducted for one academic department by a counseling center staff (Conyne, Rapin, & Berger, 1980; Rapin, Conyne, & Berger, 1980). This project began in the form of a training request to advance the group facilitation skills of student discussion group leaders in a large undergraduate course (N=480) in the department. This training continued over a three-year period, leading to an expansion of the involvement beyond (but including) the training element to a focus on the total discussion group program itself. The initial training contract was renegotiated with program planners to include assessing the ideal and real social climates of 12 discussion groups (as perceived by students, facilitators, and program planners), followed by feedback sessions, and program-centered administrative consultation to the program planners, aimed at program redesign. This project nicely demonstrated how a counseling center staff can become engaged in OD activities with an academic department program that evolved from an initial training involvement.

A second example focuses on commuter students. On many campuses today commuter students are in a majority. The campus ecology for commuter students is different than that for residential students. Likens (1982) has described it as "POP:" From "Parking Lot to Classroom to Parking Lot (p. 547)." This restricted involvement in the campus environment makes student development work with commuter students a significant challenge.

Banning and Hughes (1986) have described how the campus ecosytem design process can be applied to alter the campus environment in ways that would be more conducive to commuter student functioning. Basically, this design process represents an application of organization development principles and processes within a campus institution, giving specific emphasis to environmental considerations and change. For instance, Banning and Hughes suggested that an institution could adjust its course offerings to make more classes available in the evening, rather than always to expect that busy commuter students should modify their work schedules.

Finally, student retention is a source of large concern on many campuses and in the literature of higher education (e.g., Carnegie, 1986; Project of AAC, 1985). Recent research (e.g., Astin, 1984; Pascarella & Terenzini, 1977) has converged to suggest that the creation of involving learning environments can help stem the tide of attrition. Conyne (1986) has conceptualized an involving learning environment to provide ample opportunities for personal development, for interpersonal development, and that it affords a dynamic and interdependent set of systemic processes. Smith, Lippitt, Noel, and Sprandel (1981) proposed a "campus health check of 11 vital signs" that can be used for diagnosis and to guide campus change. Again, as is the case with the campus ecosystem design process discussed previously, these signs are consistent with organization development processes applied broadly to an institution. A related approach to student retention, called "enrollment management" (e.g., Hossler, 1985), involves the entire campus by interconnecting and directing institutional efforts in the areas of marketing, recruitment, admissions, pricing, financial aid, academic advising, orientation, and other student services.

As Hossler (1985) stated, "This requirement to *involve the entire campus* places enrollment management squarely at the door of the student affairs division (p. 3)." Organization development provides an encompassing framework to guide student affairs interventions of this kind within the institution.

USING OD IN STUDENT AFFAIRS

Crisis theory holds that emergency situations provide critical leverage points for significant advancement or decline in the organism experiencing the crisis. At such times the assistance of a skilled helper such as a crisis intervenor can intensify advancement opportunities. This analogy can be applied nearly directly to higher education today.

As has been indicated much of higher education is in a state of crisis. Campuses, some more so than others, need their own skilled crisis intervenors. Student affairs divisions can begin to conceptualize ways to become an important crisis intervention source for the campus community. It is at this point that a range of OD interventions can be of use both within the division (Levels 1 and 2 OD strategies) and outside with other campus organizations (Level 3).

Building and "OD mucleus" within student affairs that can be drawn upon by the campus at large can give student affairs an essential and critically important new mission to benefit the institution. This point is as valid today as it was in 1983 when this book was first published. Doing so, of course, is no small task and needs to be considered in respect to a panoply of local factors. However, if the decision is "go," then the challenges and potential rewards would be many.

REFERENCES

Alderfer, C. (1977). Organization development. In M. Rosenzweig & L. Porter (Eds.), *Annual Review of Psychology, 28*, 197-223.

Argyris, C. (1970). *Intervention theory and method.* MA: Addison-Wesley.

Argyris, C., Putnam, R., & Smith, D. (1987). *Action Science: Concepts, methods, and skills for research and intervention.* San Francisco: Jossey-Bass.

Astin, A. (1984). Student involvement: A developmental theory for higher education. *Journal of College Student Personnel, 25*, 297-308.

Astin, A., Comstock, C., Epperson, D., Greeley, A., Katz, Jr., & Kauffman, J. (1974). *Faculty development in a time of retrenchment.* New Rochelle, NY: Change.

Banning, J., & Hughes, B. (1986). Designing the campus environment with commuter students. *NASPA Journal, 24*, 17-24.

Beckhard, R. (1967). The confrontation meeting. *Harvard Business Review, 45*, 149-55.

Beer, M., & Walton, A. (1987). Organization change and development. *Annual Review of Psychology, 38*, 339-67.

Bennis, W. (1973). An OD expert in the cat bird's seat: An interview with Warren Bennis. In R. Boyer & C. Crockett (Eds.), Organizational development in higher education, (Special Issue) *Journal of Higher Education, 44*, 389-98.

Bennis, W., & Nanus, B. (1985). *Leaders.* New York: Harper.

Blake, R., & Mouton, J. (1976). *Consultation.* Reading, MA: Addison-Wesley.

Bolton, C., & Boyer, R. (1973). Organizational development for academic departments. In R. Boyer & C. Crockett (Eds.), Organizational development in higher education (Special Issue), *Journal of Higher Education, 44*, 352-69.

Borland, D. (1980). Organization development: A professional imperative. In D. G. Creamer (Ed.), *Student development in higher education: Theories, practices, and further directions,* (pp. 205-27). Washington, DC: American College Personnel Association.

Bowers, D., & Franklin, J. (1974). Basic concepts of survey feedback. In J. Pfeiffer & J. Jones (Eds.), *The 1974 annual handbook for group facilitators,* (pp. 221-26). La Jolla, CA: University Associates.

Boyer, R., & Crockett, C. (1973). Organizational development in higher education: Introduction. *Journal of Higher Education, 44*, 339-51.

Bradford, L., Gibb, J., & Benne, K. (Eds.). (1964). *T-group theory and laboratory method: Innovation in re-education.* New York: John Wiley.

Caple, R. (1987). The change process in development theory: A self-organization paradigm, Part 2. *Journal of College Student Personnel, 28,* 100-04.

Carnegie Foundation Survey. (Feb. 2, 1986). *College students: Who they are, what they think.* Washington, DC: Chronicle of Higher Education, 21-30.

Clark, D., & Guba, E. (1965). *Innovation in school curricula.* Washington, DC: The Center for the Study of Instruction, National Education Association.

Cochran, D. (1982). Organizational consultation: A planning group approach. *Personnel and Guidance Journal, 60,* 314-17.

Collier, J. (1945). United States Indian administration as a laboratory of ethnic relations. *Social Research, 12,* 275-6.

Conyne, R. (1975). Environmental assessment: Mapping for counselor action. *Personnel and Guidance Journal, 54,* 150-55.

Conyne, R. (1978). An analysis of student-environment mismatches. *Journal of College Student Personnel, 19,* 461-65.

Conyne, R. (1980). Resource networking on the campus: A prospective for prevention. *Journal of College Student Personnel, 21,* 573-4.

Conyne, R. (1983). Models for conducting student organization development. *Personnel and Guidance Journal, 61,* 394-97.

Conyne, R. (1986). *The involving learning environment.* Unpublished Document. University of Cincinnati.

Conyne, R., Rapin, L., & Berger, R. (April, 1980). *Consulting with academia using a collaborative research approach.* Paper presented at the annual meeting of the American College Personnel Association, Boston.

Corey, S. (1953). *Action research to improve school practices.* New York: Bureau of Publications, Teachers College, Columbia University.

Creamer, D., & Creamer, E. (1986). Applying a model of planned change to program innovation in Student Affairs. *Journal of College Student Personnel, 27,* 19-26.

Creamer, E., & Creamer, D. (1988). Predicting successful organizational change: Case studies. *Journal of College Student Personnel, 29,* 4-11.

Emery, F., & Trist, E. (1960). Socio-technical systems. In C. Churchman & M. Verhulst (Eds.), *Management sciences models and techniques (Vol. 2)*, (pp. 83-87). London: Pergamon Press.

Faucheux, C., Amado, G., & Laurent, A. (1982). Organizational development and change. *Annual review of psychology, 33*, 343-70.

Fordyce, J., & Weil, R. (1971). *Managing with people*. Reading, MA: Addison-Wesley.

French, W., & Bell, C., (1973). *Organization development*. Englewood Cliffs, NJ: Prentice-Hall.

French, W., Bell, C., & Zawacki, R. (Eds.). (1978). *Organization development: Theory, practice, and research*. Dallas: Business Publications.

Frohman, M., Sashkin, M., & Kavanagh, M. (1978). Action-research as applied to organization development. In W. French, C. Bell, & R. Zawacki (Eds.), *Organization development: Theory, practice, and research*, (pp. 137-147). Dallas: Business Publications.

Harrison, R. (1970). Choosing the depth of organizational intervention. *Journal of Applied Behavioral Science, 6*, 181-202.

Hausser, D., Pecorella, P., & Wissler, A. (1977). *Survey-guided development II: A manual for consultants*. La Jolla, CA: University Associates.

Havelock, R. (1969). *Planning for innovation*. Ann Arbor, MI: Center for Research on Utilization of Scientific Knowledge, Institute for Social Research.

Hossler, D. (1985). Enrollment management: A paradigm for student affairs professionals. *NASPA Journal, 23*, 2-8.

Huse, E. (1980). *Organization development and change*. St. Paul, MN: West.

Huse, E., & Bowditch, J. (1973). *Behavior in organizations: A systems approach to managing*. Reading, MA: Addison-Wesley.

Jones, J. (1973). The sensing interview. In J. Pfeiffer and J. Jones (Eds.), *The 1973 annual handbook for group facilitators (pp. 213-24)*. La Jolla, CA: University Associates.

Kanter, R. (1983). *The change masters*. New York: Simon & Schuster.

Kast, F., & Rosenzweig, J. (1970). *Organization and management: A systems approach*. New York: McGraw-Hill.

Katz, D., & Kahn, R. (1978). *The social psychology of organizations*. New York: Wiley.

Kirn, A., & Kirn, M. (1978). *Life work planning (4th ed).* New York: McGraw-Hill.

Lawrence, P., & Lorsch, J. (1969). *Developing organizations: Diagnosis and action.* Reading, MA: Addision-Wesley.

Lewin, K. (1946). Action research and minority problems. *Journal of Social Issues, 2,* 34-46.

Likens, J. (1982). The brown bag special—A commuter program. *Journal of College Student Personnel, 23,* 546-547.

Lippitt, R., Watson, J., & Westley, B. (1958). *The dynamics of planned change: A comparative study of principles and techniques.* New York: Harcourt, Brace, & World.

Martorana, S., & Kuhns, E. (1975). *Managing academic change.* San Francisco: Jossey Bass.

Miller, T.K., & Prince, J. (1976). *The future of student affairs: A guide to student development for tomorrow's higher education.* San Francisco: Jossey-Bass.

Pascarella, E., & Terenzini, P. (1977). Patterns of student-faculty informal interaction beyond the classroom and voluntary freshman attrition. *Journal of Higher Education, 48,* 540-62.

Patton, M. (1978). *Utilization-focused evaluation.* Beverly Hills, CA: Sage.

Project of AAC (1985). *Integrity in the College Curriculum: A report on the academic community.* Washington, DC: Association of American Colleges.

Rapin, L., Conyne, R., & Berger, R. (Sept., 1980). *Consultation and collaborative research: A new direction for counseling centers.* Paper presented at the annual meeting of the American Psychological Association, Montreal, Canada.

Reilly, A., & Jones, J. (1974). Team Building. In J. Pfeiffer & J. Jones (Eds.), *The 1974 annual handbook for group facilitators* (pp. 227-37). LaJolla, CA: University Associates.

Sarason, C., Carroll, C., Maton, K., Cohen, S., & Lorentz, E. (1977). *Human services and resource networks.* San Francisco: Jossey-Bass.

Schein, E. (1969). *Process consultation: Its role in organization development.* Reading, MA: Addison-Wesley.

Seiler, J. (1967). *Systems analysis in organizational behavior.* Homewood, IL: R. D. Irwin-Dorsey Press.

Smith, L., Lippitt, R., Noel, L., & Sprandel, D. (1981). *Mobilizing for campus retention.* Iowa City, IA: ACT.

Steele, B., Rue, P., Clement, L., & Zamostny, K. (1987). Quality circles: A corporate strategy applied in a student services setting. *Journal of College Student Personnel, 28,* 146-151.

Steele, F. (1973). *Physical settings and organization development.* Reading, MA: Addison-Wesley.

Turk, H. (1970). Interoganizational networks in urban society: Initial perspectives and comparative research. *American Sociological Review, 35,* 1-19.

Weisbord, M. (1978). *Organizational diagnosis: A workbook of theory and practice.* Reading, MA: Addison-Wesley.

SUGGESTED READINGS

Alderfer, C. (1977). Organization development. In M. Rosenzweig & L. Porter (Eds.), *Annual Review of Psychology,* 197-223.

Banning, J. (1978). *Campus ecology: A perspective for student affairs.* Cincinnati, OH: NASPA.

Beer, M., & Walton, A. (1987). Organization change and development. *Annual Review of Psychology, 38,* 339-67.

Borland, D. (1980). Organization development: A professional imperative. In D. Creamer (Ed.), *Student development in higher education: Theories, practices, and future directions.* (pp. 205-27). Washington, DC: American College Personnel Association.

Boyer, R., & Crockett, C. (1973). Organizational development in higher education: Introduction. *Journal of Higher Education, 44,* 339-51.

Faucheux, C., Amado, G., & Laurent, A. (1982). Organizational development and change. *Annual Review of Psychology, 33,* 343-70.

French, W., & Bell, C. (1973). *Organization development.* Englewood Cliffs, NJ: Prentice-Hall.

French, W., Bell, C., & Zawacki, R. (Eds.) (1978). *Organization development: Theory, practice, and research.* Dallas: Business Publications.

Hossler, D. (1985). Enrollment management: A paradigm for student affairs professionals. *NASPA Journal, 23,* 2-8.

Huse, E. (1980). *Organization development and change.* St. Paul, MN: West Publishing.

Katz, D., & Kahn, R. (1978). *The social psychology of organizations.* New York: Wiley.

Kilmann, R., Saxton, M., Serpa, R., & Associates. (1985). *Gaining control of the corporate culture.* San Francisco, CA: Jossey-Bass.

Lawrence, P., & Lorsch, J. (1969). *Developing organizations: Diagnosis and action.* Reading, MA: Addison-Wesley.

Schein, E. (1969). *Process consultation: Its role in organization development.* Reading, MA: Addison-Wesley.

Smith, L., Lippitt, R., Noel, L., & Sprandel, D. (1981). *Mobilizing the campus for retention: An innovative quality of life model.* Iowa City, IA: ACT.

Weisbord, M. (1978). *Organizational diagnosis: A workbook of theory and practice.* Reading, MA: Addison-Wesley.

Richard B. Caple, Ed.D., is Professor of Counseling Psychology in the Department of Educational and Counseling Psychology and is a Counseling Psychologist in the Counseling Center at the University of Missouri, Columbia. He received his B.A. from Cornell College and his M.A. and Ed.D. from Teachers College, Columbia University. He has previous experience in counseling and administration at New Mexico State University and was the Chief Student Affairs Officer at Northwestern State College, Oklahoma.

Dr Caple has had a long interest in social theory and its meaning for human behavior. This has led to his special interest in new paradigms and models that conceptualize about human behavior and existence. Most recently he has developed and applied new theory utilizing systems theory and self-organization theory and is conducting research in this area. He is presently Editor of the *Journal of College Student Development.*

Fred B. Newton, Ph.D., is Director of University Counseling Services and Associate Professor in Counselor Education and Educational Psychology at Kansas State University. His previous experiences include both teaching and administrative positions at Duke University, University of Georgia, and Sinclair Community College in Dayton, Ohio. He received his master's degree in student personnel in higher education at the Ohio State University and his Ph.D. in counseling psychology at the University of Missouri-Columbia. He has published several articles in student personnel and counseling journals, and co-edited the book, *Student Development Practice: Strategies for Making a Difference.*

Dr Newton's interests include the development of innovation systems for management of change in both organizations and individuals. Current research includes the function and outcome of metaphoric language in the process of change.

CHAPTER 4

LEADERSHIP IN STUDENT AFFAIRS

Richard B. Caple
Fred B. Newton*

In 1970 Alvin Toffler wrote about the phenomenon of "future shock"—the reaction to a period of technological innovation, accumulation of knowledge, and access to information that occurred so rapidly that people and systems in society were overwhelmed and under stress to make adjustments and accommodation to its impact. At about the same time, men like Prigogine, Feigenbaum, and a handful of other scientists scattered about the country were grappling with ideas that would begin to explain the nature of the change process that Toffler had noted. They were committed to the study of dynamic systems that today is referred to under the rubric "chaos" (Gleick, 1987). Science and technology have opened the way to new vision and understanding of the world, but at the same time created new complex systems that seem to require greater energy to maintain. New relationships and new ways of connecting by individuals and families with work, business, government, and social institutions are having startling and unpredictable consequences for economic, political, and social behaviors.

Old concepts of change as gradual, connected, cumulative, and progressive are no longer always valid (Kagan, 1980).

*Susan M. Scott contributed ideas to sections of this chapter.

Prigogine, a biochemist, and collaborators have developed a new theory of change for which Prigogine received the Nobel Prize for Chemistry in 1977. His theory of dissipative structure first described how order is achieved out of chaos. He later applied this theory to social change (Prigogine & Stengers, 1984). This theory postulates that when fluctuations within the system become sufficiently turbulent so that old connecting points no longer work, the system transforms itself into a higher order with new and different connecting points that are more integrated and connected than in the preceding one. But, also a larger flow of energy is required to maintain it. Not only does this theory more fully describe the process of change, but it explains the critical role of stress in change.

How does science change its mind? Kuhn (1962) noted that new paradigms, explanatory models that more effectively explain phenomena, are at first met with resistance. As the more powerful idea gains ascendance, however, a shift occurs as if the old model is suddenly replaced in a revolutionary manner. Tensions and dissonance caused by turbulence stimulate the opportunity for new ways of acting upon the world, but they may, also, frighten people to withdraw into a protective stance trying to hold on to the security of the old way of living and resisting with a last gasp for the familiar and seemingly safe world. Students in recent years have been labeled the "me generation," concerned only with achieving private ends to take care of and protect themselves (Levine, 1980). But, Boyer (1987) found undergraduates often torn between ambiguous feelings of idealism on the one hand (aspirations to reach beyond themselves) and on the other hand the temptation to pursue their private interests that could leave them politically and socially disengaged.

Indeed, a world that is undergoing transformation rather than maintenance is in need of an extraordinary form of leadership—the type of leadership that is able to inspire and create new processes of social existence. Leaders are needed who are similar to those leaders that shaped the beginnings of this country—leaders with broad knowledge, a sense of courage, a belief in a strong set of ethical and moral principles, and creative, imaginative minds capable of identifying many potentials.

LEADERSHIP THEORY

Leadership, according to Burns (1978, pp. 18-19) is "the exercise of those with power potential, to engage, mobilize, induce, and transform followers to act for certain goals which represent the values and motivations—the wants and the needs, the aspirations *of both leaders and followers.*" The leader is powerful but not a power wielder. The leader takes initiative creating links for communication. The leader is moral, raising the level of human conduct and ethical aspiration. The leader is "transforming" as followers proceed to higher levels permitting the relationship to change. The extent of the quality and power of the leader is measured by actual accomplishment toward promised change.

Leadership has been a topic of widespread interest throughout much of recorded history from Plato's discussion of the "philosopher king" and Machiavelli's description of the "Prince" to countless modern day biographies of American presidents, generals, and world leaders in nearly every walk of life. Management science programs require courses in leadership, political scientists research the nature of individual impact, and sociologists and social psychologists study the interface of individual and group dynamics. Still leadership in many ways remains an enigma, a much discussed but little understood phenomenon (Burns, 1978).

Fiedler (1967) reviewed many of the diverse descriptions of leadership enumerating phrases such as the exercise of authority and responsibility, the making of decisions, the initiation of acts leading to purposeful group solutions, the creation of change, and the direction and coordination of task relevant group activity. Leadership also has been viewed as the relationship of leader to follower: as an ability to understand human behavior, to listen, to understand, and to respond to human need (Kouzes & Posner, 1987). The relationship potentially can be one of transaction, and agreement between two levels: transformation, encouraging followers to greater potential; and transcendence, which elevates followers to leaders (Burns, 1978). The following historical development of leadership theory provides perspective for the present status of this complex and sometimes controversial subject.

Leadership Theory In The Twentieth Century

Two major explanations were used as models for the description of leadership 50 years ago. One was commonly referred to as the "Great Man" theory, which described qualities of superiority that were ascribed as the domain of certain elite. They became leaders because of a natural tendency for "the cream to rise to the top." A counter theory, the *Zeitgeist*, explained leadership as a result of the situation with factors of time, place, and circumstance as preeminent determinants in the emergence of leader behavior. In the 1930s and 1940s, early research on group dynamics attempted to isolate the behaviors and qualities that identified leadership. The White and Lippitt (1968) study of democratic, autocratic, and laissez-faire behaviors exemplified research that isolated leader behavior and its impact upon the group.

In the 1950s, a study of specific characteristics of leaders seen as effective by subordinates was carried out by researchers at The Ohio State University (Forsyth, 1983). This study was the first to identify two sets of variables that became the focus for leadership study during the sixties. The first of these variables followed a dimension that has been variously called maintenance, relationship, likability, or process. The second dimension was described as task, structure, initiation, or production (Hershey & Blanchard, 1977). Studies of relationships between variables in the leader behavior and the performance or effectiveness of the group led to the subsequent emphasis on the interaction of a situation with the leader's behavior.

The "contingency model" was an outcome of style and situation research. Fiedler (1967) considered three variables: (1) the group atmosphere, measure of the leader-group relationship, (2) the task structure, the specificity of goals, and (3) the leader power position, the authority over group members. He concluded that the favorableness of leader behavior was contingent upon the situation. Task-oriented leaders performed best in less favorable situational structure, and relationship-oriented leaders functioned best in moderately structured settings. Thus, the leader must either adapt to the situation, or the appropriate leader must be matched to the situation (Fiedler, 1967). Subsequent research has considered variations on this theme, including changing leadership styles (Fiedler & Mahar, 1979).

Tannebaum and Schmidt (1973) emphasized that a person with qualities of sensitivity, insight, and flexibility is more able to adapt and have a higher batting average in successfully assessing appropriate behavior for the setting. House and Mitchell (1974) reasoned that a leader's choice of behavior is related directly to the awareness of subordinate motivation and the influence the leader has in influencing the work goals and personal goals on a personally satisfying path.

Hershey and Blanchard (1977) took the relationship and task dichotomies and added a "life cycle" or time maturity dimension. The life cycle theory demonstrates the relationship of task and maintenance functions to the maturity level of group or follower development. As the level of maturity of the group increases, the leader behavior requires less structure and support. Four patterns of potential leader behavior are expressed on these continua: (1) dictating (telling), (2) persuading (selling), (3) facilitating (participating), and (4) involving (delegating). A leader may assume a different pattern of behavior based upon the readiness of subordinates.

House (1971) in the path-goal model of leadership theory identified the leader as the person providing a motivational function for subordinates. Leaders, by understanding the reasons for individuals' choices, facilitate the attainment of their goals by reducing obstacles and enhancing satisfaction in the path toward the goal. The leader may provide guidance and performance incentives. This model is best demonstrated in situations where goals are concrete, structure is clear, and incentives are readily identifiable.

Vroom and Yetton's (1973) decision-process model is yet another case of situational leadership theory. The emphasis in this model is on the social process in which decisions take place. The leader is advised to approach the decision process based upon the attributes that define a problem situation. Seven attributes or levels of the decision process are evaluated by a yes/no decision tree that in turn determine a prescribed set of rules to apply to the situation. These attributes consider such factors as amount of information available concerning the problem, level of acceptance with members, amount of structure, shared goals, and amount of conflict likely for a solution. Vroom (1984) pointed out that a leader in the educational environment does not operate in a closed system, the internal organization of subordinates. The leader must mediate an interaction with the forces in the surrounding environment (boards, taxpayers, granting agencies, and others) as well as charting a course for subordinates within the institutional structure.

Herzberg (1968) emphasized the leader's need to understand what really motivates followers. He maintained that the commonly assumed means of directing action (money, benefits) are "hygiene" factors that do not motivate or satisfy workers, although they are means for causing dissatisfaction. Herzberg hypothesized that the true motivators are individual responsibility, achievement, internal recognition, growth, advancement, and learning.

The description of theory and research over the past 50 years has demonstrated the interaction of variables such as style, behavior, situational structure, follower maturity, motivation, and adaptability. The interdisciplinary nature of leadership has left a wide range of philosophical, social, psychological, and political perspectives with need for a synthesizer. Burns (1978), a political scientist, presidential biographer, and ardent student of leadership theory across all disciplines, offered the most complete dynamic theory of leadership to date. He described leadership as a reciprocal and interactive relationship between leader and follower. It is a dynamic interaction that involves a continual dialectic give and take. Burns based his ideas of leadership on both motivation theory (Maslow, 1954) and developmental theory (Erikson, 1968; Kohlberg, 1981). Maslow's hierarchy of needs explains how the attainment of a lower level of need depletes the drive or motivation for that need. For example, once people feel secure in an environment, unthreatened by arbitrary or punitive intervention, they may then be willing to risk more open relationships with associates. The leader's role is to recognize continually and facilitate the follower's striving toward higher levels of personal fulfillment. Developmental theories are used to explain the process people experience when moving through crisis to equilibrium, a process leading to increased levels of personal competence and confidence in achieving potentials and moral commitment. People mature through stages in life in which personal issues are confronted and resolved and tasks mastered before advancing. Burns uses extensive case evidence of famous world leaders of the century—Churchill, Mao, Gandhi, and several American presidents—to assess and identify qualities of leadership.

A discussion of the leader-situation interaction applied to education settings was provided by Blake, Mouton, and Williams (1981). They held that by considering two functional aspects of leadership, concern for institutional performance and concern for people, as horizontal and vertical scaled continua (ranging from low 1 to high 9), an administrator's leadership style may be described as coordinates of a grid (see Figure 4.1.). Administrators that are 1,1 on the grid are called "caretakers"; they exert the minimum amount of effort required to meet minimum work expectations and demand little from subordinates. One/nine administrators (1,9 on the grid) are characterized as "comfortable and pleasant" and are concerned primarily with creating satisfying relationships and a pleasant work tempo. They display little concern for production and reaching institutional goals. Administrators whose emphasis is on efficiency in operations with little regard for the feelings of staff are 9,1 on the grid. They concentrate on getting results by the use of power and authority, and demand unquestioning obedience from subordinates. Leaders who subscribe to a "constituency-centered" approach (5,5 on the grid) attempt to balance the needs of the college to get results while maintaining good morale among the staff. The "team administrator" (9,9 on the grid) has equally high concern for institutional performance and people. This style leader encourages staff to achieve at high levels and attempts to motivate them by gaining their commitment to the college's goals.

LEADERSHIP IN HIGHER EDUCATION

Institutions of higher education, facing a period in which economic conditions, changing student populations, technological

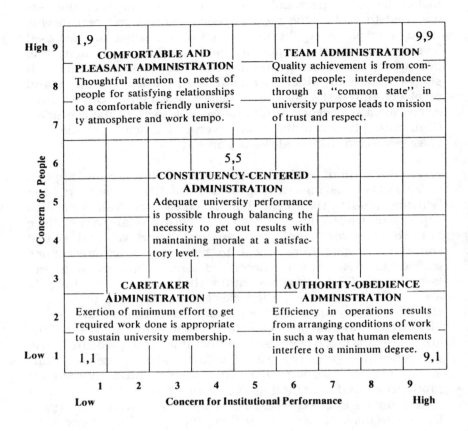

Figure 4.1. The Academic Administrator Grid.®

innovations, shifting emphases in the world of work, and enhanced methods for the storage and communication of information that have revolutionized the world, have the need to respond, to make adjustments, and to accommodate the shifts that have stressed and made obsolete many of the methods for operating an educational system in the recent past. This constant need for change presents continuing opportunity for academia to develop higher levels of functioning that will prepare more diverse populations with increased educational needs to live in a complex world.

Keller (1983) assessed the needs for managing higher education during a period of change, and indicated the importance of leadership that is willing to take the initiative and create an inevitable tension between stability and change. Leadership from the top down may be the single most important factor in managing the process of change, but Keller also mentioned that it is all too frequently found lacking on college campuses.

Most research and theory on leadership has evolved from the business field. Peters and Waterman (1982) identified management characteristic of the most successful American companies. Douglas (1981) applied these same characteristics to the college campus. These eight characteristics are summarized as follows:

1. **Hold a bias for action**—must be able to adjust and make changes more rapidly to keep institutions alive and viable; leaders must lead and take action even though the resources and structure in many institutions make it difficult.

2. **Listen closely to consumer**—form a partnership by being attentive to diverse needs of population served.

3. **Encourage autonomy and creativity**—promote an atmosphere of autonomy, entrepreneurship, allow people (staffs) to take risks, unlock creativity.

4. **Implement Theory Y of work**—appreciate people, allow for (encourage) employee growth and development.

5. ***Transmit a message of value***—integrity of organization is determined through consistency of behaviors (e.g., if an institution says rigor and standards are important then the actions of leaders must reinforce this).

6. ***Stay with what you know***—do not try to be all things to all people.

7. ***Simple organizational structure***—lean staffing, do not have too many layers of bureaucracy, and administrative "flab," keep organization streamlined and trim, but do not pare away bone and muscle along with the fat.

8. ***Simultaneous loose-tight properties***—flexible response system in which people are free to do job they are hired to do, but managers take corrective action when either crisis or opportunity determines it is necessary.

Vroom (1984) indicated that he was employed for over two decades in the academic setting without researching or even thinking about making application of leadership principles to the college setting. He indicated that the vagueness of educational mission statements, the tendency toward anarchy in the internal governing structure, and the presence of factors such as tenure create in the university setting certain unique situations not present in the business setting. Vroom's conclusion from limited study in academic settings was that this setting is best suited for forms of highly participatory leadership in which the presence of diverse ideas, research attitudes, and intellectual input can lead to greater innovation, higher levels of commitment to the institution, and greater levels of staff satisfaction.

Three universities participated in a Kellogg Foundation grant for developing institutional leadership for supporting effective change strategies during the early 1980s (Hipps, 1982). While organizational structure and methods of change were considered in the project the emphasis was placed on the people factors, such as enhancing communication, participatory problem solving methods, and preparing individuals in collaborative work efforts. On one campus over 100 faculty and administrative staff members participated in an extensive training program to prepare individuals to assume new leadership responsibilities. The conclusion of the project emphasized the input of leadership development activities as the single most important component for change on all three campuses.

NEW WAYS FOR VIEWING LEADERSHIP

Paradigms or models are tools that help conceptualize and explain certain aspects of reality. In one sense they become maps that help to explore unfamiliar territory and act as guides that permit individuals to look beyond present positions. But paradigms and models are always incomplete and invite generalizations that go beyond their original purpose. They are restrictive, too, because people tend to become accustomed to their perceptions and will not give up an old framework until circumstances demand it. This leads to the creation of new paradigms.

Generally, developmental theorists have explained developmental change to be the result of seeking a balance, and accommodation with the environment, or a state of equilibrium. They have usually perceived change as being gradual, progressive, predictable, and connected; they have viewed behavior as directed toward stability, equilibrium, and balance. New theory called *Self organization Theory* has challenged these conceptualizations and proposed that many changes are found in disequilibrium (Caple, 1987a). This theory is build on *General System Theory* (Bertalanffy, 1968), the theory of *Dissipative Structures* and a new ordering principle underlying them called *Order Through Fluctuations* (Nicolis & Prigogine, 1977; Prigogine, 1976; Prigogine & Stengers, 1984).

The central concepts in general system theory are (1) the open system model—every living system, including the human being, is an open or partially open system that maintains itself only in a continuous exchange of energy with its environment; (2) boundaries—every system has either spatial or dynamic boundaries that regulate the exchange of energy with the environment; (3) autonomy—the function of consciously managing the system's boundaries, which represents both the potential and the limitation of a human system; and (4) the developmental process—proceeds from a state of differentiation to a state of articulation and hierarchial order, and which reflects the sense of a differentiated self emerging from the environment.

Central concepts of the theory of Dissipative Structures are (1) nonequilibrium—dissipative structures originate from conditions of nonequilibrium and interact with the outside environment in such a way that they are open to reordering; (2) connections—any living or open system is connected at various points and the more complex this structure the more energy required to maintain its connections; and (3) fluctuations—the continuous flow of energy through a system creates fluctuations, many of which are absorbed or adjusted to without altering the system's structural integrity (a first-order change), but some of which, because of high levels of turbulence, result in old connecting points no longer working which produce system transformation to a higher order with new and different connecting points (second-order change).

The principles of self-organization theory apply equally well to social groups and organizations as they do to human organisms, and certain principles apply to systems in general irrespective of the nature of the entities concerned (Bertalanffy, 1968). Jantsch (1980) viewed self-organizing principles applying from the cell to society, and proposed four levels of planning that are useful as a model for leaders to follow: (1) tactical—the level of day-to-day planning for short-range goals; (2) strategic—the level at which a variety of options is created, tested, and prepared for implementation on a broad range, creating a mental structure that is not in equilibrium, with fluctuations fed into it deliberately to trigger further evolution; (3) policy—the level at which the dynamics of the system (organization or group) are considered in relation to the larger society; and (4) creative—the level that goes beyond the rational, logical responses of the other levels to effect value creation. If an organization is to evolve, upper levels must be open to the introduction and integration of creativity.

In *process-oriented management*, the role of the leader is that of a catalyst and process is emphasized rather than product. Although process is emphasized, outcomes are not altogether ignored, but are seen in relation to the process. Autonomy is basic to each concept within self-organization theory, and it increases as the organization achieves differentiation from its environment. Conflict is viewed as being inherent to the change process. The natural efforts to dampen fluctuations within systems and to perceive equilibrium as the more desirable state may lead observers to interpret the resulting conflict as negative experience. In truth, likely the fluctuations leading to change are experienced as conflict and are necessary and constructive forces in the change process (Caple, 1987b).

Self-organization theory provides student affairs practitioners with a broad theory of change from which to view the development of students. Leaders oriented toward providing services and physical facilities will emphasize and support first-order changes and resist second-order changes. Leaders who are oriented toward self-organizing principles will emphasize process and will be aware that outcomes cannot always be specified before they occur. Their emphasis will be on creating experience rather than maintaining the system and on awareness of the system's coevolution with its environment.

Kuh, Whitt, and Shedd (1987) identified similar characteristics of an emergent paradigm with implications for student affairs leaders. They indicated that situations must be viewed in complex and diverse ways rather than in simple reductionist explanations. For example, enrollment management studies are only able to factor out 20 to 30% of the variance to explain dropouts. Patterns need to be identified in what was termed as *holonomic* (that is, any part of a system, such as a department or unit, reflects in some ways the character of the whole division and even the institution). This inner relatedness and interdependence is exemplified by how curriculums are modified through a process that involves individuals, departments, divisions, other institutions in a system, consortiums, and even governing boards. Kuh and his colleagues further elaborated that this emergent model reflects an indeterminate understanding of causality in understanding human behavior. Ambiguity, subtlety, and mutual shaping of subject and context become important considerations in the establishment of an organizational response. No two students are necessarily shaped in the same way by environmental conditions. This requires strategies that can pick up the uniqueness and nuances of a situation. An individual student's academic success, for example, may be enhanced by supportive intervention, by challenge, or by appropriate doses of both (the choice of which may vary considerably with the knowledge and response of that student).

To implement the strategies of the emerging perspective described by Kuh et al. (1987), will require the preparation of student affairs professionals with vision and leadership. Good leaders will be able to generate understanding among those they lead. This requires skills in group facilitation, negotiation, and conflict management and knowledge of participative decision models, leadership theories, and planning models. But, what the leader stands for and does is far more important than what the leader says. The leader must show integrity, consistently articulate values, and adhere to principles in all that he or she does.

PROPOSITIONS FOR
EFFECTIVE LEADERSHIP

Based on reference from both the general field of leadership and the more specific area of higher education, the following seven propositions for effective leadership are proposed. Each is described and further explained by the use of student affairs related examples.

1. A leader is aware of his or her role and responsibility within a system and of the connections that relate and affect this position. A leader realizes that people, interacting in a system, will always influence one another. Recognition of this need to connect is made through the process of group cooperation and communication. Emphasis needs to be on this "process." Process is the way or manner in which people interact to accomplish a goal. The most productive leaders are aware of the process of interaction and will focus their attention on the quality of these connection points. A connected leader is not laissez faire, ignoring conflicts and avoidance behaviors, or similar signals of problems with interacting people. Instead, the leader will use strategies that bring dynamics into the open, will embrace conflict as a tool for growth, and will not hesitate to give clear and immediate feedback.

An important aspect of providing clarity in the process of communication is the ability to self-differentiate. Friedman (1985, p. 229) described a leader as one who takes "primary responsibility for his or her own position as head and works to define his or her own goals, while staying in touch with the rest of the organism." To know ones own needs, wishes, prejudices, and perceptions will at least minimize the possibility of projecting these personal predispositions on others. Heider (1985, p. 15) cited the Taoist metaphor of water as an example of this type of leadership. "Water cleanses and refreshes all creatures without distinction and judgement; water frequently and fearlessly goes deep below the surface of things; water is fluid and responsive . . . ." A leader speaks simply and honestly and intervenes in order to shed light and create harmony.

Deliberate strategies may be used in the management of student affairs units to facilitate the process of the work group. Establishing, as an explicit norm, that it is appropriate to discuss concerns about the way a staff communicates, makes decisions, and interacts together is an important initial step. Planning retreats or workshops at the beginning stage of interaction, such as the start of a school year, can provide needed discussion to establish procedures for considering process issues. On an individual basis a leader needs to consistently pay attention to his or her own connections to staff. Quality connections are dependent upon confrontation, recognition, and other forms of direct feedback that constitute open communication.

2. A leader is able to articulate and act consistently with a clear set of values. Mission statements are typically written as reflections of the values for which institutions purport to stand. However, these statements are often lost and forgotten in the hidden recesses of college catalogs. Real values are demonstrated, however, in the daily experience of the campus. The action of leaders should similarly reflect an underlying value orientation. A leader must identify a personal sense of value and then function with these values as a source of commitment and empowerment for subsequent action. In some cases, following a principled path may necessitate courage and risk taking on the part of the leader. Leaders that act in this way, however, will receive respect for their courage of conviction and need not in retrospect take a defensive stance to justify their actions.

A common example is espousal of an affirmative action, equal opportunity position in the hiring of staff. This position may be stated in job announcements due to legislated requirements, but in many instances it may only be window dressing for the actual hiring process. How often has a search taken place with a job description written for a particular individual but openly advertised, with a preferred "in-house" candidate that is unknown to other candidates, with certain characteristics being sought that are not communicated in public, or with an implication of interest in minority candidates but without the necessary initiative to actively seek them? Leaders must establish their values and implement them with their very first contacts beginning with the hiring process.

3. A leader demonstrates respect for people through actions that value human dignity. Higher education is a system that concerns people, and its product is people. Frequently the more tangible aspects of its operation—facilities, technical assistance, computer operations, research apparatus, volumes in the library—too often command the attention of budget makers. Comparisons of institutions may even focus on how well an institution keeps pace with technology, volume collections in the library, or other quantitative measures. The people, however, make the difference at all levels of campus operations. Is an institution willing to invest in the improvement of employee conditions, the accessibility of faculty advisors to students and vice versa, the growth and enhancement opportunities for support personnel, and the representation of all campus constituents on policy making committees? Are minorities given reasonable opportunity to find a place in a college environment that accepts cultural differences and enhances success potentials, or do they feel disenfranchised in an alien milieu, under represented in the decision-making process, and without successful role models to emulate? An institution must invest fully in the enhancement and development of people by setting clear priorities in the reward system; by recognition of conditions that influence the dignity of students, employees, and public; and by communicating an attitude of human concern from the top down.

4. A leader is a model for others. In many ways a leader teaches by doing, particularly for younger members of the staff. Bandura (1977) has demonstrated that many complex occupational and social requirements are learned as a result of modeling. Human development and, perhaps, survival is facilitated by the ability of individuals to acquire new responses, by watching someone else perform an activity before doing it themselves.

The most effective way to accomplish this form of leadership is rarely by assuming the "expert" role and pretending to be special. Eastern thinking may best summarize this point:

> A leader is best
> When people barely know that one exists,
> Not so good when people obey and acclaim him/her.
> Worst when they despise him/her.
>   Fail to honor people,
>   They fail to honor you.
> But of a good leader who talks little
> When his/her work is done, his/her aim fulfilled,
> They will say, "We did this ourselves."

> From the *Way of Life: Tao Te Ching*
> according to Lao-tzu, a Taoist Chinese Scholar.

Leadership done so deftly that people are barely aware of the effort made to accomplish the task is a goal worth achieving.

5. A leader knows when to assert direct or indirect influence and when to distribute power. A familiar Kenny Rogers' song about a riverboat gambler reflects the importance of the sense of timing involved in knowing when to act, when it suggests that one needs to know when to fold, or when to hold a poker hand and, perhaps more important, when to walk away from the game completely. A leader knows when to exercise power by making decisions, when to let a consensus of the work group make a decision, or when to allow a decision to "make itself." An understanding of when to use resources and when to conserve them is also important.

Power exercised in the natural order of things creates energy. "Potency comes from knowing what is happening and acting accordingly" (Heider, 1985, p. 77). On the other hand, potency is not a "calculation or manipulation, or a matter of trying to look good." A leader acts from clarity of value, consciousness of purpose and the courage of belief and not from a sense of self-aggrandizement and personal reward. A leader who exerts power in this manner will actually energize and empower followers.

Many times in the work life of a student affairs staff this form of leadership may be demonstrated. Standing up for and supporting a position that may be generally unpopular with other segments of the campus administration is an example. Initially this may be seen as risking a position of influence with significant connections in the authority structure, but when grounded in clear argument and presented with conviction, it will generally be respected by others even when holding a different opinion. Constructing and implementing a budget is another example where leadership can exert influence by putting these resources behind the implementation of decisions and goals of an organization. Frequently, budgets are perpetuated from year to year without looking for creative possibilities to redistribute some of the available resources.

6. A leader is aware of the special nature of the system in which she or he is embedded and how this system relates (exchanges) energy with its environment. At some points a leader must focus on specific detail as it applies to a given situation but at other times the leader must view the larger picture giving attention to the total organization and its relationship to the wider world. Hall and Quinn (1983) described (1) how organizations are the means by which public policy is implemented (for example, governmental agencies, groups from the private sector, political action committees), and (3) how the bulk of public policy is aimed at organizations (for example, labor relation laws, taxation). Although the interconnections between public policy and organizations is obvious, little attention is given to this fact by many leaders.

Many modern organizations have become larger and more powerful than nation-states (Morgan, 1986). As organizations function and assert their identities they can influence transitions in the social ecology to which they belong. Institutions of higher learning are public organizations, too. Student affairs leaders need to be aware of how their institutions connect, interact, and respond to other policy making organizations. Leaders need to understand and reflect on their role in this process and function as managers of change.

7. A leader is able to make transitions to higher levels of order and inspire people to achieve similar levels of functioning. Increased awareness and enhanced autonomy are basic parts of human development. Burns (1978) proposed that a leader who is able to assist others in transcending their previous mindsets and elevate goals toward higher levels is a "transforming" leader. Instead of bargaining for separate goals, based upon individual need, the transforming leader seeks the common goal of personal development of leader and follower, each wanting to move to a higher level of potential. The value of this type of leadership is to move toward ends that reflect concepts such as liberty, justice, equality, and morality as measuring rods. Burns has seen this type of leadership as sorely lacking at times in history. He cited the examples of a Ghandi or even presidential figures like Kennedy who elicited strong feeling and reactions from people, in some cases anger, that inspired and elicited greater levels of achievement and moral direction from many followers.

Within the student affairs profession, this mode of transforming leadership is especially important to deal with cultural diversity and to achieve inclusion of previously disenfranchised groups. Examples fairly common to many campus situations are (1) student government leaders and staff advisors convincing a frugal student senate and campus administration that child care for the relatively small number of students with children should be the responsibility of the entire campus and, therefore, taxing themselves for this purpose; (2) a residence hall staff initiating education and support programs for gay and lesbian students; and (3) the establishment of student behavior guidelines that provide clear sanctions against sexual discrimination and harassment that were once seen as the "harmless" behavior of "college boys."

Transforming leadership has the potential to influence the transcendence of an entire community to a level that celebrates diversity and enhances greater human understanding and acceptance.

SUMMARY

This chapter has emphasized the need for leadership in student affairs that encompasses a broad and effective range of values and behaviors. Skills in communication, budgeting, group facilitation, and computer applications are important, but even more essential are the values a leader holds with regard to human dignity and a social structure that functions with concern for the welfare and development of all people. Leaders cannot predict all changes that will occur, but they can manage change as it occurs and help prepare people for new structure in their systems that results from those changes.

Professional education is an important influence on student affairs leaders. Academic programs need to emphasize the knowledge and skill required to function as student affairs professionals, but, in addition, they also need to focus on the values of future leaders in the field. The combined efforts of practitioners, faculty in graduate training programs, and professional associations are necessary to support and encourage quality leadership in the field.

REFERENCES

Bandura, A. (1977). *A social learning theory.* Englewood Cliffs, NJ: Prentice Hall.

Bertalanffy, L. (1968). *General system theory* (rev. ed.). New York: Braziller.

Blake, A.R., Mouton, J.S., & Williams, M.S. (1981). *The academic administrator grid: A guide to developing effective management teams.* San Francisco: Jossey-Bass.

Boyer, E.L. (1987). *College: The undergraduate experiences in America.* New York: Harper and Row.

Burns, D.M. (1978). *Leadership.* New York: Harper and Row.

Caple, R.B. (1987a). The change process in developmental theory: A self-organization paradigm, Part 1. *Journal of College Student Personnel, 28*(1), 4-11.

Caple, R.B. (1987b). The change process in developmental theory: A self-organization paradigm, Part 2. *Journal of College Student Personnel, 28*(2), 100-04.

Douglas, L.H. (1981, Sept. 19). In search of excellence on college campuses. *The Chronical of Higher Education,* p. 72.

Erikson, E. (1968). *Identity, youth and crisis.* New York: W.W. Norton.

Fiedler, F.E. (1967). *A theory of leadership effectiveness.* New York: McGraw-Hill.

Fiedler, F.E., & Mahar, L. (1979). The effectiveness of contingency model training: A review of the validity of leader match. *Personnel Psychology, 32,* 45-62.

Forsyth, D.R. (1983). *An introduction to group dynamics.* Pacific Grove, CA: Brooks/Cole.

Friedman, E.H. (1985). *Generation to generation.* New York: Guilford Press.

Gleick, J. (1987). *Chaos.* New York: Viking.

Hall, R.H., & Quinn, R.E. (1983). *Organizational theory and public policy.* Beverly Hills, CA: Sage.

Heider, J. (1985). *The Tao of leadership.* Atlanta, GA: Humanics Limited.

Hershey, P., & Blanchard, K. (1977). *Management of organizational behavior: Utilizing human resources.* Englewood Cliffs, NJ: Prentice-Hall.

Herzberg, F. (1968). One more time: How do you motivate employees? *Harvard Business Review, 46*(1), 53-62.

Hipps, G.M. (Ed.). (1982). *Effective planned change strategies.* New Directions for Institutional Research. (No. 33). San Francisco: Jossey-Bass.

House, J., & Mitchell, T.R. (1974). Path-goal theory of leadership. *Journal of Contemporary Business, 3*(4), 81-98.

Jantsch, E. (1980). *The self-organizing universe.* New York: Pergamon.

Kagan, J. (1980). Perspectives on continuity. In O.G. Brim, Jr., & J. Kagan (Eds.), *Constancy and change in human development* (pp. 26-74). Cambridge, MA: Harvard, University Press.

Keller, G. (1983). *Academic strategy: The management revolution in American higher education.* Baltimore: The Johns Hopkins University Press.

Kohlberg, L. (1981). *The philosophy of moral development: Moral stages and the idea of justice.* New York: Harper and Row.

Kouzes, J.M., & Posner, B.Z. (1987). *The leadership challenge: How to get extraordinary things done in organizations.* San Francisco: Jossey-Bass.

Kuh, G.D., Whitt, E.J., & Shedd, J.D. (1987). *Student affairs work, 2001: A paradigmatic odyssey.* Alexandria, VA: American College Personnel Association.

Kuhn, T. (1962). *The structure of scientific revolutions.* Chicago: University Chicago Press.

Levine, A. (1980). *When dreams and heroes died: A portrait of today's college students.* San Francisco: Jossey-Bass.

Maslow, A.H. (1954). *Motivation and personality.* New York: Harper and Row.

Morgan, G. (1986). *Images of organization.* Beverly Hills, CA: Sage.

Nicolis, G., & Prigogine, I. (1977). *Self-organization in nonequilibrium systems: From dissipative structures to order through fluctuations.* New York: Wiley-Interscience.

Peters, T.J., & Waterman, R.H. (1982). *In search of excellence.* New York: Harper and Row.

Prigogine, I. (1976). Order through fluctuation: Self-organization and social system. In E. Jantsch & C.H. Wadington (Eds.), *Evolution and consciousness: Human systems in transition* (pp. 93-126). Reading, MA: Addison-Wesley.

Prigogine, I., & Strengers, I. (1984). *Order out of chaos.* New York: Bantam.

Tannebaum, R., & Schmidt, W.H. (1973). How to choose a leadership pattern. *Harvard Business Review, 51*(3), 162-75.

Toffler, A. (1970). *Future Shock.* New York: Random House.

Vroom, V.H. (1984). Leaders and leadership in academe. In J.L. Bess (Ed.) *College and university organization: Insights from the behavioral sciences* (pp. 129-48). New York: New York University Press.

Vroom, V.H., & Yetton, P.W. (1973). *Leadership and decision-making.* Pittsburgh: University of Pittsburgh Press.

White, R. & Lippitt, R. (1968). Leader behavior and member reaction in three "social climates." In D. Cartwright & A. Zander (Eds.). *Group dynamics: Research and theory* (pp. 318-35). New York: Harper and Row.

SUGGESTED READINGS

Blake, A.R., Mouton, J.S., & Williams, M.S. (1981). *The academic administrator grid: A guide to developing effective management teams.* San Francisco: Jossey-Bass.

Burns, D.M. (1978). *Leadership.* New York: Harper and Row.

Heider, J. (1985). *The Tao of leadership.* Atlanta, GA: Humanics Limited.

Hershey, P., & Blanchard, K. (1982). *Management of organizational behavior: Utilizing human resources (4th ed.).* Englewood Cliffs, NJ: Prentice-Hall.

Kuh, G.D., Whitt, E.J., & Shedd, J.D. (1987). *Student affairs work, 2001: A paradigmatic odyssey.* Alexandria, VA: American College Personnel Association.

Sashkin, M., & Lassey, W.R. (Eds.). (1983). *Leadership and social change (3rd ed.).* San Diego, CA: University Associates.

Don G. Creamer, Ed.D., is professor of college student personnel at Virginia Ploytechnic Institute and State University in Blacksburg, Virginia. A former president of the American College Personnel Association, he remains active in service to professional associations, in consultation with two-year colleges, and in research into student development, organization development, and academic advising. Dr. Creamer is the author of more than 50 professional papers.

Pamela M. Frederick, M.Ed., is presently a full time doctoral student in the Counselor Education and Student Personnel department at Virginia Polytechnic Institute and State University. She is also currently a Graduate Research Assistant with the Virginia VIEW occupational information system. She received her M.Ed. from the University of Virginia in counselor education. She received her B.A. in Psychology from James Madison University. Before entering the doctoral program, Mrs. Frederick was a counselor for a Special Services program at National Business College in Roanoke, Virginia.

CHAPTER 5

ADMINISTRATIVE AND MANAGEMENT THEORIES: TOOLS FOR CHANGE

Don G. Creamer
Pamela M. Frederick

Organization patterns within higher education place student affairs administrators in prominent roles to implement educational programs of the institution. They hold many titles, such as vice president, dean, director, and coordinator, but they share common responsibilities to manage one or more units of the institution. Like all other professional roles in education, administrators are more likely to be successful if they are knowledgeable about, and able to apply, theory and research in their work.

Although management theory had its origins in industry and was impelled by concerns for increased production of goods, it has evolved as a response to a changing economy and now is used in all types of organizations, including higher education, where educational service is the primary motivation. While management theory has direct application to higher education, the terms management and manager are not ordinarily used within colleges and universities where the more familiar terms administrator and administration are preferred. Keller (1983) suggested that the distinction between administration and management in higher education is that the former is concerned with day to day activities in an institution and that management is concerned with planning, setting goals, and making changes in the institution. This perspective views administration as oriented in the present and management in the future.

Both day to day operations and planning for the future are important in higher education. Those who are called administrators in higher education would be referred to as managers in other types of organizations. Pertinent information about both the administration and management functions comes from what traditionally is known as management theory and is referred to in the literature as management; however, to remain consistent with terminology used throughout this book, the terms administrator and administration will be used interchangeably with the terms manager and management.

In this chapter several schools of thought associated with management theory are briefly reviewed . Synthesizing what is known about management from the various schools of thought, fifteen basic concepts about management are presented and the implications of the basic concepts about management for student affairs professionals are discussed. Finally, a model for using theory to promote changes in organizations is presented.

SCHOOLS OF MANAGEMENT THEORY

Even though most of the literature on management theory has been written in this century, the argument could be made that the basic concepts of management were discernable even in ancient civilizations (George, 1972). Indeed, history reveals that as people learned to organize for production, efficiency, and harmony, they used many contemporary management concepts. The systematic study of management, however, was not evident until the turn of the 20th century when Taylor (1911) began his now classic work.

In Table 5.1 is summarized the evolution of management thought in this century. Five perspectives on management are presented—classical scientific, human relations, behavioral science, management process, and quantitative—citing representative theorists; basic assumptions about people, work, and management; and selected research topics. The reader will note that the separate schools of thought contain overlapping ideas. In fact, no universal agreement exists about the distinctions used in the Table. This typology was chosen to represent important, though not always discrete, differences in evolving thought.

The distinguishing feature of the **classical scientific** school of thought holds that management has the responsibility to systematically determine the optimal performance requirements of a job and to match the best trained worker to those requirements. The **human relations** perspective points to the importance of work-group relationships, whereas the **behavioral science** approach underscores the idea that people are motivated to fulfill their needs through work. The **management process** school focuses on universal processes and functions, found in all management activities. Finally, the **quantitative** school of thought focuses on the application of mathematical and logical-theoretical equations to explain patterns of interaction within an organization. This school also is concerned with predicting consequences under selected conditions.

Theorists identified with one school of thought may agree to some extent with the basic assumptions of another perspective. Similarly, contemporary managers cannot be categorized by only one position on management. Day to day management is too complex to fit neatly into a single category. Most managers can and should take into account aspects of each school of thought to enable eclectic use of ideas that fit individual situations. In this manner, managers create their own management style based upon many theories.

GENERALIZATIONS ABOUT MANAGEMENT THEORY

Certain concepts and assumptions about management have become almost universally accepted for their veracity, which may be summarized under 15 topics:

(Continued on page 140)

TABLE 5.1
Perspectives on Management Theory

Representative Theorists	Assumptions About People, Work, and Management	Typical Areas of Research
Classical Scientific		
Frederick Taylor (1911)	The best work methods can be developed through science.	Time study
Frank and Lilian Gilbreth (1917)	Workers can be scientifically selected and developed.	Standardization of tools
	Managers respond to well trained workers.	Instructions
	Work should be equally divided between managers and employees with managers responsible for planning.	Routinizing systems
		Hand/motion studies
Human Relations		
Mary Parker Follet (1941)	People are motivated by needs.	Group processes
	People gain identity through inter-personal relations.	Group problem solving
R.J. Roethlisberger and W.J. Dickson (1941)	Routine work in industry is dissatisfying to workers.	Interpersonal relations
	Employees are influenced by peer groups more than incentives and discipline.	Decision making
Elton Mayo (1933)	Management should provide for and accept the social needs of workers.	
Behavioral Science		
Chester Barnard (1938)	Worker motivation is categorized by type of need.	Human resource use
Herbert Simon (1947)	Employees seek and are capable of finding self-fulfillment on the job.	Employee satisfaction
Chris Argyris (1957)		

Table 5.1. Continued.

Representative Theorists	Assumptions About People, Work, and Management	Typical Areas of Research
Behavioral Science (Cont.)		
Douglas McGregor (1960)	Employees are self-motivated and self-regulating and are negatively influenced by controls imposed externally.	Personnel management
Abraham Maslow (1964)		Organization theory
Frederick Herzberg (1966)	People who gain fulfillment on the job will integrate their personal goals with the organization's goals.	
Rensis Likert (1967)		
William Ouchi (1981)		
Management Process		
Henri Fayol (1949)	The management process consists of four functions: Planning, organizing, actuating, and controlling.	Division of labor
James D. Mooney and A.C. Reiley (1931)		Organization structure
	The principles of organization management are universal.	Chain of command
Peter Druker (1954)	The management process is accomplished by establishing agreed upon objectives and then creating and following a plan of action for meeting the objectives.	Degree of centralization
George Odiorne (1979)		
Quantitative		
Ford Harris (Raymond, 1931)	Management can be explained by patterns of decisions within the framework of mathematical models.	Information theory
H.S. Owen (1925)		Inventory control
Benjamin Cooper (1926)	Organization consists of three factors: input, process, and output.	Game theory
Harold Hotelling (1925)		Linear programming
	Input, process, and output must be optimized for peak performance.	Replacement theory
Ellis Johnson (1953)		Symbolic logic

1. *All managerial decisions are contingent on circumstances;* therefore, no one best way exists to manage (Carlisle, 1973).

2. *Centralization, a condition of little delegation of authority, achieves conformity and coordination and avoids duplication.* Decentralization, a wide delegation of authority, motivates lower level managers, obtains quicker decisions, develops better managers and allows those closest to a situation to make decisions regarding that situation (Drucker, 1954). Decentralization is increasingly becoming the preferred means of coping within large organizations (Pfiffner & Sherwood, 1960).

3. *Division of labor, the practice of dividing work into component parts, benefits an organization by increasing productivity, profit, and efficiency although excessive division of labor can result in low worker satisfaction and motivation* (Rogers & McIntire, 1983).

4. *The scalar principle maintains that the chain of command in an organization should clearly include all members of the organization so that each person knows to whom to report and from whom to take orders* (Rogers & McIntire, 1983).

5. *Functional departmentalization is the most commonly used organization method.* This principle asserts that units should have homogeneous activities and common functions. Functional departmentalization results in greater efficiency and economy but it can lead to an overly intense focus on a single function, problems in teamwork, and interdepartmental conflicts (Rogers & McIntire, 1983).

6. *Span of control refers to the number of employees reporting directly to a manager.* Span of control can be broad when employees are capable, well-educated, and highly motivated. Span of control tends to be narrow however, in organizations with technical tasks or a great amount of regulation. Narrow spans of control result in small, cohesive groups that have good horizontal

communication. Highly motivated employees with good vertical communication and developed decision making skills are associated with broad spans of control (Carlisle, 1973).

7. *For managers, communication serves as a way to implement and coordinate activities and as a means of motivating employees.* One-way communication is from the top down, which is faster but results in less accuracy and lower morale. Two-way communication flows both up and down. Although two-way communication is slower, it results in greater accuracy and improved morale (Flippo, 1970).

8. *How an employee is compensated determines his or her status within an organization.* How compensation relates to the pay of others, especially that of peers, is important in determining status. Managers should try and balance recognition of the individual with stability and maintenance of the organization, although no compensation system can be completely balanced (Drucker, 1977).

9. *Managers make types of decisions ranging from completely programmed to completely nonprogrammed.* Programmed decisions are highly structured with a prescribed method of handling known problems. Nonprogrammed decisions involve new and ill-defined problems and result in less certain decisions (Simon, 1947).

10. *When employees participate in decision making, it can lead to greater accuracy and acceptance of decisions as well as better communication, more cooperation, and higher commitment.* Participation is associated with higher morale and motivation (Terry & Franklin, 1982).

11. *The most useful management plans are flexible enough to allow for changing as the situation changes* (Rogers & McIntire, 1983). Goals included in a management plan should supplement and be integrated well with the goals of other organization groups (Terry & Franklin, 1982).

12. *Conflict exists in every organization.* Conflict always exists because of goal differences, group interdependence and perceptual differences (Downs, 1968). Managers should recognize conflict as normal and interpret the usefulness of conflict for making goal changes, reassigning resources, or altering procedures (Terry & Franklin, 1982).

13. *Management style is affected by assumptions about human nature.* McGregor (1960) postulated two theories of management that tend to be predominant. He proposed that *Theory-X* managers believe people are indolent, unambitious, passive, self centered, gullible, and resistant to change. Therefore, employees must be persuaded, rewarded, punished, and controlled. *Theory-Y* managers believe people have the motivation and capability to assume responsibility and self-direction on the job. Managers, therefore, must create an environment in which employees can achieve goals by their own efforts (McGregor, 1960). Argyris (1971) added Pattern A and Pattern B behaviors to Theory-X and Theory-Y management assumptions. *Pattern A* behaviors reflect managers' norms of conformity, antagonism, and mistrust. Pattern B managers' behaviors reflect norms of trust, concern and individuality. Argyris believes Theory X/Pattern A organizations need to move toward Theory Y/Pattern B. More recently, Ouchi (1981) postulated an even more advanced theory. His *Theory-Z* management evolved from Japanese management style and emphasizes an integrated and supportive working environment based on trust, long-term employment, and close personal relationships. (See Chapter 4 for greater detail.)

14. *Highly cohesive groups are associated with high morals and the ability to stay together in a variety of situations.* Cohesiveness is highest when a group's members' personal goals are being advanced by the group's goals (Rogers & McIntire, 1983). Group productivity is highest when group members believe the organization's goals correspond to the group goals (Seashore, 1954).

15. *Behavior is related to the expectation of rewards.*
Employees must expect that working harder will improve
their performance on the job and that high performance
is related to desirable rewards. Reward valence is the
internal need for a reward (Vroom, 1964). Aside from
pay, motivating rewards include challenging work, added
responsibility, opportunities for advancement, recognition
and praise, and opportunities for personal growth
(Herzberg, 1966).

MANAGEMENT THEORY AND STUDENT AFFAIRS

Student affairs professionals can use these basic
management concepts and assumptions to become more aware
of how management works. Attention should be paid to the
manner in which responsibility is delegated. New professionals
should become familiar with the chain-of-command within
the institution and should determine each administrator's
span of control and devise ways he or she can fit within
the prevailing structure of the institution.

New employees in an organization should observe
communication patterns carefully. Notice who participates
in nonprogrammed decision making and whether decisions
are communicated from the top down or are the product
of two-way communication. Pay attention to how conflict
is handled. Find out what formal and informal groups exist
and then discern their levels of cohesiveness. Closely observe
the behaviors of administrators to determine which basic
assumptions about human nature they use to guide their
actions and how these assumptions affect their management
styles. Become aware of planning processes. Carefully develop
personal work goals, work groups' (departmental) goals and
the institution's goals. Discover how these goals fit together
and where incongruencies may exist.

EXPECTATIONS OF NEW PROFESSIONALS

New professionals have much to gain by observing the
behavior of managers. New professionals are expected to possess

knowledge about the theory and research in their field and to be skilled in writing, speaking, interviewing, assessing, programming, and evaluating. Other expectations of student affairs practitioners may be much less obvious.

New professionals may be expected to conduct an informal assessment of all other professionals with whom direct and immediate interaction is required. This task would be assigned to ascertain colleagues' roles and duties, professional and personal interests, perspectives on the organization and the subunits in which each person works, judgments on the formal and informal decision making structures, views on the organization culture, ideas about needed innovation, and opinions about organization politics, including who are the opinion leaders and/or the antagonists toward creative application of ideas. Learning these things about colleagues need not be stiff or formal, but it should be done fairly early.

New professionals may be expected to study the organization's goals and procedures to become thoroughly familiar with current conditions that enable and/or hinder student affairs initiatives. Being clear about organization goals also helps practitioners know which initiatives are needed most and which are of secondary priority.

New professionals may be expected to practice professional skills such as interviewing, advising, programming, employee supervision and procedures oversight, budgeting and resource management, assessment and evaluation, and data generation and research. Likely new professionals will require help in some or all of these areas so as to meet supervisors' expectations that new employees will take the initiative to ensure growing competence in all key areas of professional practice.

New professionals may be expected to receive constructive criticism on performance nondefensively and work to remove deficiencies and to sharpen strengths. Especially important is that new employees demonstrate an openness to feedback from colleagues and supervisors about their work. Openness may set the tone for future collegiality or partnerships that are crucial to advancement in the organization.

New professionals may be expected to set sensible goals for personal and professional activities and to negotiate reasonable support from supervisors. One of the principal indicators of institutional effectiveness is whether professionals' goals have been met; thus, crucial to this is that goals be explicitly stated and clear. At the same time, goals must be appropriate to the setting, reflect a mutual respect for others, and represent accurately evolving status in the profession.

No guarantees of success can be given for any professional, but new employees who meet these expectations may be in a better position to achieve and gain recognition within the organization and the profession. Those who do not may have to depend on overpowering raw talent or luck, which seldom is dependable in the long run.

Often new professionals have their sights set on becoming mid- or upper-level administrators in student affairs. This is a routine ambition in most student affairs operations and upper-level administrators are attentive to promising new professionals. Established administrators need to encourage beginning professionals to strengthen the ranks of institutional leaders and may be watching for certain indicators that signal leadership potential. New professionals who hold aspirations for administrative advancement, therefore, may wish to pay particular attention to sharpening basic skills in written and oral communication; to honing talents in basic research and evaluation; to developing competence in planning, budgeting, and supervising others; and to learning when and how to offer creative ideas for organizational transformation. Also crucial is that administrators who wish to be leaders must be knowledgeable of and able to use theories of organization change and development.

BEING AN EFFECTIVE
AGENT FOR CHANGE

Management theory and knowledge of its use in organizations has a very practical side, for professionals who understand and can use theory are more likely to become leaders than those who cannot. However, the discussion to this point has been geared primarily to individual performance in delivering direct service to students and colleagues. Note also must be taken of other factors involved in organizational change that practitioners must recognize as well.

New professionals need to know that organizations change over time for many reasons. Sometimes organizations change because of the turnover of key people. This reason may be particularly apparent when the president leaves and a new leader takes the position. Organizations also change in response to compelling pressures from outside forces, such as demands from the state or federal governments that created and continue to fund public colleges. For example, when the federal government mandates adherence to a law to qualify an institution to receive significant amounts of funds, institutional leaders typically insure at least selective adaptation to conform to regulatory requirements.

Often forces from inside the organization provide the impetus for change. Creative people with ideas for improved service or new programs may provoke a process of planning for change; that is, that certain persons assume leadership roles to design a new approach to a routine task or to add a new initiative to existing practices. These persons sometimes are called "change agents" due to their intentional and directed efforts to alter the organization in some important way. They often are administrators who already possess much responsibility for selected organizational functions.

The ability to influence the entire organization by altering its goals, policies, structures, technology, programs, culture, or problem solving capacity reflects high level skill and a supreme application of professional craft. To be truly effective, student-affairs professionals should be able to promote change consistently in both individuals and in the organization. The required knowledge for transforming organizations is planned change. In a context of well-rounded professionalism, the following can be used to guide practitioners' approaches to effecting organization change.

Like management, the processes of planning and implementing lasting change in an organization can be best understood by a knowledge of relevant theory. Unlike management, however, planned change is not well undergirded by theory. Knowledge of intents and consequences of planned change historically has been shaped by consultant reports, though such limitations are rapidly being overshadowed by emerging theoretical models and research.

One of the earliest theoretical models of change was advanced by Lewin (1948) who argued that changes in organization culture can be brought about through re-education of members. He posited that organizational conditions must first be unfrozen, then changed, then refrozen. This model is vague, but accurate, about the panoramic perspective of change. A later model, called *planned change* (Lippitt, Watson, & Westley, 1958), is characterized by practical steps to be taken by an external consultant. This model calls for phases of scouting, entry, diagnosis, planning, action, stabilization and evaluation, and termination. One might imagine this model to represent Lewin's premises in greater detail. French and Bell (1978) proposed another model called *action research* that builds on earlier models and is characterized by reliance on data generated about the organization and use of feedback to principal actors controlling a change project. (The place of planned change models in organization development is dealt with in more detail in Chapter 3.)

Until recently, most research and theory building about planned change occurred in organizations other than higher education. Knowledge of many issues germane to planning for successful change in higher education has been advanced by the work of Lindquist (1978) who explained the role of information linkages in planned change, Levine (1980) who spotlighted views of the processes used by organizations to diffuse or reject new knowledge throughout the organization, and Martorana and Kuhns (1975) who illuminated the role of selected internal factors that influence decisions to adopt innovations. Creamer and Creamer (1986a, 1986b, 1988, 1989) have more recently presented work grounded in higher education, and, for the most part, totally within student affairs. Their research led to a model called the **Probability of Adoption of Change (PAC)** model.

The essential elements of the PAC model are presented in Table 5.2. The most basic tenet of the model is that the likelihood of institutional adoption of a specific planned change project can be predicted by knowledge of nine environmental conditions. Each condition is configured by specific attributes. For example, the variable *Circumstances* assembles its force from the source of impetus for change and from the level of felt need for the change. *Value Compatibility* is indicative of success to the extent that the values of the project and those of the existing environment and culture are harmonious. The clarity of the idea and the likelihood that the goals and ways to achieve them can be communicated are the qualities of *Idea Comprehensibility* that give the condition its force. *Practicality* is a condition shaped by availability of both human and fiscal resources.

A central feature of the PAC model is the superintendency variables. *Superintendency* connotes direction or guidance given to a change project and takes three forms—*Top-Level Support*, characterized by the persistent and continuous backing of the chief executive; *Leadership*, revealed by action to marshall resources and to cultivate an initial readiness for the idea within the organization; and *Championship*, representing the persuasive advocacy of the idea by one or more persons with authority to carry out the implementation plan.

Advantage Probability in the PAC model points to the issue of whether the adoption of the idea will solve wide spread or perplexing problems of the institution. Finally, *Strategies* alerts the change agent to the need to use many approaches or methods to communicate the implementation tactics that involve as many stakeholders as possible in the overall effort.

Taken together, this model identifies for the student affairs practitioner the institutional conditions that must be controlled to varying degrees for success of innovative projects to be ensured. Thus, the model has heuristic value to the practitioner. It can serve as a guide to organized change and as a diagnostic tool for assessing the progress of change projects. The model can even serve as a framework for the initial assessment to determine the likelihood that a specific project is worth whatever effort may be required for its institutionalization.

TABLE 5.2
Probability of Adoption of Change Model

Key Variables	Variable Definitions
Circumstances	Refers to the source of impetus for change, environmental readiness, and the degree of felt need for change.
Value Compatibility	Refers to the degree of harmony between the values and procedures of the project and those of the institution.
Idea Comprehensibility	Refers to clarity and simplicity of the project goals, the ability to articulate ways to implement them, and the timing of the project.
Practicality	Refers to the adequacy of the personnel and other resources necessary to carry out the project.
Superintendency Top-Level Support Leadership Championship	Refers to three levels of authority and guidance that shepherd the project.
Advantage Probability	Refers to the likelihood that the project will solve perplexing problems of the institution.
Strategies	Refers to the adequacy of the procedures or methods used to insitutionalize the project.

Adapted from D.G. Creamer & E.G. Creamer (1986a).

Assume, for example, that a practitioner in career planning and placement at a comprehensive university wishes to modify the program of career development activities for freshmen and sophomore students. The plan is to consolidate career planning and placement with academic advising activities of the respective colleges within the university and to make both activities more developmental. The practitioner wants to offer a well integrated, comprehensive initiative to help students set goals and plan for both academic and career futures. This is a simple idea that assumes that if professionals work together toward common goals, students may be served more efficiently and effectively. The implementation of this idea, however, will not be simple. Implementation requires wide spread support of people at several levels of the university, including people who may not think the idea is worth the trouble.

The professional could use the PAC model as a tool for assessing the probabilities of achieving the goals of such an initiative by gathering answers to questions inherent in the PAC variables. Questions to be answered prior to formal planning might include the following:

1. Is there a wide spread felt need for this change? Will the source of the idea garner support from key people across the university? These questions relate to the variable, *circumstances,* and inform the innovator about the general climate for change.

2. Does the scheme to connect career planning and placement with academic advising "fit" the customs of the university? Will it be perceived as an intrusion into the sanctity of academic affairs? Answers to these questions give a fair indication of the *value compatibility* of the project activities and goals with the prevailing culture of the university.

3. To determine the degree of *idea comprehensibility,* it must be decided whether the implementation goals and the strategies can be communicated clearly. Are there many ways to achieve the goals or must everyone use the same strategies?

4. Will it require cost sharing? Will the costs of both activities rise? Will expenditures for this project compete well against all other needs of the university? These are questions that help assess the *practicality* of the project.

5. Leadership of three types may well determine whether the project can be implemented, including *top-level support, leadership,* and *championship.* Will top-level administrators support the idea? Will immediate supervisors help set the stage for the change? Is there someone who can take charge for as long as necessary to make the project work?

6. Will many people see the advantages of the project? This issue relates to *advantage probability* and is instructive about the level of energy people may be willing to give to a project of innovation.

7. Will the project require negotiation through the academic governance system of the institution or can it be handled as an administrative matter? Can cooperation be marshalled from all those necessary to plan and implement the project? These are important questions and strategies.

If these questions can be answered prior to planning for implementation, judgments can be made as to the likelihood of success and plans can be shaped to deal with questionable conditions. If the evidence gathered from these questions suggests wide spread interest and concern that the proposed change would genuinely improve educational opportunities for students and that major constituencies would help to achieve the goals of the project, then the practitioner may proceed with the confidence of support from colleagues. If the evidence suggests weak interest and concern and/or pockets of opposition, the practitioner may choose to spend more time educating colleagues about the virtues of the idea, or, if support clearly is not there, possibly to abandon the project.

The PAC model also has theoretical value. For example, outcomes from the research to date on the model suggest that level of participation of constituents is a key ingredient in change project success. Likewise, communication linkages and information flow appear to play major roles in determining success or failure. Thus, *Idea Comprehensibility, Superintendency,* and *Strategies* appear to be powerful indicators of outcomes. Hypotheses about participation, communication, and information use can be framed within the context of the theory and tested for salience. A particularly useful procedure may be to conduct research studies of the conditions that control or shape innovations or change at a specific institution.

What is the value of theory about change to new professionals, or to aspiring managers, in student affairs? The utility of change theory rests on the issue of whether professionals intend to gain dominion over their environments. Obviously, those who are content to work within surroundings as they exist or to implement only those programs already operational have little practical need for change theory. But many student affairs professionals seem discontent with existing policies, structures, programs, or general patterns of interaction with students and strive to institute change through proposing innovative ideas to leaders. The knowledge of planned change theory gives one professional an edge over another in taking actions intended to change the organization. A student affairs administrator who is unarmed with a knowledge of change theory and who is presented with competing ideas for change may have little basis for decided what to support and what to discourage. Conversely, the administrator appropriately equipped with change theory awareness is in a better situation to carry out innovative projects and to pick persons within the organization to serve in key roles, such as project champion or the person who would actually carry out plans.

SUMMARY

Student affairs professionals are involved heavily in the management of colleges and universities. Their effectiveness, therefore, is related to their knowledge and use of management theory, both in day-to-day practice and in planning for the future of their departments, divisions, and institutions. Both structural and human resource elements of management theory are important to student affairs. Sound organization structure promotes efficiency, clarity of communication patterns, and departmental or unit coordination. Sound management of human resources often encourages open communication, employee participation in decision making, group cohesiveness, high staff morale and motivation, and commitment to common goal achievement. The skillful application of both aspects of management are critical to the achievement of institutional effectiveness.

The wise use of management theory is especially critical for a manager acting as a change agent to implement innovations or to develop plans for the future. The PAC model may be useful in this case. When change is necessary in the organization, as it often is due to new demands for service, new technologies, new concepts, or new priorities, the PAC model may serve as a guide to administrators to alert them to internal forces that shape or control outcomes of planned change efforts.

REFERENCES

Argyris, C. (1957). *Personality and organization.* New York: McGraw Hill.

Argyris, C. (1971). *Management and organizational development: The path from XA to YB.* New York: McGraw Hill.

Barnard, C. (1938). *The functions of the executive.* Cambridge, MA: Harvard University Press.

Carlisle, H. (1973). *Situational management: A contingency approach to leadership.* New York: AMACOM.

Cooper, B. (1926). How to determine the economical manufacturing quantities. *Industrial Management, 72,* 228-33.

Creamer, D.G., & Creamer, E.G. (1986a). Applying a model of planned change to program innovation in student affairs. *Journal of College Student Personnel, 27,* 19-26.

Creamer, E.G., & Creamer, D.G. (1986b). The role of leaders and champions in planned change in student affairs. *Journal of College Student Personnel, 27,* 431-37.

Creamer, E.G., & Creamer, D.G. (1988). Predicting successful organization change: Case studies. *Journal of College Student Development, 29,* 4-11.

Creamer, E.G., & Creamer, D.G. (1989). Testing a model of planned change across student affairs and curricular reform projects. *Journal of College Student Development, 30,* 27-34.

Downs, A. (1968). *Inside bureaucracy.* Boston: Little & Brown.

Drucker, P. (1954). *The practice of management.* New York: Harper & Brothers.

Drucker, P. (1977). *An introductory view of management.* New York: Harper & Row.

Fayol, H. (1949). *General and industrial management.* London: Sir Isaac Pitman & Sons.

Flippo, E. (1970). *Management: A behavioral approach.* Boston: Allyn & Bacon.

Follet, M. (1941). *Dynamic administration: The collected papers of Mary Parker Follet.* New York: Harper.

French, W.L., & Bell, C.H., Jr. (1978). *Organization development (2nd ed.).* Englewood Cliffs, NJ: Prentice-Hall.

George, C. (1972). *The history of management thought.* Englewood Cliffs, NJ: Prentice-Hall.

Gilbreth, F., & Gilbreth L. (1917). *Applied motion study*. New York: Sturgis & Walton.

Herzberg, F. (1966). *Work and the nature of man*. New York: World.

Hotelling, H. (1925). A general mathematical theory of depreciation. *Journal of American Statistical Association, 22*, 340-44.

Johnson, E. (1953). *The applications of operations research to industry*. Baltimore, MD: The Johns Hopkins University Press.

Keller, G. (1983). *Academic strategy: The management revolution in American higher education*. Baltimore, MD: The Johns Hopkins University Press.

Levine, A. (1980). *Why innovation fails*. Albany, NY: State University of New York Press.

Lewin, K. (1948). *Resolving social conflicts*. New York: Harper.

Likert, R. (1967). *The human organization: Its management and value*. New York: McGraw-Hill.

Lindquist, J. (1978). *Strategies for change*. Berkeley, CA: Pacific Soundings Press.

Lippitt, R., Watson, J., & Westley, B. (1958). *The dynamics of planned change*. New York: Harcourt, Brace and World.

Martorana, S.V., & Kuhns, E. (1975). *Managing academic change*. San Francisco: Jossey-Bass.

Maslow, A. (1964). *Motivation and personality*. New York: Harper & Rowe.

Mayo, E. (1933). *The social problems of an industrial civilization*. Boston: Division of Research, Harvard Business School.

McGregor, D. (1960). *The human side of enterprise*. New York: McGraw-Hill.

Moony, J.D., & Reiley, A. C. (1931). *Onward industry!* New York: Harper & Brothers.

Odiorne, G. (1979). *MBO II: A system of managerial leadership for the 80s*. Belmont, CA: Fearon Pitman.

Odiorne, G. (1987). *The human side of management: Management by integration*. Belmont, CA: Fearon Pitman.

Owen, H. (1925). How to maintain proper inventory control. *Industrial Management, 69*, 83-85.

Ouchi, W. (1981). *Theory Z: How American business can meet the Japanese challenge.* Reading, MA: Addison-Wesley.

Pfiffner, J., & Sherwood, F. (1960). *Administrative organization.* Englewood Cliffs, NJ: Prentice-Hall.

Raymond, F. (1931). *Quantity and economy in manufacturing.* New York: McGraw-Hill.

Roethlisberger, R. J., & Dickson, W. J. (1941). *Management and the Worker.* Cambridge, MA: Harvard University Press.

Rogers, R. E., & McIntire, R. H. (1983). *Organization and management theory.* New York: Wiley.

Seashore, S. (1954). *Group cohesiveness in the industrial work group.* Ann Arbor, MI: University of Michigan.

Simon, H. (1947). *Administrative behavior.* New York: Macmillan.

Taylor, F. (1911). *Principles of scientific management.* New York: Harper.

Terry, G., & Franklin, S. (1982). *Principles of management.* Homewood, IL: Richard D. Irwin.

Vroom, V. (1964). *Work and motivation.* New York: Wiley.

SUGGESTED READINGS

Bennis, W. (1989). *Why leaders can't lead.* San Francisco: Jossey-Bass.

Creamer, D., & Associates (1990). *College student development: Theory and practice for the 1990s.* Alexandria, VA: American College Personnel Association.

Keller, G. (1983). *Academic strategy: The management revolution in American higher education.* Baltimore: The Johns Hopkins University Press.

Odiorne, G. (1987). *The human side of management: Management by integration.* Belmont, CA: Fearon Pitman.

C. Carney Strange, Ph.D., serves as Associate Professor and Chair of the Department of College Student Personnel at Bowling Green State University where he has been employed as a faculty member since 1978. Recipient of the Ralph F. Berdie Memorial Research Award from the Ameican Association for Counseling and Development, Strange completed his B.A. degree at St. Meinrad College of Liberal Arts and M.A. and Ph.D. degrees at the University of Iowa. His teaching and research has focused on student development, the impact of educational environments, needs and characteristics of returning adult learners, and factors that encourage student involvement in quality out-of-clas experiences. An active member of several professional organizations, Strange has served on the editiorial boards of both the *National Association of Student Personnel Administrators Journal* and the *Journal of College Student Development.* He now serves as a member of the directorate body of the Commission on Professional Preparation of the American College Personnel Association.

CHAPTER 6

MANAGING COLLEGE ENVIRONMENTS: THEORY AND PRACTICE

Carney Strange

Over the past fifty years American postsecondary education has witnessed a profound revolution in scale, purpose, and clientele. What was once a relatively homogeneous system, serving the few who could afford it (mostly white, middle or upper class, males) for purposes of developing student character and good moral habits, is now a multiplex of institutional types serving a vast number of students for as many different reasons. For every college student enrolled in 1940 there are now eight in nearly twice the number of institutions (Bonner, 1986). The mixture and variety of students has changed as well. "New students" (Cross, 1971) continue to bring a greater range of expectations of what colleges and universities can and should do for them. Returning adult learners look for assistance in responding to changing life goals and circumstances (Cross, 1981); previously disenfranchised minority groups seek channels of opportunity and access to social change; and traditional-age students expect marketable skills and a career-oriented curriculum that will secure a position for them in the young adult world.

This revolution in higher learning has given rise to a complex maze of state, private, and community-based institutions that is as challenging and difficult to comprehend for the faculty and administrators who work within them, as it is for those students who must choose among them. "What college should I go to?" A conveniently located regional state university? A small private college assuring personalized attention? A large multiversity promising the excitement of cutting edge research and a diverse student body? What about all the options within? Should I commute to campus or live in a residence hall? A single-sex or coed living arrangement? Should I continue to explore as an "undecided student" or commit to a major now?

From the faculty viewpoint the task is equally difficult. "Students no longer respond to my teaching the way they used to." What can I do differently? How will this approach work with older students? How can I create an exciting learning environment in a classroom of 200 students? How can I help students make better decisions about their choices of career majors?

Administrators, too, are puzzled by all the options. What "institutional image" should we project to get the type of student who will do well here? What can make our institution more attractive to minority students? How can we accommodate individual needs in a cost effective manner? What can be done to increase our student retention rate? What is needed to reduce the first semester freshman attrition rate?

An essential problem facing postsecondary institutions today is the creation and maintenance of a campus environment that attracts, satisfies, sustains, and involves students in the achievement of their educational goals. A major part of that responsibility lies in the hands of student affairs practitioners who as admissions counselors and orientation directors, recruit and acclimate new students to the campus environment; as residence hall educators, assist them in accommodating the challenges of communal living; as student activity and organization advisers, introduce students to the opportunities of campus involvement and leadership; as personal counselors, assist them in understanding the adjustments required of life transitions; and as academic, career, and placement advisers, assist in their choosing a personally fulfilling academic/occupational goal. What is needed to guide these practices is a comprehensive model of the college environment that describes its various features and sub-environments and assists the campus community (faculty, students, and staff alike) in understanding how such factors can either encourage or inhibit student development (Strange & King, 1990). Although a single comprehensive model does not exist, various environmental theories and concepts are in the literature that can prove useful in understanding the interaction of students with the college environment. This chapter surveys the major models and addresses their application to the professional practice of student development on the college campus.

OVERVIEW OF
EXTANT ENVIRONMENTAL MODELS

Four basic models or sets of concepts exist, each with a distinct corresponding literature, that examine the nature and effect of human environments: (1) *physical models* address the natural and synthetic physical features of human environments, noting the limits they set on the behavior that can occur within them; (2) *human aggregate models* emphasize that environments are transmitted through people and reflect the collective characteristics of those individuals who inhabit them; (3) *structural organizational models* underscore the importance of goals and purposes of environments, which give rise to various organizational structures that, in turn, enhance or inhibit certain environmental characteristics and outcomes; and (4) *perceptual models* acknowledge that a critical element in understanding how individuals experience an environment is their subjective interpretation of that environment. Collectively, these four sets of concepts are useful in understanding how the design of educational environments can enhance the experience and development of students on campus. Each set of concepts is summarized in the material that follows and each contains an exemplary sampling of tentative conclusions relevant to that perspective.

Models of the Physical Environment

The basic premise of these models is that all environments contain physical features, both natural and synthetic, that influence human behavior within them. Natural physical features, created primarily for purposes of shelter, include elements such as architectural design, space, amenities, and distance. Both sets of features, through various conditions of light, density, noise, temperature, and air quality, combine to create a powerful influence on an individual's attraction to and satisfaction within a setting.

At the very least, the physical environment sets broad limits on the phenomena that can occur in any given setting, making some behaviors more or less likely to occur than others—a model labeled "intersystems congruence" (Michelson, 1970, p. 25). According to his perspective, aspects of the physical environment interact with other features of the setting (e.g., social systems) to affect the probability of various phenomena occuring. For example a large theater style classroom with immovable seating may set limits on the extent to which group discussions can occur, regardless of types of students involved or the best efforts of the instructor. On the other hand, some phenomena are encouraged because of those physical limitations, as is evident on many campuses where bare paths are quickly worn through once green lawn to find the shortest distance between two points. Although the physical environment may not directly cause specific behaviors or attitudes, its limitations present challenges that must be negotiated by those within.

From the view of a prospective college student, the physical features are often among the most important factors in terms of creating a critical first impression of an institution (Sturner, 1973; Thelin & Yankovich, 1987) [See Chapter 19]. The basic layout of the campus, open spaces and shaded lawns, interior color schemes, the shape and design of a residence hall or classroom building, a library or gallery, an impressive fitness center, and even the weather on the day of a campus visit, all shape initial attitudes in subtle ways (Stern, 1986). Admissions offices have more recently begun to understand and to exploit the power of these images with the use of videotapes, offering potential students a quick, economical, and manicured tour of campus life in the privacy of their home.

The on-campus residence hall offers a classic study of the influences of the physical environment (Heilweil, 1973). The number of floors, the location of stairwells and elevators, the design of inner spaces (e.g., suites vs. traditional room arrangements, private baths vs. "gang showers"), the use of amenities, and distances to communal facilities all play an important role in the quality of a student's campus experience. These aspects also can be a positive force for development in students' lives (Strange, 1983). For example, development of relationships and consequent interpersonal skills is often influenced by conditions of physical proximity to others (Yinon, Goldenberg, & Neeman, 1977); likewise, opportunities for expression and development of personal identity lie in the flexibility students may enjoy in shaping and arranging their immediate living space. (Refer to Chapter 19 for a more detailed examination of these phenomena.)

In the interest of creating residence hall environments that enhance the student development mission of the institution, recent attention has been directed toward application of the concepts of territoriality (Schroeder, 1979a), personal space (Anchors, Schroeder, & Jackson, 1978), and the development of community (Ender, Kane, Mable, & Strohm, 1980). These approaches encourage students to assume greater responsibility for individualizing the design of and exerting control over their own living spaces.

A Sampling of Conclusions and Implications. Just as theories of human development have served as sources of awareness and insight for thinking about students and their responses (Parker, 1977), theory and research about human environments also can serve as an important source of information for understanding the design and effect of various educational practices. The following, empirically supported, tentative conclusions excerpted from Moos (1986) offer a sampling of these findings with respect to physical environments. To illustrate the connection between theory, research, and practice (Strange & King, 1990), the implications of each conclusion are examined in light of the practice of student affairs on the college campus according to Moos (1986).

1. There is a tendency for people to be rated as less attractive under hot (and subjectively uncomfortable) conditions. (p.399)

2. Interpersonal judgments may be affected by the characteristics of the room in which the judgments take place (e.g., judgments of people are more negative in ugly physical environments). (p. 402)

3. Complaints about lack of space and privacy are related to the social composition of the living unit rather than the number of occupants only. (p. 404)

4. There are consistent sex differences in reaction to crowding. Males in small crowded rooms are more competitive and harsh, feel less pleasant and friendly, and like other participants less than males in large uncrowded rooms. Female subjects produce opposite results, being more cooperative and perceiving their experience as more pleasant and other subjects as more likable and friendlier, in small than in large rooms. (p. 404)

The first two conclusions (1 and 2) focus on the comfort and condition of physical spaces and their effects on inter-personal judgments. A general implication of this connection is that faculty and student affairs staff need to be conscious of the importance of the conditions of spaces over which they have control, particularly when interacting with students. For example, perhaps to the best interest of the college community, in general, the institution's admissions, placement and alumni offices all have (and they most often do) the latest styles, decorations, and amenities, since this is where potential students, employers, and donors are likely to make judgments about the institution. Much like the function of a living room or den in a home, these offices serve to create valuable impressions for "guests" and may make a difference as to how they respond to the setting.

The second two conclusions (3 and 4) both focus on issues of density and crowding. The decision whether to expand housing facilities is currently a precarious one for some residential campuses, due to highly competitive and fluctuating enrollment trends. Many are faced with the problem of "overbooking" current residence facilities, with the expectation that not all admitted students will show. However, when matriculation rates exceed available spaced, the placement of students in lounge areas and other temporary facilities as a short term solution may result. Although such crowded conditions are never desirable, the last two conclusions in the list may yield some clues as to how best to handle such a situation. Accordingly, the keys to minimizing complaints about the lack of space and privacy lie in the social and gender composition of the group affected. If possible, students with similar characteristics (e.g., similar academic majors or hometowns) might be assigned to temporary overflow space since the potential for congruence and satisfaction is maximized in such a homogeneous grouping. Likewise, such conditions might prove more successful (questions of equity aside) with female students involved rather than male students. On the other hand, these conclusions also suggest that crowded conditions, particularly those involving males, may warrant special anticipatory interventions (e.g., additional staff, workshops on negotiating differences, or managing conflict) to prevent potential problems from arising.

In summary, the physical features of the environment influence the extent to which individuals are attracted to and satisfied within any given setting. They also set broad limits on the phenomena that can occur within them. Student affairs educators need particularly to be aware of purposes and goals of various campus environments and the appropriateness of their physical features for achieving those goals.

Human Aggregate Models

Human aggregate models focus on the collective characteristics of people within an environment. These theories assume that the characteristics of an environment are collectively transmitted through its inhabitants and, therefore, the dominant characteristic of the individuals within determines the dominant feature of that environment. Measuring and understanding the nature of an environment then involves assessing the various characteristics of its inhabitants. The works of Astin

(1968), Holland (1973), and Myers (1980) exemplify this approach.

In Astin's earlier work (1962) he assumed that the activities of individuals in the environment (regardless of their personalities or interests) constitute the only legitimate source of observable stimulus in an environment. For example, the extent to which a campus environment created a press toward intellectual or academic interests would be reflected in observable and quantifiable incidences of behaviors such as student trips to the library, formal and informal discussions, books read, and faculty-student interactions. Differences in strength of environmental press from one setting to the next are reflected in different frequencies of such behaviors. Measurement of these environmental features involves self reports of various individuals' activities and behaviors in the setting and the collective effect of these reported activities constitutes the dominant feature of the environment (e.g., 90 out of 100 students sampled reporting frequent informal discussions with faculty outside of the classroom).

Holland (1973) contended that information about individual personalities in the environment is the key to understanding its dominant feature, since individuals' activities and behaviors are assumed to be a direct reflection of their personality and interests. Assessment of those various interests represented among the environmental occupants, as is done in using the *Environmental Assessment Technique (EAT)* (Astin & Holland, 1961), provides an adequate measure of that environment. Six different environmental occupational interest patterns are identified in Holland's model: (1) **Realistic** environments demand the explicit, ordered, or systematic manipulation of objects, tools, machines, and animals (e.g., an environment dominated by engineers); (2) **Investigative** environments encourage scientific and scholarly activities and offer opportunities for observation and symbolic, systematic, creative investigation of physical, biological, or cultural phenomena (e.g., anthropology) (3) **Artistic** environments are characterized by the dominance of demands and opportunities that entail ambiguous, free, and unsystematized activities and competencies to create art forms or products (e.g., theatre); (4) **Social** environments encourage understanding, cooperation, and sociability and present opportunities that entail the manipulation of others to inform, train, develop, cure, or enlighten (e.g., counseling); (5) *Enterprising* environments demand the manipulation of others to attain organizational or self-interest goals and people to see themselves as aggressive, confident, and leading (e.g., business); and (6) *Conventional* environments entail the explicit, ordered, systematic manipulation and organization of data according to a prescribed plan, and they encourage people to see themselves as conforming and orderly (e.g., accounting).

According to Holland, environments are distinguished by their degree of *differentiation* and *consistency.* A highly differentiated (or focused) environment is characterized by the dominance of one type of individual. For example a highly differentiated *Social* environment would be in evidence in a residence hall suite where five out of six residents were social work majors. Consistency refers to the similarity of interests and opportunities in an environment. Adjacent types in Holland's hexagonal arrangement are those most similar and consistent (see Figure 6.1). For example, *Social* activities and interests are most similar and consistent with *Enterprising* and *Artistic* opportunities, but very dissimilar and inconsistent with *Conventional, Realistic,* or *Investigative* activities and interests.

Environments that are highly differentiated and consistent seem to have the most powerful effect over time, and they tend to reinforce and accentuate their own characteristics. This "press toward conformity" influences the extent to which an individual is likely to be attracted to and remain stable within an environment. Fraternities and sororities often exhibit this dynamic in the attraction and selection of new members. Rush parties or gatherings allow potential pledges to experience the dominant characteristics of the current members of the organization. Usually candidates most attracted to the particular unit (and invited to pledge) are those who already share the most similarities with the existing aggregate. By their joining they will then, in turn, reinforce the existing dominant characteristic(s) and the accentuation effect continues. This accentuation effect is also evident in the power of small homogenous institutions, e.g., single sex colleges or specialized single-purpose schools, to attract and retain a highly consistent student body.

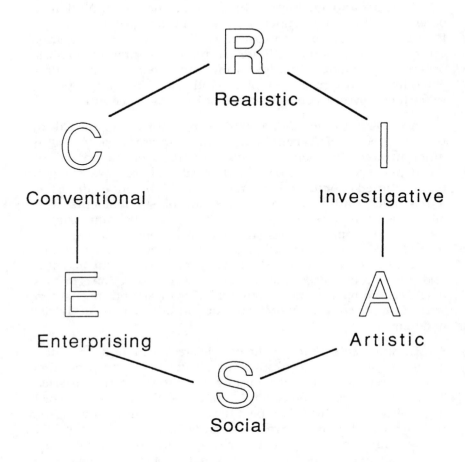

Figure 6.1. Holland's Model of Environmental Types. From *Making vocational choices: A theory of vocational personalities and work environments* by John L. Holland, 1985. Reproduced by permission of Prentice-Hall.

Holland (1973) further contended that person-environment *congruence* (e.g., a Conventional person in a Conventional environment) is the best predictor of individual satisfaction and stability in an environment. He also noted that individuals respond to situations of person-environment incongruence by (1) leaving the environment and seeking a new, more congruent environment; (2) attempting to change the current environment to make it more compatible; or (3) adapting to the current environment. Which option a person selects is usually a function of the degree of differentiation and consistency of the individual's interests and the degree of differentiation and consistency of the environment. For example, an individual with a very undifferentiated interest pattern (i.e., having many different interests of equal strength) would most likely adapt to the dominant feature of the environment. On the other hand, a highly differentiated person might attempt to change the environment if it is undifferentiated, or leave it if the environment is differentiated but inconsistent with that person's type.

Myers (1980) employed a similar set of assumptions. Through application of the *Myers-Briggs Type Indicator* (MBTI) (Myers & McCaulley, 1985) individual differences are described in terms of four dichotomous personality dimensions: extraversion (E) or introversion (I); sensing(S) or intuition (N); thinking (T) or feeling (F); and judgment (J) or perception (P). The **Extraversion-Introversion** (EI) dimensions assesses whether an individual prefers to direct mental activities toward the external world of people and things (extraversion) or toward the inner world of concepts and ideas (introversion). The **Sensing-Intuition** (SN) dimension assesses whether the person prefers to perceive the world in a factual, realistic way (sensing) or to perceive inherent, imaginative possibilities (intuitive). On one end of the **Thinking-Feeling** (TF) dimension, an individual prefers to arrive at decisions by logical analysis (thinking) or by appreciating personal and interpersonal subjective values (feeling). Finally, the **Judging-Perception** (JP) dimension assesses an individual's preference for taking either a judgmental attitude (judging) or a perceptive attitude (perceiving) toward his or her environment.

The various combinations of these dimensions yield sixteen different personality types, each with a unique set of preferences, approaches, and styles. Again, consistent with the tenets of human aggregate models, an environment dominated by the presence of a particular personality type would likely convey the characteristics of that type. For example, much like Holland's Social type, an environment dominated by Feeling types would place a premium on being aware of other people and their feelings. In contrast, an environment dominated by Sensing types would likely be distinguished by a set routine and an emphasis on detail and precision. However, this model differs somewhat from Holland's typology with respect to how each handles the problem of opposite types. Holland concludes that opposite types (e.g., Artistic and Conventional) are inherently incongruent and a source of potential stress and dissatisfaction to each other. The Myers-Briggs' model, on the other hand, emphasizes the concepts of balance and complementarity of types. Although individuals develop a dominant preference on each of these four dimensions, the opposite traits are necessary to supplement and to provide balance for the dominant trait. The same dynamic is assumed to function with respect to human aggregates. For example, a work environment dominated by Intuitive types (with their enthusiasm for new problems and solutions) will benefit from the perspective and skills of a Sensing type to keep things realistic and on track.

Tentative Conclusions and Implications. The following empirically supported conclusions reflect the principles and dynamics of the human aggregate models reviewed:

1. In general, students who are congruent with the majority are more satisfied and stable in terms of their vocational plans than are incongruent students. However . . . congruence effects may be stronger for women than for men. Congruence, homogeneity, and consistency have important effects . . . [and should be taken] into account in selecting environments. (Moos, 1986, p. 412)

2. People have a tendency to become more like their environments [progressive conformity] . . . [However, people who] do not share the dominant racial, religious, or socioeconomic characteristics of the population have high rates of mental illness and associated symptoms. (Moos, 1986, p. 413)

These two conclusions from the human aggregate literature speak directly to the importance of person-environment congruence or "fit." Assuming that successful attraction, matriculation, and retention of students are desirable goals for all campuses, those in charge of recruitment and admissions need to pay special attention to the degree of institutional fit for any potential student. Careful and accurate presentation of the institution's or various departments' dominant features is critical in encouraging an informed decision that will result in maximum consistency and congruence.

A similar dynamic is reflected in the second conclusion and is especially significant in addressing issues of minority recruitment. First, it suggests that stress and associated symptoms, due to person-environment incongruence, are additional burdens that students, who do not share the dominant characteristics of the institution's population, must carry as they matriculate into the college experience. Higher attrition rates and incidences of adjustment problems should not be unexpected under such conditions. Campus administrative models for addressing such issues range from a centralized approach, where a single "umbrella" office provides most services in a culturally focused manner (e.g., Office of Minority Student Affairs), to a decentralized approach where representative minorities are located throughout existing campus offices. Considering the foregoing conclusions, a highly focused, centralized model may be most effective in initially acclimating minority students to campus, in that such an arrangement provides a visible, homogenous unit where cultural ethnic consistency and congruence are maximized. For purposes of identity, recognition, and support, this arrangement is likely to result in the highest level of initial satisfaction and stability. A similar conclusion can be argued in support of the creation and maintenance of other specialized units on campus, organized to meet the needs of particular populations, e.g., an Adult Learner Support Service or an International Student Center. These too can offer a highly differentiated source of congruence at a critical point of transition in these students' lives.

In summary, these human aggregate models offer a useful, descriptive tool for identifying the predictable patterns environments assume as a result of the various types of people who occupy them. In a field such as student affairs, dominated by individuals who are particularly attuned to the dynamics of interpersonal interactions, the human aggregate is an especially important feature of the environment.

Structural Organizational Models

A basic premise of these approaches is that environments are purposeful, that is, they have goals, explicit or implicit, that give them direction and, in turn, give rise to organized structures that affect inhabitants' behaviors and attitudes. Most of us spend a good deal of time, from day to day, in explicitly purposeful environments (Etzioni, 1964), e.g., classrooms, offices, services, and programs. They are designed to achieve certain ends and their success is often gauged by the extent to which they do so, in other words, by their effectiveness. The tendency to "get organized" to "get things done" is a natural one and in accomplishing such a task a number of decisions must be made along the way. Who's in charge? How will decisions about spending resources be made? By what rules, if any, will we function? What must be accomplished and how fast? The decisions made with respect to these questions create a variety of organizational structures in an environment which, in turn, affect an individual's attraction to and satisfaction within that setting.

A model of complex organizations, consistent with this line of inquiry and useful in understanding these various environmental structures, is found in Hage and Aiken (1970). These authors posited that organized environments can generally be characterized along a continuum, one end of which is described as dynamic and the other end static. Dynamic environments respond to change; static environments resist it. The extent to which an organized environment is likely to exhibit dynamic or static characteristics can be determined with reference to six basic organizational structures: (1) the degree of organizational **complexity,** or the number of occupational subunits and specialities in an organization, as well as the intensity and extensity of their knowledge and expertise; (2) the degree of **centralization,** the way in which power is distributed in an organization (only very few people exert power in highly centralized units); (3) the degree of *formalization,* the number and specificity of enforced rules; (4) the degree of **stratification,** the differential distribution of rewards in a system; (5) the degree of **production,** the relative emphasis on quantity or quality of products or services; and (6) the degree of **efficiency,** the relatively high emphasis on cost reduction of organization's products or services. The structural arrangement of dynamically organized environments combines a high degree of complexity with low centralization, formalization, stratification, and efficiency, and a relatively high emphasis on the quality of products or services. According to Hage and Aiken (1970) such an environment is highly conducive to change and innovation. Static environments, which tend to discourage change and innovation, are characterized by a low degree of complexity, high centralization, formalization, stratification, and efficiency, and a relatively high emphasis on the *quantity* of products or services. The importance of this distinction lies in the notion that developmental educational environments are those that exhibit characteristics of a dynamic organization, where individual differences are appreciated, participation is expected, interactions are personal rather than functional, and risk-taking is encouraged (Strange, 1983). A critical mediating factor in all of this, of course, is environmental scale or size, with large systems generally exhibiting more characteristics of a structured static environment (or "bureaucracy") than smaller ones.

The degree to which an organized environment is static or dynamic can also affect the morale of participants in the setting, depending upon individual differences. For example, consider a static classroom environment, where the professor makes all the decisions about the timing and content of what is taught (high centralization), where assignments are governed by highly specific and inflexible rules (high formalization), where few questions or comments are encouraged for fear of wasting time (high production and efficiency), and where examinations assess simple recall of information (low complexity). While that classroom environment may be comforting to some students at one level of development, e.g., Dualism (Perry, 1970) or Dependent/Conforming (Harvey, Hunt, & Schroder, 1961), it may be very boring and unchallenging to other students with a different set of assumptions about what it means to learn, e.g., Relativism (Perry, 1970) or Independent/Self Reliant (Harvey, Hunt & Schroder, 1961). Various personality styles may respond differently to this same environment as well. Sensing types (Myers, 1980) or Conventional types (Holland, 1973) might enjoy the routine and standardization of such a class, but the consequent high structure may frustrate Intuitive and Artistic types. As another example, student organizations structured around a hierarchical model of constitutionally-based roles and powers may be less attractive to female students who are socialized in the ethic of care and "connectedness" (Forrest, Hotelling, & Kuk, 1986; Gilligan, 1982).

Tentative Conclusions and Implications. The following conclusions focus on the dynamics of organizational size:

1. The results on organizational size are highly consistent. As . . . group size increase[s], morale and attitudes become less positive, and absenteeism is more frequent. (Moos, 1986, p. 410)

2. Certain behavioral and attitudinal consequences occur when environments are "undermanned." People perform more activities in undermanned settings, and they are required to accept more positions of responsibility. These settings have a greater "claim" on people, because they require more effort and because relatively more difficult and important tasks are assigned to the occupants. It is less likely that a person will achieve great proficiency at any one task, since each person must fulfill several tasks. Each person has greater functional importance in the setting, more responsibility, and a greater feeling of functional self-identity. However, there may be greater feelings of insecurity, since each person is in greater jeopardy of failing to carry out the tasks assigned, and the tasks are more important for the maintenance of the setting. (Moos, 1986, p. 408)

The college campus offers many illustrations of the dynamics highlighted in these two conclusions. "Fighting the bureaucracy" becomes a rallying cry for students attempting to negotiate all the barriers endemic to the large organized systems of a modern day megaversity. Endless long lines, numbers instead of names, forms in quadruplicate, all take their toll on the human spirit at a time in students' lives when questions of identity and purpose (Chickering, 1969) demand, and are better served by, a high degree of personalism and support (Widick, Knefelkamp, & Parker, 1975). Even the express goals of the academy, the development of intellect and reason, are jeopardized by the limitations of size. What are the chances of any individual student posing a question, expressing a comment, exchanging a point of view, or writing a position statement, in a classroom with 600 students? The implications of this conclusion on organizational size are clear and consistent: bigger is not better when it comes to education. Perhaps it is no secret why large institutions tend to have higher attrition rates than smaller ones. The challenge to many institutions is to compensate for the inherent problems of oversizing with the intentional development of smaller sub-environments (e.g., residence hall units, student organizations, class discussion sections) that more fully engage students in meaningful ways. For example, at Iowa State University, a campus of over 26,000 students, a "house system" has been in effect for thirty years, wherein large residence halls are divided into smaller, more manageable living units ("houses"), each with a distinctive name.

The second conclusion illustrates another point about the relative size of an institution (or, for that matter, a class or student organization). An "undermanned" environment, as Barker (1960) labeled it, exists when too few people exist for too many tasks to be accomplished. The opposite condition, an "overmanned" environment, exists when too many people exist for too few opportunities for meaningful involvement and achievement. Chickering (1969) identified the latter condition as "redundancy." Generally speaking, large institutions tend to be "overmanned" and "redundant" and smaller institutions tend to be "undermanned." Consistent with Astin's (1984) observations about student involvement, smaller campuses tend to have a greater claim on students (in the same manner as small classes and small organizations) and the resultant sense of functional importance and functional self-identity is probably a significant factor in the higher retention rates experienced by these institutions. A general implication for administrative practice here is that strategies must be employed to maintain manageable campus sub-environments where individuals can experience a sense of functional importance and self-identity.

In summary, structural organizational models focus on the importance of understanding the goals and purposes of an environment and the resultant structured patterns of interrelationships that emerge through the various functional responsibilities and roles assumed by occupants of the setting. If colleges are to survive as dynamic educational institutions, the organizational structure of their various subunits must be examined in light of their ability to respond to changing circumstances and to the individual developmental needs of the students they serve (Strange, 1981; 1983).

Perceptual Models

Perceptual models of the environment operate on the premise that a consensus of individuals characterizing their environment constitutes a measure of environmental climate which, in turn, exerts a directional influence on behavior (Moos, 1986). Simply stated, environments are defined by the perceptions of the individuals within them. Unlike the three previous models described, which identify various aspects of the environment from an assumed objective and independent view, the perceptual approach focuses on the subjective view of the participant observer. Thus an environment can be measured objectively as being 70 degrees Farenheit, but seem "warm" to one person and "cold" to another. Likewise, a particular human aggregate may seem both "friendly" and "overbearing" depending upon perceptual differences, or a high degree of formalization may be reassuring to one yet confining to another. The key point demonstrated by these models is that individual and collective perceptions of an environment are critical in understanding how individuals are likely to react to that environment.

Murray, (1938), Stern (1970), and Pace and Stern (1958) are among those who established the foundational principles of this environmental approach. According to Stern (1970) an environmental "press " can be inferred from consensual self-reports of environmental activities by either participants (beta press) and/or observers (alpha press) of an environment. For example, of 90 out of 100 sampled participants in an environment report that students frequently spend time working in clubs and organizations, a press toward group life might be inferred. The various identified "presses" in an environment may or may not correspond to individual participant's "needs," or those "organizational tendencies that seem to give unity and direction to a person's behavior" (Stern, 1970) (e.g., a group life "need" is inferred from an individual's high level of club or organizational participation). A close correspondence (or congruence) between individual need and environmental press is said to be *anabolic,* or growth producing. A *catabolic* need-press combination, where significant dissonance exists between need and press, is growth-inhibiting and contributes to dissatisfaction and turnover.

Pervin's (1968) model focuses on the importance of personal goals and self-concept in understanding an individual's perception of and response to an environment. According to this "transactional approach," human behavior can best be understood in terms of the interaction (cause-effect relationships) and transactions (reciprocal relationships) between the individual and the environment. Furthermore, high performance and satisfaction are associated with environments which tend to reduce the discrepancies between the individual and the environment. Furthermore, high performance and satisfaction are associated with environments which tend to reduce the discrepancies between an individual's perceived actual-self and perceived ideal-self. Three basic assumptions underly this model (see Figure 6.2). First, "individuals find painful and unpleasant large discrepancies between their perceived actual selves and their perceived ideal selves: (a.). Second, "individuals are positively attracted toward objects in the perceived environment which hold potential for moving them toward their perceived ideal selves [b1.]; conversely, individuals are negatively disposed toward stimuli that hold potential for moving them away from their ideal selves" (b2.). Third, "similarity in regard to objects of importance to the individual is desirable where the individual has a low actual self/ideal self discrepancy [c1.] and undesirable where the individual has a high actual self/ideal self discrepancy" (c2.) (Walsh, 1973, p. 158).

Consider the example of an "undecided" student as an illustration of the dynamics in Pervin's first two assumptions. First of all, being undecided is difficult in a setting organized

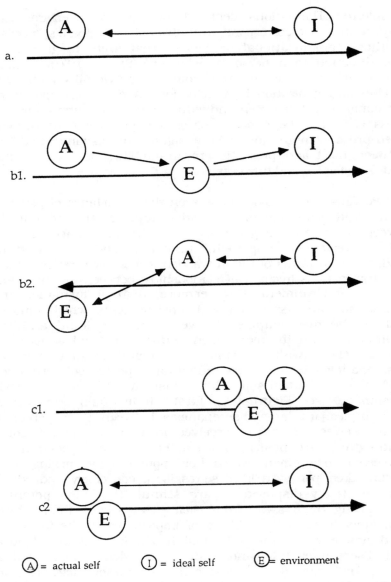

a.

b1.

b2.

c1.

c2

(A) = actual self   (I) = ideal self   (E)= environment

Figure 6.2. Pervin's Model of Person-Environment Interaction.

Source: Figure developed by author from content in Pervin, L. (1968). Performance and satisfaction as a function of individual-environment fit. *Psychological Bulletin, 69,* 56-68.

around academic and professional departments where friends often introduce themselves in terms of their majors. Not having selected a major may be tantamount to identity diffusion in the eyes of some. In such a case, the discrepancy between the actual self (i.e., "undecided") and ideal self (i.e., "decided") may be large, and a source of pain and anxiety to the individual student. The longer the indecision persists, the greater the pressure from others to make a choice, and the greater the anxiety experienced. According to Pervin's second assumption then, an undecided student would be positively disposed to an environment that would assist him or her in selecting a career or major (e.g., a Career Life Planning class) since this environment is likely to move the student toward his or her ideal self and therefore remove the source of anxiety associated with such discrepancies.

The third assumption offers an additional refinement to Sanford's (1966) classic prescriptions for challenge and support. According to Sanford's model, because of the natural tendency toward balance and stability ("homeostasis") people need to be *challenged*, or placed in situations where they must generate responses not previously used, in order for growth to occur. Since change always involves an element of risk, such a challenge is more readily accepted under conditions of *support* (e.g. personalism and structure). Pervin's third assumption suggests that the timing of challenge and support (or "similarity of objects of importance" to the individual) must be considered with respect to where students are in terms of meeting their personal goals ("ideal self"). Example c1. in Figure 6.2 illustrates the situation where an individual has reached an important set of goals, and therefore, similarity of objects of importance is appropriate. In the case of c2., where the discrepancy between actual self and ideal self is much larger, similarity of objects of importance in the environment (in other words, an overly supportive environment) would not serve to sufficiently challenge that individual toward the goal of ideal self.

Implicit in Pervin's assumptions is that individuals need accurate information about themselves (actual self) and a vision of what they want to be (ideal self) before they can judge the appropriateness or relevance of any given environment. The importance of a planned change, student development model (e.g., Miller & Prince, 1976; Morrill, Hurst, & Oetting, 1980) becomes clear in light of these assumptions, where an assessment of current level or progress (i.e., "actual self") is made, goals to be reached are set (in effect, identifying the "ideal self"), and intervention strategies (instruction, consultation, environmental management) are planned to encourage growth. The intent and effect is to reduce the actual/ ideal self discrepancy and the associated anxiety. Also implicit in Pervin's model is that individuals who have not yet defined an "ideal self" may be at risk in an environment since they lack an important referent for judging the appropriateness of the setting. The higher incidence of attrition found among students who have not yet declared a major tends to support such a claim.

Finally, Moos (1979) offers a model of **social climate** which describes the nature and effect of various "environmental personalities." Social climate, according to Moos, is comprised of three sets of dimensions found in any environment: (1) **Relationship dimensions,** which assess "the extent to which people are involved in the environment, the extent to which they support and help each other and the extent to which there is spontaneity and free and open expression among them" (Moos, 1974, p. 11); (2) **Personal Growth and Development** dimensions, assessing the "basic directions along which personal growth and self enhancement tend to occur . . . depending upon their [environments] underlying purposes and goals" (Moos, 1974, p. 13); and (3) **System Maintenance and System Change** dimensions, assessing "the extent to which the environment is orderly, clear in its expectations, maintains control and is responsive to change" (Moos, 1974, p. 14). These three dimensions manifest themselves in specific ways dependent upon the environment being examined (See Table 6.1). For example, Instructor Support is an important Relationship dimension in the classroom environment, but not a critical aspect of the family environment. On the other hand, some aspects are important across differing environments as is a Relationship dimension like Involvement, in this case, an important feature across residence, classroom, and work environments.

(Continued on page 183)

TABLE 6.1
Social Climate Dimensions Across Environments

Personal Maintenance/ Relationship System Change Dimensions Dimensions	System Development Dimensions
Residence Involvement Order and Organization	Independence

Environment
    Traditional/Social
      Orientation
    Competition
    Academic Achievement
    Intellectuality
	Emotional Support
	Student Influence
	Innovation

Classroom Involvement Order and Organization	Task Orientation

Environment
    Competition
  Instructor
    Instructor Control
  Support
    Innovation
	Affiliation
	Rule Clarity

Social/Task Cohesion Order and Organization	Independence
Oriented Leader Support Leader Control	Task Orientation
Group Expressiveness Innovation	Self-Discovery
Environment Anger and Aggression	

Source: Adapted from Moos (1974). *The social climate scales: An overview.* Reproduced by special permission of Consulting Psychologists Press, Palo Alto: CA.

Table 6.1. Continued.

Personal Maintenance/ Relationship System Change Dimensions Dimensions	System Development Dimensions
<u>Work</u> Involvement	Autonomy
Clarity	
<u>Environment</u>	Peer Cohesion
Task Orientation	Control
Supervisor	Work Pressure
Innovation	
Support	
Physical Comfort	
<u>Family</u> Cohesiveness	Independence
Organization	
<u>Environment</u>	Expressiveness
Achievement Orientation	Control
Intellectual-Cultural	
Orientation	
Active Recreational	
Orientation	
Moral-Religious Emphasis	

Tentative Conclusions and Implications. The following tentative conclusions are illustrative of the concepts of the perceptual models reviewed.

1 Students feel more secure, interested, and satisfied in classrooms that emphasize involvement, affiliation, and support. Classrooms in which students report a great deal of content learning combine an affective concern with students as people and an emphasis on working hard for academic rewards, with a coherent organized context. (Moos, 1986, p. 414)

2. Colleges that emphasize Relationship dimensions (faculty-student interaction, peer cohesion) have a positive impact on students. Colleges stressing Personal Development dimensions (e.g., humanism, breadth of interest, reflectiveness, broad intellectual emphasis, independent study, and criticism) also tend to have more productive students. (Moos, 1986, p. 414)

Perhaps the implications of these two conclusions are obvious; institutional environments most satisfying, secure, and productive to humans are those that emphasize involvement, affiliation, and other Relationship dimensions. This is particularly true of educational institutions where some degree of transformation of personal identity is almost always an expected outcome for students, whatever their age. Transformations, whether from late adolescence to young adulthood, from full-time homemaker to full-time career, or from a job in one field to a career in another, all contain elements of risk. Changing goals, unexpected barriers, or challenging opportunities are less difficult to negotiate in a personalized atmosphere of individualized acceptance and support. Consistent with the *Student Personnel Point of View* (American Council on Education, 1937; 1949), colleges that emphasize relationships and involvement, both within and outside the classroom from admissions and orientation to placement and alumni development, are those that will attract, satisfy, sustain, and retain students to a greater degree than those institutions that ignore such dimensions.

In summary, the importance of evaluative, subjective interpretations of the environment cannot be overlooked in understanding how individuals function within a setting. Participant perceptions can be an important source of information for designing responsive educational environments, and educators must be particularly sensitive to any discrepancies between their views of the institution and those of students.

SUMMARY AND INTEGRATION
OF CONCEPTS

The literature on human environments suggests that a more complete understanding of the dynamics and consequences of any environment lies in an examination of four key aspects: (1) the physical features of the setting; (2) the collective characteristics of the people within; (3) the organized structures associated with the specific goals of the setting; and (4) the subjective perceptions of the participants. Collectively, these four interactive elements can serve as a framework for describing an environment, as well as a basis for implementing environmental change.

Consider the following hypothetical case illustration. Assume that the environmental assessment data presented in Figure 6.3 were collected in an attempt to understand the functioning of a student organization on campus, and in particular, to learn more about the source of an apparent morale problem among its members. Moos' *Group Environment Scale* (GES) (Moos, 1981) offers information about the perceived functioning of organized volunteer groups along three sets of social climate dimensions (see Figure 6.3). This particular assessment example employs two forms of the GES: Form R (Real)—measuring respondent perceptions of the group's current functioning; and Form I (Ideal)—assessing respondents' perceptions of how the group should ideally function. Two general conclusions seem to be supported by these data. First, group members desire a much greater emphasis on Relationship dimensions (i.e., cohesion, leader support, expressiveness) than is currently present in their environment. Second, members further desire less of an emphasis on leader control and structure, as well as, less open conflict and expression of negative feelings (a Personal Growth and Development dimension). In terms of the four environment models reviewed here, the problem is essentially a structural organizational one, with the involvement of potentially related human aggregate and physical aspects.

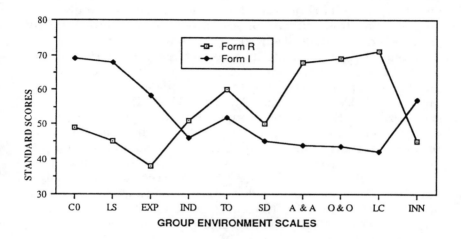

CO = Cohesiveness
LS = Leader Support
EXP = Expressiveness
IND = Independence
TO = Task Orientation
SD = Self Discovery

A & A = Anger and
    Aggression
O & O = Order and
    Organization
LC = Leader Control
INN= Innovation

Figure 6.3. Group Environment Scales (Real-Ideal).

Source: Adapted from Moos (1981). *Group environment scale manual.* Reproduced by special permission of the publisher, Consulting Psychologists Press, Inc.: Palo Alto, CA.

A closer examination of the specific dimensions involved (see Table 6.2) indicates that members perceive the group to be low in degree of involvement and commitment (Cohesion),with little freedom of action encouraged (Expressiveness), and with little concern or friendship shown by the leaders for the members (Leader Support). These findings, combined with the fact that members desire less formality and structure (Order and Organization), less of an emphasis on the leader directing the group (Leader Control), and greater emphasis on changing functions and activities (Innovation), suggest that this student organization suffers from a highly centralized, control-oriented leadership which does not understand or appreciate the collective characteristics and needs of group members. The pattern in these findings is similar to problems of static organizational environments articulated by Hage and Aiken (1970). High degrees of centralization (i.e., few have input into decision making) and formalization mitigate against innovation, which in this case, probably creates an organizational atmosphere that is incongruent with the members' style and preferences (Holland's "Social" types or Myers-Briggs ENFP's). Even physical factors, such as the shape and color of the room where meetings are conducted and the time of day at which they are held, might exacerbate these organizational problems as well, resulting in a depleted morale and low level of accomplishment.

Potential solutions to the problems also can be identified from the four environmental models. The obvious choice is that the leadership must be changed or decentralized, with greater responsibility for control and structure being placed in the hands of members, perhaps through a coordinated committee structure. Even a change of location where the meetings are usually held, and/or a change of time, could be useful in signaling a shift in leader support. From a human aggregate perspective, a team building workshop focusing on individual differences and similarities (use of Holland's model or the *Myers-Briggs Type Indicator* would be appropriate) might increase group cohesion and expressiveness, as well as assist current leaders in understanding the collective characteristics of the members (Schroeder, 1979b). Finally, from a perceptual perspective, periodic assessment and

(Continued on page 188)

TABLE 6.2
GES Subscales and Dimensions Descriptions

Relationship Dimensions

1. Cohesion   degree of involvement in and commitment ito the group.

2. Leader Support   degree of help, concern and friendship shown for the members.

3. Expressiveness   extent to which freedom of action and expression of feelings are encouraged.

Personal Growth Dimensions

4. Independence   extent to which independent action and expression among members is encouraged.

5. Task Orientation   emphasis that is placed on practical, concrete, down-to-earth tasks, decision-making and training.

6. Self-Discovery   extent to which the group encourages members' revelations and discussions of personal information.

7. Anger and Aggression   extent to which the group tolerates and encourages open expression of negative feelings and intermember disagreement.

System Maintenance and System Change Dimensions

8. Order and Organization   degree of formality and structure, explicitness of rules and sanctions.

9. Leader Control   degree of directing the group, making decisions and enforcing rules that is performed by the leader

10. Innovation   extent to which the group facilitates diversity and change in its own functions and activities.

Source: Adapted from Moos (1981). *Group environment scale manual.* Reproduced by special permission of the publisher, Consulting Psychologists Press, Inc.: Palo Alto, CA.

discussion of members' ideal expectations vs. current perceptions of the group's social climate would be helpful in monitoring the organization's functioning.

STUDENT DEVELOPMENT AND THE CAMPUS ENVIRONMENT: A CONCLUSION

Perhaps unique to this system, American postsecondary education has historically demonstrated an interest in the holistic development of students. However, the extent to which that role is endorsed by any specific college is a function of its mission, history, and campus culture. Recent critiques of the undergraduate experience (Boyer, 1987; The Study Group on the Conditions of Excellence in American Higher Education, 1984) have called for some fundamental changes in many institutions, for purposes of achieving a more personalized atmosphere and an educational environment capable of truly engaging students. Knefelkamp, Widick, and Parker (1978) offer the metaphor of a "developmental community" as a model for accomplishing these goals. They suggested that the creation of such a community requires a theoretical knowledge base which describes:

(1) Who the college student is in developmental terms. We need to know what changes occur and what those changes look like.

(2) How development occurs. We need to have a grasp of the psychological and social processes which cause development.

(3) How the college environment can influence student development. We need to know what factors in the particular environment of a college/university can either encourage or inhibit growth.

(4) Toward what ends development in college should be directed. (p.x)

Concerning their first two points, a reasonably comprehensive literature has evolved over the past two decades describing the nature and processes of human development during the college years (Chickering & Associates, 1981; Rodgers, 1989, 1990; Knefelkamp, Widick, & Parker, 1978). Only recently though, in reference to their third point, has the literature on human environments begun to emerge on a comparable scale. We now know some of the basic features of functional human environments and are beginning to understand their implications for the design of educational systems and practices.

Moos (1979) suggested five fundamental applications of this environmental knowledge base to the college campus. Each is considered in light of the functions and practices of student affairs work, and the role that student development educators can play in creating a more engaging institutional environment.

1. Maximizing Educational Information

The knowledge base on human environments reviewed here can serve as a conceptual framework for organizing information about a college and its various sub-environments, and for giving and taking feedback from students. Communicating to prospective students the nature of the social climate dimensions of the institution, from the student, faculty, and staff perspectives, may serve to better educate them about the dimensions of the environment that are likely to have a significant effect on their satisfaction, as well as assist them in making a more informed decision about college choice. The same type of information could be prepared and communicated for various sub-environments within the institution such as specific academic departments and residence halls.

Too often, information is collected from students, through surveys and questionnaires, but is rarely fed back to them for purposes of discussion and insight as to potential action and understanding. Using these environmental models to communicate to students their collective perceptions of the respective living environments can prove helpful in their initial adjustment to college. For example, a residence hall director could administer the *University Residence Environment Scale* (URES) (Form E or Form I) (Moos & Gerst, 1974) to assigned residents prior to their arrival on campus, or during the orientation process, for purposes of understanding students' expectations of what on campus living will be like. This consensual report or profile can serve as and important source of information for organizing programming that will meet their needs or for correcting those expectations that may be unrealistic. Following up that assessment, six to eight weeks into the term, with the URES (Form R) (or simply engaging in a guided group discussion of the URES subscale framework and definitions) can help identify sources of discrepancy between what the students expected (or ideally sought) and what they found. This simple give and take of information and feedback, which can be organized from floor to floor, accomplishes several important learning goals: (a) students learn about the nature and design of their environment in terms of a conceptual framework that will continue to prove helpful to them as they make decisions about living environments in the future; (b) students learn how they individually may differ from and share perspectives with their group of peers on what they perceive to be the desirable aspects of a living environment; (c) residence hall staff members gain an important source of information for purposes of planning and programming in the discrepancies students perceive between what they expected and what they found to be the case; and finally (d) students learn that you value their perspective as one source for planning a living learning experience and that they must become involved in the processes of community change and goal setting.

2. Facilitating and Evaluating Environmental Change

This knowledge base on human environments, Moos argued, is helpful in facilitating and evaluating the consequences of environmental change on campus, whether that involves changing social climate, or changing architectural and organizational characteristics. Campus change is sometimes unexpected and at other times intentional. It can be both revolutionary and evolutionary. The importance of these environmental models lies in their descriptive value for monitoring the nature and direction of those changes. In concert with some of the established environmental process models, e.g., ecosystem design (Aulepp & Delworth, 1976; Huebner, 1979; Western Interstate Commission for Higher Education, 1973) they can serve as a powerful tool for facilitating desired changes. For example, most campuses, at one time or another, have shared the experience of one institution that attempted to alter the environment of a particularly troublesome residence hall on campus (the proverbial "zoo"). In this hypothetical illustrative case, new paint, carpeting and furniture, was met with little change in behavior or attitude by the all-male residents. What was overlooked in this situation (as an integrated model of the environment suggests) was the significant influence of the human aggregate and organizational features in shaping the nature of the environment. The following year, in addition to the previous cosmetic physical improvements, the hall composition was changed to include females (an aggregate change strategy) and residents were engaged in an experimental model for self governance and territorial design (an organizational change strategy). Consequently, over a period of a few years the social climate of the hall evolved into an entirely different pattern.

3. Implementing Educational Consultation

The lives of many students are significantly influenced during the college years by their participation in one or more campus groups. Here they learn the lessons of interdependence and group life, critical tools for later survival and success in the world of work. Also in these groups many student affairs educators have the opportunity to do their "teaching." As the preceding case of the student organization group analysis suggests, the framework provided by these environmental models can be helpful in sorting out issues of group functioning and in responding to needs of students who participate in them. Similar to the example already noted, where students' expectations of a residence hall environment were assessed and fed back to them, application of these models accomplishes several important learning goals. Students learn about the nature of effective group environments, they learn how their views compare with others, and they learn that you value and expect their involvement in making decisions about their learning environments.

4. Formulating Ecologically Relevant Case Descriptions

Students arrive on campus as part of an already intact life ecology, bringing with them interacting systems of family, peers, culture, and hometown. To that they join the existing ecology of the campus, which usually includes a residence hall environment, various classroom environments, a social or task group environment, and very often a work environment. Table 6.1 and Figure 6.4, in combination, offer a framework for advisors and counselors to understand the nature of each student's ecology. For students experiencing transitional adjustment problems, the various social climate dimensions listed in Table 6.1 catalogue specific concerns and issues relevant to personal functioning in any of these environments. Figure 6.4 recognizes that environments can exert a powerful positive influence as well as a powerful negative influence. While Table 6.1 describes the content of a student's social ecology, Figure 6.4 focuses on the processes involved. Is the issue primarily a relationship dimension concern? Which subenvironment(s) is (are) involved? Is the concern one of active stress requiring immediate relief (a powerful negative influence) or a matter of normal anxiety and frustration in response to a developmental challenge (a powerful positive influence)? Such probes can help advisors and counselors build a more complete and relevant picture of how students are adapting to and coping with the campus environment.

5. Enhancing Environmental Competence

In this final application, Moos (1979) talks about teaching students how to create, select, and transcend environments, how to maximize person-environment congruence when support is the goal, or to seek an appropriate amount of challenge and incongruence when the goal is personal growth. The overall intent is to help students understand more fully the impact of the environment on their lives.

Enhancing environmental competence is a goal that encompasses the basic purposes and outcomes of higher education. From a developmental perspective the typical entering student might be characterized by a simplistic, categorical

(Continued on page 194)

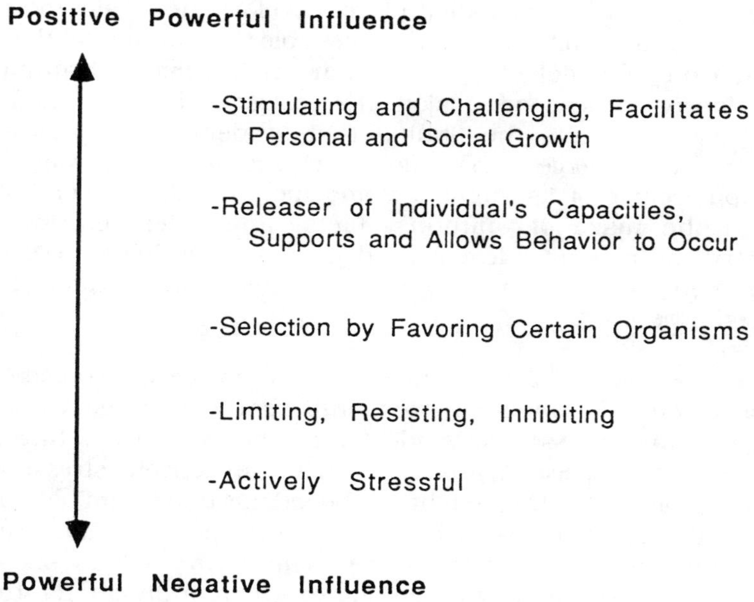

Positive Powerful Influence

-Stimulating and Challenging, Facilitates
   Personal and Social Growth

-Releaser of Individual's Capacities,
   Supports and Allows Behavior to Occur

-Selection by Favoring Certain Organisms

-Limiting, Resisting, Inhibiting

-Actively Stressful

Powerful Negative Influence

Figure 6.4. Influence of the Environment on the Process of Individual Adaptation, Adjustment, and Coping.

view of the world, dependent on external authorities for certainty, and lacking both the motivation and skill for self-directed learning (e.g., Perry's "Dualist"; Harvey, Hunt, & Schroder's "Dependent/Conforming" stage). Some may argue that such a posture is incompatible and ineffective in a world environment where little is certain and change is constant. Through a general education core, students are challenged to examine the world environment in all its contexts (historical, cultural, physical, and interpersonal) and to develop the basic tools of inquiry and communication to be able to pursue further examination of a select part of that environment through completion of an academic major. The college outcome research consistently supports the finding that students who persist in this process emerge with a more complex view of the world, more appreciative of its subtleties, and more capable of sorting through the maze of opinions, facts, and interpretations necessary for making adequate judgments about life and the environment surrounding them (Kitchener, King, Wood, & Davidson, 1989).

The challenge to higher education today is the development of institutional learning environments that encourage these developmental processes in students. At the very least, those aspects of the college environment that are actively stressful or limiting and resisting ought to be changed or eliminated. However, the ultimate goal is to be a powerful positive influence in students' lives where the campus and its various sub-environments stimulate and challenge them individually to personal and social growth. Student affairs educators, with their focus on the whole student, their professional commitment to human development, and their knowledge of these developmental processes in educational environments, can play a critical role in bringing this perspective to the campus community.

REFERENCES

American Council on Education. (1937). *The student personnel point of view.* American Council on Education Studies, Series 1, Vol. 1, No. 3, Washington, DC: Author.

American Council on Education, Committee on Student Personnel Work. (E.G. Williamson, Chmn.) (1949). *The student personnel point of view* (rev. ed.). American Council on Education Studies, Series 6, No. 13. Washington, DC: Author.

Anchors, S., Schroeder, C., & Jackson, S. (1978). *Making yourself at home: A practical guide to restructuring and personalizing your residence hall environment.* Washington, DC: ACPA Media Publications.

Astin, A.W. (1962). An empirical characterization of higher educational institutions. *Journal of Educational Psychology, 53,* 224-35.

Astin, A.W. (1968). *The college environment.* Washington, DC: American Council on Education.

Astin, A.W. (1984). Student involvement: A developmental theory for higher education. *Journal of College Student Personnel, 25,* 297-308.

Astin, A.W., & Holland, J.L. (1961). The environmental assessment technique: A way to measure college environments. *Journal of Educational Psychology, 52,* 308-16.

Aulepp, L., & Delworth, U. (1976). *Training manual for an ecosystem model: Assessing and designing campus environments.* Boulder, CO: Western Interstate Commission for Higher Education.

Barker, R.G. (1960). Ecology and motivation. In M. Jones (Ed.), *Nebraska Symposium on motivation.* (pp. 1-49). Lincoln: University of Nebraska Press.

Bonner, T.N. (September/October, 1986). The unintended revolution in America's colleges since 1940. *Change,* 44-51.

Boyer, E.L. (1987). *College: The undergraduate experience in America.* New York: Harper & Row.

Chickering, A.W. (1969). *Education and identity.* San Francisco: Jossey-Bass.

Chickering, A.W., & Associates. (1981). *The modern American college.* San Francisco: Jossey-Bass.

Cross, K.P. (1971). *Beyond the open door: New students to higher education.* San Francisco: Jossey-Bass.

Cross, K.P. (1981). *Adults as learners.* San Francisco: Jossey-Bass.

Ender, K., Kane, N., Mable, P., & Strohm, M. (1980). *Creating community in residence halls.* Washington, DC: ACPA Media Publications.

Etzioni, A. (1964). *Modern organizations.* Englewood Cliffs, NJ: Prentice-Hall.

Forrest, L., Hotelling, K., & Kuk, L. (1986). The elimination of sexism in the university environment. Pingree Park, CO: Student Development through Campus Ecology Second Annual Symposium. ERIC Document Reproduction Service #ED267 348.

Gilligan, C. (1982). *In a different voice: Psychological theory and women's development.* Cambridge, MA: Harvard University Press.

Hage, J., & Aiken, M. (1970). *Social change in complex organizations.* New York: Random House.

Harvey, O.J., Hunt, D.E., & Schroder, H.M. (1961). *Conceptual systems and personality organization.* New York: John Wiley & Sons.

Heilweil, M. (1973). The influence of dormitory architecture on residence behavior. *Environment and Behavior, 5,* 377-412.

Holland, J.L. (1973). *Making vocational choices: A theory of careers.* Englewood Cliffs, NJ: Prentice Hall.

Holland, J.L. (1985). *Making vocational choices: A theory of vocational personalities and work environments.* Englewood Cliffs, N.J.: Prentice-Hall.

Huebner, L.A. (1979). Redesigning campus environments. *New Directions for Student Services,* No. 8. San Francisco: Jossey-Bass.

Kitchener, K.S., King, P.M., Wood, P.K., & Davison, M.L. (1989). Sequentiality and consistency in the development of reflective judgment: A six-year longitudinal study. *Journal of Applied Developmental Psychology, 10,* 73-95.

Knefelkamp, L.L., Widick, C., & Parker, C.A. (Eds.). (1978). Applying new developmental findings. *New directions in student services,* No. 4. San Francisco: Jossey-Bass.

Michelson, W. (1970). *Man and his urban environment: A sociological approach.* Reading, MA: Addison-Wesley.

Miller, T.K., & Prince, J.S. (1976). *The future of student affairs.* San Francisco: Jossey-Bass.

Moos, R.H. (1974). *The social climate scales: An overview.* Palo Alto, CA: Consulting Psychologists Press.

Moos, R.H. (1979). *Evaluating educational environments.* San Francisco: Jossey-Bass.

Moos, R.H. (1981). *Group environment scale manual.* Palo Alto, CA: Consulting Psychologists Press.

Moos, R.H. (1986). *The human context: Environmental determinants of behavior.* Malabar, FL: Robert E. Krieger.

Moos, R.H., & Gerst, M. (1974). *The university residence environment scale manual.* Palo Alto, CA: Consulting Psychologists Press.

Morrill, W., Hurst, J., & Oetting, E. (1980). *Dimensions of intervention for student development.* New York: John Wiley & Sons.

Murray, H. (1938). *Exploration in personality.* New York: Oxford University Press.

Myers, I.B. (1980). *Gifts differing.* Palo Alto, CA: Consulting Psychologists Press.

Myers, I.B., & McCaulley, M.H. (1985). *Manual: A guide to the development and use of the Myers-Briggs Type Indicator.* Palo Alto, CA: Consulting Psychologists Press.

Pace, C.R., & Stern, G.G. (1958). An approach to the measurement of psychological characteristics of college environments. *Journal of Educational Psychology, 49,* 269-77.

Parker, C.A. (1977). On modeling reality. *Journal of College Student Personnel, 18,* 419-25.

Perry, W.G. (1970). *Forms of intellectual and ethical development in the college years: A scheme.* New York: Holt, Rinehart & Winston.

Pervin, L. (1968). Performance and satisfaction as a function of individual-environment fit. *Psychological Bulletin, 69,* 56-68.

Rodgers, R.F. (1989). Student development. In U. Delworth, G.R. Hanson, & Associates. *Student services: A handbook for the profession* (2nd ed.) (pp. 117-164). San Francisco: Jossey-Bass.

Rodgers, R.F. (1990). Recent theory and research underlying student development. In D.G. Creamer & Associates. *College student development: Theory and practice for the 1990s* (pp. 27-79). Alexandria, VA: American College Personnel Association.

Sanford, N. (1966). *Self and society: Social change and individual development.* New York: Atherton Press.

Schroeder, C.C. (1979a). Designing ideal staff environments through milieu management. *Journal of College Student Personnel, 20*(2), 129-35.

Schroeder, C.C. (1979b). Territoriality: Conceptual and methodological issues for residence educators. *Journal of College and University Housing, 8,* 9-15.

Stern, G. (1970). *People in context: Measuring person-environment congruence in education and industry.* New York: Wiley & Sons.

Stern, R.A. (1986). *Pride of place: Building the American dream.* New York: Houghton Mifflin.

Strange, C. (1981). Organizational barriers to student development. *National Association of Student Personnel Administrators Journal, 19*(1), 12-20.

Strange, C. (1983). Human development theory and administrative practice in student affairs: Ships passing in the daylight? *National Association of Student Personnel Administrators Journal, 21*(1), 2-8.

Strange, C.C., & King, P.K. (1990). The professional practice of student development. In D.G. Creamer & Associates. *College student development: Theory and practice for the 1990s.* (pp. 9-24). Alexandria, VA: American College Personnel Association.

Sturner, W.F. (1973). The college environment. In D.W. Vermilye (Ed.), *The future in the making (pp. 71-86).* San Francisco: Jossey-Bass.

The Study Group on the Conditions of Excellence in American Higher Education. (1984). *Involvement in learning: Realizing the potential of American higher education.* Washington, DC: National Institute of Education.

Thelin, J.R., & Yankovich, J. (1987). Bricks and mortar: Architecture and the study of higher education. In John C. Smart (Ed.), *Higher Education: Handbook of Theory and Research, Vol. III,* (pp. 57-84). New York: Agathon Press.

Walsh, W.B. (1973). *Theories of person-environment interaction: Implications for the college student.* Iowa City: American College Testing Program.

Western Interstate Commission for Higher Education. (1973). *The ecosystem model: Designing campus environments.* Boulder, CO: WICHE.

Widick, C., Knefelkamp, L., & Parker, C. (1975). The counselor as developmental instructor. *Counselor Education and Supervision, 14*(4), 286-96.

Yinon, Y., Goldenberg, J., & Neeman, R. (1977). On the relationship between structure of residence and formation of friendships. *Psychological Reports, 40,* 761-762.

SUGGESTED READINGS

Boyer, E.L. (1987). *College: The undergraduate experience in America.* New York: Harper & Row.

Creamer, D.G., & Associates. *College student development: Theory and practice for the 1990s.* Alexandria, VA: American College Personnel Association.

Stern, R.A. (1986). *Pride of place: Building the American dream.* New York: Houghton Mifflin.

Part II

PARAMETERS
OF
PROFESSIONAL
PRACTICE

Robert F. (Bob) Rodgers, Ph.D., is an associate professor of higher education and psychology at The Ohio State University. He specializes in the study of college student development and campus ecology. Bob initially studied systems engineering at Texas Tech University. He received his Masters of Arts degree in Counseling Psychology from The Ohio State University. He worked for ten years in the field of student affairs and subsequently received a Ph.D. in Higher Education from The Ohio State University. He has been teaching and doing research for the past twenty years.

7

USING THEORY IN PRACTICE IN STUDENT AFFAIRS

Robert F. Rodgers

In this chapter is examined the use of theory in practice in student affairs. The assumptions, values, general character, and specific and general operational principles of using theory to guide the design of environments intended to help students learn and develop are examined and illustrated. The examination begins by reviewing the basic values and assumptions underlying the use of theory in practice.

FOUNDATIONS FOR APPLYING THEORY TO PRACTICE

A basic educational value is enhanced when one uses theory to inform practice by designing and providing environments (i.e., programs, services, facilities, policies, and procedures) that help students to both learn and mature. That is, well-rounded development of the whole personality is valued and is a primary goal of higher education. Primary goals are not limited to intellectual development alone, or to the life of the mind in the classroom.

The efficacy of this primary educational value has been debated by philosophers, scholars, student affairs staff members, and the public. Many in these groups support it; but some do not. Those who do not, often view the basic purpose of higher education to be one of professional or vocational preparation and/or scientific and scholarly inquiry rather than for promoting well-rounded development of students (Kerr, 1962). From these points of view the role of student affairs is seen as being supplementary to the life of the mind in the classroom, and focused on providing basic services to student consumers and solving problems so that students can perform well in the classroom. From this perspective, student affairs does not have a direct, primary educational role.

The second important value underlying the use of theory in practice centers on the question of whether the practice of student affairs is best served by *professionals* using applied social and behavioral science, or by *craftsmen* using disciplined intuition and common sense. A professional uses a knowledge base and its measurement techniques to assess persons, environments, and their interactions. A craftsman on the other hand, does not and cannot use such knowledge for it is not known. Thus, for example, a dentist uses knowledge in his or her field to diagnose dental health needs during regular check-ups. Hopefully one's dentist reads professional journals and keeps up with advancements in dentistry and is ready to take preventive action to extend the life of one's teeth rather than prescribe extractions or dentures prematurely. Theory and knowledge of dentistry, therefore, guide the dentist's assessment of the condition of teeth and help the professional take appropriate actions that prevent unnecessary or premature problems. Similarly, residence hall staff members who know theory and research on personality type can assess residents' types and then prescribe roommate assignment strategies designed to prevent unnecessary roommate conflicts and facilitate maturation. Or, a dean of students who knows comprehensive theoretical models of student-environment interactions and how to use them to assess both students and the environment can plan a retention program relevant for particular student constituencies. A residence director who is not thoroughly grounded in personality type theory and assessment techniques cannot use knowledge of type in making roommate assignments. A dean who does not know comprehensive models of person-environment interaction and related assessment techniques cannot use this knowledge to develop a campus retention plan. In short, professionals, as contrasted to craftsman or amateurs, know in-depth both the theories and assessment techniques relevant to their field. Practice based upon this knowledge, it is argued, leads to better outcomes than practice that is not based upon such knowledge. Before illustrating professional practice in student affairs, however, arguments that stand in opposition to the use of theory in practice need to be examined and carefully analyzed. Such opposition comes from both within and outside the field of student affairs and the issues raised deserve careful reflection.

Some critics have rejected the linking of formal theory and practice on the grounds that it is manipulative, seems like "human engineering," and therefore may be unethical (Barbie, 1980). Others charge student development advocates with the excesses of "true belief" (Bloland, 1986a, 1986b), that is, the use of developmental theory in practice is touted as the only way to do the work of student affairs. Developmental theory is seen as the knowledge base to be shared by all specialties in the field. In short, a dualistic orthodoxy is created.

Finally, still other student affairs critics have found the theory in practice approach to be overly complex. They have asked for a simpler or reductionistic way of using theory in practice. Rhatigan (1975, 1987), for example, believed Rodgers and Widick's (1980) and Rodgers' (1983) grounded formal theory approach to be too complex for general use. Lipsetz (1975) has asked for a simple, easy approach to using theory in student affairs, something that can be taught easily and applied quickly. Benjamin (1986) and Drum (1980) have sought unifying perspectives for integrating the various kinds of developmental theory and their use in practice.

Let us examine and analyze the issues raised by these critics. The charge that the student development approach is manipulative human engineering raises ethical questions. Is it manipulatively unethical to use theory to design environments intended to help students to learn and develop? Is the use of theory to guide practice manipulative of human freedom or dignity or free will? In order to respond to these questions, a useful procedure is to examine the distinctions between *formal* and *informal* theory (Parker, 1977). *Formal* theories are explicit conceptualizations of a given phenomena. The constructs in formal theories are explicitly related to each other and a research base exists which is partially supportive of both the constructs and the relationships. *Informal* theories are the tacit theories-in-use that everyone has. *One cannot act without implying a tacit informal theory.* These tacit informal theories guide how we think and what one does in everyday life and often in one's professional work (Argyis & Schon, 1974). All human action implies such theories-in-use. Hence, in one sense the charge that the use of formal theories is manipulative is also a universal charge against all human action. If action implies a theory-in-use and if a theory-in-use is a theory, then to act is to be manipulative in the sense of this criticism. The heart of this criticism, therefore, must be found elsewhere.

As we look elsewhere an important note is that usually we do not make informal theories-in-use explicit. Hence, neither student affairs staff members nor students are clearly aware of the assumptions or bases for existing programs and actions. Usually, one tends to accept what supports his or her views and ignore what does not. Theories-in-use may be good theories; however, they need to be made explicit in order to make judgments about goodness. When they are made explicit, they can be tested formally. As a consequence, they become formal theories. The heart of the issue, therefore, is not the use of theory *per se,* but the ethical use of theory. Perhaps to use untested and tacit theories-in-use is more questionable ethically than to use formal theories. Formal theories, however, also can be used unethically. Stamatakos (1988), for example, questioned whether our formal theories are adequate for use with some populations or in some contexts. This is a basic and legitimate question. If a staff member uses a theory generated from one population (e.g., males) to plan practice for another group (e.g., females), then such a use of theory in practice is questionable. Similar issues can be raised for age and ethnic groups.

Fortunately progress has been and is being made both in theoretical formulations and research on women and black students. Branch-Simpson (1984), for example, has generated psychosocial vectors of development from research on black colleges students. She found much overlap with and some differences from Chickering's (1969) vectors. Similarly, Straub (1987) and Straub and Rodgers (1986) have focused on the vector development of women. Nevertheless, when adequate theory and research do not exist for a given population or context, practitioners can help generate new insights and theory by using naturalistic and aphorismic techniques as Winston (1990) has advocated.

A third group of student affairs critics appears to raise *ideological* objections to student development. Bloland (1986a, b) for example, has questioned the validity of well-rounded development as a primary goal for higher education. He followed Plato (1978) in saying that expertise in college student development has not been requested by colleges and universities and is not sought by students. Hence, expertise in designing environments that help students develop may be neither wanted nor desired.

One can easily imagine faculty members who view the primary purpose of higher education to be research or even professional/vocational preparation and administrators who view the role of student affairs to be *in loco parentis* and/ or auxiliary service raising the question of "whoever asked you to develop students anyway?" Well-rounded development is not viewed as a goal central to the mission of the college from these perspectives. The academic program is the central mission and student services are supplemental at best. Hence, once again are value issues raised. Is oen of the fundamental purposes of higher education well-rounded development of students? A reasonable case can be made for either position.

If this value question is answered in favor of well-rounded development, the *means* to the desired end also can be debated. Some faculty of the liberal arts tradition, a tradition purporting to honor well-rounded development, often criticize the legitimacy and centrality of the means used by professionals in student affairs. These criticisms may derive from the fact that the liberal arts can be taught as scholastic research specialties as Kuh, Shedd, and Whit (1987) have argued. Or, they may derive from the fact that only empirical or rational research and teaching are seen as legitimate means to the end. For example, Scott Buchanan (1970), the eminent educator from St. John's College, Annapolis, Maryland, has argued that *rationality* is the one and only means for education. He said,

> What is the whole man? When you define man as a rational animal you are giving a substantial form for the whole man . . . This means that no matter what a man does the rational permeates his whole being . . . Our emotions are under the reason and so are other things, like perception.
>
> The rational soul is leading and controlling . . . . in the sense of realizing completely what the whole nature of man is. So if you're educating anybody the channel, the medium, by which you do this will be rational. And you'll have as a result a refining of emotion (Buchanan, 1970, p. 65).

Another rationalist, John Silber (1971), the controversial liberal arts educator and president of Boston University, contrasted a college orientation program emphasizing small group acquaintance and other personal and intimate interactions on a social issue with a program emphasizing small group intellectual discussions of a social issue. He found favor with the later but not the former. He believed the relationships of the former are pseudo-relationships and have no place in education. Further, he argued that almost all applied psychology may be invalid for it has inadequate theoretical and philosophical grounding, and only rarely, he believed, does it benefit anybody.

For Buchanan and Silber, therefore, rationality is the guiding center of wholeness and all proper educational methods are rational. Refined emotions are rationality's by-product. Equal status to emotional reality is not granted. Hence, to the extent that applied forms of psychology focus on emotions, intra and interpersonal self-examination, and aesthetic appreciation, they are not trusted as legitimate means for learning or inquiry (Silber, 1971). Using theory in practice is applied psychology, and questionable methodologies are often used. Hence, the whole approach is suspect.

This rationalistic bias underestimates the importance of aesthetic and emotional reality. As French philosopher Roger Garaudy (1973, p. 39-40) wrote,

> If, since Socrates, we have gotten into the habit, . . . , of underestimating the importance of whatever escapes our purely intellectual procedures, hypotheses, deductions, verifications, concepts, and language, then aesthetic experience can help us see the value of these other realities. When I have analyzed a picture, I cannot demonstrate scientifically that it is beautiful and ought to move us. At best what I can do is bring you to the point where you, and you alone, can test all that I have not been able to express. . .The anguish of death or love; the faith that makes the believer, as well as the militant revolutionary, joyfully confront sacrifice; the emotion evoked by the beauty of a landscape or another human being - all these are irreducible to the notion of "concept."

The rationalistic bias within higher education also may be an example of the overemphasis of *one voice of development* to the *exclusion or detriment of another voice.* Gilligan (1982a, b), described this bias by contrasting the voice of *autonomy and justice* with the voice of *care and responsibility.* The former may be characterized as cognitive, objective, rational, and intellectual; the latter, as sensitive, empathic, and oriented toward feelings. If the care voice is excluded from education, it remains untutored and may sound naive because it is underdeveloped. If the "care" way of asking questions and doing inquiry is suspect or rejected, then obtaining status and acceptance within the academy for those who embrace it will be difficult. Student affairs, therefore, may be a care-oriented ship negotiating a turbulent, rationalistic or positivistic sea. Consequently, student affairs' values and methodologies often may be in conflict with assumptions and methodological biases of its host environment.

In addition, the argument may be made that many of the problems that colleges and students face today—abuse of alcohol and other drugs, racism, sexism—are not solved by rational interventions. If the guiding center of these problems were rational, then they already would have been solved by the rational educational efforts that have previously taken place. The guiding center of these problems may be emotional, affective, and psychological and may require intensive and prolonged educational programs or therapeutic relationships of the kind that President Silber found suspect and developmental theory-in-use found central.

Somewhat similarly, but from the obverse of the coin, Rhatigan (1975, 1987) has questioned whether the use of developmental theory unintentionally will lead student affairs away from its humanistic heritage in favor of behaving like objective, impersonal technocrats. In other words, is using theory to inform practice as advocated by the student development approach overly impersonal or even mechanistic?

The use of theory in practice is not unlike any other means to an end. It can be used in mechanical ways, or it can be used with human warmth and concern, empathetic support, and humanistic care. Student development approaches are not inherently one or the other. Indeed, the question of whether student affairs efforts are humanistic or mechanistic may be more a function of the voice orientation or personality type of staff members than whether or not they have internalized formal theories for informing practice. Nevertheless, as Garaudy (1973) has pointed out, a *rational* chapter such as this one cannot demonstrate cognitively that the use of the theory-in-practice approach ought to be adopted or that it can be used humanistically. At best the hope is that this chapter provides readers with basic understandings of the use of theory in practice so that they, and they alone, can individually decide whether to take the time and energy to learn the theories and student development approaches to the extent necessary to internalize them and make them part of the reader's theory-in-use.

Finally, the plea for an easy-to-use, less complex, or reductionistic model for using theory in practice is at best a fanciful dream. This is the case for at least two reasons. First, a single or reductionistic model is not a theory. A model can inform a practitioner on the steps one needs to take in order to use theory in practice; it can broadly conceptualize the domains of development or the dimensions of relating theory to practice; but it cannot provide substantive content or program guidance. Models are basically substanceless. Formal or informal theories are needed in order to give models flesh or content. Secondly, not one grand theory exists to describe human development. Often these aspects are interdependent but they cannot be reduced to a single theory. Specific theories are needed to assess, design, and evaluate student development efforts. *Student development is a complex task requiring complex methods using multiple specific theories.* Reductionistic integration or the desire to find a simple unified student development model to replace complex theories is misplaced energy and an ill-advised goal. They rest on two faulty assumptions: (1) all development is similar in nature and commensurable; (2) the use of theory in practice has to be quickly grasped and easily applied.

CONTINUUM FOR UNDERSTANDING THEORY

As previously indicated, in-depth knowledge of specific theories is needed in order to use theory in practice. No substitute exists. Although new professionals cannot be expected to know a vast number of theories-in-depth, they can be expected to have intimate knowledge and understanding of a few selected theories and to work continuously to broaden their repertoire of competence. In order to characterize the degree of in-depth knowledge needed, the following continuum of degrees of understanding are reviewed.

Location 1

This is an amorphous, almost distinctionless understanding of a theory or a construct. For example, a person may have just heard or read the terms "managing emotions" (Chickering, 1969) and may be inclined to wonder, "What is that?" The person may only recognize Chickering's name and the name of the construct but not know the theory or construct. This degree of knowledge and understanding is not sufficient for using theory in practice.

Location 2

At this location a theory or a construct has more meaning. *A person at this level of understanding is able to recognize or give a brief description or definition of a construct.* For example, a person is able to indicate that "managing emotions" is a developmental task common to young adults between the ages of 17 and 25 in which the control of emotions moves from rigid adherence to external rules of one's heritage through external control by the norms of primary peer groups to internal flexible control. This degree of knowledge and understanding also is *not* sufficient for using theory in practice.

Location 3

A person at Location 3 has achieved a greater degree of knowledge and understanding of the theory or construct than at Locations 1 and 2. For example, the person at Location 3 knows that the concept "managing emotions" focuses on controlling the emotions of sex and aggression in the 17 to 25 age range and that it involves a process of development. (See Figure 7.1).

Managing the emotions of sex and aggression moves through the following: Phase A, release of rigid controls over emotions by the external rules of one's heritage or peer group; Phase B, achievement of an awareness and acceptance that these emotions are legitimate and normal; Phase C, trust in one's feelings as a basis for action—that is, appropriate action is often an integration of logic and these emotions; Phase D, acting on these emotions, both vicariously and actually and receiving feedback; Phase E, acting and receiving feedback repeatedly; and Phase F, reflecting on one's experience with sex and aggression and integrating and internalizing personalized control.

Phases A, B, and C involve awareness and trust and are differentiation tasks, while Phases D, E, and F involve both differentiation and integration of tasks. Programs which respond to Phases A, B, and C should reflect awareness, trust and differentiation. Programs responsive to Phases D, E, and F should reflect support as a person lives through new behaviors and learns their meaning.

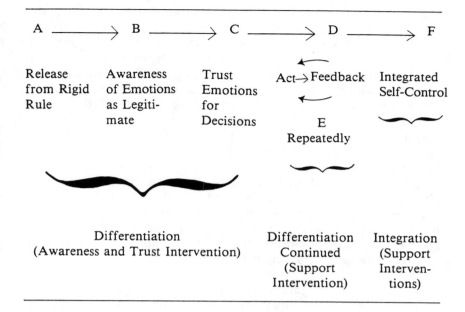

Figure 7.1. Managing Emotions.

In Location 3 the person's knowledge and understanding of "managing emotions" are no longer amorphous or superficial. The concept has taken on shape, structure, and meaning. This degree of knowledge and understanding of the construct is sufficient for using theory in practice.

Location 4

A person who has this level of understanding and knowledge of a theory or construct is best able to use theory in practice. This is the level of knowledge and understanding possessed by sophisticated professionals in the field. In this location, a professional person not only knows the construct as defined in Location 3, but also knows the intimate and detailed relationships between "managing emotions" and all of the other constructs in the general theory of which it is part. That is, the professional knows the relationships between managing emotions and the other six vectors (i.e., establishing competence, autonomy, establishing identity, freeing interpersonal relationships, establishing purpose, and developing integrity) of Chickering's (1969) theory (Figure 7.2). These relationships are known in sufficient detail so that a person is able to reconstruct "managing emotions" within the general developmental themes of values and moral development, intimacy and sexuality, and career and vocational growth. A person at Location 4 can relate any one vector to any of the others in diagnosing a problem or in designing an intervention. This person also is familiar with and experienced in using the various means of measuring all the constructs in the theory. The person also can discuss the advantages and disadvantages of each method of measurement. Finally, this professional has kept up with recent research findings and knows, for example, that women are ahead of men in resolving some of these issues (Branch-Simpson, 1984; Straub, 1987; Straub & Rodgers, 1986). Differential programming, therefore, may be needed for groups of women and groups of men.

In summary, a professional at Location 4 has (1) intimate familiarity with the constructs covered by a theory and the interrelationships among the constructs and subconstructs of the theory; (2) knowledge of how developmental change takes place in terms of the constructs of the theory; (3) an intimate familiarity with the means of measuring the constructs and the advantages and limitations of each; and (4) knowledge that is updated with the findings of recent research. This is the level of in-depth knowledge and understanding of selected social and behavioral science theories that ideally a professional needs to attain in order to maximize the use of theory in practice.

PRACTICE-TO-THEORY-TO-PRACTICE APPROACH

The practice-to-theory-to practice approach to student development programs is potentially applicable to a broad range of practice areas. The essential character of the approach can be summarized as follows: given a context of practice, formal theories plus procedural process models can lead to more professionalized practice. That is,

(Continued on page 216)

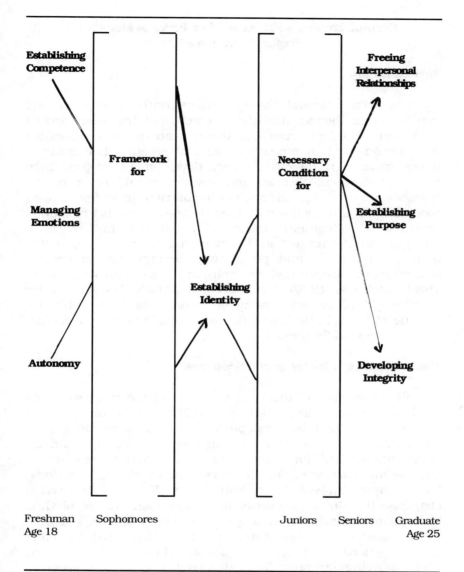

Figure 7.2. Chickering's (1969) seven vectors in chronological, directional, and age-related order.

Formal Theory + Procedural or Process Models → Professional Practice

Formal Theory

The term "formal theory" refers both to *content* and *developmental* theories and the research that has been derived therefrom. "Content" refers to theories about, and associated research on, a given problem or area of practice. For example, if one were working on a career development project, then career development theories and research would be "content." If one were working on conflict resolution problems among roommates in a residence hall, then theories of conflict resolution would be the "content" theories. "Developmental" refers to developmental theories and associated research applicable to a given content and population. Several general reviews of development theory and research have been published (Drum, 1980; Rodgers, 1980). Professionals should become aware (Location 2) of the wide array of theories listed in Table 7.1 and develop in-depth knowledge and understanding (Location 3 or 4) of selected theories.

The Concepts of Challenge and Response

All the families of theory and individual theories mentioned in this chapter share Sanford's (1967) concepts of challenge and response. That is, developmental change seems to require an environment that offers an *appropriate challenge* and an environment that *invites response* due to the presence of *appropriate supports.* On the vector of managing emotions, for example, Phases A, B, and C (see Figure 7.1) need a challenge that invites students to release rigid control of their feelings of sexuality and aggression, helps students accept these emotions as legitimate, and facilitates trust in using these emotions as a basis for action. These challenges need accompanying support from the environment if responses that help students resolve these issues are to occur. Relevant support can include encouragement, lack of ridicule, and genuine acceptance when awkward expressions of emotions first occur.

(Continued on Page 218)

TABLE 7.1

Selected Developmental and Related Theories

Psychosocial	Cognitive-Structural Developmental	Person-Environmental Interaction	Topological
White (1966)	Harvey, Hunt, & Schroeder (1961)	Lewin (1936)	*Jung/Meyers (Myers, 1980; Myers & McCaulley, 1985)
Sanford (1967)	Piaget (1965)	Clark & Trow (1960)	
*Erickson (1968)	*Perry (1970)	Pace & Baird (1966)	
*Heath (1968)	*Kohlberg (1984)	Newcomb et al. (1967)	
*Chickering (1969)	Loevinger (1976)	*Pervin (1967)	*Kiersey & Bates 1978
Keniston (1970)	*Kegan (1982)	Astin (1968)	*Kolb (1976)
Havighurst (1972)	Selman (1980)	Barker (1968)	Heath (1974)
Sheehy (1974)	Fowler (1981)	Stern (1970)	Witkin (1976)
Neugarten (1975)	*Kitchener & King (1981)	Chickering (1972)	Furhmann & Grasha (1983)
Vaillant (1977)	*Gilligan (1982a,b)	*Holland (1973)	
Gould (1978)	Nucci (1985)	*Moos (1979)	
Levinson et al. (1978)	Belenky, Clinchy, Goldberger, & Taruk (1986)	*Aulepp & Delworth (1976)	
Baltes, Reese, & Lipsitt (1980)		*Milieu Management (Schroeder, 1976, 1980)	
*Baruch, Barnett, & Rivers (1983)			
*Farrell & Rosenberg (1981)			
McAdams (1985)			
Josselson (1987)			
Rubin (1981)			

* Recommended for in-depth knowledge and understanding

Generally, challenges need to be appropriate, neither too great nor too small. Supports likewise need to be appropriate, neither too much nor too little. Each theory provides the professional student affairs staff member with definitions of appropriate challenges and responses for persons at different levels on its content. Hence, in-depth knowledge of the theory and how change takes place are needed in order to give Stanford's general concepts specific meaning. The three possible conditions of person-environment interaction are summarized in Figure 7.3. Knowledge of the theory helps staff members provide appropriate challenge/response environments rather than overly challenging or overly supportive ones.

Briefly, a person can be thought of as having a range of dissonance that is developmentally appropriate for him or her. This is illustrated in Figure 7.3.

The location and range of developmental dissonance of a person are functions of the challenge to support ratio of the person-environment interaction in a given setting (see Figure 7.3). Three cases illustrate this point.

The person-environment interaction may be characterized as *balanced*. This means that the degree of challenge and support falls within an individual's range of developmental dissonance. Typically some tension and anxiety exist, therefore, the person is challenged to develop new skills, insights, differentiations, ways of making meaning, and also is supported to deal with difficulties and anxieties created by these experiences. This is a developmental person-environment interaction.

The second interaction may be characterized as *overly challenging*. The degree of challenge in the environment compared to support for the person is over-balanced in favor of challenge. As a result, the person's range of developmental dissonance shrinks and shifts downward. Typically the person polarizes, hardens his/her position, tries to flee the environment, and experiences high levels of tension and anxiety. This challenge to support ratio is not developmental.

(Continued on page 220)

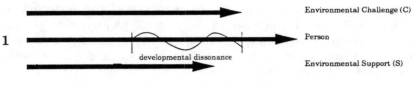

Environmental Challenge (C)

Person

developmental dissonance

Environmental Support (S)

Balanced - In Range C/S Ratio

• Some stress, but can handle it
• Appropriate environment for learning and development

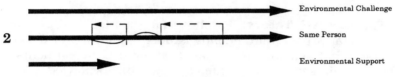

Environmental Challenge

Same Person

Environmental Support

Overly Challenging C/S Ratio

• Learning-developmental dissonance range shrinks and movers downward
• Not developmental; not good for learning
• Tend to *escape* the environment; polarized into "we-they" and blame "they";
  or become apathetically uninvolved if have to stay in environment

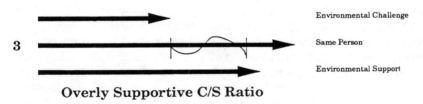

Environmental Challenge

Same Person

Environmental Support

Overly Supportive C/S Ratio

• Developmental dissonance range returns to normal
• Not enough challenge to stimulate development or new learning
• Tend to form elite, "I'm better than you" attitudes

Figure 7.3. Schematic of a person-environment interaction: Degree of challenge and support.

The final person-environment interaction may be characterized as overly supportive. The degree of support in the environment compared to challenge is over-balanced in favor of support. As a result, the demands of the environment never challenge the person to develop. Typically, the person in this environment may become complacent or bored and may develop elitist attitudes. This challenge-support ratio is not developmental either.

Theoretical Constructs

Let us now examine the families of theory that give substance to the ideas previously introduced.

Psychosocial Theory. Psychosocial theories and research are especially useful in helping student affairs professionals understand developmental tasks that preoccupy students at different phases of the life cycle. This knowledge and understanding can provide the basis for designing programs and services that help people mature and resolve developmental issues. For example, Figure 7.2 presents Chickering's vectors in chronological, directional, and age-related order. Briefly, many freshmen and sophomores are developmentally involved with resolving the first four vectors, while many juniors, seniors, and graduate students are more involved with resolving the latter three. Further, within a given vector the beginning content often can be differentiated conceptually and chronologically from the more advanced levels. A residence hall director, therefore, can use Chickering's theory as a map for locating vectors that were emphasized by the educational, social, and related developmental programs offered to students during an academic year and to determine to what degree the content of a given vector was addressed. Then, given an assessment of the population, a director could evaluate the appropriateness of both the content and the variety of the programs offered. At the Ohio State University, for example, a director of a freshman residence hall mapped his previous year's programs and found that 77% of the programs could be categorized under Developing Competence, one of the vectors theoretically appropriate for freshmen. Some of the programming (23%) was considered to be inappropriate for freshmen because it dealt with the developmental tasks of Freeing Interpersonal Relationships, Developing Purpose, and Developing Integrity. These issues usually are more developmentally appropriate for juniors, seniors, and graduate students. Before the hall director congratulated himself, however, he analyzed his omissions and the scope and variety of the 77% of the programming that seemed to be appropriate developmentally. The omissions were obvious. No deliberate efforts had been made to offer programming consistent with the developmental vectors of Managing Emotions, Developing Autonomy, or Establishing Identity. Only two percent of the programs dealt with intellectual competence. The analysis of the scope and variety of the programming was also revealing. The variety and scope of athletic and other physical-manual programming were excellent. In the area of social-interpersonal competence, however, programming was limited in scope. Even though a large number of social programs were sponsored (30%), opportunities to learn and use a variety of social-interpersonal competencies were not provided. Basically, the social programming taught and required students to use the same social skills over and over again. The director summarized the situation himself when he exclaimed, "We flunked! We offered the same social programs over and over. The students did not learn anything new" and their social competencies were not broadened.

Cognitive Structural Theory. The second family of useful developmental theories in student affairs practice is cognitive structural theories. These theories are useful in planning how student affairs practitioners can "package" effective developmental programs and services. That is, persons who reason or make meaning at different cognitive structural stages apparently learn and develop best in different kinds of environments. Information on how cognitive-structural developmental change takes place provides cues and criteria for designing appropriate environments for different students. In the Perry (1970) scheme of intellectual and ethical development, for example, students reasoning in positions of dualism apparently learn best, are more satisfied, and develop their ability to reason more complexly more quickly if their environments (1) provide encounters with moderate degrees of diversity (in terms of content) through (2) highly structured and (3) experiential learning processes. These encounters need to be (4) followed by analytic processing with an emphasis on differentiation and analysis. Finally, all of these processes need to take place in a (5) warm, personal atmosphere (Widick, Knefelkamp, & Parker, 1975). Students making meaning in the positions of *relativism* may learn best, however, if their environments provide (1) encounters with many points of view on a subject and (2) exposure to abstract or experiential learning processes. Relativistic students should have (3) extensive degrees of freedom to influence both the content to be learned and the process to be used. Similar to dualistic reasoning students, an environment that is (4) warm and personal is also helpful (Widick et al., 1975). Recent research (Baxter-Magolda, 1986-87, Winter, 1987a, 1987b; Benack, 1982) indicates that although structural differences may not exist between men and women on intellectual development, some stylistic differences may exist within which the structures are expressed. When compared to men, for example, many women students who reason in dualistic ways prefer more collaborative and less competitive learning experiences. Hence, a program requiring students to debate two points of view would be more appropriate for the learning style of many men and only a few women.

Person-environment Interaction Theory. The third family of theories relevant to the theory-in-practice approach is person-environment interaction theories (see Table 7.1). These theories require student affairs staff members to focus on three questions:

- Who are the students and what are relevant ways to conceptualize their characteristics?

- What is the nature of the environment or social setting in which the students live and/or learn, and what are the relevant ways to conceptualize the environment?

- How do the student and the environment interact? Is it Congruent? Incongruent? To what extent?

These questions can be applied to a variety of person-environment settings in order to better understand the situation and intervene to change the environment, the student, or both (Banning & McKinley, 1980; Paul, 1980). In the in-depth case study that follows person-environment models provide a basic framework for examining the problem of roommate conflicts in a residence hall and for designing an effective conflict resolution program.

Topological Theories. The final family of theories summarized here are topological theories. These theories are not developmental *per se,* and they have no unified theoretical heritage. What these theories share is an attempt to explain preferred or habitual patterns of mental functioning, that is, one's learning and functioning *style or type.* These style preferences are important because they can be used (1) to differentiate program designs for persons with different learning and communication styles, (2) to inform team building in student organizations where different styles need to be appreciated in order to work together productively, and (3) to match closely interacting persons such as roommates. To illustrate, Schroeder (1976l, 1980) and Kalsbeek, Rodgers, Marshall, Denny, and Nicholls (1982) have used Myers-Briggs types for residence hall roommate assignments; Schrader (1982) has used types to differentiate assignments within a career development workshop; and Provost (Provost & Anchors, 1987) has used different styles in couples and family counseling.

Procedural or Process Models

Procedural or process models are the second element in the formula of the practice-to-theory-to-practice approach. *These models describe sets of steps that can be used to guide the use of theory in student development practice.* These models are not theories; rather, they are rules of thumb or steps that can be taken when theory is to be used in practice. For example, the Council of Student Personnel Associations (COSPA) (Cooper, 1971) outlined 10 steps that should be taken when designing and implementing student development programs:

1. Assess behaviors the student has already deveeloped.

2. Formulate the student's behavioral objectives.

3. Select college programs that build on existing behaviors to accomplish the student's objectives.

4. Foster student growth within the context of his or her own cultural background and encourage his/her appreciation of the cultural backgrounds of the educational institution and of other students.

5. Develop physical environments, human groups, institutional organizations, and financial resources most conducive to the student's growth.

6. Integrate concurrent experiences outside the institution with the student's educational program as an aid in achieving the student's objectives.

7. Modify existing behaviors that block the further growth of the student.

8. Give visibility to a value system that enables the student to judge the worth of behavior patterns.

9. Record the student's progress as a means of facilitating his or her growth.

10. Identify appropriate environments for continued development before and after the student leaves his or her present educational setting. (pp. 2-3)

These steps do not provide a definition of development, information on how development can be assessed, how developmental change takes place, or criteria for determining whether environments are developmentally appropriate. Only theories can provide this information. A model, however, can provide student affairs professionals with a structure and a set of steps for defining what one should do and the order in which one should do it as student developmental programs are created.

Table 7.2 references several procedural or process models. Student affairs professionals are encouraged to learn all of these models because different models may be useful in different programmatic or environmental settings.

The symbol → represents the phrase "can lead to" in the theory-to-practice formula. This is an important phrase because many people in student affairs are seeking fool-proof

(Continued on page 226)

TABLE 7.2
Currently Available Procedural and Process
Models and Source Theorists

Name of Model	Source Theorists and Date
Model for Behavioral Change	Blocker & Shaeffer (1971)
COSPA Model	Cooper (1971)
Deliberate Psychological Education	Mosher & Sprinthall (1971)
Model for Creating a Democratic Society	Crookston (1974)
BPE Analysis	Hunt & Sullivan (1974)
Deliberate Psychological Instruction	Widick, Knefelkamp, & Parker (1975)
Ecosystems Model	Aulepp & Delworth (1976)
Eco-mapping Model	Huebner & Corazzini (1976)
THE Student Development Model	Miller & Prince (1976)
Developmental Transcripts	Brown & Citrin (1977)
Multiple Perspective Model	Paul & Huebner (1978)
Seven-Dimensional Model	Drum (1980)
Conceptual Model of Intervention Strategies	Morrill & Hurst (1980)
Grounded Formal Theory Model	Rodgers & Widick (1980)
Practice-to-Theory-to-Practice	Knefelkamp (1984) Rodgers (1985)
Intentionally Structured Group Model	Winston, Bonney, Miller, & Dagley (1988)

recipes for student development programs. Such recipes do not exist. The phrase "can lead to" is deliberately used because the combination of formal theories with process models does not automatically result in appropriately challenging and supportive programs. The design cues and criteria provided by content and developmental theories may be more or less specific; however, usually a creative translation is required in order to design an appropriate program. In addition, multiple programs can be generated for the same problem and setting using the same theories and design criteria. There exists no one single *correct* program for each situation. Many environments are equally valid in principle and similar in empirical outcome.

Professional Practice

Finally, the phrase "professional practice" in the formula refers to the intervention or student development program actually designed and selected for implementation from an array of possible programs. The term "professional" is used because the practice-to-theory-to-practice approach is logically consistent with criteria for defining professional activity. The term serves as a reminder that no substitute can occur for an in-depth knowledge and understanding of theories, process models, and interventions if student affairs staff members are to practice professionally.

A CASE STUDY

This case study concerns roommate conflicts in a university residence hall and how a developmental response was created that achieved effective conflict resolution, student satisfaction, and enhanced development of students involved. The Grounded Formal Theory (Rodgers & Widick, 1980) process model was used, and the person-environment interaction approach was selected as a basic framework for understanding and defining the problem. Conflict resolution theories also were used as content theories for defining the problem and planning an intervention.

Phases in the Grounded Formal Theory (GFT) model are

Phase I—Focus on practice: a problem, a context, and a population;

Phase II—Select useful and usable formal theories to enlighten or define the problem in principle;

Phase III—Assess the population, context and interaction using the formal theories;

Phase IV—Formulate goals and objectives from the assessment data and formal theories;

Phase V—Design interventions (programs) using the theories and assessment data; and

Phase VI—Evaluate the intervention/program.

Problem Area, Context, and Population

Phase I in the GFT model starts with practice, not theory. It directs staff to develop a common sense description of the problem, context or setting, and population under consideration. This provides a data base for selecting relevant *content* and *developmental* theories for use in the process and begins one's understanding of the problem and the realities in which it operates.

Problem. Roommate conflict is a common problem faced by almost every professional who works in a residence hall. Like the common cold, this problem has not received the attention it deserves. A systematic application of the GFT approach to roommate conflict therefore was undertaken.

Population. The residence hall staff at The Ohio State University identified roommates who were having difficulty, and 32 pairs (16 female and 16 male) or 64 persons were randomly selected from the total pool of subjects and agreed to participate in Phases I and III of the GFT process. The sample was composed of 70% freshmen and 30% sophomores; their ages ranged from 18 to 20. The mode was 18. The group was 10% Black and 90% White. The group was culturally diversified, with 50% coming from metropolitan centers (15%

from inner cities and 35% from suburbs), 20% from rural homes, and 30% from moderate to small towns. Five percent came from families earning more than $50,000 per year, 25% between $30,000 and $49,000; 50% between $20,000 and $29,000; and 20% less than $19,000.

The second population relevant to this problem was the Resident Advisors (RA) who served as floor staff members. At Ohio State these staff members are undergraduate juniors and seniors ranging in age from 20 to 23. In this case, 5% were Black and 95% were White. The group included 60% juniors and 40% seniors. The modal age was 21. Sixty percent were from large metropolitan centers (5% from the inner cities and 55% from suburbs), 35% from moderate to small towns, and 5% from rural areas.

Setting. All the students lived either in double rooms (70%) or triple rooms (30%). The RA to student ratio was 1:40. The community unit was a floor with rooms on both sides of the hall. The halls involved were coed with men on one side of the hall and women on the other. The general population of these halls was 50% freshmen, 30% sophomores, and 20% juniors and seniors.

Select Theories

Phase II focuses on defining and understanding the problem in terms of content and theory. The task is to select relevant content and developmental theories and to apply them in principle to the problem, setting, and population.

In the residence hall example, the staff examined the conflict resolution works of Deutsch (1969), Eiseman (1977), Thomas (1976), Jones and Banet (1976), Pfeiffer and Jones (1981), Porter (1981), Sherwood and Glidewell (1973), and Kurtz and Jones (1973). Finding criteria for discriminating among these content theories was difficult without adding the insights of developmental theory. In this case, the theories of Perry (1970) (cognitive-structural) and Chickering (1969) (psychosocial) were used to analyze the situation and to derive criteria for evaluating the models of conflict resolution.

In terms of Perry's (1970) scheme, if the students involved in roommate conflicts reason primarily in dualistic ways, then the method or processes used in conflict resolution would need to be characterized by the following: (1) high degrees of structure, (2) limited degrees of freedom to change the purpose(s) or process(es) used, (3) an agenda controlled and facilitated by an authority figure and/or by the structure, (4) encounter with the other person's point of view followed by structured processing that focuses on awareness and differentiation, and (5) an atmosphere as warm and personal as can be created under the circumstances (Widwick, Knefelkamp & Parker, 1975).

When these criteria were applied to different theories and models of conflict mediation, Walton (1969), Pfeiffer and Jones (1981), and Porter (1981) were found to be more compatible with the criteria in principle than were other models.

If students reason in relativistic ways, however, the criteria alter radically. In this case, the conflict resolution processes used would need to be characterized by the following: (1) high and then low degrees of structure, (2) higher degrees of freedom to alter the process or agenda, (3) encounter with the point of view of the other, (4) self generation of alternatives to control or solve the problem areas, (5) a commitment to a program of control or resolution, and (6) a personal environment (Widick et al., 1975). These criteria were more characteristic of Eiseman's (1977) and Jones and Banet's (1976) models than other theories or models.

In terms of Chickering's theory (1969), if students are dealing with the first four vectors, then they may not have developed the social skills necessary for unaided interpersonal negotiation, and may not be emotionally autonomous enough to handle interpersonal conflict resolution *on their own.* In addition, emotions of anger and aggression could be aroused, and a student might still be managing emotions through external rules of heritage or peer group. If so, winning the conflict in order to save face, rather than negotiating in order to solve a problem, may be more important from the student's perspective. If an appropriate environment for conflict resolution can be designed and used, conflicts can become the medium for helping students learn these new skills and perhaps resolve the tasks of these first three vectors.

In contrast, if students are dealing with the last four vectors, then they probably already have developed interpersonal skills, emotional autonomy, and senses of self to handle interpersonal conflict without the aid of resident advisors.

Combining analyses of the problem from points of view of both Perry (1970) and Chickering (1969) and applying their theories to the three questions of person-environment interaction, the following can be hypothesized in principle: If the students are primarily dualistic (Perry) and working on the first four vectors (Chickering), then the person-environment interaction would be congruent if current practice is consistent with Perry's dualism and Chickering's vectors 1 through 4 as criteria for defining a developmental environment for such students. If current RA practice varies more-or-less from the criteria recommended for Perry dualists and Chickering first four vectors, then current practice would be incongruent more-or-less.

If, on the other hand, students with roommate problems are primarily relativistic and operating on the last three vectors, then the person-environment interaction would be congruent if current practices of RAs are consistent with Perry and Chickering criteria for relativists and persons involved with freeing interpersonal relationships, developing purpose, and developing integrity. The interaction would be partially-to-totally incongruent if practices and behaviors vary from the criteria.

Given these two theoretical hypotheses, actual RA practices and student behavior need to be assessed. Perry and Chickering levels of both RAs and students also need to be assessed. Actual practices and behaviors of both RAs and students need to be classified in terms of both Perry and Chickering criteria and then compared to the students' personal Perry and Chickering levels. The degree of congruence or incongruence between the persons and the environment then can be determined by comparing the actual personal development levels of students with assessed characteristics (in terms of

Perry and Chickering) of the actual conflict resolution practices of the RAs.

Ground the Formal Theories in the Context by Doing the Assessments

Phase III of the GFT Model generates a data base for interpreting the problem in terms of the hypotheses developed in Phase II. Both RAs and students were assessed using the Perry (1970) scheme and Chickering (1969) vectors, and they were interviewed concerning their *real* behaviors in roommate conflicts and also how they thought they *should behave* in these situations.

Student Data. Data provided by students on how they behaved in roommate conflicts are outlined in Table 7.3. Most students in the case study campus *do nothing* when they have a roommate conflict, and the situation either stabilizes at a given level of conflict or gradually worsens. Some of the students appealed to their RAs to solve the problem or they applied for room or hall changes. Most RAs refused to get involved in solving the problem until the students tried to solve their conflicts on their own. Students reported that they usually did nothing after being told to try to resolve their conflicts on their own. Hence, the RA usually did not see the students again and may have assumed that conflicts were resolved when they were not. A few students tried to confront roommates as the RA recommended. These confrontations would be called "win-lose" rather than "win-win" (Wiley, 1973) encounters, and the situation in their rooms usually got worse rather than better. For a few students, however, the conflicts were apparently resolved.

The students were assessed as still developing capacities for empathy and assertiveness. They usually tried "to prove that I'm right and you are wrong." All of the students also were assessed as reasoning in positions of dualism on the Perry (1970) scheme. On Chickering (1969) vectors, 90% were still coping with vectors one through four. They were not yet autonomous, and they worried about how they were perceived by peers. They could not yet manage aggressive emotions autonomously; they were still developing interpersonal skills of empathy, assertiveness, and negotiation.

Resident Advisor Data. The RAs espoused and were taught that roommates should not avoid their conflicts. The best method of resolution was to have students deal with their conflicts themselves if possible. The RA was not to become involved until students have tried to settle their conflicts by themselves.

TABLE 7.3
Student Data: Actual Behavior and Outcome in Roommate Conflict Situations

Actual Behavior in	Frequency of	Outcome
1. I avoid the conflict and do nothing.	usually	Things get worse or stay at the same level of conflict.
2. I appeal to my RA to solve the problem. It's his/her job, isn't it?	sometimes	RA usually refuses and then tells the student to try to settle the conflict on his/her own first. If the student tries and it does not work, then the student is told to see the RA. After hearing this from the RA, students usually do nothing.
3. I confront my roommate and we try to work out our conflicts.	rarely	A few students try to resolve their conflicts on their own. They report behaviors that would be called WIN-LOSE, and the situation tends to get worse.

The RA's actual behavior was sometimes inconsistent with the espoused ideal as shown in Table 7.4. In 60% of the cases, the behavior matched the espoused ideal; however, in 40% of the conflict situations, the RA took charge and told students what to do to solve their problems. In the former case, the RAs felt satisfied and thought they had taken the proper and expected action. In the latter, they felt somewhat guilty for taking charge and violating the system's expected behavior for RAs in roommate conflicts; however, they also felt powerful because their strategy sometimes worked.

On the Perry (1970) scheme, RAs were more advanced in intellectual development than were the students who reported roommate conflicts, with 30% being dualistic, 65% multiplistic, and 5% relativistic.

TABLE 7.4
Resident Advisor Data: Actual Behavior and
Self-evaluation in Conflict Situation

Self Report Action Taken	Frequency	Feelings and Evaluation
1. I make them deal with each other first.	60%	Satisfied that I did what is best, and this is what I was taught to do.
2. I step in, listen to them separately, and then tell the students what to do, and we solve the problem.	40%	Guilty for taking responsibility for the situation and powerful because I did something important and had influence in the situation.

In terms of Chickering's (1969) vectors, 60% of the RAs were assessed as being involved in resolving the last three vectors, while 40% were still involved with the first four.

When student data and environmental data were compared, the person-environment interaction at the case study university was basically incongruent. Students reasoned in dualistic ways and were still resolving the tasks of vectors one through four. The environment for resolving roommate conflicts, on the other hand, was basically relativistic. That is, when the RAs ask students to try to solve their problems themselves, the environment assumed that students already had achieved the skills, competence, and attitudes of vectors one through four. This method of resolution would require students to be relativistic and competent with interpersonal confrontation and negotiation in order to have a reasonable chance of success. The "successes" seemed to be the occasions where the RAs took charge and told students what to do. This would be consistent with students' levels according to Perry and Chickering, but would not provide encouragement of development as well. What is needed is a procedure for conflict resolution with a reasonable probability for successfully resolving conflicts that also provide students with opportunities to advance their cognitive structural and psychosocial development.

The desired environment would contain elements of both support and challenge. it would be structured, authority facilitated, involve encounter and diversity through actual experience, be processed with the authority, and be mutually respectful. The facilitator would model and teach assertion and negotiation, help the student to learn to control anger and aggression, and help to develop emotional and instrumental autonomy.

Formulate Goals and Objectives for an Intervention

Phase IV focuses on establishing both content and developmental goals and objectives using both the theories and data generated in the previous Phase.

Goals in the case study were as follows: (1) to control or resolve roommate conflicts, (2) to feel satisfied with the processes used in the conflict management process, and (3) to foster psychosocial and cognitive structural development through the conflict management process.

Content objectives were to control or resolve 50% of the roommate conflicts and to have students report satisfaction with the process at least 70% of the time.

Developmental objectives were as follows: (1) to design a conflict management process to meet both challenge and support criteria for defining a developmental environment for dualists, (2) to teach negotiation skills in the process, (3) to learn to control emotions of anger and aggression in constructive ways, and (4) to facilitate development of emotional and instrumental autonomy.

Design Intervention

In order to design such a conflict resolution process, the student affairs staff used the goals and objectives (Phase IV) and information about the general political and organizational realities in which these specific residence halls operated (Phase I of the GFT Model) and they also sought to identify interventions (Phase II) characteristics that would be consistent with the developmental levels of students (Phase III).

The staff began by brainstorming the following questions: What should be done with whom? When? and Why? As indicated, many interventions are logically consistent with the goals, objectives, and realities of a setting. The quality and variety of interventions generated depend upon the repertoire of professional interventions known to a staff and the quality of their creativity. In the case study, a partial list of interventions generated in the brainstorm session is presented in Table 7.5. Three interventions ultimately were used by the staff; however, only one program is described. This program focused on teaching RAs to use Walton's (1969) model of third party mediation in dealing with roommate conflicts, and, through use of Walton's model, to try to achieve the goals and objectives outlined in Phase IV.

TABLE 7.5
Brainstorm on Possible Interventions
in Roommate Conflict Situations

all students on floor	hall orientation	roommate conflict lecturettes on data from process 1 through 4 and then an appeal to use RA if needed to mediate conflicts. Explain procedures RA will use.	preventative maintenance create expectation of using the RA
all students on floor	after first big conflict	human relations lab on lifestyle differences and conflict resolution skills	first big conflict provides motivation and readiness for internalizing aware-ness and skills learned in such a lab.
all students on floor	monthly floor meetings	reinforce the skills, norms, and expectations of human relations lab mentioned above	behavior change takes repeated experience and reinforcement.
students in conflict	as conflicts occur	use Walton's model of third party conflict mediation	Walton's model is consistent with the goals and objectives; is teachable to RAs; is useable by RAs
RAs	Spring course or Fall orientation	conflict resolution workshop to teach Walton's model	to teach RA's to use Walton's model and explain *why* changing from "have them do it" to Walton's third party mediation
RAs	Spring course or Fall orientation	teach RAs to design and facilitate human relations workshops	so RAs can do workshops for entire floor
RAs	in-service training	assertion workshop	so RAs can develop assertion skills and have a basis for calling on senior staff to do a similar workshop for the floor, if needed.

Walton's (1969) model of third party conflict mediation was selected because its characteristics are consistent with dualistic challenge and support criteria for environmental design and the skills taught in the process are consistent with those associated with vectors one through four.

Briefly, Walton's model has a mediator (e.g., the R.A.) meet separately with each party in a conflict in order to learn the issues from each person's point of view and to negotiate the follow-up process to be used. During the negotiation of the follow-up process, the mediator makes sure the following conditions are met:

1. The mediation session between or among the parties takes place in a neutral physical environment.

2. The mediator will control the agenda, structure the discussion, and make sure all issues are discussed.

3. The mediator will model and teach appropriate interpersonal behaviors such as assertion and negotiation skills and empathetic listening.

4. The goal is the resolution or at least the control of the conflict.

During the mediation session itself, the mediator controls the agenda and the order in which items are discussed, keeps both parties on the topic, structures the interaction, and models and teaches appropriate skills. Hence, in terms of Perry (1970) criteria, Walton's model uses an authority figure to pre-structure the environment and control the number, nature and timing of confrontations. In terms of Chickering's (1969) vectors, the mediator models and teaches the skills and attitudes needed to express and yet to control anger, to negotiate from a "win-win" perspective, and to move toward a greater capacity for autonomous, responsible behavior. Organizational realities also provided opportunities to teach this model to RAs. All new RAs take a course to prepare them for their positions during the spring before their service in the autumn, and all attend two weeks of training just before the halls open in the autumn. Walton's model and associated skills could be taught on either or both occasions. Hence, Walton's model logically seemed to be consistent with all of the goals; that is, control or resolution of roommate conflicts, a higher level of student satisfaction than the level expressed by the students who were assessed in Phase III, opportunities to learn interpersonal negotiation skills, to learn to control the emotions of anger and aggression, to learn emotional and instrumental autonomy, and to do all of the above in an environment appropriate for dualists.

The autumn training was used to teach RAs the Walton model. Objectives of the workshop were (1) to learn Walton's model and skills needed to use it, (2) to learn Chickering's vectors well enough to understand *why* a third party mediator and a method like Walton's may be needed when helping students who reason primarily in dualistic ways, (3) to design the training consistent with the dualistic and multiplistic developmental levels of the majority of the RAs, and (4) to help those RAs dealing with the first four vectors to make progress on these vectors.

The Rodgers, Bryer, and Hollingsworth (1976) teaching-learning model, which uses the following steps, was used to teach the Walton model:

1. *Provide Cognitive Understanding:* (a) define the model or skill including both what it is and what it is not, and (b) relate the model and the needs of the persons who are in conflict and the mediator's role.

2. *Model the Process and Skills:* (a) model appropriate use of the model and skills needed to use it, and (b) model inappropriate uses of the model and skills.

3. *Practice Using the Model and Skills:* (a) practice using the model and skills in a structured skill-building setting and (b) receive positive and corrective feedback from observers.

4. *Evaluate level of achievement:* (a) via behavioral criteria and (b) give feedback on level of achievement.

This teaching-learning model is structured and experiential, introduces moderate to high degrees of complexity, and processes interactions through feedback and evaluation. Hence, the method is consistent with the dualistic and multiplistic levels of most of the RAs. In addition, learning Walton's model and the skills needed to use it would, in itself, help to develop interpersonal competence and autonomy for RAs who have not yet resolved these vectors. The design of the workshop is outlined in Table 7.6.

Evaluate Outcomes

In Phase VI the intervention designed in Phase V is implemented and evaluated.

In this case a pilot study involved teaching a random sample of RAs to use the Walton model and then monitoring the RA's use, modifications, or failure to use the model. These steps were followed by obtaining data on resolution outcomes, students' levels of satisfaction with the process, and post-test Perry and Chickering levels. These data would then be compared to the data obtained in the grounding (Phase III) in order to determine if the intended objectives were achieved.

In a pilot evaluation involving live modeling rather than videotapes, the Walton trained RAs used the Walton method 80% of the time during the Autumn Quarter, while 20% of their behavior in roommate conflicts was not consistent with Walton's model. Control or resolution of conflicts was achieved in 67% of the cases using Walton's method compared to 25% for a comparison group using regular methods. Similarly, student satisfaction with the Walton process was significantly higher than for regular practices. No significant differences were found in Perry levels between the two groups of students on pre- and post-tests. Differences in favor of the Walton group occurred in obtaining negotiation and assertion skills.

Case Study Summary

This case study illustrates the practice-to-theory-to-practice approach to using theory. The approach emphasizes the use of procedural or process models as the guiding structure.

(Continued on page 243)

TABLE 7.6
Design of Resident Advisor Workshop on Roommate Conflict Resolution

1. to model three approaches to roommate conflict resolution. to inform RA's on *why* a new conflict resolution approach is being adopted.	1-1 Introduce videotapes of three approaches and outcomes (5 min). Materials: psychodrama videotapes of the three models and results developed originally by residence hall staff using staff as actors. 1-2 Approach #1 (a) "do it yourself first" with result that students do nothing or they try and WIN-LOSE makes matters worse; (b) discuss and analyze; (c) present data from Phases I to III of the GFT applicable to this approach (10 min) 1-3 Approach #2 (a) "do it for them" with result of control or resolution but no development; (b) discuss and analyze; (c) present data from Phases I to III of GFT applicable to this approach (30 min) 1-4 Approach #3 (a) "Walton's method" with result of control or resolution and some progress on developmental goals; (b) discuss and analyze; (c) compare Walton's model and other two approaches (45 min)
2. break	2-1 Break and refreshments (20 min)
3. to learn Chickering's vectors with concentration on one through four	3-1 Lecturette on Chickering's vectors, especially one through four and related behaviors in videotapes to Chickering's vectors [transparencies, screen, overhead projector, and handouts] (30 min)
4. eat and free time	4-1 Lunch (2 hours)
5. to learn the basics of Perry's scheme and environmental design criteria for dualists	5-1 Lecturette on Perry's stages and design criteria and relate criteria to behaviors in videotapes [transparencies, screen, overhead projector, and handouts] (50 min)

Table 7.6. (Continued)

6. to learn the elements of Walton's model and to identify skills required to use it.	6-1 Lecturette to describe the model, what it is and is not, skills needed to use it [transparencies, screen, overhead projector, and handouts] (30 min)
7. to model the process in appropriate and then in "common errors" ways	7-1 Replay videotape of Walton's model or another videotape of a second person using Walton's model (45 min) 7-2 Play videotape of an RA making common errors in using Walton's model 7-3 Analyze, discuss and relate to Chickering's and Perry's criteria [videotape player, screen] (20 min)
8. break	8-1 Break (15 min)
9. to practice using Walton's model and skills it requires	9-1 Role-play and feedback (three RAs and one senior staff person work together—there are three role play situations involving an RA and two roommates—each RA serves once as the RA. The other RAs play the students. The senior staff person acts as coach to the RAs preparing to be the RA in the role play and gives feedback on positive and corrective behaviors. 9-2 After one role play, dismiss for the day [role play materials, semi-private space] (1 hr role play)
10. warm-up and introduction	10-1 Some ice breaker and brief lecturette on previous day's and current day's activities.
11. to practice using Walton's model and skills continued	11-1 Same three RAs and 1 senior staff member do the two remaining role plays as described in 9 above. [role play materials, semi-private space] (2 hr)
12. eat and free time	12-1 Lunch and break ($1^1/_2$ hr)

Table 7.6. Continued.

13. to practice and to evaluate the level of competence in using Walton's model	13-1 Rotate and use a different set of three RAs with a different senior staff member. Do three more role plays. Each RA serves as RA in a role play once. Senior staff evaluate performances and give positive and corrective feedback. [role play materials, semiprivate space] (3 hr)
14. to reinforce use of the model in actual practice	14-1 Closing assembly and lecturette by director of training to reinforce the purpose of the workshop (15 min)

The approach also uses formal social and behavioral science theories, research on those theories and various means of measuring their constructs in order to give substance to the steps in the process model. Initially, formal theories provide a basis for defining and understanding the problem in principle. When the theory is grounded with the real people involved, a data base is generated that provides a concrete basis for defining and understanding the problem, and provides a basis for defining appropriate content and developmental goals and objectives. Finally, theories also provide criteria for designing developmentally appropriate interventions and for defining and measuring outcomes.

USING THEORY
IN PRACTICE SUMMARY

Using developmental and related social and behavior science theories in the practice of student affairs assumes that well-rounded development of the whole personality is a primary goal of higher education. In addition, it requires that professionals possess in-depth (Location 3 or 4) understanding and knowledge of (1) process models, (2) selected content and developmental theories, and (3) means for measuring persons and environments for all theories used. It requires professional competence.

Both *process models* and *formal theories* are needed in order to use theory in practice. Neither can do the job without the other. Process models provide the order and nature of the considerations used in linking theory and practice. Formal theory and its related measurement technologies provide substance to the steps recommended by process models.

Planning practice based upon theory is a complex task. In many cases, multiple kinds of theory (psychosocial, cognitive-structural, person-environment interaction, and topological) can be used together to increase both the individuation of programs and services and the desired outcome. Staff members are encouraged to learn and internalize theories in each category of theory.

Using theory in practice also requires a very personal decision. Individual staff members must decide whether or not to learn multiple kinds of theory to the degree necessary (Location 3 or 4) to internalize the theories in their personal theory-in-use (Argyris & Schon, 1974). An affirmative decision implies certain values and requires time and effort to implement. Apparently only a few student affairs staff members have done so to date (Heineman & Strange, 1984; Strange, 1983).

Even with an affirmative personal decision and the achievement of competence in one's theory-in-use, organizational and political factors affect the degree to which one can use theory in practice. Organizations with values and structures opposed to the educational values inherent in using developmental theory in practice can discourage, fail to support or reward, and even punish staff members who engage in such efforts. Hence, sometimes staff members must work for organizational change as well as the use of theory in practice.

Finally, the use of theory in practice in student affairs involves ethical issues. Staff members must be careful, for example, not to impose theories generated from one population (e.g., whites) on another population (e.g., blacks). Fortunately, progress is being made in terms of gender, racial, age, and ethnic similarities and differences on many of the most relevant theories. When adequate and relevant theory does not exist, however, then student affairs staff members can follow Winston's (1990) recommendations and use qualitative and aphorimic methodologies in grounding their practice and generating new formal theories.

REFERENCES

Argyris, C., & Schon, D.A. (1974). *Theory in practice: Increasing professional effectiveness.* San Francisco: Jossey-Bass.

Astin, R.W. (1968). *The college environment.* Washington, DC: American Council on Education.

Aulepp, L., & Delworth, U. (1976). *Training manual for an ecosystem model: Assessing and designing campus environments.* Boulder, CO: Western Interstate Commission for Higher Education.

Baltes, P.B., Reese, W.E., & Lipsitt, L.P. (1980). Life-span developmental psychology. *Annual Review of Psychology, 31,* 65-110.

Banning, J.H., & McKinley, D.E. (1980). Conceptions of the campus environment. In W.H. Morrill & J.C. Hurst (Eds.) *Dimensions of intervention for student development* (pp. 39-57). New York: Wiley.

Barbie, M. (1980). Personal conversations at University of New Mexico, Albuquerque.

Barker, R.G. (1968). *Ecological psychology: Concepts and methods for studying the environment of human behavior.* Stanford, CA: Stanford University Press.

Baruch, G., Barnett, R., & Rivers, C. (1983). *Lifeprints.* New York: Signet.

Baxter-Magolda, M.B. (1987a). *Measuring gender differences in intellectual development: A comparison of assessment methods.* Paper presented at annual convention, American College Personnel Association, Chicago.

Baxter-Magolda, M.B. (1987b). The affective dimension of learning: Faculty-student relationships that enhance intellectual development. *College Student Journal, 22,* 46-58.

Baxter-Magolda, M.B. (1986-1987, Winter). Experiential learning and student development theory as guides to developing instructional approaches. *International Journal of Social Education, 1,* (3). 28-40.

Benack, S. (1982). The coding of dimensions of epistemological thought in young men and women. *Moral Education Forum, 7,* 3-23.

Benjamin, M. (1986). *Developmental theory as a guide to policy and research: Critique and reformulation.* A discussion paper by Student-Environment Study Group. Guelph, Canada: University of Guelph.

Belenky, M.F., Clinchy, B.M., Goldberger, N.R., & Tarule, J.M. (1986). *Women's ways of knowing: The development of self, voice, and mind.* New York: Basic Books.

Blocker, D.H., & Shaffer, W.F. (1971). Guidance and human development. In O.R. Cook (Ed.) *Guidance for education in revolution (pp. 117-45).* Boston: Allyn & Bacon.

Bloland, P.A. (June, 1986a). Student development: The new orthodoxy? Part I. *ACPA Developments. 13*(3), 1, 13.

Bloland, P.A. (August, 1986b). Student development: The new orthodoxy? Part II. *ACPA Developments. 13*(4), 1, 22.

Branch-Simpson, G. (1984). *A study of the pattern in development of Black seniors at The Ohio State University* (unpublished doctoral dissertation). Columbus, OH: The Ohio State University.

Brown, R.D., & Citrin, R.S. (1977). Student development transcript: Uses and formats. *Journal of College Student Personnel. 18,* 163-68.

Buchanan, S. (1970). *Embers of the world: Conversations with Scott Buchanan. H. Wofford, Jr. (Ed.).* Santa Barbara: The Center for the Study of Democratic Institutions.

Chickering, A.W. (1972). Undergraduate academic experience. *Journal of Educational Psychology, 63,* 134-43.

Chickering, A.W. (1969). *Education and identity.* San Francisco: Jossey-Bass.

Clark, B.R. & Trow, M. (1960). *Determinants of college student subcultures.* Berkeley: Center for the Study of Higher Education.

Cooper, A.C. (1971). *A proposal for professional preparation of the college development educators.* Report from the Commission of Professional Development, Council of Student Personnel Associations.

Crookston, B.B. (1974). Design for an intentional democratic community. In D.A. DeCoster & P. Mabel (Eds.), *Student development and education in college residence halls* (pp. 55-67). Washington, DC: American College Personnel Association.

Deutsch, M. (1969). Conflicts: Productive and destructive. *Journal of Social Issues, 25,* 7-41.

Drum, D. (1980). Understanding student development. In W.H. Morrill & J.C. Hurst (Eds.), *Dimensions of intervention from student development* (pp. 14-38). New York: Wiley.

Eiseman, J.W. (1977). A third-party consultation model for resolving recurring conflicts collaboratively. *Journal of Applied Behavioral Science, 13*, 303-14.

Erikson, E. (1968). *Identity, youth and crisis.* New York: Norton.

Farrell, M.P., & Rosenberg, S.D. (1981). *Men at midlife.* Dover, MA: Auburn House.

Fowler, J. (1981). *Stages of faith.* New York: Harper & Row.

Furhmann, B., & Grasha, S. (1983). *Designing classroom experiences based on student styles and teaching styles: A practical handbook for college teaching.* Boston: Little, Brown, & Co.

Garaudy, R. (1973). We can learn from Africa. *The Center Magazine. VI (2),* 38-41.

Gilligan, C. (1982a). *In a different voice: Psychological theory and women's development.* Cambridge: Harvard University Press.

Gilligan, C. (1982b). New maps of development: New visions of maturity. *American Journal Orthopsychiatry, 52,* 199-212.

Gould, R. (1978). *Transformations.* New York: Simon and Schuster.

Harvey, D.J., Hunt, D.E., & Schroeder, H.M. (1961). *Conceptual systems and personality organization.* New York: Wiley.

Havighurst, R.J. (1972). *Developmental tasks and education* (3rd ed.). New York: McKay.

Heath, D.H. (1968). *Growing up in college: Liberal education and maturity.* San Francisco: Jossey-Bass.

Heath, R. (1974). *The reasonable adventurer.* Pittsburgh, PA: University of Pittsburgh Press.

Heineman, D., & Strange, C. (1984). Uses of human development theory by entry-level practitioners in student affairs. *Journal of College Student Personnel 25,* 528-33.

Holland, J.L. (1973). *Making vocational choices: A theory of careers.* Englewood Cliffs, NJ: Prentice Hall.

Huebner, L.A., & Corazzini, J.G. (1976). *Ego-mapping: A dynamic model for intentional campus design.* (Student Development Staff Papers.) Fort Collins, CO: Colorado State University.

Hunt, D.E., & Sullivan, E.V. (1974). *Between psychology and education.* Hinsdale, IL: Dryden Press.

Jones, J.E., & Banet, A.G. (1976). Dealing with anger. In J.W. Pfeiffer & J.E. Jones (Eds.), *Annual handbook for group facilitators* (pp. 111-14). La Jolla, CA: University Associates.

Josselson, R. (1987). *Finding herself: Pathways to identity development in women.* San Francisco: Jossey-Bass.

Kalsbeek, D., Rodgers, R., Marshall, D., Denny, D., & Nicholls, G. (1982). Balancing challenge and support: A study of degrees of similarity in suitemate personality type and perceived difference in challenge and support in a residence hall environment. *Journal of College Student Personnel, 23,* 434-42.

Kegan, R. (1982). *The evolving self: Problems and process in human development.* Cambridge: Harvard University Press.

Keniston, K. (1970). Youth: A "new" stage of life. *American Scholar, 39,* 631-54.

Kiersey, D., & Bates, M. (1978). *Please understand me: Character and temperament types* (3rd ed.). Del Mar, CA: Prometheus Nemesis Books.

Kitchener, K.S., & King, P.M. (1981). Reflective judgment: Concepts of justification and their relationship to age and education. *Journal of Applied Developmental Psychology, 2,* 89-116.

Knefelkamp, L. (1984). *Practice-to-theory-to-practice: Models and families of theory.* (Videotape, 2 volumes). Generativity project. Washington, DC: American College Personnel Association.

Kohlberg, L. (1984). *Essays on moral development (Vol. II). The psychology of moral development: The nature and validity of moral stages.* New York: Harper and Row.

Kolb, D.A. (1976). *Learning styles inventory: Technical manual.* Boston: McBer.

Kuh, G.D., Shedd, J.D., & Whitt, E.J. (1987). Student affairs and liberal education: Unrecognized (and unappreciated) common law partners. *Journal of College Student Personnel, 28,* 252-60.

Kurtz, R.R., & Jones, J.E. (1973). Confrontation types, conditions and outcomes. In J.W. Pfeiffer & J.E. Jones (Eds.), *Annual handbook for group facilitators.* (pp. 135-38). LaJolla, CA: University Associates.

Levinson, D.J., Darrow, C.N., Klein, E.B., Levinson, M.H., & McKee, B. (1978). *The seasons of a man's life.* New York: Knopf.

Lewin, K. (1936). *Principles of topological psychology.* New York: McGraw-Hill.

Lipsetz, A. (1975). *Student development: Make it simple and easy to use.* Paper presented at the annual convention of National Association of Student Personnel Administrators.

Loevinger, J. (1976). *Ego development.* San Francisco: Jossey-Bass.

McAdams, D.P. (1985). *Power, intimacy, and the life story: Personological inquiries into identity.* Homewood, IL: Dorsey Press.

Miller, T.K., & Prince, J. S. (1976). *The future of student affairs: A guide to student development for tomorrow's higher education.* San Francisco: Jossey Bass.

Moos, R.K. (1979). *Evaluating educational environments: Procedures, measures, findings, and policy implications.* San Francisco: Jossey-Bass.

Morrill, W. H., & Hurst, J. C. (Eds.). (1980). *Dimensions of intervention for student development.* New York: Wiley.

Mosher, R. L., & Sprinthall, N. A. (1971). Psychological education: A means to promote personal development during adolescence. *Counseling Psychologist, 2,* 3-82.

Myers, I.B. (1980). *Gifts differing.* Palo Alto, CA: Consulting Psychologists Press.

Myers, I.B., & McCaulley, M.H. (1985). *Manual: A guide to the development and use of the Myers-Briggs Type Indicator.* Palo Alto, CA: Consulting Psychologists Press.

Neugarten, B.L. (1975). Adult personality: Toward a psychology of life cycle. In W.C. Sze (Ed.), *The human life cycle* (pp. 379-94). New York: Jason Aronson.

Newcomb, T.M., Joenig, K.E., Flacks, R., & Warwick, D.P. (1967). *Persistence and change: Bennington College and its students after 25 years.* New York: Wiley.

Nucci, L. (1985). Children's conceptions of morality, social convention, and religious prescriptions. In C. Harding (Ed.), *Moral dilemmas; Philosophical and psychological issues in the development of moral reasoning* (pp. 137-74). Chicago: Precedent Press.

Pace, C.R., & Baird, L.L. (1966). Attainment patterns in the environmental press of college subcultures. In T.M. Newcomb & E.K. Wilson (Eds), *College peer groups* (pp. 215-42). Chicago: Aldine.

Paul, S.C. (1980). Understanding student environment interaction. In W.H. Morrill & J.C. Hurst (Eds.), *Dimensions of intervention for student development* (pp. 58-82). New York: Wiley.

Paul, S.C., & Huebner, L.A. (1978). *Persons in their contextual systems of consumers in the market place.* Paper presented at the annual convention of the American College Personnel Association, Detroit, MI.

Parker, C.A. (1977). On modeling reality. *Journal of College Student Personnel, 18,* 419-25.

Perry, W., Jr. (1970). *Intellectual and ethical development in the college years.* New York: Holt, Rinehart, & Winston.

Pervin, L.P. (1967). Satisfaction and perceived self-environment similarity: A semantic differential study of student-college interaction. *Journal of Personality, 35,* 623-34.

Pfeiffer, J.W., & Jones, J.E. (1981). *Intergroup meeting: An image exchange. Structured experiences for human relations training.* La Jolla, CA: University Associates.

Piaget, J. (1965). *The moral judgment of the child.* New York: The Free Press.

Plato, K. (1978). The shift to student development: An analysis of the patterns of change. *NASPA Journal, 15,* (4), 32-36.

Porter, L.C. (1981). Intergroup clearing: A relationship building intervention. In J. W. Pfeiffer & J.E. Jones (Eds.), *Annual handbook for group facilitators* (pp. 48-49). La Jolla, CA: University Associates.

Provost, J.A., & Anchors, S. (1987). *Applications of the Myers-Briggs Type Indicator in higher education.* Palo Alto, CA: Consulting Psychologists Press.

Rhatigan, J.J. (1975). Student services vs. student development: Is there a difference? *The Journal of the National Association for Women Deans, Administrators, and Counselors, 38,* (2), 51-59.

Rhatigan, J.J. (1987). Personal conversation at national convention of National Association of Student Personnel Administrators, Chicago.

Rodgers, R.F. (1980). Theories underlying student development. In D.G. Creamer (Ed.), *Student development in higher education: Theories, practices and future directions* (pp. 10-95). Washington, DC: American College Personnel Association.

Rodgers, R.F. (1983). Using theory in practice. In T.K. Miller, R.B. Winston, & W.R. Mendenhall (Eds.), *Administration and leadership in student affairs* (pp. 111-44). Muncie, IN: Accelerated Development.

Rodgers, R.F. (1985). *Practice-to-theory-to-practice: Using theories of Lee Knefelkamp and Arthur Chickering to create developmental programs.* Videotape (2 volumes). Generativity Project, Washington, DC: American College Personnel Association.

Rodgers, R.F., Bryer, J., & Hollingsworth, R. (1976). *Helping skills for paraprofessionals (3rd ed.).* Columbus, OH: The Ohio State University Office of Student Services.

Rodgers, R.F., & Widick, C. (1980). Theory to practice: Uniting concepts, logic and creativity. In F.B. Newton & K.L. Ender (Eds). *Student development practices: Strategies for making a difference* (pp. 3-25). Springfield, IL: Thomas.

Rubin, L. (1981). *Women of a certain age.* New York: Harper & Row.

Sanford, N. (1967). *Where colleges fail.* San Francisco: Jossey-Bass.

Schrader, D. E. (1982). *Intellectual development: Myers-Briggs and Perry Scheme applications in career development seminars.* Unpublished master's thesis, The Ohio State University.

Schroeder, C. (1976). New strategies for structuring residential environments. *Journal of College Student Personnel, 17,* 386-91.

Schroeder, C. (1980). Student development through environmental management. In F.B. Newton and K.L. Ender (Eds.), *Student development practices: Strategies for making a difference* (pp. 52-79). Springfield, IL: Thomas.

Selman, R.L. (1980). *The growth of interpersonal understanding.* New York: Academic Press.

Sheehy, G. (1974). *Passages: Predictable crises of adult life.* New York: Dutton.

Sherwood, J.J., & Glidewell, J.C. (1973). Planned renegotiation: a norm-setting OD intervention. In J.W. Pfeiffer & J.E. Jones (Eds.), *Annual handbook for group facilitators* (pp. 195-202). La Jolla, CA: University Associates.

Silber, J. (1971). *Masks and fig leaves.* Center audio tape. Santa Barbara: The Center for the Study of Democratic Institutions.

Stamatakos, L. (1988). *Comments on the adequacy of student development theories.* Paper presented at American College Personnel Association National Convention, Miami.

Stern, G.G. (1970). *People in context.* New York: Wiley.

Strange, C.C. (1983). Human development theory and administrative practice in student affairs: Ships passing in the daylight. *NASPA Journal, 21* (1), 2-8.

Straub, C. (1987). Women's development of autonomy and Chickering's theory. *Journal of College Student Personnel, 26,* 198-205.

Straub, C., & Rodgers, R.F. (1986). An exploration of Chickering's theory and women's development. *Journal of College Student personnel, 27,* 216-24.

Thomas, K. (1976). Conflict and conflict management. In M.D. Dunnette (Ed.), *Handbook of industrial and organization psychology* (pp. 889-935). Chicago: Rand McNally.

Vaillant, B. (1977). *Adaptation to life.* Boston: Little, Brown & Co.

Walton, R.E. (1969). *Interpersonal peace making: Confrontation and third party consultation.* Reading, MA: Addison Wesley.

White, R.W. (1966). *Lives in progress (2nd ed.).* New York: Holt, Rinehart, & Winston.

Widick, C., Knefelkamp, L.L., & Parker, C.A. (1975). The counselor as a developmental instructor. *Counselor Education and Supervision, 14,* 286-96.

Wiley, G.E. (1973). Win/lose situations. In J.W. Pfeiffer & J.E. Jones (Eds.), *Annual handbook for group facilitators* (pp. 105-07). La Jolla, CA: University Associates.

Winston, R.B., Jr., (1990). Using theory and research findings in everyday practice. In D.D. Coleman & J.E. Johnson (Eds.), *The new professional: A resource guide for new student affairs professionals and their supervisors* (pp. 30-55). Washington, DC: National Association of Student Personnel Administrators.

Winston, R.B., Jr., Bonney, W.C., Miller, T.K., & Dagley, J.C. (1988). *Promoting student development through intentionally structured groups.* San Francisco: Jossey-Bass.

Witkin, H.A. (1976). Cognitive style in academic performance and in teacher-student relations. In S. Messick & Associates (Eds.), *Individuality in learning* (pp. 38-72). San Francisco: Jossey-Bass.

SUGGESTED READINGS

Belenky, M.F., Clinchy, B.M., Goldberger, N.R., & Taruk, J.M. (1986). *Women's ways of knowing: The development of self, voice, and mind.* New York: Basic Books.

Creamer, D.G., & Associates (1990). *College student development: Theory and practice for the 1990s.* Alexandria, VA: American College Personnel Association.

Fowler, J. (1981). *Stages of faith.* New York: Harper & Row.

Kegan, R. (1982). *The evolving self: Problems and process in human development.* Cambridge: Harvard University Press.

Winston, R.B., Jr., Bonney, W.C., Miller, T.K., & Dagley, J.C. (1989). *Promoting student development through intentionally structured groups.* San Francisco: Jossey-Bass.

D. Stanley Carpenter, Ph.D., a native of Texas, received the baccalaureate degree in mathematics from Tarleton State University (Texas) and the Master's degree in student personnel and guidance from East Texas State University. He worked in residence halls at Oglethorpe University in Atlanta, Georgia before moving to the University of Georgia where he earned the Ph.D. in counseling and student personnel services. His dissertation on professional development in student affairs earned the dissertation of the year award from the National Association of Student Personnel Administrators. He served as Dean of Students at the University of Arkansas at Monticello and Assistant Director of Development at Texas A & M University before assuming a position as Associate Professor of Educational Administration and Coordinator, Higher Education Specialization at Texas A & M.

CHAPTER 8

STUDENT AFFAIRS PROFESSION: A DEVELOPMENTAL PERSPECTIVE

D. Stanley Carpenter

This chapter provides a comprehensive examination of professionalism and professional development in the field of student affairs, and briefly traces the development of the profession historically and the place of professional development therein. To avoid confusion, a few definitions are important. First, the term **profession** is used in a sociological sense. That is, the assumption is that a generalized continuum exists with some jobs classified as occupations (at one end of the continuum) and some as professions (at the other end) with all other jobs classified somewhere in between. The location of a particular job on the continuum is dependent upon criteria such as feeling of community, formal and informal sanctions, and enforced codes of ethics (Pavalko, 1971). Based upon these criteria, the field of student affairs is seen as being on the profession end of the continuum.

Second, **professional development** is considered to be a universal process analogous to human development with many of the same elements involved. It is not narrowly defined as simply in-service education or professional association activity. Rather, it includes aspects such as developmental tasks and stages common to student affairs professionals, and a case can be made in this chapter for use of a developmental model to support this view of professional growth. In addition, one conception of such professional growth is offered, and the implications of professionalism and professional development for the field are examined.

EMERGENCE OF STUDENT AFFAIRS PROFESSIONALS

The English Influence

In the earliest colleges in America, nearly everyone had some type of student affairs responsibility. The colleges were imitations of the English residential model and by definition had to be concerned with extracurricular activities. One has only to consider the histories of such cities as Athens (Georgia and Ohio); Cambridge, Massachusetts; Oxford (Ohio and Mississippi); and numerous other college communities to deduce that the founders of early institutions were interested in insulation and isolation from the outside world. Colleges were largely self-contained units in terms of residence, food, and social life. Religious and moral developments were as important as cognitive development—often more important. Students were typically quite young, often as young as 11 (Rudolph, 1962). The president, faculty, trustees, and all other college officials took an active hand in the control and guidance of students (Leonard, 1956). For control it was. Often one of the most important duties of the president was his series of moral lectures to seniors.

The legal doctrine of *in loco parentis*, while not truly established as law until 1913 (*Gott v. Berea College*, 161 S.W. 204. Court of Appeals of Kentucky, 1913) was not a debated abstraction, but a useful paradigm. Care must be taken in generalizing because, as Appleton, Briggs, and Rhatigan (1978) pointed out, *in loco parentis* is an incomplete and often inaccurate way to look at total educational practice in early colleges. What existed then would today be termed developmental concern, but it was of a directive judgmental nature and involved very little student volition.

The English model predominated until about the Civil War when the pendulum began to swing. New forces were shaping higher education. Curricula, and indeed entire colleges, began to be secularized. Science and technology began to be legitimated as fields of study. The land grant movement aided the proliferation of "nonreligious" institutions.

The German Influence

In the middle of all this change, an aberration appeared. During the 19th century, more and more faculty members completed formal study in Germany, and the influence of German university thinking spread throughout American higher education. The German system was viewed by many as the best in the world with its emphasis upon scholarship, graduate education, and research and thus thought worthy of emulation. The best minds in higher education began to take the attitude that students' behavior out of class was of no concern to the institution. This laissez-faire attitude was reinforced by faculty reaction to the old control model of their youth (Cowley, 1964). Also, faculty and administrators were having too many other demands put on their time to continue 24-hour a day surveillance and concern for students.

The Emergence of Student Affairs Administrators

When these factors were added to the increasing presence of women students (who educational leaders believed needed additional supervision) and the burgeoning of extracurricular activities, such as fraternities, literary societies, and sports activities, the stage was set for the entrance of the student affairs officer. Just as the German movement was in part a reaction to the earlier emphasized English model, the proliferation of student affairs officers was a response to the German influence. Obviously these time periods were not sharply defined. Historians agree that the positions of **Dean of Men** and **Dean of Women** increased rapidly on American campuses during the period from 1870 to 1910. During the latter part of this time period, vocational counseling, mental hygiene, and psychological testing were gaining credence on campuses, also. During the early 20th century, the increased emphasis upon student services contributed to student affairs administration as a field (Lloyd-Jones, 1954).

Interesting to note is that only in America did the Dean of Men/Women movement surface. Even then, deans were nearly always appointed from the teaching faculty, which often resulted in a confusing and sometimes humorous lack of specific duties for early appointees. The first academic course in student affairs was conducted at Columbia University in 1915 (Appleton, Briggs, & Rhatigan, 1978).

Formal associations for student affairs practitioners were established and gained strength during the first quarter of the 20th century. Groups such as the *National Association of Deans and Advisers of Men* and the *National Association of Women Deans* were formed as were organizations for college physicians, college union directors, appointment secretaries (placement directors), and vocational guidance personnel. These fragmented organizations provided identity for practitioners in specific areas, but a more generalized and comprehensive conception of student affairs administration was coming. In 1937, the *American Council on Education* published the "Student Personnel Point of View" and revised it in 1949. These statements made three basic assumptions; (1) each student is unique; (2) each student is an integrated whole and the development of this whole person is mandatory; and (3) all development begins at the individual student's level and not at some mythical mean. This introduction of non-academic areas of development and the necessary tailoring of developmental experiences for different students implied out-of-class education conducted by knowledgeable professionals. Student affairs practitioners now had a philosophy to guide their work with students.

The "Profession" Controversy

Given the diversity of student affairs practice and the more or less peripheral structure of student affairs on many campuses, not surprisingly consensus among practitioners on the efficacy of the "Student Personnel Point of View" did not accrue overnight. The post World War II period has been characterized by active disagreement among the authorities in the student affairs literature. Many authors engaged in breast-beating and bemoaning the state of student affairs. Wrenn (1949) analyzed student affairs administration from a sociological perspective and concluded that it did not meet the criteria for being a profession. Shoben (1967) chided the field for being essentially contentless and urged it to stay out of areas belonging to other fields such as counseling. Koile (1966) was disappointed that student affairs had neither a clear body of knowledge, skill, and ethics, nor a central place in American higher education. Penney (1969) pointed out that student affairs had had time to prove itself as a profession and had not done so. He was concerned with the housekeeping emphasis apparent in much of the student affairs literature and the failure of the literature to promote areas of exclusive practice for the field. For some of these authors an apologetic or *mea culpa* attitude appears to have been present concerning the very existence of student affairs.

Fortunately, other authors challenged these negative viewpoints. Williamson (1958) left little doubt that he considered student affairs administration to be an identifiable field with its own preparation and professional characteristics. Miller (1967) called for an increased awareness of the student affairs practitioner as an educator, implying the professionalization of the field. He further proposed that practitioners should function as scholar-administrators with the creation of total learning environments as one of their primary tasks. Penn (1974) assumed he was writing to a professional field in calling for more collegial control of preparation programs. Bloland (1974) suggested that the personal development of students should be viewed as a major point of unity for the field. Trueblood (1966) made a case for the exclusivity of student affairs preparation and practice, and Nygreen (1968) noted that student affairs had many aspects of a profession and should be so amended in the future. A growing acceptance of human development theory as a foundation for practice (Miller & Prince, 1976), increasing emphasis upon professional preparation programs (Knock, 1977), and concern with the nomenclature of the field (Crookston, 1976) are examples in the literature of powerful, positive influences toward greater professionalism.

During this time of professional controversy, the 1960s and early 1970s, the entire higher education establishment was in ferment. While initially being criticized for not controlling student dissent, student affairs practitioners often came to be viewed as the only persons on campus truly able to deal with student disaffection. As the liaison between students and administrations, student affairs professionals often gained much respect. Further, the educational reforms that resulted from student demonstrations and the humanizing of the college environment necessitated by the student demands were often carried out by the student affairs staff.

Also during the 1960s came formal death of the *in loco parentis* doctrine as a cornerstone of student control. With the new legal requirements of due process for students and the lowering of the age of majority nationwide came necessity for a new relationship with students. Colleges could (and can) still require certain behaviors, but the new emphasis was upon collaboration with adults (rather than control of children) to maintain and enhance the educational community. Student affairs practitioners have been at the forefront in negotiating and administering this new relationship.

No conclusion has been reached in the profession controversy (Knock 1988; Kuk, 1988; Moore, 1988; Rickard, 1988a & b; Williams, 1988; Young, 1988). According to the usual criteria, the field of student affairs cannot be called a profession in the classic sense of the word (Stamatakos, 1981, 1987; Bloland, 1987; Komives, 1988). On the other hand, it has been argued that student affairs is an "emerging profession" (Carpenter, Miller, & Winston, 1980, p. 21). In any case, the field may be a profession "at least in practice. . .if not in theory. . ." (Trueblood, 1966, p. 80) and it is certain that professional attitudes, practice, and behavior are already expected and achieved by practitioners (Stamatakos, 1987). Stamatakos (1981) had earlier written about an underlying assumption "As individuals and as groups, we believe ourselves to be 'professionals,' and we believe our calling and colleagues with whom we work and with whom we have established formal organizations to be professional" (p. 105). This implies that student affairs exists as a field of endeavor only in the context of a larger institution, that of higher education. This calls into play the concept of professionals in bureaucracies. Like higher education faculty, or physicians in hospital settings, student affairs workers never operate in an atmosphere of unbounded autonomy, regardless of their status as professionals. A fair amount of sociological literature is related to this idea, which is beyond treatment here, but the fundamental theme is that professionals in organizations (or bureaucracies) experience values conflict with the host institutions resulting in a blurring of pure professionalism in that quality control (from a practice standpoint) is at least partially in the hands of lay persons.

This brief historical review has traced the development of student affairs administration from a series of parental oriented chores to a complete set of educational responsibilities involving difficult academic, psychological, and legal issues. Student affairs professionals increasingly are filling the role of valued partners with the faculty in an evolving educational mission of intentional student development. Professionalism, then, is an essential ingredient of both preparation and practice in the field of student affairs.

PROFESSIONALISM AS DEVELOPMENT

The specific application of principles of human development as articulated in Chapter 1 requires a knowledge of both the culture and community within which the individual lives and works. Human development theory, of course, has value in analyzing the comprehensive psychosocial, cognitive, and psychomotor development of individuals. It also can be applied to modular portions of total development, if such modules are defined by a community. Developmental principles, for example, may be applied specifically to the content and process of career development. This component of total development may be examined in light of its unique developmental tasks and stages that can be identified, verified, and discussed as separate units. Similarly, an even smaller area of human growth, development as a professional, can be profitably analyzed if a community can be defined within which such development occurs. Student affairs administration, like any profession, represents such a community (Carpenter, Miller, & Winston, 1980).

A professional community may be largely defined by three main sets of commonalities. First, *a group of professionals must share goals and objectives.* For student affairs professionals, the most common goal is the structuring of a campus environment in which students may maximize their growth in all possible ways. Ways to influence this environment or developmental milieu range from the most mundane services such as food and shelter to the most esoteric sensitivity training, but all are means to the common end. Student affairs staff and programs exist to promote student development.

A second attribute of professional community is **the existence of formal and informal sanctions.** That is, certain practices are rewarded and others are punished. For example, consider resumes. While resumes vary in style and content, most are expected to conform to relatively narrow norms. Generally, they should be neat, succinct, and honest. Deviations are punished by the simple expedient of "violators" neither being hired nor interviewed. On the positive side, persons who publish their work in books or professional journals are rewarded with respect, consulting jobs, and sometimes increased chances for better jobs or promotions, especially in professional preparation programs. Willingness to participate in and contribute to professional association activities is usually rewarded by the opportunity to assume more responsibility and leadership.

As student affairs has evolved as a profession, more attention has been paid to formal sanctions, as well. For a treatment of the place of professional ethics in this context, see the next chapter of this book.

Any community must **attend to socialization and regeneration,** the third set of processes considered. Socialization has both formal and informal forms. Informally, the lore of student affairs is communicated by more experienced professionals to new and less experienced ones. Proper ways to work with students, to communicate appropriately orally and in writing, to behave at conventions, to obtain or change positions, and many other things are taught by example, dialogue, and experience. Many of these same professional traits or activities are dealt with more formally in professional preparation programs, professional literature, and periodic job performance evaluations. An example of such formal codification of the field is Rentz and Saddlemire's (1988) descriptive book that examines the functions of the profession.

Regeneration is related closely to socialization in that certain of the processes are quite similar. However, the focus is more upon the actual bringing of individuals into the field. In order to continue to be vital, the profession must have new blood and the new blood should share the values, goals, and skills of the field after a brief orientation or preparation period. Therefore this preparation period needs to be a relatively common or similar experience for all the new recruits. Assurance of this commonality of training is the responsibility of practitioners and educators alike and is accomplished informally through communication and formally through accreditation, research, and professional association guidelines for training. While no real level of control of professional preparation has been achieved in student affairs, efforts have continued and seem to be bearing fruit. The CAS Standards, published in 1986 and the revised CACREP Standards (1988) which are included as Appendices and examined in another chapter in this book are the most promising recent developments in this area.

One important implication of the existence of a professional community is the concomitant developmental milieu thereby defined. However one must keep in mind that professional development also takes place in the context of global personal development. Hence, from time to time attention must be paid to ongoing life issues to the detriment of strict professionalism, as when one chooses to spend another year or two in an already mastered position in order to respond to a spouse's preferences, for example. Relatedly, some find that a good fit does not exist between preferred career reward structures and the field of student affairs. Schein (1978) and DeLong (1981) proposed the existence of career orientations and career anchors. DeLong discussed values and career needs in terms of career anchors including technical competence, managerial competence, security, creativity, autonomy, identity, service, and variety. Wood, Winston, and Polkosnik (1985) found evidence that autonomy and geographical security orientations were related to attrition in student affairs. Some combination(s) of these career anchors could interact negatively with any given job setting or supervisory style, or even with perceptions of the field as a whole. The picture that emerges, then, is what might be called "macro" processes of development for any given person, against which the "micro" process of professional development plays itself out, sometimes interactively, sometimes almost independently.

MODEL OF PROFESSIONAL DEVELOPMENT IN STUDENT AFFAIRS

Accepting that the student affairs profession is a community with shared goals, sanctions, and socialization/regeneration criteria, and believing that principles of human development have direct application to professional development, Miller and Carpenter (1980) suggested five propositions for consideration:

1. Professional development is continuous and cumulative in nature, moves from simpler to more complex behavior, and can be described via levels or stages held in common.

2. Optimal professional development is a direct result of the interaction between the total person striving for positive professional growth and the environment.

3. Optimal professional preparation combines mastery of a body of knowledge and a cluster of skills and competencies within the context of personal development.

4. Professional credibility and excellence of practice are directly dependent upon the quality of professional preparation.

5. Professional preparation is a lifelong learning process. (p. 84)

These propositions have many implications and offer a number of testable hypotheses. One such hypothesis, the existence of developmental stages, can be derived from Proposition 1. Four stages have been proposed: Formative, Application, Additive, and Generative. These four stages provide the basis for the postulation of developmental tasks of student affairs professionals (Carpenter, 1979). These tasks were formulated on the basis of Pavalko's (1971) profession-occupation continua:

- knowledge of theory and levels of skill,
- clarification of motivation and relevance to society,
- decisions regarding preparation and career,
- autonomy of professional behavior,
- developing a sense of professional community (professional association activity and colleague relationships),

- activities related to professional publications, and

- developing a sense of ethical practice.

Tasks were sorted by expert judges and are listed by stages in Figure 8.1 a factor analysis of responses to an instrument created from these tasks yielded four professional development factors (Carpenter & Miller, 1981):

1. contributions to the professional community,

2. institutional leadership and practice,

3. professional preparation, and

4. career awareness.

A Composite Career Path

A good way to synthesize all this stage, task, continuum, and factor information is to look at a career ladder composite for the student affairs professional.

Consider a hypothetical college student—John Johnson. He or his counterpart Jane Johnson (J.J.) probably became aware of student affairs administration as a career option through a positive relationship with one or more professionals. Maybe J.J. was a resident assistant, active in student government, a student activity board member, an orientation assistant, or filled some other paraprofessional role. Usually, as J.J. considers a student affairs career, the next step is to enter a master's degree program in counseling, student affairs practice, student development, or higher education administration. J.J. concurrently gets a graduate assistantship in housing, student activities, or some other area as a financial and experiential supplement to his/her education. Parenthetically, it is possible to enter the student affairs field without a master's degree, usually at smaller institutions, but this is becoming rare.

During the **Formative Stage,** J.J. is accomplishing several specific tasks related to acquiring knowledge of the field of

(Continued on Page 286)

Stage 1
Formative

1. Getting enough education and/ or skill training to obtain and hold a position in student affairs.

2. Tailoring learnings and experiences to meet the criteria and expectations of teachers or supervisors.

3. Attaining a knowledge of the theory and skills necessary for facilitating the development of students.

4. Reading journals and other professional publications in order to learn about the field and become aware of basic approaches.

5. Internalizing the values of student affairs professionals.

6. Attending regional and national conferences to make contacts and obtain a position.

Stage 2
Application

1. Beginning to apply the skills and competencies involved with student affairs practice.

2. Learning to take responsibility for professional decisions.

3. Attaining the respect of the campus community.

4. Making a firm commitment to student affairs as a profession.

5. Applying established ethical standards in direct contact work with students.

6. Contributing to newsletters that report on current practices in specific student services.

7. Taking part in inservice education, workshops, and other methods of gaining knowledge and skills to aid performance in one's current position.

Figure 8.1. Proposed four stages of developmental tasks of student affairs professionals.

Stage 3
Additive

1. Creating and devising new approaches to student development.

2. Taking responsibility for the professional activities and ethics of one's administrative subdivision and the professionals one supervises.

3. Contributing to professional publications in order to share current thinking and practice techniques.

4. Interpreting the rationale of student affairs to the larger community.

5. Encouraging younger professionals to take responsibility for their own professional efforts, while still providing them with support, input, and feedback.

6. Helping to welcome and orient young professionals to the field by "showing them the ropes" and encouraging the continued professional development of all colleagues.

7. Consulting with, directing, and/or supervising those responsible for accomplishing practical student development goals.

8. Taking part in the leadership of local, regional, and national professional associations.

Stage 4
Generative

1. Judging the merits of, and otherwise criticizing new student development/student affairs theories.

2. Contributing broad-scale "think pieces" concerning current and future student development theory and student affairs practices.

3. Sharing one's wealth of experience in student affairs with the profession as a whole.

4. Being heavily involved in the upper level leadership of and helping to shape the direction of professional associations.

5. Encouraging involvement of and being a mentor to less experienced student affairs workers in professional association leadership.

student affairs administration. Course work, books, and journals are all used to gain knowledge, and supervised practice is used to gain necessary skills. Students begin to become more committed to values of the student affairs field (if they decide to stay with their studies) as their learning increases. Professional associations are seen primarily as placement vehicles. Standards for knowledge, skills, practice, ethics, career awareness, and all other facets of professionalism are derived from and dependent upon the views of the instructors and practicum/internship/assistantship supervisors.

The **Application Stage** begins with the first professional position. Possible job titles include Head Resident or Resident Director, Programming Assistant, Counselor, Career Counselor, or sometimes (usually at smaller schools) Assistant Dean of Students, Assistant Director of Housing, Assistant Director of Student Activities, and so forth. J.J. still has much to learn. Education and training continue through in-service workshops, conference sessions, informal consultations with colleagues, journals and newsletters, and supervisors. However, the best teacher in this stage is experience. For entry level professionals, almost every decision is a "first." Most people try to follow all the rules and get input from supervisors and handbooks in dealing with situations that arise in practice. This is good for a while, but in an ideal setting, the budding professional is able (indeed required) to test theories and practice skills with students. J.J. finds that student affairs practice is idiosyncratic in some ways and that personal style contributes a part. Gaining respect from colleagues, students, and the academic community is important. Ethics are tested—and sometimes altered. Flexibility is critical—but in a firm context. Procedures are important—but so are exceptions. Student are unique—with predictable similarities.

On the career front, J.J. needs to decide whether to change jobs and campuses after two or three years in an initial position. Should central office or specific service area work be a goal? Also, a decision must be made about continuing in student affairs as a career as J.J. moves into the later Application Stage (after three to five years in the field). If a student affairs career is to be pursued, then J.J. must either decide to seek more formal education, or middle-management positions with increasing responsibility. These activities reflect the transition to the next stage.

The **Additive Stage** is not as easily or sharply defined. It can be said to start when J.J. obtains a policy-making position, although senior-level counseling and staff positions exist that are very influential without having final decision power. Sample position titles include Dean of Students, Vice-President for Student Affairs, Director of Housing (or Career Planning and Placement, Student Activities, Counseling, Financial Aid, Recruitment and Orientation), Counseling Psychologist, Coordinator for Minority Programs, or Associate Vice-President or Director. Additive Stage professionals are generally quite knowledgeable, highly skilled people who are in a position to supervise others. As such, they are creative and take a holistic view of student affairs. J.J., in such a position, must take responsibility for the ethical practices of the staff members of that administrative sub-unit as well as be accountable for achieving its goals and purposes. Additionally, the Additive J.J. will often take leadership in regional and national professional associations and contribute to professional journals, books, and convention programs. J.J. is seen more and more as a role model and leader in the campus and community by colleagues as evidenced by consulting opportunities, and particularly by younger staff members who look to J.J. for guidance. J.J. will usually have made a decision about continued practice as an administrator or moving into the teaching ranks by the early Additive Stage. (This hypothetical composite career is based upon an administrative practitioner, but fits a teacher with minor modifications such as substituting students for subordinates.) J.J., as an Additive professional, is a leader by example, by job description, by activity, and by temperament.

If J.J. stays in student affairs administration through a long and productive career, passing appropriately through the previous stages, the time will come when achievement of the pinnacle of professional practice, the **Generative Stage,** will be within reach. In this stage, J.J. has earned the professional respect of others and is frequently called upon for consulting activities, invited presentations, broadranging articles or books charting the future of the field, and top association leadership, task force, and editorial positions. Only a relatively few Generative professionals exist and their titles are often those of Vice-President, full Professor, Executive Director, or they may even have emeritus status. J.J. as a

Generative professional would be an assertive and able elder spokesperson for the profession and function as a mentor and guide to many of the more youthful professionals. Note that often difficulty occurs in distinguishing between the advanced additive and the Generative professionals as many of the behaviors and characteristics of the two stages tend to be somewhat similar. In many instances, the years of service and the recognition factors reflect the greatest distinction.

On a somewhat more specific level and based upon many recent studies of career patterns (Grant & Foy, 1972; Brooks & Avila, 1974; Paul & Hoover, 1980; Kuh, Evans, & Duke, 1983; Harder, 1983; Ostroth, Efrid, & Lerman, 1984; Burkhalter, 1984; Rickard, 1985; Paterson, 1987), several statements appear warranted.

- There are avenues for advancement in student affairs and the steps are identifiable.

- As in most fields, the career ladder in student affairs has a pyramidal shape. That is, some number of entry level jobs exist, a smaller number of mid-level positions, and so on with the number of chief students affairs administrator (CSAA) slots bounded by the number of higher education institutions.

- Some career path variability is attributable to practice setting. Specific differences need to be considered in getting and holding positions in community colleges as opposed to four-year and four-year/graduate institutions, for example. Similarly, central office administration has some different requirements from specialized areas such as housing, financial aid, etc.

- Constraints related to geographical preferences, dual career decisions, "stop out" periods for child bearing or rearing, adverse economic conditions, and many others often have large impact upon personal and professional development.

- Research indicates that CSAA's are staying in their positions longer and have more education and experience than ever before (Paterson, 1987). This is an apparent consequence of the increasing professionalization of student affairs, but it tends to create something of an "aspirational logjam." (Carpenter, Guido-DiBrito, & Kelly, 1987, p. 8)

These trends and facts should not frighten or discourage, but rather make clearer the necessity to continue to develop in intentional ways in order to survive and thrive in a professionally competitive environment.

PROFESSIONAL IMPLICATIONS OF A DEVELOPMENTAL MODEL

Perhaps the most important concept in this developmental framework of professional growth is that in each area of professionalism are different levels of tasks. That is, the crises or turning points for a beginning professional in the areas of ethical practice or association activity (for example) are different from those of the seasoned practitioner. However, if earlier tasks are not mastered, later ones are unlikely or even impossible. Once again, development is cumulative and continuous.

Career Implications

To get "too much, too soon" can occur in student affairs work. Some evidence has been presented in this chapter that development in practice-related knowledge and skills is a process occuring over time, as is professional association leadership. Persons who take on professional or associational positions beyond their capabilities or beyond their developmental level are likely doomed to failure or at least mediocrity of performance. This implies that individuals must keep a developmental awareness of the consequences of professional activities as they move up the ladder of responsibility in practice and associational participation. While some people experience professional growth more rapidly than others, care must be taken to accomplish tasks and gain skills in a timely fashion. Taking a position totally disparate from one's skills and abilities will result in frustration, disappointment, and stalled growth. Similarly, failure to advance to positions of greater responsibility when they are appropriate is to cease developing. The knowledge of when career moves are appropriate or not comes from assessing and actively working on one's own professional development.

At its base, professional development is the responsibility of the individual. The profession and the employer should provide systematic opportunities, but the practitioner must take advantage of such opportunities. Professionals should engage in continual clarification of values. If two-year college administration is a goal, then appropriate academic or workshop education and proper experience should be obtained. If practitioners feel inadequately prepared to work with budgets, then exposure to certain books, courses, or supervised experiences may be indicated. Appropriate professional growth is possible only through stringent self-assessment, goal setting, and action. All position or responsibility shifts should be made with an eye toward professional growth.

This is not to say that all ambition is bad, that individuals can know everything about the future, or that professional growth is mechanistic. However, very few newly minted masters degree recipients are ready to be chief student affairs officers. Careful, individualized, and planned professional development is crucial to any successful career.

Professional Preparation Implications

Separate and apart from personal career considerations, developmental aspects of professionalism in student affairs require a rethinking of professional preparation. If developmental principles can be applied to student affairs professional growth, then such growth *must* be recognized as continuous and cumulative. That is, from the time that a person decides to enter student affairs, a process begins of continual upgrading in skills, knowledge of student development theory, and personal/professional awareness. While initial preparation (masters or paraprofessional level) is not the end of preparation by any means, it is the basic foundation. Student affairs professional educators, then, have an enormous responsibility. Professional development is best facilitated if it takes place in an environment in which change is planned and anticipated. Initial preparation should, therefore, concentrate not only on skills required for meeting the needs of entry-level professional positions, but also upon an awareness of professional development stages and tasks and factors of professional development that come into play as careers continue. Rather than being nebulous or too narrowly focused, masters (and even doctoral) programs should identify developmental tasks and stages (those suggested and others) and endeavor to increase student knowledge and awareness of them. Further, systematic, developmental-based continuing education in the form of workshops, courses, and publications must become a focus for professional associations, preparation programs, and practitioners alike.

Professional preparation is a career-long process. If one stops intentionally growing and preparing, then more complex and higher-level developmental tasks will be impossible to accomplish or master. What must be recognized by the student affairs profession is that continuous preparation and education at all levels are too important to be left to chance or whim and must be addressed systematically.

Professional Practice Implications

Professional awareness in preparation should be mirrored in practice. The ability to perform ever more complex duties in student affairs positions is related to professional development level. At the beginning of their careers, new professionals need careful supervision and mentors to aid them in beginning their career-long development auspiciously, so as not to get in over their heads immediately. As experience and professional development increase, student affairs practitioners are able to take more and more responsibility for their activities and decisions as well as for those of their administrative subdivisions and subordinates. The responsibility of both individual practitioners and their supervisors is to create and maintain an environment encouraging professional growth.

The importance of personal mentors at all levels cannot be overemphasized as a key component of continued professional development. Without support, encouragement, help, and role modeling, stagnation and retarded development will occur. Professionals, then, are responsible not only for their own development, but also for that of less experienced practitioners.

Professional Association Implications

Professional associations have a major responsibility to the profession of student affairs if a developmental model is accepted as a paradigm for professional growth. If professional preparation is to be considered career-long and hierarchical in nature, then associations must take a much more serious approach to their instructional function than has heretofore been apparent. Workshops and interest sessions at national and regional conferences, while given importance currently, are not offered with anything approaching regularity or singleness of purpose. The American College Personnel Association (ACPA) focuses upon new professionals with content sessions and encouragement of involvement as do several other associations. Also, ACPA cosponsors or sanctions numerous campus-based skill-building workshops and conferences designed to address various levels of concern. The National Association of Student Personnel Administrators has for years sponsored a summer program for new chief student affairs officers and is moving toward a "level" concept in conference content sessions. Most professional associations are doing an increasingly effective job of placement and career orientation for their members. However, these halting steps are not enough. Many instructional avenues have gone unexplored to date. Modular instruction, for example, with specific goals and objectives over a long term is only one way to approach "leveled" instruction. Specific "tracks" based upon strong research could be offered at both annual conferences and year-round locations in such areas as budgeting, personnel management, theory intensive service delivery, ethical practice, and many other topics at each of the four professional stage levels. Such goals will not be met by adopting standards for masters programs alone, however, but must be tied into a continuing education format by professional associations with appropriate recognition and reward systems. Obviously, in order for such a scheme to be functional, the associations must first lead the way in research and reeducation concerning professional development.

Additionally, and more specifically, a developmental process occurs with respect to associational leadership and publication activity. However, systematic effort is made by few professional associations to induce, encourage, and develop younger and lower-level professional leadership. While some attempts are made in this area, they are relatively irregular and disorganized. In a very real sense the persons who need the least help, the higher level professionals, find it far easier to participate in associational leadership, while those lower-level persons who could best benefit are often discouraged by the seeming impenetrability of the bureaucracy. This is not to say that experience is unnecessary in association leadership, but rather that appropriate levels of leadership exist for persons in all stages of development, and that consistently using only high level professionals for all leadership is expedient but ultimately damaging to everyone concerned, including the association. Some efforts are being made in this area, but these efforts are neither widespread nor consistent. Professional associations must lead the way in an organized, systematic fashion, and younger professionals must take advantage of available opportunities.

SUMMARY

This chapter has argued that student affairs is an emergent profession, despite predictable controversy. As such, great opportunities exist for those willing and able to control their own destinies and intentionally create the future. To be sure, concerns are present. Student affairs still has a problem of credibility born of ignorance on many campuses. People are still hired for responsible positions in the field who have little or no professional awareness or training. An ongoing need is still present to educate and even indoctrinate numerous constituencies such as faculties, students, and other administrators. The theory base of the profession must be refined and supported by research.

However, powerful forces are in favor of student affairs professionalism. Efforts related to the CAS Standards and other credentialing and accreditation processes are gaining strength. Increased attention to student assessment, retention and recruitment, quality of campus life, and student involvement demands the expertise of experienced, dedicated, theory-based professionals. The literature and associations of student affairs are more and more dominated by respected, capable, and aware professionals. Fewer and fewer practitioner positions are being filled by "laypersons."

Imperative, then, student affairs as a field must begin to practice what it preaches. The consequences of continuing to ignore the developmental nature of professional growth are significant. If individual professionals ignore their personal growth, they will stagnate and become ineffective, thereby hurting their employing institutions and the profession of student affairs as well as the students they serve. If institutions, associations, and preparation programs do not systematically and energetically set about insuring professional development, the entire profession will suffer, and indeed in an era of cutbacks and retrenchment, may not survive. And, if student affairs as a profession falters, weakens, or perishes, then higher education, all college students, and, at the risk of sounding melodramatic, the nation will have lost valuable resources. The growing understanding about the nature of professional development and the individual's responsibilities and opportunities inherent therein will enhance the profession of student affairs administration in the years ahead.

REFERENCES

American Council on Education. (1937). *The student personnel point of view.* American Council on Education Studies Series (Series 1, Vol. 1, No.3). Washington, DC: Author.

American Council on Education. (1949). *The student personnel point of view.* American Council on Education Studies Series (Series 6, Vol. 13, No.13). Washington, DC: Author.

Appleton, J.R., Briggs, C.M., & Rhatigan, J.S. (1978). *Pieces of eight: The rites, roles, and styles of the dean by eight who have been there.* Portland, OR: NASPA Institute of Research and Development.

Bloland, P.A. (1974). Professionalism and the professional organization. In T.F. Harrington (Ed.), *Student personnel work in urban colleges* (pp. 244-67). New York: Intext Educational Publishing.

Bloland, P.A. (1987, March). *Are we a profession?* Paper presented at the joint national conference of the American College Personnel Association and the National Association of Student Personnel Administrators. Chicago, IL.

Brooks, G., & Avila, J. (1974). The chief student personnel administrator and his staff: A profile. *NASPA Journal, 11*(4), 41-47.

Burkhalter, J.P. (1984). Career patterns of chief student personnel administrators. (Doctoral dissertation, University of Georgia, 1984). *Dissertation Abstracts International, 45,* 425A.

Carpenter, D.S. (1979). The professional development of student affairs workers: An analysis. (Doctoral dissertation, University of Georgia, 1979). *Dissertation Abstracts International, 40,* 3645A-3646A.

Carpenter, D.S., Guido-DiBrito, F., & Kelly J.P. (1987). Transferability of student affairs skills and competencies: Light at the end of the bottleneck. *NASPA Journal, 24*(3), 7-14.

Carpenter, D.S., & Miller, T.K. (1981). An analysis of professional development in student affairs work. *NASPA Journal, 19*(1), 2-11.

Carpenter, D.S., Miller, T.K., & Winston, R.B. (1980). Toward the professionalization of student affairs. *NASPA Journal, 18* (2) 16-22.

Cowley, W.H. (1964). Reflections of a troublesome but hopeful Rip Van Winkle. *Journal of College Student Personnel, 6,* 66-73.

Crookston, B.B. (1976). Student personnel—All hail and farewell. *Personnel and Guidance Journal, 55,* 26-9.

Council for Advancement of Standards for Student Services Developmental Programs (CAS). (1986). *Standards and guidelines for student services/development programs.* Iowa City, IA: Author.

Council for the Accreditation of Counseling and Related educational Programs (CACREP). (1988). *Accreditation procedures manual and application.* Alexandria, VA: Author.

DeLong, T.J. (1981). *Career anchors: A new concept in career development for the professional educator.* Paper presented at the annual meeting of the American Educational Research Association, Los Angeles, CA. (ERIC Document Reproduction Service No. ED 209 545).

Grant, W.H., & Foy, J. (1972). Career patterns of student personnel administrators. *NASPA Journal, 10*(2), 106-13.

Harder, M.B. (1983). Career patterns of chief student personnel administrators. *Journal of College Student Personnel, 24,* 443-48.

Knock, G.H. (Ed.). (1977). *Perspectives on the preparation of student affairs professionals.* Washington, DC: American College Personnel Association.

Knock, G.H. (1988). More things considered: A response to Scott Rickard. *Journal of College Student Development, 29,* 395-97.

Koile, E.A. (1966). Student affairs: Forever the bridesmaid. *NASPA Journal*, *4*, 65-72.

Komives, S.R. (1988, March). *The art of becoming professional.* Paper presented at the annual conference of the American College Personnel Association. Miami, FL.

Kuh, G.D., Evans, N.J., & Duke, A. (1983). Career paths and responsibilities of chief student affairs officers. *NASPA Journal*, *21*(1), 39-47.

Kuk, L. (1988). Professional existence—a path of knowing. *Journal of College Student Development*, *29*, 397-400.

Leonard, E. (1956). *Origins of the personnel services.* Minneapolis, MN: University of Minnesota Press.

Lloyd-Jones, E. (1954). Changing concepts of student personnel work. In E. Lloyd-Jones & M.R. Smith (Eds.), *Student personnel work as deeper teaching* (pp. 1-14). New York: Harper & Brothers.

Miller, T.K. (1967). College student personnel preparation: Present perspective and future directions. *NASPA Journal*, *4*, 171-78.

Miller, T.K., & Carpenter, D.S. (1980). Professional preparation for today and tomorrow. In D.G. Creamer (Ed.), *Student Development in Higher Education: Theories, Practices, and Future Directions* (pp. 181-204). Washington, DC: American College Personnel Association.

Miller, T.K., & Prince, J. (1976). *The future of student affairs: A guide to student development for tomorrow's higher education.* San Francisco: Jossey-Bass.

Moore, L.V. (1988). Movin' on. *Journal of College Student Development*, *29*, 400-02.

Nygreen, G.T. (1968). Professional status for student personnel administrators. *NASPA Journal*, *5*, 283-91.

Ostroth, D.D., Efrid, F.D., & Lerman, L.S. (1984). Career patterns of chief student affairs officers. *Journal of College Student Personnel*, *25*(5), 443-47.

Paterson, B.G. (1987). An examination of the professional status of chief student affairs officers. *College Student Affairs Journal*, *8*(1), 13-20.

Paul, W.L., & Hoover, R.E. (1980). Chief student personnel administrator: A decade of change. *NASPA Journal*, *18*(1), 33-39.

Pavalko, R.M. (1971). *Sociology of occupations and professions.* Itasca, IL: F.E. Peacock.

Penn, J.R. (1974). Professional accreditation: A key to excellence. *Journal of College Student Personnel, 15,* 257-59.

Penney, J.F. (1969). Student personnel work: A profession stillborn. *Personnel and Guidance Journal, 47,* 958-62.

Rentz, A.L., & Saddlemire, G.L. (1988). *Student affairs functions in higher education.* Springfield, IL: Charles C. Thomas.

Rickard, S.T. (1985). Titles of student affairs officers: Institutional autonomy or professional standarization? *NASPA Journal, 23*(2), 44-49.

Rickard, S.T. (1988a). Toward a professional paradigm. *Journal of College Student Development, 29,* 388-95.

Rickard, S.T. (1988b). Response to Knock, Kuk, Moore, Remley, and Williams. *Journal of College Student Development, 29,* 405-07.

Rudolph, F. (1962). *The American college and university: A history.* New York: Random House.

Schein, E.H. (1978). *Career dynamics: Matching individual and organizational need.* Reading, MA: Addison-Wesley.

Shoben, E.J. (1967). Psychology and student personnel work. *Journal of College Student Personnel, 8,* 239-44.

Stamatakos, L.C. (1981). Student affairs progress toward professionalism: Recommendations for action. *Journal of College Student Personnel, 22*(2 & 3), 105-13, 197-205.

Stamatakos, L.C. (1987, March). *Are we a profession?* Paper presented at the Joint National Conference of the American College Personnel Association and National Association of Student Personnel Administrators. Chicago, IL.

Trueblood, D.L. (1966). The educational preparation of the college student personnel leader of the future. In G.J. Kloph (Ed.), *College student personnel in the years ahead* (pp. 77-84). Washington, DC: American College Personnel Association.

Williams, T.E. (1988). Toward a professional paradigm: In search of a philosophy. *Journal of College Student Development, 29,* 403-05.

Williamson, E.G. (1958). Professional preparation student personnel workers. *School and Society, 86,* 21-3.

Wood, L., Winston, R.B., & Polkosnik, M.C. (1985). Career orientations and professional development of young student affairs professionals. *Journal of College Student Personnel, 26,* 532-39.

Wrenn, C.G. (1949). An appraisal of the professional status of student personnel workers, Part I. In E.G. Williamson (Ed.), *Trends in student personnel work* (pp. 264-80). Minneapolis: University of Minnesota Press.

Young, R.B. (1988). The professionalization of student affairs. *NASPA Journal, 25,* 262-66.

SUGGESTED READINGS

Appleton, J.R., Briggs, C.M., & Rhatigan, J.S. (1978). *Pieces of eight: The rites, roles, and styles of the dean by eight who have been there.* Portland, OR: NASPA Institute of Research and Development.

Crookston, B.B. (1976). Student personnel—All hail and farewell! *Personnel and Guidance Journal, 55,* 26-9.

Leonard, E. (1956). *Origins of the personnel services.* Minneapolis, MN: University of Minnesota Press.

Miller, T.K., & Carpenter, D.S. (1980). Professional preparation for today and tomorrow. In D.G. Creamer (Ed.), *Student development in higher education: Theories, practices, and future directions* (pp. 181-204). Washington, DC: American College Personnel Association.

Nygreen, G.T. (1968). Professional status for student personnel administrators. *NASPA Journal, 5,* 283-91.

Paterson, B.G. (1987). An examination of the professional status of chief student affairs officers. *College Student Affairs Journal. 8*(1), 13-20.

Pavalko, R.M. (1971). *Sociology of occupations and professions.* Itasca, IL: F.E. Peacock.

Wood, L., Winston, R.B., & Polkosnik, M.C. (1985). Career orientations and professional development of young student affairs professionals. *Journal of College Student Personnel, 26,* 532-39.

Barbara Jacoby, Ph.D., is Director of the Office of Commuter Affairs at The University of Maryland College Park. She also serves as Director of the National Clearinghouse for Commuter Programs, the only national organization which exists solely to provide information and assistance to professionals in designing programs and services for commuter students. Jacoby received her Ph.D. degree from The University of Maryland at College Park in 1978, and is an Affiliate Assistant Professor of College Student Personnel Administration. She has had experience in resident life and financial aid. Jacoby has held leadership positions in the American College Personnel Association and the National Association of Student Personnel Administrators and is on the Board of Directors of the Council for the Advancement of Standards for Student Services/Development Programs. She has written and consulted extensively and has made numerous presentations around the country. She has been recognized by her institution and by professional associates for her outstanding work on behalf of commuter students.

CHAPTER 9

TODAY'S STUDENTS: DIVERSE NEEDS REQUIRE COMPREHENSIVE RESPONSES

Barbara Jacoby

The demographics of students in American higher education have been changing and are continuing to change dramatically. The diversity of students at all institutions of higher education is increasing in regard to age, race, gender, living arrangements, attendance patterns, nationality of origin, and disabilities. Today's students have a wide range of needs and confront a multiplicity of developmental issues.

The performance of student affairs functions is sometimes hampered by the fact that most professionally trained student affairs practitioners were prepared in programs that emphasize— both in classroom and field experiences—"traditional" college students. The literature and research about college students generally focus on students in the 18 to 22 year old age span. Several prevalent theoretical models of college student development are based on the experiences of traditional-age students, many of whom were white, middle-class males who attended mainly private four-year residential institutions. The considerable body of literature on traditional college students does not necessarily help in addressing the developmental concerns of the diverse students present on campuses today (Stewart, 1983; Stodt, 1982; Wright, 1987).

Incumbent upon student affairs professionals is the need to understand the demographics and needs of all college students so that appropriate services and programs can be provided. A major challenge is how to deliver quality educational experiences to an increasingly diverse student population.

DIVERSITY OF
TODAY'S COLLEGE STUDENTS

To help recognize the diversity of contemporary college students, several key groups can be identified: commuters, adults, women, minorities, internationals, and students with disabilities. Two groups represent a *majority* of college students nationwide: commuters (over 80%) and women (over 50%). On a number of campuses, "minority" students actually comprise a majority of the student body. Each of these groups is by no means homogeneous; therefore, one must avoid stereotyping and overgeneralization. To further complicate matters, the groups overlap to create a bewildering variety of students.

Student affairs administrators have an obligation to familiarize themselves with the literature about individual differences among college students and to incorporate that knowledge into the design of services and programs. A brief description of several key groups is presented here as an introduction to some of those individual differences. Sources of further information for each group are included as suggested readings.

Commuter Students

Commuter students, those students who do not live in housing owned and operated by the college, are by far the largest and most varied student population (Stewart & Rue, 1983). Their numbers include representatives of all the other student groups described in this chapter. For residential students, home and campus are synonomous; for commuter students, the campus is a place to visit, sometimes for only short periods. Place of residence, therefore, is a key factor in defining the nature of the relationship between students and their colleges (Likins, 1988). Commuter students may live near the campus or far away; they may commute by car, bicycle, walking, or public transportation.

To clarify the different types of commuter students, Stewart and Rue (1983) identified three variables that are most useful for determining the characteristics of the population: (1) dependence versus independence in living arrangements, (2) traditional or nontraditional age, and (3) full-or part-time enrollment status. Dependent students live at home with parents or other close relatives who assume parental responsibilities; independent students live alone, with peers, or with their own families. Commuters of traditional college age share many of the developmental needs of their residential counterparts. Older commuters may be returning to school after a break in their education, having been employed in a career positions, and having spouses and children. Commuters' attendance patterns often reflect their other life roles and commitments and affect the degree to which they may concentrate on their education.

The interactions among these three variables yield eight distinct types of commuter students. These are listed in Table 9.1, together with examples of students who might fit into each category (Stewart & Rue, 1983). The number of each type of commuter students varies considerably from campus to campus. Although commuter students are extraordinarily diverse, a common core of needs and concerns can be delineated (Wilmes & Quade, 1986).

Mobility Issues. The most obvious concerns commuters share are those related to transportation to campus: parking, traffic, fixed transportation schedules, inclement weather, car maintenance, transportation costs, and finding alternative means of transportation. Whether they walk, use public transit, or drive, commuting is demanding in terms of time and energy.

TABLE 9.1
Commuter Students

CATEGORY	EXAMPLE
Dependent, traditional, full time	An 18-year-old freshman who lives at home because of family responsibilities or financial constraints
Dependent, nontraditional, full time	A divorcee with children who has returned to her parents' home so she can attend college full time
Dependent, nontraditional, part time	A veteran who lives with parents or other relatives and attends part time
Dependent, traditional, part time	A 19-year-old student who lives at home and works
Independent, traditional, full time	An international student who attends full time with full support of the home government and lives in a rented room
Independent, nontraditional, full time	A retiree who has returned to school full time and is supported by a pension
Independent, nontraditional, part time	An adult with a full-time position and a family who takes courses for career enhancement
Independent, traditional, part time	A 20-year-old student who lives in a rented apartment, works to support herself, and attends college part time

Frequently, commuters concentrate their classes into blocks and have little free time on campus. Convenience of services and programs that fit into commuters' schedules is of paramount importance.

Multiple Life Roles. For young and old commuters alike, being a student is only one of several important and demanding roles. Most commuters work; many have responsibilities for caring for children or older relatives and for managing households. By necessity commuters select their campus involvements carefully. Student affairs professionals must be certain that thorough and timely information reaches commuters about campus options and opportunities. The perceived value of an activity becomes crucial in their decisions about whether to participate.

Integrating Support Systems. The support networks for commuter students generally exist off the campus: parents, spouses, children, employers, coworkers, and friends in the community. Each term, students must negotiate with family, employers, and friends to establish priorities, responsibilities, and time allotments. These negotiations are more difficult if significant others are unaware of the challenges and demands of higher education. An important responsibility for colleges is to provide opportunities for these individuals to learn about and to participate in campus life.

Developing a Sense of Belonging. All too often, colleges perpetuate a variety of roadblocks to commuters' ability to develop a sense of belonging on the campus. At the most basic level, services such as lockers, transportation and housing assistance, study and lounge areas, and eating facilities are essential. In addition, social, cultural, and recreational programs that meet the needs of different types of commuter students as far as topic, time, and location are important.

Student affairs professionals need to assure that the institution values commuter students as individuals, recognizes their contributions to the campus and the community, and does not judge them in comparison to their traditional, residential counterparts. Practitioners can take a leading role in assisting commuter students to obtain accurate and timely information about the campus and its opportunities; to identify with the institution; to interact with peers, faculty, and staff; and to integrate their lives on and off the campus.

Adult Students

A variety of terms has been used to refer to adult students in higher education, including returning students, nontraditional students, stop-outs, re-entry students, older students, and adult learners. Age has generally been used as the determination of "adult" or "nontraditional" student status (Hughes, 1983). Nearly 40% of college students are age 25 or older, and projections suggest that the percentage will rise to over 50% by the early 1990s (Commission on National Challenges in Higher Education, 1988). Morstain and Smart (1977) identified five distinct types of adult learners: (1) non-directed learners who have no specific goals; (2) social learners who wish to improve their social interests and personal associations; (3) stimulation-seeking learners who want to escape from routine and boredom; (4) career-oriented learners who learn because of occupational needs and interests; and (5) life-change learners who seek to enhance several facets of their lives—career, intellectual, and social (Aslanian & Brickell, 1980).

Research on adult students has provided some differences between adult learners and younger (18 to 22 year old) students. Adult students are more likely to be financially independent and often carry additional financial and emotional responsibilities as a result of their roles as spouses and/or parents. They bring to the campus a wide range of life and career experiences and often seek to integrate their education with those experiences immediately rather than in the future. Their education usually competes with their job, family, community, and personal commitments. They have developed a variety of problem-solving skills through their life experiences, but may have rusty academic skills or a lack of confidence in their academic abilities (Aslanian & Brickell, 1980; Hughes, 1983).

Cross (1981) sheds light on adults' attitudes towards further education in her classification of perceived barriers to adult learning. Her research has led her to classify such barriers under three headings:

- **Situational barriers** are those arising from one's situation in life at a given time, such as finances, lack of time as a result of job and home responsibilities, and opposition of family or friends.

- **Dispositional barriers** are those related to perceptions of oneself as a learner, including feeling too old, lack of confidence, and lack of understanding of today's educational environment.

- **Institutional barriers** consist of all those policies, practices, and procedures that exclude or discourage working adults from participating in education: inconvenient schedules or locations, unavailability of financial aid, inappropriate courses of study, "red tape" in the admissions process, failure to recognize prior learning, and so forth.

In addition to such institutional barriers, colleges do not always make adults feel welcome as full members of the campus community. Their basic needs, such as married student housing and child care, frequently are not met adequately. Adults often find that career counseling, academic advising, health services, and social and recreational activities are geared for traditional-age students. Opportunities to interact with peers may be limited, services may not be available at hours when most adults are on campus, and family-oriented activities are often lacking.

Cross (1981, p. 12) coined the phrase "blended life plan" to suggest that work, education, and leisure are concurrent, rather than alternating, at all points throughout life. A variety of literature on the adult life cycle describes life stages or phases that necessitate biological, psychological, and social adaptations as adults mature (Aslanian & Brickell, 1980). More and more adults are seeking education at key transition points throughout their lives. Practitioners must acquire an understanding of adult development if student services, most of which were originally designed to attend to the needs and interests of traditional students, are to be appropriate for students of all ages.

Women Students

Women students are higher education's "new majority" (Hall & Sandler, 1982, p.1). Recent studies of the lives of women demonstrate that important gender differences exist and that these differences are influenced by changing values concerning the role of women in society (Evans, 1985; Gilligan 1982). For example, women tend to define themselves in terms of their relationships to others. While maturity in men is viewed as a process of developing autonomy, for women it is meeting responsibilities within relationships (Gilligan, 1982). Men generally view occupation as separate from marriage and parenthood, while women perceive the three roles as linked (Belenky, Clinchy, Goldberger, & Tarule, 1986; Evans, 1985). Women have been found to possess a less positive self-image than men, particularly prior to midlife (Lowenthal, Thurnher, Chiriboga, & Associates, 1975). Studies suggest that women students are more likely than men to doubt their abilities and to attribute their success to luck or hard work rather than to skill (Hall & Sandler, 1982).

As a result of the feminist movement, the norms for young college women have become more varied. Role expectations, while more open, are also more confusing. Today's college women have watched older role models try to "have it all," with varying degrees of success and happiness. Life planning and career decision making are critical issues.

Older, or returning, women students are the fastest growing segment of the entire postsecondary student population. Too often, they are stereotyped as "bored, middle-aged women who are returning to school because they have nothing better to do" (Hall & Sandler, 1982, p. 12). The population of returning women can be better understood by dividing it into three groups: (1) working women (single or married) without children who return to college to enhance already existing skills, (2) working women with children who return to college with a specific vocational goal in mind in order to enhance the family's financial situation, and (3) women who discontinued their education in order to become homemakers and are re-entering college to finish their degree or to pursue vocational skills (Wheaton & Robinson, 1983). More and more returning women are from minority groups with lower incomes and are single-parent heads of households.

Hall and Sandler (1982, 1984) described the effects of a "chilly" campus climate for *all* women students both inside and outside the classroom. Faculty, administrators, and student affairs professionals—both men and women—may overtly, but more often, inadvertantly, treat women students differently from men. Subtle behavioral biases in which women students are either singled out, differentiated, or ignored may seem so normal that they often go unnoticed. Student affairs professionals must be vigilant in identifying and eliminating these patterns because they discourage women from participating fully in classes and in other aspects of campus life, making the best use of student services, or seeking help with academic or personal concerns (Hall & Sandler, 1982, 1984).

Minority Students

Minority students enter higher education from diverse cultural backgrounds. As individuals and as groups, they share some similar needs and concerns but differ substantially by ethnicity, customs, and level of acculturation. Differences among individuals within the same minority group may be even greater than differences between groups. Although debate surrounds the appropriateness of the term "minority," it is nevertheless generally used to simplify mutual recognition of American ethnic minority groups.

All minorities have in common the experience of varying degrees of discrimination, racism, and prejudice. In addition, many Blacks, Hispanics, Asians, and American Indians believe in maintaining a strong sense of community in which norms, values, customs, and cultural traditions are shared and reinforced. Related to this sense of community is the central role of the family. Within minority cultures, decisions are more often made based on their potential outcome for the family (Wright, 1984).

Many minority students entering college find themselves for the first time in a setting without significant numbers of minority peers and role models. Thus, they find themselves caught in a struggle between assimilation which necessitates relinquishing their ethnic or cultural identity and moving fully into the larger society, or integration which entails becoming an integral part of the larger societal framework while maintaining a strong cultural identity (Quevedo-Garcia, 1987).

Black Students

Currently, over 80% of black students in higher education are enrolled in predominantly white institutions (Wilson, 1986). Black college students today are different from and more heterogeneous than preceding generations. Pounds (1987) described five key factors in the college experience of black students:

1. They have diverse social, cultural, and economic backgrounds; these differences are often not appreciated or acknowledged by faculty, staff, and students. Many maintain close ties to their extended as well as nuclear families. Some may be the first of their families to attend college, while others have college-educated parents. They come from rural and urban environments, racially segregated or integrated communities, military installations, and plush suburbs.

2. Many come to college underprepared academically and disadvantaged financially. A high percentage of black students attended understaffed, underfunded, and ill-equipped public schools. Far too often, black students' parents have low incomes and little or no savings available to meet the expenses of a college education. A disproportionate number of blacks come from single-parent families.

3. They are less satisfied with and less involved in campus life. Often, black students do not find activities that relate to their life experiences.

4. Black students often find the college environment to be confusing and hostile. Incidences of racism and problems in residence halls are regularly reported.

5. Blacks feel isolated and alienated on white campuses. When the ratio of black to white students is low, blacks tend to turn to other blacks for social interaction. Their sense of loneliness and isolation is increased in the absence of black role models among faculty and staff.

Hispanic Students

Hispanics, the minority population of most rapid growth in the United States, are severely underrepresented in higher education (Astin, 1982). The term "Hispanic," which is generally used to refer to U.S. citizens whose countries of ethnic origin were colonized by Spain and are now Spanish-speaking, reflects little of the enormous complexities and diversities of the population (Payton, 1985; Quevedo-Garcia, 1987).

One general cultural value that is attributed to Hispanics is the importance of the family. The family unit, including the immediate blood relatives and the extended family, is regarded as the single most important element in Hispanic culture (Payton, 1985). Students who come from a traditional cultural environment may view themselves as representatives of their communities and families first and as individuals second (Quevedo-Garcia, 1987).

Strong identification with the family and low average income influence most Hispanic students to attend college close to home. A high percentage of Hispanics attend college part-time (most often at community colleges) so that they can work to cover their educational expenses. Many Hispanic parents have little understanding of higher education, and students who attend college away from home may suffer feelings of guilt at having "abandoned" the family. Traditional Hispanic culture regards assertive behaviors as rude, especially when directed towards elders; thus, Hispanic students may have trouble functioning in competitive college environments. As far as the curriculum, proportionately fewer Hispanics choose majors in the fields of science, technology, and business than the overall student population (Duran, 1983).

Asian-American Students

Asian-American students come from a variety of countries of origin, including China, Japan, Korea, India, the Pacific Islands, the Philippines, and Viet Nam. Each ethnic group has distinct subcultures with unique values and customs (Chew & Ogi, 1987).

Besides diversity of country of origin, Asian-Americans may be differentiated by a number of other dimensions such as area of residence in the United States, socioeconomic status, degree of acculturation, level of family education, and English language ability.

Despite these differences, some similarities can be identified among Asian-American students. Often they are confused by the conflict between their cultural values and those of other Americans. Traditional Asian values emphasize reserve and formality in interpersonal relationships, humility, restraint and inhibition of strong feelings, obedience to authority, filial piety and sense of obligation to the family, high academic and occupational achievement, and use of shame and guilt to control behavior (Chew & Ogi, 1987; Payton, 1985). Asian-American students can easily perceive colleges' goals of promoting critical thinking and questioning of established views as incongruent with their traditional values. From the values of humility and reserve come the image of the quiet, shy, and introverted Asian-American student. However, because of their formality and restraint of emotional expression, these students often experience difficulties in interpersonal relationships and a higher degree of tension and anxiety than may be recognized by many student affairs professionals (Chew & Ogi, 1987; Minatoya & Sedlacek, 1981).

Asian-Americans have experienced a long history of racism and discrimination. Anti-Asian sentiment is still quite high, even on many college campuses. The "model-minority myth," which has become a much-used catch phrase for the notion that Asians are superior to other minorities in their work ethnic and social values, is adding to the resentment felt towards Asians (Greene, 1987). Such views, combined with

Asian-American students' reticence to seek help, have impeded the diagnosis of needs and the delivery of services to this group (Minatoya & Sedlacek, 1981).

Native American Students

Native Americans, or American Indians, are dispersed among several hundred tribes. They are quite diverse culturally, ranging from urban to rural, from matrilineal to patrilineal (La Counte, 1987; Payton, 1985). Increasing numbers of native Americans are seeking higher education as a direct result of economic pressures. For many Indian students, enrollment in college is their first long-term exposure to a non-Indian environment.

Most native Americans enter higher education underprepared in traditional academic skills. Nearly all receive some form of financial aid. Approximately one-half are over 25-years-old; many are married or are single parents. They tend to commute to campus from nearby reservations or to live in college towns.

Native American students on campuses are often in the process of resolving for themselves issues related to maintaining their traditional lifestyles versus assimilation into the majority culture. Many Indian students express interest in earning a degree so they can go back to the reservation and help their people. Thus, they aspire to occupations visible on or near their reservations, such as agriculture (La Counte, 1987). The needs of native American students include high levels of personal contact, monitoring of academic progress, tutorial support, financial assistance, and career counseling.

American ethnic minorities are extremely heterogeneous in terms of customs, values, linguistic styles, and socioeconomic status (Wright, 1987). The efforts of student affairs practitioners on their behalf should reflect this diversity. Astin (1984) used the term "pluralism" in American education to suggest

> something beyond the mere *combining* of different student
> subgroups: it suggests that somehow the special needs

and concerns of these groups should be attended to, and that in adapting to the campus community, these groups should not necessarily be forced to give up all of their history, tradition, and cultural heritage in the interest of creating a student "melting pot" which blurs all differences and distinctions among different student subgroups. (p.2)

Student affairs professionals should be prepared to assist minority students to define their identities based on realistic self-appraisal and in the context of culture-specific issues and values.

International Students

More than 400,000 international students are enrolled in American institutions of higher education (Arndt, 1988). They are extremely difficult to characterize as a population in that they come from more that 150 nations (Manese, Leong, & Sedlacek, 1985). International students bring with them a complicated set of culturally based values, attitudes, expectations, assumptions, perceptions, and modes of behavior. Considerable adjustments on their part are required; the nature of the adjustments depends on the nature of the differences between the original and the new culture and on the goals they seek to achieve in the new culture (Foust, 1981; Stewart & Hartt, 1987).

Most international students experience considerable stress during much of their period of study in the United States. Meeting the basic needs of food, shelter, and transportation are often stressful because of vast cultural differences between students' home countries and the college community. Homesickness and loneliness are pervasive; depression is common. Achieving academic success in a foreign language and adapting to differences in teaching and learning modes are complicating factors. Further, most international students feel tremendous pressure from their governments and their families to succeed academically. Some are under financial strain which is compounded by legal restrictions on working off-campus (Wehrly, 1988).

The language barrier and cultural differences often impede international students' social interactions with American students and their ability to seek help. Faculty and staff have the responsibility to recognize and meet international students' special needs for assistance, advice, and support.

Students with Disabilities

Students with disabilities are an increasingly visible and vocal minority. Although students with disabilities have always attended college, the passage of Section 504 of the Rehabilitation Act of 1973—which requires colleges to provide equal educational opportunities for them—has stimulated their enrollment (Sprandel & Schmidt, 1980).

Like other student groups, students with disabilities are a heterogeneous population. Unlike other minorities, however, they do not share a common heritage of values and experiences. Students with disabling conditions are of many types including (1) mobility impairments—students who use canes, crutches, wheelchairs, or walk unaided but with difficulty; (2) visual impairments—students who are blind or partially sighted; (3) hearing impairments—students who are hearing impaired or deaf; (4) learning impairments—students with average or above average intellectual potential but who have mild to severe difficulties in reading, calculation, listening, writing, or relating socially; and (5) speech impairments—students with articulation problems, stuttering, esophageal speech, or aphasia (Hameister, 1984).

Students with disabilities have a wide range of feelings about their disabilities and varying degrees of understanding of their strengths and limitations. They share the same developmental tasks as able-bodied students, along with some unique concerns. Usual apprehensions about handling college-level academic work, interpersonal relationships, sexual identity and intimacy, career choice, and health may be even more complicated for them. Some may not wish for their disability to be overtly recognized, and to respect their desire for privacy is important. Student affairs professionals can and should assist students with disabilities with what is perhaps their greatest challenge: dealing with the stereotypes, patronizing sympathy, and myths of ineffectiveness perpetuated in the minds of well-meaning able-bodied people (Patterson, Sedlacek, & Scales, 1988).

A COMPREHENSIVE APPROACH
TO MEETING STUDENTS'
DIVERSE NEEDS

A comprehensive approach to meeting the educational and developmental needs of diverse student populations begins with a question: If a college truly wanted to create an optimum educational experience for its students, what would it have to do? Substantial change would be necessary in most colleges in order to create such an environment. Institutional responses to the increased presence of different groups of students have generally been fragmented attempts to deal with immediate, specific problems rather than long-range and comprehensive. Sheer numbers have not been sufficient to bring about substantive change in programs, practices, and policies.

In the late 1960s and early 1970s, many colleges created new offices or departments to serve the needs of what were often termed "special populations" (blacks, women, commuters, adults, and students with disabilities). A number of these offices were funded by federal or other grants recognizing the emergence of "new" student groups on campuses. Usually underfunded, placed at lower levels of the administrative hierarchy, and staffed by individuals with relatively little experience in effecting change in higher education, these offices were charged with "doing everything" for a specific student group.

Operating under an unrealistic set of expectations, many of these offices failed to make a measurable difference in the experience of the populations they attempted to serve. Institutional retrenchment, together with evaporation of grant funding and little apparent outcome, has led to the dissolution of "special" services on many campuses. The concept of "mainstreaming" is often invoked to account for decisions to abandon the special services. On other campuses, population-specific offices continue to exist with widely varying levels of institutional support and effectiveness.

THE SPAR MODEL

Jacoby and Girrell (1981) created a model that serves as a framework for the development of a comprehensive approach to meeting the needs of the diverse groups of students. Because it is organized around basic functions rather than administrative units, the model works as well in colleges where population-specific offices or departments exist as in those where they do not. It assumes that student affairs professionals—no matter where they fall within the organizational structure—will work for, with, and on behalf of all groups of students. Further, it demands that the institution as a whole changes to accommodate the diversity of the students it has admitted.

The variety of functions which should be performed to enhance the educational experience of each of the student groups described earlier can be sorted into four areas that are essential to a comprehensive effort: *services, programs, advocacy,* and *research.* The approach is referred to as the *SPAR Model.*

Services

Services, or functions performed *for* students, are both general to the entire student body and specifically designed for particular groups. Each student affairs unit should ask itself: (1) How can all services be made more accessible and appropriate for all students? and (2) What specific services can be provided to identified groups of students? In responding to the first question the hours of operation should be ascertained as to whether they are convenient for all students, including evening and part-time students. Offices should be open when commuter students with tight schedules can utilize them (early mornings and lunch hours). Service delivery methods should accommodate the full range of students with disabilities.

Services that are provided to traditional students should be expanded to include others (housing for adults, financial aid for part-time students).

In addition to assuring general access to its services, each department should provide services to meet population-specific needs. The career center, for instance, should be prepared to serve mid-career changers as well as students seeking their first job. Learning assistance centers need to offer services to meet the needs of international students having difficulty with the English language or in adapting to American pedagogical methods. Likewise, health services should be prepared to respond to the particular health needs of women and ethnic minorities. Counseling should be available in a variety of formats to accommodate different interpersonal style preferences.

Some population-specific services may be offered by offices set up to serve particular student groups. Colleges often designate an office to provide or coordinate interpreters, personal care attendants, and assistance to blind and partially sighted students. International education departments may be appropriately charged with providing visa and immigration assistance. Specialized tutoring is often offered by offices of minority student services, while commuter services meet the fundamental needs for housing and transportation information and referral.

Programs

Programs are activities carried on *with* rather than *for* students; the emphasis is on interaction and the process is two- rather than one-directional. Programs are generally more staff-intensive than services. As with services, student affairs professionals should encourage the participation of all students in a broad range of programs *and* should provide programs specific to the needs and interests of each student group. Programs need to be offered at times and locations convenient for all students. Information about programs should be disseminated in multiple ways and in a timely manner so that students with complex schedules can plan to attend. Programs should be designed to promote interaction within student groups, with different types of students, and with faculty and staff.

Agencies responsible for general programming as well as population-specific units should be charged with developing programs for each group within the student body. Activities offices and program boards should provide educational, cultural, social, and recreational programs designed for specific populations. Orientation programs should include components that focus on the unique transition needs of each student group. Family-oriented activities and individualized fitness programs often appeal to adult students. On-campus activities that bring together members of ethnic minorities in traditional ways can elevate students' comfort levels with the institutional environment. General programs on career or financial aid opportunities should be supplemented by information sessions targeted for specific groups, such as re-entry women or native Americans. Programs that are usually held on evenings and weekends can be scheduled for lunch hours when many daytime commuter students can attend without making an additional trip to campus.

In addition to focusing programming efforts on members of student groups, programs should be developed to affect faculty, staff, and other students through positive endorsement of diversity. If colleges are to become multicultural and multigenerational environments, all members of the campus community must be educated about diversity and about the values associated with diverse environments. Thus, programs aimed at assisting Hispanic students to adjust to the institution could be supplemented by programs to introduce other students, faculty, and staff to various aspects of Hispanic cultures. International days or fairs can accomplish the dual purposes of bringing groups of students together in a context of mutual support and of exposing the community at large to the richness of its many cultures.

Advocacy

The mere addition of services and programs for the various student groups is necessary but not sufficient to improve the quality of campus life. **Advocacy** functions *on behalf* *of* students to insure that their needs and educational goals are recognized and integrated in planning, policy making, and practice at all levels of the institution. To be most effective, change must occur from the inside out and from the top down. Students' diverse needs should be incorporated into decisions regarding construction and renovation of facilities, allocation of revenues, scheduling of classes, organization of services and programs, and so forth. Advocacy can be as complex as the creation of advisory boards to the president on issues related to women or minority students or as simple as a telephone call to a department head to suggest a more effective method of reaching adult students with essential information.

In addition, student affairs professionals should take the lead in educating campus colleagues about the diversity of students and the implications of that diversity. Faculty should be encouraged to consider the multiplicity of student learning styles as they develop curricular and teaching strategies. Student affairs professionals can increase the sensitivity of clerical and service workers to the cultural norms and expectations of different students they will encounter. In addition to on-campus advocacy, work needs to be done with community agencies to ensure that students' needs are considered in the development of transportation, housing, and child care policies and programs, to name but a few.

Research

Research on student characteristics, satisfaction, and success is necessary in order to determine the types of services, programs, and advocacy that are needed most. Closely related to research is the evaluation of both services and programs. Research and evaluation provide a vital foundation for practice, substantiate calls for action, support requests for funds and staff, and justify services and programs in times of fiscal constraint.

Such research and evaluation may appear on first review to be overwhelming tasks, especially because most colleges do not have institutional research programs capable of implementing all the various types of research activities that are desirable. However, if each unit conducts research related to its functions, the task becomes less burdensome and the data are more likely to be used in planning and evaluation. Activities staff can determine whether programs are attended by commuter or minority students in proportion to their presence within the student body. Counselors can keep track of the kinds of issues raised by students in specific groups. And the student union can determine which entrance and hallways have the most student traffic so that bulletin boards and information racks can be placed there.

Valuable data can be gathered by the simple addition of key variables to institutional data already collected upon admission or at registration (age, employment status, place of residence, ethnic origin). Examination of existing data can reveal helpful information. For example, studying the class schedules of commuter students reveals the best times for programming, and comparing the retention rates of students in different majors can determine where academic assistance and career support are most needed. Formal assessments of needs and studies of satisfaction with aspects of the college experience are highly desirable. However, informal methods of research and evaluation, such as telephone surveys and focus groups, can yield much useful anecdotal as well as quantifiable date. (See chapter 22 for more detail.)

Table 9.2 represents an example of how the SPAR Model can be applied to a particular student group. The four functions—services, programs, advocacy, and research—appear across the top, and several student affair areas are listed on the left. Each box represents a function that can be performed by a specific unit for, in this example, adult students. (The chart is not intended to be complete either in the list of agencies or in the specific applications of the four functions to each agency.)

In Table 9.3, an example is offered of how student affairs professionals, no matter what their affiliated area, can apply each aspect of the SPAR Model to the various student groups.

This chapter highlighted the diversity of today's students and the varied nature of the needs, goals, and concerns that

(Continued on Page 304)

TABLE 9.2
An Example of How the SPAR Model
Can Be Applied to a
Particular Student Group
ADULT STUDENTS

	Services	Programs	Advocacy	Research
Orientation		Programs to orient parents, spouses, children	Encourage all academic depts. and student services to offer programs for new students	
Activities	Provide child care during activities	Family-oriented activities		Assess adult students' needs and preferences for programs
Counseling	Train adult peer counselors		Promote faculty awareness of adults' preferred learning styles	Compile data on adults' counseling issues so that groups can be formed to address them
Union	Lounge set aside for adult students to mingle and relax			Measure use of union services by adults
Career Planning		Programs for mid-career changers	Encourage hiring of adult students in career-related on-campus jobs	
Financial Aid	Aid available to part-time students	Programs on financial management and retirement planning	Encourage local banks to offer loans to adult students	
Health	Clinics on age-related problems (menopause, backache)			Survey adults to determine health-related concerns

Source: Adapted from B. Jacoby and K. Girrell, 1981. Reprinted by courtesy of the *NASPA Journal.*

TABLE 9.3
**An Example of How Student Affairs Professionals
Can Apply Each Aspect of the
SPAR Model to the Various Student Groups**

ADVOCACY

Women	Encourage women students to consider majors and careers in "nontraditional" fields
Minorities	Advocate for faculty and staff hiring policies to increase representation of minorities
Adults	Encourage faculty awareness of adults' preferred learning styles
Commuters	Work to assure that recreational facilities are open at hours convenient for students with limited time on campus.
Internationals	Promote campus-wide activities which recognize and celebrate international cultures
Students with disabilities	Work to make facilities and programs accessible and welcoming.

Source: Adapted from B. Jacoby and K. Girrell, 1981. Reprinted by courtesy of the *NASPA Journal.*

they bring to college campuses. No easy solutions exist to the complex issues generated by this diversity. In order to assure that all students have the highest quality educational experiences possible, student affairs professionals must make the commitment to reshape the educational environment as new challenges are encountered.

REFERENCES

Arndt, R.T. (1988). Developing all its people: The university's next challenge. In J.M. Reid (Ed.), *Building the professional dimension of education exchange* (pp. 9-24). Yarmouth, ME: Intercultural Press.

Aslanian, C.B., & Brickell, H.M. (1980). *Americans in transition: Life changes as reasons for adult learning.* New York: College Entrance Examination Board.

Astin, A. (1982). *Minorities in American higher education.* San Francisco: Jossey-Bass.

Astin, A. (1984). A look at pluralism in the contemporary student population. *NASPA Journal, 21,* 2-11.

Belenky, M.F., Clinchy, B.M., Goldberger, N.R., & Tarule, J.M. (1986). *Women's ways of knowing.* New York: Basic Books.

Chew, C.A., & Ogi, A.Y. (1987). Asian American college student perspectives. In D.J. Wright (Ed.), *Responding to the needs of today's minority students.* (pp. 39-48). New Directions for Student Services (No. 38). San Francisco: Jossey-Bass.

Commission on National Challenges in Higher Education. (1988). *Memorandum to the 41st president of the United States.* Washington, DC: American Council on Education.

Cross, K.P. (1981). *Adults as learners.* San Francisco: Jossey-Bass.

Duran, R.P. (1983). *Hispanics' education and background: Predictors of college achievement.* New York: College Entrance Examination Board.

Evans, N.J. (Ed.). (1985). *Facilitating the development of women.* New Directions for Student Services (No. 29). San Francisco: Jossey-Bass.

Foust, S. (1981). Dynamics of cross-cultural adjustment from pre-arrival to re-entry. In G. Althen (Ed.), *Learning across cultures* (pp. 7-29). Washington, DC: National Association for Foreign Student Affairs.

Gilligan, C. (1982). *In a different voice.* Cambridge, MA: Harvard University Press.

Greene, E. (18 November 1987). Asian-Americans find U.S. colleges insensitive, form campus organizations to fight bias. *Chronicle of Higher Education,* pp. 1, 34, 38.

Hall, R.M., & Sandler, B.R. (1982). *The classroom climate: A chilly one for women?* Washington, DC: Association of American Colleges.

Hall, R.M., & Sandler, B.R. (1984). *Out of the classroom: A chilly climate for women?* Washington, DC: Association of American Colleges.

Hameister, B.G. (1984). Orienting disabled students. In Upcraft, M.L. (Ed.), *Orienting students to college* (pp. 67-78). New Directions for Student Services (No. 25). San Francisco: Jossey-Bass.

Hughes, R. (1983). The non-traditional student in higher education: A synthesis of the literature. *NASPA Journal, 20*(3), 51-64.

Jacoby, B., & Girrell, K. (1981). A model for improving services and programs for commuter students. *NASPA Journal, 18*(3), 36-41.

La Counte, D.W. (1987). American Indian students in college. In D.J. Wright (Ed.), *Responding to the needs of today's minority students* (pp. 65-80) New Directions for Student Services (No. 38). San Francisco: Jossey-Bass.

Likins, J.M. (1988). *Knowing our students: A descriptive profile of commuter students at a large, public, mid-western university.* Unpublished manuscript. Columbus, OH: The Ohio State University.

Lowenthal, M.F., Thurnher, M., Chiriboga, D., & Associates. (1975). *Four stages of life: A comprehensive study of women and men facing transitions.* San Francisco: Jossey-Bass.

Manese, J.E., Leong, F.T.L., & Sedlacek, W.E. (1985). Background, attitudes, and needs of undergraduate international students. *College Student Affairs Journal, 6,* 19-28.

Minatoya, L.Y, & Sedlacek, W.E. (1981). Another look at the melting pot: Perceptions of Asian-American undergraduates. *Journal of College Student Personnel, 19,* 328-36.

Morstain, B.R., & Smart, J.C. (1977). A motivational typology of adult learners. *Journal of Higher Education, 48,* 665-679.

Patterson, A.M., Sedlacek, W.E., & Scales, W.R. (1988). The other minority: Disabled student backgrounds and attitudes toward their university and its services. *Journal of Postsecondary Education and Disability, 5,* 87-94.

Payton, C.R. (1985). Addressing the special needs of minority women. In N.J. Evans (Ed.), Facilitating the development of women (pp. 75-90). *New Directions for Student Services, No. 29.* San Francisco: Jossey-Bass.

Pounds, A.W. (1987). Black students' needs on predominantly white campuses. In D.J. Wright (Ed.), *Responding to the needs of today's minority students* (pp. 28-38). New Directions for Student Services (No. 38). San Francisco: Jossey-Bass.

Quevedo-Garcia, E.L. (1987). Facilitating the development of Hispanic college students. In D.J. Wright (Ed.), *Responding to the needs of today's minority students* (pp. 49-64). New Directions for Student Services, No. 38. San Francisco: Jossey-Bass.

Sprandel, H.Z., & Schmidt, M.R. (Eds.). (1980). *Serving handicapped students.* New Directions for Student Services (No. 10). San Francisco: Jossey-Bass.

Stewart, G.M., & Hartt, J. (1987). *Promoting a multicultural environment through college activities, services, and programs.* Proceedings of the 67th ACU-I annual conference. Bloomington, IN: Association of College Unions-International.

Stewart, S.S. (Ed.). (1983). *Commuter students: Enhancing their educational experiences.* New Directions for Student Services (No. 24). San Francisco: Jossey-Bass.

Stewart, S.S., & Rue, P. (1983). Commuter students: definition and distribution. In Stewart, S.S. (Ed.), *Commuter students: Enhancing their educational experiences* (pp. 3-8). New Directions for Student Services (No. 24). San Francisco: Jossey-Bass.

Stodt, M. (1982). Psychological characteristics of 1980's college students: Continuity, changes, and challenges. *NASPA Journal, 19*(4), 3-8.

Wehrly, B. (1988). Cultural diversity from an international perspective, Part 2. *Journal of Multicultural Counseling and Development, 16*, 3-15.

Wheaton, J.B., & Robinson, D.C. (1983). Responding to the needs of re-entry women: A comprehensive campus model. *NASPA Journal, 21*(2), 44-51.

Wilmes, M.B., & Quade, S.L. (1986). Perspectives on programming for commuters: Examples of good practice. *NASPA Journal, 24*, 25-35.

Wilson, R. (1986). Minority students and the community college. In L.S. Zwerling (Ed.), *The community college and its critics* (pp. 61-70). New Directions for Community Colleges (No. 54). San Francisco: Jossey-Bass.

Wright, D.J. (Ed.). (1987). *Responding to the needs of today's minority students.* New Directions for Student Services (No. 38). San Francisco: Jossey-Bass.

Wright, D.J. (1984). Orienting minority students. In M.L. Upcraft (Ed.), *Orienting students to college* (pp. 53-66). New Directions for Student Services (No. 25). San Francisco: Jossey-Bass.

SUGGESTED READINGS

Commuter Students

Jacoby, B., & Burnett, D. (Eds.). (1986). *NASPA Journal* (special issue), *24*, 1-67.

Stewart, S.S. (Ed.). (1983). *Commuter students: Enhancing their educational experiences.* New Directions for Student Services (No. 24). San Francisco: Jossey-Bass.

Adult Students

Cross, K.P. (1981). *Adults as learners.* San Francisco: Jossey-Bass.

Hughes, R. (1983). The non-traditional student in higher education: A synthesis of the literature. *NASPA Journal, 20*(3), 51-64.

Women Students

Evans, N.J. (Ed.). (1985). *Facilitating the development of women.* New Directions for Student Services (No. 29). San Francisco: Jossey-Bass.

Gilligan, C. (1982). *In a different voice.* Cambridge, MA: Harvard University Press.

Hall, R.M., & Sandler, B.R. (1984). *Out of the classroom: A chilly climate for women?* Washington, DC: Association of American Colleges.

Minority Students

Fleming, J. (1985). *Blacks in college.* San Francisco: Jossey-Bass.

Wright, D.J. (Ed.). (1987). *Responding to the needs of today's minority students.* New Directions for Student Services (No. 38). San Francisco: Jossey-Bass.

International Students

Althen, G. (Ed.). (1981). *Learning across cultures.* Washington, DC: National Association for Foreign Student Affairs.

Jenkins, H.M., & Associates. (1983). *Educating students from other nations.* San Francisco: Jossey-Bass.

Students with Disabilities

Schmidt, M.R., & Sprandel, H.Z. (Eds.). (1982). *Helping the learning-disabled students.* New Directions for Student Services (No. 18). San Francisco: Jossey-Bass.

Sprandel, H.Z., & Schmidt, M.R. (Eds.). (1980). *Serving handicapped students.* New Directions for Student Services (No. 10). San Francisco: Jossey-Bass.

Roger B. Winston, Jr., Ph.D., is Professor in the Student Personnel in Higher Education Program, College of Education, at The University of Georgia. He was awarded the A.B. in history and philosophy from Auburn University and the M.A. in philosophy and Ph.D. in counseling and student personnel services from The University of Georgia. Prior to joining the faculty at The University of Georgia in 1978, he was Dean of Men and Associate Dean of Students at Georgia Southwestern College.

Sue A. Saunders, Ph.D., is the Dean of Students at Longwood College in Virginia. She received her doctorate in counseling and student personnel services at the University of Georgia. Her bachelor's degree in journalism and master's degree in counseling are from Ohio University. She has worked with residence halls, counseling and placement centers, fraternities and sororities, student activities, and academic affairs administration. Dr. Saunders' research interests include inquiry into nonintellective factors related to academic success and investigation of effective strategies for promoting development among student groups.

Dr. Saunders has published chapters and articles on mentoring, academic advising, factors related to the academic success of scholarship athletes, student development theory implications for sororities and fraternities, leadership development programs for freshmen, and career decision-making processes. She was a member of the Task Force that coordinated development of the American College Personnel Association Statement of Ethical and Professional Standards and is currently developing strategies to teach ethical decision-making to college freshmen.

Chapter **10**

ETHICAL PROFESSIONAL PRACTICE IN STUDENT AFFAIRS

Roger B. Winston, Jr.
Sue A. Saunders

If student affairs administrators are to be justified in being considered professionals, as many have argued (Carpenter, Miller, & Winston, 1980; Miller & Carpenter, 1980; Stamatakos, 1981; Trueblood, 1966; Wrenn 1949), then they must possess commonly recognized ethical standards that are clearly defined and backed by sanctions. Without such functioning guidelines and canons, the profession is open to the justified criticism that it, especially in its culpable professional organizations, is "much more concerned about the welfare of its membership than the protection of those whom the profession is to serve" (Stamatakos, 1981, p. 201). The student affairs profession, when compared to more established fields such as law and medicine, is still in its infancy with regard to establishing and enforcing standards of professional behavior.

However, the field has not been without its attempt to promulgate standards. As Stamatakos (1981) stated, a number of statements have been proposed in the past 30 years. For example, the American Personnel and Guidance Association adopted its first statement in 1961 which was primarily directed at counselor-client relationships. The National Association of Student Personnel Administrators (NASPA) (1960) adopted a rather narrow statement without enforcement mechanisms. The American College Personnel Association (1976) adopted a statement related to working with students in groups and and its first comprehensive set of ethical standards in 1981 and revised it in 1989. In 1985 NASPA adopted a somewhat more comprehensive standards statement. Neither ACPA's nor NASPA's standards, however, have enforcement provisions or formal means of addressing alleged violations by individual practitioners or institutions that can result in sanctions for violations of specific provisions of their statements.

ACPA's most recent standards statement provides means for its members and institutions to receive consultation in solving ethical problems. When ethically inappropriate conduct appears to have occurred, the ACPA *Statement of Ethical Principles and Standards* (1989) recommends that (1) the student affairs professional initiate a private conference with the practitioner thought to be behaving unethically about the conduct or policy in question as the first step; (2) if the private consultation does not produce desired effects, then the professional should pursue institutional channels for addressing alleged ethical misconduct; (3) if needed, the ACPA Ethics Committee also will provide an opinion based on written information about the ethical appropriateness of certain behavior; (4) if an institution wants assistance, ACPA will provide on-campus (non-binding) consultation in addressing the ethical concerns; and (5) if other approaches fail and the alleged violator is a member of the American Association for Counseling and Development (AACD), formal charges can be initiated through that body.

A number of specialized student affairs associations such as the College Placement Council, Association of College and University Housing Officers, National Association of Foreign Student Advisors, Association of College Unions-International, and National Association of Campus Activities have standard statements that are at various levels of sophistication and specificity. The area of admissions, records, and student recruitment has received considerable attention as reflected in the *Joint Statement on Principles of Good Practice in College Admissions and Recruitment* (American Association of Collegiate

Registrars and Admissions Officers, College Entrance Examination of Collegiate Registrars and Admissions Officers, College Entrance Examination Board, National Association of College Admissions Counselors, and National Association of Secondary School Principals, 1979) and in statements on fair practices by the Carnegie Council on Policy Studies in Higher Education (1979). Without question issues of ethical and professional practice will receive increased attention in the decade of the 1990s.

This chapter offers schemata for viewing professional ethics in the student affairs field from both theoretical and historical perspectives. A paradigm for ethical decision making is presented, along with some vignettes depicting application of an ethical decision-making process. Finally, recommendations are offered for enhancing ethical practice in student affairs.

ETHICS: A DEFINITION

For most student affairs administrators the idea that they should be *ethical* is often accepted as a given, but is seldom analyzed and only vaguely understood. "Ethics" from a philosophical point of view is concerned with determining what acts or behaviors are "right," or "ought to be done/ not done," as well as determining the epistemological justifications for ethical statements or assertions. From the philosophical perspective, the first sense of ethics is normative in that the concerns are in specifying rules or principles which can guide individual decisions about conduct. The second sense of ethics has to do with asking questions about what does it mean to say "one ought to" or "that is good" and is known a metaethics. "Ethics" is also used to describe the activity of specifying how and why some particular group of people decide a given behavior is right or wrong and then acts upon these decisions. This sense of ethics is descriptive of human behavior and seeks to find empirical explanations for such conduct. This area is typically thought the province of anthropology, psychology, and sociology (Bruening, 1975). The concern in this chapter is with **normative ethics,** that is, what behaviors fit within a code of professional ethics for student affairs administrators.

Bruening (1975) has proposed a broad framework that specifies four different levels of ethical codes (See Table 10.1). Levels 1 and 2 are based either on some fundamental philosophical principles—such as the utilitarian principle of *promote the greatest good for the greatest number* or the egoistic hedonism principle of *in the present moment I should always do what will give me the most pleasure* (Hospers, 1972)— or some religious tenet or doctrine (such as, *do unto others as you would have them do unto you*) which is sanctioned by appeal to some supernatural authority. These two levels are of interest primarily to philosophers and theologians. While these considerations are both interesting and important and need to be more thoroughly investigated in relationship to the student affairs profession, for the purposes of this chapter attention will be focused on identifying some of the commonly shared philosophical values and underpinnings of the profession, but shall not attempt to formulate them into any principles or laws.

Level 3 is the category in which one would place codes of professional ethics. Student affairs administrators, to paraphrase Golightly's (1971) comment about counselors, are professional makers of value judgments and ethical decisions within a given social context. In other words, they are concerned with application of Level 3 ethical codes. They are asking questions such as what are the rules; do they apply here; can there be a justification for violating the rules? For many years the student affairs profession has struggled because a comprehensive statement of ethical rules was lacking. Practitioners have been required to construct their own set of standards and then repeatedly to justify and defend them against challenges from other members of the academic community or the general public, generally without support or guidance from their professional associations.

Level 4 overlaps with law in that many ethical rules have been felt to be crucial to the protection of the public and, therefore, governmental bodies have given them the added sanctioning power of the state's judicial system. (This overlap of ethics and law will be explored later.)

TABLE 10.1
Levels of Ethical Codes

LEVEL 1: ULTIMATE MORAL PRINCIPLES

Characteristics of this level are (a) the principle(s) always hold(s) and always apply(ies) and (b) there is usually only one principle, but if there are more, then they can never conflict.

EXAMPLE: Promote the greatest good for the greatest number.

LEVEL 2: ETHICAL LAWS

Characteristics of this level are (a) the laws always hold, but do not always apply and (b) they cannot conflict with the ultimate principle(s) or with other ethical laws.

EXAMPLE: Lying is wrong.

EXAMPLE: Degrading the worth or dignity of any person is wrong.

LEVEL 3: ETHICAL RULES

Characteristics of this level are (a) the rules usually hold, but do not always apply, (b) violation must be justified, and (c)the rules cannot conflict with either laws or ultimate principles.

EXAMPLE: Lying is wrong.

EXAMPLE: Revealing information about a student received in confidence is wrong.

LEVEL 4: LEGAL RULES/LAWS

Characteristics of this level are (a) the rules usually hold, but do not always apply, (b) violation must be justified, and (c) the tules cannot conflict with either laws or ultimate principles.

EXAMPLE: One should honor copyright restrictions.

Note: Adapted from Bruening, 1975.

With this framework in mind, it can be seen that professional ethics is a set of rules devised through a consensus of the profession that guides or specifies the parameters of the conduct of members of the profession when fulfilling professional responsibilities and roles. Ethical standards statements serve seven basic purposes (Winston & Dagley, 1985);

- **Pedagogical Tool.** Ethical standards are a concise statement of ideals that instruct students preparing to enter the field and can make them aware of potential ethical problem areas.

- **Guidelines for Practical Decisions.** By specifying a certain conduct as unethical and another as encouraged, practitioners have a tool which can be used on a daily basis to inform their decisions. "One of the primary reasons for having a code of professional ethics is to shift some of the responsibility for ethical decision making from the individual practitioner to the larger group or, more specifically, to the profession. . . . It is psychologically comforting to know that other responsible persons will support one's ethical stand" (Winston & Dagley, 1985, p.50).

- **Clarification of Responsibilities.** A mark of a profession is the steps that are taken to assure that those who claim the status of a "professional" possess at least minimum levels of competence. Ethical standards promote the concept of maximum competence.

- **Protection of the Profession.** Ethical standards provide some criteria that can be used by members of the profession to maintain a watchful eye for those who perform incompetently or bring discredit on the profession.

- **Public Affirmation.** Standards statements are concise ways that practitioners can communicate the role and function of student affairs in higher education to others in the academic community and to the public.

- **Protection of Individual Practitioners.** Standards statements can be used to defend practitioners when they are unjustly attacked. Likewise, student affairs staff members are sometimes requested by institutional superiors to perform acts that are unethical. Standards statements can serve to inform the "boss" that refusal to perform a particular act is not insubordination, but is based on the considered judgment of the profession.

- **Performance Appraisal Tool.** By specifying desirable behavior, standards statements can serve to help supervisors and staff members alike identify appropriate goals and activities for individuals and can serve as criteria for structuring performance evaluations.

ETHICS, LAW, SOCIETY, AND THE PROFESSION

Professional ethics cannot be discussed in a social vacuum. Codes of professional ethics are intimately intertwined with social mores, professional norms, and law. What then are the connections among these different ideas and social entities?

Social Mores and Values

Any given society shares a collection of moral attitudes or mores, that is, some generally accepted beliefs defining right and wrong conduct (See Figure 10.1). For example, in this country it is a generally accepted belief that to kill another person or to steal something belonging to another is wrong. Likewise, for a professional to take advantage of or to fail to provide reasonable service to his/her clients who are depending on the professional for expertise is considered wrong. Society then can be seen to have certain expectations of those who label themselves as "professionals." Generally, the public expectation is that professionals in higher education will provide nurturant care to students, even though they appear to be mature and are legally classified as adults. Despite the legal burial of in loco parentis, student affairs professionals reason that

(Continued on Page 317)

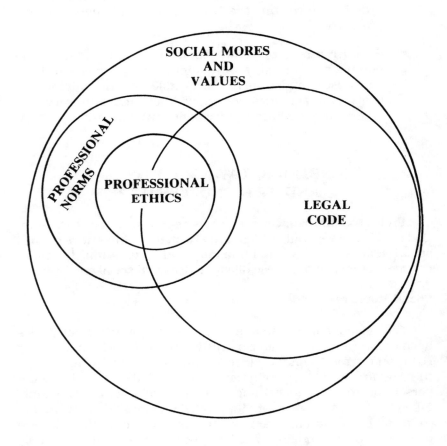

Figure 10.1. The context of professional ethics.

most college students are still searching for their life goals and are steadily forming personal values and beliefs. Consequently, many students are susceptible to exploitation, abuse, manipulation, or simple neglect by college personnel who . . . remain powerful role models for young minds. (Chambers, 1981, p. 2)

Professional Norms

A profession can be thought of as a community within the larger society that has influence and sanctioning power, both formal and informal, over its members. This professional community exercises influence through selection, training, and socialization of new members. It establishes norms of behavior for its members, violations of which may be classified as either "unprofessional" or "unethical." A behavior can hence be called "unprofessional," but not "unethical," but all unethical conduct is by definition unprofessional. For example, failure to extend common courtesies such as returning fellow professionals' telephone calls, appearing promptly for appointments, or failure to support to one's full capacity the endeavors of the employing institution is unprofessional conduct, but may not be unethical. Typically, violations of professional norms are sanctioned informally through social ostracism and by withholding rewards such as membership in professional societies or offices or recognitions within those societies. Formal sanctioning often occurs at the institutional level by reducing or withholding salary increments, transferring the offender to a menial position, or terminating employment.

Ethical Code

The existence of a regulative code of ethics is a common attribute of any profession (Greenwood, 1957; Wilensky, 1964). Rather universal standards of ethical behavior in all professions include (1) maximum competence; (2) lack of self-interest as a motivator; (3) colleague relationships characterized as cooperative, egalitarian, and supportive; and (4) sharing new information rather than using it to gain a competitive edge as in business (Greenwood, 1957).

Professional associations can perform a valuable and necessary function by serving as the formal mechanisms for enforcement of the ethical code. Their ultimate sanction is to exclude an individual from membership. Informally, members of the profession can and should apply social pressure to assure conformity to the ethical code.

The student affairs field lacks an ethical code that is both generally accepted throughout the field and has sanctioning mechanisms in place. This lack of a code with a means for enforcing it is one of the reasons the student affairs field must still be classified as an emerging profession (Carpenter, Miller, & Winston, 1980).

Professional Ethics and the Law

Law may be thought of as a subset of ethical practice that society, through its governmental bodies and agencies, has decided is so important to community welfare that the coercive power of the state is required to maintain it. No exact dividing line exists between legal and ethical principles, however. Governments are always writing new laws that redefine boundaries. Nevertheless, "an illegal act is, within the context of the given society, an unethical act" (Chambers, 1981, p. 4). However, in the narrow sense of professional ethics, much of the law is only distantly related; for example, driving 66 miles per hour down an interstate highway is a violation of the 65 miles per hour speed limit, but would not be classified as unethical professional behavior. On the other hand, for a residence hall director to divulge a student confidence without a compelling reason would generally be considered unethical, but not illegal since no statute requires the protection of that confidence.

From a more pragmatic point of view, Fargo (1981) has observed that government has moved into the province of professional ethics when the profession has acted in its own self-interest rather than the public interest. "Law fills ethical vacuums. When . . . [a profession] insists on acting on the basis of self-interest," Fargo (1981, p. 73) asserts that "law is the responsive social mechanism that mediates . . . conflicts." An excellent example is Title IX of the Education Amendments of 1972 (PL 92-318) which prohibited sex discrimination in higher education. The government decided to influence this area of higher education because professional administrators had been unable or unwilling to change age-old, unfair attitudes and practices toward women. El-Khawas (1981) has argued that if colleges wish to maintain their autonomy and minimize governmental regulation, then they must take seriously self-regulation, which includes well-defined and enforced codes of ethical conduct that assure fair and equitable treatment for all of higher education's constituencies.

VALUES AND THE STUDENT AFFAIRS PROFESSION

Before one can hope to establish a code of professional ethics, one must seek to identify values that the profession holds consensually (Peterson, 1970). However, with a few exceptions, the student affairs profession has not been introspective, nor analytical, concerning its philosophy and values. Generally speaking, student affairs professionals have been "doers," not "thinkers." As a consequence no first-rate philosophical analysis of the field's assumptions, beliefs, and values has yet appeared. Three documents have served as basic statements of values and philosophy: (1) *The Student Personnel Point of View* (American Council on Education, 1937), (2) *The Student Personnel Point of View, Revised Edition* (American Council on Education, 1949), and (3) "Student Development Services in Post Secondary Education" (Council of Student Personnel Associations in Higher Education, COSPA, 1975). Four diverse philosophical traditions—holism, humanism, pragmatism, and individualism—are woven throughout the profession's fundamental literature (Appleton, Briggs, & Rhatigan, 1978; Saddlemire, 1980).

Holism means, in the words of the 1937 Student Personnel Point of View (American Council on Education), that colleges have

> the obligation to consider the student as a whole—his intellectual capacity and achievement, his emotional make-up, his physical condition, his social relationships, his

vocational aptitudes and skills, his moral and religious values, his economic resources, his aesthetic appreciation . . . . [This philosophy] puts emphasis . . . upon the development of the student as a person rather than upon his intellectual training alone. (p. 1)

This commitment to dealing with the person in the totality of her/his selfhood was reaffirmed in the COSPA (1975) statement with the added dimension of advocating a developmental perspective for conceptualizing students and for designing interventions. Some student development advocates (Brown, 1972, 1980; Ender, Winston, & Miller, 1982; Miller & Prince, 1976) have applied the concept of holism to the institution by asserting that the whole college—students, faculty, administrators, and other student affairs staff—must collaborate in creating a positive learning environment.

Humanism makes three basic assumptions about the nature of humankind: (1) belief in human rationality, (2) possibility of human perfectibility, and (3) insistence on the importance of self-awareness and self-understanding (Appleton, Briggs, & Rhatigan, 1978). Belief in rationality and belief in human perfectibility are cornerstones of education; without these assumptions there is no point to the education enterprise. The student affairs field has its historical roots in vocational guidance, which emphasized the necessity for students to identify their aptitudes and skills and then to match them to an occupation. As the COSPA (1975) student development statement asserts, "the potential for development and self-direction is possessed by everyone. Education is a way of assisting in developing these potentials" (p. 525). One very important result of a humanistic view is a basic optimism about the profession's clientele—students—and its setting—the college environment.

Pragmatism, the "American philosophy," first expressed itself in higher education through the shift from classical and liberal arts education to more vocational and technical-scientific training. As Saddlemire (1980) observed "Dewey's position that knowledge is a consequence of combining thought and action provided a solid theoretical base for the evolution for a student services approach to involving students in many campus roles" (p. 26). Student affairs administrators have always been viewed as the persons whose responsibility it is to make things work—whether through control and discipline or through facilitating the institution's meeting the needs of students. The Student Personnel Point of View (American Council on Education 1937, 1949) assigned student affairs professionals the roles of interpreter of the institution and its policies, coordinator, facilitator, counselor, supervisor, institutional researcher, record keeper, disciplinarian, cheerleader (maintainer of morale), and employer.

Individualism is another philosophical cornerstone. "Human beings express their life goal as becoming free, liberated, self-directed, and they seek it through a process variously called self-actualization, full functioning, and behavioral development" (COSPA, 1975). The touchstone of the student affairs profession is a recognition of individual differences in backgrounds, abilities, interests, and goals (American Council on Education, 1949). Only through recognizing these differences and then taking appropriate action to meet the diversity of needs can a college provide quality education; otherwise it is simply broadcasting information. Student affairs historically has seen as its mission identification of individual uniqueness and provision of individualized attention.

The 1989 ACPA statement provides ethical standards with explicitly stated values related to the four principal constituencies with whom student affairs professionals work: fellow professionals, students, educational institutions, and society.

1. ***Professional Responsibility and Competence.*** Student affairs professionals are responsible for promoting students' learning and development, enhancing the understanding of student life, and advancing the profession and its ideals. They possess the knowledge, skills, emotional stability, and maturity to discharge responsibilities as administrators, advisors, consultants, counselors, programmers, researchers, and teachers. High levels of professional competence are expected in the performance of their duties and responsibilities. They ultimately are responsible for the consequences of their actions and inaction. (ACPA, 1989, p. 5)

2. **Student Learning and Development.** Student development is an essential purpose of higher education, and the pursuit of this aim is a major responsibility of student affairs. Development is complex and includes cognitive, physical, moral, social, career, spiritual, personality, and educational dimensions. Professionals must be sensitive to the variety of backgrounds, cultures, and personal characteristics evident in the student population and use appropriate theoretical perspectives to identify learning opportunities and to reduce barriers that inhibit development. (ACPA, 1989, p.7)

3. **Responsibility to the Institution.** Institutions of higher education provide the context for student affairs practice. Institutional mission, policies, organizational structure, and culture, combined with individual judgment and professional standards, define and delimit the nature and extent of practice. Student affairs professionals share responsibility with other members of the academic community for fulfilling the institutional mission. Responsibility to promote the development of individual students and to support the institution's policies and interests require that professionals balance competing demands. (ACPA, 1989, p.8)

4. **Responsibility to Society.** Student affairs professionals, both as citizens and practitioners, have a responsibility to contribute to the improvement of the communities in which they live and work. They respect individuality and recognize that worth is not diminished by characteristics such as age, culture, ethnicity, gender, disabling condition, race, religion, or sexual/affectional orientation. Student affairs professionals work to protect human rights and promote an appreciation of human diversity in higher education. (ACPA, 1989, p.9)

The profession values service to individuals and society. The conflict for student affairs professionals comes when individuals and institutions differ. Brown (1977) suggested three value conflict areas repeatedly encountered by student affairs professionals: (1) dissonance between individual liberty and social responsibility, (2) conflict between hedonistic needs/

desires and altruism, and (3) search for meaning to human existence. Ethical codes are needed by the profession, not to solve these problems, but to lay out the parameters of acceptable solutions.

ISSUES AND PRINCIPLES

Although a historical understanding of the philosophical underpinnings of the student affairs profession is a necessary prerequisite to defining a clear set of ethical principles, also necessary is to identify ethical questions faced by student affairs professionals and ways in which these issues may be resolved. While general ethical issues are covered, ethical standards references will be to the ACPA Standards (1989) for simplicity sake. (A copy of the ACPA Ethical and Professional Standards can be found in Appendix A.)

Ethical standards, such as those cited in this chapter, define behaviors which ought to or ought not to be performed by student affairs professionals. Although standards are essential and helpful as guides to behavior, they do not solve all individual ethical problems (Van Hoose & Kottler, 1977). In writing about the ethics of counselors/therapists, Barclay (1968) stated that the ultimate safeguards for ethical practice are individual professionals' sense of integrity and responsibility. This statement may well apply to student affairs professionals as well. Wrenn (1966) stated that although many professionals have established codes of ethics, the application of such principles may require courage and depth of conviction as well as a reliance on the "great values and principles of the human race" (p.135). Oftentimes, the entering professional is faced with ambiguous, nonspecific standards and also lacks a clear understanding or his/her personal values in relation to professional issues and situations. Therefore, because ethical issues are not usually resolved in a simplistic, "cookbook" fashion, in this chapter a process model for ethical decision making is explored.

No clear answers exist for all the ethical and professional behavior issues faced on a daily basis by student affairs professionals. A sometimes bewildering array of facts, codes, personal values, social norms, moral principles, and theories affect the process one uses to determine the appropriate course of action when confronted with an ethical dilemma. Particular facts of any given ethical dilemma have implications for its resolution, as do the codes of ethics to which professionals subscribe. Individual factors, such as theoretical orientation, religious belief, previous education, ethical behavior of significant mentors or others in the institution, and personal values all affect the ways in which practitioners choose to cope with decisions involving ethical issues. Generally, accepted ethical principles, such as preventing harm, loyalty, justice, and benefiting others, guide decision making in ways more fundamental than do ethical codes or even laws. The task of making ethical decisions becomes more problematic when principles, values, or institutional needs are in conflict, as they frequently are. How, then, does one develop a workable, utilitarian scheme for dealing with these intellectually-complex and emotionally-laden situations?

Kitchener (1985) proposed a conceptualization based on the work of Beauchamp and Childress (1979) and Drane (1982) that is useful for practitioners as they work through ethical dilemmas. Kitchener identifies three increasingly more abstract levels of reasoning in an hierarchical model. The first line of reasoning is to consult professional ethical standards statements. (This can be equated with Level 3 in the Bruening conceptual framework discussed earlier.) If those statements do not provide reasonably specific direction for resolving the problems, then practitioners should call upon general principles of ethical conduct (Level 2 in the Bruening conceptualization). If conflict among ethical principles or competing interests exist, then general theories of ethical conduct or ultimate principles should be called upon for guidance—Level 1 in the Bruening conceptualization. (For religiously affiliated institutions, Level 1 principles may be derived from the teaching of the sponsoring sect. For public institutions and nonsectarian private colleges, Level 1 principles are more subject to individual interpretation and may vary widely among staff members.)

Ethical codes are standards of conduct for a particular profession and can in many cases provide definitive guidance for the practitioner. For example, clearly from the ACPA Standards (1989) a supervisor who pressures staff members to participate in a workshop activity that requires relatively high levels of self-disclosure would be violating Standard 1.15. (See Appendix A.) Yet, in many instances, ethical codes may be silent on a given issue, or may fail to address specifically the circumstances of a given problem. These circumstances require use of general, or more fundamental, ethical principles.

Kitchener (1985) identified five general, fundamental principles (which were subsequently adopted in the 1989 ACPA Statement [See Appendix A]) that underlie the student affairs profession (and its ethical standards) which may be called upon in situations in which the ethical standards statements do not provide specific guidance:

- **Respect Autonomy.** This principle involves respecting one's right to make choices about life issues and freedom of thought and expression. These rights and freedoms are, however, limited by the need to respect the rights of others—including students, professionals, and others in the academic community and society in general.

- **Do No Harm.** This principle includes refraining from activities that have a high potential to harm another physically or psychologically. Because the risks of psychological harm are often subtle and difficult to predict accurately, decisions based on this principle must be made carefully, giving due recognition of the level of error inherent.

- **Benefit Others.** This principle is fundamental to the student affairs profession because of its mandate to assist students in their personal development. It may, however, frequently conflict with the first principle (respect autonomy) when related to issues such as confidentiality when one is required to examine conflicting claims or "goods."

- **Be Just.** This principle refers to fair and equitable treatment of individuals and groups in the higher education environment. The student affairs practitioner is often called upon, however, to balance the rights of competing groups and individuals. Justice is not simply a matter of equal treatment, equal access, or due process. It is a complex concept that must take into account individual differences and the effects of the action taken. For instance, handicapped student services are good examples of a circumstance in which "unequal," special treatment is necessary in order to be just.

- **Be Faithful.** This principle embodies concepts of loyalty, keeping promises, truthfulness, and basic respect. Without this, professionals would lack the basic credibility necessary to help others. Kitchener (1985, pp.25-26) argued that "this special ethical obligation can be thought of as an implicit contract or agreement between professionals and those with whom they work not to exploit, lie to, or otherwise deceive those in their professional care."

Kitchener's conceptualizations do not address ethical theories in detail but do point to the prevailing notion among many twentieth-century ethicists (Abelson & Nielson, 1967; Baier, 1958; Toulmin, 1950) that ethical decisions should be generalizable. That is, these decisions should be consistent with decisions made for ourselves, our loved one, and others facing the same situation.

In using Kitchener's model, student affairs practitioners face a myriad of conflicting values, principles, and loyalties. As with any individual facing an ethical or moral decision, *not to decide* is to decide. Simply failing to take action may be as unethical as any other voluntary action. Ross (1930) held that the task of being moral was to discern which conflicting principle takes precedence in any given situation. Student affairs professionals, because of their responsibilities involve concern for individuals, organizations, and programs alike, are faced with many complex and intricate ethical dilemmas. For example, when a student affairs practitioner disciplines a student, the prescribed penalty specified by the institution's conduct regulations may not appear to enhance the development of that individual student. That action, however, may serve to prevent harm to other students, maintain the reputation of the institution, and may enhance other students' opportunity for learning about the nature of personal responsibility.

Part of this clash stems from the conflict inherent with being a professional in the context of a bureaucratic organizational structure. Because one cannot practice this profession independent of higher education institutions, it will always require a careful balancing of interests and benefits (Winston & Dagley, 1985). As Standard 3 of the *ACPA Statement of Ethical Principles and Standards* (1989) highlights, student affairs professionals have dual responsibilities to individuals and to institutions. The student affairs professional, in order to make decisions congruent with the ACPA *Standards,* must evaluate each situation carefully and determine an appropriate balance between the needs for individual growth, organizational demands, and the integrity of institutional programs.

The student affairs professional operating at the more advanced levels of ethical development has a clear understanding of her/his ethical values. Ethical decisions reflect an internal orientation, rather than immediate and automatic responses to external pressures and demands. These higher levels of ethical development should, for the student affairs professional, reflect cognizance of consequences for organizations, for the institution, and for society at large, as well as for individuals.

In the real world of student affairs practice, professionals are presented with literally dozens of situations that have ethical implications each day. Seldom is sufficient time available to examine painstakingly the complex factors involved in each situation and to consider all the possible ethical ramifications and consequences of each course of action. Given these limitations, to create a general process model for use in making ethical judgments in everyday practice is plausible. A model was constructed by Van Hoose and Kottler (1977) for use by counselors, and an adaptation for student affairs practitioners is presented in Figure 10.2.

The effective use of the decision-making model is dependent on the practitioner's willingness and ability to (1) confront personal values related to ethical decisions; (2) tolerate ambiguity and a lack of clear external directives; (3) analyze ethical

(Continued on Page 329)

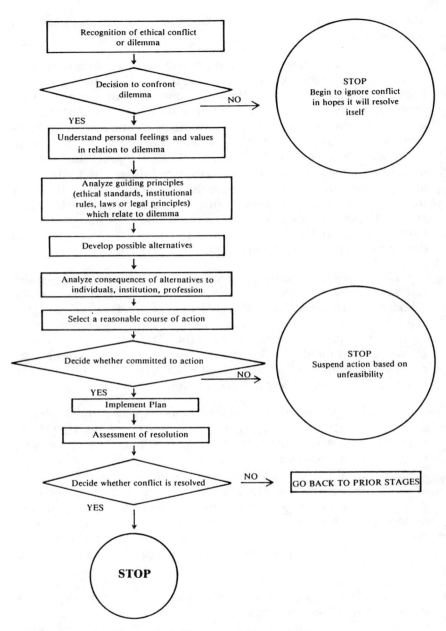

Figure 10.2. Paradigm of ethical decision-making process.

Note: Based on and modified from Van Hoose & Kottler, 1977.

standards, institutional rules, legal principles; (4) assess results of ethical judgments in a nondefensive manner; and (5) take positions that may be unpopular or that may be detrimental to career advancement.

Particularly for beginning professionals, to be thrust into situations that require quick and competent resolution of an ethical dilemma is often confusing and anxiety producing. Through personal questioning and confrontation development of a personal style of ethics can be enhanced . Answers to the following questions adapted from Van Hoose & Kottler (1977) may help one to develop confidence with complex ethical decisions.

- How congruent are ethical standards and institutional rules with personal values? How does one confront incongruities?

- What criteria would one use to decide about ambiguous ethical problems, such as divulging confidential material, sharing test results, confronting an unethical colleague, or deciding what constitutes a significant contribution to research?

- In which situations might one provide services in which he/she has not had adequate training?

- With what types of students and colleagues is one most effective?

- What personal "payoffs" (such as prestige, power, responsibility, helpfulness, money) does one receive from work and how important are each of these rewards?

- What criteria does one use to evaluate the effectiveness of one's work and professional development?

These questions obviously have no clear and universal answers. The purpose of such questions is to help professionals assess their values—a first step toward ethical development.

APPLICATION OF ETHICAL DECISION-MAKING MODEL

Perhaps the most effective way to understand ethical decision-making principles is to identify hypothetical ethical problems and to apply the ethical decision-making model. This section focuses on the application of the ethical decision-making model in three hypothetical situations. The reader should be forewarned that the alternative resolutions listed herein do not constitute a complete, or, in fact, a recommended list. Each student affairs professional can use these examples as stimuli for further questioning, rather than as definitive answers.

The Dilemma of Jane Smith

Jane Smith was in her second year as a residence hall director. During that time she had written a research study investigating the relationship of hall activities to academic performance. The housing director, Dr. Jones, had helped Jane gather information by contacting the Registrar and by informing Jane of the institution's educational record policy. Jane conceived, designed, and wrote the study. When Jane showed the completed study to Dr. Jones, he demanded that he be included as a coauthor because he had made the essential contacts with the appropriate college officials. How might Jane respond to this situation?

Practitioner's Feelings and Values. Jane Smith has experienced several heated disagreements with Dr. Jones and wants to smooth over any conflicts with him. Jane believes that any and all collaboration should be noted. However, she defines major contributions as those that involve collaboration in the design and writing of research.

Ethical Conflict. Should Dr. Jones be included as a coauthor, even though his contribution was not nearly as significant as Jane Smith's? Was Dr. Jones' contribution *major*, and was it, in fact, essential to completion of the study?

Guiding Principles. ACPA Ethical and Professional Standards (1989)—Standard 1.20—states that student affairs professionals will "acknowledge major contributions to research projects and professional writing through joint authorship, with the principal author listed first. They will acknowledge minor technical or professional contributions in notes or introductory statements." In addition, Standard 1.2 holds that professionals will "not demand co-authorship of publications when their involvement was ancillary or unduly pressure others for joint authorship."

The general ethical principle of **promoting justice** assumes reciprocity, which means that individuals are given the benefits due them. In addition the principle of **being faithful** means that a special ethical obligation or contract exists between supervisor and employee that implies an agreement not to exploit or deceive, particularly when one party is in a less powerful position.

Alternative Actions. Actions open to Jane include (1) Jane tells Dr. Jones that he will not be included as a coauthor because his contributions were minor; (2) Jane informs Dr. Jones that his assistance will be noted in a footnote, but that he will not be listed as a coauthor; (3) Jane agrees to include Dr. Jones as a coauthor; and (4) Jane asks Dr. Jones to carefully consider each of their contributions. She could propose using a scheme for addressing these issues, which weighs various contributions made to research projects and the resulting report, suggested by Winston (1985). He proposed that each contributor, using preestablished weights, independently complete a worksheet assigning points to each person involved in various categories and then compare results. The decision about whether to include Dr. Jones would rest on whether he accumulated enough points, according to the Winston scheme, to justify joint-authorship.

Evaluation of Alternatives. In this particular situation, two criteria should be used to evaluate alternatives: (1) the consequences of a particular action for Jane's relationship with her supervisor and (2) the consequence of the action chosen for Jane's sense of professional integrity.

The Dilemma of Bill Brown

Bill Brown is a new dean of students on a small, private college campus. Shortly after his arrival in July a vacancy occurs in a residence hall, and Bill is named chairperson of the search committee to find a replacement before the beginning of the fall term. The screening committee receives applications and one applicant appears far superior in terms of education and experience and is invited for an on-campus interview. After a poll of all interviewers, the consensus was to offer the applicant the position. Bill sought the president's approval to offer the position and was refused. When pressed, the president stated that although he had not interviewed the candidate, he felt that a Black person from a public school background could not project the kind of image the college should have.

Practitioner's Feelings and Values. Bill is committed to anti-discriminatory practices in all aspects of higher education. Furthermore, Bill feels that the candidate chosen by the committee would serve as an excellent role model for minorities. Because Bill is new to his job, he is uncertain of the most effective ways to voice disagreements. Also, Bill is too new to his position to have amassed much political support.

Ethical Conflict. How can one be certain whether or not this action was, in fact, based on racial discrimination? How can one most effectively work to modify discriminatory practices?

Guiding Principles. In Standard 4.3, the ACPA *Statement of Ethical Principles and Standards* (1989) specifies that student affairs professionals will "not discriminate on the basis of age, culture, ethnicity, gender, disabling condition, race, religion, or sexual/affectional orientation. They will work to modify discriminatory practices."

The general principle of *being just* suggests that all individuals should receive fair and equitable treatment. The ACPA *Statement* specifically holds that "A crucial aspect of promoting justice is demonstrating an appreciation of human differences and opposing intolerance and bigotry concerning these differences. Important human differences include . . . characteristics such as age, culture, ethnicity, gender . . ." (p.4). The principle of *being faithful* is likely to be in conflict with the justice principle in this situation. Faithfulness implies that employees are loyal to their employers and protect the reputation of the institution that employs them.

Alternative Actions. Actions available include the following: (1) Bill would contact the candidate directly, inform the candidate of the racial bias used in decision making, and encourage the candidate to take legal action; (2) Bill would confront the president directly, ask for a clear-cut explanation of the decision, share reasons for wanting to hire the candidate, and encourage the president to reverse his position; and (3) Bill would accept the decision, say nothing and immediately begin seeking another candidate.

Evaluation of Alternatives. In this particular situation, three criteria should be used to evaluate alternatives: (1) What will be the effect of the action on the institution's programs, students, and integrity? (2) How will the action taken affect Bill's sense of upholding standards of professional behavior and fair play? (3) How will the action affect Bill's future effectiveness at the institution?

The Dilemma of Pat Martin

Pat Martin is responsible for the orientation and admission of transfer students at a small, regional university. Pat possesses a M.A. in counseling, but she has not worked in a counseling capacity for five years. After leading an orientation seminar for several weeks, Pat is contacted by one of the women students enrolled in the seminar. The young woman, Sheila, shares that she is lonely and homesick and wants to drop out. Pat and Sheila spend much time talking about Sheila's adjustment difficulties. At the end of the first term, Sheila starts to become verbally abusive with Pat. She also begins talking about past violent behavior and her hostility towards her roommate. As time progresses, Sheila's hostility becomes more intense, and she threatens to push her roommate out of the window.

Practitioner's Feelings and Values. Pat is aware that Sheila regards her relationship with Pat as a counseling or therapeutic one. Sheila has opened up to Pat about a variety of deep personal issues and says that she has not exposed herself like this before. Pat feels that her counseling skills are somewhat rusty and is concerned about her ability to deal with the intense nature of Sheila's problem. Pat is also aware that Sheila is likely to stop talking to her if the hostility is exposed to a third party.

Ethical Conflict. Should Pat break confidentiality in light of the threats made against the roommate?

Guiding Principles. Two provisions in the ACPA *Statement* seem particularly appropriate for this situation. Standard 4.5 maintains that professionals will "report to the appropriate authority any condition that is likely to harm their clients and/or others." Standard 2.5 requires professionals to "inform students of the conditions under which they may receive assistance and the limits of confidentiality when the counseling relationship is initiated."

The general principle of *respecting autonomy* has implications for this dilemma. Sheila has a right to freedom of thought and expression, as long as this does not negatively affect the rights of others. If, however, Sheila is irrational to the point of being incompetent to make her own decisions, respecting autonomy becomes less important than the principle of *doing no harm.* If Sheila is serious about her threats, her roommate runs a high risk of being harmed. Also, the principle of being faithful also has implications in this case. Sheila may have assumed an agreement of confidentiality, because of the "counseling" nature of her relationship with Pat. Failing to clarify the limits of the relationship is likely to upset the implicit contract between Pat and Sheila.

Alternative Actions. Actions available include the following: (1) Pat would contact the campus psychologist for consultation and would refer Sheila to the psychologist. Pat would also inform Sheila that unless she sees the psychologist, Pat will take further action. (2) Pat would inform Sheila's resident director of the situation and recommend that Sheila's roommate be changed. (3) Pat would contact campus security with the information she possesses. (4) Pat would take no action and continue to keep what is said strictly confidential. (5) Pat would inform the roommate she may be in danger.

Evaluation of Alternatives. In this particular dilemma, the following criteria should be used to evaluate alternatives: (1) the effect of Sheila's threats on the roommate and other residents, (2) the effect of disclosure on Sheila's personal development, (3) the possible physical harm which could occur, and (4) the effect of this intense relationship on Pat's effective performance as orientation director.

While of little assistance in resolving the present dilemma but with implications for future actions, had Pat paid close attention to Standard 2.5 and explicitly addressed the issues related to the limits of confidentiality when she first began to work with Sheila, then fewer difficult ethical decisions would be facing Pat now. Generally, as a practical matter, "strict confidentiality" cannot be maintained outside of a formal counseling setting such as a center where the professional does not have other institutional responsibilities that could conflict with the therapist role. Professionals and students should be fully aware of limitations prior to initiating a relationship.

RESPONSIBILITIES OF ALL STUDENT AFFAIRS PROFESSIONALS

The fundamental responsibility of all student affairs professionals is to be knowledgeable of the existing ethical standards statements and to assess their conduct in relation to those standards. As part of the assessment, student affairs professionals must become aware of implications of their behavior and be reflective and introspective about their motivations in working with students and community members. Ethical behavior is contingent upon a high level of self-awareness.

Each student affairs staff member has a primary responsibility to model high levels of ethical and professional conduct for fellow professionals and students alike. Brown (1985, p.68) emphasized the importance of this responsibility by stating that "The common mission of the student services profession is being the moral conscience of the campus. Staff responsibility is to promote and support ethical behavior on campus and to recognize and confront unethical behavior." That responsibility, without a mutually supportive staff environment that fosters discussion and a caring resolution of ethical issues, could be extraordinarily burdensome. Yet, staff teams must begin their discussions on ethics with the assumption that all are "traveling companions" on the rocky road to dealing with ethical dilemmas and that discussions of these issues are not license to parade self-righteousness. Canon and Brown (1985) dismissed the myth that "personal ethical perfection (or near perfection) is prerequisite to any serious ethical inquiry" (p.82). A staff team needs to develop a climate of mutual trust and a clear process for discussing these issues, because these types of inquiry force examination of values and sensitive issues. Brown (1985) outlined an agenda for creating an ethical community that could be translated for staff development activities.

With the sometimes lamented demise of *in loco parentis*, some have argued that the traditional charge to higher education for responding to the character development of students has been abandoned. This is true to a large extent when viewed from a prescriptive perspective. However, student affairs staff members probably can have a much greater impact on students' ethical development by modeling a concern for and adherence to a set of publicly owned standards than they ever could have when prescribing rigid rules for students. Other powerful techniques for enhancing the ethical development of students include (1) student affairs professionals directly confronting students about conduct that has ethical implications when it occurs and (2) stimulating dialogue and critical analysis of situations that present ethical or moral questions, whether in response to issues related to campus activities or to societal concerns.

Chief Student Affairs Administrator Responsibilities

All student affairs administrators bear responsibilities in the area of professional and ethical conduct. However, the chief student affairs administrator has some additional responsibilities by virtue of his/her leadership position.

The chief student affairs administrator has the responsibility to assure that staff members are aware of ethical standards. This may be most effectively addressed by insisting that ethical standards are given regular attention in staff development activities. At least once a year every staff member should be reminded about ethical concerns and assisted in examining his/her behavior. Even more importantly, ethical behavior should be one category addressed in the formal staff evaluation process. If ethical behavior is a serious concern of the profession, then simply giving lip service is inadequate. Ethics must be directly applied to the day-to-day operations with students and staff.

The recently adopted CAS *Standards* (1986) mandate that each functional area in a student affairs division publish and disseminate a statement of ethical standards that guide the conduct of staff. However, for each area to begin *tabla rosa* in this process is unnecessary. The statements adopted by various professional organizations should be starting points. These statements, however, should be supplemented with more detailed guidelines for ethical conduct that are based on the shared values of the particular student affairs staff in question and the institution's goals and ideals. The chief student affairs administrator has the primary responsibility to make sure that this occurs in each functional area of the division— even in areas that may not constitute a separate office—and that these statements are reviewed at least annually and changed as experience with their use dictate.

Another major responsibility of the chief student affairs administrator is to monitor, either personally or through assignment to a specific staff member, the institution's policies, procedures, and practices as they relate to the profession's statements of ethical standards. When violations or inconsistencies are recognized, the institution's leadership should be informed. Only when student affairs professionals are willing to confront unethical behavior (particularly when institutionalized) will the field in fact become a true profession. By placing concern for its clientele (students) and protection of the public interest ahead of personal gain or loyalty to individual institutional leaders, the profession will preserve its integrity and will gain the respect from other members of the academic community that it has often felt lacking.

Each student affairs division should have an established procedure through which staff members and students can have addressed any alleged violations of ethical standards. The 1989 ACPA *Statement of Ethical Principles and Standards* states that "All student affairs divisions should have a widely-publicized process of addressing allegations of ethical misconduct" (p.2). The process might well resemble the procedures that many institutions have created to address allegations of sexual harassment or violations of civil rights. The procedure should allow questioning the ethical conduct of individuals and the effects of institutional policies.

RECOMMENDATIONS TO IMPROVE ETHICAL CONDUCT IN THE PROFESSION

Two areas require attention in order to improve ethical practice in the profession: professional association activities and professional preparation programs.

Professional Associations

Profession-wide Statement of Standards. A statement of ethical standards that addresses student affairs practice in a generic or general sense and that has the approval of all or most student affairs professional associations is badly needed. Once adopted, such a statement would require wide dissemination and a vigorous educational campaign. Workshops, newsletter columns, a standards casebook, and convention programs could all be used in the educational effort.

Support and Consultation. Professional associations need to develop task forces or commissions that will provide consultation to members in dealing with questions about ethical conduct. Also the need exists to provide support to members who elect to take action against either individuals or colleges who are unethical in their treatment of students and/or staff.

Sanctioning Mechanisms. Ethical standards that have no consequences if violated have limited value for a profession. Some would argue that such standards are only a facade, designed to give student affairs practitioners a cosmetic appearance of being professionals. Professional associations, either in concert or independently, need to establish processes through which alleged violations of ethical standards can be quickly investigated and sanctions applied when violations have been established. A process for admonishing higher education institutions that disregard or refuse to alter practices found to violate principles of ethical practice is also needed.

Professional Preparation Programs

Student affairs preparation programs bear a heavy responsibility for improving ethical practice in the profession. Graduate students need to become very familiar with the statements of ethical standards. During practicum and internship supervision sessions, preparation program faculty should help students examine their behavior, as well as that of the professionals in the setting, for ethical implications. Even before students enter practicum sites they should have spent time discussing potential ethical dilemmas. Without having time to reflect on how one might deal with an ethical problem before it is encountered, because of the press of time and circumstances, one may take an unethical course of action that could have been avoided.

One question that students need to consider carefully before the practicum placement is the distinction between the ethics in counseling and other student affairs functions. As a counselor, one's primary responsibility is to the individual receiving attention, provided the actions are not dangerous to themselves or others. What is said in the counseling session is confidential, and the counselor's attention and concern are focused on the welfare of that individual student. However, in settings outside the counseling session, the student affairs practitioner has a major responsibility to the institution, as well as to the student. In some senses this issue can be seen as a matter of accountability. In a counseling relationship, the counselor is primarily accountable to, or responsible to, his/her client; however, in the student activities office or housing department, for instance, the student affairs professional has a responsibility to protect the integrity of the institution and the best interests of all students and must therefore work with individual students within that context. This issue is further complicated by the fact that hall directors who possess counseling skills may establish counseling relationships with residents. (All counseling does not occur in the counseling center, nor should it.) Graduate students and professionals alike need to consider carefully these issues before being thrust into the middle of them and to develop a set of personal guidelines, within the boundaries of the established ethical standards statements, that can be used to guide their conduct in such situations.

Preparation program faculty members must model appropriate ethical behavior, instruct students about ethical standards, create a climate that evidences a concern about ethical issues, and provide stimulation and support to students as they explore ethical issues. However, faculty cannot accomplish the task alone; practitioners as they have contact with students in preparation programs have a responsibility to help students confront the ethical issues of the profession.

A concern for the ethics of student affairs practice in a formal sense is relatively recent. Whether the profession chooses to accept the challenge to deal with these important issues will determine whether student affairs will move beyond its emerging professional status to become a true profession.

REFERENCES

Abelson, R., & Nielson, K. (1967). History of ethics. In P. Edwards (Ed.), *The encyclopedia of philosophy (vol.3)*, (pp. 520-32) New York: Macmillan.

American Association for Counseling and Development. (1988). *Ethical standards.* Alexandria, VA: Author.

American Association of Collegiate Registrars and Admissions Officers, College Entrance Examination Board, National Association of College Admissions Counselors, & National Association of Secondary School Principals. (1979). *Joint statement on principles of good practice in college admissions and recruitment.* Authors.

American College Personnel Association [ACPA]. (1976). The use of group procedures in higher education: A position statement by ACPA. *Journal of College Student Personnel, 17,* 161-68.

American College Personnel Association [ACPA]. (1981). American College Personnel Association statement of ethical and professional standards. *Journal of College Student Personnel, 22,* 184-89.

American College Personnel Association [ACPA]. (1989). *A statement of ethical principles and standards.* Alexandria, VA: Author.

American Council on Education. (1937). *The student personnel point of view.* American Council on Education Studies (Series 1, Vol. 1, No. 3). Washington, DC: Author.

American Council on Education. (1949). *The student personnel point of view.* *American Council on Education Studies* (Series 6, Vol. 13, No. 13). Washington, DC: Author.

Appleton, J.R., Briggs, C.M., & Rhatigan, J.J. (1978). *Pieces of eight: The rite, roles, and styles of the dean by eight who have been there.* Portland, OR: NASPA Institute of Research and Development.

Baier, K. (1958). *The moral point of view.* Ithaca, NY: Cornell University Press.

Barclay, J. (1968). *Counseling and philosophy: A theoretical exposition.* Boston: Houghton Mifflin.

Beauchamp, T.L., & Childress, J.F. (1979). Principles of biomedical ethics. Oxford: Oxford University Press.

Brown, R.D. (1972). *Student development in tomorrow's higher education: A return to the academy.* Washington, DC: American College Personnel Association.

Brown, R.D. (1977). Professional development and staff development: The search for a metaphor. In R.P. Wanzek (Ed.), *Staff development.* DeKalb, IL: Northern Illinois University.

Brown, R.D. (1980). Student development and the academy: New directions and horizons. In D.A. DeCoster & P. Mable (Eds.), *Personal education & community development in college residence halls* (pp. 79-95). Washington, DC: American College Personnel Association.

Brown, R.D. (1985). Creating an ethical community. In H.J. Canon & R.D. Brown (Eds.), *Applied ethics in student services* (pp. 67-80). New Directions for Student Services (No. 30). San Francisco: Jossey-Bass.

Bruening, W.H. (1975). Ethics and morality. In W.R. Durland & W.H. Bruening (Eds.), *Ethical issues: A search for the contemporary conscience* (pp. 1-12). Palo Alto, CA: Mayfield.

Canon, H.J., & Brown, R.D. (1985). How to think about professional ethics. In H.J. Canon & R.D. Brown (Eds.), *Applied ethics in student services* (pp. 81-88). New Directions for Student Services (No. 30). San Francisco: Jossey-Bass.

Carnegie Council on Policy Studies (1979). *Fair practices in higher education: Rights and responsibilities of students and their colleges in a period of intensified competition for enrollments.* San Francisco: Jossey-Bass.

Carpenter, D.S., Miller, T.K., & Winston, R.B., Jr. (1980). Toward the professionalization of student affairs. *NASPA Journal, 18*(2), 16-22.

Chambers, C.M. (1981). Foundations of ethical responsibility in higher education administration. In R.H. Stein & M.C. Baca (Eds.), *Professional ethics in university administration* (pp. 1-13). New Directions for Higher Education, (No. 33). San Francisco: Jossey-Bass.

Council for the Advancement of Standards for Student Services/Development Programs [CAS]. (1986). *CAS standards and guidelines for student services/development programs.* Washington, DC: Author.

Council of Student Personnel Associations in Higher Education. [COSPA]. (1975). Student development services in post secondary education. *Journal of College Student Personnel, 16*, 524-28.

Drane, J.F. (1982). Ethics and psychotherapy: A philosophical perspective. In M. Rosenbaum (Ed.), *Ethics and values in psychotherapy.* New York: Free Press.

El-Khawas, E. (1981). Self-regulation: An approach to ethical standards. In R.H. Stein & M.C. Baca (Eds.), *Professional ethics in university administration* (pp. 55-62). New Directions for Higher Education, (No. 33). San Francisco: Jossey-Bass.

Ender, S.C., Winston, R.B., Jr., & Miller, T.K. (1982). Academic advising as student development. In R.B. Winston, Jr., S.C. Ender, & T.K. Miller (Eds.), *Developmental approaches to academic advising* (pp. 3-18). New Directions for Student Services, (No.17). San Francisco: Jossey-Bass.

Fargo, J.M. (1981). Academic chivalry and professional responsibility. In R.H. Stein & M.C. Baca (Eds.), *Professional ethics in university administration* (pp. 63-82). New Directions for Higher Education, (No. 33). San Francisco: Jossey-Bass.

Golightly, C.L. (1971). A philosopher's view of values and ethics. *Personnel and Guidance Journal, 50,* 289-294.

Greenwood, E. (1957). Attributes of a profession. *Social Work, 2,* 45-55.

Hospers, J. (1972). *Human conduct: Problems in ethics.* New York: Harcourt Brace Jovanovich.

Kitchener, K.S. (1985). Ethical principles and ethical decisions in student affairs. In. H.J. Canon & R.D. Brown (Eds.), *Applied ethics in student services* (pp. 17-30). New Directions for Student Services (No.30). San Francisco: Jossey-Bass.

Miller, T.K., & Carpenter, D.S. (1980). Professional preparation for today and tomorrow. In D.G. Creamer (Ed.), *Student development in higher education: Theories, practice, and future directions* (pp. 181-204). Washington, DC: American College Personnel Association.

Miller, T.K., & Prince, J.S. (1976). *The future of student affairs: A guide to student development for tomorrow's higher education.* San Francisco: Jossey-Bass.

National Association of Student Personnel Administrators. [NASPA]. (1960). *Statement of principles and ethical practices of student personnel administrators.* Portland, OR: Author.

National Association of Student Personnel Administrators [NASPA]. (1985). Standards of professional practice. In H.J. Canon & R.D. Brown (Eds.), *Applied ethics in student services* (pp. 99-101). New Directions for Student Services (No.30). San Francisco: Jossey-Bass.

Peterson, J.A. (1970). *Counseling and values: A philosophical examination.* Scranton, PA: International Textbook.

Ross, W.D. (1930). *The right and the good.* Oxford: Clarendon Press.

Saddlemire, G.L. (1980). Professional developments. In U. Delworth, G.R. Hanson, & Associates, *Student services: A handbook for the profession* (pp.25-44). San Francisco: Jossey-Bass.

Stamatakos, L.D. (1981). Student affairs progress toward professionalism: Recommendations for action. *Journal of College Student Personnel, 22,* 105-12, 197-207.

Toulmin, S. (1950). *An examination of place and reason in ethics.* Cambridge: Cambridge University Press.

Trueblood, D.L. (1966). The educational preparation of the college student personnel leader of the future. In G.J. Klopf (Ed.), *College student personnel in the years ahead* (pp. 77-84). Washington, DC: American Personnel and Guidance Association.

Van Hoose, W.H., & Kottler, J.A. (1977). Ethical and legal issues in counseling and psychotherapy. San Francisco: Jossey-Bass.

Wilensky, H.L. (1964). The professionalization of everyone? *American Journal of Sociology, 70,* 137-58.

Winston, R.B., Jr. (1985). A suggested procedure for determining order of authorship in research publications. *Journal of Counseling and Development, 63,* 515-18.

Winston, R.B., Jr., & Dagley, J.C. (1985). Ethical standards statements: Uses and limitations. In H.J. Canon & R.D. Brown (Eds.), *Applied ethics in student services* (pp.49-66). New Directions for Student Services, No. 30. San Francisco: Jossey-Bass.

Wrenn, C.G., (1949). An appraisal of the professional status of personnel work, Part I. In E.G. Williamson (Ed.), *Trends in student personnel work* (pp. 264-79). Minneapolis: University of Minnesota Press.

Wrenn, C.G. (1966). The ethics of counseling. In B. Ard (Ed.), *Counseling and psychotherapy* (pp. 120-32). Palo Alto, CA: Science and Behavior Books.

SUGGESTED READINGS

Baca, M.C., & Stein, R.H. (Eds.). (1983). *Ethical practices and problems in higher education.* Springfield, IL: Thomas.

Canon, H.J. (1989). Guiding standards and principles. In U. Delworth & G.R. Hanson (Eds.). *Student services: A handbook for the profession* (pp. 57-79). (2nd ed.) San Francisco: Jossey-Bass.

Canon, H.J., & Brown, R.D. (Eds.). (1985). *Applied ethics in student services.* New Directions for Student Services (No. 30). San Francisco: Jossey- Bass.

Doromal, Q.S., Jr., & Creamer, D.G. (1988). An evaluation of the ethical judgment scale. *Journal of College Student Development, 29,* 151-57.

Stein, R.H., & Baca, M.C. (Eds.). (1981). *Professional ethics in university administration.* New Directions for Higher Education (No. 33). San Francisco: Jossey-Bass.

Phyllis Mable (M.S.Ed.) has been involved with college students, student affairs programs and services, and higher education for over 25 years and has provided leadership promoting change from student adjustment themes to human development themes. She has held student affairs professional positions over the years including the University of Florida and Virginia Commonwealth University. She is currently the Vice-President for Student Affairs at Longwood College (Virginia). She has co-edited several books dealing with student development, residence education, and student life and is in demand as a speaker at professional meetings. She is the recipient of several prestigious awards including the ACPA Distinguished Service Award.

A past president of the American College Personnel Association, Mable has been active in the Council for the Advancement of Standards for Student Services/Development Programs (CAS) during the past decade and represents the American Association for Counseling and Development on that body. In 1989 she was elected president of CAS.

She holds a B.S. degree from Cornell University and a M.S. in education in College Student Personnel Administration from Indiana University. She also holds a certification from Harvard University Institute for Educational Management.

Theodore K. Miller, Ed.D., is Professor of Counseling and Human Development Services at the Univesity of Georgia in Athens, Georgia in the Division of Counseling, Educational Psychology, and Educational Technology in the College of Education. He is currently the Director of the University of Georgia Southern Association of Colleges and Schools (SACS) Accreditation Reaffirmation Self-Study and is Chairman of the Self-Study Steering Committee. He was president of the Council for The Advancement of Standards for Student Services/Development Programs (CAS) from 1979 to 1989.

CHAPTER 11

STANDARDS OF PROFESSIONAL PRACTICE

Phyllis Mable
Theodore K. Miller

The practice of student affairs can be traced to the earliest days of higher education in America (Leonard, 1956; Rudolph, 1962). Yet both those concerned about and those responsible for personal aspects of student life have had no clearly defined criteria to judge the quality of their efforts and activities through the first three quarters of the 20th Century. As noted in Chapter 8, this lack of minimum professional standards for both the practice and the preparation of its members has limited seriously the establishment of student affairs as a recognized profession (Larson, 1977).

Although a number of authorities have focused attention upon the importance of standards for preparation program accreditation, little attention was paid until recently to standards of professional practice (Penn, 1974). As Penney (1969; 1972) strongly implied, the field of student affairs has lacked congruence and consistency of practice essential to the existence of a profession. Thus, even though the lack of professional standards caused concern, relatively little activity designed to establish standards of practice or preparation for the field had been initiated prior to the 1980s. Recent events have brought an abrupt change to this situation however.

NOMENCLATURE

Certain terms are basic to understanding the concept and application of professional standards. Although some terms occasionally are used interchangeably, the professional practitioner must be able to distinguish their varied meanings and nuances.

Accreditation

Accreditation represents both a concept and a process used throughout postsecondary education. The ***concept of accreditation*** is defined as the formation of voluntary organizations of institutions, practitioners, or educators that encourage and assist institutions or their specialized subunits such as colleges, schools, departments, or programs in evaluating and improving their educational endeavors. These organizations publish the names of institutions or programs that meet or exceed acceptable standards of educational quality.

The ***process of accreditation,*** on the other hand, is defined as a periodic evaluation of the educational activities of an institution or its subunits and is therefore an independent judgment by peers, specialists, or other professionals that determines whether the stated educational mission is being achieved. This process typically involves a concise statement of educational objectives, a self-study to examine the extent to which those objectives have been met, an on-site peer review, and a judgment by the accrediting body. *Accreditation is applied to institutions and educational programs,* not to individuals. Accreditation functions for the benefit of the public as an accounting of the quality of services rendered.

According to the Council on Postsecondary Accreditation (COPA, 1989), the functions of accreditation at the postsecondary level have been and are to

- foster excellence in postsecondary education through the development of uniform national criteria and guidelines for assessing educational effectiveness;

- encourage improvement through continuous self-study and review;

- assure the educational community, the general public, and other agencies or organizations that an institution or program has clearly defined and appropriate objectives, maintains conditions under which there achievement can reasonably be expected, is in fact accomplishing them substantially, and can be expected to continue to do so;

- provide counsel and assistance to established and developing institutions and programs; and

- endeavor to protect institutions against encroachments which might jeopardize their educational effectiveness or academic freedom. (p.4)

Accreditation Standards and Guidelines. Accreditation, when conducted through nongovernmental organizations, provides a major means for determining and fostering standards of quality and integrity. Standards reflect criteria established or adopted by an accrediting body to articulate its expectations of an institution or program. Standards provide a frame of reference or context within which the accreditation process can be implemented. Other terms such as *criteria, requirements,* or *essentials* are sometimes used in lieu of the term *standards.* Because standards reflect requirements, auxiliary verbs *shall* and *must* are used in their wording.

Guidelines are used to explain and amplify standards and frequently provide examples of flexible interpretations that are acceptable to, or even encouraged by, the accrediting body. The auxiliary verbs *should* and *may* are used in interpretive guidelines.

Presently, at least two of six regional accrediting associations have published standards and guidelines related to the practice of student affairs on their member campuses. The Commission on Colleges of the Southern Association of Schools and Colleges (1988) has issued Standard 5.5, *Student Development Services;* The Northwest Association of Schools and Colleges has prepared guidelines for evaluation committee members. In addition, the Association of Independent Colleges and Schools recognizes student services in its standards.

Credentialing

Institutions of higher learning, whether accredited or not, typically issue **credits** upon satisfactory completion of academic or technical work. When the specified number and type of credits are earned, a **diploma, certificate,** or **degree** is granted as evidence of successful mastery of required knowledge and skills. These requirements are based on professional standards of preparation and ethical practice and represent the minimum criteria established for entrance into a particular field or endeavor. Resulting "credentials awarded by institutions gain 'legitimacy' for third parties through their value in the marketplace and through accreditation by nongovernmental institutional and specialized accrediting agencies" (Miller & Boswell, 1979, p. 219). Noteworthy in relation to these factors is the fact that whereas accreditation is applied to institutions and programs, credentialing is applied to individuals.

In addition to institutional endorsements by diplomas and degrees, at least two other major forms of individual endorsement are common to many professions: **certification** and **licensure.** Increasingly, these alternative forms of endorsement are influencing employment practices in institutions of higher learning.

Certification. This type endorsement can take several forms but basically involves a process by which an authorizing agency or organization officially certifies that an individual, voluntarily seeking such recognition, has met certain predetermined qualifications specified by that authorizing body. Typically, the authorizing agency publishes a **registry** of the names and qualifications of those who meet the criteria for certification. In addition to formal academic preparation and supervised practice requirements, satisfactory performance on examinations also may be required. Certification is usually monitored on a regular basis by the authorizing body.

State certification of school teachers, counselors, and administrators are familiar examples of this procedure, although not all certifying agencies are governmentally sponsored or limited to a state or other localized area. Examples of non-governmental agencies that grant certification on the national level are the Commission on Rehabilitation Counselor Certification, the National Academy of Certified Mental Health Counselors, and the National Board of Certified Counselors.

Licensure. Professional licensure is a process by which an agency of government, usually on the state level, grants permission to individuals who meet predetermined qualifications to engage in a specified profession or occupation and/or to use a particular title (for example, counselor, psychologist) in their work. Through licensure, governments legally define and regulate the practice of a variety of professions. Licensure legislation sets standards of training and practice to protect the public from unqualified practitioners and better assures practitioner protection under the law in the application of skills. Licensing typically involves some type of standardized examination procedure and is common in the fields of medicine and law and more recently in the practice of psychology and counseling. In recent years higher education institutions have increasingly included reference to state licensure qualifications as criteria for employment in counseling centers and on counselor education faculties.

Peer Endorsement

In student affairs practice, formal endorsement procedures such as certification and licensure are emphasized much less than endorsement and sponsorship by peers. In many instances it is peer endorsement in the form of letters of reference or interviews with former professors, employers, supervisors, and colleagues that institutions emphasize when selecting new staff members. Building a professional reputation as a knowledgeable and skilled practitioner who works well in situations that require high levels of collaboration and team work may, in many instances, represent one's best professional credential.

FOUNDATIONS OF ACCREDITATION

Higher education exists within the context of a larger community. To be viable, higher education must be responsive to changing social realities. The nongovernmental, voluntary accreditation process organized under the Council on Post-secondary Accreditation (COPA) umbrella is the means by which the U.S. higher education community seeks to assure viability over time. Two critical developments have challenged accreditation and guided its existence in recent years (Thrash, 1979): (1) the reliance of the federal government on nongovernmental accrediting agencies as reliable authorities in determining the eligibility of schools and colleges to participate in federal education assistance programs and (2) the exploding educational universe that has caused higher education to expand its program offerings, missions, and accessibility to nontraditional student populations. Federal government influence has been increasingly obvious since World War II. The Veterans' Readjustment Assistance Act of 1952 (Korean GI Bill) and the parallel establishment of the Division of Eligibility and Agency Evaluation (DEAE) within the U.S. Office of Education brought about a unique triad of two governmental agencies and one nongovernmental entity concerned with the quality of postsecondary education institutions. As the federal government pressed to assure that funds designated for veterans' educations would go to institutions offering quality educational experiences, the DEAE was faced with making judgments about institutional eligibility. The voluntary accrediting agencies became the vehicle for DEAE to carry out its mission. As the years passed, and the federal government increased its involvement in higher education, the importance of a more highly organized accreditation system to assure quality education grew as well.

Nongovernmental Accrediting Agencies

For many decades a number of independent accrediting bodies offered institutional and academic program accreditation with little or no coordination among the groups. In 1949, seven national organizations that accredited educational institutions and programs merged and created the National Commission on Accrediting (NCA). This commission both recognized and monitored the various groups that awarded accreditation to specialized educational programs (for example, academic units such as colleges, and departments). In 1964, the Federation of Regional Accrediting Commissions of Higher Education (FRACHE) was organized to coordinate the work of the postsecondary commissions of the six regional accrediting associations. These two bodies represented, at the national level, both the regional institutional and the programmatic accreditation bodies then in existence. In addition, four other national groups were concerned with the accreditation of over 1000 specialized institutions such as Bible colleges, independent colleges and schools, trade and technical schools, and home-study institutions. The Council on Postsecondary Accreditation (COPA) was organized early in 1975 as the result of a merger of FRACHE, NCA, and the four specialized institutional accrediting groups. With this merger, COPA became the lead agency for establishing policies and practices in postsecondary accreditation (COPA, 1989).

In 1981, COPA reorganized the major accrediting groups into three constituent assemblies. These were (1) the Assembly of Institutional Accrediting Bodies (AIAB), which currently has 14 national and regional accrediting body members; (2) the Assembly of Specialized Accrediting Bodies (ASAB), which numbers 39 program area accrediting agencies; and (3) the Presidents Policy Assembly on Accreditation (PPAA). The latter assembly is a consortium of higher education organizations made up of college and university presidents "which do not sponsor accreditation but which currently participate in COPA: The American Association of Community and Junior Colleges, the American Association of State Colleges and Universities, the American Council on Education, the Association of American Colleges, the Association of American Universities, the Association of Governing Boards, and the National Association of State Universities and Land-Grant Colleges" (COPA, 1989, p. 5).

In 1982 the COPA Board adopted the *Policy Statement on the Role and Value of Accreditation* which outlines the purposes of voluntary accreditation and its inherent value to the public, students, institutions, and professions. Accordingly, accreditation has two fundamental purposes: (1) to assure the quality of the institution or program and (2) to assist institutions or programs to improve. According to COPA (1982), the accreditation process serves professions by both providing opportunity for practitioners to set requirements for those seeking entrance to the field and promoting unity by bringing practitioners, teachers, and students together in activities designed to improve professional preparation and practice.

Accrediting Student Affairs Practice

Accreditation is important to professional student affairs practitioners in that it concerns both their professional practice and formal academic preparation. Currently, however, only two of the regional and one of the specialized institutional accrediting associations have specifically addressed student affairs, student services, or student development in their published accreditation standards. At best a great inconsistency exists in the criteria used to judge the effectiveness and quality of these programs. Lack of uniform standards of practice for accreditation purposes has hindered the professional growth and recognition of student affairs programs throughout the country.

Special Program Accreditation. Several specialty program areas of student affairs practice have established accreditation bodies. The International Association of Counseling Services (Garni et al., 1982) created criteria and implemented accreditation procedures for college student counseling centers, while the Accreditation Association for Ambulatory Health Care and The Joint Commission on Accreditation of Health Care Organizations provide accreditation for college student health centers. This trend for specialized professional interest groups to create specialty area standards and accrediting bodies tends to encourage an already fragmented field of student affairs to become even more segmented, a consequence of which will be territorial conflicts and adversary relationships among its constituent members. Without a concerted effort to establish coordinated accreditation standards and procedures for the field as a whole accreditation on a specialized or programmatic basis will certainly increase. If student affairs is to function as an integrated whole, then efforts must be made to deal with its practice in a holistic fashion. This is a key issue facing student affairs professionals that requires immediate and increased attention. Although the Council for the Advancement of Standards for Student Services/Development Programs (CAS) has developed a comprehensive set of standards (1986), no official or direct CAS tie exists to any of the accrediting agencies currently in existence. One proposed solution to the issue of fragmentation would be to encourage regional accrediting associations to encourage their member institutions to use the *CAS Standards and Guidelines* (1986) as criterion for accreditation self-studies.

Accrediting Preparation Programs

Until recently, a similar problem existed in the area of accreditation of student affairs professional preparation programs. Although the American College Personnel Association adopted a set of preparation standards in 1979, it was not until 1985 that they were recognized and adapted for accreditation purposes by the Council for the Accreditation of Counseling and Related Educational Programs (CACREP). This body, which is a recognized member of COPA's ASAB and is a consortium of divisional associations of the American Association for Counseling and Development (AACD), incorporated the ACPA preparation standards into its criteria for the accreditation of masters level college student affairs preparation programs with emphases in (1) counseling, (2) student development, or (3) administration. Prior to that action, CACREP had been accrediting student affairs preparation programs with the same standards used to accredit programs of counselor education. In 1986 CAS published an adaptation of the ACPA preparation standards and those standards were later used by CACREP when that body revised its accreditation standards (CACREP, 1988). Presently, any student affairs preparation program seeking accreditation through CACREP must meet the preparation standards that have evolved over the past decade via ACPA and CAS.

These accreditation activities bode well for the future of professional student affairs preparation although much work is yet to be accomplished. For instance, through 1988 no preparation programs with an administrative emphasis have been accredited by CACREP. One important variable underlying this is the fact that such programs are usually housed in departments of higher education administration, academic units not typically associated with counseling or counselor education. Because CACREP is primarily a counseling-oriented accrediting agency, higher education administration departments are disinclined to seek them out for accreditation purposes. Likewise, the CACREP leadership by and large does not understand the unique needs or special concerns of higher education administration programs as they differ from programs of counselor education. All of these factors merge to cause consternation and uncertainty in the area of student affairs preparation program accreditation. Though fraught with difficulties, professional practitioners and educators must continue to work on these important issues in the search for a unified accrediting process that can allow for everyone involved to have a voice in its creation and evolution.

PURPOSE AND PRACTICALITY
OF STANDARDS

Meaning and Importance of Standards

Recently, considerable emphasis has been placed on the significance of institutional effectiveness. Accrediting agencies, students and their parents, leaders in the academic community, government officials, potential employers, concerned citizens, and tax-payers are demanding new forms of accountability. In years past, accreditation criteria tended to place greater emphasis upon the *quantity* of resources available within an institution (for example, number of books in the library, amount of classroom space, number of faculty members with terminal degrees) than upon the *quality* of the educational experienced by students. The concept of institutional effectiveness, although still in the process of being defined, focuses more attention upon evaluation and assessment of the quality of educational life than upon the amount of resources available. An example of a representative statement intended to focus attention upon the importance of effectiveness assessment in accreditation is presented in the criteria of one of the six regional accrediting associations.

> It has usually been assumed that, if an institution has certain resources and uses certain processes, effective education will occur. A comprehensive approach to accreditation, however, takes into account not only the resources and processes of education (such as faculty and student qualifications, physical plant, fiscal resources, and

other elements addressed in the *Criteria*) but also the evaluation of the results of education and plans for the improvement of the institution's programs. (Southern Association of Colleges and Schools, 1988, p.13)

As a result of this new emphasis, institutions must define their purposes more clearly, and they must use assessment and evaluation methods to assure themselves and their publics that they are accomplishing what they say they are accomplishing. Therefore, critical for those responsible for implementing the higher education process is to help students acquire the knowledge, skills, attitudes, and values identified in the institution's mission and goals.

Over the years, student affairs and its functional areas have had few published standards to use to guide self-studies and to make recommendations about an institution's effectiveness relevant to its purpose and to student performance and satisfaction. This situation eventually caused student and academic affairs professional associations to join together to collaboratively formulate a set of professional standards of practice. An increased realization of the pressing need for profession-wide standards of practice and preparation has occurred during the past decade, which resulted in a sometimes surprising amount of individual and association involvement to produce professional standards and guidelines. These standards were developed under the auspices of the Council for the Advancement of Standards for Student Services/ Development Programs (CAS) (1986).

The 20 professional associations that hold membership in CAS have publicized these standards, and basically have agreed on the following initiative: high quality student affairs efforts require student services/development programs that enhance each student's opportunity for development in cognitive, affective, and practical ways. Increasing numbers of student affairs practitioners are discovering the value of the standards, with their consistent definitions and their focus on a direction that shapes the student affairs mission within an institution— as a complementary or integral part of the liberal education curriculum, along with general education courses, the academic major, and electives. In the words of Stamatakos, "the task before us is to accept and respond cooperatively, systematically, and vigorously to the constant challenge of becoming a profession" (1981, p. 202). As the expectation for institutional effectiveness and accountability becomes increasingly evident, student affairs will be required to demonstrate that it does in fact make a difference in the learning and performance evidenced by students. Student affairs staff members must substantiate the extent to which students are growing, developing, and becoming involved in and realizing satisfaction from their college experiences.

Institutional effectiveness is realized to the extent that carefully formulated educational goals are achieved, as evidenced in student learning and performance, or an understanding of what students can do with what they know. The CAS *Standards* require an analysis and account of what student affairs contributes to that educational process.

Implications of Standards for the Profession

With deepening economic problems, priorities in higher education may be required to shift from offering many different programs to providing fewer but higher quality programs. As compromises are hammered out between planning and budgeting committees, student affairs programs can and will gain credibility if their leaders clearly articulate the programs' needs, values, and requirements. Given the pecuniary pinch and realignment of priorities that confront all educational institutions, student affairs administrators must be assertive and creative in determining the rightful place of the field in higher education during the coming decades.

The field of student affairs cannot afford to wait for "outsiders" to develop and force upon it unacceptable models for evaluation and assessment. The task and responsibility of its collective associations is to assure the profession that it will be assessed or evaluated on its own merits, not upon others' philosophies or terms (Stamatakos, 1981).

Management of standards for the profession must be regarded as even more important than the standards themselves. Professionals who are competent managers with savvy political sense can fuel the development of the profession by sorting out the more likely winning service and program designs from those that will be predicted to almost certainly fail. By using professional standards for service and program implementation and evaluation, practitioners can open entirely new areas of influence, involvement, and innovation. Professionals who find and foster the standards' intent will develop the capacity to design new student affairs programs that can increase meaning and purpose in students' lives and that will increase productivity in the student affairs services and programs of the Twenty-First Century.

Also, basic to standards of professional practice is the ability and willingness of student affairs practitioners to engage in the continuing self-study processes necessary for institutional effectiveness, student development, and program success. Standards of professional practice support Young's assertion that "colleges and universities will be expected to ask and answer what it is, specifically, that they are about as educational institutions, and how they know they are achieving their objectives" (1979, p. 136). Professionals expect and demand standards that keep their purpose high, preserve hope and honor, and ignite student learning. As applications of the professional standards grow, and as increasing numbers of institutions realize that student affairs programming involves far more than recreation and entertainment, student affairs leaders can increasingly use professional standards to express values that buttress their commitments to student learning. Here is a grand opportunity to marshal leadership, creativity, and energy from a creditable base in order to meet the challenges of shaping student service programs and students' development in the future. If educational excellence is defined as the development of human talent as Astin (1985) has proposed, then institutional effectiveness evaluation that focuses attention upon accurately assessing the developmental outcomes experienced by students must of necessity be developed and implemented.

The success of an institution, the success of student affairs, and the resulting success of the students themselves represent combined efforts, initiatives, and commitments. Goals for student learning, development, and outcomes are vital.

Ultimately, program development and institutional effectiveness rest on two anchor points: (1) the academic knowledge, personal skills, and social values which an institution's leaders desire for students to learn and exhibit as an outcome of matriculation, and (2) the extent to which all components of the institution can muster and marshal their collective resources to make these desires a reality.

The *CAS Standards and Guidelines* are a marvelous vehicle for shaping the influence of student affairs in many areas: mission, program, leadership and management, organization and administration, human resources, funding, facilities, legal responsibilities, equal opportunities and access, affirmative action, campus and community relations, multicultural programs and services, ethics, and evaluation. These standards can contribute to the institution's success in seeking quality in student learning and performance, as well as the enhancement of student development in distinctive ways. An immediate and decisive need is for managing student affairs as it takes its place as part of the liberal education process, but an even more preeminent need is for an ideology that shapes the substantive aspects of student affairs specified by the *CAS Standards.* The student affairs passion for student development may in sum represent simply the human need for being generative and society's need for change that verifies and validates the presence of education in specific value-directed ways.

Note that the *CAS Standards and Guidelines* provide a foundation that can help student affairs to become a significant part of the liberal education process through applying knowledge to life's challenges and concerns; building communities of educational excellence that expect and encourage student learning, development, and involvement; designing programs for students to apply competence to their commitments; focusing attention on educational goals that will bring distinctiveness to both students and student affairs programs; gaining an understanding of the needs of new students and meeting them promptly; and creating a student-centered environment where genuine care and enthusiasm are expected, rewarded, and generated. Nevitt Sanford (1982, P.xxii) said it well when he wrote "intelligence, feeling, emotion, and action can be separated conceptually but no one of them functions independently of the others." Herein lies the challenge for student affairs, a challenge that is inherent in the CAS *Standards and Guidelines* (1986) and the *Self Assessment Guides* (Miller, Thomas, Looney, & Yerian, 1988a). Importantly, these standards have the capacity to help practitioners shape a comprehensive student affairs perspective, one which is relevant to the total institution and which can help generate an environment of care and concern for the population of diverse students who are striving to meet their multiple developmental needs.

Use of Standards

The CAS *Standards* have been widely circulated, and they are frequently on the minds of student affairs leaders who are preparing to respond to the need to implement self-examinations and studies. Chief executive officers, governing boards, accrediting agencies, and state legislators are increasingly expecting and even requiring these studies, and student consumers may soon be demanding them as evidence that institutions are providing their constituents ample opportunity to be successful. These standards speak to the quality of the student services/development programs, to the contributions of these services and programs to student motivation required for shaping and completing educational goals, and to the accountability of student affairs as a part of the liberal education process and the institution's effectiveness. Appropriately used, these standards have great utility to aid student affairs leaders in the areas of program evaluation and program development. An effective accountability procedure that can be implemented in any institution is the use of the standards as a framework for the annual report. By collecting data and documenting, on a continuing basis, the extent to which programs and projects achieve their stated objectives and aid students to accomplish their developmental needs, the annual report can reflect all relevant aspects of a comprehensive self-study. Such an approach saves great amounts of staff time, energy, and hair pulling when time comes to initiate the decennial reaccreditation self-study or otherwise report and document accountability upon demand.

These standards also provide a framework that enables student affairs programs to positively influence student learning and involvement within the academic community. The CAS general standards and related functional area standards and guidelines provide practitioners with both direction and encouragement for helping students attain academic knowledge and skills; for making a positive difference in their social, cultural, and personal development; and for adding value to each student's desire to achieve success in humane and intellectual endeavors.

Fortunately, graduates of many student affairs preparation programs were exposed to the CAS Standards during their courses of study, and they are eager to enter institutions and to use the standards in program evaluation and development. Chief student affairs administrators have received copies of the CAS Standards and Guidelines (1986)—compliments of the American College Testing Program—and are thereby stimulated to charge their staff members to use the standards to implement program development activities. A refreshing level of enthusiasm and commitment exists for designing programs as CAS directs, which often means that goals of programs (functional areas) must be reviewed, reconsidered, and sometimes changed. Program goals, and missions as well, must focus on student outcomes and also on areas that will bring distinction to the institution, and to student affairs as an integral part of the liberal education process. As the CAS Standards are used for program development, imperatively appropriate changes must be made in order for the programs to comply with the standards and, potentially, the guidelines. Student affairs leaders should give a great deal of thought to making their programs distinct in the minds of students, the institution, and the public-at-large. A competitive, distinct advantage has enormous benefits for pride, success, and contribution to student learning and outcomes.

The presence of the CAS Standards significantly affects student affairs programs, as rising productivity and increased excellence combine to enhance the quality of student affairs and to diminish institutional losses from student attrition and budget cuts. As Young (1979) stated, higher education is "moving into a time when institutions, for their own purposes (survival) as well as for socially induced reasons (accountability, consumer information), will engage in a continuing process of self-evaluation" (p. 136). As a result of this process, students will know precisely what to expect from an institution. Communications about services and programs will be increasingly accurate, reliable, and valid according to the goals that guide student learning and outcomes. Therefore, student affairs leaders will be even more responsible for shaping student services and developmenting character (in accordance with the *CAS Standards*) that is clear, distinctive, and purposeful.

The *CAS Standards* were designed so as to encourage student affairs staff members to analyze the effectiveness of their functions on regular and continuing bases. Although the accreditation self-study is crucial, and the *CAS Standards* provide criterion measures for evaluation not previously available, these standards have utility that goes well beyond this purpose alone. These standards can serve as a reliable, credible, and valuable means to measure student affairs' influence on students' development, success, learning, satisfaction, and performance. They also have the capacity to provide an ongoing means to study student affairs in the following ways: to clarify goals related to student outcomes, to collect and analyze information that speaks to student success and outcomes, and to collaborate in an institutional planning process that places student affairs squarely within the institution's primary educational efforts. The *CAS Standards* can be used to guide good planning and effective management efforts. Therefore, the professional standards of practice relate well to regular and continuing data collection that can be used to determine the extent to which the various student affairs functions are accomplishing what they purpose to accomplish, and can contribute much to the analytical resources available for strategic planning initiatives.

Using the Self Assessment Guides

CAS has recently published, under the auspices of the American College Testing Program, *Self Assessment Guides* (Miller et al., 1988a) for the general standards and each of the nineteen functional area standards and guidelines. Each *Guide* states that it "translates the *CAS Standards and Guidelines* (1986) into a format for self-study purposes. By following this *Guide*, an institution can gain an informed perspective on strengths and deficiencies and then plan for program improvement" (p. iii). Those who propose to use the *Guides* must make clear distinctions between the *CAS Standards* and their accompanying guidelines. Likewise, they must realize that simply rating the assessment criteria in the *Guides* is inadequate for comprehensive self-study purposes. In addition, the self-study process requires relevant documents and related materials be collected that demonstrate compliance with the standards prior to considerations about any program changes or improvements. The self-study part of each *Guide* is presented in a very usable rating and worksheet format that is related clearly and directly to the standards under consideration. The *Self Assessment Guides* provide criterion measures for each of the standards' component parts which allows users to be assured that all specifics included in the standards are taken into account when implementing self-study activities.

The worksheet format includes several sections that enable individuals, staff member groups, and assessment committees to study the various student services and development programs with clarity, substance, and vision. These sub-sections include space for (1) identifying any *CAS Guidelines* to be assessed as an institutional criterion for the self-study, (2) identifying documents that support criterion measure ratings, (3) listing discrepancies between the standards and current practice, (4) listing actions required for compliance, and (5) listing actions that will enhance the program to levels beyond those called for in the standards.

The Self Assessment

The *Self Assessment Guides* (Miller et al., 1988a) provide examples of materials that are necessary for giving credence to evaluative judgments. These include publications (for example, mission statements, catalogs, handbooks, staff manuals, annual reports); descriptions of existing programs and interventions (such as, Career Development Center, alcohol awareness workshop, text anxiety reduction groups, new student orientation, Advising Center); relevant institutional and other data (for example, student profiles, quantitative data; student needs assessment; theory-based assessments; and state, regional, and national data for comparisons); program evaluation data (such as, surveys, ratings, interviews, reports, summaries); self-study initiated research and evaluation data (for instance, student surveys, ratings, follow-ups, and theory-based research studies designed to evaluate various aspects of the program/ department/division using *CAS Standards* as measurement criteria; and resources, job descriptions, performance evaluations, budgets, organizational charts, and similar documents. The *Self Assessment Guides* provide a valuable structure for guiding activity in both creative and critical ways. Professionals will be challenged to think, to learn, and to change as the worksheet format is used along with documentation and assessment in the self-study activity.

Basically, the *Self Assessment Guides* were prepared for evaluating programs using the *CAS Standards*. These activities include gathering evidence about the effectiveness of the student affairs functional areas and rating the assessment criteria in terms of compliance. The *Guides* provide ways to judge levels of student affairs initiative and involvement within the institutional learning environment. Throughout the *Guides* and the standards themselves, student affairs is expected to know itself and to be consistent and persistent in its professional practice. Once again, understanding the student affairs functional areas and evaluating their effectiveness based on standards, evidence, and vision are essential to student affairs' participation in the institution's liberal education effort. The guides will stimulate and shape improvements in student services and development programs which in turn will raise the levels of student involvement, learning, and satisfaction. Stated simply, the *Guides* provide a very direct way to determine the effectiveness of student affairs programs and practice.

In effect, the primary purposes of the self-study process are (1) to ask important questions about student affairs and its place in the institution; (2) to review in depth some meaningful information related to these questions; and (3) to use the information to develop follow-up plans designed to make corrective changes required for achieving compliance with the standards and for other program enhancements. Using the *Self Assessment Guides* with strong institutional and student affairs involvement should create a collective and continuing initiative to determine how effectively student affairs is meeting its goals, influencing the institution, and consequently, improving the teaching/learning effort with students, particularly in areas that contribute richly to student performance and satisfaction. The final section of this chapter focuses attention upon the activities and procdures common to applying the self-study process in practice.

SELF-STUDY APPLICATIONS

CAS Standards and Guidelines

Organization. A total of 20 *CAS Self Assessment Guides* exist, 19 of which represent functional areas of practice and one, the Division Level, which is based upon the *CAS General Standards* only. The 19 functional areas of practice for which both standards and assessment guides have been developed include (1) Academic Advising, (2) Admission Programs and Services, (3) Career Planning and Placement, (4) College Unions, (5) Commuter Student Programs and Services, (6) Counseling Services, (7) Disabled Student Services, (8) Fraternity and Sorority Advising, (9) Housing and Residential Life Programs, (10) Judicial Programs and Services, (11) Learning Assistance Programs, (12) Minority Student Programs and Services, (13) Recreational Sports, (14) Religious Programs, (15) Research and Evaluation, (16) Student Activities, (17) Student Orientation Programs, and (18) Women Student Programs and Services; and (19) Alcohol and Other Drug Programs.

Each set of CAS functional area standards and guidelines is organized into 13 component parts. These are (1) Mission, (2) Program, (3) Leadership and Management, (4) Organization and Administration, (5) Human Resources, (6) Funding, (7) Facilities, (8) Legal Responsibilities, (9) Equal Opportunity, Access, and Affirmative Action, (10) Campus and Community Relations, (11) Multi-Cultural Programs and Services, (12) Ethics, and (13) Evaluation.

From an operational perspective, these professional standards and guidelines cover most of the functional areas common to student services and student development programs on most college campuses and include the primary component parts that go to make up such programs. This combination of functional areas and component parts have great utility for accomplishing the self assessment process, whether for program development or institutional accreditation purposes.

Interpreting the Standards and Guidelines. A definitive difference exists between professional standards and guidelines. A **standard** is viewed as an essential element expected of any institution and its student services and student development programs. For purposes of the CAS Standards, all standards are printed in **bold type** and are represented by the auxiliary verbs **must** and **shall.** In other words, any program that is in compliance with the standards is able to show evidence of its ability to meet or exceed the expectations implicit within the standards.

Guidelines, on the other hand, are designed to amplify and enhance the standards and should be viewed as examples and suggestions that are consistent with quality professional practice, but which exceed the expectations implicit within the standards. For purposes of the CAS Standards and Guidelines, all guidelines are printed in regular type and are represented by the auxiliary verbs should and may. In the broadest sense, the CAS professional standards are viewed as being the minimal expectations for any student service or student development program of practice whereas the guidelines are viewed as suggestions and recommendations which will, if implemented, raise the program to even higher levels of compliance and quality.

Applying the CAS Self Assessment Guides

Organization of the Guides. Self Assessment Guides have been developed for each of the functional areas recognized in the CAS Standards and Guidelines. An introduction section explains how the Guide is organized and how to use it for self-study purposes. The Guide itself is presented in a workbook format with space provided for inserting ratings, identifying guidelines that are to be assessed as institutional criteria for self-study purposes, documentation information to support the ratings, and statements describing observed discrepancies and corrective actions needed. The *Guides* are organized on the bases of the 13 component parts previously identified. Within this 13 part structure, more than 80 assessment criterion statements are presented, each of which can be used by raters to judge the extent to which an institution and its programs are in compliance with a particular segment of a given standard. At the close of the self assessment workbook, space if provided for assessors to present a statement of the overall action needed to bring the program into compliance with the standards and/or enhance the capacity of the program to accomplish its purposes to an even greater extent. This is referred to as the **Follow-Up Action Plan** and is an important consideration for any self-study.

With the foregoing as a base, readers may wish to work through the actual steps for using the *Self Assessment Guides* in preparation for initiating an actual self-study. For students in training, implementation of the self assessment process can greatly enhance any student services or student development practicum or internship experience. For beginning professionals entering their first professional position, such a self-study approach will give them not only an excellent understanding of the program(s) with which they will be working, but an in depth understanding as well of the types of actions required to make the institution's program(s) even more viable to the benefit of the students served. For those wishing a more definitive description of how to use the *Self Assessment Guides*, Yerian (1989) has developed a training manual that goes into considerable detail on the specifics involved.

A Self-study Example. Let us assume that one is assigned the task of initiating a comprehensive self-study of the student activities program on campus. How might one proceed? First of all, it would be incumbent upon the evaluator to determine two things: (1) what are the primary purposes of the program as to its role, function, and mission within the institution? and (2) what criterion measures exist to judge the extent to which the program is accomplishing its goals? In the past the probability was great that one or both of those questions would be difficult if not impossible to answer in a ready fashion for even if a written mission statement existed, the standards on which to make judgments were extremely difficult to determine and even more ambiguous to interpret. Program evaluation has been made much simpler with the establishment of the *CAS Standards and Guidelines,* for now the criterion measures on which judgments can be made are easily accessible to professionals at all operational levels.

The very first assessment criterion statement presented in the *CAS Student Activities Standards Self Assessment Guide* (Miller et al., 1988b, p.1) is stated as follows:

Part 1: Mission

> 1.1 There exists a well developed, written set of student activities program goals that are consistent with the stated mission of the institution.

This assessment criterion statement is based on the *Student Activities Standards and Guidelines* presented in the document's appendix. An excerpt from those standards upon which the criterion statement is based reads as follows:

> The institution and its student activities program must develop, review, and disseminate regularly their own specific goals for student services/development, which must be consistent with the nature and goals of the institution and with the standards in this document. (p. 21)

Note that the standard herein quoted does not specify the specific nature or direction of the mission, but rather indicates that each institution's student activities program must have a statement of purpose based on specific program goals. Further, the standard requires that such a mission statement must be consistent with that of the institution in which the program is housed. Also note that the stated standard includes requirements that exceed criterion Statement 1.1. Therefore, three additional criterion statements are designed to deal with the standard in total. These are

> 1.2 Student activities has a well developed, written set of goals that are consistent with the stated student services/development goals of the institution.

1.3 Student activities goal statements are reviewed and disseminated on a regular basis.

1.4 Student activities goals and objectives are consistent with the CAS Standards.

In effect, because of the comprehensive nature of the standard involved, it required four separate criterion statements to incorporate all aspects of that single standard statement for evaluation purposes. The *Self Assessment Guide,* through this approach to covering all aspects of every standard, presents each criterion measure for the sole purpose of judging one single observable part of the standard. Through this detailed approach, the over 80 criterion statements involved assure that each part of each standard can be observed separately and adequately judged on its own merits. Each criterion measure is designed to be rated on a five point scale by one or more evaluators who are asked to judge the extent to which the program is in compliance with that particular criterion. A rating of 1 would indicate that the program is in no way in compliance with that part of the standard while a rating of 5 indicates that the program is presently in or even exceeds compliance. Ratings of 2, 3, and 4 reflect judgments that the program is somewhere between noncompliance and compliance with a particular standard.

Note that the assessment criterion statements are not concerned directly with the guidelines which are published in conjunction with the standards. This does not mean that the guidelines are unimportant, but it does indicate that for evaluation purposes concerned with compliance, the guidelines are explanation and amplification as opposed to substance. However, a particular program may wish to view one or more of the guideline statements as a criterion measure for the self-study. For example, Part 2, PROGRAM of the student activities standards and guidelines includes a guideline statement that reads: "The development of an activities program should be based on a regularly scheduled assessment of student needs" (p. 21). Because this statement is printed in regular type and uses the auxiliary verb *should* rather than *must,* it becomes a criterion measure only if and when someone in authority concerning the self assessment process decides that it should be so utilized. Assuming such a decision has been made, the guideline statement is treated as if it were a standard statement with the auxiliary verb *should* being changed to *must* for judgment purposes. The statement might then be reworded to read: *Each and every student activities program offered is based on the most recent assessment of students' needs.* This statement would then be written in the space provided immediately following assessment criterion 2.15 on page 4 of the *Self Assessment Guide* and treated as any other assessment criterion statement for rating purposes.

Before making final rating judgments concerning the various assessment criterion statements, the available documentation that will support the ratings as well as provide a rationale for them must be identified. The evaluative evidence and related support documents must be clearly identified and made available to those who will complete the rating prior to the rating process itself. The 1.1 assessment criterion measure example previously noted requires that a "well developed, written set of student activities program goals" be in existence. This implies a formal statement of some type that defines and describes the goals, objectives purpose, and mission of this institution's student activities program at this point in time. Such a statement may possibly be found in the institution's published catalog, or in its student handbook, or in the student activities program's policies and procedures manual, or in a drawer of the program director's desk. On the other hand, it may not be found at all and furthermore a question may be raised as to whether such a statement was ever in existence. The documenting requirement reflects the need to be accountable and the ability to support, with tangible evidence, that which is called for in the standards.

If a mission statement cannot be found, either because it does not exist or because no one knows where it can be located, no clear way would exist to support the proposition that the program was in compliance with this particular standard. Even if a purpose statement is available and printed in an institutional publication, that fact alone does not reflect compliance with the standard. Several possible limitations may be in evidence as well, such as the statement may be considerably out of date, or it may be out of sync with the institution's statement of purpose, or it may be limited in scope, or it may be known to only a few, or any one of many other factors that limit its use and effectiveness. In other words, the quality of the evidence used to document a particular criterion measure is an important consideration when it comes to making judgments about compliance. If, after careful review, what clearly appears is that the standard is not being met, whether in fact or in spirit, then those responsible for doing the ratings need to note the discrepancies found between actual program practice and the stated assessment criteria that represent standards of good practice. If discrepancies concerning goal statements are found to exist, they should be listed in the space provided on page 2 or expanded elsewhere. What has been accomplished to this point is determination of the fact that the program does not, does partially, or does fully meet the required level of practice denoted in the standards. At this point the judgment process should be complete and a rating made on the criterion measures that reflect the particular standard under consideration.

If discrepancies between current program practice and the written standards are not found to exist, then no actions will be required for achieving compliance. On the other hand, if discrepancies are noted, actions are to be identified that will be required to bring the program into compliance. For instance, assume that a program mission statement is found, but that it is woefully out of date and has not been reviewed for several years. What can be done to overcome this discrepancy between the program and the standards? Several actions may be possible that could be initiated to deal with such contingencies. Actions deemed necessary to overcome the noted discrepancies can be listed in the space provided in the *Self Assessment Guide* (p. 2). Examples of such actions include establishing a committee to study the current statement, revise it as necessary, and initiate a campus-wide review process for the revised statement. The bases for such actions are a direct consequence of the raters' ability to identify and obtain appropriate documentation, the evaluative evidence made available, and the competence of those responsible to interpret that evidence objectively and accurately.

Even though the judgment might be that the program is in compliance with standards, often additional actions can be taken to enhance the program even more. In our example, such actions might be to increase the regularity of initiating the program mission review or to expand the number of constituent groups provided opportunity to review the goal statements. These and other enhancement type action proposals may be written in the space provided in the *Guide* (p.2).

Obviously, a comprehensive self assessment process requires considerable time and campus resources. The example presented outlined the procedures needed to evaluate one standard statement and only one of four assessment criterion measures used to evaluate that standard. This standard and criterion measure is actually simpler than many to evaluate because no data are necessary to collect in addition to documentation that currently exists. Many of the other student activities standards focus attention upon issues and concerns that will require additional data collection procedures to be implemented. For instance, assessment criterion statement 11.3 of Part 11: MULTI-CULTURAL PROGRAMS AND SERVICES (p.13) focuses attention on an area that will very likely require additional data that is not currently available to evaluate. This assessment criterion statement reads as follows:

> 11.3 Student activities assists minority students to identify, prioritize, and meet their unique educational and developmental needs.

Would raters be able to go to a current data base or published document to evaluate this statement in an objective fashion? Not very likely. Evaluation of this criterion will almost certainly require some careful data collection, probably both quantitative and qualitative in nature. What, if any, programs currently exist that have the capacity, let alone the purpose, to assist minority students accomplish their unique educational and developmental needs? What are those needs? How have they been determined? What special initiatives are currently operative within the student activities program designed for particular minority student populations? How many different minority groups have been identified as existing on campus and how many students have been identified as belonging to each particular group? In many instances an accurate rating would necessitate initiating some basic data collection procedures to determine the current status of the populations under consideration, let alone their particular needs. Perhaps accurate information could be obtained from campus data bases on the number of African-American, Native American, and international students on campus; but what about the nontraditional aged students, the returning students, the single parent students, or students with homosexual preferences? With the increasing diversity evident in institutions of higher learning throughout the country comes increased complexity when it comes to even identifying the various unique cultures and heritages involved. Consequently, those responsible for guiding student activities and other student affairs' assessment initiatives may need to obtain data not only from currently available data bases and other campus resources, but also from special self-study initiated research and evaluation data collection processes as well. These data may come from current and former student surveys, ratings, and follow-ups as well as theory-based research studies designed to evaluate various aspects of the program using CAS Standards as measurement criteria. Perhaps the "bottom line" in self-study documentation is that no self-study is complete without relevant data and related documentation to support rater judgments. A basic characteristic of the self-study process is that it typically requires the collection of additional data.

Upon completing a comprehensive evaluation of the program, the whole thing must be brought into focus by creating a self-study follow-up action plan. Such a plan takes into account all aspects of the self-study and is based on three of its primary outcomes. These are (1) the self-study identified areas of program excellence, (2) the actions required to overcome the discrepancies judged to exist between the program as practiced and the standards' criterion measures, and (3) the voluntary actions proposed to enhance the program beyond actions required for compliance. Using these three outcomes as a foundation, the follow-up action plan is designed to initiate and implement the changes required to bring the program into compliance with the standards and to strengthen it beyond compliance. Such a plan will prioritize the desired actions so that adequate and appropriate resources can be brought to bear, establish a time schedule for bringing about the required changes, identify responsible parties to complete the action tasks, and ascertain the criteria to be used to evaluate whether the changes are actually accomplished. Once the follow-up action plan is completed it will very likely be time to begin the self-study process all over again as a normal part of the natural recycling process common to all higher education organizational development and change.

REFERENCES

American College Personnel Association. (1979). *Standards for the preparation of counselors and college student affairs specialists at the masters degree level.* Washington, DC: Author.

Astin, A.W. (1985). *Achieving educational excellence: A critical assessment of priorities and practices in higher education.* San Francisco: Jossey-Bass.

CACREP (1985). *Accreditation procedures manual and application for counseling and related educational programs* (rev. ed.). Alexandria, VA: Council for the Accreditation of Counseling and Related Educational Programs.

CACREP (1988). *Accreditation procedures manual and application.* Alexandria, VA: Council for the Accreditation of Counseling and Related Educational Programs.

CAS (1986). *CAS Standards and guidelines for student services/development programs.* Washington, DC: Council for the Advancement of Standards for Student Services/Development Programs.

Council on Postsecondary Accreditation. (COPA) (1982). *Policy statement on the role and value of accreditation.* Washington, DC: Author.

Council on Postsecondary Accreditation. (COPA) (1989). *The COPA Handbook.* Washington, DC: Author.

Garni, K., Gelwick, B.P., Lamb, D.H., McKinley, D.L., Schoenberg, B.M., Simono, R.B., Smith, J.E., Wierson, P.W., & Wrenn, R.L. (1982, October). Accreditation guidelines for university and college counseling services. *Personnel and Guidance Journal, 61,* 116-121.

Larson, N.S. (1977). *The rise of professionalism: A sociological analysis.* Berkeley: University of California Press.

Leonard, E. (1956). *Origins of personnel services in American higher education.* Minneapolis: University of Minnesota Press.

Miller, J.W., & Boswell, L.E. (1979). Accreditation assessment, and the credentialing of educational accomplishment. *Journal of Higher Education, 50,* 219-25.

Miller, T.K., Thomas, W.L., Looney, S.C., & Yerian, J. (1988a). *CAS self assessment guides.* Washington, DC: Council for the Advancement of Standards for Student Services/Development Programs.

Miller, T.K., Thomas, W.L., Looney, S.C., & Yerian, J. (1988b). *Student activities self assessment guide.* Washington, DC: Council for the Advancement of Standards for Student Services/Development Programs.

Penn, J.R. (1974). Professional accreditation: A key to excellence. *Journal of College Student Personnel, 15,* 257-9.

Penney, J.F. (1969). Student personnel work: A profession stillborn. *Personnel and Guidance Journal, 47,* 958-62.

Penney, J.F. (1972). *Perspective and challenge in college personnel work.* Springfield, IL: Charles C. Thomas.

Rudolph, F. (1962). *The American college and university: A history.* New York: Random House.

Sanford, N. (1982). Foreword. In J.M. Whitely, and Associates. *Character development in college students* (xxii). Schenectady, NY: Character Research Press in association with the American College Personnel Association.

Southern Association of Colleges and Schools. (1988). *Criteria for accreditation* (rev. 5th ed.). Atlanta: Author.

Stamatakos, L.C. (1981). Student affairs progress toward professionalism: Recommendations for action (part 2). *Journal of College Student Personnel, 22,* 197-207.

Thrash, P.A. (1979). Accreditation: A perspective. *Journal of Higher Education, 50,* 115-20.

Yerian, J.M. (1989). *Putting the CAS standards to work: Training manual for the CAS self assessment guides.* Washington, DC: Council for the Advancement of Standards for Student Services/Development Programs.

Young, K.E. (1979). New pressures on accreditation. *Journal of Higher Education, 50,* 132-144.

SUGGESTED READINGS

Banta, T.W. (Ed.).(1988). *Implementing outcomes asessment; Promise and perils.* New Directors for Institutional Research, (No. 59). San Francisco: Jossey-Bass.

Council on Postsecondary Accreditation (1986). *A guide to COPA recognized accrediting bodies.* Washington, DC: Author.

Ewell, P. T., & Lisensky, R. P. (1988). *Assessing institutional effectiveness: Redirecting the self-study process.* Washington, DC: The Consortium for the Advancement of Private Higher Education.

Jacobi, M., Astin, A., and Ayala, F., Jr. (1987). College student outcomes asessment: A talent development perspective. *ASHE-ERIC Higher Education Report No. 7.* Washington, DC: Association for the Study of Higher Education.

Kells, H. R. (1983). *Self-study processes: A guide for postsecondary institutions.* New York: American Council on Education and Macmillan.

Thrash, P. A. (Ed.). (1979). *Journal of Higher Education* (whole issue), *50,* 115-232.

Yerian, J. M. (1989). *Putting the CAS standards to work: Training manual for the CAS self asessment guides.* Washington, DC: Council for the Advancement of Standards for Student Services/Development Programs.

Young, K. E., Chambers, C. M., Kells, H. R., & Associates. (1983). *Understanding accreditation: Contemporary perspectives on issues and practices in evaluating educational quality.* San Francisco: Jossey-Bass.

Donald D. Gehring, Ed.D., is Professor of Higher Education at the University of Louisville. He was awarded the B.S. degree in industrial management from Georgia Institute of Technology, the M.Ed. in mathematics education from Emory University, and was the first graduate of the doctoral program in higher education at the University of Georgia. Dr. Gehring has also completed post doctoral study in adult education at the University of Georgia.

He has held numerous administrative positions in higher education including Director of Housing, Assistant to the Dean of Men, and Dean of Student Development. He has authored numerous articles and chapters on legal issues. Currently, he edits all state higher education cases for the *School Law Reporter* and serves as Co-Editor of *The College Student and the Courts.* Dr. Gehring was cited by NASPA for his outstanding contribution to research and literature in 1985 and received the Mel Hardee Award for Outstanding Service to the Student Affairs Profession in 1987 from the Southern Association of College Student Affairs.

Chapter 12

LEGAL ISSUES IN THE ADMINISTRATION OF STUDENT AFFAIRS

Donald D. Gehring

WHY STUDY LEGAL ISSUES?

Student affairs professionals must have a basic understanding of the law as it affects their relationships with students. Programs, policies, and practices that are well grounded in developmental theory, but fail to take into consideration legal rights of students can result in personal liability suits and create adversarial relationships with students.*

Student affairs professionals need not be lawyers, but an understanding of the legal aspects of their work and their relationships to students can be helpful. They will be better able to recognize circumstances and situations that raise legal questions and that need to be brought to the attention of the institution's counsel. Because these lawyers are not usually familiar with every policy or practice of the institution, they

---

*Appendix B, An Introduction to Legal Research, provides an explanation of how to read legal citations and to locate and use legal sources in research.

appreciate administrators who can spot the warning flags and raise legal questions with them before an action is taken that could be filled with potential liability.

Another reason for studying legal issues is that administrators need to consider students' basic rights as they develop institutional policies, procedures, and practices. Student affairs can assist in educating and sensitizing other policy groups on campus to the rights and responsibilities of students. This may even be an area in which student affairs professionals, by exhibiting expertise where faculty need help, may gain recognition from the faculty. Interpreting the legal rationale underlying institutional policy to the college community and external constituents also can be facilitated by a basic knowledge of the law. It is not unusual for policies to be called into question by faculty, other administrators, trustees, and external constituents. The student affairs administrator can respond to the legitimate concerns of other members of the community.

One of the most important reasons for understanding legal relationships that exist between the institution and the student, and knowing the legal rights and responsibilities of each is that the student affairs professional is in a better position to provide students the information they need to make decisions. Developmentally, young adult college students are at a period where they are confronting a whole series of questions concerning values, relationships to others, and careers. These questions must be answered in the context of a society that affords certain rights and imposes certain responsibilities. However, most students are not taught these concepts. The student affairs staff member has an excellent opportunity to provide developmental education in this respect.

Finally, the student affairs professional has a responsibility to learn the basic legal aspects of the profession in order to guard against potential liability. This responsibility is not only to protect the individual, but also to protect the institution as one's employer.

THE STUDENT-INSTITUTION RELATIONSHIP: PUBLIC v. PRIVATE

Relationships students have with institutions define individual rights. Thus, it is imperative for student affairs professionals to understand various legal relationships that exist between students and the institutions they attend. These relationships are determined by the facts and circumstances of each situation, but generally can be classified as constitutional, statutory, and contractual.

Public Colleges and the Constitution

The Constitution of the United States provides in its amendments certain rights that guarantee citizens protection against certain actions by the government or its agencies. Most state constitutions provide similar protections. State supported colleges and universities are agencies of the government and, therefore, students have a constitutional relationship to these institutions. This means that in its dealings with students, a public college or university must afford the rights guaranteed under the federal and state constitutions. While that may not be very revolutionary, it has been accepted practice only for the past thirty years *(Dixon v. Alabama State Board of Education)*. Prior to that time, colleges and universities generally took the attitude that students only had the rights that the institution gave them. If students did not agree, then they were free to attend another institution. Those days have passed, and the United States Supreme Court has decided that students do not shed their constitutional rights when they enter a college *(Tinker v. Des Moines)*.

Private Colleges and Contracts

Students attending private institutions, however, do not enjoy protections of the Constitution in their relationships with colleges and universities. The Constitution only protects citizens against actions by the government or its agencies but "erects no shield against purely private conduct" *(Shelly v. Kraemer)*. If a private institution is found to be closely linked to the state, then it could be required to provide constitutional guarantees. This concept of a private institution being involved in "state action" has seldom been applied to a private college by the courts. Examples of factors that have been used in unsuccessful attempts to show that private institutions have been engaged in state action include receipt of state money that did not constitute a significant proportion of operating funds *(Torres v. Puerto Rico Junior College)*; receipt of federal funds *(Grossner v. Trustees of Columbia University)*; contracts with the state *(Powe v. Miles)*; tax exempt status *(Browns v. Mitchell)*; serving a public function *(Counts v. Voorhees College)*; being chartered by the state and being granted powers of eminent domain *(Blackburn v. Fisk University)*; use of local police as campus security *(Robinson v. Davis)*; state approval of courses *(Rowe v. Chandler)*; and state accreditation *(Berrios v. Inter American University)*. The Supreme Court has said that only by "sifting facts and weighing circumstances" can the imperceptible involvement of the state in the affairs of a private institution be determined *(Burton v. Wilmington Parking Authority)*. Thus, "state action" is very elusive and will be determined by the facts of each case. Courts, however, have found state action in business involving racial discrimination *(Hammond v. Tampa)*. Although private institutions are not required to provide constitutional safeguards for students, it seems antithetical to the purpose of a liberal education to deny such rights. Only where religious tenets would preclude granting constitutional rights should they be denied.

CONSTITUTIONAL PARAMETERS

The constitutional relationship that students have with their institutions emerges in many student affairs functions. The relationship is given expression for students primarily as a result of three constitutional amendments—the First, Fourth, and Fourteenth. Courts have provided a series of decisions giving guidance to the administrator in the application of each of these amendments on the campus.

First Amendment

The First Amendment includes several clauses that directly affect the operation of various student development programs. As stated in the Amendment:

> Congress shall make no laws respecting the establishment of religion or prohibiting the free exercise thereof; or abridging the freedom of speech or of the press; or the right of the

people peaceably to assemble; and to petition the Government
for a redress of grievances.

The first two clauses are generally referred to as the Establishment Clause and the Free Exercise Clause. Taken together, they constitute the concept of separation of church and state so fundamental to this country's social system.

Separation of Church and State. In higher education, the concept of separation of church and state applies to a whole range of internal and external activities. The Supreme Court has supplied a test to serve as a guide in determining if particular activities or actions violate the separation concept. The test seeks to ascertain whether the law, program, policy, or practice (1) reflects a clearly secular legislative purpose; (2) has a primary effect that neither advances nor inhibits religion; and (3) avoids excessive government entanglement with religion *(Lemon v. Kurtzman)*. Most often the test is applied to situations in which state or federal financial aid is being provided to private, church related institutions or to the students who attend them. Where such financial assistance is not used for sectarian purposes and does not violate other specific provisions of state or federal constitutions, courts have found the aid programs to be permissible *(Tilton v. Richardson; Roemer v. Board of Public Works;* and *Americans United v. Rogers)*.

Financial assistance programs are not the only activities affected by the concept of separation of church and state. The use of state college facilities by religious groups has also been litigated, but with differing results. In Delaware the state supreme court held a university prohibition against the use of a residence hall lounge for religious services to violate the free exercise clause *(University of Delaware v. Keegan)*. A similar university prohibition at the University of Missouri-Kansas City was upheld by a federal district court, but reversed on appeal *(Chess v. Widmar)*. The Supreme Court has agreed to hear this controversy. Campus regulations of this type should be reviewed thoroughly by institutional counsel. Whether to permit the distribution of religious material on campus is another issue that is affected by the Establishment Clause. Recently, Ohio State University was temporarily enjoined from restricting the distribution of a religiously oriented publication on its campus *(Solid Rock Foundation v. Ohio State University).*

Speech and Expression. The First Amendment prohibition against abridging freedom of speech or press can become an issue in a variety of student development programs. Campus lecture series, student newspapers and other media, individuals who speak out on topics of interest, and groups banded together to advocate a particular position are all activities protected by the First Amendment. While no absolute right exists to engage in such activities, once an institution opens its doors to one group, establishes a newspaper, or provides a forum for one individual, then all others must be treated under constitutionally valid principles. Institutions may, however, impose reasonable time, place and manner restrictions on the exercise of First Amendment rights.

One constitutional principle that applies to speech, expression, or advocacy is definite—such occasions may not be regulated based upon the content of the message. The editor of the student newspaper cannot be terminated simply because the administration does not like the editorials. Students cannot, under the First Amendment, be denied the right to invite controversial speakers based on the fact that the administration does not like what the speakers will say or have said, or on their political or idealogical positions. The same principle is also true for other student media and student organizations. In one instance a graduate student was suspended from a public university for distributing a newspaper on campus that included a picture of policemen raping the Statue of Liberty, the Goddess of Justice, and which also contained allegedly obscene language. The basis for the suspension was violation of a university rule prohibiting indecent conduct or speech. The United States Supreme Court, however, noted that while public institutions are free to enforce reasonable rules governing student conduct consistent with their mission, they "are not enclaves immune from the sweep of the First Amendment" *(Papish v. Board of Curators of University of Missouri).* The Supreme Court further pointed out "that the mere dissemination of ideas—no matter how offensive to good taste—on a state university campus may not be shut off in the name alone of 'conventions of decency.'" The student was dismissed because of disapproved "content" of the publication, and such action violated rights guaranteed by the First Amendment.

No absolute rights exist, and if an expression in any form, including symbolic expression, would "materially and substantially disrupt the work and discipline of the school," present a clear and present danger, or exhort others to imminent violence, only then may the expression be regulated (*Tinker v. Des Moines*). However, those attempting to regulate expression have a heavy burden to show convincing evidence that a danger exists. The mere speculation that the expression will present danger is not enough. A Federal District Court upheld the disciplining of one student who spoke to a large gathering of his classmates urging them to make it "costly" for the university to erect a particular fence. The court said that "utterances in a context of violence, involving a definite and present danger can lose [their] significance as an appeal to reason and become part of an instrument of force . . . unprotected by the Constitution" (*Siegel v. Regents of the University of California*).

Expression which is symbolic is also protected under the First Amendment. In recent years, students have erected shanties on their campuses to protest the South African policy of apartheid and their universities' investments in that country. Courts have consistently found these shanties to come within the scope of protected First Amendment activity (*University of Utah Students Against Apartheid v. Peterson* and *Students Against Apartheid Coalition v. O'Neil I & II*). Institutions have, however, been permitted to impose reasonable time, place, and manner restrictions on the erection of these shanties, but those restrictions are only valid " . . . provided that they are justified without reference to the content of the regulated speech, that they are narrowly tailored to serve a significant governmental interest, and that they leave open ample, alternative channels for communication of the information" (*Students Against Apartheid Coalition v. O'Neil I*).

Student Organizations. "While the freedom of association is not explicitly set out in the [First] Amendment, it has long been held to be implicit in the freedoms of speech, assembly, and petition. No doubt denial of official recognition, without justification, to college organizations burdens or abridges that associational right" *(Student Coalition v. Austin Peay State University)*. With this statement, a federal district court held invalid a decision of a university to deny recognition to a group organized to promote gay rights. Student organizations, deriving their right of association from the First Amendment, are protected in ways similar to those already mentioned. While no absolute right exists to be granted official recognition, once one organization has been so recognized or registered all others must be accorded similar privileges under constitutionally valid principles. Official registration or recognition, however, does not mean that the organization gains any new rights *(National Strike Information v. Brandeis)* nor that the institution takes on any new responsibilities to assist the organization in exercising its constitutional rights. The Fourth Circuit Court of Appeals noted this principle when the student chapter of the Maryland Public Interest Research Group, a recognized campus organization challenged the university policy of withholding activity funds from organizations that the policy violated their First Amendment rights, but the court said, "there is no affirmative commandment upon the university to activate Mary Pirg's exercise of First Amendment guarantees; the only commandment is not to infringe there enjoyment" *(Maryland Public Interest Research Group v. Elkins)*.

An institution cannot withhold recognition simply because it disagrees with the organization's philosophy. That would be a type of impermissible censorship *(Healy v. James)*. An institution may, however, require the organizaiton to provide a statement of purposes, names of officers, and an assurance that the group will comply with reasonable and valid rules of the college *(Eisen v. Regents; Merkey v. Board of Regents)*. The Supreme Court of Washington has also pointed out that the constitutional right of association carries with it a corresponding right to not associate. That court had "no hesitancy in holding that the state, through the university, may not compel membership in an association, such as ASUW (the student government type of organization), which purports to represent all the students at the university" *(Good v. Associated Students)*.

Activity Fees. Activitiess such as lecture series, campus newpapers, and organizations that sponsor these activities are generally funded by fees assessed all students. Challenges have been made regarding the assessment, collection, and use of these fees. Some students have argued that they are forced to pay activity fees that are used to support speakers and media whose philosophies are repugnant to their own. This, they argue, is a violation of their own right to free speech and association. Courts have disagreed and permitted the assessment of mandatory activity fees to provide a forum for the expression of political and personal opinions (*Veed v. Schwartzkoph*). Fees may not, however, be used to support only one particular philosophy, and equal access to the fees should be provided. Equal access to the activity fee does not, however, guarantee that each student organization requesting funds will receive all or even part of their request or that all organizations will be funded equally. A certain amount of discretion and subjective judgment may be exercised in funding student organizations so long as the process is fair and democratic. Decisions to fund student organizations also may not be made on the basis of the viewpoint expressed by the group. That would consitute a violation of the First Amendment. In *Gay and Lesbian Student Association v. Gohn*, the Eighth Circuit Court of Appeals noted that "Every claim of viewpoint discrimination requires, by its nature, that the purposes or motives of governmental officials be determined. When the body involved has many members, the question is harder to answer, but it still must be faced." The body in this instance was the student senate which had denied funding to the Gay and Lesbian Student Association. Many student senators freely admitted that they voted against the funding because of the views expressed by the gay student group. The court found this constitutionally unacceptable.

Assembly Rights and Demonstrations. The final clause of the First Amendment that emerges as an area of concern to the student affairs administrator is "the right of the people peaceably to assemble." Campus demonstrations still take place, and like other activities protected by the First Amendment, they cannot be regulated on the basis of the message to be conveyed. Reasonable time, place, and manner restrictions may be imposed, and prior registration may be required for scheduling purposes. However, prior restraint is impermissible *(Sword v. Fox; Bayless v. Martine)*. Disruption of the ongoing functions of the university may be prohibited *(Esteban v. Central Missouri)*. A good example of the line drawn between time, place, and manner restrictions and prior restraint arose at Mississippi State University. Regulations at the University required that students receive authorization for demonstrations, rallies, or parades at least three days prior to the event, and only those activities of a "wholesome nature" would be approved. The court held the regulation to be an impermissible prior restraint on First Amendment freedoms. The prior notice aspect of the regulation was acceptable to the court, but the "wholesome nature" language was unacceptable. The court said, "the point of this language converts what might have otherwise been a reasonable regulation of time, place, and manner into a restriction on the content of speech. Therefore, the regulation appears to be unreasonable on its face" *(Shamloo v. Mississippi State Board of Trustees, Etc.)*.

Fourth Amendment

Application of the law concerning the Fourth Amendment rights of students on campus is controversial *(Morale v. Grigel)*. This Amendment guarantees, in part, "the right of the people to be secure in their persons, houses, papers, and effects against unreasonable searches and seizures shall not be violated, and no warrants shall be issued but upon probable cause . . . ." The controversy surrounding search and seizure on campus concerns whether college officials are required to obtain a warrant before a search of a student's room can be conducted. Several courts have argued that if college officials had "reasonable cause to believe" that activity was taking place in a student's residence hall room that was in violation of college regulations, a warrantless search could be conducted. The basis for this rationale was that a search to maintain good order and discipline on campus was considered a *reasonable* search because criminal prosecution was not contemplated—thus the application of a "reasonable cause" standard as opposed to the "probable cause" standard required by the Fourth Amendment *(Moore v. Troy State; United States v. Coles;* and *Keene v. Rodgers)*. The United States Supreme Court also has upheld a warrantless search by high school officials *(New Jersey v. T.L.O.)*. The court said school officials are justified in undertaking a warrantless search "when there are reasonable grounds for suspecting that the search will turn up evidence that the student has violated or is violating either the law or the rules of the school." In allowing a search of the student's purse for drugs in this case, the court was attempting to strike a balance between the student's legitimate expectation of privacy and the administration's legitimate need to maintain a safe environment for learning. However, where police have sought evidence for a criminal prosecution rather than a mere disciplinary proceeding, courts have required a warrant and held that college administrators could not delegate their lower "reasonable cause" standard to the police *(Piazzola v. Watkins)*. Subsequently, the "reasonable cause" standard was rejected by another federal district court *(Smythe and Smith v. Lubbers)*. Thus, until the Supreme Court provides guidance with respect to the applicable standard to be used, administrators would be well advised to review their search and seizure policy with institutional counsel.

The "plain view" and "emergency" doctrines are still legally sound. In essence, the plain view doctrine holds that any contraband that is in plain view may be seized. Thus, where entry to a room has been made legally, such as maintenance checks either requested by the occupant or carried out as an announced routine, and an illegal substance is seen in plain view, it may then be seized and used for disciplinary purposes *(State v. Kappes)*. Plain view means exactly that— if something must be moved or opened to see the substance, then it is not in plain view. An "emergency" does not demand a warrant to search. If someone credible reported in good faith that a bomb was in locker 319 in the university student center, to attempt to obtain a warrant would be ridiculous. Once that locker is legally opened, as in the case of an emergency, anything illegal that is in plain view may be confiscated *(People v. Lanthier)*.

Finally, several courts have interpreted the privacy rights contained in the Fourth Amendment to support a denial of door-to-door canvassing or voter registration in the residence halls *(National Movement v. Regents; Brush v. Penn State University; American Future Systems, Inc. v. Penn State)*. The upper floors of a residence hall have been held to be private living quarters, and prohibiting door-to-door registration and canvassing is not a Fourth Amendment violation where other alternatives exist.

Fourteenth Amendment

Due Process. Two classes of Section 1 of the Fourteenth Amendment, the Due Process Clause and the Equal Protection Clause, have particular significance for the student affairs professional. The due process clause was the basis for one of the most significant decisions in higher education. The *Dixon* case set forth the principle that students attending state colleges or universities were entitled to due process. A natural question that arises, however, is "What process is due?" The answer lies in an understanding of due process as a flexible concept rather than a fixed standard. Due process is fundamental fairness, and therefore, depends upon individual circumstances. A fair summary of due process is that the greater the right sought to be deprived, the greater the process due. Thus, a deprivation of some social privileges would not demand the degree of procedure required for an expulsion. Both the *Dixon* decision and *General Order on Judicial Standards of Procedure and Substance in Review of Student Discipline in Tax Supported Institutions of Higher Education* provide excellent guidelines for the administrator involved in disciplinary affairs. Courts have held consistently that college discipline is not a criminal procedure, and thus, is not required to conform to the rules of criminal jurisprudence.

Courts have stated that three general standards must be met in order to satisfy the minimum requirements of due process in instances of student discipline: students must be given adequate notice, an opportunity must be given for a hearing, and decisions must be based upon substantial evidence. The Supreme Court has recently held that academic dismissals do not, however, require the same procedural safeguards demanded by disciplinary dismissals *(Board of Curators v. Horowitz)*. Situations involving allegations of academic dishonesty are disciplinary in nature since they involve a question of fact—whether the student accused of academic dishonesty should, therefore, be provided with some measure of due process rather than summarily being given a failing grade or dismissed (see *Kibler, Nuss, Patterson, & Pavela, 1988*). Over the years the standards in disciplinary cases for notice, hearing, and decisions based upon substantial evidence have been refined by the courts and are summarized:

1. **Notice:** Students charged with infractions should be provided with a notice that (1) is written *(Esteban v. Central Missouri State College)*; (2) contains the charges against them in enough detail to permit the preparation of a defense against the charges *(Esteban v. Central Missouri)*. The regulations the students are charged with violating should also be specific enough to give a reasonable person notice of what is prohibited *(Soglin v. Kauffman)*; (3) includes the nature of the evidence supporting the charge *(Dixon v. Alabama State Board of Education)*, and (4) provides a time, date, and place of hearing in enough time after delivery of the notice that the student can prepare a defense *(Dixon v. Alabama State Board of Education)*. Reasonable efforts to deliver the notice are all that are required, and the student cannot frustrate this process by moving or failing to accept mail *(Wright v. Texas Southern University)*.

2. **Hearing:** The hearing should provide an opportunity to hear both sides of the controversy. (1) The hearing is to be conducted by an impartial person or persons *(Dixon v. Alabama State Board of Education)*. That a panel or board conduct hearings is not a general requirement. One person may conduct the hearing so long as that individual is impartial. (2) The student must be provided with an opportunity to present a defense against the charges, including presenting witnesses and oral, written, or physical evidence *(Dixon v. Alabama State Board of Education)*. (3) The hearing process must be fair and impartial. For example, allowing the student an attorney is not a general requirement *(Dixon v. Alabama State Board of Education)*, however, if the institution is represented by an attorney or if the student faces similar charges in criminal court, then it would be only fair to allow the student to have counsel *(French v. Bashful)*. Similarly, there is no absolute

right to cross-examine witnesses *(Dixon v. Alabama State Board of Education)*, but where there are real questions or witness credibility, cross examination of witnesses might be essential to a fair hearing *(Blanton v. State University of New York)*.

Hearings should not be open to the public since doing so would violate the terms of the Family Educational Rights and Privacy Act by exposing part of a student's record to the public without the student's consent. Allowing others to have access while the record is being developed is no less intrusive than opening the record to inspection after it has been developed *(Marston v. Gainesville Sun Publishing Co., Inc.)*. As long as the university maintains a copy of the proceedings which is open to the student's inspection, the student has no absolute right to record the hearing *(Gorman v. University of Rhode Island.)*

3. **Evidence:** Decisions in student disciplinary cases must be based upon "substantial" evidence, and if the hearing is not conducted by the decision-making body, then "the results and finding of the hearing should be presented in an open report to the student's inspection" *(Dixon v. Alabama State Board of Education)*.

These due process requirements may seem cumbersome, but they are designed to ensure that each student is accorded "a day in court" without being overly legalistic. The procedures do take time; in most instances this is beneficial because time has a way of adding a measure of objectivity. However, one cannot always take the time required by these standards when a possible rapist, arsonist, or other offender, who constitutes a threat to self, to property, or to others remains on campus. This individual must be dealt with immediately. In instances in which a student's continued presence on the campus poses a threat to the welfare of the student, property, or others, an interim suspension may be imposed. The student could be suspended immediately, with a hearing set at a later time *(Gardenhire v. Chalmers)*. This is a very serious action, however, and should be reserved for actual threats.

Two final aspects of due process of interest to the student affairs administrator involve double jeopardy and proceeding with campus hearings before civil or criminal charges are settled in court. If a student has been charged by civil authorities, the on-campus hearing need not wait until the case has been settled in court. The Supreme Court of Vermont decided a case where a student, charged with burglary, attempted rape, and simple assault and whose campus hearing preceded his criminal prosecution, alleged that his due process rights were violated. The court upheld the right of the college to proceed first.

> Educational institutions have both a need and a right to formulate their own standards and to enforce them; such enforcement is only coincidentally related to criminal charges and the defense against them. To hold otherwise would, in our view, lead logically to the conclusion that civil remedies must, as a matter of law, wait for determination until related criminal charges are disposed. (*Nzuwe v. Castleton State College*)

Equal Protection. The Fourteenth Amendment also contains equal protection guarantees that apply to a variety of student development programs. Equal treatment under the law does not necessarily mean that everyone must be treated exactly the same. For example, many states have laws that permit an 18 year old to drink beer, but require that one be 21 to drink liquor. This is not a violation of the equal protection clause, yet citizens are being treated differently on the basis of age. Similarly, colleges and universities may treat different classifications of students differently, but institutional officials must be prepared to bear the burden of showing that the classifications so established are justified.

The courts generally apply either a "strict scrutiny" or a "rational relationship" test to situations in which some people are treated differently based upon a particular classification scheme. The test used is determined by the rights being deprived by the classification used. If the classifications create a "suspect" class—one based on race, alienage, or national origin, then the court will demand "strict scrutiny" to determine if a "compelling state interest" will be served by the classification. Thus far the Supreme Court has not chosen to specify sex as a suspect category. The "strict scrutiny" test also will be applied if one of the classes created will be deprived of a fundamental right. A college education is not a fundamental right *(Mauclet v. Nyquist)*, nor is the pursuit of a graduate degree *(Purdie v. University of Utah)*. Living in college housing also has been held not to be a fundamental right *(Bynes v. Toll)*. However, voting, interstate travel, marriage, procreation, and freedom from wealth distinctions in criminal prosecution have been held to be fundamental rights. Thus, a deprivation of any of these rights would require that a "compelling state interest" exist.

If the classifications are not suspect and if no fundamental rights are involved, then the courts apply a less demanding standard called the "rational relationship" test, which requires that a rational relationship be shown to exist between the classifications established and the legitimate interests of the state. The two tests, while certainly not restricted to these areas, are often applied to "housing and admissions".

Frequently equal protection challenges to on-campus living regulations have been made. Those students required to live in college residence halls complained that they were discriminated against by being required to pay rents to amortize loans on the buildings. Because classifications were usually based upon academic class (freshmen and sophomores required to live in residence halls), which is not suspect, and no fundamental rights were involved, the "rational relationship" test was applied in these cases. In one instance all women students, but only male freshmen, were required to live on campus because that was the number required to fill the residence halls. The institution failed its "rational relationship" test *(Mollere v. Southeastern Louisiana College)*. While the court would not uphold such an arbitrary classification without some rational relationship, it pointed out that an institution might require all or certain categories of students to live on campus to promote the education of those students. That hint did not go unnoticed. A year later an institution defended successfully its required on-campus residence regulation on the basis of the educational benefits to be derived from on-campus living *(Pratz v. Louisiana Polytechnic Institute)*. Courts have since held that even where one of the reasons behind the regulation may be amortization of loans on the buildings, "so long as the state purpose upholding a statutory class is legitimate and non-illusionary, its lack of primacy is not disqualifying" (*Schick v. Kent State University*).

Admissions also can be fertile ground for equal protection suits. The Supreme Court of Utah found no rational relationship to exist between the legitimate interest of the state and the age of a 51 year old applicant to a graduate program. She had been denied admission because the department to which she applied preferred younger students (*Purdie v. University of Utah*). Admissions also provides an excellent example of a "strict scrutiny test." During the time hostages were being held in Iran, the Board of Regents of New Mexico State University passed a regulation denying subsequent enrollment to any student whose home government holds or permits the holding of U.S. citizens as hostages. Several Iranian students successfully challenged the constitutionality of the regulation. The court found the regulation to be based on alienage and national origin, both "suspect" cases. The Regents only basis for the regulation was that Americans were "angry and fed up with Iranians and, therefore, Iranian students shouldn't get any benefits from New Mexico taxpayers." Lacking a compelling state interest, the regulation was held to violate the equal protection clause (*Tayyari v. New Mexico State University*). Finally the fact that even constitutionally valid rules may be implemented in ways that offend the Constitution must be realized (*Cooper v. Nix*). For this reason practices, procedures, programs, and policies should be reviewed systematically with legal counsel.

CONTRACTUAL RELATIONSHIP

The discussion of contractual relationships has focused on those rights of students that are derived from the constitutional relationship of the student to the college or university. Also what has been pointed out is that only students at public institutions have such a relationship with their institutions, unless "state action" can be shown. However, students also have contractual rights and the exercise of those rights derived from the contractual relationship with the institution is often referred to as educational consumerism. In essence, the students and the college enter into a contract in which the institution offers certain educational services and a degree and the student agrees to abide by the rules and regulations and pay a specified tuition. This relationship between the student and the institution applies equally at public and private colleges and universities. The college catalog, student handbook, and the variety of brochures published by an institution of higher education all constitute part of the terms of the contract. The Illinois Supreme Court provided a good example of the contractual relationship when it said,

> . . . the description in the brochure containing the terms under which an application will be appraised constituted an invitation for an offer. The tender of the application, as well as the payment of the fee pursuant to the terms of the brochure, was an offer to apply. Acceptance of the application and fee constituted acceptance of an offer to apply under the criteria the defendant (medical school) had established. (*Steinberg v. Chicago Medical School*)

The court also held that the $15 application fee was sufficient consideration to support the agreement. Contracts are not chipped in concrete, and with proper notice, terms can be modified (*Jones v. Vassar; Pride v. Howard*), even to the extent of substantially increasing tuition (*Eisele v. Ayers*) or making changes in academic requirements. The latter point was concisely stated by the Fifth Circuit in a case involving a graduate student who was notified that a change in requirements for the master's degree would require that she take a final comprehensive exam. She was first notified of this requirement six weeks prior to completion of her course work and two weeks before the exam was to be administered. The exam was not mentioned as a requirement in the catalog. The student alleged that requiring the exam breached the "implied contract" she had with the institution. The court, concluded that "implicit in the student's contract with the university upon matriculation is the student's agreement to comply with the university's rules and regulations, which the university definitely is entitled to modify so as to properly exercise its educational responsibilities" (*Mahavongsana v. Hall*).

Some terms of the contract are not explicitly stated, but rather are implicit understandings. An Ohio court stated that students have an implied contractual right to receive accredited instruction *(Behrend v. State)*. Once the student fulfills the reasonable requirements set forth by the institution, the degree must be awarded *(Tanner v. Board of Trustees)*. Students also have contractual arrangements with the institution for housing, meals, and other services. These contracts should be examined by an institutional counsel before they are executed by the institution and should be reviewed every few years to keep abreast of changing conditions. In recent years, suits, based upon contractual obligations, both expressed and implied, have surpassed in number those based on civil rights violations in the student area.

REGULATORY RELATIONSHIPS

In recent years, the federal government has enacted several laws or statutes specifically designed to aid students. These statutes have generally prohibited discrimination in any program or activity receiving federal financial assistance. Because almost every college and university receives some form of federal aid, these statutes apply to both public and private institutions. The aid can be made directly to the college or given directly to the student for the school to qualify as a recipient *(Grove City College v. Bell)*. Furthermore, "program or activity" is defined to include *all* operations of a college or university. Hence, if an institution is a recipient of federal financial assistance, then every one of its operations must comply with the law regardless of whether that specific operation receives any federal funding *(Civil Rights Restoration Act of 1987, P.L. 100-259)*. Thus, student affairs administrators at both public and private institutions need to become familiar with the rights students derive from this statutory relationship. In some instances, statutes and regulations implementing them set higher standards than do constitutional rights. For example, a curfew for female students without a corresponding restriction for men was upheld under the "rational relationship" test for equal protection under the Fourteenth Amendment

(Robinson v. Eastern Kentucky University). This same rule, however, would violate a student's statutory rights, as defined by federal regulations, under Title IX (34 C.F.R. 106).

Primary federal statutes affecting student affairs administration are Title VI, Title IX, Section 504, and the Buckley Amendment. Title VI of the Civil Rights Act of 1964 (42 *U.S.C.* 2000d) prohibits discrimination on the basis of race, color, or national origin in any educational program or activity receiving federal financial assistance. Title IX of the Education Amendments of 1972 (20 *U.S.C.* 1681) was modeled after Title VI and prohibits discrimination on the basis of sex. Section 504 of the Rehabilitation Act of 1973 (29 *U.S.C.* 794) is also modeled after the language of Title VI but prohibits discrimination on the basis of a handicap.

Statutes provide general guidance, but specific regulations are issued to effectuate the intent of statutes. Regulations for Title IX can be found in Title 34 of the *Code of Federal Regulations* at part 106; Section 504 regulations also can be found in Title 34 but at part 104. Title VI regulations appear at 34 *C.F.R.* 100. These regulations contain detailed specifications of policies, practices, and procedures permitted and precluded by law. These laws and their implementing regulations cover everything from pre-admission inquiry to placement services.

Although Title VI was originally designed to benefit minority students, it also is being used to prevent reverse discrimination. The constitution of the student government association at the University of North Carolina-Chapel Hill specified that a specific number of minorities must be elected to the Campus Governing Council. It also stated that student defendants had the right to demand four of the seven honor court justices be of their race or sex. These sections of the constitution were challenged under Title VI and found to be in violation *(Uzzell v. Friday).* The admissions area also has been held up to Title VI scrutiny. Probably the most famous case in postsecondary education since *Dixon* was the *Bakke* case, which held that an admissions quota specifically reserved for minorities violated Title VI. The Supreme Court did state, however, that colleges and universities may consider race or ancestry factors in the selection process to obtain diversity in the student body *(Regents v. Bakke)*. Two institutions that have since given consideration to race in their admission process have been upheld by their respective state supreme courts *(McDonald v. Hogness; DeRonde v. Regents of University of California)*.

Title IX also has provided a graduate admissions case. In *Cannon* the Supreme Court was asked to decide whether an applicant who alleged that she was being denied admission on the basis of her sex had a private right of action *(Cannon v. University of Chicago)*. The Supreme Court answered affirmatively. Because Title IX and Section 504 are both modeled after Title VI, all three statutes probably allow a student to bring suit directly against the college without going through the federal administration procedures outlined in the regulations. Title IX also has significant application to student organizations, housing, counseling, and placement, but these areas have not been tested judicially.

Making physical changes to facilities would seem to have been the most significant aspect of Section 504. However, two other areas have had greater impact. Several courts have ordered colleges to provide sign language interpreters for deaf students under the Section 504 regulations *(Barnes v. Converse College; Crawford v. University of North Carolina)*. This requirement is under "auxiliary aids" section of the regulations. One most interesting case involved a controversy between Illinois Institute of Technology and the Illinois Department of Rehabilitative Services over who would pay the interpreter's salary; the institution was willing to provide an interpreter but believed that the Department of Rehabilitative Services had primary responsibility to pay the interpreter's salary. The court agreed with the college when it found the Department was not precluded from paying for the service and the intent of the federal government when it promulgated the regulations was "that the bulk of auxiliary aids will be paid for by the state and private agencies, not colleges or universities" *(Jones v. Illinois Department of Rehabilitation Services)*. Also see *Schornstein v. New Jersey Division of Vocational Rehabilitational Services*.

Another Section 504 decision involved admissions and held that the regulations implementing the Section may not be interpreted to require curricular modifications. In this instance, a licensed practical nurse was denied admission to a nursing education program on the basis that her hearing loss would make it impossible to participate safely in the program *(Southeastern Community College v. Davis)*. Finally, administrators should be aware the United States Supreme Court has held that contagious diseases constitute a handicap under Section 504 *(School Board of Nassau County, Florida v. Arline)*. Although the decision involved an individual with tuberculosis, the holding would clearly apply to persons suffering from symptomatic AIDS and, thus, also define their rights under Section 504.

The fourth federal statute involving student affairs programs is the Buckley Amendment, formally known as the Family Educational Rights and Privacy Act of 1974 (20 *U.S.C.* 1232g). Regulations implementing the act appear in 34 *C.F.R.* 99. This law and its regulations guarantee students access to their educational records and, with a few exceptions, prohibit release or review of those records to anyone without the student's written consent. The law has not been interpreted to mean that students who leave the institution owing money must be furnished copies of the official transcripts. However, if students who attended state institutions discharge their outstanding debts in bankruptcy, the institution may not withhold transcripts *(Handsome v. Rutgers)*. Private institutions, on the other hand, may withhold transcripts under similar circumstances *(Girardier v. Webster College)*. Finally, under the Buckley Amendment disciplinary hearings must be closed unless the defendant student waives that right *(Marston v. Gainesville Sun)*. To prohibit students access to their records, if the disciplinary hearings of the institution were open to the college community, would be illogical. The regulations also require that each institution have a written policy concerning specific points outlined in the regulations and students receive annual notification that such policy exists and where to find it.

TORT LIABILITY

Because of their potential for personal and institutional liability, administrators should also be familiar with the area of torts. Certain minimum standards of conduct exist for our relationships with others, and, where those standards are not met, the relationships "twisted" or a tort is committed. A tort is a civil wrong, as opposed to a criminal wrong (violation of a law) other than the breach of a contract, for which the courts will provide a remedy. Usually the remedy consists of financial damages against the one who failed to meet the standard. These damages may be **compensatory** (to compensate the person injured in an amount deemed adequate to make them "whole" again) and **punitive** (assessed as a punishment where one's behavior was willful and with a total disregard for the other person). Although many types of torts exist, administrators should be primarily aware of the two that pose the greatest potential for suits in higher education settings—negligence and defamation.

Negligence

Negligence involves the failure to meet a prescribed standard of conduct for the protection of others. This definition includes several elements which must be met for liability to be assessed. First, one must have a duty to the other person. If there is no duty, there can be no negligence, nor liability. Second, one must breech the duty owed either by an act of omission or commission. Third, an injury must be suffered by another to their person or property. Even if a breach of a duty is owed, no liability can be assessed if no injury occurred. Finally, the breach of the duty must be the proximate cause of the injury. If a duty was breached and an injury was suffered but that injury was caused by an intervening variable rather than the breech of the duty, generally no liability would be assessed. These elements are illustrated by a case in which a young woman was raped in here residence hall. The night watchman saw large footprints in new snow leading up to the dormitory's locked doors and no footprints leading away from the building, but he subsequently saw tracks on the roof. He limited his search to basement storage rooms since he was not permitted on the upper halls of the women's building. The court stated that "a reasonably prudent man charged with the protection of the dormitory's young female residents (duty) would have taken some measures to avert the likelihood that one (or more) of them would be physically harmed. The jury could reasonably conclude that the failure of the watchman to do so was a violation of a duty owed the plaintiff (student) and such violation was a proximate cause of her injuries" (Schultz v. Gould Academy).

Although tort liability is a matter of state law, the various courts generally agree on the standard of care or duties owed to others. Some of the more common duties defined by the courts (common law) include the duty to provide proper supervision, proper instruction, and to maintain equipment and premises in a reasonable state of repair. These duties are especially important for those who manage physical facilities or supervise intramurals or field trips. The degree of supervision depends upon the age of the student, the nature of the activity, and the foreseeability of risk. College students require less supervision than younger elementary and secondary students, but still may require supervision where a reasonably forseeable risk exists (Mintz v. State). Several courts have held that, absent a special relationship creating a dependency of one person on another, no custodial duty or duty to control the conduct of students exists (Bradshaw v. Rawlings; University of Denver v. Whitlock).

The duty to provide proper instruction goes beyond the classroom and can include any activity in which students are engaged from knowing how to exit a building in case of fire to knowing how to operate a fog machine for a drama production (Potter v. North Carolina School of the Arts). Maintaining equipment is particularly important for those who have facilities to manage such as college unions or residence halls (Lumbard v. Fireman's Fund; Shetina v. Ohio University). Those who enter campus facilities are usually business invitees while residential students have a landlord-tenant relationship with the institution. In both instances, the university has a duty not only to maintain its facilities in a reasonable state of repair but to protect those who enter from foreseeable danger (Duarte v. State; Mullins v. Pine Manor College; Miller v. State).

Several jurisdictions also recognize a counselor or therapist's duty to warn *(Tarasoff v. Regents of University of California; McIntosh v. Milano)*. The *Tarasoff* case involved a client, Mr. Poddar, who told his therapist that he intended to kill another student when she returned to the country. Although the therapist attempted to have Mr. Poddar taken into custody by the campus police, his supervisor ordered the officers not to place Poddar in a short-term confinement facility for treatment and evaluation. The client discontinued therapy and no one ever warned the other student that her life was in danger. When she returned to the country, Poddar killed her. In a wrongful death suit California held that the therapists had a "duty to warn." In order to trigger this duty, three conditions must be met. First, a special relationship must exist either to the person whose conduct needs to be controlled (usually a client) or to the foreseeable victim. A special relationship has been found to exist in a counseling relationship. The second condition requires that a determination is made that the client's conduct needs to be controlled. Here the counselor is free to exercise professional judgment without fear of liability. To determine if a client's conduct needs to be controlled, courts will apply a standard of reasonableness to the facts of the case or "that reasonable degree of skill, knowledge, and care ordinarily possessed and exercised by members of (that professional specialty) under similar circumstances" *(Tarasoff)*. Finally, in most jurisdictions there must also be a foreseeable victim. The Supreme Court of Vermont has held that even where the danger was to property rather than to a person, the duty to warn still existed *(Peck v. Counseling Service of Addison County, Inc.)*. Also note that Section 4.2 of the ACPA ethical standards imposes a duty to warn under certain circumstances (see Appendix A).

Defamation

Defamation is a false statement made by one person to another about a third person that holds the third person up to hatred, disgrace, ridicule, or contempt. **Libel** is written defamation while slander is oral defamation. Student newspapers are potentially vulnerable to libel *(Ithaca College v. Yale Daily News Publishing Co., Inc.)* and student editors are responsible for what they publish *(Mazart v. State; Brooks v. Stone)*.

Defamation is like negligence in that it has similar elements: (1) a duty to speak and write the truth about people; (2) a breach of that duty by making false statements; (3) an injury of holding the person up to ridicule, contempt, hatred, or disgrace; and (4) the statement to another about the third person was the proximate cause of the injury. In many jurisdictions accusing someone of a crime, of having a loathsome social disease, or of being unchaste is injury *per se* and the individual need not show that the false statement injured their reputation *(Wardlaw v. Peck; Melton v. Bow)*.

Alcoholic Beverages

Since the federal government passed 23 USC 158 tying the receipt of highway funds to a minimum drinking age of 21, every state has raised its legal age to 21 years. Thus, most college students, while adults for many purposes, are now under the legal age to possess or consume alcoholic beverages, thereby creating a potential for criminal or civil liability. Alcoholic beverage laws vary widely from one state to another. For example, providing alcohol to an underaged drinker in Iowa results in a $15 fine while the same offense in Oklahoma is a felony subjecting the violator to a fine of up to $5,000 or imprisonment for five years or both! Most states prohibit anyone from providing alcoholic beverages to underage persons or those who are intoxicated. A violation of these laws constitutes a crime, but even more important, a violation could lead to civil liability.

Most, but not all states have civil damages acts or case law which holds a licensed furnisher of alcoholic beverage liable for injuries caused to innocent third persons by intoxicated customers. This is especially important for those who have licensed pubs on campus or social organizations that obtain temporary permits to sell alcoholic beverages during homecoming and other special events. An increasing number of states also have social host liability which holds a gratuitous provider of alcohol liable to third persons injured by an intoxicated guest. Usually, this liability is triggered when a host serves an underage consumer or a person already intoxicated.

Alcohol is a very powerful depressant drug and certainly not something to play with. In Illinois where an 18 year-old fraternity pledge suffered neurological damage after being required to consume vast amounts of alcoholic beverages, the fraternity was held liable for his injuries and that such organizations have the *duty* to refrain from requiring pledges and others from consuming excessive amounts of alcohol *(Quinn v. Sigma Rho Chapter Beta Theta Pi Fraternity)*. In South Carolina, a similar incident resulted in the death of an initiate. In that case, the court held that fraternities have a duty not to cause harm to their initiates and, since they breached that duty, thereby causing the initiate's death, they were negligent *(Ballou v. Sigma Nu General Fraternity)*. The point in these cases is that "duty is not socrosanct in itself, but only an expression of the sum total of those considerations of policy which lead the law to say that a particular plaintiff is entitled to protection" (Prosser, 1971).

Tort Liability Defenses

The exposure to tort liability is not as fearsome as it may sound. While specific duties and standards do exist to which one must adhere (such as the duty to warn), the law generally holds you to the standard of acting as a reasonable person under the circumstances. Good "common sense" and "fair play" will remove most of the risk of liability, but there are also specific defenses of sovereign immenity (available only to state institutions), assumption of risk and contributory negligence. These defenses are discussed in the following chapter. The best defense, however, is to do your duty and tell the truth. Where the duty is met, no negligence exists and where the statement is the truth (factual truth, not opinion) then no defamation exists.

SUMMARY

A basic understanding of the law related to postsecondary education is a necessity for student affairs practitioners at every level as this knowledge can benefit the practitioner in policy development, in relations with internal and external constituents, in facilitating students' educational and personal development, and in avoiding personal and institutional liability.

With the average age of students increasing, a lowered age of majority, and economically hard times, the amount of litigation brought against administrators and institutions they represent will continue to increase. Through a better understanding of the relationships that exist between students and institutions, the student affairs practitioner can prevent time consuming and financially draining legal battles.

These relationships depend, first, upon whether the student is attending a public or a private institution, and to what extent the state is involved in its affairs. Students at public colleges or universities have been recognized to be full beneficiaries of the rights guaranteed by the United States Constitution. The rights most frequently exercised on campus are embodied by the First, Fourth, and Fourteenth Amendments—religion, speech, press, assembly, association, search and seizure, due process, and equal protection. Aspects of one or more of these rights are involved in almost every student development program.

Students at public as well as those at private institutions generally have a relationship to their college or university that is based upon a series of public laws or statutes enacted during the past two decades. These statutes and the regulations designed to implement them essentially guarantee students the right to be free from discrimination based upon race, sex, national origin, and handicap in educational programs and activities. Privacy rights of students and their records also are a subject of statutory and regulatory control that must be fully understood by the practitioner.

The student affairs practitioner also needs to understand the contractual relationship between the student and the institution. These contractual rights apply to both public as well as private institutions and are generally defined by terms contained in the catalog and other official publications. Oral agreements may also bind as implicit understandings. To know what has been promised and to fulfill those obligations is therefore most important. Students, too, may be held to their part of the contract; and when they breach terms of the agreement, the contract may be set aside or considered invalid.

Finally, administrators must have an understanding of duties to which they are required to conform under the law. The area of torts presents a tremendous potential for personal and institutional liability, and without a knowledge of one's legal duties the practitioner is particularly vulnerable to suit. Although tort law is interpreted differently in each state, practitioners must generally provide proper supervision and instruction and maintain their equipment and premises in a state of reasonable repair. What is "proper" and "reasonable" will depend upon the situation and the foreseeable risk involved. False statements which ridicule another or hold them up to contempt, disgrace or hatred are not only unprofessional, but can provide the basis for a defamation action. The best advice to keep from being negligent or defaming anyone is still to treat others as you would have them treat you.

Understanding these basic legal relationships can provide a firm foundation for creating student affairs programs. The adversarial relationship, so common to criminal law, is antithetical to the purposes of higher education. Through professional study and understanding of the law as it affects the work of student affairs practitioners, adversarial relations may be eliminated and programs that facilitate educational and personal development may be enhanced while maintaining the rights of all.

CASE CITATIONS
and REFERENCES

American Future Systems, Inc. v. Penn. State, 618 F.2d 252 (3rd Cir., 1980).

Americans United v. Rogers, 45 L.W. 3429 (1976).

Ballou v. Sigma Nu General Fraternity, 352 S.E. 2d 488 (S.C. App. 1986A)

Barnes v. Converse College, 436 F.Supp. 635 (D. S. C., Spartanburg Div., 1977).

Bayless v. Martine, 430 F.2d 873 (5th Cir., 1970).

Behrend v. State, 379 N.E. 2d 617 (Ct. App. Oh., Franklin Cty., 1977).

Berrios v. Inter American University, 535 F.2d 1330 (1st Cir., 1976).

Blackburn v. Fisk University, 443 F.2d 121 (6th Cir., 1971).

Blanton v. State University of New York, 489 F.2d 377 (2nd Cir., 1973).

Board of Curators v. Horowitz, 46 L.W. 4179 (1978).

Bradshaw v. Rawlings, 612 F. 2d 135 (3rd Cir. 1979)

Brooks v. Stone, 317 S.E. 2d 277 (Ga. App. 1984)

Browns v. Mitchell, 409 F.2d 593 (10th Cir., 1969).

Brush v. Penn State University, 414 A.2d 48 (Pa., 1980).

Burton v. Wilmington Parking Authority, 365 U.S. 715 (1961).

Bynes v. Toll, 512 F.2d 252 (2nd Cir., 1975).

Cannon v. University of Chicago, 99 S.Ct. 1946 (1979).

Chess v. Widmar, 480 F.Supp. 907 (W.D. Mo. W.D., 1979); rev'd 635 F.2d 1310 (8th Cir., 1980).

Cooper v. Nix, 496 F.2d 1285 (5th Cir., 1974).

Counts v. Voorhees College, 312 F.Supp. 598 (D.S.C. Charleston Div., 1970).

Crawford v. University of North Carolina, 440 F.Supp. 1047 (M.D.N.C., Durham Div., 1977).

DeRonde v. Regents of University of California, 172 Cal. Rptr. 677 (Ca., 1981).

Dixon v. Alabama State Board of Education, 294 F.2d 150 (5th Cir., 1961); cert. den. 386 U.S. 930 (1961).

Duarte v. State, 148 Cal. Rptr. 804 (Ca. App. 4th Dist. 1978)

Eisele v. Ayers, 381 N.E. 2d 21 (App. Ct. Ill., 1st Dist., 3rd Div., 1978).

Eisen v. Regents, 75 Cal. Rptr. 45 (Ct. App., 1969).

Esteban v. Central Missouri State College, 277 F.Supp. 649 (W.D. Mo., 1967).

Esteban v. Central Missouri, 415 F.2d 1077 (8th Cir., 1969).

French v. Bashful, 303 F.Supp. 1333 (E.D. La. No. Div., 1969).

Gardenhire v. Chalmers, 326 F.Supp. 1200 (D.Ks., 1971).

Gay and Lesbian Student Association v. Gohn, 57 L.W. 2007, July 5, 1988 (8th Cir. 1988)

General Order on Judicial Standards of Procedure and Substance in Review of Student Discipline in Tax Supported Institutions of Higher Education, 45 FRD 133 (W.D. Mo., 1968).

Girardier v. Webster College, 563 F.2d 1267 (8th Cir., 1977).

Good v. Associated Students, 542 P.2d 762 (Wa., 1975).

Gorman v. University of Rhode Island, 837 F. 2d 7 (1st Cir. 1988)

Grossner v. Trustees of Columbia University, 287 F.Supp. 535 (S.D.N.Y., 1968).

Grove City College v. Bell, 104 S. Ct. 1211 (1984)

Hammond v. Tampa, 344 F.2d 951 (5th Cir., 1965).

Handsome v. Rutgers, 445 F.Supp. 1362 (D. N.J., 1978).

Healy v. James, 92 S.Ct. 2338 (1972).

Ithaca College v. Yale Daily News Publishing Co., Inc., 433 N.Y.S. 2d 530 (S. Ct. 1980)

Jones v. Illinois Department of Rehabilitation Services, 504 F.Supp. 1244 (N.D. Ill. E.D., 1981).

Jones v. Vassar, 299 N.Y.S. 2d 283 (S.Ct. Dutchess Cty., 1969).

Keene v. Rodgers, 316 F.Supp. 217 (D. Me. N.D., 1970).

Kibler, W., Nuss, E., Patterson, B., & Pavela, G. (1988). *Academic integrity and student development: Legal issues and policy perspectives.* Asheville, N.C.: College Administration Publications, Inc.

Lemon v. Kurtzman, 403 U.S. 602 (1971).

Lumbard v. Fireman's Fund, 302 So. 2d 394 (La. App. 1st Cir. 1974)

Mahavongsana v. Hall, 529 F.2d 448 (5th Cir., 1976).

Marston v. Gainesville Sun, 341 So. 2d 783 (Dist. Ct. App. FLA., 1st Dist., 1976).

Maryland Public Interest Research Group v. Elkins, 565 F.2d 864 (4th Cir., 1977).

Mauclet v. Nyquist, 406 F.Supp. 1233 (W.D. N.Y., 1976); aff'd. 97S.Ct. 2120 (1977).

Mazart v. State, 441 N.Y.S. 2d 600 (Ct. Clms. 1981)

McDonald v. Hogness, 598 P.2d 707 (Wa., 1979).

McIntosh v. Milano, 403 A. 2d 500 (N.J. Super. Law 1979)

Melton v. Bow, 247 S.E. 2d 100 (Ga. 1978)

Merkey v. Board of Regents, 344 F.Supp. 1296 (N.D. FLA., 1972).

Miller v. State, 478 N.Y.S. 2d 829 (1984)

Mintz v. State, 362 N.Y.S. 2d 619 (App. 3rd 1975)

Mollere v. Southeastern Louisiana College, 304 F.Supp. 826 (W.D. Ark., Fayetteville Div., 1969).

Moore v. Troy State, 284 F.Supp. 725 (M.D. Ala N. Div., 1968).

Morale v. Grigel, 422 F.Supp. 988 (D. N.H., 1976).

Mullins v. Pine Manor College, 449 N.E. 2d 331 (Mass. 1983)

National Movement v. Regents, 123 Cal. Rptr. 141 (Ct. App. 2nd Dist., Div. 1, 1975).

National Strike Information Center v. Brandeis, 315 F.Supp. 928 (D. Mass., 1970).

New Jersey v. T.L.O., 105 S. Ct. 733 (1985)

Nzuve v. Castleton State College, 335 A.2d 321 (Vt., 1975).

Papish v. Board of Curators of University of Missouri, 93 S.Ct. 1197 (1973).

Peck v. Counseling Service of Addison County, Inc., 449 A. 2d 422 (Vt. 1985)

People v. Lanthier, 97 Cal. Rptr. 297 (CA., 1971).

Piazzola v. Watkins, 442 F.2d 284 (5th Cir., 1971).

Potter v. North Carolina School of the Arts, 245 S.E. 2d 188 (N.C. App. 1978)

Powe v. Miles, 407 F.2d 73 (2nd Cir., 1968).

Pratz v. Louisiana Polytechnic Institute, 316 F.Supp. 872 (W.D. La., 1970); cert. den. 401 U.S. 1004 (1971).

Pride v. Howard, 384 A.2d 31 (D.C. Ct. App., 1978).

Prosser, W. (1971). *Law of torts (4th ed.).* St. Paul, MN: West Publishing.

Purdie v. University of Utah, 584 P.2d 831 (Ut., 1978).

Quinn v. Sigman Rho Chapter Beta Theta Pi Fraternity, 507 N.E. 2d 1193 (Ill. App. 4th Dist. 1987)

Regents v. Bakke, 98 S.Ct. 2733 (1978).

Robinson v. Davis, 447 F.2d 753 (4th Cir., 1971).

Robinson v. Eastern Kentucky University, 475 F.2d 707 (6th Cir., 1973); cert. den. 416 U.S. 982 (1973).

Roemer v. Board of Public Works, 96 S.Ct. 2337 (1976).

Rowe v. Chandler, 332 F.Supp. 336 (D. Ks., 1971).

School Board of Nassau County, Florida v. Arline, 55 L.W. 4245 (1987)

Schornstein v. New Jersey Division of Vocational Rehabilitational Services, 519 F. Supp. 773 (D.N.J. 1981).

Schultz v. Gould Academy, 332 A. 2d 368 (Me. 1975)

Shetina v. Ohio University, 459 N.E. 2d 587 (Ohio App. 1983)

Shick v. Kent State University, 74-646 (N.D. Oh. E.D., 1975).

Shamloo v. Mississippi State Board of Trustees, Etc., 620 F.2d 516 (5th Cir., 1980).

Shelly v. Kraemer, 334 U.S. 1 (1947).

Siegel v. Regents of the University of California, 308 F.Supp. 832 (N.D. Cal., 1970).

Smythe and Smith v. Lubbers, 398 F.Supp. 777 (W.D. Mich., 1975).

Soglin v. Kauffman, 418 F.2d 163 (7th Cir., 1969).

Solid Rock Foundation v. Ohio State University, 478 F.Supp. 96 (S.D. Oh. E.D., 1979).

Southeastern Community College v. Davis, 99 S.Ct. 2361 (1979).

State v. Kappes, 550 P.2d 121 (Ct. App. Az., Div. 1 Dept. A, 1976).

Steinberg v. Chicago Medical School, 371 N.E. 634 (Ill., 1977).

Student Coalition v. Austin Peay State University, 477 F.Supp. 1267 (M.D. Tenn., Nashville Div., 1979).

Students Against Apartheid Coalition v. O'Neil I, 660 F. Supp. 333 (W.D. VA. 1987).

Students Against Apartheid Coalition v. O'Neil II, 838 F. 2d 735 (4th Cir. 1988).

Sword v. Fox, 446 F.2d 1091 (4th Cir., 1971).

Tanner v. Board of Trustees, 363 N.E. 2d 208 (App. Ct. Ill. 4th Dist., 1977).

Tarasoff v. Regents of University of California, 551 P. 2d 334 (Cal. 1976)

Tayyari v. New Mexico State University, 495 F. Supp. 1365 (D.N.M. 1980)

Tilton v. Richardson, 403 U.S. 627 (1970).

Tinker v. Des Moines, 393 U.S. 503 (1969).

Torres v. Puerto Rico Junior College, 298 F.Supp. 458 (D. P.R., 1969).

United States v. Coles, 302 F.Supp. 99 (D.Me. N.D., 1969).

University of Delaware v. Keegan, 349 A.2d 14 (Del., 1975); cert. den. 424 U.S. 934 (1975).

University of Denver v. Whitlock, 744 P. 2d 54 (Colo. 1987).

University of Utah Students Against Apartheid v. Peterson, 649 F. Supp. 1200 (D. Utah, C.D. 1986).

Uzzell v. Friday, 591 F.2d 997 (4th Cir., 1979).

Veed v. Schwartzkoph, 353 F.Supp. 149 (D. Neb., 1973); aff'd. 478 F.2d 1407 (8th Cir., 1973); cert. den. 414 U.S. 1135 (1973).

Wardlaw v. Peck, 318 S.E. 2d 270 (S.C. App. 1984)

Wright v. Texas Southern University, 392 F.2d 728 (5th Cir., 1968).

SUGGESTED READINGS

Appenzeller, H., & Appenzeller, T. (1980). *Sports and the courts.* Charlottesville, VA: Michie Co.

Bender, L. (1977). *Federal regulation and higher education.* Washington, DC: American Association of Higher Education.

Bickel, R. (1988). *The college administrator and the courts, (2nd ed.)* Asheville, NC: College Administration Publications.

Hammond, E., & Shaffer, R. (1979). *The legal foundation of student personnel services in higher education.* Washington, DC: American College Personnel Association.

Kaplin, W. (1985). *The law of higher education: A comprehensive guide to legal implications of administrative decision making.* San Francisco: Jossey-Bass.

Weistart, J., & Lowell, C. (1979). *The law of sports.* Charlottesville, VA: Michie Co., 1979.

Young, D. P., & Gehring, D.D. (1986). *The college student and the courts (3rd ed.).* Asheville, NC: College Administration Publications.

Patricia A. Hollander, J.D., is an attorney in Buffalo, New York, and serves as General Counsel of the American Association of University Administrators. She was both an administrator and faculty member at the State University of New York at Buffalo, and was Visiting Professor at the University of Virginia where she taught a doctoral course in higher education law. She is the author of *Legal Handbook for Educators*, an editor of *The Computer Law Monitor*, co-author of *A Practical Guide To Legal Issues Affecting College Teachers*, author of *Computers in Education*, and co-author of *A Guide For Successful Searches For College Personnel*. Her B.S. and J.D. degrees are from St. Louis University and she did additional study at Harvard Law School.

D. Parker Young, Ed.D., is Professor of Higher Education in the Institute of Higher Education at the University of Georgia teaching doctoral courses in college law and the two-year college. He has had extensive experience as an administrator and faculty member and is a nationally known scholar in the field of college law. He conducts many conferences each year concerning higher education and the law. In addition, he has written widely and edited numerous books, monographs, and articles. He is co-editor of the *College Student and the Courts* and *The College Administrator and the Courts*. Young is a well recognized speaker who is in demand to address and chair sessions of state, regional, and national professional groups.

Chapter 13

LEGAL ISSUES AND EMPLOYMENT PRACTICES IN STUDENT AFFAIRS

Patricia A. Hollander
D. Parker Young

Student affairs administrators frequently are called upon to make decisions relating to staff employment, tort liability, and civil rights liability. In order to make effective and appropriate decisions, they need to understand the legal parameters within which these decisions must be made.*

Administrators may be expected to deal with staff employment practices such as determining job descriptions and job qualifications; recruiting candidates for positions; interviewing; negotiating salaries; and making recommendations or decisions regarding appointments, promotions, tenure or continuing appointment, or about nonrenewal or dismissal. Employment issues concerning evaluation of staff, appropriate review and due process procedures for termination of staff from the institution, and handling the consequences of financial exigency also need to be considered in light of legal requirements and pertinent court decisions.

---

*Appendix B, An Introduction to Legal Research, provides an explanation of how to read legal citations and to locate and use legal sources in research.

Student affairs administrators also should be aware that their actions may lead to claims based upon tort liability, as for negligence or defamation, and upon civil rights liability, as may arise if staff are deprived of constitutional rights.

THRESHOLD QUESTIONS

A number of threshold questions must be explored by student affairs administrators in order to make appropriate decisions relating to staff. Among the most important are (1) Is the institution private or public? (2) What are the essential employment and tort liability concepts that apply to each type institution? (3) What is the chief student affairs administrator's job description, including authority to hire and fire staff? (4) Are student affairs staff positions administrative, faculty, or a combination of both? What are their job descriptions and qualifications?

Private-Public Distinction

At both private and public institutions, sources of employment rights of student affairs administrators and their staff members may be found in statutes, contracts, policies of governing boards, faculty or staff handbooks, college catalogues, and customs and practices at the institution. In addition, professional standards promulgated by groups such as the American Association of University Professors and the American Association of University Administrators are considered by many courts to be appropriate standards to which institutions should adhere. However, at public institutions the federal and/or state constitutions are additional sources of employment rights. In other words, employees at private institutions have employment rights and obligations based principally on statutes and contracts, while employees at public institutions are affected additionally by constitutional rights, such as freedom of expression and due process.

Tort Liability

Regarding tort liability, employees at private institutions need to be concerned about negligence and defamation, and employees at public institutions, in addition to negligence and defamation, must be aware of constitutional torts that may occur in connection with violations of constitutional protections, such as constitutionally impermissible dismissals from employment. Student affairs administrators often function as Vice-Presidents or Deans of Student Affairs and report to the President or Executive Vice-President of the institution. They may have delegated to them the authority to hire and fire their own staffs, particularly if their staff members do not receive concurrent faculty appointments. In the latter case, the faculty appointment would normally be subject to peer scrutiny by faculty committees, as well as ultimate approval by the top hiring authority of the institution.

Delegation of Authority

The kinds of staff positions that student affairs administrators generally are authorized to fill include the following: admissions, positions related to student disciplinary codes, veteran services, foreign student programs, student financial aid, services for the handicapped, student activities and programs, student testing and research, personal counseling of students, career planning and placement, student publications, student housing, and student records. Sometimes medical services may be included, but at large institutions these may be placed under the jurisdiction of an office of business affairs or health services. Basically, the kinds of staff positions for which a student affairs administrator is responsible are those involving student matters after a student has been admitted to the institution and which do not relate to a student's academic program. A number of clerical, graduate or undergraduate assistantships, and other miscellaneous support positions also may be the responsibility of a student affairs administrator.

Classification of Positions

The various student affairs staff positions may be filled by persons classified only as administrators, only as faculty, or as a combination of both. How the job is classified is crucial to knowing what legal rights and responsibilities are involved. For instance, if a position is one classified purely as administrative, the person hired for that position may or may not have a written contract, be hired for a definite period of time, serve at the pleasure of his/her supervisor, be periodically evaluated, have a right to review of decisions regarding employment, have a right to some stated period of notice prior to nonrenewal or termination, or have a clearly stated job description.

By contrast, some members of the student affairs staff are also faculty members assigned certain administrative duties, such as publications advising or supervising athletics. The assignment may be on a voluntary basis that can be discontinued at the pleasure of either the board or the chief administrator to whom the employee reports. These purely faculty positions usually carry with them normal faculty employment conditions, such as peer review prior to hiring, written contracts of appointment for a certain length of time with a stated period of notice prior to nonrenewal, regular evaluation, and an opportunity for career advancement in their disciplinary departments.

A third classification is the position that may be part-time administrative and part-time faculty. For example, the job may involve implementing the student disciplinary procedure as the administrative part of the position, and an appointment as a tenured faculty member in journalism with teaching duties as the faculty part of the position. Each of these positions confers different rights and obligations regarding employment, as has been presented.

EMPLOYMENT ISSUES

Employment issues normally relate to the following: deciding upon job descriptions and qualifications, advertising for the position, interviewing candidates, hiring, setting salaries, evaluation, promotion, and termination.

At a private institution employment practices generally are affected by very few statutory constraints. The employment statutes that affect private institutions the most are those that prohibit certain specific employment practices such as discrimination based on race, sex, or religion. These statutes apply to public institutions as well. They have nothing to do with the fact that the employer is an educational institution, but cover many employers in the country. Exceptions would be employers with very few employees or those who may be covered by a similar state law rather than a federal law.

Public institutions, in addition to statutes and contract law, are usually considered to be units of government. Therefore, those who act on behalf of public institutions may be considered to be public officials. As such, their actions are subject to certain constraints set forth in the U.S. Constitution. Public officials may not refuse to hire persons, nor may they terminate persons, for constitutionally impermissible reasons, such as exercising their rights under the First Amendment protection of free speech.

Selection, Appointment, and Retention of Staff

Selection of staff should be done according to a standard set of procedures adopted in advance that take into account the job description developed for the position and the job qualifications set forth as requirements to meet the job description. All applications should be processed in a similar and nondiscriminatory fashion.

A critical issue, from the standpoint of preventing legal challenges, is that a strong rationale be presented for whatever job qualifications are set. For example, a position of program director of a student center may be advertised as requiring three years experience in administration and supervision related to student activities or a student center. Under Title VII of the Civil Rights of 1964, a court may be asked to examine the qualifications required by other colleges for similar positions in their student centers and determine whether in fact the requirement of three years experience was job-related.

Appointment procedures should be made absolutely clear, especially with regard to who has the authority to hire. If in a college handbook the governing board authority to hire is stated clearly, an applicant for employment may be expected to know that the authority to hire has been placed in that particular body and, therefore, has no right to rely on statements of anyone else, such as an associate dean. Only rarely have courts recognized that past custom and practice may clothe someone other than the designated individual or group with apparent authority to hire or promote.

Retention problems often may be the result of a lack of mutual understanding about the basic terms of the appointment that occurred between parties at the very beginning of the employment relationship. A clear understanding should be made definite about the following matters: Is the person being hired as an administrator, a faculty member, or a combination of both? Is a written contract involved? Is it for a definite term, such as one year or three years? Is there a possibility of continuing appointment or tenure thereafter?

First of all, the employment contract may consist of more than the basic document itself. By implication or by reference, other institutional documents may be incorporated as part of the contract, including policies of the governing board, the administrator or faculty handbook, the college catalogue, and the institution's customs and practices.

At a private institution, if a contract is breached, the injured employee may sue for breach of contract and recover lost wages. This is true also at a public institution. However, a public institution as a unit of the government is bound also to recognize constitutional rights of employees.

In *Board of Regents v. Roth* the U.S. Supreme Court held that where a faculty member was hired on a one-year contract and notified of nonrenewal during the appropriate period, there was no requirement under the Fourteenth Amendment Due Process Clause of the Constitution that Roth be given notice of a reason for the nonrenewal or an opportunity for a hearing.

A companion case to *Roth* was decided differently. In *Perry v. Sindermann* the U.S. Supreme Court held that the faculty handbook and the state system guidelines at a Texas college were sufficient to create the possibility of *de facto* tenure.

The faculty member, therefore, was to be given the opportunity to prove such *de facto* tenure. If he were able to do so, then he would have a property interest entitled to Constitutional protection, and would have a right to be told the reason for nonrenewal, and given the opportunity for a hearing to rebut the charges.

Regarding nonrenewal decisions, in two kinds of situations an appropriate form of due process should take place: first, where the institution, in connection with the nonrenewal, makes some publicly known charge, such as dishonesty or immorality, that imposes a stigma on the individual and forecloses other employment opportunities, or that seriously damages the individual's reputation or standing in the community; second, where statutory, or contractual law, or the existing rules or practices of the situation create a mutual understanding between the employee and the institution regarding an expectation of continued employment.

The form of due process required in a nonrenewal situation usually should consist of some appropriate process that provides the individual with notice of the reason for the nonrenewal and an opportunity for a hearing to rebut charges. If a tenured individual, or person on a continuing appointment, is being dismissed, more formal procedures are required. In *Ferguson v. Thomas* the Fifth Circuit Court of Appeals set forth a minimal procedural process to be provided in a tenured termination hearing for cause:

- The teacher be advised of the cause or causes for termination in sufficient detail to fairly enable teacher to show any error that may exist.

- The teacher be advised of the names and the nature of the testimony against him/her.

- At a reasonable time after such advice, the teacher must be accorded a meaningful opportunity to be heard in his/her own defense.

- A hearing should be held before a tribunal that both possesses some academic expertise and has an impartiality toward the charges.

Evaluation. Evaluation of student affairs administrators and staff for purposes of contract or appointment renewal, promotion, and salary increases is a process that only recently has become one for research and study. Faculty evaluation has a long history and tradition associated with promotion and tenure; evaluation of administrators has little history to serve as a guide. Courts have routinely held that faculty evaluations made by peers, according to accepted standards and in a nonarbitrary and nondiscriminatory manner, should not be tampered with by the courts.

Standards for evaluating administrators have only recently been developed. The American Association of University Administrators (AAUA) adopted "Professional Standards for Administrators in Higher Education" in 1978 (Hollander). These standards specify that

> an administrator has the right to be free from arbitrary or capricious action on the part of the institution's administration or governing board, especially in those decisions affecting continuation or termination of office . . . . An administrator has the right, under conditions established by the institution's board, to regular and formal evaluation of job performance, to participation in the evaluation process, and to receipt of timely knowledge of the results of such evaluation. (Stein & Baca, 1981, p. .90)

Other associations of administrators also have developed professional standards. One of these is the ethical standards statement concerning employment practices of the American College Personnel Association listed in Appendix A.

The purpose of an evaluation must be clear. Evaluation may be principally for the purpose of assisting administrators and faculty in improving performance and becoming more skilled and valued members of an academic community. What also must be emphasized, however, is that evaluation may be done by institutions on two levels. One level has to do with the performance of the individual. The other level has to do with the needs of the institution. Thus, it may happen that an individual may receive a positive personal evaluation, yet be dismissed because the institution no longer has a need for the services of an individual with this particular set of skills.

An institution also may change its evaluation criteria from time to time. Persons hired under the new criteria should expect to be measured by them rather than by any earlier criteria.

Those who are asked to do the evaluations usually are protected from defamation suits, even when they communicate information that is false, so long as there is no proven malice or ill will.

Separation. Separation of student affairs staff members from employment at an institution raises various legal issues related to the kind of appointment the person had, whether the institution was private or public, and whether the person allegedly was deprived of any constitutional rights.

Where a student affairs administrator or staff member was serving at the pleasure of the employer, generally there would be no right to notice, a reason for dismissal, or a hearing. Many employers have believed that this arrangement gave them great freedom and flexibility. However, now the realization is that this so-called freedom also may lead to unnecessarily high costs associated with turnover, new hiring, and new training periods. The American Association of University Administrators reacted to this concern about better management of human resources by including the following in its 1975 Professional Standards for Administrators in Higher Education:

> an administrator has a right to a written statement of the conditions of employment, including, but not limited to, statements on salary and fringe benefits, term of office, process of review, date of notification of action regarding renewal or continuance, and responsibilities of the position. (Stein & Baca, 1981, p. 89)

Where an employee has a contract for a specified term, the employment relationship ceases at the end of the contract period. If the employer chooses to dismiss the employee during the contract period, the employer would have to show just cause or else the employee could sue for breach of contract.

If the employer is a public institution, or if a private institution is sufficiently involved in "state action" (see Chapter 9), and an employee can show an expectancy of continued employment by statute, contract, or custom, most employment decisions would be subject to challenge by the employee on the ground that the action was not based on job-related performance, but on the employee's exercise of some constitutionally protected activity.

Without question, public employees have a right to free expression protected by the First Amendment. But it is not an absolute right. In *Pickering v. Board of Education,* the U.S. Supreme Court held that a teacher could not be dismissed for making public statements upon matters of public concern in the exercise of First Amendment rights, unless the statement could be shown to (1) impede the teacher's proper performance of classroom duties, (2) disrupt substantially the regular operation of the school, (3) violate an express need for confidentiality, or (4) undermine the effectiveness of the working relationship between the superior and the subordinates. This decision has become known as the "Pickering Rule". In *Mt. Healthy City School District Board of Education v. Doyle,* the U.S. Supreme Court held that where a dismissed teacher claimed his conduct was protected by the First and Fourteenth Amendments (he had made a telephone call to a radio station about school business), but his employer claimed that he was dismissed for other permissible reasons (among them, making obscene gestures to students in the school cafeteria), the trial court should determine whether the employer had shown by a preponderance of the evidence that the employee would have been dismissed even if no constitutionally protected conduct had occurred. Two years later the Supreme Court, in *Givhan v. Western Line Consolidated School District,* ruled that the free speech rights of public employees is protected in any private communication with an employer. Finally, 1984 the Supreme Court in *Connick v. Myers,* reaffirmed that public employees have the right under the First Amendment to comment on matters of public concern; however, this right, the Court reiterated, must be balanced against the state's interest, as an employer, in promoting the efficiency of the public services it performs through its employees. The Court held that where the time, place, and manner of expression may disrupt relations and threaten the efficiency of the workplace, courts should refrain from interfering with a management decision sanctioning the employee.

Financial Exigency. Bona fide financial exigency has been upheld by courts as just cause for separation of employees on term contract as well as those on continuing contracts or tenure. Sometimes the financial crisis may affect the whole institution, only one school or program within an institution, or just one department. Assuming the financial crisis to be valid, courts usually have sustained layoffs so long as there was proof that the decision as to which specific employees were to be dismissed was reached in some rational fashion. In the case of public institutions, once again, the principal reason would have to be financial distress and not the employee's exercise of some constitutionally protected right. Where a bona fide budgetary exigency exists, a tenured faculty member may be terminated and a nontenured person kept on the payroll. For instance, accreditation may be lost in the tenured person's area, and growth may be occurring in that of the nontenured faculty member.

Legal Implications of Nondiscrimination Statutes. Prominent among statutes that may affect both private and public institutional employers are nondiscrimination statutes, such as (1) Title VII of the 1964 Civil Rights Act, 42 *U.S.C.* A. Sec. 2000, as amended by the Equal Employment Opportunity Act of 1972, the Pregnancy Discrimination Act of 1978, and the Equal Employment Opportunity Commission (EEOC) Regulations of 1980 regarding Sexual Harassment; (2) the Equal Pay Act of 1963, 29 *U.S.C.* A. Sec. 206(d); (3) the Age Discrimination in Employment Act of 1967, 29 *U.S.C.* A. Sec. 621, as amended in 1986 (P.L. 99-592); and (4) the Rehabilitation Act of 1973, 29 *U.S.C.* A. Sec. 701 as amended.

A serious question arose in connection with colleges and universities receiving federal aid: do prohibitions against discrimination based on race, sex, age, and handicap apply to all of the operations of an institution or are they limited to the specific departments that receive federal aid. This question finally was answered by passage of the Civil Rights Restoration Act of 1987, P.L. 100-259, 56 LW 45. It stated that all of the operations are covered. It made clear, however, that "No provision of this Act or any amendment made by this Act shall be construed to force or require any individual or hospital or any other institution, program, or activity receiving Federal Funds to perform or pay for an abortion."

Title VII of the 1964 Civil Rights Act affects such employment practices as hiring, promotions, upgrading, salaries, fringe benefits, training opportunities and terminations. Title VII prohibits employers from discriminating in employment on the basis of race, religion (except religious institutions regarding a particular religion), national origin, and sex. The first cases to arise under Title VII often alleged discrimination on the basis of race. Many of those cases did not involve educational institutions, but decisions in the cases certainly applied to colleges and universities as employers. For instance, where a job candidate is given a test, or must meet stated job qualifications, the test or the qualifications must be related to the job. It is not enough that the test of qualifications measure the candidate in the abstract, they must measure in relation to criteria needed to do the job *(Griggs v. Duke Power Company)*. Racial discrimination may be proved in a *prima facie* sense by producing statistics showing a substantial lack of minorities in the employer's labor force *(McDonnell Douglas Corporation v. Green)*. An employer then may rebut such statistical evidence by articulating some legitimate, nondiscriminatory reason for the rejection of the candidate *(Furnco Construction Company v. Waters)*. In a significant case involving an allegation of sex discrimination at a college, regarding nonpromotion on a timely basis, the female faculty member proved to the court's satisfaction that the college's reasons for the delay were based on pretext and were discriminatory. The Court ordered back pay for the period of delay regarding the promotion *(Sweeney v. Board of Trustees of Keene State College)*.

Parenthetically, note that while employment discrimination based on race and national origin may be attacked under Title VII, another statute may be available as well—the 1866 Civil Rights Act, 42 U.S.C. sec. 1981. The Supreme Court has interpreted the 1866 Civil Rights Act, which grants to all persons including blacks the same right to make and enforce contracts (e.g., employment contracts) as is enjoyed by white citizens, to include all persons who are intentionally discriminated against because of ancestry or ethnicity. This includes Arabs and Jews. *(Saint Francis College v. Al-Khazraji; Shaare Tefila Congregation v. Cobb)*

Regarding Title VII's prohibition against discrimination based on religion, the Supreme Court held that an employer's duty to reasonably accommodate employees' religious beliefs does not require it to accept an employee's own preferred accommodation *(Ansonia Board of Education v. Philbrook)*.

Religious organizations are exempt from Title VII's prohibition against religious discrimination in employment. In that connection, the Supreme Court held that it is not a violation of Title VII for religious employers that run secular non-profit operations, such as a church that runs a non-profit gymnasium, to make religion a condition for employment for jobs in their non-profit operations. *(Corporation of the Presiding Bishop of the Church of Jesus Christ of Latter-Day Saints v. Amos)*

Title VII was amended to include the Pregnancy Discrimination Act of 1978. EEOC's final guidelines for this act will be found in 44 *Federal Register 13278*, March 9, 1979. The Pregnancy Discrimination Act makes it a violation of Title VII for an employer to discriminate on the basis of pregnancy, childbirth, or related illnesses in employment opportunities, health or disability insurance programs, or sick leave plans. Under this act pregnancy-related conditions must be treated the same as any other disability. Health insurance that covers pregnancy-related conditions of male employee dependents also must cover pregnancy-related conditions of female employees. This act is meant principally to affect attempts by employers to terminate pregnant employees rather than giving them leaves of absence, to refuse to reimburse an employee's pregnancy costs under health or disability income insurance plans, or to penalize a female employee returning from pregnancy leave by denying her access to her former position at her regular pay. In 1987 the U.S. Supreme Court upheld a California statute that requires employers to provide unpaid leave and reinstatement to employees disabled by pregnancy; the Court held that the California statute is not preempted by Title VII. *(California Federal Savings & Loan Association v. Guerra)*

Sexual harassment regulations under Title VII were published by EEOC on November 10, 1980, in 45 *Federal Register*, at page 25024. These rules generally apply to all employers, including colleges and universities, having more than 15 employees.

Essentially, the sexual harassment regulations require an employer to (1) develop a policy statement (see sample, Figure 13.1); (2) develop sanctions; (3) inform employees of their rights; (4) develop grievance procedures; and (5) investigate and take appropriate action against harassers of either sex. Examples of harassing behavior include unwanted sexually explicit language, physical contact, and the creation of a hostile work environment *(Bundy v. Jackson).* This may be interpreted to mean that regulations cover not only behavior of persons with authority to affect hiring, salaries, training, promotions, or terminations, but also the behavior of co-workers, and in some instances, nonemployees.

Where sexual harassment has been found, evidence often demonstrates that repeated offences are corroborated by witnesses.

An institution generally will be liable for sexual harassment of an employee by a supervisor where the supervisor is acting as the institution's agent or where the supervisor's advances are so pervasive and continuous that the institution must have been conscious of them, yet the institution failed to take prompt corrective action *(Meritor Saving Bank v. Vinson).*

At least one court has upheld the validity of a personnel rule prohibiting consenual sexual relations between managers and subordinates, on the grounds that *such* a rule helps avoid both the appearance of favoritism created by romantic relationships and possible claims of sexual harassment should the relationship sour *(Crosier v. United Parcel Service, Inc.).* Some colleges and universities have developed similar rules, not only regarding employees but also regarding faculty and staff in their relationships with students.

The Equal Pay Act affects not only an employee's initial hiring salary, but rates of pay for subsequent promotions

Sample Policy Statement on Sexual Harassment

The policy of this organization always has been that all our employees should be able to enjoy a work environment free from all forms of discrimination, including sexual harassment.

Sexual harassment is a form of misconduct which undermines the integrity of the employment relationship. No employee—either male or female—should be subjected to unsolicited and unwelcome sexual overtures or conduct, either verbal or physical.

Sexual harassment does not refer to occasional compliments of a socially acceptable nature. It refers to behavior which is not welcome, which is personally offensive, which debilitates morale, and which therefore interferes with our work effectiveness.

Such conduct, whether committed by supervisors or nonsupervisory personnel, is specifically prohibited. This includes repeated offensive sexual flirtations, advances or propositions; continued or repeated verbal abuse of a sexual nature; graphic or degrading verbal comments about an individual or his or her appearance; the display of sexually suggestive objects or pictures; or any offensive or abusive physical contact.

In addition, no one should imply or threaten that an applicant or employee's "cooperation" of a sexual nature (or refusal thereof) will have any effect on the individual's employment, assignment, compensation, advancement, career development, or any other condition of employment.

Any questions regarding either this policy or a specific fact situation should be addressed to the appropriate supervisor or personnel officer or to _____.

Figure 13.1 Sample policy statement on sexual harassment.

as well. It provides that females and males employed in the same establishment receive equal pay for substantially equal work. Legal challenges by females usually allege that the work they are doing is substantially equal to the work being done by males, but that their pay is not. One of the earliest cases based on the Equal Pay Act was *Corning Glass Works v. Brennan*, in which the U.S. Supreme Court held that equal work will be rewarded by equal wages. The defense raised by employers in most cases is that the particular job being performed by a female is not in fact equal to the job to which it is being compared and for which a male is being paid a higher wage. More specifically, the Act requires that men and women employed in the same establishment receive equal pay, including fringe benefits, for jobs that involve substantially equal skill, effort, and responsibility, and are performed under similar working conditions. Comparison of actual job content, not job titles, determines whether the work is substantially equal. Four exceptions are permitted by this Act. They are unequal payments based on other factors, specifically (1) a seniority system, (2) a merit system, (3) a system that measures earnings by quantity or quality of production, or (4) a differential based on any factor other than sex.

Equal pay cases turn on the facts and evidence in each case. The burden of proving that two jobs are substantially equal is a heavy one. For example, different pay scales have been found appropriate for female custodians doing lighter cleaning work than that done by males. Similarly, the initial salary of a male faculty member may be higher than that of a female hired at the same time for an equal job, where the male had other job offers at a higher starting wage, and the institution merely was meeting market conditions.

Comparable worth is a concept that looks beyond equal pay for equal work. Comparable worth deals with sex-based wage discrimination under Title VII in instances when the jobs typically assigned to men and women, though not the same, arguably could be classified as comparable regarding skill or worth. For example, secretarial jobs in an organization may have been assigned typically to women. Where the secretarial job pay scale is less than that of the janitorial job, a Title VII claim might allege that an analysis of two jobs would show that the secretarial job required as much or more education, experience, and skill as the janitorial job, and that the sole reason for its lower pay scale was that it was typically held by women. An employer can defend Title VII claims concerning wage differentials on the basis of the same four exceptions set out in the Equal Pay Act, namely, seniority, merit, quality or quantity of production, or any other factor other than sex. A number of states, cities, and counties, are doing comparable worth studies of their jobs and modifying their pay scales accordingly.

The Age Discrimination in Employment Act of 1967 as amended in 1986 is one of the most critical new statutes with which educational institutions must deal. This Act affects hiring, promotion, fringe benefits, and termination, among other employment conditions.

The Age Discrimination in Employment Act of 1967 was amended in 1986 to cover employee's age 40 and above, thereby removing the act's prior upper age limit of age 70. In effect, the act prohibits mandatory retirement of employees at any age. Certain exceptions exist. Until December 31, 1993, tenured faculty members may be retired involuntarily at age seventy, and law enforcement officers at public institutions, if part of a unit of local government, may be retired involuntarily upon reaching the retirement age prescribed by state or local law. At present regarding non-faculty employees, and at the appropriate date regarding tenured faculty and law enforcement officers as indicated above, federal regulations also prohibit the automatic elimination of health, life, and disability insurance at age seventy.

Several examples may be instructive relative to this Act. For instance, a *prima facie* case of age discrimination may be proved by showing that the complainant is in the protected age group, that his/her job performance meets appropriate expectations of employers, that someone else was hired to perform the same work after the complainant was terminated, and that age was shown to be the determining factor in the termination decision.

The question of what remedy is available to persons who believe they have been discriminated against in employment on the basis of age has been litigated in the courts for some time. Generally, the appropriate remedy is the repayment of lost wages, including lost minimums and overtime, but not damages for pain and suffering or punitive damages.

The Rehabilitation Act of 1973 (Section 504) prohibits covered federal contractors from discriminating in employment against qualified handicapped persons. Employment practices covered by this Act include recruiting, hiring, compensation, job assignment, classification, and fringe benefits. Employers must make affirmative efforts (Section 503) to employ and advance in employment qualified persons with handicaps. Structural barriers must be modified as well.

Employers are expected to make reasonable accommodations for qualified handicapped employees, such as modification of work schedules, use of ramps, and the shifting of some nonessential duties to other employees. Employers are not expected to make accommodations that would be an undue hardship, based on business necessity. Persons handicapped by alcohol or other drugs are covered by this Act, but institutions may take into account the actual behavior of handicapped individuals in deciding whether they are qualified in spite of such handicap.

Employers are urged to make employment decisions regarding persons with handicaps on a case by case basis, taking care to make a fair determination whether the individual is qualified in spite of the handicap. If an employer requires medical exams of handicapped applicants or employees, exams must be required for the nonhandicapped as well.

The Supreme Court was asked to review a case questioning whether a teacher with a contagious disease, tuberculosis, may be considered "handicapped." The Court held that she could. An individual with a contagious disease coupled with a physical impairment, in this case to her respiratory system, which limits major life activities is "handicapped" within the meaning of the act. The Court also held that in determining whether a person so afflicted is "otherwise qualified" for the job, courts should seek medical judgments in considering the nature, duration, and severity of the risk of contagion; the probabilities that the disease will be transmitted; and whether the employer can reasonably accommodate the employee. Though this case does not involve AIDS, its holdings may apply to persons with active AIDS's, but not a person who merely is an asymptomatic carrier of AIDS (*School Board of Nassau County, Florida v. Arline*).

To further clarify whether persons with contagious diseases may be deemed "handicapped," The Civil Rights Restoration Act of 1987 provides that "such term does not include an individual who has a currently contagious disease or infection and who, by reason of such disease or infection, would constitute a direct threat to the health or safety of other individuals or who, by reason of the currently contagious disease or infection, is unable to perform the duties of the job" (Section 9 of the Civil Rights Restoration Act of 1987, P.L. 100-259, 56 LW 45, amending Sec. 7(8) of the Rehabilitation Act of 1973).

Affirmative Action

The principles involved in affirmative action came into vogue in the 1970s. The guiding principle behind affirmative action plans is to provide opportunities for members of minority groups and women who in the past have been deprived of equal opportunity. Much controversy and debate has arisen from implementation of affirmative action plans, with opponents claiming that affirmative action is often synonymous with reverse discrimination.

Educational institutions that qualify as federal contractors or subcontractors are subject to Executive Order 11246, as amended. The institution's attorney should be consulted as to whether the college must adhere to this Executive Order. If so, the essential purpose of this Executive Order is to prohibit discrimination in employment on the basis of race, color, religion, sex, and national origin in hiring, upgrading, salaries, fringe benefits, training, and other conditions of employment.

The institution generally is required to analyze its work force to see if minorities and women are being underutilized. If they are, the employer is to create an affirmative action plan setting forth a timetable within which goals of hiring certain numbers of minorities and women are set. The employer then is obligated to make a good faith effort to reach the goals within the timetable.

The legality of affirmative action has been challenged often. However, two early U.S. Supreme Court decisions regarding affirmative action in employment have supported the basic concept. They are *Weber v. Kaiser Aluminum Co.* and *Fullilove v. Klutznick.* The *Weber* case involved a legal challenge to private, voluntary affirmative action plans. The *Weber* opinion upheld a collective bargaining agreement that reserved for Black employees 50 percent of the openings in an in-plant craft training program until the percentage of Black craft workers in the plant was commensurate with the percentage of Blacks in the local labor force. A white employee, Brian Weber, challenged the plan. The Supreme Court found that employers and the unions in the private sector were free to take such voluntary race-conscious steps to eliminate manifest racial imbalance in traditionally segregated job categories. The Court specifically noted that the plan did not necessarily trammel interest of white employees; the plan was a temporary measure and was not intended to maintain race balance, but simply to eliminate a manifest racial imbalance.

The *Fullilove* case upheld the provisions of the Public Works Employment Act of 1977. That Act provides that 10 percent of all federally funded public works projects shall be awarded to minority contractors.

The Supreme Court has taken a different stance concerning layoffs as compared with hiring, assigning, and promotions. It is reluctant to deprive current employees of their livelihoods.

Regarding hiring, assigning, and promotions, the Supreme Court upheld a court order that a union not only cease its discriminatory conduct, but also adopt an affirmative action program including a special fund to recruit and train minority workers and a 29% minority membership goal *(Local 28 of the Sheet Metal Workers' International Association v. EEOC).*

Regarding promotions, the Supreme Court upheld a court ordered affirmative action plan establishing a one-for-one racial quota for promotions *(U.S. v. Paradise).*

Also regarding promotions, the Supreme Court upheld a public employer's voluntary affirmative action plan designed to get more women and minorities into jobs where they traditionally have been underrepresented. From a group of seven candidates qualified for promotion to highway repair road dispatcher, a woman with a score of 73 was selected over a man with a score of 75 *(Johnson v. Transportation Agency, Santa Clara County, Calif.).*

Regarding layoffs, however, the Supreme Court struck down a layoff clause in a school board's collective bargaining agreement that provided for the possible layoff of nonminority teachers having less seniority than minority teachers. Here there was an unacceptable desire to redress "societal discrimination" rather than an acceptable desire to redress an employer's past discrimination. The Supreme Court was reluctant, as well, to deprive present employees of their jobs *(Wygant v. Jackson Board of Education).*

The emphasis given to affirmative action is subject to change due to the changes in philosophy of different national government administrations and the philosophy of administrators who enforce civil rights laws. Because of these periodic shifts in governmental philosophy, student affairs administrators need to be aware continually of parameters governing affirmative action issues.

LEGAL LIABILITY

Student affairs administrators often are faced with two major kinds of legal liability—tort liability and civil rights liability. Tort liability refers to most wrongful, civil, injurious acts that occur between individuals, except for acts involving contracts or crimes. Civil rights liability arises when government, through public officials, causes an injury by deprivation of Constitutional or statutory rights.

Tort

Four elements generally must be present for tort liability to exist. First, there must be a duty to use due care under the circumstances to prevent an unreasonable risk of harm. Second, there must be a breach of that duty. Third, there must be proved a direct, causal relationship between the behavior and the alleged injury. Fourth, there must be proof that an actual injury occurred. Common examples of torts include negligence, such as an injury to an employee that is caused by ice allowed to remain on the steps of a campus office building, and defamation, such as an injury to an employee's reputation that is caused by a news story in the college paper falsely and knowingly accusing him/her of theft of funds.

Sovereign Immunity. One defense against tort liability available to some public institutions is based on the premise that a government may not be sued without its consent. This defense is referred to as sovereign or governmental immunity. However, the concept of sovereign immunity has been abrogated by statute in some states and by judicial decisions in others. Student affairs administrators should not rely upon sovereign immunity as a defense without checking carefully with their attorneys. Also, even where the public institution itself may be protected by sovereign immunity, an individual administrator may not be.

Proprietary Functions. Even where sovereign immunity ordinarily might be available—as in the case of a public university in a state where such immunity still exists—the particular behavior that caused the injury may be characterized as a proprietary function rather than a governmental function, and sovereign immunity may not apply. For example, courts have found in some instances that jobs performed by doctors and nurses at public university hospitals did constitute proprietary rather than governmental functions, because they were the same jobs as those performed by doctors and nurses in private practice. Big time college football, similarly, has been held a proprietary function.

Negligence. Student affairs administrators must know that negligence may consist of either doing an act or failing to do an act, such as neglecting to remove snow and ice from stairs and walks. Generally the institution itself is liable for damages caused by torts if the individual administrator who caused the injury was acting within the scope of employment. Even then, however, the administrator may be sued as well and will be protected only if he/she can show no lack of reasonable care. If an administrator acts outside the scope of employment, the individual administrator alone may be liable.

Assumption of the risk is a defense against a claim of negligence. For instance, staff members who are employed as athletic coaches or assistant coaches would be expected to have assumed the normal risks attendant to employment duties associated with their particular athletic activities. Probably no remedy for negligence is available to them if they are injured at work. There may be a basis for relief under Workers' Compensation Laws, however.

Contributory negligence is another defense against liability for negligence. If a student affairs staff member were aware, for example, that his/her office door handle was loose and then was injured when the handle fell off and broke a toe, the staff member may be found contributorily negligent. In such a situation, the injured party may recover only part of the costs of the damages suffered.

Defamation. Defamation is a false and injurious statement about another person. If the statement is an oral statement, it is called slander. If it is written, broadcast, or televised, it is called libel. There are a number of defenses against a charge of defamation, such as that the statement is true, that the statement is privileged, or that the injured person is a "public figure" in which case malice must be proved. In order for a statement to be found slanderous or libelous, it must be communicated to some one, not merely to the complaining party. Where a third party overhears or reads a statement, communication has taken place.

Some communications to others about a person are considered to be privileged. The nature of privilege may be absolute, as in the case of judges' communications from the bench, or qualified, as in the case of persons authorized to perform a certain function and making otherwise defamatory statements in the course of performing that function. In an academic setting a person chairing a personnel committee deciding whether or not to continue staff members' employment may be in such a situation.

If a person is a "public figure," he/she must prove malice in an action for defamation. A well-known case that arose in an academic setting involved an adjunct professor at Western Michigan University. He received the notorious "Golden Fleece Award" from U.S. Senator William Proxmire and thereafter was adversely affected as to employment and research funding. He sued Senator Proxmire for defamation. Ultimately the U.S. Supreme Court held that a U.S. Senator is not immunized from suit for allegedly defamatory statements that he makes in press releases and newsletters, in contrast to actions and statements made on the floor of the Senate. More to the point of this discussion, the Supreme Court also ruled that Hutchinson, the professor, was not a public figure merely because he received public grants for research and published his work in professional journals. Hutchinson and Proxmire then reached an out of court settlement. Basically, Proxmire was to pay Hutchinson $10,000 damages out of personal funds and issue a public apology to Hutchinson on the floor of the Senate and through the same media and newsletters initially used to disseminate the falsehoods *(Hutchinson v. Proxmire)*.

Civil Rights Liability

Civil rights liability generally refers to the liability that emanates from guarantees of due process in the U.S. Constitution, particularly from an implementing statute referred to as 42 U.S.C. Sec. 1983 that provides

> every person who, under color of any statute, ordinance, regulation, custom or usage, or any State or Territory, subjects or causes to be subjected, any citizen of the United States or other person within the jurisdiction thereof to the deprivation of any rights, privileges, or immunities secured by the Constitution and laws, shall be liable to the party injured in an action at law, suit in equity, or other proper proceeding for redress.

Civil rights liability also may refer more broadly to a whole range of liabilities arising under civil rights statutes such as Title VII. The discussion here will be confined largely to liability under 42 U.S.C. Sec. 1983, which seeks to redress acts by public officials *who knew or should have known* that their actions would deprive persons of their constitutional rights without due process *(Wood v. Strickland)*. Public officials may be personally liable in such situations. Where a procedural due process requirement is violated and no actual financial loss is proved, a nominal award, such as one dollar, may be ordered *(Carey v. Piphus)*.

42 *U.S.C.* Sec. 1983 protects administrators, faculty, and other staff members at public institutions who allege they were suspended or disciplined or terminated without due process for exercising a constitutional right, such as participation in political activities.

Regarding searches of a public employee's desk, the Supreme Court held that a state employer's search of a state employee's desk and file cabinet in his private office without a warrant or probable cause may not violate the Fourth Amendment to the U.S. Constitution where the search is initiated appropriately and is reasonable in scope, and is conducted for a non-investigatory, work-related purpose or to investigate work-related conduct. In this case the employee was a physician-psychiatrist who was suspected of irregularities regarding his acquisition of a computer; charged with possible sexual harassment of female hospital employees; and inappropriate disciplinary action against a resident *(O'Connor v. Ortega)*.

A New York court held that the testing for drugs of public school teachers who are about to be promoted from probationary to tenured status violates the New York State Constitution as well as the U.S. Constitution *(Patchoque-Medord Congress of Teachers v. Board of Education of Patchoques-Medford Union Free School District, 517 NYS 2d 456).*

In addition to claims for violations of constitutional rights, 42 *U.S.C.* Sec. 1983 has been recently interpreted by the U.S. Supreme Court to encompass claims based solely on statutory violations of federal law, such as the Social Security Act *(Maine v. Thiboutot).*

Award of Attorneys' Fees. The Civil Rights Attorneys' Fees Awards Act of 1976, 90 Stat. 2641, 42 U.S.C. Sec. 1988 is one of some 50 statutes that give courts discretionary or mandatory power to award reasonable attorney's fees to prevailing parties in suits filed under federal statutes. Other such statutes are Title VII, the Fair Labor Standards Act, the Employees Retirement Income Security Act (ERISA), the Age Discrimination in Employment Act, and the Equal Pay Act. Under Title VII, for example, prevailing plaintiffs' attorneys may submit their bills to courts, and the courts examine them carefully regarding time and labor required, difficulty of the legal questions, skill required, and other criteria to determine the award of attorney's fees that may be approved. Occasionally, a prevailing defendant's attorney may be awarded fees where the plaintiff's suit was shown to be vexatious, in bad faith, and characterized by abusive conduct or attempts at harassment. Amounts of fees awarded range widely. Prevailing attorneys have been awarded as much as $160,000 based on actual hours spent by the attorney in the office and in court.

The first step for an attorney seeking the awarding of fees from a public employer is, as has been suggested already, to overcome the doctrine of sovereign immunity under the Eleventh Amendment of the Constitution that would prohibit paying damages from public funds without some express language from Congress in the pertinent statute permitting such payment. The trend appears to be to permit such awards in accordance with a Supreme Court decision in a Title VII case *(Fitzpatrick v. Bitzer).* Attorney's fees also may be awarded to a party who prevails through settlement rather than through judicial determination *(Maher v. Gagne).*

Guidelines for Student Affairs Administrators

1. Student affairs administrators should familiarize themselves with an institution's corporate and organizational structure as it affects employment matters, that is, whether it is a private or public institution, and what employment-related constitutional and statutory mandates apply to it at both the federal and state levels.

2. Official documents of the institution should be read and understood. These include policies of the governing board; various faculty, staff, and student handbooks; and college catalogues and bulletins. In addition, the institution's past practices and customs regarding employment should be reviewed.

3. Each individual student affairs administrator should reach a mutual understanding with the proper hiring authority at the institution regarding term and conditions of his/her own employment. This understanding preferably should be in writing. The understanding should be clear about all employment responsibilities and rights, including the following:

- Job description:
  administrative or faculty
  part-time or full-time
  authority to hire or terminate subordinates
  authority regarding budget

- Salary

- Fringe benefits, including sabbatical and leaves of absence

- Term of office

- Process of evaluation

- Date of notification of action regarding promotions, renewals, or continuance

- Due process procedures regarding review of institutional actions affecting employment

- Other relevant employment-related issues, such as: attendance at professional meetings; personal rights to free expression, privacy, and outside activities; assistance in seeking new employment in cases of reallocation of institutional resources; permissible outside employment; and seeking funds for research.

4. Student affairs administrators should ascertain what are institutional policies regarding risk management: what insurance coverage or other mechanisms exist for handling tort, civil rights, or statutory claims, particularly costs of defense of claims and payment of court or other awards?

CASE CITATIONS
and REFERENCES

Ansonia Board of Education v. Philbrook, S.Ct., November 11, 1986k, 55 LW 4019

Board of Regents v. Roth, 408 U.S. 564 (1972)

Bundy v. Jackson, 49 U.S.L.W. 2453 (1981)

California Federal Savings & Loan Association v. Guerra, 1075 S.Ct. 683 (1987)

Carey v. Piphus, 98 S. Ct. 1042 (1978)

Connick v. Myers, 103 S. Ct. 1684 (1983)

Corning Glass Works v. Brennan, 417 U.S. 188 (1974)

Corporation of the Presiding Bishop of the Church of Jesus Christ of Latter Day Saints v. Amos, S.Ct., June 24, 1987, 55 LW 5005

Crosier v. United Parcel Service, Inc., 198 Cal. Rpt. 36 (1983)

Ferguson v. Thomas, 430 F. 2d 852 (1970)

Fitzpatrick v. Bitzer, 427 U.S. 445 (1976)

Fullilove v. Klutznick, 100 S. Ct. 2758 (1980)

Furnco Construction Company v. Waters, 98 S. Ct. 2943 (1978)

Givhan v. Western Line Consolidated School District, 99 S. Ct. 693 (1979)

Griggs v. Duke Power Company, 401 U.S. 424 (1971)

Hollander, P.A. (1978). *Legal handbook for educators*. Boulder, CO: Westview Press.

Hutchinson v. Proxmire, 99 S. Ct. 2675 (1979)

Johnson v. Transportation Agency, Santa Clara County, Calif., S.Ct. March 25, 1987, 55 LW 4379

Local 28 of Sheet Metal Workers' International Association v. EEOC, 106 S. Ct. 3019 (1986)

Maher v. Gagne, 100 S. Ct. 2570 (1980)

Maine v. Thiboutot, 100 S. Ct. 2502 (1980)

McDonnell Douglas Corporation v. Green, 411 U.S. 792 (1973)

Meritor Savings Bank v. Vinson, 106 S. Ct. 2399 (1986)

Mᵗ. Healthy City School District Board of Education v. Doyle, 429 U.S. 274 (1977)

O'Connor v. Ortega, S.Ct., March 31, 1987, 55 LW 4419

Patchoque-Medford Congress of Teachers v. Board of Education of Patchoque-Medford Free Union School District, 517 NYS 2d 456 (1986)

Perry v. Sindermann, 408 U.S. 593 (1972)

Pickering v. Board of Education, 391 U.S. 563 (1968)

Saint Francis College v. Al-Khazraji, 107 S. Ct. 2022 (1987)

Shaare Tefila Congregation v. Cobb, 107, S. Ct. 2019 (1987)

School Board of Nassau County, Florida v. Arline, S. Ct. March 3, 1987, 55 LW 4245

Stein, R.H., & Baca, M.C. (Eds.). (1981). *Professional ethics in university administration* New Directions for Higher Education (No. 33). San Francisco: Jossey-Bass, 1981.

Sweeney v. Board of Trustees of Keene State College, 604 F. 2d 106 (1979)

U.S. v. Paradise, S. Ct. February 25, 1987, 55 LW 4211

Weber v. Kaiser Aluminum Co., 99 S. Ct. 2721 (1979)

Wood v. Strickland, 420 U.S. 308 (1975)

Wygant v. Jackson Board of Education, S. Ct. May 19, 1986, 54 LW 4479

SUGGESTED READINGS

Beckham, J.C. (1988). *Faculty/staff nonrenewal and dismissal for cause in institutions of higher education.* Asheville, NC: College Administration Publications.

Bickel, R.D., & Brechner, J.A. (1978). *The college administrator and the courts (and quarterly updating supplements).* Asheville, NC: College Administration Publications.

Higgins, J.M., & Hollander, P.A. (1987). *A guide to successful searches for college personnel.* Asheville, NC: College Administration Publication.

Hollander, P.A. (1978). *Legal handbook for educators.* Boulder, CO: Westview Press.

Hollander, P.A. (1980). A mediation service for administrators. In J. McCarthy (Ed.), *New directions for higher education: Resolving conflicts for higher education (No. 32).* San Francisco: Jossey-Bass.

Hollander, P.A. (1986). *Computers in education: Legal liabilities and ethical issues concerning their use and misuse.* Asheville, NC: College Administration Publications.

Hollander, P.A., Young, D.P., & Gehring, D.D. (1985). *A practical guide to legal issues affecting college teachers.* Asheville, NC: College Administration Publications.

Young, D.P., & Gehring, D.D. (1977). *The college student and the courts (and quarterly updating supplements).* Asheville, NC: College Administration Publications.

Part III

STRATEGIES
FOR
ADMINISTRATION
AND
LEADERSHIP

Roger B. Winston, Jr., Ph.D., is Professor in the Student Personnel in Higher Education Program, College of Education, at The University of Georgia. He was awarded the A.B. in history and philosophy from Auburn University and the M.A. in philosophy and Ph.D. in counseling and student personnel services from The University of Georgia. Prior to joining the faculty at The University of Georgia in 1978, he was Dean of Men and Associate Dean of Students at Georgia Southwestern College.

Theodore K. Miller, Ed.D., is Professor of Counseling and Human Development Services at the University of Georgia in Athens, Georgia in the Division of Counseling, Educational Psychology, and Educational Technology in the College of Education. He is currently the Director of the University of Georgia Southern Association of Colleges and Schools (SACS) Accreditation Reaffirmation Self-Study and is Chairman of the Self-Study Steering Committee.

Chapter **14**

HUMAN RESOURCE MANAGEMENT: PROFESSIONAL PREPARATION AND STAFF SELECTION

Roger B. Winston, Jr.
Theodore K. Miller

Student affairs administration can be conceptualized as designing an institutionally unique formula combining money, physical facilities, ideas, and people to produce programs and services that meet student needs. Of these components, the people ingredient is the most critical because without staff, programs and services cannot exist. The importance of the staffing element is obvious when the budgets of most student affairs divisions reflect that from 75% to 85% is expended on personnel costs. Lack of the other three elements can and do limit programs, but will not necessarily preclude them. (Many student affairs professionals, for instance, are distinguished for their ability to create programs with limited financial resources. This can explain, in part, the extensive use of student paraprofessionals and even allied professionals in some student affairs programs.) This chapter examines preparation for professional practice and the process for selecting professional and support staff members.

THE STUDENT AFFAIRS STAFF

Many assume that "student affairs staff" refers to residence hall directors, counselors, activities advisors, directors of placement, deans, and vice-presidents for student affairs. However, if a student affairs division were composed only of these professional employees, it would function very poorly, if at all. Secretaries, maintenance workers, computer programmers, bookkeepers, receptionists, resident assistants, physicians, peer counselors, and others are essential to the functioning of an effective student affairs division. When thinking about the personnel of a student affairs division, all those who make contributions toward accomplishment of division goals must be considered a part of the division. A division's personnel can be divided into five categories: professional, allied professional, support, paraprofessional, and volunteer.

Professionals

"Professional staff" are persons who hold at least a master's degree in student affairs, counseling, or higher education administration; who hold membership in and ascribe to the ethical and professional standards of one or more student affairs professional associations; and who have responsibility for outside-the-classroom education of students in post-secondary institutions. This category includes those traditionally thought of as the "staff," ranging from entry level residence hall directors and student activity advisors through middle management department directors to chief student affairs administrators (CSAA). Their formal education, speciality training, and work experiences give them a clear understanding of the purposes of student affairs administration and a firm commitment to the growth and development of college students.

Allied Professionals

Persons responsible for performing or directly supporting outside-the-classroom educational functions but who possess extensive education in specialized professions other than student affairs are allied professionals in student affairs (Delworth & Aulepp, 1976). Personnel in this category come from a wide array of fields. Included are physicians, accountants, computer systems designers, clergy, statisticians, editors, and attorneys. Although they bring highly developed skills and expertise, they nevertheless require special training and supervision in the areas of college student development and student affairs administration designed to aid them in applying their skills and knowledge in furthering the goals of the student affairs division. Expecting these kinds of specialty trained people to make the maximum contribution to the division's goals without a clear understanding of and commitment to the underlying philosophy of student development is a mistake. Effective allied professionals must appreciate the division's goals and must view themselves as a part of that structure, not as isolated specialists within it.

Support Staff

The third category of staff is support. Support staff members are persons who perform the myriad of activities that enable the professionals and allied professionals to provide essential services and educational interventions. They are vital to the student affairs division because they complement and supplement divisional goals. "Receptionist," "clerk," "secretary," "keypunch operator," "computer programmer," "security officer," and "printer" are examples of support staff job titles. Generally, these jobs require some specialized training, but seldom a college degree.

Work-study and other part-time student workers who perform tasks such as typing, key punching, duplicating, filing, and maintenance also fit into this category. Although they often need on-the-job training and require more supervision than do full-time support staff, they are important division personnel, especially in an era of limited resources. Employing student workers has an additional payoff: the college is investing in itself because students use much of their earnings to pay tuition and fees. If adequately managed, a part-time employment program can enhance students' educations by providing "hands on" work experience through which marketable skills can be learned.

Support personnel occasionally are referred to as the "nonprofessional staff," an unfortunate selection of words because it reflects a lack of appreciation for the importance of these staff members to the effective functioning of a department. Support staff members are often the first and only contact students have with a particular student affairs office. Frequently, they are the first exposed to digruntled or troubled students, faculty, parents, and members of the public. How well that contact is negotiated may determine whether a student remains in college and receives the help and services needed or whether potentially emotionally explosive situations are resolved with the skill and diplomacy demanded (Eble, 1979; Williams, 1973).

Paraprofessionals

Paraprofessionals are individuals, usually students, who are selected, trained, and supervised in the performance of specific functions that generally would be accomplished by professionals and who are paid compensation in money or kind. Examples of paraprofessionals found on many campuses include resident assistants, peer counselors, peer academic advisors, orientation leaders, and tutors. Graduate assistants may be classified as paraprofessionals or professionals-in-training (distinguished from professionals primarily by responsibilities, status, and pay) depending on assigned tasks, the nature of their education, and the goals for the position they hold.

Student Volunteers

Finally, students who perform volunteer services are another important source of human resources. Organizationally, these students may function autonomously as recognized student organizations. Such groups may assume responsibility for certain activities such as providing visitors guided tours of the campus, operating nonprofit book exchanges, or serving as ushers and ticket takers for campus cultural events. Students also may provide volunteer services through programs initiated, supervised, and supported by a student affairs department. For example, the admissions office may use volunteer orientation leaders; the counseling center may staff a crises line with volunteers; the international student office may organize volunteer hosts for newly arrived international students.

Student affairs administrators must consider many factors when deciding to use student volunteers. First, how critical is the service? Volunteers are using their free time to provide the service. When the amount of their free time is diminished, especially near midterm and final examinations, volunteer activities usually, and rightfully, become secondary. If the service is critical (such as a crisis line), then a backup means of providing services must be planned, or other staff members over whom one has more influence should be utilized. Second, how qualified are the volunteers? Volunteers should be systematically trained before they provide the service and must be supervised thereafter. Simply because one uses student volunteers does not mean that there are no costs. Failure to provide adequate training and supervision is to flirt with disaster and is unfair to and exploitive of the volunteers. Third, what are the legal liabilities? When a college uses volunteers to fulfill a college function, the institution should exercise great care to assure that the student volunteers are qualified to render the services offered, that their work activities are closely monitored, and that their responsibilities do not exceed their level of competence. Volunteers can be a valuable complement to the paid staff, and the experiences can be rewarding for the students involved. However, student affairs administrators should carefully evaluate their use in an objective and critical fashion.

PROFESSIONAL PREPARATION

An essential aspect of being a profession is the control of entrance criteria of prospective practitioners. In other words, a certain minimal level must exist of generally agreed upon academic preparation over established content domains and skill areas (Carpenter, Chapter 8; Miller & Carpenter, 1980; Winston, 1990). Practitioners seeking to employ entry-level staff members need to be assured that applicants have mastered certain knowledge areas, have had supervised practice in applying theories and models to work with students, have been enculturated to the basic values and ideals of the profession, and posses personality characteristics that permit them to work effectively with students within a bureaucratic organization. This is only possible when standards are accepted for professional education.

Considerable progress in this regard has been made since the first preparation program for deans of women was established at Teachers College, Columbia University in 1913, which was expanded to admit men in 1928 (Johnson & Sandeen, 1988). However, it was 65 years later before a set of widely-accepted standards for professional preparation was created.

In 1979 the American College Personnel Association adopted a set of preparation standards, which served as the impetus for the creation of the Council for the Advancement of Standards for Student Services/Development Programs (CAS). In 1986 preparation standards were published by CAS. Concurrently, under the leadership of the American Association for Counseling and Development, the Council for the Accreditation of Counseling and Related Educational Programs (CACREP, 1989) was established, adopted standards and began to accredit programs, including student affairs preparation programs at the master's degree level (See Mable and Miller, Chapter 11).

Unfortunately, universal acceptance has not taken place for professional education with a specified core content for employment in the field. Even today "talented amateurs" and allied professionals are employed at entry-level and even as CSAAs by college presidents who do not understand or appreciate the goals of student development and the sophistication required to accomplish them. At the entry-level this can be explained by several factors: (1) preparation programs have been unable to produce enough graduates to meet the entry-level practitioner needs of the field (2) many practitioners who entered the field without benefit of rigorous professional preparation do not see the need; (3) entry-level salaries have been so depressed that some institutions have found it impossible to attract well qualified graduates of preparation programs; and (4) entry-level job assignments at some institutions (which have been basically clerical and organization maintenance in nature) have not required professional preparation.

Preparation Standards

Three basic approaches to professional preparation have been accepted by both CAS and CACREP: counseling, administration, and student development. This classification of emphases was basically established *de facto*, that is, it was based on Rodgers' (1977) survey findings about what existed in the field rather than on a careful consideration about what is the most effective preparation for the field. The tripartite approaches to professional preparation standards, however, share a certain amount of common ground.

Content Areas. In addition to practica and internships in college student affairs settings, 11 academic content areas appear as requirements in one or more of the CAS preparation standards. (Letters following each content domain indicate which approach or emphasis requires this area: C = counseling, A = administration, and SD = student development.)

1. ***Human Development Theory and Practice*** (C, A, SD) includes development theories appropriate for students from age 17 through adulthood and process models for translating that theory into applications or interventions. Theories of which students should be knowledgeable include phychosocial, cognitive, moral, person-environment interaction, humanistic, and socio-cultural foundations, as well as instruments to assess development or status in each of the areas.

2. ***Higher Education and Student Affairs Functions*** (C, A, SD) includes study of the history of higher education and the student affairs profession, legal parameters of practice, traditional functional areas in student affairs, professional ethics, professional standards, and supervised practice in student affairs settings.

3. ***Research and Evaluation*** (C, A, SD) includes study of research design, elementary statistical procedures, computer literacy, proposal writing, and evaluation models and methodologies.

4. **Organization Behavior and Development** (A,SD) includes study of organization behavior, leadership, naturalistic inquiry methods, process consultation, organizational design, decision making, conflict resolution, and planned organization change.

5. **The Helping Relationship and Career Development** (C,SD) includes study of counseling theories and techniques, development of self-awareness and counseling skills, theories of career development, cultural differences, career decision-making, and supervised practice in application of counseling skills and techniques.

6. **American College Student and College Environment** (SD) includes investigation of the attitudes and characteristics of students and their cultures. Areas of study include the effects of college on students, environmental assessment, and contemporary problems such as attrition, cultural differences, and sexual behavior.

7. **Administration** (A) includes study of budgeting and finance, governance and policy making, human resource development, management information systems, and collective bargaining.

8. **Performance Appraisal and Supervision** (A) includes study of job analysis; performance appraisal; theories and applications of supervision of professional, paraprofessional, and support staff; and management techniques.

9. **Administrative Uses of Computers** (A) includes programming, use of computers for forecasting, budgeting, planning, and resource allocation.

10. **Group Counseling** (C) includes study of group dynamics, intervention strategies, theories of group counseling, facilitation skills, and supervised practice.

11. **Appraisal of the Individual** (C) includes study of framework for understanding the individual, interpretation

of psychological tests, use of case studies, test construction, and individual differences.

Practitioners and students alike should keep in mind that the CAS standards specify *minimum* requirements. Optimum professional preparation will exceed these standards.

Brown (1985) has proposed that students should progress through three levels of learning in these content areas: Level I involves acquiring basic knowledge principally through reading the literature and discussion with classmates and faculty members; Level II involves knowledge of intervention or change strategies through application and analysis (reality testing; experimentation under somewhat controlled conditions or simulations); and Level III involves experiential learning often through internships and practica. Only graduates who have significant learning experiences at each of these levels can be adequately prepared for professional practice.

Employer Expectations of Entry-level Professionals' Skills. Walter (1988) conducted a survey of the employers of recent graduates of professional preparation programs to determine which skills were thought essential. The following skills were classified as "very important" by over one-half of the respondents:

- Teach students to take responsibility for their decisions

- Teach students to deal with the consequences of their behavior

- Confront destructive, unhealthy or counterproductive behavior of students

- Communicate and establish rapport with students

- Assist students to identify behaviors that are desired or should be changed

- Understand institutional objectives, expectations, and policies

- Communicate effectively on a one-to-one basis with students

- Listen to students' perceptions of feelings

- Assess student needs

- Use effective communication skills

- Understand the institutional structure

- Initiate contact with the appropriate resource people

- Make appropriate referrals

- Develop positive public relations

- Promote effective team work

- Maintain student confidentiality

- Provide in-service training and staff development programs

- Establish priorities

- Bridge the gap between theory and practice

- Use effective decision-making strategies

- Evaluate staff performance

- Establish rapport with administrative staff

- Perform duties in accordance with professional ethical standards

- Perform duties in accordance with professional practice standards

- Write clear concise memos and reports

- Draw realistic conclusions and recommendations from available data

- Evaluate programs to determine their effectiveness

A quick survey of this list of expected skills reveals that persons who enter the field without benefit of professional preparation very likely will be unable to perform at the same level as graduates. Different preparation emphases will better prepare new professionals to perform some tasks than they will others. A careful analysis is required to ascertain the knowledge and skills needed to function successfully in a particular position. Potential employers, however, should keep in mind that individual differences exist among graduates of programs and that it is unwarranted to assume, because a program does not emphasize certain skills in its curriculum, that a graduate has not developed those skills through internships or practica. Competent student affairs professionals enter the field with a combination of knowledge, personality traits or affective attitudes, and skills that are suited to the requirements of the position (Bair, 1985).

When called upon to employ entry-level professionals, student affairs administrators should ask themselves several questions: (1) Is this truly a professional position? If the answer is "yes," then only graduates of "good quality" preparation programs (that is, those who at least meet the *minimum* preparation standards adopted by CAS) should be interviewed. (2) What skills am I as the supervisor willing to teach a new professional on the job, and what skills must an entry-level professional possess upon entry into the institution? In effect, a major additional responsibility exists when one decides to employ an underqualified staff member. Ethically and professionally the student affairs administrator must assume the responsibility to teach the new professional the skills and knowledge that are lacking at employment. Most student affairs practitioners do not have sufficient time to take on the systematic "basic education" of staff members as well as perform the myriad of other assigned duties.

STAFFING THE STUDENT AFFAIRS DIVISION

This section presents considerations and processes involved when staffing the student affairs division with professional, allied professional, and support personnel. Staffing should not be thought of as being synonymous with employment or personnel selection. It "includes all the methods of matching the skills available with the tasks to be performed" (Albright, 1974, p. 4-2), namely organizational analysis, personnel planning, position analysis, recruitment, selection, job/organization restructuring, promotion/demotion, and termination.

Personnel Planning and Forecasting

Whether an institution and its student affairs division are growing, leveling off, or declining, student affairs administrators are under constant pressure to obtain maximum results from the human and financial resources available. Consequently, careful planning, monitoring, and inventorying of personnel needs and changes are essential.

Personnel planning is a systematic process for analyzing an organization's present makeup in terms of categories of people within its work force and its future needs for staff based on both internal and external conditions (Butteriss & Albrecht, 1979).

Forecasting is based on the assumption that, while the future is indeterminable, it will contain extensions of many conditions or forces working in the present and immediate past. In other words, present trends can be projected into the future. Forecasting forms the basis upon which assumptions can be made and, hence, with which uncertainties can be dealt. Personnel forecasting must take into account conditions both internal and external to the college.

Internal Conditions. Internal conditions that need to be considered in personnel forecasting include: (1) the institution's mission as defined by institutional leaders or as assigned by governing bodies; (2) institutional goals, programs, and priorities; (3) present enrollment trends; (4) institutional political issues such as power, authority, and territory (Baldridge, 1971; Barr & Keating, 1979); (5) available funds within existing budget structures; (6) changing demands of internal constituencies such as student groups, faculty governance structures, and collective bargaining units; and (7) career advancement, promotion, and retirement schedules.

Personnel planning must be keyed to fit institutional long-range goals and objectives. For example, if a college plans to emphasize graduate programs as a means of off-setting a projected decline in traditional age undergraduate students, then student affairs staff members will need to be reassigned to programs and services required by such students. However, by custom many assume that graduate students do not need the support provided to traditional age undergraduates. Because of this mistaken idea the student affairs administrator will need to build a data base that can document graduate student needs, begin an educational campaign designed to dispel the conventional (though uninformed) view of graduate students, and initiate staff development activities to prepare staff members for different roles. Also, because most entry-level positions can be expected to be vacated every two to four years as young professionals make their career ladder ascent, (or unfortunately leave the field), the comprehensive personnel planning program must assure that staff with appropriate backgrounds, skills, and experiences are available to meet the changing needs of the division. Just because a vacancy exists in the fraternity advisor's position, for example, does not mean that one automatically seeks another person to perform exactly the same functions. Each position vacancy should be viewed within the overall personnel needs. Without a clear picture of future needs, the division will always be in the position of playing "catch up" or "making do" with inadequately or inappropriately trained staff.

External Conditions. Conditions outside the institution also have an influence on personnel planning and forecasting. Such conditions include (1) governmental funding; (2) changing demographic characteristics of the student population both current and potential; (3) standards and requirements of accrediting agencies; (4) legislative actions such as affirmative action mandates, minimum wage laws, civil service classification systems and regulations, and social security taxes, (5) general economic conditions; and (6) demands and needs of various constituencies such as alumni, trustees, students' parents, the news media, and business and industry.

For example, Deegan (1981) described student affairs practices at a university projecting a 20% decline in enrollment.

The vice-president "claims" all positions that become vacant. A needs assessment then is conducted of personnel needs within the division; the personnel inventory and forecast are consulted, and only then are decisions made about filling the position. Because of the projected enrollment decline, the student affairs division has adopted a policy of attempting to fill vacancies with existing personnel. If that is possible, then the number of staff members can be gradually reduced through attrition, because the termination process tends to have a deteriorative effect on staff morale and productivity. Only through systematic personnel evaluations and projections can needed reductions be accomplished without adding unnecessary hardships for staff while maintaining high quality services for students. As Sprunger and Bergquist (1978) noted, personnel forecasting in a period of reduction or no growth is critical particularly because it in large measure determines the institution's flexibility in meeting changing needs and circumstances.

Position Analysis

In order to have an effective personnel planning program, gaining a clear understanding of the responsibilities of each position is essential. "The process of position analysis addresses the relatedness of duties and responsibilities to experience, skills, knowledge, and abilities required for the tasks to be performed" (Fortunato & Waddell, 1981, p. 43). Every position in the student affairs division should be reviewed at least once a year (regardless of whether a vacancy is expected).

A number of different schemata has been developed for analyzing positions. The U.S. Training and Employment Service developed a process for analyzing jobs that is related to the *Dictionary of Occupational Titles* known as Functional Job Analysis (FJA) (Fine & Wiley, 1971). Under this approach a position can be divided into three "primitives": data, people, and things (McCormick, 1974). How a worker functions in relation to things (physical manipulation), people (interpersonal relationships), and data (mental processes) can describe a job or position. Each hierarchy under people, data, and things provides two measures: (1) level, a measure of relative complexity, and (2) orientation, a measure of relative involvement with people, data, and things. Data for analyzing a position are obtained from experienced workers or by FJA trained personnel through observations and interviews (Fortunato & Waddell, 1981; McCormick, 1974).

Other commonly used analysis methods include the (1) Job Element Method developed by the U.S. Civil Service Commission, (2) U.S. Department of Labor Method, and (3) Comprehensive Occupational Data Computer Program developed for the Air Force and used primarily by the military (Fortunato & Waddell, 1981; McCormick, 1974). All of these methods require specific training for their use. Depending upon the scope and sophistication of an institution's personnel department, the student affairs administrator may be able to call upon that department for assistance in analyzing the positions within the division. If staff expertise is not available, faculty from the college or department of business may be of assistance.

The position analysis approaches identified previously are most appropriate for support staff positions that typically reflect a relatively high level of standardization and transferability from one campus office to another. The positions assumed by student affairs professionals, however, are often unique in that a campus may have only one or two persons with the same duties. These positions are often extensively influenced by tradition and eccentricities of the institution. Consequently, a less formalized position analysis process that can be performed by one not trained in the technology of position analysis may be more appropriate.

One begins by determining the role definition, that is a description of the outcomes expected from the person filling the position (Sprunger & Bergquist, 1978). For example, a partial role definition for a director of housing might include the following:

- To participate with the Vice President for Student Affairs and other department heads in a team management approach to the campus;

- To provide leadership for the area directors and administrative staff by

(1) building a cohesive team in the department,

(2) calling upon individual expertise to assist in accomplishing objectives,

(3) encouraging participation in division task forces and professional organizations, and

(4) promoting and supporting innovation;

- To establish mechanisms for the continual development of staff (professional, allied professional, support, and paraprofessional);

- To create residential environments that stimulate and support the intellectual, emotional, and social development of students;

- To relate institutional trends, direction, policies, procedures, and problems to the departmental staff;

- To direct and monitor business and maintenance operations to assure sound fiscal practices and a safe and healthy environment; and

- To create a diversity of living arrangements within the housing facilities to accommodate the full range of student needs.

Once a complete role definition for a position has been developed, an inventory of knowledge, abilities, and skills can be used to identify critical attributes needed. Zion (1977) identified six aspects of administration that may be applied to the role definition in determining the level of skills and abilities needed to be successful: needs assessment, planning, goal setting, selection/training, delineating tasks, and evaluation. Because different roles require different levels of abilities and expertise, identifying them serves as an informal, but effective way to analyze a position. A position's role definition and the profile of requisite skills and abilities should not be viewed as a one-time operation. As institutions change, the requirements of the various positions need to reflect those changes, thus requiring reevaluation at least annually.

Job Specifications and Position Descriptions

Upon completion of the position analysis, job specifications for the position should be formulated. Included in the specifications are (1) an accurate position title, (2) an outline of the scope of activities involved, (3) a description of duties, (4) a statement of responsibilities and authority, (5) a description of expected relationships with others, and (6) the minimum education, experience, and skills required. Job specifications may be different from those of the previous jobholder. Close examination of job specifications when a vacancy occurs is particularly important so as to determine whether a new staff member should have responsibilities different from his/her predecessor.

A position description may be developed from the position analysis, which includes role definition, survey of skills and abilities, and job specifications. Position descriptions differ from job specifications in that the latter defines and lists desired skills, experiences, and characteristics and is intended to be used as a source document during hiring activities, while the former is (1) based on the job specifications, (2) a public document made available to job candidates, and (3) a part of the contractual documents (Sprunger & Bergquist, 1978).

An adequate position description should include the following (Fortunato & Waddell, 1981; Sims & Foxley, 1980; Sprunger & Bergquist, 1978):

- position title;
- division in which position is located and the title of supervisor for the position;
- goals of the position (why the position exists);
- work activities and procedures (including duties, responsibilities, scope of authority, materials used, and equipment operated—when appropriate—and a statement such as "performs duties as assigned");
- position requirements including minimum education, knowledge, and experience needed; and

- conditions of employment (wage structure, working hours, permanency of position, and description of benefits).

Position descriptions should be carefully drawn and periodically updated. Berenson and Ruhnke (1966) pointed out that position descriptions have multiple uses, including to (1) reassign or fix functions and responsibilities within an organization, (2) evaluate employee performance, (3) help orient new employees to their positions, (4) delineate lines of authority, and (5) communicate with prospective employees during the selection process.

FILLING POSITION VACANCIES

Professional and
Allied Professional Positions

When a position becomes vacant, a number of predetermined steps should be followed by the CSAA: (1) consult personnel plan, (2) determine budget availability, (3) consult position analysis and job specification and compare with student needs assessment data, and (4) decide whether to continue the position as is, to restructure, abolish, or transfer it to another department with different duties and responsibilities.

Vertical Staffing. If the plan is to employ a person to fill a position, then a decision must be made either to transfer an existing staff member (vertical staffing) or seek someone from outside the student affairs division (horizontal staffing). Arguments exist on both sides of the issue of promoting from within. On the pro side, divisions that provide in-house staff with promotion opportunities build morale (provided the process is perceived as fair and equitable), commitment and loyalty to the institution, and continuity for programs and services. On the con side, opponents argue that internal promotion (1) retards efforts to increase the representation of minorities and women on the staff, (2) tends to encourage inertia by limiting the input of new ideas, and (3) tends to promote conformity and superficial agreement, while stimulating internecine backbiting. Each division should have a published policy about vertical staffing to which it strictly adheres.

Should a college elect to employ vertical staffing, several procedural rules may lessen the disadvantages. First, announcement of the vacancy should be published in a widely read institutional publication that all eligible employees receive weekly or biweekly (Fortunato & Waddell, 1981). Second, deadlines for application, as well as specified decision making criteria and procedures, should be communicated to all applicants. Deadlines should be as short as possible, yet ensure reasonable opportunity to apply and sufficient time to evaluate candidate qualifications. If the unit or job classification shows an underutilization of minorities or women, special recruiting efforts may be necessary. The college affirmative action officer can help determine whether external recruiting is necessary. Third, all candidates should be treated the same even if external recruiting is used.

Horizontal Staffing. Following is a model process for recruiting and selecting professional and allied professional staff. Effort has been made to conform to definitions of good practice as specified in Risch (1977), the *American College Personnel Association Statement of Ethical Principles and Standards* (1989), and equal employment opportunities and affirmative action laws and executive orders* (See Chapter 13).

1. *Prepare the job specifications and position description.* The chief student affairs officer or department director

---

*Five major pieces of legislation and two executive orders are the legal bases for equal employment opportunity and affirmative action: Title VII of the Civil Rights Act of 1964 and a 1971 amendment; Executive Orders 11246 and 11375; Equal Pay Act of 1963 and a 1972 amendment; Age Discrimination in Employment Act of 1967; Rehabilitation Act, Sections 503 and 504; Vietnam-Era Veterans Readjustment Act of 1974. Fortunator & Waddell (1981), Stanton (1977), and Commerce Clearing House (1979) are excellent sources of information on these legal matters.

has responsibility for preparing these documents, ideally in consultation with other staff members.

2. *Appoint and charge a search committee.* A search committee of three to nine persons should be appointed to coordinate the recruitment and selection process. When possible, departments in addition to the one in which the vacancy occurs should be represented. For upper level administrators, care should be exercised to assure broad representation of programs and departments within the student affairs division. Having knowledgeable students and faculty members on the committee is desirable but not essential. Committee members must be well acquainted with the duties and responsibilities of the vacant position if they are to be contributors. To appoint students and faculty is a disservice to all concerned unless they are in a position to be equal partners in the search process. The ACPA *Statement of Ethical Principles and Standards* (1989) holds that a professional responsibility is to educate or train members of search and screening committees who are unfamiliar with the profession before they begin their work on the committee.

A written, formal charge of duties, responsibilities, and expectations should be made to the committee. The charge may be to (a) screen applications and accumulate credentials, (b) screen and select a specified number of candidates for in-depth interviews, (c) screen, interview, and recommend either a rank-ordered or unranked list of names, or (d) screen, interview, and offer the position. Confusion and accusations of betrayal have resulted from unclear charges to committees who felt that administrators were manipulating them or withdrawing authority because of displeasure with the committee's decisions. Affirmative action guidelines or preferences for the position should be communicated to the committee at the outset along with the position specifications and description.

3. *Establish working rules of the committee, a detailed description of the selection process, and appropriate*

deadlines. The committee should decide the rules under which it will function. Must decisions be unanimous or by a simple majority vote? What constitutes a quorum; how often and when will the committee meet? Will meetings be confidential or considered public?

Deadlines should be established, not only for candidates making application, but also for various stages in the selection process. A clear, concise statement of this process should be formulated and shared with all applicants.

4. *Announce the position and specify application requirements.* Position announcements should include the following: (a) position title, (b) responsibilities and duties, (c) necessary qualifications, specifically education and previous experience, (d) salary range, and (e) application procedure and deadline. Applicants should also be provided information about the institution, the student affairs division, and any special requirements or restrictions such as live-in requirements, night work, or travel.

A variety of means are needed to communicate the position announcement. Recommended means include advertisements in publications such as *Chronicle of Higher Education, Affirmative Action Register,* and professional association newsletters and placement publications. Letters to university placement offices and preparation programs can be particularly effective for entry level positions. Numerous professional student affairs associations have placement services that provide periodic announcements to their membership and subscribers. The Higher Education Administrative Referral Service (HEARS) is an agency formed by several associations to serve as a year-round liaison for colleges and candidates. Vacancies known in the early spring can find a large applicant pool at the annual conventions of national professional student affairs associations. Preliminary screening can also be done during short interviews at the conventions.

Initial applications should require a résumé or curriculum only. Requiring letters of recommendation, transcripts, and placement credentials during the initial screening process is unnecessary. Initial screening can be adequately accomplished with the information found in résumés and vitae.

5. *Complete initial screening.* Applicants obviously lacking necessary credentials or the experience specified should be notified immediately that they are no longer being considered. Each committee member should independently evaluate all remaining applications on a predetermined set of criteria. Use of a simple rating scale based on criteria from the job specifications is recommended. After the independent evaluations, each committee member should rank the top 10 candidates to create the short list. The committee as a group can then select its top candidates for further investigation. Candidates eliminated from consideration, as well as those still being considered at this point, should be notified of their status.

6. *Collect and evaluate additional data on the short list candidates.* Each of the candidates on the short list should be contacted by telephone and asked (a) if he/she is still interested in the position, (b) to answer specific questions raised by the committee when reviewing resumes, (c) to submit credentials (and a philosophy statement and/or a portfolio of work samples—if the committee deems that desirable), and (d) for permission to contact identified references and other persons not listed as references. Designated committee representatives should contact by telephone at least one identified reference and one other person on the campus where the candidate is located to solicit evaluations and answers to a short list of questions devised by the committee. References should also be asked to verify and evaluate previous work experiences related to the position. McIntire and Carpenter (1981) in a survey of colleges in the south central United States reported that the primary considerations used in evaluating letters of reference were (a) evidence of ability to fit into a work

group, (b) evidence of adaptability, (c) position of reference writer (superior, subordinate, or peer), (d) performance-based (behavioral) statements, and (e) personal knowledge of the writer.

7. *Select candidates from the short list for on-campus interviews.* Once the committee has accumulated and evaluated the data requested, candidates for on-campus interviews should be selected. The number of candidates to be invited to campus may be determined by the amount of travel funds available and by the charge to the search committee. The committee may have been charged to submit a list of five to ten unranked or ranked candidates from which the CSAA, department director, or president will select, or it may have been charged to invite a specified number of candidates. McIntire and Carpenter (1981) found that the modal number of candidates invited to campus was three, with a tendency to invite five for department heads and chief student affairs officers.

8. *Interview the candidates.* Before candidates arrive on campus, they should be provided written materials to acquaint them with the college, its goals, philosophy, and general mode of operation. Helpful materials include catalogues, student newspapers, student affairs staff manuals, departmental operating manuals, annual report summaries, and maps and descriptive material about the local community. If the candidate would be living off campus, general real estate information should be provided.

The on-campus interview should be planned carefully so that the college can get an accurate picture of the candidate both in terms of skills and knowledge as well as personality and style. Equally important, the candidate should be given opportunity to gain an accurate picture of the college, both strengths and weaknesses. The candidate should have opportunity to meet persons with whom he/she will work, including people outside the division in areas such as business affairs and academic affairs.

The interview process, according to Sprunger and Bergquist (1978), should be designed to determine whether the candidate is able (competency criterion) to perform the job and willing (interest criterion) to do the job. To be qualified is not enough. A useful form that interviewers may use to help systematize the analysis of candidate qualifications is shown in Figure 14.1.

In order to make the interview situation constructive and efficient as a data collection technique that can lead to a satisfactory personnel decision, careful planning and preparation are needed before the candidate arrives for interviews. Sprunger and Bergquist (1978) identified five categories of information that should be sought during the interview process: (a) previous jobs, (b) future career goals, (c) attitude and experience with supervisors, peers, and subordinates, (d) perceptions of colleges at which he/she has worked (were they positive or negative and why), and (e) past compensation record. For student affairs positions, other categories of information to be ascertained during the interview process that generally facilitate making good employment decisions include: (a) knowledge of professional literature, especially student development theory, (b) philosophy of and commitment to the student affairs profession, (c) involvement in professional organizations, and (d) style of relating to students.

Legal limitations exist on the kinds of information that may be sought either on applications or during interviews. Generally speaking, asking questions that do not have a direct and *bona fide* bearing on the performance of the job or asking different questions of applicants based on gender, race, religion, marital status, national origin, age, or status as a Vietnam-era veteran is impermissible. A summary of various antidiscrimination rules and regulations pertaining to employment interviewing is provided in Figure 14.2.

Student affairs professionals can use several guidelines to avoid pitfalls that may be encountered during the interview process.

- *Clearly define each interviewer's role and responsibilities.* Never ask someone to interview a candidate and then

(Continued on Page 480)

Candidate's Name_____

Position Applying For_____

There are two critical questions that must be considered in promoting, interviewing, and selection. They are "Can the person perform up to the expected level?" and "Will the person perform?" The first question deals with qualifications, abilities, and experience. The second question deals with motivation and desire. Using the rating scale, indicate your assessment of the candidate on these two factors.

Not Applicable	High Ability and Potential			Average Ability and Potential			Low Ability and Potential		Don't Know
NA	8	7	6	5	4	3	2	1	X
Can Do	Will Do								

_____ _____ 1. Is professionally competent as evidenced by degrees and experience, and will continue to develop professional competence by attending conferences, doing research, writing, etc.

_____ _____ 2. Is intelligent and has academic ability and potential for continued development.

_____ _____ 3. Is physically healthy and is interested in maintaining health.

_____ _____ 4. Shows ability for this position and will grow into it.

_____ _____ 5. Is professionally active in associations and will continue or become more active.

_____ _____ 6. Cooperates with superiors, peers, students.

_____ _____ 7. Is able to motivate students.

_____ _____ 8. Is skilled in organization of subject matter and the teaching/learning process.

_____ _____ 9. Understands the importance of planning, follow-through, and performance of himself and others.

_____ _____ 10. Is and will be positive, empathetic, and fair.

(continued)

Figure 14.1. Selection and analysis form: Used by interviewers to systematize the analysis of candidate's qualifications.

Note: From *Handbook for college administration* by B.E. Sprunger and W.H. Berquist, Washington, DC: Council of Independent Colleges (then the Council for the Advancement of Small Colleges), 1978, pages 163-4. Reprinted by permission of the publisher.

Figure 14.1. Continued

_____	_____	11. Is able to motivate others to high achievement.
_____	_____	12. Is able to verbalize, write, and illustrate effectively.
_____	_____	13. Is able to develop rapport with others.
_____	_____	14. Maintains employment for acceptable length.
_____	_____	15. Is able and willing to work in excess of minimal demands.
_____	_____	16. Is able to develop loyalties to institution.
_____	_____	17. Is self-reliant and perseverant.
_____	_____	18. Exercises leadership even in difficult situations.
_____	_____	19. Works with others, but is not dependent.
_____	_____	20. Is able to make decisions and accept consequences.
_____	_____	21. Is self-disciplined.
_____	_____	22. Is unselfish and sharing with others.
_____	_____	23. For the most part, is free of cynicism and negative attitudes.
_____	_____	24. Is able and willing to excel and strive for perfection.
_____	_____	25. Needs status and power.

A cumulative score is less important than matching the responses on the various items with the job specifications and requirements for the position for which the candidate is being considered.

List the candidate's strengths:

List the candidate's weaknesses:

Recommendation to employ: Yes _____   No _____

Reasons:

Rating by _____ Date _____

The following list summarizes various antidiscrimination rules and regulations pertaining to employment interviewing. This is not an all-inclusive list of permissible and nonacceptable questions; however, it covers the major areas of questioning relevant to interviewing.

Permissible	Questionable or Prohibited
Name and Address	
One may ask the applicant his or her name and address.	One should not ask an applicant whose name has been changed for his or her original name.
Age	
One may ask the applicant if his or her age complies with applicable institutional policies, such as minimum and maximum age for employment, employment certificate, working papers, and the like.	One should not ask questions that imply a preference for a specific age group.
One may ask for proof-of-age card (issued by an applicant's high school) to verify minimum age requirements.	
Birthplace	
	One may not inquire into the birthplace of the applicant, spouse, parents, or other close relatives.

Figure 14.2. Permissible and impermissible interview questions.

Note: From *Personnel administration in higher education: Handbook of faculty and staff personnel practices* by R.T. Fortunato and D.G. Waddell, San Francisco: Jossey-Bass, 1981, pages 122-5. Reprinted by permission.

Figure 14.2. Continued

Permissible	Questionable or Prohibited

Birthplace

	One may not ask the applicant to disclose ancestry or national origin.

Height and Weight

One may ask about an applicant's ability to perform the job requirements.	One should not ask about the height and weight of an applicant, unless they are bona fide job requirements.

Physical Disabilities

One may ask if the applicant has a physical disability that would prevent satisfactory performance on the job. One may ask about the applicant's general health.	One should not ask about a general physical disability that has no direct bearing on performance of the job in question.

Education and Experience

One may ask about schooling, both academic and vocational. One may inquire into work experience.	

Military Experience

One may inquire into the applicant's experience in the U.S. armed forces or state militia.	One should not inquire into the foreign military experience of the applicant.

Figure 14.2. Continued.

Permissible	Questionable or Prohibited

Military Experience

	One should not require the applicant to produce his or her military discharge papers before employment. (Such papers show birthdate, place of birth, and the like.)

Citizenship

One may ask if the applicant is a U.S. citizen or intends to become one. One may ask an applicant, who is not a U.S. citizen, about the type of visa possessed.	One should not inquire whether the applicant or applicant's spouse or parents are naturalized or native-born citizens nor ask for the dates of naturalization. One should not require the applicant to produce naturalization papers or first papers.

Marital Status

	One may not ask about the applicant's marital status. Women should not be asked if their social title is Miss or Mrs.

Family or Relatives

One may ask for the name, address and relationship of persons to be notified in case of accident or emergency.	

Figure 14.2. Continued.

Permissible	Questionable or Prohibited

Family or Relatives

One may inquire if the applicant has any relatives employed by the institution. However, such information should be used only to avoid placements in which supervisory lines or the handling of confidential information could influence rates of pay, promotions, or the granting of tenure or if an awkward work situation might result.

One should not ask about the place of residence of the applicant's spouse, parents, or other close relatives.

One should not ask the applicant about the maiden name of his or her mother. Male applicants should not be asked their wife's maiden name.

One should not ask the applicant to identify dependent children. If, by chance, this information is volunteered by the applicant, one should not pursue with questions such as, "What plans can you make for childcare, if you are employed?" (Historically, questions regarding dependent children have been shown to have adverse impact on women. Thus, questioning along such lines should be avoided.)

Religion

One may not ask about the applicant's religion, church, parish, or pastor, nor about the religious holidays the applicant observes.

Figure 14.2. Continued.

Permissible	Questionable or Prohibited
Language	
One may ask the language(s) the applicant speaks, reads, or writes, and the degree of fluency.	One should not ask the applicant's native tongue nor the language commonly used at home. One should not ask how the applicant acquired the ability to read, write, or speak a foreign language.
Photographs	
	One should not require an applicant to submit a photograph before an offer of employment is made.
Memberships	
One may ask the applicant about membership in organizations, the nature of which do *not* disclose race, religion or national origin. One may ask if the applicant belongs to an organization that advocates the violent overthrow of the U.S. government.	One should not ask the applicant to disclose memberships in organizations, the nature of which would indicate religion, race, or national origin.
Arrest and Conviction Record	
One may ask if the applicant has been convicted of a crime, and the nature of crime. (In this instance, one may inquire if conviction record is under a different name than the applicant now uses.)	One should not ask the number and kinds of arrests the applicant may have had.

fail to request feedback. If selected personnel are asked only to give the candidate a "feel for the college," and not intended to be involved in the evaluation process, they should be so informed. The candidate also has a right to know who is going to be involved in the decision-making process.

- *Establish an interview format that will maximize gaining significant information.* A full day of half hour interviews is very fatiguing for the candidate and tends to produce only superficial knowledge.

- *Allow time in the interview schedule for the candidate to rest or to talk with whomever he/she desires.* If there are persons or departments with whom the previous jobholder had difficulty working, make sure the candidate learns of the conflict and meets the antagonist(s). Difficult or unpleasant situations should not come as a surprise *after* the person is on the job.

- *Make sure the candidate knows what is changeable or negotiable and what is not.* For example, if the present rules about alcoholic beverages on the campus are not open for discussion or if an opportunity to replace certain staff or to hire new staff will not exist, the candidate should be made aware of these factors.

Kaplowitz (1986) pointed out that interviews basically assess sociability and verbal fluency but do not predict administrative success. The most entertaining and interesting conversationalist often may not be the most effective staff member over the long haul. "In an interview, learning why a candidate took a particular course of action is more revealing than what was done"(p.iv). An important procedure is to place interview data in the context of all the information, including academic performance, letters of recommendation and work samples.

9. *Evaluate candidates and make a decision about offering the position.* The search committee should collect and organize the data and evaluations on each candidate

into a short summary based on the job specifications. The decision on the candidate should be based upon the plan developed when the search committee was appointed and charged.

Once the decision is made, the candidate should be contacted by telephone, offered the position at a specific salary, and given a reasonable period to make a decision (generally two to seven days). The offer should also be made in writing and forwarded to the candidate. The other candidates should be informed by letter that they will be given a decision by a given date (usually two to three weeks). If the first choice candidate accepts, the remaining candidates, both interviewed and uninterviewed, should immediately be notified that the position has been filled. It is highly unprofessional for colleges to fail to notify promptly candidates who are no longer under consideration.

When the applicant accepts the position, she or he should be requested to confirm in writing the acceptance and date of employment, provide transcripts from all degree-granting colleges or universities attended, and complete a formal job application provided by the institution's personnel office.

If the first choice candidate declines the offer, a decision must be made whether to (a) offer the position to another interviewed candidate, (b) interview more candidates from the short list, or (c) reopen the search process beginning again at step 1. Once that decision is made, all parties should be promptly notified. (Figure 14.3 provides a checklist for important activities to be accomplished during the selection process.)

Support Staff Positions

Many of the same procedures for filling professional positions apply when support staff vacancies occur. However, some differences deserve comment. Steps to be followed in filling support staff positions include: (1) consulting personnel planning and forecasting documents, (2) verifying position analysis, (3) developing job specifications and position description, (4) deciding on vertical or horizontal staffing, (5) announcing the position, (6) receiving applications, (7) screening applications

(Continued on page 484)

Professional Staff Search Check List

Date

_____ 1. Job specifications and position announcement prepared

_____ 2. Appoint search/screen committee

_____ 3. Written charge transmitted to search/screen committee

_____ 4. Committee establishes

    a. Working rules
    b. Detailed description of selection process and deadlines
    c. Draft of position announcement

_____ 5. Committee submits proposed working rules, selection process, and draft of the position announcement to appointing authority and Affirmative Action Office for review

_____ 6. Receive clearance from Affirmative Action Office and appointing authority to announce position

_____ 7. Publish position announcement after incorporating feedback

8. Acknowledge receipt of applications and inform candidates of selection process and tentative deadlines for making decisions

_____ 9. Inform candidates eliminated from consideration because of lack of basic qualifications

_____ 10. Screening of applications completed

_____ 11. Establish "short list" of candidates

Figure 14.3. Professional staff search check list.

Figure 14.3. Continued.

_____ 12. Notify persons not on the "short list" that they are no longer under consideration

_____ 13. "Short list" candidates contacted to determine continued interest

_____ 14. Request additional data and references on "short list" candidates

_____ 15. Recommend/select list of candidates for on-campus interviews

_____ 16. Contact candidates to arrange on-campus interviews

_____ 17. Establish feedback mechanisms for persons conducting interviews

_____ 18. Establish on-campus interview schedule and communicate expectations/requirements to persons to conduct interviews

_____ 19. Appoint coordinator/host of interview visit (duties may be passed among committee members for each candidate)

_____ 20. Collect feedback from interviewers and share in committee

_____ 21. Submit recommendations(s) for hiring to the appointment authority based on charge to the committee

_____ 22. Transmit all data collected to the appointment authority for disposition according to institutional policies (Generally the appointing authority or immediate supervisor has the responsibility to contact candidates to make position offers and to notify candidates who were not selected of the employment decision.)

and selecting the list to be interviewed, (8) checking references, (9) interviewing candidates, and (10) offering position.

Consult Personnel Forecast. As with professional and allied professional staff members, the student affairs division should maintain a current inventory of support staff with both short and long range personnel plans. When a vacancy occurs, the forecast should be consulted before making any decision about filling the position.

Verify Position Analysis. If possible every support position in the student affairs division should be analyzed by a personnel management specialist using a method similar to those identified earlier. Ideally, this should be a service provided by the college's personnel office to all divisions of the institution. If this has been accomplished, the student affairs administrator would need to verify that the position still requires the same skills and abilities previously identified. Should changes in duties be desirable, the personnel specialist could assist in ascertaining the levels of skills and knowledge the reconstituted position would require.

Develop Job Specifications and Position Description. After the position analysis has been completed, development of the job specifications and position description is a relatively simple matter. Because of the possibility of legal action, one needs to be especially careful to assure that the job specifications are directly related to the work to be performed. Stanton (1977, p. 40) noted that "in stipulating the requirements of a position, the frame of reference is [often] unduly influenced by the present or last person who happened to have held the particular position. However, such a person may possess qualifications that exceed those actually required." Using systematic position analyses as the basis for job specifications can lessen or eliminate this concern.

Decide on Vertical or Horizontal Staffing. Many of the disadvantages of vertical staffing in filling professional positions are not considerations with support staff. Within the frame of reference of the whole institution it is preferable to promote from within when possible. It allows the college to keep qualified personnel. Internal transfer or promotion is easier when dealing with support staff because the skills needed such as typing, key punching or shorthand are transferable. A secretary in the Office of the Dean of the School of Business needs the same basic skills as a secretary in the Dean of Students' Office.

However, caution should be exercised in making internal promotions. At universities, especially those with large graduate programs, there is often a large pool of highly qualified people who must work at whatever is available to support their family while a spouse earns a graduate degree. Because often these persons are overqualified for the position for which they are hired, positions are sometimes reclassified to administrative or special assistant simply because the persons are talented, intelligent, and capable of assuming responsibility for routine, detailed tasks that professionals once performed. Such reclassifications can become problematic by slowly consuming the personnel budget with support staff when professionals are needed to direct service and programs to students.

Announce the Position. Position vacancies should be announced in a wide variety of media. The student affairs administrator either directly, or through the college's personnel department, should make sure position vacancies are listed with the state employment service, local technical or community colleges, and the house organ. In some cases, newspaper advertisements may be necessary.

Receive Applications. Depending upon institutional policy, applications may be received directly by the office with the vacancy or preferably by the personnel office. If the personnel office receives applications, it can also test applicants to determine skill level (typing speed and accuracy, knowledge of spelling and grammar, etc.), and screen candidates who do not possess the requisite skill level. A formal application should be completed by all applicants.

Screen Applications and Select List to be Interviewed. Since reimbursement for travel is not typically involved when interviewing support staff, one has the freedom to interview a large number of applicants. Applications should be rated based on the job specifications with certain criteria serving as cutoff points. For example, if the job requires typing 50 words per minute with 95 percent accuracy, and the applicant has been tested at 35 words per minute, he or she would not have reached the cutoff and would be eliminated from further consideration.

Stanton (1977) has suggested several danger signals that can be spotted on applications. These danger signals should tip one off to investigate further, not to eliminate an applicant.

1. Has the applicant a sketchy and erratic job history, with many periods of unemployment or brief employment?

2. Has the applicant moved frequently from region to region or from one type of work to another, suggesting a lack of personal stability or maturity?

3. Do reasons given for leaving previous positions suggest the applicant has a tendency to be an undesirable or troublesome worker? Did she or he often leave positions over "personality conflicts" or disagreements with supervisors?

A final list of three to ten candidates should be identified for further screening.

Check References. Three types of references exist: (1) personal or character, (2) academic, and (3) work. Several personnel management authorities (Flippo, 1976; Megginson, 1977) maintain that character references seldom produce useful information and are not worth pursuing. Academic references, on the other hand, can be valuable, especially for applicants who have short work histories. Work references are considered the most important because they provide a measure of the applicant's actual accomplishments including productivity and ability to work with others.

Generally, the most efficient and effective means for checking references is by telephone. Ideally, one would wish to interview the applicant's immediate supervisor and others who had daily contact. When calling to check a reference, interviewers should identify themselves and explain the specific reason for calling and assure the person of confidentiality. Briefly describe the job to be filled and ask the referent's opinion of how the applicant would fit. Other questions that often produce useful information include the following:

> How did the applicant get along with others with whom he or she worked?
>
> How did the applicant get along with supervisors?
>
> Did the applicant have any personal habits that you consider to be negative?
>
> How was the applicant's attendance?
>
> Did the applicant meet commitments?
>
> Why did the applicant leave [if that has in fact occurred]?
>
> Would you reemploy the applicant?
>
> What was the nature of the applicant's work with you?
>
> What are the applicant's strengths and weaknesses?
>
> Is there anything else [relevant to the applicant's work] you'd like to tell me . . .? (Fortunato & Waddell, 1981, p. 127)

Interview Candidates. Persons who appear to possess the necessary skills, experiences, and personal attributes for the position should be invited for an interview to determine whether the applicant possesses ability for and interest in the position. Especially important for support staff is the determination of whether the applicant will fit in the situation, work well with other employees, and meet the demands of the environment. Because it is often critical that the new employee work closely with other support staff and because support staff are often more familiar with procedures and equipment, it is wise to include support staff in the interview process and decision making.

Offer Position. After receiving impressions and/or evaluations from all who interviewed candidates, a decision to offer the position must be made. If the offer is not accepted, as with professional staffing, a decision must be made to offer it to another candidate or begin the process over. Unsuccessful candidates should be notified promptly.

ROLE OF THE PERSONNEL OFFICE

The role of the college personnel office in staffing varies widely across institutions. It is typical for this office to serve a major role in recruiting a pool of support staff applicants, testing applicants, maintaining employment records, supervising staff benefits, and coordinating support staff evaluations. Its involvement with professional and allied professional staff is usually less extensive.

As a general rule, chief student affairs officers seek the same kind and degree of support and involvement in selecting and evaluating professional and allied professional staff as the personnel department has with faculty selection and evaluation. Specialists in the personnel office can be valuable consultants and sources of technical advice in regard to all levels of staff, and, therefore, a compatible working relationship between student affairs and the personnel office needs to exist.

SUMMARY

Management of human resources is a critical function for the student affairs administrator. To be accomplished effectively and efficiently, staff resources must be objectively evaluated and inventoried and staff needs determined. Armed with a personnel forecast and plan that are consistent with the institution's resources and an appreciation for the relevant legal and ethical parameters, the student affairs administrator can begin the staffing process. The goal of the staffing process is to employ the best people available at all staff levels (professional, allied professional, support, and paraprofessional), and to place them in positions that allow them to make the greatest contribution to the accomplishment of the division's goal.

Selecting professional staff members is perhaps the single most important determinate of successful student affairs programs. At the entry-level the quality of professional preparation determines how quickly the new staff members can begin making contributions to the program and may ultimately determine whether or not they master the basic skills and the institution-specific information that will allow them to become contributing members of the staff.

REFERENCES

Albright, L. E. (1974). Staffing policies and strategies. In D. Yoder & H. G. Henaman, Jr. (Eds.), *ASPA handbook of personnel and industrial relations (Vol. 1): Staffing policies and strategies* (pp. 4/1-4/34). Washington, DC: Bureau of National Affairs.

American College Personnel Association. (1989). *A statement of ethical principles and standards.* Alexandria, VA: Author.

Bair, J.L. (1985). Recruiting and training competent staff. In M.J. Barr & L.A. Keating (Eds.), *Developing effective student services programs: Systematic approaches for practitioners* (pp. 212-233). San Francisco: Jossey-Bass.

Baldridge, J. V. (1971). *Power and conflict in the university.* New York: John Wiley & Sons.

Barr, M. J., & Keating, L. (1979). No program is an island. In M. J. Barr & L. Keating (Eds.), *Establishing effective programs* (pp. 13-28). New Directions for Student Services, No. 7. San Francisco: Jossey-Bass.

Berenson, C., & Ruhnke, H. O. (1966). Job descriptions: Guidelines for personnel management. *Personnel Journal 45*:(1), 14-19.

Brown, R.D. (1985). Graduate education for the student development educator: A content and process model. *NASPA Journal, 22*(3), 38-43.

Butteriss, M., & Albrecht, K. (1979). *New management tools: Ideas and techniques to help you as a manager.* Englewood Cliffs, NJ: Prentice-Hall.

Commerce Clearing House. (1979) *Topic law reports.* Chicago: Author.

Council for the Accreditation of Counseling and Related Educational Programs, (CACREP). (1989). *CACREP team member handbook.* Alexandria, VA: Author.

Council for the Advancement of Standards for Student Services/Development Programs (CAS). (1986). *CAS standards and guidelines for student services/ development programs.* Washington, DC: Author.

Deegan, W. L. (1981). *Managing student affairs programs: Methods, models, muddles.* Palm Springs, CA: ETC Publications.

Delworth, U., & Aulepp, L. (1976). *Training manual for paraprofessional and allied professional programs.* Boulder, CO: Western Interstate Commission for Higher Education.

Eble, K.E. (1979). *The art of administration.* San Francisco: Jossey-Bass.

Fine, S. A., & Wiley, A. W. (1971). *An introduction to functional job analysis: A scaling of selected tasks from the social welfare field.* Kalamazoo, MI: W. E. Upjohn Institute for Employment Research.

Flippo, E. B. (1976). *Principles of personnel management (4th ed.).* New York: McGraw-Hill.

Fortunato, R. T., & Waddell, D. G. (1981). *Personnel administration in higher education: Handbook of faculty and staff personnel practices.* San Francisco: Jossey-Bass.

Johnson, C.S., & Sandeen, A. (1988). Relationship of guidelines and standards of student affairs preparation programs to current and future trends. In R.B. Young & L.V. Moore (Eds.), *The state of the art of professional education and practice* (pp. 79-89). Alexandria, VA: American College Personnel Association Commission on Professional Education in Student Personnel.

Kaplowitz, R.A. (1986). *Selecting college and university personnel: The quest and the questions.* Washington, DC: ASHE-ERIC Higher Education Reports.

McCormick, E. J. (1974). Job information: Its development and applications. In D. Yoder & H. G. Henaman (Eds.), *ASPA handbook of personnel and industrial relations (Vol. 1): Staffing policies and strategies.* (pp. 4/35-4/83). Washington: DC: Bureau of National Affairs.

McIntire, D. D., & Carpenter, D. S. (1981). Employment practices in student affairs. *NASPA Journal, 18*(3), 18-24.

Megginson, L. C. (1977). *Personnel and human resources administration (3rd ed.).* Homewood, IL: Richard D. Irwin.

Miller, T.K., & Carptenter, D.S. (1980). Professional preparation for today and tomorrow. In D.G. Creamer (Ed.), *Student development in higher education: Theories, practices, and future directions* (pp. 181-204). Cincinnati: ACPA Media.

Risch, T. J. (Task Force Chairperson). (1977). Placement ethics position statement. *ACPA Developments, 4*(4), 12, 16.

Rodgers, R.F. (1977). Student personnel work as social intervention. In G.H. Knock (Ed.), *Perspectives on the preparation of student affairs professionals* (pp.12-34). Washington, DC: American College Personnel Association.

Sims, J. M., & Foxley, C. H. (1980). Job analysis, job descriptions, and performance appraisal systems. In C. H. Foxley (Ed.), *Applying management techniques* (pp.41-54). New Directions for Student Services, No.9. San Francisco: Jossey-Bass.

Sprunger, B. E., & Bergquist, W. H. (1978). *Handbook for college administration.* Washington, DC: Council for the Advancement of Small Colleges.

Stanton, E. S. (1977). *Successful personnel recruiting and selection.* New York: AMACOM.

Walter, T.G. (1988). *Administrative, developmental, and counseling emphases in student affairs preparation programs and employment settings.* Unpublished doctoral dissertation, University of Georgia.

Williams, W. G. (1973). Memo to a college student personnel secretary. *NASPA Journal, 10,*(3), 206-210.

Winston, R.B., Jr. (1990). Using theory and research findings in everyday practice. In D.D. Coleman & J.E. Johnson (Eds.), *The new professional: A resource guide for new student affairs professionals and their supervisors* (pp. 30-55). Washington, DC: National Association for Student Personnel Administrators.

Zion, C. (1977). Role definition training. *Journal of the College and University Personnel Association, 22,* 5-12.

SUGGESTED READINGS

Council for the Accreditation of Counseling and Related Educational Programs (CACREP). (1989). *CACREP team member handbook.* Alexandria, VA: Author.

Council for the Advancement of Standards for Student Services/Development Programs (CAS). (1986). *CAS standards and guidlines for student services/ development programs.* Washington, DC: Author.

Delworth, U., & Hanson, G.H. (1989). Future directions: A vision of student services in the 1990s. In U. Delworth & G.H. Hanson (Eds.), *Student services: A handbook for the profession* (2nd ed.). (pp. 604-618). San Francisco: Jossey-Bass.

Fortunator, R.T., & Waddell, D.G. (1981). *Personnel administration in higher education: Handbook of faculty and staff personnel practices.* San Francisco: Jossey-Bass.

Sprunger, B. E., & Bergquist, W. H. (1978). *Handbook for college administration.* Washington, DC: Council for the Advancement of Small Colleges.

Young, R.B., & Moore, L.V. (Eds.). (1988). *The state of the art of professional education and practice.* Alexandria, VA: American College Personnel Association Commission on Professional Education in Student Personnel.

John H. Schuh, Ph.D., is Associate Vice President for Student Affairs and Professor of Counseling and School Psychology at The Wichita State University. Previously, he was Associate Dean of Students at Indiana University-Bloomington where he directed the residence life program. Additionally, he taught regularly in the higher education and student affairs graduate program at Indiana University.

He has served two terms as a member of the Exectutive Board of the Association of College and University Housing Officers-International, and is the current chair and editor of American College Personnel Association Media Board. He is the author of a number of books, monographs, chapters, articles and technical reports on various topics related to student affairs administration and college students.

Wayne Carlisle, M.A., is Director of Placement and Career Services at The Wichita State University. He received his M.A. in College Student Personnel from Bowling Green State University. Previous positions have included responsibilities in career planning and placement, financial aid, residential life, counseling and academic advising. His professional activities have included being the Chairperson for the NASPA National Career Development and Professional Standards Division and frequent coordination of Career Services for NASPA and ACPA National Conferences.

Wayne is currently participating in an interdisciplinary project called the Research Group on Women and Work. The emphasis of his research is on dual-career issues. He also is active in making presentations and conducting consultations in educational, corporate, and government settings.

CHAPTER 15

SUPERVISION AND EVALUATION:

Selected Topics for Emerging Professionals

John H. Schuh
Wayne Carlisle

Fuhrmann (1987), in describing careers in higher education compared with those in the corporate world, stated:

> A career is a sequence of work-related positions occupied throughout a person's life. It reflects the individual's needs, motives, and expectations, as well as societal and organizational expectations and constraints. A successful career is one in which the individual and organizational perspectives have been meshed through appropriate role adjustments, developments, and changes in response to both individual and organizational characteristics. Research in corporations has shown that a worker's performance is facilitated when organizational values and individual values are compatible and when individual growth is encouraged. Human resource professionals in the corporate world are charged with the task of assuring the best possible fit between organizations and individual values, and they actively intervene in both organizational and individual planning to assure the best matches. We in academia need to do the same. (p.24)

This chapter takes the position that supervision and evaluation have not received adequate attention as key elements for a career in student affairs. Few practitioners have received adequate preparation as supervisors or evaluators, and frequently pay little attention to those roles after entering the field. Perhaps as frustrating for many student affairs professionals is the tendency for some practitioners to fail to provide consistent, on-going supervision and evaluation to subordinates, on the one hand, while expecting or demanding more thorough supervision and evaluation for their own career development.

To learn more about various aspects of student affairs administration, a good place of reference is the *CAS Standards and Guidelines for Student Services/Development Programs* (CAS, 1986). In regard to supervision and evaluation, the standards state: "All functional areas must have a regular system of staff selection and evaluation, and must provide continuing professional development opportunities for staff . . ." (CAS, 1986, p.6). This statement requires staff evaluation, but provides neither direction for performing the function nor guidance for appropriate supervision.

The question then becomes, How will the supervision and evaluation functions in student affairs be carried out? Who is responsible for them? And perhaps even, why should staff members be evaluated at all?

Both the supervisor *and* the staff member are responsible for these functions and the process should not be viewed as a passive one. This process involves a great deal of personal interaction, and all parties can and should use evaluation information in considering career development. Although administrators are increasingly being held accountable for their subordinates' careers (Kaye, 1981), individuals are responsible for their own career development and young professionals who expect supervisors to plan career development for them are naive.

Individuals should continually negotiate how they wish to be supervised and evaluated. Needs for information, clarity of responsibility, feedback and direction differ from person to person throughout the developmental stages. Maccoby (1988) referred to people who are keenly aware of their need for new skills, changing responsibilities, opportunities for success and failure, and in-depth performance reviews as *self-developers.* These people represent an increasing proportion of the work force. Their principal loyalties are to the quality of their work and to the opportunity for meaningful and rewarding work. They are not, therefore, as loyal to organizations or institutions as has been the ideal and frequently are not interested in traditional upward mobility.

For the self-developers in student affairs, opportunities must be provided for professional development, flexible responsibilities, and in-depth performance reviews. If the trends in corporate work are in fact reflected in student affairs, even more emphasis on supervision and evaluation will be required.

SUPERVISION

In the business community the term "supervisor" frequently refers only to first line managers who work with classified, union, or production personnel. To supervise implies that the employee must be watched, judged, motivated, or taught (Phillips, 1985). For purposes of this chapter, the term supervision is used in a broader sense to include any relationship where one person has the responsibility to provide leadership, direction, information, motivation, evaluation, or support for one or more persons. In student affairs, many terms are used when referring to the person to whom a practitioner reports including boss, manager, budget review officer, director, dean, department head, and even a few terms that may be best not printed. In this chapter, the **supervisory relationship** is defined as the interaction that transpires as one staff members provides opportunities, structure, and support to another.

Motivation Issues

Over the years motivation has been considered an important factor in employee productivity, and employees have operated either by fear or as a result of fresh enthusiasm (Blake & Mouton, 1981). In effect, "people tend to do the things for which they are rewarded and to avoid what is not rewarded"

(Blake & Mouton, 1985, p. 139). The competent administrator's task is to understand various theories of motivation and apply them in ways that are consistent with the organization's mission. Peterson and Tracy (1979) have summarized three theories of motivation.

Conditioning Theory. This simple theory of motivation states that behavior is driven by needs, and that if needs are satisfied by a particular action, then the behavior tends to be repeated. Rewards or punishments must closely follow particular behavior so that positive behaviors are encouraged and negative ones are discouraged.

Expectancy Theory. Put in elementary terms, expectancy theory indicates that the strength of any particular action is motivated by what the person expects to gain from that action. If people expect to gain large rewards from a particular action, they will work hard toward that end. If the benefits are perceived to be limited, so will be the effort.

In a student affairs setting, if the advisor to a student group expects to get little reward from attending meetings of the organization, he or she may attend few of the meetings. On the other hand, if the advisor expects to be recognized in a major way for the efforts expended on behalf of the organization, such as an opportunity to attend a national conference or personal gratification through interpersonal relationships with members of the organization, the advisor may put in tremendous effort on the organization's behalf.

Motivator-hygiene Theory. This theory is drawn from the work of Herzberg (Herzberg, Mausner, & Snyderman, 1959) who suggested that some factors associated with work will facilitate employees' enjoying their efforts, while the absence of others will cause them to become dissatisfied. Recognition, responsibility, and a sense of achievement were perceived to be satisfiers, while pay, working conditions, and job security were dissatisfiers. Peterson and Tracy (1979) indicated that Herzberg's theory has not been supported by research entirely, although it appears to be congruent with Maslow's (1954) hierarchy of needs and McGregor's (1960) Theory Y of management. Theory X and Theory Y are ways of viewing individuals in the context of organizational life. The central principle of organization which derives from Theory X is that of direction and control through the exercise of authority—what has been called the "scalar principle." The central principle of organization which derives from Theory Y is that of integration—the creation of conditions such that the members of the organization can achieve their own goals best by directing their efforts toward the success of the enterprise (McGregor, 1960). Hersey and Blanchard (1982) warned that one should avoid assuming that Theory X is bad and that Theory Y is good. Theory X and Theory Y are simply different ways of viewing human behavior. Regardless of whether a practitioner subscribes to a particular theory, what is most important is that she or he realize that no consensus exists about how to motivate people. Practitioners in supervisory roles need to adopt an approach that is consistent with their values and beliefs, and try to develop ways of working with staff members that are congruent with the theory of motivation to which they subscribe and which has been tested and proved to produce desired results consistently.

Supervisory Styles

While the suggestion has been that every practitioner needs to develop a personal supervisory style, and will work with colleagues who possess very different styles, several classical styles are worth examining. Peterson and Tracy (1979) have identified three of these.

> **One-dimensional Supervision.** This general style assumes that leadership follows a continuum that ranges from the highly autocratic to the laissez-faire. On the one end of the supervisory continuum is the very directive leader who makes all the decisions for subordinates leaving no room for individual decision making or initiative. At the other end, the supervisor provides staff members with little structure or pressure.

> **Two-dimension Leadership.** Two dimensions of supervisory behavior references include initiating structure, which deals with activities like assigning work, encouraging overtime work, criticizing poor work,

and exerting pressure toward greater effort, and consideration, which involves helping behaviors, such as helping others with personal problems, being receptive to disagreements, and consulting with subordinates about change. This approach has been so pervasive that it was influential in the development of Blake and Mouton's Managerial Grid (1974) and Hersey and Blanchard's Life Cycle Leadership Theory (1977).

Facilitating Development. Behaviors that facilitate development include such activities as designing challenging jobs, assigning challenging tasks, and asking subordinates to set high goals. At the other end of the continuum are behaviors that do not facilitate development, such as designing jobs that are overly simple or impossible to accomplish, encouraging poor quality work in order just to get finished, or rejecting all ideas from subordinates. Clearly these behaviors destroy good morale and discourage staff members from putting forth strong efforts on behalf of the organization.

As with motivation theory, no specific supervisory theory will meet all needs of all employees, so one must select elements that can be used to develop a theory that fits his or her personality, the composition of the staff, and the particular work setting. Entry-level practitioners, in many cases, supervise at least two types of staff members: paraprofessionals and clerical/technical. At a minimum, the entry level practitioner needs to recognize that the motivation for work by members of these two groups varies considerably and require distinctive supervisory approaches. Paraprofessionals, such as orientation leaders, peer counselors, or resident assistants, work for a variety of reasons that complement their academic curricula, but the primary reason that they are on campus is to complete their courses of study. In short, work is a supplementary activity. Clerical and technical staff members, on the other hand, are associated with the campus community because of their employment. Their views of work, and their expectations of supervisors are considerably different from those of their paraprofessional colleagues. A host of implications are suggested by this dichotomy, and the new professional must plan carefully when interacting with these different employee groups. As supervision of professional staff increases during a career, continued adjustment to individual developmental needs becomes even more crucial.

After establishing a personal style of supervision, the next step is to examine the elements essential to supervisory effectiveness.

Elements of Supervisory Success

Elements that promote supervisory success according to Peterson & Tracy (1979), are briefly discussed.

Managerial Philosophy. Organizations have explicit and implicit philosophies that guide how they will be managed. Some organizations are direct and autocratic, whereas others appear unfocused and laissez-faire. In a college's student affairs division, much of the administrative philosophy will depend on the chief student affairs administrator (CSAA) and the campus' chief executive officer (president or chancellor). If the CSAA decides that an autocratic organization is best, then that will be the pervasive philosophy. That is not to imply that some departure from this approach may occur within various departments, but what will be rewarded in the CSAA's eyes is a supervisory style consistent with that person's philosophy. By and large, research findings do not tend to support a highly autocratic approach. Job satisfaction studies suggest that giving people independence in deciding how to go about their work increases job satisfaction (Teas, 1981). Most likely professionals will encounter a wide variety of managerial philosophies during the course of their careers.

Staff Needs and Values. Even though a CSAA has a philosophy of management that tilts in one direction, that does not mean that other staff members cannot have countervailing needs and values. Possibly the CSAA may view the world from one perspective while staff members view it from another. When this occurs, middle managers often find themselves in awkward positions. As a result, a certain degree of compromise on the part of all concerned may be required, if the organization is to effectively accomplish its mission. For example, the CSAA may believe that the agenda for the division places student growth as the organization's highest priority, while some staff members believe that controlling student behavior is paramount. Consequently, compromises are needed, and the middle managers must interpret what the leader needs while simultaneously identifying the needs of each staff member and responding to those needs in individual ways. This juggling act is not easy, but it is an important component of effective supervision. Perhaps the key to success here is supervisor flexibility and the ability to understand the motives and values that drive fellow staff members.

CAREER DEVELOPMENT

Part of a supervisor's responsibility is to provide opportunities for staff members' career development. Open communication about individual goals is crucial before the supervisor can provide opportunities for skill building, information gathering, and formal or informal education. The evaluation process can provide the supervisor with knowledge about areas of weakness that can be strengthened through a career development plan. Opportunities for inservice education in functional areas other than the one to which a practitioner is assigned are fairly rare. More commonly encouragement and training opportunities are provided for upward mobility within the assigned functional area. A broader view of career development by both practitioners and supervisors can provide greater flexibility in assigning responsibilities and training opportunities across the student affairs spectrum.

Private enterprise corporations are increasingly offering career development programs for employees (Barkhaus, 1983). The primary goals of these programs are to increase employees' work satisfaction and productivity, to help the organization change, and to retain the most valued employees. Likewise, student affairs leaders can increase the provision of career development opportunities for staff members. To utilize the institution's career services staff members as resources and to encourage continuing education on campus is particularly appropriate. Because professional career development programs are at a premium on college campuses, an important procedure is for new staff members to request the establishment of systematic career development programs. (See also Chapter 17 for discussion sof professional development.)

MENTORING

While many articles exist in the business literature about mentoring relationships, far less has been published in the higher education and student affairs literature (Kelly, 1984). A definition of **mentor** was proffered by Moore and Salimbene (cited in Kelly, 1984) who stated that a mentor is "a more experienced and powerful individual who guides, advises, and assists in any number of ways the career of a less experienced, often younger, upwardly mobile protégé in the context of a close professionally-centered relationship usually lasting one year or more" (p. 50).

Purposes of Mentoring Relationships

Kram (1986) identified two broad categories that subsume the purposes of a mentoring relationship: career functions and psychosocial functions.

Career Functions. Five functions are included in the career category. (1) **Sponsorship functions** are those related to opening doors of opportunity. This might mean that the mentor provides introductions to specific activities and people in a professional organization or on campus. (2) **Coaching functions** refer to "teaching a person the ropes." This includes providing information and feedback on performance. How well did the meeting go with students? What could be done to improve one's performance? (3) **Protection** is provided by the mentor for dealing with problems that are outside one's span of control or personal experience. The mentor may act as a buffer in this kind of situation. (4) **Exposure** means that one is provided special opportunities to grow. For instance, one might accompany the mentor to a meeting with the vice president or president and simply act as an observer. Not only would one have a chance to learn from this experience, but he or she would be introduced to others as a competent person whose career is on the move. (5) Finally, the mentor may **assign challenging tasks** that provide opportunities to develop work skills beyond what would normally be expected.

Psychosocial Functions. Included in this category are such activities as role modeling, counseling, acceptance, and confirmation. (1) When mentors serve as role models they demonstrate attitudes, behaviors, and skills that will aid in developing competence, confidence, and clearer professional identity. (2) Counseling refers to the provision of opportunities for mutual reflection on professional dilemmas, ethical concerns, and other sensitive issues that one encounters. The mentor can provide advice and guidance, and the new professional's role is to sort out the various approaches that might be taken so that one's behavior is compatible with one's belief system.

A new professional's self-confidence will be strengthened when the mentor provides continuing support, respect, and admiration. These functions are characterized as acceptance and confirmation.

Good Mentors

Not everyone can be or desires to be a good mentor. Normally, the decision to enter into a mentor-protégé relationship is mutual, but it is entirely possible that the protégé will have to initiate the contact with the potential mentor even though mentoring is currently seen as being a much more important component in managers' job descriptions than ever before (Derr, 1986). What, then, are the characteristics of good mentors? Odiorne (1984) suggested five qualities that characterize good mentors.

When looking for a mentor, one should look for a person with these five qualities and make sure that the person is an individual who is not too exacting, hostile, overly judgmental, or punitive (Odiorne, 1984). These last four characteristics can be destructive to a mentoring relationship.

Excellence. Good mentors are winners themselves in the sense that they tend to have been successful in their own professional endeavors. There is no value in imitating a loser, so young practitioners should find a person who has been very successful and they will be on the right track to finding a mentor.

Excellent Example. The person who serves as a good mentor realizes that she or he will be serving as an example. Good mentors behave in ways worthy of emulation.

Supportive. Good mentors are supportive in their work with subordinates. They are patient, slow to criticize, and willing to work with those who are less well developed in their careers.

Delegators. Top candidates for mentors are those who are not afraid to delegate tasks to colleagues and are not threatened by others who exhibit talent and initiative. The good mentor provides support for the protégé who has been unsuccessful, and provides plenty of praise for those who have been successful.

Feedback. Finally, the good mentor provides periodic, detailed, and honest feedback to the protégé.

Issues Related to Gender.

Kram (1986) listed a series of issues related to gender and mentoring relationships. This is an extraordinarily sensitive subject, and while the hope is for change in the future, the present situation is replete with problems. Among the problems listed by Kram were the following: (1) Increasing intimacy and sexual attraction frequently characterize these relationships. (2) Both men and women tend to rely on traditional sex-role stereotypes in these relationships. (3) Frequently cross-gender mentoring relationships are unsatisfactory to the junior person and at times to the senior person as well. (4) Cross-gender relationships are open to public scrutiny and may be viewed with suspicion. Rumors, innuendo, and gossip may result from a cross-gender relationship. (5) Peers may resent these relationships as well. Possibly women may run the risk of resentment if they appear to be the "chosen" one of a senior male in the organization.

Suggestions for dealing with these issues, which are built on an awareness that this kind of relationship is very sensitive, include travel arrangements, social occasions, and non-work related activities must be evaluated in terms of appearances.

While same-gender mentor relationships are less likely to have these concerns, all mentoring relationships should be based on the career development of the junior person. Both persons need to acknowledge the professional limits of the relationship. One should not conclude that problems will automatically result from a cross-gender mentoring relationship. What is important to note, however, is that this kind of relationship requires particularly clear communication, extra preparation, and a mutual awareness of its sensitive nature.

Issues Related to Race

Odiorne (1984) indicated that barriers do continue to exist for members of minority groups who seek mentoring relationships with those outside their racial groups. One would hope that such is a vestige of the past, but he wrote that some people "simply can't see themselves doing anything special for a minority person" (1984, p. 141). That is a lamentable social commentary. Beginning minority practitioners should seek mentors from senior student affairs staff members (regardless of race) who are inclined to base supervision on competence and potential. Members of minority groups are placed in an extraordinarily difficult situation if they feel that they must compromise their values to "fit in" with other staff members. Odiorne suggested that an alternative would be to use networks, support groups, and caucuses as vehicles for networking. These groups can focus on social and professional barriers that group members will be required to overcome if they are to be successful in their careers.

Ethical Issues

A number of ethical issues are involved in the mentoring process. Odiorne (1984) put forward these cautions and caveats: (1) Favoritism is not mentoring. (2) The mentoring relationship should be temporary, not permanent, and should be reviewed at least annually. (3) Gratitude, repayment, or services should not be extracted from a protégé. (4) The protégé should be worthy of the relationship. Not all people should be on a fast track for promotion, and there is no point in a mentor entering into such a relationship unless the protégé can benefit from it. (5) Having more than one protégé at a given time is better for all concerned. This is a way of avoiding charges of the mentor playing favorites or entering into a special relationship with one person to the detriment of others on the staff. (For additional discussion of these issues, see Chapter 17).

EVALUATION

Evaluation is a particularly complex issue with much literature devoted to it; consequently, only the more salient issues for the young professional are addressed here. For the purposes of this discussion, the evaluation of a student affairs practitioner by a qualified supervisor is the primary referent. Other forms of evaluation exist including peer reviews, client feedback, and program and departmental reviews. Because of space limitations, however, discussion is limited to supervisor-supervisee evaluations alone.

Business Models and Theories

Business approaches to evaluation are diverse and rapidly changing as management theory, competition, and mergers influence decision. In general, business leaders use evaluation techniques more frequently and take the process more seriously than do most higher education administrators. While significant differences do exist between the settings and the goals in areas of measurable progress, compensation, and promotion, features of evaluation can be learned from the corporate community and transferred to higher education. Penn (1979, p. 152) noted that: "A division or department of student affairs with sound staff evaluation procedure recognizes the value of people, helps staff feel they are being treated fairly, and demonstrates a commitment of the effective delivery of services and programs as well as the utilization of human resources."

Two trends in the work place make supervision and evaluation especially crucial. One trend is an increase in the amount of discretion employees have in how they do their work, and the other trend is an increase in the expectation that work is a primary means to promote personal growth and satisfaction (Yankelovich & Immerwahr, 1984). Higher education professionals have long held work discretion and personal growth as important values, but are experiencing increased pressures to plan for them more systematically in supervision and evaluation procedures. Many student affairs practitioners view higher education as a particularly attractive employment setting precisely because of these factors. However, as businesses increasingly provide similar opportunities, the desirability edge for higher education settings will lessen and thereby require increased efforts on the part of CSAAs to articulate the advantages of their work environment to emerging professionals.

Naisbeth and Aburdene (1985) stated that organizations that create the most nourishing environments for personal growth will attract and retain the most talented people. What follows then is that a thorough, fair, and developmental approach to supervision and evaluation will help create the kinds of environments most conducive to personal growth.

In white collar careers, Americans are experiencing an ever increasing desire for self-determined expectations and standards for performance (Hallett, 1987). This approach assumes collaboration, the opportunity to provide ideas, and the evaluation of the supervision being provided. Participative management approaches change the whole concept of supervision and increase the time that needs to be committed to the process.

The evaluation of college personnel, including student affairs staff members, is often more complicated than for positions in business settings. Responsibilities of student affairs practitioners frequently are not clearly defined; require interactive support; and often cross office, department, or unit distinctions (Lynton & Elman, 1987). These factors make the evaluation processes more difficult and crucial for effective performance. In many instances the clearest messages sent by supervisors are what they elect to evaluate (Waterman, 1987). The employee rightfully assumes that the criteria for evaluation must reflect those things that are most important. Therefore what becomes imperative is that supervisors provide accurate information about the relative importance (weighting) of the areas to be evaluated. In higher education, administrators usually define the goals and boundaries whereas discretion for how task responsibilities will be accomplished usually is assigned to the individual. Since discretion is so broad, clarity of goals and boundaries is even more important than in more structured environments.

Higher education institutions and student affairs practice obviously are different in many respects from the business world, and those differences are often the reason individuals choose the profession. Based on Belker (1978), business management emphasizes aspects of evaluation that differ from what is commonly experienced in student affairs.

1. In business, compensable factors are often used to measure exactly how an employee performs the specific tasks that the organization decides are most important. In student affairs, a much broader approach is used to decide how a staff member is meeting the goals and standards.

2. In business, retention is more often a goal for evaluation than it is in student affairs. Even though keeping the best people is important, student affairs leaders also encourage career development that includes helping staff members move to positions in other settings. In business, that help would either never be offered or would be a thinly veiled way of removing an unwanted employee.

3. Compensation issues are much different since most colleges do not rely on merit or bonus systems. In business, frequent direct compensation rewards are often based on performance. The private sector has such tools as bonuses, year-end gifts, and special perquisites to reward employees for exceptional service. Most institutions of higher education simply cannot match these rewards. In student affairs success or failure is often measured by verbal or written comments with an indirect relationship to salary or promotion.

4. Higher education usually provides more opportunity for upward evaluation. Student affairs practitioners more often influence how they are supervised and

evaluated than for their counterparts in business. Student affairs staff members often have direct access to supervisors' written evaluations, a practice uncommon in most businesses.

5. Supervisors in business may not be particularly well trained to do evaluations, but they are usually offered more and better training than is common in student affairs programs. The whole evaluation process also tends to be better organized and endorsed in the business world.

Purposes of Evaluation

A number of purposes have been identified for the evaluation process. Two principal reasons for performance appraisals were reported by Watson (1981) as being judgmental and developmental. The *judgmental issues* are related to pay, promotion, training needs, demotions, and separations. *Developmental issues* refer to such categories as improving individual performance, selection, placement, and training policies and practices. Peterson and Tracy (1979) viewed the purposes of evaluation in much the same way, although they were more straightforward in their characterizations. They indicated that evaluations are conducted to determine wages and salaries and to make career decisions. Evaluations are conducted for multiple reasons, including resources planning and development and human resources administration (Caruth, Noe, & Mondy, 1988; Tyer, 1983). Brown (1988) defined evaluation (or performance appraisal) as "the process of assessing and recording staff performance for the purpose of making judgments about staff that lead to decisions" (p.6).

The supervisor and the employee need to acknowledge which of the purposes are intended in the evaluation process. Organizations and their individual supervisors frequently have different goals for the evaluation process.

One area of evaluation that is frequently overlooked is its use for initiating change. The evaluation process can be a way to encourage change that the organization desires. For example, a student affairs division may desire to move toward a goal of more leadership training opportunities for students. Each director of a functional area might then be expected in the evaluation process to discuss ways the department has contributed to that general goal. Group participation in deciding appropriate ways to implement changes to meet the goal is crucial. The inclusion of a particular goal in the evaluation process clearly sends a message of the significance for the expectation for change. Kanter (1985) presented reasons why individuals may resist change including uncertainty about goals, fear of more work, fear of failure, loss of control, and surprise. The clearer the information about the changed expectations and the greater the participation in collaborative goal setting, the greater the chances for success.

Benefits of Evaluation

A number of benefits directly result from conducting routine employee evaluations. Morrisey (1983) categorized the benefits into two groups: loss avoided and value added. **Losses avoided** refer to problems that are averted and **value added** to that which is enhanced by conducting evaluations. The organization, the supervisor, and the employee can all gain from the evaluation process. The organization is likely to avoid litigation and can reduce employee turnover while developing more motivated employees and improving the internal communications of the organization. Even though no evaluation procedure guarantees that litigation by employees can be avoided, having direct observations of work performance in writing in an employee's file can help provide a record for the inspection of disinterested third parties, such as members of a jury or a judge. Each evaluation ought to focus on specific work-related behaviors. Some of these might reflect on the fact that an employee is chronically late to work, or fails to complete tasks in a reasonable time frame, or abuses sick leave or vacation time. Matters of opinion are harder to document, including such factors as whether or not the person is pleasant over the telephone, or conveys a professional image to the public. Careful, systematic evaluations also may reduce conflicts and avoid misunderstandings about what the job entails. The employee is more likely to obtain a clear picture of the supervisor's expectations and gain greater personal satisfaction from the employment situation when the criteria for evaluation are clearly stated and communicated.

An Effective Evaluation System

Caruth, Noe, and Mondy (1988) identified eleven characteristics of an effective evaluation system. Their ideas are helpful for developing a system designed to meet the needs of an organization as well as the needs of individual staff members. The characteristics listed hereafter provide the basis of an effective system.

Formal. An effective system is formal, with written policies and procedures. A copy of the written material is made available to all those subject to the evaluation system.

Job Related. The evaluation that is conducted pertains to the job itself, and not to extraneous factors such as personal characteristics, family matters, or hobbies. Blake and Mouton added that "the importance of rewarding contribution based on merit remains undiminished" (1985, p. 136).

Valid. The standards established measure what they purport to measure.

Reliable. The appraisal system consistently yields the kind of information that is desired. Excellent performance should generate excellent evaluations, and poor performance should consistently lead to poor evaluations.

Open Communication. The evaluation interview provides a formal process whereby the supervisor and staff member can exchange ideas on the staff member's performance, but that does not substitute for routine feedback or interaction between them. Infrequent, formal discussions are not sufficient to meet the needs of either person.

Trained Appraisers. The fact that a person functions in a supervisory role is not an adequate reason to believe that the person is an expert evaluator. A good system will provide periodic training so that supervisors' evaluation skills are finely honed.

Ease in Use. The evaluation system should be easy to use and free of complexities. In fact, it should be based firmly on standards and measurements that result in greater validity and reliability.

Employee Access. Employees should have access to evaluation results and be provided with copies of written materials or have access to files where the materials are kept. If employees cannot see the written results, the process may become suspect.

Review Mechanism. As is the case in the military an automatic review of the performance evaluation should be done by the next level of supervision in the organization. This will provide a check of the process to assure fairness and equity.

Appeal Process. If an employee disagrees with the results of an evaluation, an appeal should be available. The appeals process protects employees from being treated unfairly, and also ensures that supervisors will do their jobs more conscientiously.

Brown (1988) has offered further criteria for defining an effective performance appraisal system in student affairs: (1) The staff to be evaluated should be involved with the evaluators in developing and evaluating the system. (2) A purpose statement for the system, which links the system to the unit's mission, should be developed and communicated. (3) Job standards provide the guidelines for determining what is an "adequate" performance. (4) Evaluators and staff members engage in an ongoing process of setting goals and providing feedback, rather than depending solely on end-of-the-year review sessions. (5) The central orientation of the system is on education and developmental processes.

Student Affairs Staff Evaluation Components

Only general evaluation characteristics have been identified to this point. The following represents a list of more specific evaluation components that are integral to an evaluation system in student affairs. A sound performance appraisal instrument or tool should:

- be based on an accurate position description;

- be specific to tasks;

- coincide with academic term or annual reports;

- use a broad Likert-type scale of from 5 to 7 points;

- include weighting of responsibilities;

- include both ongoing job responsibilities and ad hoc projects that arose or were implemented during the evaluation period;

- be related to office, division, and institutional goals;

- be interactive, with about one half of the evaluation focusing on employee self-evaluations, comments, and future plans; and

- include a section concerning how the employee feels about the quality of supervision.

A future direction for business that would be beneficial if adopted by student affairs is described by Peters (1988, p. 283) as "achieving flexibility by empowering people." Listening to employees' ideas and concerns, involving more people in decision making, and creating more team projects are all increasingly suggested by management experts. Increased responsibility for self-management and cooperative work relationships should be hallmarks for student affairs. Unfortunately, turf protection, hierarchy of decisions, and bureaucracy still are prevalent.

Student affairs could improve its supervision and evaluation processes by providing clearer and more complete information, listening to staff concerns and suggestions, giving increased responsibility to individual and project teams, and recognizing excellence. The cost in time to improve these areas is repaid many times over in staff satisfaction, retention, and productivity. The financial cost may be minimal since recognition can be individual or public, and compensation changes are not necessarily expensive. A sample evaluation instrument that can be used in student affairs divisions is presented in Figure 15.1.

Types of Evaluation Instruments

A number of different approaches are available for conducting evaluations, and the content contained in these instruments can very widely. A study of state-wide performance appraisals conducted by Feild and Holley (1975) indicated that more than 40% of the respondents were interested in such variables as quality and quantity of work, initiative, and human relations. Other factors that have been examined on appraisal forms are judgment, job knowledge, work habits, dependability, organizing and planning, and supervisory ability. Tyer (1983) identified eight different types of evaluation formats.

1. ***Rating Scales.*** This approach requires the evaluator to check a box or place a mark along a continuum which describes a particular characteristic of the employee. It is the most common approach, but is ambiguous and subjective in nature. The definition is left to the supervisor which can create problems (Odiorne, 1984). Feild and Holley (1975) found that 62% of 39 respondents used this format.

2. ***Essay Reports.*** The essay requires that the evaluator prepare an open-ended report on the employee. If the evaluator does not prepare a thoughtful report, then this approach will not work well. On the other hand, it forces the evaluator to reflect on the employee's performance and results. Thirteen percent of the respondents to the Feild and Holley (1975) survey reported using essay reports.

3. ***Checklists.*** In this situation the evaluator checks those statements that describe an employee from a list of statements. This approach is more person-based than performance-based.

(Continued on page 521

Student Affairs

Goals

A comprehensive and fair review of each student affairs member's performance of responsibilities is the primary objective. The purposes of evaluation are to provide opportuity for clarifying expectations, giving constructive criticism, setting professional growth objectives, and giving support for quality performance.

Components

The evaluation should primarily focus on the position description and the quality of performance of assigned tasks. Both standard expectations for normal ongoing responsibilities *and* additional expectations of yearly goals and new expectations should be evaluated. The weighting of components must be clear prior to initiating the evaluation process. The supervisor and the staff member should both complete evaluation forms and should share equally in oral discussions about progress.

Timing

Supervision assumes regular discussion of performance. Formal evaluations should be conducted at least yearly with a semi-annual format best for new professionals or newly hired staff. The best procedure is to combine the evaluation process with a review of current year goals, and the preliminary setting of goals and professional development plans for the next period.

Suggested Format

Name: _____

Title: _____

Date: _____

Period Evaluated: _____

Figure 15.1. Sample Evaluation System.

Figure 15.1. Continued.

Score	Rating Definitions
5. Excellent	Performance is consistently well above expectations.
4. Above average	Performance is above acceptable level.
3. Average	Performance is acceptable.
2. Below Average	Performance is below acceptable expectations.
1. Unsatisfactory	Significant improvement is required.

I. RATINGS ON INDIVIDUAL FACTORS

Using the Rating Definitions, indicate the appropriate numerical rating and enter comments under each factor which follows. If the factor does not apply, enter N.A. in the Rating Column.

Rating

_____ A. ***Work Accomplishment:*** Accomplishment of primary mission of position or function; achieving results in a timely fashion. Comments: _____

_____

_____ B. ***Communication:*** Oral and written expression; keeping associates informed, maintaining appropriate relationships; persuasiveness. Comments: _____

_____

Figure 15.1. Continued.

_____ C. ***Decision-making:*** Promptness; clarity, quality; consideration of all facts, willingness to assume responsibility. Comments: _____

_____ D. ***Planning and Organizing:*** Developing plans; estabishing priorities; completion and follow-up of assigned tasks. Organizing work to complete responsibilities. Comments: _____

_____ E. ***Problem-solving:*** Analytical ability; resourcefulness; overall awarenss of cost implications; anticipating problems and solving them early. Comments: _____

_____ F. ***Initiative and Creativity:*** Suggesting new approaches to problems; originality of approach; desire for new responsibility. Comments: _____

_____ G. ***Budgeting:*** Setting realistic budget; effective use of people and funds; careful planning for new financial resources. Comments: _____

_____ H. ***Delegation of Responsibility:*** Delegating authority in unit; ensuring effective coordination of subordinate units, supervisors and employees. Comments: _____

_____ I. ***Leadership:*** Motivating subordinates to work in harmony for unit goals and objectives; ability to gain confidence and respect. Selection, training, and development of staff. Comments:

_____

_____

Figure 15.1. Continued.

_____ J. ***Overall Performance Rating:***
Comments: _____

_____

_____

II. YEARLY GOALS AND ADAPTATIONS

Rating

_____ A. Performance of current year individual goals.
Comments: _____

_____

_____ B. Performance on contributions to unit and/
or student affairs goals for the evaluation
period. Comments: _____

_____

_____ C. Ability to adapt to and perform unexpected
tasks that arose during the evaluation period.
Comments: _____

_____

_____ D. Contributions to the professsion through
associations, presentations and writing.
Comments: _____

_____

_____ E. Contributions to the college and local
community. Comments: _____

_____

Figure 15.1. Continued.

III. STRENGTHS, IMPROVEMENT NEEDED, AND ACTION PLAN

1. Describe the person's most significant strengths: _____

   _____

2. Describe the person's development needs: _____

   _____

3. Identify specific professional development goals that are to be accomplished in the coming year and the support that will be provided to meet those goals: _____

   _____

   _____

IV. GENERAL COMMENTS

1. Staff Member

   By my signature below, I confirm that this evaluation report has been discussed with me, however, it does not indicate my agreement or disagreement with the results except as I have commented here. Comments: _____

   _____

   _____

   Staff Member's Signature _____

   Date: _____

2. Supervisor Summary Comments: _____

   _____

   _____

   Supervisor's Signature _____

   Date: _____

   Position Description Reviewed: Date _____

   (If changes made, please attach revised position description and forward to the Vice President of Student Affairs).

4. **Critical Incidents.** This is an approach that uses anecdotal records that are kept on employees. The supervisor lists positive and negative incidents that pertain to certain aspects of the employee's work. This can be very time consuming, but pertains to actual behaviors and performance rather than personal characteristics.

5. **Forced Choice.** From a list of positive and negative statements about an employee, the supervisor is asked to make an evaluation. It is easy to administer but does not provide much useful feedback to the employee.

6. **Ranking.** This is fairly easy to complete, and can be conducted in a number of ways. Employees can be ranked from best to worst in a department, or they can be paired by comparing each employee with every other employee.

7. **Forced Distribution.** This is a variation on the ranking approach. Employees are ranked by percentiles or quartiles, for example. The major problem with this kind of approach is that the criteria for placing employees in various categories often is unclear, which can lead to employee suspicion and morale problems.

8. **Management by Objectives (MBO).** This approach refers to the supervisor and employee mutually agreeing upon a set of objectives that are quantifiable and measurable. This approach, while expensive, focuses on results. Hollmann (1979) observed that superiors must learn how to accurately assess and respond to the numerous factors determining how frequently feedback should be provided to each subordinate. According to Odiorne (1984) MBO is the most complex system, but is worth the effort in terms of outcomes.

One other type of evaluation instrument worth noting is behaviorally anchored rating scales (BARS). BARS work well on lower-level jobs where requirements are well known, but are less helpful for professional and managerial positions (Odiorne, 1984). This approach was particularly attractive in some management circles, but research findings indicated that very little reason exists to believe that BARS are superior to alternative evaluation instruments (Schwab, Heneman, & DeCotis, 1979).

Difficulties in Evaluation

A number of problems are associated with evaluation, which can, in fact, seriously damage the value of the process.

Evaluator Errors. The person conducting the evaluation can make a number of mistakes, which affect the evaluation adversely. Common problems in this general classification include lack of the skills required of evaluators, the difference between day-to-day management skills and employee development skills, and the different frames of reference brought to the evaluation process (Tyer, 1983). Additionally, the "halo and horns effects" can influence the process. The **halo effect** is the tendency for the supervisor to place a positive aura or halo over the rating of a subordinate, while the **horns effect** refers to the tendency to rate people lower than their performance actually justifies (Odiorne, 1984).

Fortunato and Waddell (1981) pointed to several other evaluator errors, including leniency (supervisors being lenient to avoid facing the unpleasant task of confronting an employee), evaluating on the basis of potential (rating on the basis of the employee's potential rather than actual accomplishments), and associating (assuming an employee is proficient in all areas of responsibility because some are done very well). Other evaluator errors include tendencies to rate all employees as average, make a best guess, exhibit personal biases (Caruth, Noe, & Mondy, 1988), *and* not evaluating a staff member as being extremely good or bad, even when the performance is actually at such a level (Watson, 1981).

Instrumental Errors. If the instruments used in the appraisal have flaws, obviously barriers will be present to effective appraisals (Tyer, 1983). Establishing effective standards and measurements is difficult and challenging, but this must be accomplished if the performance of employees is to be measured accurately (Caruth, Noe, & Mondy, 1988). Other errors occur when goals or standards are not clearly articulated or understood before the evaluation occurs (Watson, 1981).

Process Problems. Tyer (1983) identified a number of problems related to the evaluation process. Among these are the tendencies to try to achieve too many objectives with a single evaluation instrument, some of which may be in conflict with others such as combining career development with salary adjustments, to be excessively formal, view evaluation as an annual activity, and to play the ***zero-sum game.*** The zero-sum game refers to the view that if one employee moves toward the top of the organization, then another must move down the ladder. In this regard, Penn (1979) added that "The primary goal of the [evaluation feedback] session should be to encourage improved performance, not to discourage or alienate the employee. Also, as noted earlier, the evaluation interview is not the time to discuss issues concerning salary adjustment or employee benefits" (p. 159).

Organizational Climate. Tyer (1983) referred to one other category of barriers to effective evaluation as those associated with the organizational climate. "Climate is determined importantly by characteristics, conduct, attitudes, expectations of other persons, by sociological and cultural realistics" (Gibson, Ivancevich, & Donnelly, 1973, p. 313).

Misconceptions about Performance Standards

Phillips (1985) identified a number of misconceptions about performance standards. "Performance standards represent a type of goal-setting process. In simple terms, a written performance standard is defined as a statement of the conditions that will exist when a job has been or is being satisfactorily performed" (p. 126). One's work will highly likely be evaluated against performance standards. "People are rewarded primarily for their contributions to goal attainment. Work habits and personal characteristics are relevant only to the extent that they influence or are related to organizational goals" (Penn, 1979, p. 156). For example, the change in emphasis of a department might be reflected in performance standards. In the recreational sports department, because of an increasing number of older students, the emphasis may change from providing an intramural programs based on competitive teams and tournaments to more individualized fitness programs. Staff responsible in that area may have their performance goals adjusted to reflect the change in emphasis of the department. Among the problems that are associated with performance standards are the following (Phillips, 1985):

1. failure on the part of staff to realize the advantages of standards,

2. supervisors becoming overly involved in the mechanics of the process and forgetting the purpose of performance standards,

3. viewing performance standards as a mechanism for identifying failure,

4. failure to set realistic standards against which performance can be judged,

5. taking shortcuts so as to manipulate the evaluation process,

6. developing so many standards that the process becomes confused, and/or

7. hoping that the standards are a fad or gimmick and that they will go away.

Without appropriate standards of performance, the evaluation process will be badly flawed and unsuccessful. Therefore, whether one is being evaluated or serving as an evaluator, one needs to work diligently in setting appropriate standards and working toward making the total process successful.

Legal Considerations

A number of legal considerations are important to the evaluation process that should be recognized by everyone concerned with the evaluation process. Odiorne (1984) indicated that a number of groups may not legally be discriminated against. That is not to say that it is acceptable to discriminate against members of non-protected groups, but the force of law makes it criminal to discriminate against racial minorities including African-Americans, Native Americans, and those of Hispanic descent; women; older workers; and the handicapped. Depending on state and local laws, Vietnam-era veterans also may have certain protected rights, as may homosexuals. Some states are moving toward passing "comparable worth" legislation, which means that employees doing work of a certain worth should be paid the same as the employees performing different, but similarly-valued work. How far this concept will extend is not clear but supervisors and practitioners alike should know the laws of their jurisdiction and the implications such legislation has for supervision.

In the final analysis the recommendation is that the most useful guidelines are for supervisors to treat all staff members fairly, to be aware of any special legal requirements incumbent upon members of their jurisdiction, and to seek help from the institution's legal counsel should questions arise. (See Chapter 13 for further discussion of the legal issues related to employment.)

Civil Service Issues

Those employed in private colleges will not be confronted with the requirements of the state civil service commission or a similar body. Obviously, this does not mean that staff members should be treated poorly because they are not state employees. What it does mean is that supervisors will not encounter legislated aspects of supervising public employees. Morrisey (1983) pointed out "that there are some significant differences in the way performance appraisals must be handled in the public sector when compared to the private sector" (p. 26). Among these differences are substantially more media attention, elected officials focusing on state-assisted institutions, relationships with employee unions, and taxpayer revolt. Although beginning professionals seldom have to address these issues, to realize that significant distinctions do exist between public and private institutions and that one's work will be affected accordingly is important.

Equity Issues

Supervisors must conduct both supervision and evaluation as equitably as possible. Since everyone is subject to both positive and negative bias, the more objective the expectations and evaluations the better. Included in the process is the necessity for providing challenging work in conjunction with support for success. Low expectations are as discriminatory as an inequitable set of performance measurements. Caution is particularly necessary when gender, race, and age differences add to the supervisor's need to understand individual goals, skills, and preferences. To act on the assumption that one can be more straight forward in providing constructive criticism to male staff members denies female staff members an equal opportunity to receive clear signals, to grow toward the goals, and to learn the "system." In some situations, another level of supervision may need to be added to insure equity.

Equity should not be construed to mean literally that the same expectations and responsibilities exist for everyone. All supervision and evaluation should be individualized, but the criteria for individualization should be based on skill, potential, experience, and goals rather than on gender, race, age, or any other personal circumstance.

A further equity problem can occur in the area of mentoring or sponsorship, a topic addressed earlier. Because the process of mentoring may be (usually is) initiated by a supervisor, the decision regarding who is singled out for special time and attention is of concern. While subjective criteria are unavoidable, the selection should be based on observed potential, past performance, individual goals and motivation, and the opportunities available to provide the staff person with experiences that will benefit his or her career progress.

Training Supervisors to Conduct Evaluations

Even in student affairs settings where a fair, complete evaluation process is used, a major problem may occur when those responsible for the supervision are not trained to implement the evaluations. At the point of hiring and at every promotion (change of responsibility) the supervisor needs to be taught the importance of and the process of implementing the evaluation system. Inconsistent evaluations among supervisors or between departments are unfair and a major cause of low staff morale. A seminar on conducting the evaluations should be offered annually and a team consisting of staff members at all levels should review the entire evaluation process at least every three years. A corollary to the training process is that all candidates for positions in a student affairs division should be clearly informed about the supervision and evaluation processes in use.

SUMMARY

Information has been presented on issues and trends in supervision and evaluation. The responsibility for the quality and content of the supervision and evaluation processes is mutually shared by the institution, the student affairs division, the individual supervisor, and the individual staff member. Excellent supervision and evaluation contribute to work satisfaction, productivity, employee retention, and staff cooperation.

Student affairs staff members expect broad discretion to determine how they will accomplish their responsibilities and significant involvement in setting task priorities. They deserve clear information on the performance expectations and the relative significance of each responsibility. Student affairs professionals should take leadership in adapting recent trends in human resource management to higher education.

Ethical and professional considerations must be considered in designing a fair and equitable evaluation system. Training of supervisors is crucial for consistent application of performance reviews.

REFERENCES

Barkhaus, R. (1983, Summer). Career development in the corporation. *Journal of College Placement*, pp. 29-32.

Belker, L.B. (1978). *The first-time manager.* New York: AMACOM.

Blake, R.R., & Mouton, J.S. (1974). *The managerial grid.* Houston: Gulf.

Blake, R.R., & Mouton, J.S. (1981). *Productivity: The human side.* San Francisco: Jossey-Bass.

Blake, R.R., & Mouton, J.S. (1985). *The managerial grid III.* Houston: Gulf.

Brown, R.D. (1988). *Performance appraisal as a tool for staff development.* New Directions for Student Services (No. 43). San Francisco: Jossey-Bass.

Caruth, D.L., Noe, III, R.M., & Mondy, R.W. (1988). *Staffing the contemporary organization.* New York: Quorum.

Council for the Advancement of Standards for Student Services/Development Programs (CAS) (1986). *CAS standards and guidelines for student services/ development programs.* Washington, DC: Author.

Derr, C.B. (1986). *Managing the new careerists.* San Francisco: Jossey-Bass.

Feild, H.S., & Holley, W.H. (1975). Performance appraisal—An analysis of state-wide practices. *Public Personnel Management, 4*(3), 145-150.

Fortunato, R.T., & Waddell, D.G. (1981). *Personnel administration in higher education.* San Francisco: Jossey-Bass.

Fuhrmann, B. (1987). Career paths in higher education: Lessons from the corporate world. *National Forum, 67*(1), 22-24.

Gibson, J.L. Ivancevich, J.M., & Donnelly, Jr., J.H. (1973). *Organizations: Structure, process, behavior.* Dallas: Business publications.

Hallett, J.J. (1987). *Worklife vision: Redefining work for the information economy.* Alexandria, VA. American Society for Personnel Administrators.

Hersey, P. & Blanchard, K. (1977). *Management of organizational behavior: Utilizing human resources (3rd ed.).* Englewood Cliffs, NJ: Prentice-Hall.

Hersey, P., & Blanchard, K. (1982). *Management of organizational behavior: Utilizing human resources (4th ed.).* Englewood Cliffs, NJ: Prentice-Hall.

Herzberg, F., Mausner, B., & Snyderman, B.B. (1959). *The motivation to work.* New York: Wiley.

Hollmann, R.W. (1979). Applying MBO research to practice. In P.S. Greenlaw (Ed.), *Readings in personnel management* (pp. 140-147). Philadelphia: Saunders.

Kanter, R.M. (1985, April). Managing the human side of change. *Management Review*, pp. 52-56.

Kaye, B.L. (1981). Up is not the only way. *Supervisory Management, 25* (2), 2-9.

Kelly, K.E. (1984). Initiating a relationship with a mentor in student affairs. *NASPA Journal, 21*(3), 49-54.

Kram, K.F. (1986). Mentoring in the workplace. In D.T. Hall (Ed.), *Career development in organizations* (pp. 160-201). San Francisco: Jossey-Bass.

Lynton, E., & Elman, S. (1987). New priorities for the university. San Francisco: Jossey-Bass.

Maccoby, M. (1988). *Why work: Leading the new generation.* New York: Simon and Schuster.

Maslow, A.H. (1954). *Motivation and personality.* New York: Harper.

McGregor, D. (1960). *The human side of enterprise.* New York: McGraw-Hill.

Morrisey, G.L. (1983). *Performance appraisal in the public sector.* Menlo Park, CA: Addison-Wesley.

Naisbeth, J., & Aburden, P. (1985). *Re-inventing the corporation.* New York: Warner.

Odiorne, G.S. (1984). *Strategic management of human resources.* San Francisco: Jossey-Bass.

Penn, J.R. (1979). Staff evaluation. In G.D. Kuh (Ed.), *Evaluation in student affairs* (pp. 149-160). Cincinnati, OH: ACPA Media.

Peters, T. (1988). *Thriving on chaos: Handbook for a management revolution.* New York: Knopf.

Peterson, R.B., & Tracy, L. (1979). *Systematic management of human resources.* Menlo Park, CA: Addison-Wesley.

Phillips, J.J. (1985). *Improving supervisors' effectiveness.* San Francisco: Jossey-Bass.

Schwab, D.P., Heneman, III, H.G., & DeCotis, T.A. (1979). Behaviorally anchored rating scales: A review of the literature. In P.S. Greenlaw (Ed.), *Readings in personnel management* (pp. 148-159). Philadelphia: Saunders.

Teas, R.K. (1981). A test of a model of department store salespeople's job satisfaction. *Journal of Retailing 57*(1), 3-25.

Tyer, C.B. (1983). Employee performance appraisal: Process in search of a technique. In S.W. Hays and R.C. Kearney (Eds.), *Public personnel administration: Problems and prospects* (pp. 118-136). Englewood Cliffs, NJ: Prentice Hall.

Waterman, R.H. (1987). *The renewal factor: How the best get and keep the competitive edge.* New York: Bantam Books.

Watson, C.E. (1981). *Results-oriented managing: The key to performance.* Menlo Park, CA: Addison-Wesley.

Yankelovich, D., & Immerwahr, J. (1984). The emergence of expressivism will revolutionize the contract between workers and employers. In L. Chiara & D. Lacey (Eds.), *Work in the 21st century* (pp. 11-24). Alexandria, VA: American Society for Personnel Administration.

SUGGESTED READINGS

Baird, L.S., Beatty, R.W., & Schneier, C.E. (Eds.). (1982). *The performance appraisal sourcebook.* Amherst, MA: Human Resources Development Press.

Brown, R.D. (1988). *Performance appraisal as a tool for staff development.* New Directions for Student Services (No. 43). San Francisco: Jossey-Bass.

Council for the Advancement of Standards for Student Services/Development Programs (CAS). (1986). *CAS standards and guidelines for student services/ development programs.* Washington, DC: Author.

Fortunato, R.T., & Waddell, D.G. (1981). *Personnel administration in higher education.* San Francisco: Jossey-Bass.

Morrisey, G.L. (1983). *Performance appraisal in the public sector.* Menlo Park, CA: Addison-Wesley.

Steven C. Ender, Ed.D., received his doctorate and M.Ed. from The University of Georgia in counseling and student personnel services and his B.S. from Virginia Commonwealth University in business. He is presently serving as an Assistant Vice President for Student Affairs at Indiana University of Pennsylvania.

His publications include several articles and books including co-authoring *Students Helping Students: A Training Manual for Peer Helpers on the College Campus* and co-editing and writing chapters in *New Directions for Student Services: Developmental Approaches to Academic Advising, New Directions for Student Services: Students as Paraprofessional Staff*, and *Development Academic Advising.* He has extensive consultation experience in the areas of student development programming, academic advising, developmental education, and peer helper training and programming.

Carmy Carranza, M.A., received her B.S. in mathematics education and her M.A. in English from Indiana University of Pennsylvania. She is presently serving as the Tutorial Coordinator and Math Specialist for the Learning Center at IUP. She has previously been an instructor in mathematics, English, and writing at both the secondary and college levels, most recently at the University of Pittsburgh at Greensburg.

She has given numerous conference presentations in the areas of remedial mathematics for developmental students, tutorial program models, and paraprofessional training and also has consulting experience in each of these areas.

CHAPTER 16

STUDENTS AS PARAPROFESSIONALS

Steven C. Ender
Carmy Carranza

Employment of undergraduates to function in a variety of paraprofessional roles in student affairs departments and programs is expanding rapidly. Professional literature provides little in the way of a definitive definition for the student paraprofessional. This void may be due to the multiplicity of roles students now perform on college campuses (Ender, 1984; Winston & Ender, 1988) or, perhaps, to the rapidly expanding scope of the paraprofessional movement in higher education.

Delworth and Aulepp (1976) defined the paraprofessional as a person willing to give time and talent to assist others. When this person is identified, selected, and trained to assume tasks usually performed by certain professional staff members, this student becomes a paraprofessional. Ender, Schuette, and Neuberger (1984) defined the student paraprofessional as a student employed by a division of student affairs for purposes of providing direct services to other students on a paid or voluntary basis. Also, Ender, McCaffrey, and Miller (1979) have defined the paraprofessional as "an undergraduate or graduate student who has been trained to assist fellow students in adjusting to, and successfully functioning within, the higher education setting" (p. 12).

In light of these definitions, *paraprofessionals are students who have been selected and trained to offer educational services to their peers. These services are intentionally designed to assist in the adjustment, satisfaction, and persistence of students toward attainment of their educational goals. Students performing in paraprofessional roles are compensated for their services and supervised by qualified professionals.*

RATIONALE

Impact of the Peer Group

A strong rationale for students functioning as paraprofessionals is the powerful impact peers have on one another. Chickering (1969) maintained that relationships with close friends and peer groups are primary forces that influence student development on college campuses. Heath (1968), in research on variables that affect the maturity of college students, concluded that one powerful source of impact is interpersonal relationships with other students. More specifically, Feldman and Newcomb (1970) noted that the peer group assists students in the resolution of many developmental tasks including independence from parental authority, clarification of values, and acceptance of differences in others.

The strong impact students have on peers' growth and development occurs through intrapersonal and interpersonal dynamics of stimulation, psychic dissonance, and the regaining of emotional equilibrium (Chickering, 1969; Heath, 1968). Student growth in intellectual, psychosocial, moral, and ethical areas can be attributed largely to the challenges to ideas and values they experience. These challenges come primarily from other students, forcing reflection and consideration of present behavior. In many instances, reflection results in behavioral change to higher levels of academic, personal and interpersonal functioning. Student paraprofessionals have a distinct advantage regarding their potential to influence their peers if they have an understanding of the maturation process and are trained to implement developmental dynamics.

Administrators who utilize students in paraprofessional roles are intentionally maximizing the developmental impact students have on each other. Student paraprofessionals serve not only as challengers and supporters in the developmental process but also are role models for others. Behaviors that student paraprofessionals model are often characteristic of successful, responsible, and self-directed college students. As Miller and Prince (1976) indicated, development can be fostered by creating a developmental milieu whereby students are able to observe and interact with others who effectively model the characteristics, values, and processes that best represent the outcomes to which the environment is committed.

Impact on Student Paraprofessionals

Developmental dynamics created by the implementation of student-staffed programs have a major effect on participating paraprofessionals. This outcome has been overwhelmingly endorsed by coordinators of paraprofessional programs across the country (Ender, 1984; Winston & Ender, 1988). Administrators who implement such programs should realize that the program itself is a developmental intervention for the participating paraprofessional. This is especially true during the training, interviewing, delivery, and evaluating phases of the program. Heath (1980) asserted that personal development of college students can be enhanced through programs that expect and encourage students to take responsibility for growth in others and provide opportunities for students to assume alternative roles. These concepts are underlying principles upon which student paraprofessional programming is based.

Budget Restrictions

Institutional budget restrictions and the conflicting need to offer developmental-based programming to large and divergent populations provide another strong rationale for student paraprofessional programming (Ender & McFadden, 1980; Ender, 1984; Winston & Ender, 1988). In many instances student affairs administrators may be able to increase student development programming by using student staff, while minimizing budget increases. This is often possible by utilizing already existing institutional resources such as college work-study budgets, room or board waivers, and academic credit for the work experience. Additionally, student volunteers who want work experiences documented in developmental transcripts (Brown, 1980) or for letters of recommendation can be utilized as peer helpers at low cost.

Enhancing Skill of Professionals

Not only can more students be reached through paraprofessional programming, but such programming affords professional practitioners the opportunity to provide services that require higher levels of education and skills (Delworth & Yarris, 1978). For instance, professionals employed in settings that use paraprofessionals can often accomplish more by training, supervising, and evaluating peer helpers than by limiting their activity to only working directly with students. And, students with more serious concerns can be referred to the professional. Many students with personal problems seek help from friends first. Through paraprofessional referrals, professionals can likely achieve a wider campus impact than through most traditional approaches. Because paraprofessionals are representatives of many different student subcultures, student affairs practitioners can increase their insight and impact regarding the needs of diverse student groups.

Paraprofessional Effectiveness

Literature on student paraprofessional effectiveness suggests that peer helpers may be more effective or as effective as professionals when dealing with many developmental concerns (Barron & Hetherton, 1981; Brown & Myers, 1975; Ender, 1984; Frisz & Lane, 1987; Getz & Miles, 1978; Winston & Ender, 1988). For instance, studies concerning the use of undergraduates as study-skills counselors found that freshmen counseled by student paraprofessionals made significantly greater use of the information received during counseling than did those counseled by professionals (Zunker & Brown, 1966). Likewise, Carkhuff and Truax (1965) contended that paraprofessionals can be as effective as professionals in facilitating constructive change in people over relatively short periods of time. Harrar & Ender (1987) provided research results which suggests that students receiving tutoring from undergraduate peer helpers overwhelmingly concluded that the assistance was positive in regard to raising their grade point averages in the tutored course.

ROLES, GOALS, AND LIMITATIONS

Roles

In many student affairs programs students currently are employed as paraprofessionals in a variety of roles (Ender, 1984; Winston & Ender, 1988). The beginning of this movement perhaps can be traced to residence halls where students have been assisting other students as resident assistants, proctors, hall counselors, or advisors since the turn of the century (Powell, Pyler, Dickerson, & McCallan, 1969). Brown's (1972) pioneering study-skills-counseling model was based on 18 years of testing and counseling research. More recent literature suggests the use of student paraprofessionals in a host of program settings (Ender, 1984; Winston & Ender, 1988). Smith (1981) reported that students at the University of the Pacific are working in new student orientation; academic advising; learning center; admissions, international services, registrar and financial aid offices, as well as in the Upward Bound and community involvement programs. Other examples of campus roles in which student paraprofessionals are being utilized include peer counselors (Lucian, 1977; Delworth & Johnson, 1984; Holly, 1987), peer tutors (Ender & McFadden, 1980; Harrar & Ender, 1987; Kelley & Nolan, 1980), student leaders (DuVall & Ender, 1980; Frigault, Maloney, & Trevino, 1986; Newton, 1980), assistance in career planning and placement (Delworth & Johnson, 1984; Johnston & Hansen, 1981), peer consultants to student organizations (Presser, Miller & Rapin, 1984), and peer workshop leaders addressing student development topics (Croteau & Tinsley, 1984).

Goals and Expectations

Even though expectations placed on paraprofessionals change from setting to setting and are somewhat dependent on the particular role the student is being asked to assume, certain guidelines need to be considered as specific paraprofessional expectations are being formulated by the professional staff. Ender, Schuette, and Neuberger (1984) proposed six objectives for paraprofessional programs that administrators should consider:

- provide direct services to college students,

- maximize the potential positive effects of peers interacting with peers,

- provide guidance and developmental support services and programs rather than counseling/therapeutic interventions,

- provide a wide range of developmental services at reduced cost,

- provide positive role models for other students to emulate, and

- provide educational and developmental experiences for students serving in the paraprofessional positions.

Other expectations might include serving as ombudsman in regard to campus resources, understanding developmental stage and task theory for particular age groups, and utilizing goal setting and assessment strategies in their lives as well as in their work with others.

The guiding expectation of students serving in these positions is the developmental nature of the programming thrust. The paraprofessional is expected to perform educational, advising, and preventive services rather than focus on intensive counseling issues or remedial concerns for which they are not qualified to deal.

Limitations

Several issues affect both roles and limitations of student paraprofessionals. Administrators need to consider the following when formulating role definitions.

Length, degree, and quality of training have a direct bearing on how realistic the professional's expectations are of paraprofessionals. A training program that meets for a weekend cannot possible teach helping skills one could only realistically expect to master in an intensive semester-long training experience. Also, trainer qualifications must be considered. One cannot expect paraprofessionals to develop helping skills that exceed those of the trainer. Careful consideration of training resources available on campus must be made when considering both expectations and limitations for the paraprofessional position.

Time available and physical proximity of professional staff members for supervision need consideration also. If the supervisor can meet with the paraprofessional on a biweekly basis only, the paraprofessional should not be allowed to offer services requiring daily observation and consultation. Likewise, the physical proximity of the supervisor to the paraprofessional work site is important. A rule of thumb is that the greater the responsibility of the paraprofessional, the closer and more immediately available must be the supervisor. For example, if the paraprofessional is assisting another student with personal concerns, the supervisor should be in immediate easy access. On the other hand, paraprofessionals offering tours of the career library do not need such close supervision. Also remember that tasks and duties assigned paraprofessionals must fall within the professional expertise of the supervisor. A paraprofessional working in the tutorial center and supervised by a member of the English faculty should not be asked to function as a personal counselor.

The stated goals and objectives of the student affairs division employing paraprofessionals provide guidelines for limitations. A paraprofessional trained to offer services that address one department's goals and objectives cannot move to another unit without additional training.

The number of contact hours between the paraprofessional and the target population is also an important factor to consider. Paraprofessionals should be able to accomplish their work activities within reasonable or designated work hours.

Administrators should be careful not to burden paraprofessionals with unrealistic work expectations.

Developmental or maturity levels of the participating paraprofessional also will govern to a certain extent the limitations of the role. For example, freshman and sophomore students working in the career counseling center are, in most instances, in a position to help other students with their career exploration. On the other hand, in most situations they are not in a position, developmentally, to assist students who wish to make decisions concerning career choices, if they have not themselves mastered this developmental task.

A final limitation concerns policies and procedures of the department within which a paraprofessional works. These helpers should not be put in the position of having to formulate or interpret policies to other members of the campus community. That responsibility belongs to administrators and other professionals.

IMPLEMENTING PARAPROFESSIONAL PROGRAMS

Three major program phases with corresponding program components need consideration as administrators implement paraprofessional programs. Phase one provides focus and direction for the paraprofessional campus role; phase two identifies recruitment and selection techniques; and phase three attends to training and rewarding the paraprofessional.

Phase One: Focus and Direction

Identification of Campus Role. Role identification is the first step when implementing a paraprofessional program. Careful consideration should be given to the needs of the population to be served. Factors such as location of paraprofessional work stations, training and supervising new personnel, and acceptance and endorsement of the paraprofessional program by affected professionals all need careful consideration. As these issues are resolved, the paraprofessional job description can be refined.

Developing Job Descriptions. The job description must be grounded in behavioral language that specifies what the paraprofessional is expected to do (Ostroth, 1981). This attention to actual behaviors assists in all subsequent phases of program development. By having a list of behaviors describing the position, students can assess their abilities to perform as paraprofessionals, and faculty and staff can refer potential paraprofessionals to the program administrator with greater ease. The recruitment process can be enhanced greatly with job descriptions that are written in behavioral language. Additionally, trainers need a definite idea of training areas and helping skills that must be addressed in the training program, and supervisors will be in much better positions to evaluate paraprofessional effectiveness.

Establishing Selection Criteria. Criteria for selection are a natural outgrowth of the behavioral job description and should be disseminated to all recruitment agents (faculty, staff, administrators, and students) on the campus. Ender, Schuette and Neuberger (1984) suggested generic criteria, which include academic records; recommendations from faculty, staff, and employed paraprofessionals; past and present persons in positions of leadership; and desire and willingness of the prospective paraprofessional to assist and help other students. Ostroth (1981) and Smith (1981) suggested that participation in training programs by students interested in the paraprofessional position should be included as one criterion for selection. Some paraprofessional training should take place before selection and employment. By participating in training before selection, students are given the opportunity to make decisions concerning their ability to serve in the position, and professional staff members are able to observe the student functioning in role-related activities before employment.

Phase Two: Identification and Selection

Recruitment Procedures. Student affairs administrators should strive to include as many representatives as possible from the college community in the recruitment process. The representation includes faculty, staff, students, and other administrators. The development and dissemination of behavioral job descriptions and well-defined selection criteria to potential referral agents will aid in the recruitment process and also should result in a pool of well qualified and possibly pretrained students desiring the position, if the selection criteria include participation in training. Administrators need to recruit a heterogeneous group of students who represent the diversity of the population they will be assisting. Factors such as age, gender, race, socioeconomic background, and other demographic characteristics of the target population need to be given careful consideration during the recruitment process. Successful paraprofessionals are able to empathize with concerns of the target population and can model adaptive behaviors that they have learned in overcoming similar concerns.

Selection Procedures. The literature pertaining to selection of paraprofessionals presents a wide range of alternatives for administrators to consider. German (1979) conducted an intensive review of selection procedures used to hire paraprofessional student counselors. The procedures he described included the use of personality inventories (*Edwards Personal Preference Schedule* and *Minnesota Multiphasic Personality Inventory*), direct evaluation of actual performance (leaderless group discussion, role plays using rating scales, and sociodrama techniques), and standardized selection interviews.

Ostroth (1981') discussed techniques used to select resident assistants that also seem appropriate for other types of paraprofessionals. He pointed out that many traditional selection processes, such as resumés, recommendations, and unstructured interviews, have proven to be biased, unreliable, and invalid. Other selection procedures that have greater utility for selecting paraprofessionals include peer ratings, performance of tasks, role play situations, participation in leaderless group discussions, apprenticeships, and participation in training programs before selection.

Ender and McFadden (1980) suggested initial selection procedures using traditional methods, including application forms, letters of recommendation, and individual interviews. The applicant pool derived from those who completed this process then participated in a training course, followed by group interviews. Paraprofessionals were then selected by a team of staff members.

Phase Three: Training and Rewards

Training Program. A wealth of information exists regarding the training of paraprofessionals for their campus roles. Also, now available are several published manuals related to training undergraduates to serve in paraprofessional positions (Arkin & Shollar, 1982; Blimling & Miltenberger, 1981; D'Andrea & Salovey, 1983; Ender et al., 1979; Upcraft & Pilato, 1982). Training can be thought of in two stages. Stage one, pre-service training, occurs before actual employment, and stage two, in-service training, is provided throughout the program.

The training program during the pre-service stage provides opportunities for students to gain information pertaining to the role, participate in personal growth opportunities, and learn specific helping skills. Training, during the pre-service stage, should include such topics as knowledge of the role, awareness of self and power of role modeling behavior, creating and maintaining support groups, student (human) development theory, communication skills, goal setting strategies and the identification of behavioral objectives, assessment skills and techniques, cross-cultural relations, problems of gender stereotyping, study skills techniques, knowledge of campus and community resources, and referral techniques (Ender, Schuette & Neuberger, 1984). The main focuses of the pre-training experience are personal exploration and development of helping skills. Minimally, peer helpers should complete the pre-service stage of training with adequate self-insight regarding their strengths and weaknesses as a helping person and minimum skill development regarding student development assessment, communication/human relation skills, and the ability to make appropriate referrals to campus and community resources. Helpers, at this stage of training must understand their power and influence as a campus role-model, be able to offer facilitative helping interventions rather than control oriented advice giving, be knowledgeable regarding those student problems with which peers can provide assistance, and be knowledgeable regarding other concerns which must be referred to a more knowledgeable and skilled staff member.

The second stage of training concerns in-service or job-functional training. This stage of training initially concentrates on areas such as divisional goals and objectives; policies and procedures; ethical concerns, such as confidentiality; and job-specific knowledge and skills (Delworth & Yarris, 1978). Other areas of in-service training expand on the skill areas presented earlier in pre-service training and offer additional topics and programs as needed.

Several other issues to address include the amount of time needed for training, methods of reimbursement for participation in training, and training as a prerequisite for employment. Training, at the highest level of quality and effectiveness, should be offered for a minimum of one academic term and should earn academic credit. By spreading the experience over a period of several months, trainees have many opportunities to test their abilities to master helping skills and to become better role models. In many instances, training challenges individuals to change their behavior: for example, moving from an advice-giving perspective to a helping frame of reference. Short, intense training experiences, such as the weekend retreat, generally will not result in significant levels of behavioral change and skill development on the part of the paraprofessional.

For maximum effectiveness, training needs to be a prerequisite for obtaining the position. Research by Upcraft and Pilato (1982) and Winston and Buckner (1984) has demonstrated that those trained prior to beginning the actual work experience function more effectively in their paraprofessional roles than do those with no pre-service training. Students who choose to participate in this type of experience, with no assurance that they will be employed, are publicly expressing their belief in the importance of learning about themselves in relationship to a helping role. Just as one could not expect competence from a professional staff person who has had no formal preparation, competence cannot be expected from a paraprofessional who has had no training for the paraprofessional role.

Reward System. Administrators and other staff members must understand the necessity for establishing reward systems for students working in paraprofessional positions. Such systems can include pay, fee/tuition waivers, room and board remissions, and course credit. Other reward options include recognition at award ceremonies and documentation of services rendered in the students' permanent records or developmental transcripts.

AN ILLUSTRATION OF THE THREE PHASE MODEL: PARAPROFESSIONAL TUTORS/ STUDY SKILLS COUNSELORS

The following description is of a specific undergraduate staffed paraprofessional program. It illustrates a tutorial study skills service that utilizes student paraprofessionals as tutors and study skills counselors and is based on the three phase model previously described.

Phase One: Focus and Direction

Campus Role. This program offers free tutorial and study skills assistance to all students taking general education and remedial courses at a moderate sized university. These servies are available on individual and group appointment basis. The tutorial/study skills assistance is provided to enhance the learning experience of undergraduates and is not intended to be used to offer last minute cramming in preparing for tests and examinations or to be the sole campus intervention for students experiencing severe remedial problems related to academic preparation for college.

Job Description. The paraprofessionals selected to work in the Center are responsible for providing tutorial assistance in subject areas on both a one-on-one and/or a small group basis; providing basic study skills assistance; leading study skills workshops; developing and nurturing a rapport with peers and faculty members; making referrals when needed; being present at scheduled hours whether assigned to a tutorial duty or not; and participating in in-service paraprofessional activities such as staff meetings, on-going training and discussion sessions, lab responsibilities, clerical activities, and preparation responsibilities.

Selection Criteria. All program staff are trained paraprofessionals. They are required to complete a three-credit training course, entitled "Guidance for the Paraprofessional," in order to be eligible to work in the Center. Candidates are selected according to the following advertised criteria: presently enrolled as a sophomore or junior; enrolled as major or minor in the academic area in which they will tutor; exhibit confidence in their academic area; consider themselves an above average student with good study habits; and view helping others as an important activity with mutual benefits to both the students seeking help and the student paraprofessional.

Students selected for the position are required to enroll in the training course during the spring term prior to beginning the work experience the following fall.

Phase Two: Identification and Selection

Recruitment Procedures. Recruitment begins early in the fall term. In an attempt to recruit a heterogeneous group of students representing the diversity of the campus population and in order to include as many representatives as possible from the college community in this process, several types of recruitment efforts are employed. These include the following:

1. Full or one-half-page position ads featured in the campus newspaper.

2. Shorter announcements and ads made through various other channels (news stories, building marquees, classifieds, flyers, bulletins, etc.).

3. Letters to deans and chairpersons requesting referrals and enclosing position ads to post and distribute.

4. Letters to select groups of students, such as honorary societies, club and campus groups, and former student-clients of the center.

5. Phone calls and letters to the core of faculty who work closely with the Tutorial Center and the tutor trainees.

6. Recruitment efforts solicited from existing tutorial staff.

7. Information and orientation sessions arranged and announced through all of the initiatives outlined in Items 1 through 6. These sessions present interested candidates with necessary information regarding the position and the application requirements.

Selection Procedures. All candidates with complete application files are considered for the positions. A complete application file must include an application form, two completed faculty recommendation forms, and an interview rating form.

The application form, besides gathering a demographic profile, asks candidates to comment on their interest and/ or experience in a helping position, the role of tutoring and study skills assistance within the higher education environment, and the advantages and benefits to them personally if hired for the position.

Recommendation forms are provided by the Tutorial Program. Of the two required recommendations, at least one must be from a faculty member from the academic area in which the candidate wishes to tutor. The form asks for ratings of the candidate in the areas of academic performance, communications, initiative, responsibility, personality, social sensitivity, and assertiveness.

During the interview process, the interviewer assesses the applicant's ability to relate to others, enthusiasm to be a peer-tutor, knowledge of the position, self-confidence during the interview, and ability to be a role-model to other students.

In general, the selection of undergraduate students to serve as peer-tutors is based on the following criteria:

1. evidence of strong academic skills in the area to be tutored (based upon transcripts and faculty recommendations),

2. previous leadership experience and involvements in working with people (replies and application),

3. reliability and dependability (based upon faculty recommendations, applications, and interview), and

4. desire and willingness to work with undergraduate students (interview and application).

Phase Three: Training and Rewards

Training Program. Enrollment in a pre-service training course is required. This is a three-credit, semester-long course of forty-two contact hours. The purpose of the course is to focus on the role and function of undergraduate students serving as paraprofessional helpers within the higher education environment. Goals of the course include:

1. the student will understand his/her role(s) as a paraprofessional student helper,

2. the student will understand the impact paraprofessionals can have on other students' cognitive and psychosocial development,

3. the student will be able to assist others through one-to-one contact,

4. the student will be able to model appropriate college study skills and assist others in the development of those skills,

5. the student will be able to demonstrate appropriate referral strategies and will understand the purpose of various college resources, and

6. the student will demonstrate skills and competencies necessary to provide appropriate tutorial/helping interventions in the assigned content area.

These goals are accomplished through three course components which include: (1) a generic training unit that covers topics such as paraprofessionals in higher education and paraprofessional standards, the helping person, the paraprofessional as a role model, student development theory, cognitive development theory, communication skills, goal setting and assessment, and campus resources and referrals; (2) a study skills component that prepares the paraprofessional to assist other students in the implementation of a study system focusing on time management, note-taking, textbook reading, and text/exam preparation; and (3) a content-training component of fourteen contact hours that focuses on specific issues, goals, objectives, and endorsed activities of the academic area being served. Faculty members from the representative departments are employed to provide this portion of the training.

Training requires that students attend class regularly and participate actively, read all material assigned, write five reaction papers and one personal development autobiography, prepare a study skills project, a marketing handout, and an oral presentation and paper on the content training component.

Reward System. The position entails a work commitment of from eight to twelve hours weekly and is a paid position at minimum wage. Students are paid for two administrative hours per week beyond their scheduled work commitment. These additional hours are compensation for preparation time, project development, early arrival for appointments, and meetings. Other non-monetary rewards consist of recognition awards, early registration privileges, banquet and socials, and employment recommendations.

PROGRAM EVALUATION

Well planned and implemented programs include formative and summative evaluations (Miller & Prince, 1976) throughout each program phase and, in addition, evaluate the strengths and weaknesses of student participants.

Formative Evaluation

Formative evaluation focuses on each phase and component of the program and is intended to provide immediate feedback to the program administrator and staff so changes can be made to improve the program as it develops (Brown, 1979). This evaluation does not require high levels of sophistication. Simple questionnaires, surveys, and interviews can provide much of the information needed.

The implementation of formative evaluation procedures assists the administrator with the fine tuning aspects of program development. The outcome desired is a stronger, more viable program that is both efficient and effective. Basically, questions to be answered through formative evaluation are procedural and process oriented in nature. Questions may include: Was the job description understandable to recruitment agents and potential student paraprofessionals? Did the training program address the essential skill areas? Was training comprehensive— did the peer helpers develop the necessary helping and informational skills to perform in the position?

Summative Evaluations

Summative evaluation, or evaluation that focuses on accomplishing program goals and objectives, should take place at least annually, but preferably more often. From a program perspective this evaluation answers questions pertaining to the accomplishment of program goals and objectives and will typically be reported to administrators who are faced with budgetary decisions (Brown, 1979). The life, depth, and expansion of the program, in many instances, will be influenced strongly by summative evaluation data.

Interesting to note, although difficult to understand are research findings of Ender (1984), which indicated that 45% of all paraprofessional programs nationally fail to evaluate the effectiveness of their programs. This is an alarming statistic. Program administrators must be able to provide other administrators, faculty, student paraprofessionals, and student clients formal evidence of the effectiveness of the program. The inability to answer questions related to accountability and effectiveness are indications of program neglect, mismanagement, and possibly even unethical professional behavior.

Paraprofessional Evaluation

Quality programs provide both formal and informal evaluation sessions for individual paraprofessionals throughout the academic year. Typically, informal evaluation sessions are conducted by program supervisors. These evaluations should not threaten the paraprofessional's self-esteem, but rather should focus on strengths utilized to implement the role. Additionally, evaluation provides identification of training strategies and alternative programs to offset weaknesses.

These evaluation sessions should be viewed as developmental interviews. This means that the primary purpose of the interview is to focus on the growth and development of the paraprofessional as a person working in a helping position. The interview should be highlighted by establishing personal and work-related goals, helping the student to assess readiness for completing these goals, developing behavioral objectives for goal accomplishment, and identifying appropriate learning opportunities on campus or in the community.

End of the year evaluations for student paraprofessionals take a different perspective than the developmental procedures previously described. During this evaluation session paraprofessionals receive specific information regarding how they have performed in their roles, and are informed about decisions concerning their continuance on the staff. If the paraprofessional and the supervisor have a good rapport throughout the year, with ample opportunity for participation in additional skill development, this evaluation session should be constructive for both participants.

Supervisors perform three additional functions as they interact with student paraprofessionals. These include consultation, instruction, and mentoring.

Consulting. In a consulting role the supervisor works closely with the paraprofessional in reviewing the progress of clients in the target population. The supervisor should assist the paraprofessional in identification of appropriate interventions to deal with client problems and serve as a referral agent for client' concerns that go beyond the paraprofessional's realm of expertise.

Teaching. In this role the supervisor provides additional training opportunities for the paraprofessional staff. These sessions may address helping skills previously covered in pre-service training, or they may cover new areas that are identified through program assessment and evaluation. Development and implementation of in-service training programs are a primary function of the supervisor in the teaching role.

Mentoring. In the mentoring role the supervisor serves as a confidant and friend to the paraprofessional. The relationship is one in which the paraprofessional feels comfortable sharing the discussing personal, academic, and work-related concerns. In this mentoring role the supervisor models helping skills that are expected of paraprofessionals, in addition to those essential to a helping relationship.

ROLE OF THE SUPERVISOR—
IMPACT ON PROGRAM

As previously contended, the quality of any program utilizing paraprofessionals is dependent upon the supervisor's plans, implemented evaluation procedures, and actions in the capacity of counselor, teacher, and mentor to paraprofessional staff members. In each of these capacities, the supervisor is the authority; he or she is the professional who must provide needed guidance and leadership to the paraprofessional. However, the paraprofessional must be given opportunities to assume positions of leadership and authority. In many ways, the paraprofessional is the authority and is often in the best position to provide valuable input concerning program policies and practices. A supervisor who allows for a certain measure of collegiality in dealings with staff and who plans activities that involve the paraprofessional in program coordination and development is tapping a valuable source of knowledge, energy, and expertise. The impact on the program can be considerable; the impact on the paraprofessional, immeasurable.

Involvement of Paraprofessionals
in Program Coordination

Assignments that involve the paraprofessional in the coordination of various facets of the program can relieve the professional of many of the details of operation, enhance the quality and scope of the program, provide for the effective use of the paraprofessional's position and skills, and increase the paraprofessional's opportunities for growth. For example, paraprofessionals can be responsible for coordinating the recruitment and selection procedures for new staff members, designing and disseminating position ads, conducting information sessions for prospective applicants, and arranging for their interviews. Placing the responsibility for the coordination and performance of these initial screening tasks in the hands of the existing staff of paraprofessionals not only relieves the supervisor of these duties, but puts prospective candidates in touch with the best source for explaining the position and answering questions. Also the recommendation is that members of the paraprofessional staff be included where possible in the actual interviewing process and that they be in charge of the initial orientation procedures for newly-selected staff.

Program quality and effectiveness is greatly enhanced when support exists from other institutional sources and coordination with the efforts of other campus personnel. Here again, skills and position of the paraprofessional can be put to effective use. Paraprofessionals may function as liaisons, establishing ties among various programs, agencies, and departments and providing an exchange of information and ideas. Individual tutors may, for example, coordinate the responsibilities of their role in their service agency with the goals and objectives of the academic department they represent, establishing support and communication ties with individual faculty members in the process.

Involvement of Paraprofessionals in Program Development

The supervisor, and other professionals as well, must not ignore the potential of paraprofessionals to affect program change and development. By the very nature of their roles, paraprofessionals are in a prime position to identify strengths and weaknesses of the program, isolate problems, and make suggestions for improvement. Plus, they will be most eager for the opportunity to do so, their own interest and enthusiasm sustained and strengthened by this reliance on their input.

Staff meetings and in-service programs should include opportunities to discuss problems, brainstorm for new ideas, share experiences, and in general exchange information. A standing assignment for paraprofessionals to work on during preparation times and idle hours might be to complete a project related to the activities in their role—one that will facilitate their performance of their role, as well as benefit those who will eventually replace them. New models of intervention can be developed, for example, by peer-tutors working in conjunction with faculty to offer tutorials geared to particular course content and requirements or particular target populations, such as probationary students. Additionally, the evaluation process should be extended to include a reverse approach from that previously described. That is, paraprofessionals should regularly complete both formative and summative evaluations of their own, evaluations designed to elicit information about the program as they experience it.

In general, every effort should be made to include paraprofessionals in program development, invite and encourage their input, and respect their ability to provide it. Consider the following case in point: During a sharing session, several math tutors expressed a concern that many students were wasting valuable appointment time by arriving unprepared for sessions, expecting to do the homework as the tutor looked on. A discussion by paraprofessionals and professionals followed. The outcome was a solution offered by a peer-tutor: a special kind of tutorial intervention, called a Homework Helper, offered nightly for any math course, where students may convene to do homework with staff of tutors available to give immediate assistance. The idea became a successful program feature and was extended to include other disciplines. This kind of creative problem solving is limited only by the time and imagination of those involved. In this example, the problem could only have been identified by the paraprofessionals providing the direct service.

SPECIAL ISSUES

Four special issues concerning paraprofessional staff programs need consideration: (1) the ratio of paraprofessionals to student contacts and professional staff members; (2) staff qualifications for training; (3) developing professional staff commitment for the program; and (4) legal parameters.

Ratios

Student to Paraprofessional. Ender, Schuette, and Neuberger (1984) proposed a paraprofessional to student ratio of no greater that 1:35. This ration would be high if paraprofessionals were expected to have regular sessions with each student weekly, but quite appropriate if they were working in a residence hall or conducting tours of the institution for the admissions office. The ratio is dependent upon the nature of the job description and specific responsibilities of the paraprofessional. This ratio also is predicated on the number of hours per week the paraprofessional works. Given that this person is also a student, 10 to 12 work hours weekly seems an appropriate maximum. If the work required primarily one-to-one interaction, the program administrator could expect each paraprofessional to have no more than 10 to 12 student contacts weekly.

Paraprofessional to Professional. The number of paraprofessionals the professional can supervise is largely dependent on the formal organizational structure of the program. In programs where supervisors are employed full time to coordinate the program and supervise paraprofessionals, they generally can work adequately with a staff of up to 25.

If the supervisor also is performing other responsibilities, (e.g., career counseling or teaching in the learning center), an appropriate ratio for supervision might be one to five. Working in small groups or individually, the professional should plan to spend between two to four hours per week in supervisory sessions with these five paraprofessionals. This is not a sacrifice of professional time considering the fact that each paraprofessional supervised represents between 10 to 35 student contacts weekly.

Staff Qualifications for Training

Guidelines prescribing qualifications are necessary for trainers of paraprofessionals. Possessing an advanced degree may not qualify one to provide adequate training. Very few individuals have had formal education in the area of training undergraduate students to function as paraprofessionals. Staff members should seek educational experiences at professional meetings and workshops that address this critical area or pertinent formal training programs.

Minimally, trainers should have an in-depth knowledge of the student affairs division for which the paraprofessional is being trained. Also, professionals should be able to model skills the paraprofessional is expected to learn. Other trainer skills include expertise in student development theory, communication skills, group dynamics, values clarification, and problem-solving methodologies. On many campuses co-training approaches could be utilized in order to achieve quality training. (Consult Winston et al. [1988] for discussion of issues related to co-leadership.)

Developing Staff Commitment

Faculty and staff members may be threatened by paraprofessional staffed programs. Administrators must be careful to highlight the many advantages of paraprofessionals, but assure professionals that they are not being replaced by paraprofessionals. Professionals must understand that the paraprofessional is being employed to perform duties that do not require the full expertise of professional training. Also, professionals should be urged to develop training and supervisory skills as part of their professional development. Administrators should support this development through as many channels as possible including attending workshops and bringing consultants to campus to provide in-service training. Most professionals will support this type of programming if they understand its purposes and scope and the unique opportunities it offers for their professional development.

Legal Liabilities

Colleges and universities exist to offer a service—education. Faculty, staff, and administrators must make every attempt to assure that this service is one of quality, offered by competent professionals, and for our purposes here, student paraprofessionals.

Higher education has not been ignored in this "age of litigation." Today's student consumers are not reticent to bring civil charges against their institutions if they believe they have been victimized by negligent educational practices. Paraprofessional-staffed programs provide educational services. The program supervisor's responsibility is to ensure that those services are of quality, offered by qualified and competent staff.

Safeguards against litigation include well-developed behavioral job descriptions; training programs of sufficient depth, length, and quality to assume student mastery of expected skills and competencies; continuing and systematic supervision; and evaluation of paraprofessionals. An institution and program facing litigation must be able to demonstrate that student staff members have been adequately trained to perform their assigned duties and that all safeguards which one usually can expect to be implemented by program professionals (e.g., supervision, evaluation, in-service training) are in place and are systematically implemented. Evidence of training in the areas of confidentiality, ethics, and issues/concerns of students that paraprofessionals should not address are other safeguards against litigation problems.

The supervisor's formal relationship with the paraprofessional staff will be a critical variable if one is to successfully defend a program facing litigation. Supervisors must be able to demonstrate on-going, formal supervisory relationships with peer helpers. Also, supervisors must be physically accessible to paraprofessionals as they work with student-clients. Paraprofessionals should have quick and easy access to more knowledgeable and sophisticated helpers in the event that a crisis occurs during their work with students. All these safeguards demonstrate the institution's and program's concern for the well-being of students seeking services.

SUMMARY

Student paraprofessionals present one vehicle for implementing student development approaches on the college campus. Based on research, students who desire these roles are both mature and self-confident (Ender, 1981). They possess many personal characteristics that will strengthen their role-modeling capabilities. Administrators need to consider advantages of implementing paraprofessional programs because they represent a powerful strategy that can affect the intellectual and personal development of college students.

REFERENCES

Arkin, M., & Shollar, B. (1982). *The tutor book.* New York: Longman.

Barron, J., & Hetherton, C. (1981). Training paraprofessionals to lead social anxiety management groups. *Journal of College Student Personnel, 22,* 269-273.

Blimling, S., & Miltenberger, J. (1981). *The residence assistant: Working with college students in residence halls.* Dubuque, IA: Kendall/Hunt Publishing.

Brown, C.R., & Myers, R. (1975). Student verses faculty curriculum advising. *Journal of College Student Personnel, 16,* 226-231.

Brown, R.D. (1972). *Student development in tomorrow's higher education: A return to the academy.* Washington, DC: American College Personnel Association.

Brown, R.D. (1979). Evaluator roles and evaluation strategies: A consumer's introduction. In G.D. Kuh (Ed.), *Evaluation in student affairs* (pp. 33-50). Washington, DC: American College Personnel Association.

Brown R.D. (1980). Developmental transcript mentoring: A total approach to integrating student development in the academy. In D.G. Creamer (Ed.), *Student development in higher education: Theories, practices, and future directions* (pp. 239-256). Washington, DC: American College Personnel Association.

Carkhuff, R.R., & Truax, C.B. (1965). Lay mental health counseling: The effects of lay group counseling. *Journal of Counseling Psychology, 29,* 426-31.

Chickering, A.W. (1969). *Education and identity.* San Francisco: Jossey-Bass.

Croteau, J.M., & Tinsley, D.J. (1984). Training paraprofessionals in programming: An experimental course incorporating developmental theory. *Journal of College Student Personnel, 25,* 553-554.

D'Andrea, V., & Salovey, P. (1983). *Peer counseling skills and perspectives.* Palo Alto, CA: Science and Behavior Books.

Delworth, U., & Aulepp, L. (1976). *Training manual for paraprofessionals and allied professional programs*. Boulder, CO: Western Interstate Commission for Higher Education.

Delworth, U., & Johnson, M.M. (1984). Student paraprofessionals in counseling and career centers. In S.C. Ender & R. B. Winston, Jr. (Eds.), *Student as paraprofessional staff* (pp. 81-90). New Direction for Student Services (No. 27). San Francisco: Jossey-Bass.

Delworth, U., & Yarris, E. (1978). Concepts and processes for the new training role. In U. Delworth (Ed.), *Training competent staff* (pp 1-15). New Directions for Student Services (No. 2). San Francisco: Jossey-Bass.

DuVall, W.H., & Ender, K.L. (1980). A training model for developing leadership awareness. In F.B. Newton, & K.L. Ender (Eds.), *Student development practices: Strategies for making a difference* (pp. 145-169). Springfield, IL Charles C. Thomas.

Ender, S.C. (1984). Student paraprofessionals within student affairs: The state of the art. In S.C. Ender & R.B. Winston, Jr., (Eds.). *Students as paraprofessional staff* (pp 3-21). New Directions for Student Services (No. 27). San Francisco: Jossey-Bass.

Ender, S.C., McCaffrey, S.S., & Miller, T.K. (1979). *Students helping students: A training manual for peer helpers on the college campus*. Athens, GA: Student Development Associates.

Ender, S.C., & McFadden, R.B. (1980). Training the student paraprofessional helper. In F.B. Newton & K.L. Ender (Eds.), *Student development practices: Strategies for making a difference* (pp. 127-142). Springfield, IL: Charles C. Thomas.

Ender, S.C., Schuette, C.G., & Neuberger, C.G. (1984). Proposed standards on use of student paraprofessionals in student affairs. In S.C. Ender & R.B. Winston, Jr., (Eds.), *Student as paraprofessional staff*, (pp. 99-106). New Directions for Student Services (No.27). San Francisco: Jossey-Bass.

Feldman, K.A., & Newcomb, T.M. (1970). *The impact of college on students: An analysis of four decades of research* (Vol 1). San Francisco: Jossey-Bass.

Frigault, R., Maloney, G., & Trevino, C. (1986). Training paraprofessionals to facilitate leadership development. *Journal of College Student Personnel, 27*, 281-282.

Frisz, R.H., & Lane, J.R. (1987). Student user evaluations of peer adviser services. *Journal of College Student Personnel, 28*, 241-245.

German, S.C. (1979). Selecting undergraduate paraprofessionals on college campuses: A review. *Journal of College Student Personnel, 20*, 28-34.

Getz, H.G., & Miles, J.H. (1978). Women and peers as counselors. *Journal of College Student Personnel, 19,* 37-41.

Harrar, W.R., & Ender, S.C. (1987). Assessing students' perceptions of tutorial services. *Journal of College Student Personnel, 28,* 276-277.

Heath, D.H. (1968). *Growing up in college.* San Francisco: Jossey-Bass.

Heath, D.H. (1980). Wanted: A comprehensive model of healthy development. *Personnel and Guidance Journal, 58,* 391-399.

Holly, K.A. (1987). Development of a college peer counselor program. *Journal of College Student Personnel, 28,* 285-286.

Johnston, J.A., & Hansen, R.N. (1981). Using paraprofessionals in career development programming. In V.A. Harren, M.H. Daniels, & J.N. Buck (Eds.), *Facilitating students' career development,* (pp. 81-97). New Directions in Student Services (No. 14). San Francisco: Jossey-Bass.

Kelly, L.P., & Nolan, T.W. (1980). Identifying student paraprofessional training needs: An analytical approach. *Journal of College Student Personnel, 21,* 431-436.

Lucian, J. (1977). Training college peer counselors: A behavior contract model. *Journal of College Student Personnel, 18,* 66-67.

Miller, T.K., & Prince, J.S. (1976). *The future of student affairs: A guide to student development for tomorrow's higher education.* San Francisco: Jossey-Bass.

Newton, F.B. (1980). Community building strategies with student groups. In F.B. Newton & K.L. Ender (Eds.), *Student development practices: Strategies for making a difference* (pp. 80-104). Springfield, IL: Charles C. Thomas.

Ostroth, D.D. (1981). Selecting competent residence hall staff. In G.S. Blimling & J.H. Schuh (Eds.), *Increasing the educational role of residence hall* (pp. 65-80). New Direction for Student Services (No. 13). San Francisco: Jossey-Bass.

Powell, J.R., Pyler, S.A., Dickerson, B.A., & McClellan, S.D. (1969). *The personnel assistant in college residence halls.* New York: Houghton Mifflin.

Presser, N.R., Miller, T.B., & Rapin, L.S. (1984). Peer consultants: A new role for student paraprofessionals. *Journal of College Student Personnel, 25,* 321-326.

Smith, B. (1981). Orientation aids paraprofessional development. *Orientation Review, 11,* 1-7.

Upcraft, M.L., & Pilato, G.T. (1982). *Residence hall assistants in college: A guide to selection, training, and supervision.* San Francisco: Jossey-Bass.

Winston, R.B., Jr., Bonney, W.C., Miller T.K., & Dagley, J.C. (1988). *Promoting student development through intentionally structured groups: Principles, techniques, and applications.* San Francisco: Jossey-Bass.

Winston, R.B., Jr., & Buckner, J.P. (1984). The effects of peer helper training and timing of training on reported stress of resident assistants. *Journal of College Student Personnel, 25,* 430-436.

Winston, R.B., Jr., & Ender, S.C. (1988). Use of student paraprofessionals in divisions of college student affairs. *Journal of Counseling and Development, 66,* 466-473.

Zunker, V.G., & Brown, W.F. (1966). Comparative effectiveness of student and professional counselors. *Personnel and Guidance Journal, 44,* 738-743.

SUGGESTED READINGS

Blimling, G.S., & Miltenberger, L.J. (1981). *The resident assistant: Working with college students in residence halls.* Dubuque, IA: Kendall/Hunt.

Brown, W.F. (1977). *Student-to-student counseling: An approach to academic achievement (rev. ed.).* Austin: University of Texas Press.

Delworth, U. (Ed.) (1978). *Training competent staff.* New Directions for Student Services (No. 2). San Francisco: Jossey-Bass.

Ender, S.C., McCaffrey, S.S., & Miller, T.K. (1979). *Students helping students: A training manual for peer helpers on the college campus.* Athens, GA: Student Development Associates.

Ender, S.C., & Winston, R.B., Jr., (Eds.). (1984). *Students as paraprofessional staff.* New Directions for Student Services (No. 27). San Francisco: Jossey-Bass.

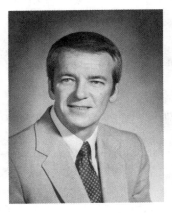

David A. DeCoster, Ph.D., is currently Vice President for Student Affairs at Indiana University of Pennsylvania (IUP). He completed the B.S. and M.A. degrees at the University of Michigan and received the Ph.D. from the University of Florida. He has served as an editorial board member of three professional journals and as associate editor of the *Journal of College Student Development.* His publications include four co-edited books: *Mentoring-Transcript Systems for Promoting Student Growth, Understanding Today's Students, Personal Education and Community Development in College Residence Halls,* and *Student Development and Education in College Residence Halls.* Additional publications include frequent contributions as author of chapters and articles in a variety of books and professional journals. He makes frequent annual appearances at state, regional, and national professional meetings and serves institutions and agencies involved in postsecondary education as a consultant, speaker, and external evaluator. Before accepting his present responsibilities at IUP he was affiliated with the University of Nebraska, Lincoln, Indiana University, the University of Georgia, the University of Florida, and the University of Michigan in various roles as a student affairs educator, administrator, and faculty member.

Suzanne Brown, Ph.D., is Associate Vice Chancellor for Academic and Student Affairs for the Pennsylvania State System of Higher Education, which comprises the state's fourteen regional comprehensive universities. Her responsibilities include coordination of a System-wide faculty development program, liaison work with chief academic and student affairs officers, advising of the System's Board of Student Government Presidents, and staffing for the Association of University Trustees. Previously, Dr. Brown served as Assistant to the Vice Chancellor for Student Affairs and Assistant Director of the Nebraska Union at the University of Nebraska-Lincoln. She has served two terms on the NASPA Board of Directors, chaired that Association's Communication Services Division, and recently served as Guest Editor for a special issue of the NASPA Journal devoted to relations between academic and student affairs. Dr. Brown holds a B.S. in Speech from Northwest University, a M.A. in English from the University of Nebraska.

Chapter 17

STAFF DEVELOPMENT: PERSONAL AND PROFESSIONAL EDUCATION

David A. DeCoster
Suzanne S. Brown

Perhaps one reason for the scarcity of research on staff development for student affairs practitioners is that the need for continuous professional growth seems self-evident. Antagonists to this concept are few, and their arguments generally are limited to such subsidiary issues as methodology, cost effectiveness, time requirements, and degree of responsibility that should be assumed by staff members. No one seems to dispute the basic rationale underlying personal and professional developmental efforts.

PHILOSOPHICAL FOUNDATION

Staff development programs are a systematic response to two developmental patterns that occur simultaneously whenever an individual's activities are intertwined with functions of a group, community, or organization. These phenomena—

human development and organization development—are not, however, simply parallel processes. For each process to achieve its goals, the two must be integrated. This interdependence assumes many forms as the following analysis of the two basic elements suggests.

Human Development

The student development concept currently incorporated within the educational mission of student affairs was borrowed from the broader body of literature relating to general human development. Briefly summarized, the concept of continuous human growth and maturation contains three major components (DeCoster & Mable, 1980):

Education is Communication. Human beings learn through communication and through interaction. As Dewey (1916) observed long ago, not only are knowledge and values transmitted through community life, but also a society continues to exist only to the extent that common understandings about self and environment are shared and communicated. Open communication and shared understandings are no less important for smaller human groups that function as subunits within a larger society, including institutional, divisional, and departmental organizations.

Learning is a Process. Education is a process, not a product. "Ends" never justify "means," and, in fact, the two cannot be meaningfully separated. Research relating to classroom teaching as well as that based on psychotherapeutic relationships reveals that the quality of the educational process is the important variable in determining the extent of constructive change and meaningful growth in the learner. Student affairs professionals must understand that generally the way in which they accomplish a task has greater educational significance than the successful completion of the task itself.

Education Means Total Development. Education is not synonymous with cognitive growth; thus, nonintellectual and affective dimensions must be perceived as not only legitimate but essential ingredients of the learning process. Cultural, spiritual, psychological, physical, and social variables must be addressed along with intellectual growth as human beings move toward increasing levels of personal competence and self-reliance. Thus, the total scope of a staff member's personal and professional life provides the potential agenda for staff development experiences. Moreover, although the study of growth and development was once focused almost exclusively on the earlier stages of the life span, psychological research in recent years has enhanced the understanding of mature adult development and has led to the concept of "lifelong learning." (Cross & McCartan, 1984). Two bestsellers, *Passages* (Sheehy, 1974) and *The Seasons of a Man's Life* (Levinson, Darrow, Klein, Levinson, & McKee, 1978), have increased public understanding for viewing human development as continuous and evolutionary throughout an individual's life.

More directly relevant to this discussion, Chickering and Associates (1981) noted:

> By understanding how students from 18 to 80 meet life cycle challenges and grow in terms of intellectual competence, ego development, moral and ethical development, humanitarian concern, interpersonal competence, capacity for intimacy, and professional development, educators can examine the potential contributions of various disciplines, area of professional preparation, and educational practices. Program changes and professional development activities can be undertaken to address dimensions of adult development and at the same time respond to the more immediate educational needs of diverse students. (pp. xxvii-xxviii)

Continuous adult learning and renewal activities will often find their origins in the context of career choice, preparation, and advancement which provides the impetus for systematic professional development programs (Arnold, 1982; McDade, 1987; Morse, 1984). After reviewing the adult development theories of Erikson, Levenson, Lowenthal, and Loevinger, Thomas (1985) summarized the direct implications of these theories to issues for staff development: identity, intimacy, generactivity, integrity, setting priorities, decision-making, assertiveness, and stress management. Developmental activities based upon adult development theory, he concluded, will benefit by being more informed, intentional, and goal-directed.

Organization Development

Human organizations are dynamic, fluid systems that not only involve people, but also are characterized by specified goals, procedural frameworks, and operational methods (Kurpius, 1980). Thus, strategies for organization development generally include structural or procedural modifications along with growth-producing experiences. Positive change results from new combinations of human and structural variables that are consistent with goals of both the organization and the individuals within it. Throughout literature, the symbiotic relationships between individual and group needs is stressed (Kurpius, 1980; Mable, Terry, & Duvall, 1980; Tripp, 1977).

For example, Richardson (1975) outlined six stages of organization development beginning with individual and small group learning experiences, but including such processes as analysis and revision of administrative and governance structure and establishing goals and priorities for the institution. Regardless of how lavish the budget or exciting the activities provided for staff development, Richardson insisted that "changed behavior by administrators will not occur unless the institutional environment and its governance procedures support the concept of a community in which everyone grows and learns" (p. 306).

Staff development, then, is not merely a matter of exposing new ideas and experiences to people. Staff development to be effective must be conceived and implemented in terms of the development of the organization. Enhancement of individual performance must be integrated with the institution's needs and goals. According to Nejedlo (1977), the process of organization development ideally culminates in self-directed and continuing "renewal activities" collaboratively designed by organization members.

After a review of the literature, Creamer and Shelton (1988) concluded that two distinct perspectives are most often offered as a conceptual framework for staff development: institutional effectiveness (organizational development) and staff effectiveness (human development). The present writers, however, prefer the view that these two orientations must be combined and integrated into one philosophical foundation to support a comprehensive staff development program. Cox (1985) provided further discussion on the relationships among staff, organizational, and program development as well as how these components interact to influence student learning.

Staff Development in Student Affairs

Brown (1977) provided an excellent perspective regarding the dimensions of evolutionary change in postsecondary education and the roles of student affairs professionals in this process. He suggested three broad areas of professional development needed for effective performance of these roles. First is the need to confront the basic issues of human existence. On the basis of his analysis of the major issues that have confronted student affairs staff members during the past ten years, Brown concluded that three predominant "universal and timeless" themes have a direct bearing on student affairs practice: (1) tension between personal liberty and social interdependence, (2) conflict between hedonistic needs and altruism, and (3) search for meaning to human existence.

The second area is the need for the knowledge and skills required to influence total student development. Brown warned against the compartmentalization of the organizational structure that may produce some efficiencies but cannot replace personal, individual relationships. And the third area is the need to promote the integration of academic and personal development. This integration involves learning how to work with faculty toward achieving a more humanized learning environment and an integrated curriculum.

In more pragmatic and specific terms, a number of staff development objectives and intended outcomes can be summarized in six categories (Arseneau & Terrell, 1985; Baier, 1985; Beeler, 1976; Beeler & Penn, 1978; Canon, 1981; Cox, 1985; Cox & Ivy, 1984; Leafgren, 1980; McIntire, 1985; Merkle & Artman, 1983; Meyerson, 1974; Miller, 1975, 1980, 1985; Stamatakos & Oliaro, 1972; Wanzek & Canon, 1975; Winston, Hebert, & McGonigle, 1985). As a composite, they represent the potential curriculum for student affairs staff development.

1. *Facilitating interaction with colleagues and associates:* exchange of ideas; team building and staff interdependence; giving and receiving feedback; promoting positive attitudes and sensitivity toward others; sharing information about the organization; enhancing internal staff communication; improving institutional accountability.

2. *Developing functional skills and specific competencies:* evaluation and analysis; organizational, administrative, and management skills; communication and consultation.

3. *Promoting self-understanding and self-actualization:* helping individuals increase their levels of awareness, autonomy, general wellness, and self-reliance; and refine personal value systems.

4. *Exposure to innovative programs:* encouraging proactive service and program development and active responses to student issues.

5. *Providing opportunities for professional renewal:* developing a professional style; enhancing commitment, accountability, and self-esteem; preventing burn-out; offering new challenges as well as chances for reflection, reassessment, and rehabilitation.

6. *Conveying theoretical and philosophical knowledge:* enhancing understanding of total student affairs programs through examination of developmental research and literature and discussion of issues in postsecondary education and society.

From many of these same authors, a list of common staff developmental activities and methods is easily abstracted: (1) academic coursework; (2) national, regional, and state convention attendance; (3) on-campus programs utilizing either internal or external consultants; (4) off-campus workshops, seminars, and institutes; (5) staff orientation and social functions; (6) organizational newsletters and other written communications; (7) organizational staff meetings, special research and program grants, committee and task force participation; (8) ongoing supervision, performance evaluation, mentoring and general relationships with colleagues; and (9) administrative fellowships and internships.

In terms of the philosophical foundation for staff development set forth earlier, the problems associated with this list are readily apparent. Many of these frequently mentioned methods, whether on- or off-campus, are structured programs and experiences that tend to emphasize "products" rather then "process." Moreover, the typical cluster of planned events, packages, or programs puts the emphasis primarily on individual development, somewhat independently from the organizational environment.

COMPONENTS OF STAFF DEVELOPMENT

A gap in the literature exists between the understanding of professional development as a process that occurs within the context of organization development and the kinds of staff development strategies most often advocated. The latter tend to create the impression for many student affairs administrators that staff development is a "professional agenda" that occurs as a separate, ancillary function to people's organizational roles and daily responsibilities. In the following discussion of five broad components of staff development, the focus shifts back and forth from the needs of the individual to the priorities of the organization; but the underlying principle is that professional development is a continual process that should be anchored in performance expectations and day-to-day, on-the-job behavior. The five strategies that constitute an effective staff development effort are (1) individual motivation and self-assessment, (2) supervision and performance evaluation, (3) mentoring relationships, (4) structured learning opportunities, and (5) professional participation, service, and contributions.

Individual Motivation and Self-Assessment

The ideal framework for professional development is built by interlocking individual initiatives with organizational opportunities, by interfacing individual and organizational goals. But when organizational components are flimsy, the motivated individual is still likely to find or create a means for continuous development. And, conversely, the person who lacks initiative, interest, or self-confidence is unlikely to respond very heartily to even the most systematic efforts initiated by the organization. Individual motivation, then, is the cornerstone of a successful staff development structure.

Long before career planning workshops, self-assessment inventories, and modern systems of goal-setting were commonplace, people were actively engaged in expanding their professional knowledge, sharpening their job-related skills, and cultivating personal qualities needed to succeed in their chosen fields. Often the process was, as it still is for many, largely haphazard and almost unconscious. Some highly motivated people, much like healthy plants, seem to grow naturally without predetermined direction or conscious deliberation and somehow bloom at just the right time and place.

Then others plot their development and advancement with meticulous precision. For centuries, class-based, profession-based, and individual-based prescriptions have guided people through specified sequences of learning followed by certain structured experiences or professional positions to some predetermined pinnacle of expertise, status, or authority. The education of a prince or the preparation of a priest in earlier days, the making of a "military man" or the lockstep climb up the corporate ladder in modern times are examples of this approach to professional development.

Somewhere between risks of undirected growth and rigidity of prescribed patterns of development is the approach best suited to today's rapidly changing world and to the student affairs profession. Self-assessment is a primary method for cultivating a systematic, yet flexible, approach to staff development. It may be employed in many ways: through interest and aptitude inventories, checklists, performance rating forms, discussions with one's supervisor or colleagues, life or career planning workshops, or simply through quiet, but deliberate introspection. The approach suggested might be supplementary to any of the previous activities. Like many similar career "mapping" or self-assessment models, it is simply a tool to help focus analysis and guide thought processes. Because this kind of exercise is rarely easy for the individual, some such form or prefabricated process is often helpful.

As shown in Figure 17.1, the model posits two dimensions: (1) career time frame, and (2) types of personal and professional development needed. Time categories are the present (current position), approximately five years hence (perhaps the next professional position), and, finally, the more distant future or the individual's ultimate career ambition. These time frames readily translate into immediate, short-term, and long-term goals, and the model can help people examine relationships or, perhaps, discrepancies between their self-determined career objectives and level of development that is required to reach them.

Individuals, then, assess areas of knowledge, skills, and personal qualities needed for their present position and for the type of position they plan to attain in each of the other time frames. If a person is considering two or more career paths, then a matrix would be completed for each option and the results compared. It is important to distinguish between competencies and qualities already developed and those requiring further development.

A few words about developmental categories themselves may provide guidance for use of this model and also lay groundwork for examination of other components of staff development that bear some relationship to these developmental areas.

Knowledge, in this context, refers both to theoretical knowledge and to concrete information needed to fulfill various job responsibilities. Generally speaking, the more responsibility an individual assumes within an organizational structure, the broader the scope of knowledge required. For example, entry-level residence hall coordinators or student activity advisors need to know about the policies and procedures of their agencies and about specific resources available to them. In addition, they would also benefit from a basic knowledge of student development theory and group dynamics.

Career Time Frame	Types of Personal and Professional Development Needed (List levels of expertise or functioning required to reach each career goal)		
	Knowledge	Skills	Personal Qualities
Current Position (immediate goals)			
Possible Next Position (Short-term goals)			
Career Objectives (Long-term goals)			

Figure 17.1. Self-assessment model for staff development related to career objectives.

In order to move into higher positions, beginning student affairs professionals need to become familiar with workings of larger organizational units and develop a foundation of knowledge in such areas as supervision, financial management, and public relations. Through their experience in working with students, they also should have deepened their understanding of developmental principles, student characteristics, and problem-solving strategies.

Increasing professional responsibilities require still broader knowledge of student affairs objectives, roles, and functions, as well as an in-depth understanding of particular areas—facilities management, food service operations, student financial aid, or political and legal ramifications of student affairs administration, for example. Knowledge of the organization, administration, traditions, and contemporary problems of postsecondary education also becomes increasingly important as one assumes greater responsibility within the profession. In short, as the scope of activity expands, so does the range of knowledge expected and required to be successful.

In terms of skill development, people often speak of sharpening or refining present abilities rather than of broadening or expanding total competencies, though both kinds of development may be required for career advancement. Skills are simply one's ability to do things that must be done—write letters and reports, communicate with a variety of constituent groups (students, colleagues, supervisors, faculty), speak before an audience, lead a committee, organize a publicity campaign, compose a handbook, prepare a questionnaire, interpret statistics, manage time, delegate responsibility, set goals—the list could go on. Skills may be very specific, like bookkeeping or menu-planning, or quite broad, like negotiating, counseling, or supervising. Some skills are used throughout a person's career, though it is to be expected that the quality of skill performance will be enhanced with experience. Other skills may be specific to a given level or type of work and thus be of little benefit in a different position.

Clearly, the first two developmental categories set forth in the model overlap at many points. Knowledge and skills often are so intertwined as to seem inseparable. How does one categorize something like public relations, for example, which involves both knowing and doing? However, because the point of the exercise is self-assessment, individuals can make such distinctions in a way that makes sense to them.

The difficulty is compounded by the third category, which is an aggregate of important intangibles. Personal qualities, including a variety of attitudes and values, are affected by one's knowledge and skills. Professionalism, for example, is a most important personal quality, but it is also one of the most difficult to define. It involves a seasoned integration of knowledge, skills, attitudes, values, and personality characteristics.

Equally complex are some of the other qualities likely to be included in this third category: self-confidence, assertiveness, tact, sensitivity to the feelings and intentions of others, loyalty, self-control, motivation, and the ability to work under pressure and manage stress, to integrate personal and professional values, and to achieve a balance between personal and professional goals.

Three observations, then, emerge from this survey of the major developmental categories to be considered in self-assessment. First, just as it is difficult in many instances to distinguish among the three categories, it is also difficult to distinguish between personal and professional development. Indeed, the two are never totally distinct. Improving one's skills in listening to others and in communicating effectively on the job, for example, is bound to have repercussions in one's personal life. Learning to control frustration or anger in personal circumstances will carry over into the way professional problems are negotiated. However specific a bit of knowledge, a skill, or even an attitude might be, the person is the one who integrates the knowledge, develops the skill, or assumes the attitude. Furthermore, the motivation for growth and the direction it takes may derive from relationships with family, friends, organizations, or interests completely apart from the job.

Second, self-assessment is not something to be done once and forgotten. It must be a continual process. The model suggested may provide a starting point leading to other techniques, or it may be reviewed, revised, or totally revamped periodically. Whatever the approach adopted, it must be recognized that few people grow and develop along the neat, tidy lines that models presuppose. Thus, the major prerequisite for self-assessment is self-awareness, keeping up with oneself, with shifts in interests, attitudes, and desires, as well as with growth in knowledge, skills, and experience.

Finally, in spite of efforts to focus on the individual's responsibility to assess strengths and weaknesses and to formulate personal and professional goals, most people need assistance in accomplishing these important tasks. Self-assessment is, in itself, a skill; it is not a capability that people inherit or are likely to acquire in school where assessment has traditionally been the prerogative of teachers. It can be approached in different ways, but the process of self-assessment will be most meaningful when individuals can incorporate information either from others' perceptions of them or when they can count on encouragement and support from others who have an interest in their personal and professional development.

So, again, the joint responsibility of the organization and the individual for professional development is underscored. Even the initial step, individual motivation and self-assessment, depends, to some extent, on the attitudes and actions of the organization. In most instances, the obvious and immediate link between the individual and the organization is the supervisor, the person within a given organizational structure to whom an individual reports.

Supervision and Performance Evaluation

The term "supervision" has negative connotations for some student affairs professionals. It suggests monitoring, critiquing, or even disciplining actions often viewed as incongruous with a positive developmental philosophy. Most people generally prefer to think in terms of working *with* colleagues, rather than for superiors.

The term "evaluation," as applied to staff performance, is anathema not only among some student affairs administrators, but to managers in many other fields as well. If self-assessment is a skill that must be learned, assessment of others is an even more sophisticated and demanding skill that few supervisors have been taught or even encouraged to learn. Unless glaring problems occur in staff performance, many people prefer to keep supervision to a minimum and to relegate performance evaluation to a perfunctory annual ritual.

Yet these two managerial functions, supervision and evaluation, are crucial to total professional development. Just as self-assessment is the starting point for the individual, performance evaluation is the most basic contribution of the organization to the development of its staff members. In Fisher's (1978) terms, there is an

> inherent relationship between personnel evaluation and professional development. While still usually treating them as discrete processes, higher education is beginning to consider both sides of this same coin, realizing that they are concurrent and continuously interacting processes, whether systematic or informal, and whether public or personal. (p. 2.)

Perhaps one reason administrators often encounter resistance to performance evaluation is that the emphasis is usually placed on its formal, systematic aspect. Performance evaluation systems, however carefully designed and objectively implemented, can be threatening and counterproductive unless they are introduced into a climate in which assessment and development flourish year round. Supervisors are the key people in the creation of such a climate, and there are a number of strategies they can use for this purpose.

Effective supervision and evaluation require, first of all, awareness of people's strengths, weaknesses, problems, interests, and aspirations. Developing this kind of awareness does not require special interviews or extra supervisory efforts. It can be derived from informal conversation and observation that are part of the daily routine. It does require, however, attention, openness, and a genuine interest in the individuals supervised. In discussing how managers motivate people, Quick (1976) emphasized the importance of being sensitive to implicit as well as explicit needs that employees communicate about their responsibilities, work environment, and professional associates.

Second, by providing frequent informal feedback, both positive and negative, a supervisor can create a climate in which performance evaluation is expected and even welcomed. "Psychologists have found that feedback on performance should be given frequently, and the closer the feedback to the action, the more effective it is" (Glueck, 1978, p. 295). Such feedback should be friendly and genuine, rather than carping or patronizing. Moreover, it should be specific rather than general. Telling people that they are "doing a great job" or that their performance "leaves something to be desired" gives them very little to go on—or to grow on. Praise or constructive criticism focused on specific tasks or actions, on the other hand, shows people that someone notices and cares and thus provides incentive to repeat the positive or improve the negative performance.

Third, the use of staff meetings or special meetings to assess group performance and to establish group goals for a given period of time reinforces the importance of evaluation. If formal or informal assessment is regularly applied to the operation of the office or program as a whole, assessment of individual performance will seem more natural. Moreover, this strategy highlights the relationship between individual performance and the realization of organizational goals.

If a supervisor involves staff members in evaluating the overall performance of the organization, why should these people not also be involved in the evaluation of individual performance, including that of the supervisor? Peer evaluation, the fourth strategy, is highly touted by some and roundly rejected by others, but in a professional setting it is an effective method for obtaining constructive feedback. Indeed, Fisher (1978, p. 5) defined the evaluation process as a review of performance vis-a-vis goal expectations and individual potential through the use of appropriate assessment techniques that involve those persons with whom the individual interacts so as to determine areas of needed and desired professional development. (In addition, Chapter 15 identifies several evaluation formats.)

Inevitably, the perspective of supervisors will be based on the areas of job behavior they directly observe. Performance on important aspects of many student affairs positions may be more accurately assessed by others. Students, for example, can provide valuable feedback regarding the effectiveness of counseling, teaching, or advising functions. Likewise, subordinates can provide relevant information about their supervisors' leadership and delegation skills. Working with professional colleagues is an important part of most student affairs positions, and people can benefit from knowing how their performance is perceived by colleagues.

A word of caution is in order concerning this strategy. Obviously, such feedback must be obtained through an evaluation process that provides for confidentiality and professionalism. The process works best in an atmosphere characterized by a high level of trust, the absence of staff rivalry, and shared interest in growth and development. With these prerequisites, a peer evaluation process can greatly benefit both supervisors and staff.

Performance evaluation contributes to staff development most directly when the input from both supervisors and peers, along with a person's self-assessment, is used for setting personal and professional goals. Most people perform more effectively when they are working towards specific objectives, a fact that has led to the implementation of elaborate goal-setting systems in both corporate and educational institutions. For most student affairs professionals, however, periodic conferences with supervisors will probably suffice to establish objectives and communicate organizational support. However formal or informal, such individual conferences should include position descriptions, general expectations, evaluation criteria, specific job assignments, working relationships, career aspirations, present job satisfaction, and, ultimately, goals or objectives agreed upon by both parties.

Organizations and individuals move from goal-setting, to finding a means for achieving goals. Before leaving the role played by supervisors in staff development, some very specific developmental resources are commanded almost exclusively by supervisors. People need not plead that they cannot promote professional development because no resources have been made available for this function. Concern, commitment, and a bit of creativity are all the following techniques require:

1. Shifts in job assignments—trade-offs with other people or simply different emphases for a period of time— can often provide people with an opportunity to practice new skills or learn new functions.

2. Special projects to be accomplished during the summer months or delegation of leadership responsibility for a specific undertaking may expand the scope of a person's knowledge or experience, while providing useful service for the agency.

3. Appointment to an interdepartmental committee or task force may enable staff members to gain new perspectives, contacts, and visibility.

4. Availability of professional journals and current books in the office, coupled with informal discussion of ideas and information in the professional literature, will help people realize the significance of this avenue to development and encourage the habit of reading professional materials.

5. Devoting portions of staff meetings to developmental activities is an easy way to underscore the importance of professional development while, at the same time, imparting useful information and generating ideas regarding specific issues (Shaffer, 1972).

6. Role-modeling of important attitudes, behaviors, and skills by the supervisor is another valuable aid to development. Few supervisors will be expected to exhibit the full range of exemplary professional qualities and skills, but all supervisors should be aware that their staff members are more likely to do as they do than as they say.

7. Release time or rearrangement of schedules to enable people to take a course, attend a workshop, write for publication, or spend some time working in another office can contribute markedly to staff development.

8. Recognition in as many different forms as possible is one of the most effective ways to promote growth. While monetary rewards are not always available, other inexpensive forms of professional recognition may have more meaning. Success breeds success, and for most individuals recognition of achievement spurs further achievement.

Obviously, not all of these approaches are possible or desirable in all situations. The important point, however, is that fostering staff development is a major managerial responsibility for which supervisors at all levels should be held accountable.

Mentoring Relationships

Professional relationships, although seldom recognized as a formal mechanism for staff development, constitute the most powerful source for day-to-day learning and growth. In addition to the supervisory relationship, individual staff members have opportunities to form meaningful relationships with a full constellation of colleagues at various organizational levels. While the present discussion focuses on the impact of mentoring relationships, it is necessary to examine this complicated role in the context of other functions performed by professional colleagues. (See also Chapter 15 for a discussion of mentoring issues.)

In Figure 17.2 is provided a continuum of functional roles, adapted from Shapiro, Haseltine, and Rose (1978). At the left end of the continuum, colleagial relationships with peers in the organization tend to be informal and are characterized by the elements of mutuality and egalitarianism. The traditional roles of counselor, teacher, tutor, and advisor, while generally viewed as "caring relationships," begin to define movement toward associations in which one person in the dyad has greater knowledge or experience than the other. In general terms, the shift of power within a relationship becomes

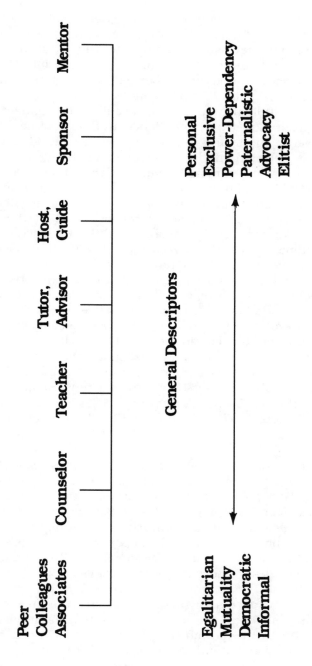

Figure 17.2. Functional roles within professional relationships.

Note: Based on and modified from Shapiro, Haseltine, & Rose, 1978.

increasingly evident as one approaches the right half of the continuum. A "host" or "guide," for example, plays a special role in introducing a new staff member to the traditions, resources, and values of the organization. This process initiates the organizational socialization of a younger, less experienced colleague. The role of sponsor implies an even greater degree of direct power and influence applied on behalf of the initiate. Sponsors will often use their experience and expertise to promote and advance the status of a younger colleague. Finally a mentor-protege relationship is recognized as being more intese, paternalistic, and personal than are the other roles. While this relationship contains mutual admiration, caring, and respect, the mentor is clearly the power figure who usually directs and controls the relationship. Levinson et al., (1978) characterizes the mentor as representing skill, knowledge, virtue, and accomplishment, thereby exemplifying the qualities that the aspiring young professional wants to attain. The mentoring role often becomes so personal and intense that the mentor becomes an "internal figure" who provides a combination of love, admiration, and support while also serving as the novice's advocate and patron. This role, then, encompasses all of the functions on the continuum. Additional terms that have been used in this regard emphasize both the personal and paternalistic nature of the traditional mentoring relationship: coach, godfather, rabbi, mother-figure, or patron (Business Week, 1978; Collins & Scott, 1978; Fury, 1980; Hennig & Jardim, 1977; Kanter, 1977; Roche, 1979; Shapiro et al., 1978).

Thus, the traditional mentoring process, as it has evolved in the corporate world as well as within professional groups such as law, medicine, and education, carries some negative political and social implications as well as offers developmental advantages. In order to utilize mentoring relationships to enhance staff development efforts, it is important to recognize the possible liabilities and construct a system that will minimize their impact. Three of these disadvantages are glaring.

The first liability or disadvantage concerns the use of organizational and political power implicit in the traditional mentoring role. The same power that is used to advance a person's career can also become an insidious force that robs a young professional of self-reliance, personal autonomy, and unique personality traits. It is critical that developmental, collaborative relationships be fostered among student affairs colleagues that emphasize mutual learning and diminish the likelihood of dehumanizing partnerships, unhealthy dependencies, or outright manipulation.

A second disadvantage that requires attention is the elitist, undemocratic characteristic of the traditional mentor role. Colleagial relationships that support professional development must be structured on an egalitarian basis. Staff members within an organization must have equal opportunities to contribute to organizational goals.

Perhaps the most destructive aspect of the traditional mentoring role is identified by Moore (1980) as the unspoken law of homogeneity-homophyly within self-selected relationships. Simply stated, this is the likelihood that individuals will recognize and promote the merits of talented young professionals who reflect values and attitudes acceptable to the mentor and to the current leaders. More often than not, this tendency includes commonality of sex, race, religion, and cultural background. Thus, the phenomenon often referred to as the "old boys' system" generally works to the advantage of people who think, behave, and look alike and to the detriment of people who do not fit the mold—women and ethnic minorities, for example.

Not surprisingly, then, mentoring has received a good deal of attention in the literature analyzing the plight of women and minorities seeking advancement in academe (Fowler, 1982; McNeer, 1986). Some writers encourage women and minorities to find a mentor to help them up the ladder (Scott, 1979; Holt, 1986). But a publication issued by the Project on the Status and Education of Women devoted to "Academic Mentoring for Women Students and Faculty: A New Look at an Old Way to Get Ahead" (Hall & Sandler, 1983) outlines a number of barriers to traditional mentoring for women on college campuses. Senior men may hesitate to mentor women either because a woman's failure may reflect negatively on their own reputation (the failure of a male protege is less likely to attract attention) or because they fear rumors of sexual involvement. The numbers of potential women mentors in positions to be truly helpful are limited. And some junior women tend to exclude themselves from the mentoring process either because they are more hesitant than men to mix friendship and the possibility of gain or because they object, on principle, to a process traditionally associated with favoritism rather than merit.

The Project paper suggests a number of alternatives for women to mentoring in the traditional sense: multiple mentors, i.e., seeking different kinds of advice, guidance, and support from a number of different people both on and off campus; paper mentors or publications which provide much of the nitty-gritty, how-to information about a particular organization or institution that might be communicated by a mentor; career counseling workshops or "mentoring" sessions for small groups of women; and networking (Green, 1986; Perry, 1983).

Networking is the alternative most frequently touted. In the past decade or so, women and minorities alike have created professional networks, formal and informal, within institutions, communities, and professions. Most professional associations have built such networks into their organizational structures. Women and members of minority groups generally derive both professional and personal benefits from the friendships formed in these loosely knit groups, which also facilitate further involvement in the professional association. But two male writers, while recognizing both the importance and the value to its members of groups of persons of the same gender or ethnicity, issued this research-based caveat: "when such support groups decrease communication with white males, they are likely to be perceived by the dominant culture as divisive" (Menges & Exum, 1983, p. 136).

Discussions and studies of the merits of mentoring and networking as strategies for advancement have perhaps reached a point of diminishing returns. What is clear, though, is that personal relationships among professional colleagues offer a dynamic mechanism for staff development, one which will probably operate whether or not it is designed or monitored with this objective in mind. But the benefits are likely to be greater, as well as more evenly distributed, if student affairs organizations deliberately foster helping relationships among individuals for the express purpose of assisting staff members to meet their personal and professional development needs. In short, an organization must minimize favoritism and cultivate a climate that reinforces collaboration, sharing, and mutual problem-solving as organizational expectations for staff members.

Structured Learning Opportunities

Structured opportunities for professional development range from academic courses to staff meetings, from week-long workshops to brown bag discussion groups. According to Miller's (1975) survey, student affairs professionals rank off-campus professional development workshops as the most valuable type of structured program and academic courses offered by graduate education programs as the least valuable.

The typical kind of structured staff development program, however, is the short, one-shot session that is utilized for a vast range of organizational and professional topics. Whether as part of a professional conference in a distant city or a session conducted in the local student center, these programs have a number of common characteristics. In length, they range anywhere from an hour to three hours; usually they include a factual presentation or the introduction of new information plus some time for discussion or small group activities.

This more or less standard format for what many people associate almost exclusively with the term "staff development" has some definite advantages, as well as distinct drawbacks. Certainly, it offers people an expedient way to gain background information or new insights regarding a topic of interest. It usually requires no preparation on the part of participants, and they can often remain comfortably passive during the session itself. People seem to enjoy programs of this type both for the change of pace they offer and the knowledge or skill development that may be gleaned from them. Sometimes, of course, such programs lead to lively conversations in conference hotel hallways or at cafeteria tables on campus —and sometimes even to action.

One of the most serious drawbacks to this form of professional development, however, is lack of follow-up. Good intentions may exist, but too often upon returning to the job after a few hours or days of this kind of activity, the good intentions, along with the new ideas and information, begin to evaporate. Given the brevity of such programs and the fact that participants often vary greatly in the amount of prior knowledge they have of the subject, the content tends to be superficial and the impact short-lived.

In some instances, this inherent disadvantage is exacerbated by people's attitudes toward structured professional development programs. Some experienced professionals regard the opportunity to attend such programs (particularly those held at national and regional meetings) as a sort of fringe benefit, rather than as a means of fulfilling their obligation to learn and grow professionally. Others complain that staff development programs are not really relevant to their everyday work situations. Sometimes, of course, this is not true; but often people fail to make the extra effort required to apply new knowledge, incorporate innovative approaches, or practice new job skills— or organizations fail to encourage and reward such effort.

Academic coursework may be the surest way to overcome some of the drawbacks associated with professional development sessions. Although this approach is stressed for people whose career advancement depends on advanced degrees, it is often overlooked as a means to enhance knowledge and skills for specific jobs. Business writing, accounting, public budgeting and finance, management, marketing, research methodology, speech communication, personnel administration, and evaluation strategies are just a few of the courses available in most institutions that could contribute significantly to professional development, whether or not they apply to a degree program. Plans that provide for tuition subsidy or remission for staff members, of course, make academic courses an even more attractive option.

On-campus staff development programs, consisting for the most part of workshops and short information sessions, are becoming increasingly common. In their *Handbook on Staff Development in Student Affairs*, Beeler and Penn (1978) summarized a number of different models and provided detailed guidelines for the design, implementation, and evaluation of division-wide staff development programs. Low budget programs generally can be planned by an interdepartmental staff development committee utilizing campus and community resources, rather than external consultants (Brown, 1979) and can have a strong positive impact on staff morale (Wanzek & Canon, 1975). The extent to which they also contribute to genuine professional development depends on a number of individual and organizational variables. Following are a few suggestions for making local, on-campus staff development programs effective.

Integrate Staff Development with Organizational Objectives. Staff development programming should be explicitly linked to student affairs goals and priorities. Stamatakos and Oliaro (1972) maintained that "in-service development is more a *function* of an effective student personnel [sic] program than a service to staff members" (pp. 270-1). Staff development activities should grow directly from current organizational objectives and be integrated with divisional efforts to support the institutional mission and meet the expressed needs of students.

Although this particular suggestion may seem to give higher priority to organizational goals than to the interests of individuals, it can help bring the two together. Moreover, if workshops, coffee hour presentations or short, in-house courses focus on topics of immediate and well-known concern within student affairs (institutional budget, confronting campus racism, relations with faculty, improving student retention, combatting alcohol abuse among students, affirmative action, and program evaluation), they are likely not only to be relevant to people's jobs, but also to garner the support of administrators. Deliberately planning, publicizing, and presenting staff development programs within the framework of student affairs goals and objectives can enhance both their appeal and their impact.

Relate Staff Development Programs to Self-assessment, Supervision, and Performance Evaluation. One approach to this task is to offer a series of self-assessment workshops at the beginning of the year to help people define their own professional development objectives and examine ways by which they might meet those objectives. A needs assessment form listing a number of possible topics for structured programs could then be completed to guide the staff development committee in program selection. Items on such a form might be derived from student affairs goals or from issues or problem areas identified by supervisors. If cooperation of student affairs managers and supervisors is forthcoming, staff development planning can also be linked to the performance evaluation process. The evaluation form itself, assuming it bears some relevance to actual performance expectations, can even be transformed into a needs assessment instrument on which supervisors and individuals can indicate needs for formal training. Only rarely is the process this explicit, but the principle is important. Additional means for linking the performance evaluation process with the planning of structured staff development programs should be explored.

Emphasize Comprehensive, In-depth Development Experiences. The mini-university format, for example, provides an opportunity to treat areas of knowledge and skill development in greater depth than the more typical one-shot session. This approach involves offering a series of short courses, each consisting of three or four sessions over a period of as many weeks and possibly including some reading assignments as well (Beeler, 1977; Meyerson, 1974; Wanzek & Canon, 1975). Course objectives need to be clearly spelled out in advance and participants need to make a commitment to attend all sessions. Obviously, the cooperation and support of supervisors are crucial to the success of this kind of program.

Target Staff Development Programs to the Interests and Needs of Particular Staff Groups. Although some people maintain that staff morale is better served by making all staff development programs open to interested staff members, including clerical staff (Wanzek & Canon, 1975), this approach can result in a watered-down program and lack of participation and support by many professionals. Perhaps a mixed approach—provision of some well-tailored programs targeted to clerical staff, food service personnel, or executive staff, along with other more general programs open to everybody—offers the best solution to this problem.

Use the Retreat Format as an Effective Method for Combining Individual and Organization Development. Generally held off-campus for a period of 24 to 48 hours, retreats offer the advantage of intensity. At one end of a continuum is the task-centered session. A staff group may, for example, take up weekend residence in a resort or camp lodge for the primary purpose of evaluating a year's work, formulating goals, or engaging in long-range planning. Usually, their objective will be to return to campus with a comprehensive plan of action.

At the opposite end of the continuum are retreat formats that focus almost exclusively on process, on team-building and developing awareness of the human relationships that enhance or impede group functioning. A particularly imaginative model for this type of retreat is the "wilderness" or "adventure" program in which participants attempt to solve a physical problem or complete an unusual physical task requiring a high degree of teamwork (Schroeder, 1976). More common methods are those of laboratory education in which, as Reynolds (1980) pointed out, "the involvement level attained through relatively low personal risk required soon leads to intimate communication, cohesive group feelings, and positive feelings about the total experience" (p. 252). Provided a professional facilitator is used and the goals and parameters of the experience are understood in advance by all participants, this kind of retreat can provide invaluable learning.

Harvey, Helzer, and Young (1972) described a model near the midpoint of the continuum, a staff retreat focusing on both tasks and process. During a weekend program, small groups or teams explore specific issues in depth and develop detailed plans. At the same time, throughout the retreat, consultants use facilitative strategies to help participants get a better understanding of individual behavior and of the group process.

Regardless of the purpose or mode of a retreat, thorough planning and carefully designed follow-up are essential if the full potential for staff development is to be realized. In terms of time, energy, and money, retreats require a substantial commitment, but their developmental impact on both individuals and organizations can be dramatic.

Professional Participation, Service, and Contributions

A full range of developmental experiences is available to student affairs professionals through active involvement in state, regional, and national professional associations. Membership and participation in such organizations provide individuals with an identifiable professional community, as well as with opportunities to develop new competencies. Perhaps most importantly, professional associations deliver systematic exposure to the literature, research, and contemporary thought that constitute the body of knowledge that gives meaning and direction to the profession. Many professional development strategies can be created or facilitated through involvement in professional student affairs associations.

Convention, Conference, and Workshop Attendance. Many types of structured learning opportunities are typically available through annual conferences and regional workshops sponsored by professional associations. Conference programs and workshop presentations generally focus on five important areas that contribute to professional development: skill development, innovative programs and services for students, current research findings, the theory and philosophy of human development, and contemporary issues in postsecondary education. Consultants and presenters are identified nationally who have a high level of expertise as well as an experiential base different from that of local colleagues. Additionally, annual attendance at association conferences provides opportunities for interaction with a broad group of professional colleagues. This acquaintance process takes place in the structured learning activities that provide a forum for exchanging ideas and sharing concerns. Dialogue and interaction are also achieved through informal discussions and social gatherings where professional friendships are expanded and solidified. Such relationships create communication networks with colleagues on a national basis and can make a substantial contribution to an individual's professional development. They also contribute to a professional consciousness and a sense of identity with a broad community of colleagues who can provide the same type of supportive relationships that are available with institutional colleagues. In one study, this very experience, "discussions with student affairs colleagues at institutions other than my own," was ranked as the most helpful professional development activity by practicing administrators (Rhatigan & Crawford, 1978).

Individual Reading, Research, and Learning. Professional associations, through journals, learning packages, media aids, research reports, newsletters, and other professional publications, provide individuals with systematic exposure to current literature and research. Unfortunately, some student affairs practitioners rely almost entirely on experiential learning opportunities and fail to enhance their professional growth by implementing a personal program of reading and study. For instance, Rhatigan and Crawford (1978) reported that the six items on their survey involving professional reading received the lowest ratings as staff development activities.

Career Development and Placement. Typically, professional organizations provide a career planning and placement service both for members who are exploring new job opportunities and for those who are seeking candidates for positions at their institutions. Workshops for developing career-related skills such as self-assessment, resume preparation, and interviewing techniques are often also available at annual conferences.

Leadership Development. Since associations provide professional leadership for their constituents, they also challenge members to become involved, to accept leadership roles, and to share responsibility for the organization's effectiveness. Such opportunities include task force membership, acting as chairperson for a standing committee, and actively seeking election as an executive officer. A large organization offers literally hundreds of possibilities for members to exercise their special talents or simply to devote time and energy on behalf of their colleagues. Such contributions and activities not only generate individual growth and renewal, but also offer a unique personal reward and the feeling of participation in the overall direction and movement of the profession.

Professional Contributions. As individuals mature professionally and develop areas of special expertise, opportunities to share their knowledge or insights become yet another type of professional development. Presenting a program or delivering a paper in the context of a conference or workshop, for example, requires a new set of skills and reflects a still deeper professional commitment. Developing research and writing skills that culminate in professional publications is another method of sharing knowledge that also produces significant professional growth for the individual. Finally, an individual can contribute expertise to colleagues by serving as a consultant or external evaluator for another institution. Each of these activities involves an instructional or sharing process that always creates growth for the teacher as well as for the learner.

Thus, various levels of involvement within the structure of professional associations provide rich sources for individual staff development. These learning experiences touch all of the basic objectives of professional development, and must be recognized as a major component for a total staff development program. Before accepting a position, an individual must clearly understand the institution's posture toward active participation in professional associations, the level of financial support available to attend meetings, and the degree to which professional contributions beyond the institutional structure are encouraged or rewarded.

THE CONTEXT FOR STAFF DEVELOPMENT

Understanding the philosophical foundation and the various components of staff development provides guidance to both the individual and the organization in planning for professional development. A third crucial area of consideration is context or, more precisely, a whole series of contexts ranging from the national climate to the personal circumstances of an individual at a particular time. Political, social, economic, organizational, educational, and personal issues—some of which have already been identified in appropriate sections of this chapter—may affect the substance and the form of professional development for student affairs staff.

Major Issues in Higher Education

Just as individual institutions form the immediate context for all student affairs activities, so the larger, national higher education enterprise forms the context for the student affairs profession in this country. As indicated earlier, staff development objectives and strategies must grown out of and address the needs of the particular organization—the student affairs division and the educational institution with which the staff members are associated. But if student affairs is, indeed, a profession, its professional staff must be well aware of and prepared to respond to the major issues with which American higher education as a whole is grappling.

Almost without exception, the issues that emerged in higher education in the 80s, most of which are likely to continue into the 90s, have significant implications for student affairs professionals. Only occasionally, however, are these implications spelled out by the university presidents, academic officers, and higher education researchers who publish and pontificate on such issues. Recognizing the new dilemmas, demands, and opportunities in higher education and developing strategies for bringing student affairs expertise to bear upon them should be a major focus for professional development in the field.

Improvement of Teaching and Learning. Ernest Boyer (1987), K. Patricia Cross (1976, 1987, 1988), Russell Edgerton (1988), and the Study Group on the Conditions of Excellence in American Higher Education (1984), among others in recent years, have called loud and clear for the improvement of teaching in the college classroom. As the segments of society from which college students come have expanded over the past quarter century, the traditional modes of college teaching seem to have become less and less effective. Research has documented differences in learning styles, academic values, and personal characteristics between the "new students" and the more affluent and academically-oriented college students of the 50s and 60s (Cross, 1976; Davis & Schroeder, 1983). Instructional development centers, intended to help faculty become better teachers, have sprung up on college campuses across the country (many have been in existence since the mid 70s). Yet, as late as 1987, the Carnegie Foundation for the Advancement of Teaching found widespread evidence of a mismatch between faculty and student expectations, a gap that left both parties unfulfilled (Boyer, 1987).

Three domains of knowledge must be brought into play, according to Edgerton (1988), if teaching is to be effective: knowledge of the subject matter; knowledge of the students— who they are, "where they are at," and how they learn; and knowledge of a variety of pedagogical techniques that can help bridge the gap between the subject matter and the student (p. 7). Student affairs professionals, presumably, are the experts on the second of these and should know something about the third as well. Faculty, as a whole, have shown remarkable resistance to moving beyond the first. How can student affairs professionals contribute to solving this pervasive problem in higher education?

Reform of the General Education Curriculum. Intense attention to the curriculum, especially to the liberal arts core that has traditionally distinguished collegiate institutions, seems to be a cyclical phenomenon. The "vocationalism" of the 70s and early 80s has since been called into question, as have been the fragmentation and superficiality of the General Education curriculum and the lack of coherence of the entire baccalaureate program (Boyer, 1987; Gaff, 1983; Select Committee of the Project on Redefining the Meaning and Purpose of Baccalaureate Degrees, 1985).

Committees to review and revise General (or Liberal) Education requirements have been appointed on campus after campus and have generally found both the task and the process to be far more challenging than originally anticipated. They have found it necessary, first of all, to reach a consensus on the desired outcomes of General Education for their students, and then to figure out what combination of disciplinary content and instructional strategies would be most likely to produce those outcomes.

The lists of objectives for General Education that have emerged, although not carbon copies, bear remarkable resemblances to one another. Competence in reasoning and critical thinking, effective communication skills, ability to make decisions, tolerance of ambiguity, understanding of different cultures and recognition of global interdependence, aesthetic appreciation, clarification of and commitment to values, and dedication to lifelong learning—these are some of the commonalities among General Education goals. They bear a remarkable resemblance as well to the goals of student development.

If the most cherished ends of liberal education and of student affairs work are so similar, why are student affairs staff so little involved in efforts to support and to reform general education? Indeed, if student affairs professionals are educators, why are they so rarely called upon to participate in discussions of curricular issues? Kuh, Shedd, and Whitt (1987) offer a number of answers, both historical and contemporary, to these questions. While their arguments are beyond the scope of this chapter, the questions and the answers, as well as the whole matter of the General Education curriculum, are well within the scope of professional development for student affairs staff.

Outcomes Assessment. Along with (and not unrelated to) the calls for improvement of teaching and reform of curriculum has come the call for accountability through the definition and measurement of outcomes. Unlike the others, however, this call has come from without, as well as from within, the higher education establishment. Governors, legislators, state commissions of higher education, and the federal Department of Education, along with the President of Harvard University, have called upon colleges and universities to document their performance, to demonstrate what differences they make in the knowledge, skills, and attitudes of their students (Bok, 1986; Marchese, 1987).

In the early 80s, Alexander Astin (1982) suggested that the traditional measures of institutional quality—resources, academic reputation, recognition accorded to faculty by their disciplinary community, and achievements of graduates—missed the point with regard to undergraduate education. Using an economic analogy, Astin argued that quality should be assessed by looking at the "value added" to students' intellectual and personal development as a result of attending a particular college. The argument makes sense to many student affairs professionals and has both reinforced and led to such innovations as the "student development transcript." Two student affairs professionals (Smith & Weith, 1985), who have been deeply involved in an institution-wide translation of Astin's theory into practice, believed that the value-added concept should be adopted as "an alternative to student development as a unifying theme in student affairs" (p. 24) because it offers the opportunity to form a true partnership with faculty, to create a more unified experience for students and to demonstrate accountability to numerous constituencies.

Assessment, however, is far more than a student affairs issue. And it has proved to be an extraordinarily complex issue, one that is testing and taxing the intelligence of faculty and academic administrators across the country (McMillan, 1988). Few have been well-prepared either by training or experience to cope with this challenge, although student affairs professionals as a whole may be better prepared than their academic colleagues. In any case, the business of determining what to assess and how to do it has provided—and will continue to provide—a fertile field for professional development for all concerned. (See Chapter 22.)

Values Education. The issue of assessment may be even further complicated if yet another current call to action is heeded. Increasing national concern about ethics is business, government, medicine, and even religion, coupled with the proliferation of value-laden personal choices—of vocation, friends, life-style, and leisure activity—that confront today's youth, have combined to prompt the call for greater attention to values education. "Education that stresses issues of values and questions of ethics—for a pragmatic and materialistic generation, this is essential" according to Arthur Levine (1986, p. 4).

No one is suggesting a return to the early days of American higher education when a major mission was to inculcate particular values. Rather, the point, as Morrill (1984) explained, is to make "a conscious effort to make students aware of the values they hold, of the values implicit in the subjects they are studying, and of the values at work in the larger society," and then to carry it one step further and "ask questions about whether the values are consistent, coherent, adequate to the situation, comprehensive, authentic, and so on." In this manner, students learn "how to value" (p. 14).

Once again, student affairs professionals may be ahead of the game. In a 1985 monograph, Dalton provided a thorough exposition of both theory and practice pertaining to values development in college students. Referring to the work of Lawrence Kohlberg, William Perry, Carol Gilligan and others, he suggested that "student personnel professionals now have a much better empirical base from which to approach values development in college students than perhaps at any time in their history" (p. 22). In the monograph also are ample models for practice within the profession, as well as issues to address in values education.

Professional development for student affairs staff on this subject should, however, go beyond the models and matters most immediately relevant to the profession, i.e., how to develop workshops and training sessions for students on personal values clarification, alcohol, drugs, sexuality, leadership, and the like. In addition to helping students analyze ethical issues that arise in roommate relationships, Welty (1988) suggested that student affairs professionals take the lead in focusing campus-wide attention on ethical issues inherent in politics, economics, technological advances, and world events.

Professional development activities, which might take the form of reading, research, or discussion, also should provide insights into and promote examination of "how values are taught—and caught—in the ordinary course of campus life" (Edgerton, 1986, p. 22). The kinds of issues raised in the context of the different disciplines, the ways in which classes are taught and students are encouraged (or discouraged) from participating, the attention (or lack thereof) paid to academic integrity on the part of both faculty and students, the type and calibre of guest speakers and artists brought to campus, the manner in which the college goes about its business and makes decisions, relations between the college and the community—through all of these facets of the institution, for better or worse, values are conveyed. If colleges and universities are to take values education seriously, they must be much more self-conscious about what is—and what should be—being taught.

Dealing with Diversity. Among the values about which higher education has become a good deal more self-conscious are those of diversity and equity. Equity is hardly a new issue, dating back (in its current form at least) to the civil rights and feminist movements of the 60s. But in the late 80s, the trends in minority student enrollment, the statistics on the employment and advancement of women and minorities in institutions of higher education, and the research, as well as the media reports, on "campus climate" all make it clear that institutions have not yet learned much that they need to know about dealing with diversity and insuring equitable treatment of all members of the academic community. In the announcement of the Eighth Annual Conference Series of The Freshman Year Experience (National Center for the Study of the Freshman Year Experience, 1988), five "critical issues areas" to be considered at the conferences were identified. Four of the five reinforce this point: warming the chilly climate for women, learning from historically Black colleges, combating the rising tide of racism, and promoting moral and character development.

Recruitment and retention of minority students, the "why" and "how" of affirmative action, and the development of sensitivity to a variety of racial and gender issues have long been among the staples of student affairs staff development programs, both on campus and at regional and national conferences. To a much greater degree than their academic colleagues, student affairs professionals have been exposed to issues and have studied and tried—indeed, created—the strategies for helping minority students and staff succeed in predominantly white institutions and for making college campuses more comfortable for minorities and women.

The time is now to develop the advanced professional development courses on this subject and to do the reading, reflection, and research, individually and collectively, that will provide new insights into this complex problem and produce new strategies desperately needed for further progress toward the still elusive goal of equity. Now also is the time for student affairs professionals to find ways of sharing their expertise with faculty, of contributing to the professional development of others on campus concerning this major issue.

Community. The term "academic community" is still part of the higher education lexicon, but many argue that a sense of community—either as a value upheld or as a quality experienced by faculty, staff, and students—is sadly lacking in most colleges and universities. Astin (1987) attributed this problem, along with a number of other problems confronting higher education today, to the dominance of the "competitive world view." While administrators and faculty may extol the value of cooperation and call upon colleagues and/or students to unite in cooperative efforts, traditional approaches to teaching, testing, grading, promotion and tenure, recruitment of students, allocation of resources, and relations with other institutions involve and promote competition.

Community is also impeded by the size of the institutions that most students attend, by the fragmentation and departmentalization of knowledge, by the intense vocationalism of students, by the lack of connection between the classroom and campus life, and by the very diversity we value. But whatever—and however many—the causes of the problem, Ernest Boyer (1987), among others, stressed that the ideal of a "community of learners" is too important to relinquish: "At a time when social bonds are tenuous, students, during their collegiate years, should discover the reality of their dependency on each other. They must understand what it means to share and sustain traditions. Community must be built" (p. 195).

Most student affairs professionals, by virtue of both personality and training, place a premium on the values of cooperation and empathy. Many have a good deal of experience in building community in residence halls, Greek organizations, and other student groups, as well as within their own staff. Building a campus community in which all aspects of undergraduate life are somehow interrelated and "contribute to a sense of wholeness," as Boyer (p. 8) put it, is a much larger challenge. Student affairs people should be prepared to contribute to that effort.

Commitment. Not only are stronger connections among individuals and groups needed to restore a sense of community within colleges and universities; stronger links between the campus and the larger community also are being called for by higher education leaders (Kennedy, 1986; Boyer, 1987), as other voices describe and decry an apparent decline in the sense of social responsibility which is fundamental to the functioning of American democracy (Bellah, Madsen, Sullivan, Swindler, & Tipton, 1985; O'Connell, 1985).

The annual survey of freshmen, conducted by the ACE-UCLA Cooperative Institutional Research Program for over 20 years, reveals dramatic changes in college students' values over that period of time. Endorsements of self-serving values having to do with money, power, and status have steadily increased since 1967, while more altruistic values having to do with helping others, being involved in the community, promoting racial understanding, and keeping up with current political issues have correspondingly declined in appeal (Astin, 1984).

Recognizing that "a central fact of life in this society is the symmetry between individual rights and personal freedoms, on the one hand, and public obligations and responsibilities on the other," Stanford president Donald Kennedy (1986) has called upon the higher education community to draw out, enlarge, and channel what he believes is a "large reservoir of social responsibility in contemporary students" (p. 5). To facilitate the process, Kennedy and several presidential colleagues created the national *Campus Compact.* Among other things, Compact members develop networks that will match students seeking opportunities to local and regional needs.

The implications of this concern for student affairs seem obvious (although only rarely noted in the literature). To be most effective in their response, however, student affairs professionals might well devote some professional development time to examining the meaning of social responsibility in our society, how the concept fits into student development theory, the source and nature of students' attitudes in this regard, the role of higher education in producing conscientious citizens, and the many ways in which institutions might fulfill that role.

Internationalizing the Campus. Along with the renewed concern about service and citizenship, the concept of "global citizenship" has emerged as yet another urgently needed outcome of higher education. After many months of studying undergraduate education first-hand across the country, Boyer (1987) and his colleagues at the Carnegie Foundation concluded that "a dangerous parochialism pervades many higher learning institutions. While some students have a global perspective, the vast majority, although vaguely concerned, are inadequately informed about the interdependent world in which they live. They lack historical understanding and remain shockingly ignorant about their own heritage and about the heritage of other nations" (p. 281).

Ample evidence is available that colleges and universities recognize this need: foreign language requirements are being increased or reinstated; new General Education curricula frequently require some exposure to a non-Western culture or course taught from an international perspective; agreements between American and foreign universities are proliferating, and more and more faculty members and students are taking advantage of opportunities to teach or study abroad; the numbers of foreign student and foreign visiting scholars have increased significantly, even at smaller, regional institutions; and many universities have designated a single administrator to inventory and coordinate the dozens of different international activities on campus (Wilkins, 1988).

For years student affairs staff have tried to promote ongoing interaction between American and foreign students (too often, with limited success). Today, much more is needed. Just as faculty members have been called upon to enlarge the international dimension in the curriculum, student affairs professionals must come up with new strategies for insuring that global awareness and concern are part of students' development during their college years. This task is likely to involve a good deal of professional development.

In his "Thoughts on Career Advancement" for student affairs professionals, Birch (1984) suggested that while a place may always be in student affairs for the person with good management and counseling skills and a commitment to students, "the future student affairs professional will need to better understand global issues in higher education and precisely where student affairs fits into the broad institutional picture" (p. 51).

Relations Between Academic and Student Affairs

Other professionals with whom student affairs people work, especially the faculty, form a crucial part of the context for the student affairs staff development. The student development model encourages involvement of faculty in the mission of student affairs, although some maintain that efforts to implement this thrust of the model have largely failed (Smith, 1982). Only rarely do either academic or student affairs administrators seek to involve student affairs professionals in carrying out the academic mission for which faculty mainly (but not necessarily solely) are responsible. This failure stems at least partly from the perceptions that student affairs professionals lack understanding of (or interest in) academic issues, that they lack rigorous preparation in an academic discipline, and that they are "relatively uncontemplative," even "anti-intellectual" (Young, 1985, pp. 52, 56).

Clearly, the weakness in relationship between academic and student affairs also stems from corresponding lack of confidence on the part of student affairs staff. Out of 40 items included on a recent survey of staff development needs of student affairs professionals working at eight different universities, four of the five highest ranking items related to competencies in communicating and working with others in the institution included top-level decision-makers and "academicians" in particular, while the five lowest ranking staff development needs (presumably, because they had already been met) related to competencies in working with students (Cox & Ivy, 1984).

Faculty may be invited to serve as leaders for student affairs staff development programs or, better yet, as participants in ongoing discussions designed to deepen student affairs professionals' understanding of faculty values and attitudes and of how they regard the academic mission of the university.

Obviously, this kind of activity can serve to enlighten faculty about the values and roles of student affairs as well. Student affairs professionals may plan and implement professional development programs intended to assist faculty in understanding—and thus in "reaching"—students, as Schroeder, DiTiberio, and Kalsbeek (1988) have done at St. Louis University. Student affairs staff members may propose joint research projects related to student learning, retention strategies, or the academic climate. And faculty and student affairs staff could build collegiality and lay foundations for collaborative activities through joint professional development programs focusing on some of the major issues in higher education as outlined previously (and others yet to emerge), which command institution-wide attention.

Personal and Professional Circumstances

Part of the philosophical foundation for professional development, as noted near the beginning of this chapter, is human development and, more specifically, adult development theory. Thus, the personal needs and the particular stages of personal and professional growth through which individuals are passing also form part of the context for student affairs staff development. In response to this recognition, increased attention seems to be occurring, both in research and the resulting literature and in professional conference programs, to the special needs of "entry-level professionals," "middle management" people, "experienced student affairs professionals," and those who are "burned out," as well as to the needs of particular groups, e.g., women and minorities (Arnold, 1982; Forbes, 1984; Harter, Moden, & Wilson, 1982; Wiggers, Fornay, & Wallace-Schutzman, 1982; Young, 1985).

Moreover, several trends have combined to produce both the need and the general expectation that job-related benefits and activities will address the total scope of a person's life. First is the now widespread recognition that the pressures of employment have a direct impact upon a person's health, emotional well-being, and family relationships—just as the latter factors have an impact on job performance. Second is the dramatic increase over the past decade or so in two-career families—a phenomenon which puts pressure on both spouses who are trying to assume parental and household responsibilities as well as to advance in their careers, and which also greatly complicates job mobility. Third is the full emergence of student affairs as a career field—one that many women and men alike train for and plan to pursue for a lifetime, rather than as an interim occupation prior to full-time parenting, graduate work in another field, or movement into another profession. Since the career ladder in student affairs is limited, this trend has led to frustrated ambitions, underemployment, burn-out from doing the same job for too long and, in some cases, feelings of entrapment and loss of self-esteem. (See Chapter 8.)

Obviously, professional development cannot be all things to all people, but program planners and supervisors should be aware of both the personal and the professional circumstances of the people with whom they are working and realize that the separation of the two, like the separation of individual and organizational development discussed earlier, is impossible to achieve.

Institutional Commitment and Resources

Finally, student affairs staff development is shaped by the context of institutional commitment and the institutional resources allocated to it. In a national survey of student affairs staff members conducted in 1975, 80% of respondents reported that their institutions had no definitive policy regarding staff development responsibilities or expectations (Miller, 1975). One hopes that things have changed since then. Rhetoric about professional development is fine, but institutional commitment is expressed, most meaningfully, through explicit policy and budgeted funds (however limited the latter might be).

Staff development policy should address questions of how available resources should be allocated among various levels and groupings of staff and among various components of staff development. It should also establish a link between staff development and long-range plans, as well as current goals, of the particular college or university.

Kuh (1985) made a provocative suggestion with regard to the first of these issues. In discussing "What Is Extraordinary About Ordinary Student Affairs Organizations," he asserted that "Extraordinary student affairs units make opportunities for professional growth available to all, but concentrate resources on those most likely to benefit" (p. 34). Admitting that his prescription "smacks of blasphemy," he goes on to explain that about one-third of the staff in a typical student affairs division are outstanding professionals who will continue to acquire knowledge, develop their skills, and make significant contributions to the organization, regardless of the opportunities or the obstacles they encounter. Another one-third are not likely to improve their performance or change their attitudes much, no matter to how much professional development they are exposed. The middle one-third consists of those individuals eager to expand their professional capacities or ripe for re-focusing or renewal. Although all three groups should have access to professional development opportunities, Kuh argued that opportunities specifically targeted to the "middle third" are "more likely to pay dividends for both the individual and the institution" (p. 35).

Kuh's rather radical approach may not be widely adopted, but it should be noted that share-and-share-alike policies, e.g., so many dollars per person per year to engage in whatever kind of activity the individual chooses, avoids rather than addresses the issue of how to allocate staff development resources most effectively.

A common approach to planning for staff development is needs assessment—talking with staff individually or surveying the entire group to find out what people feel they need in terms of professional development. This approach is useful, providing its limitations are recognized. As in any needs assessment, respondents may not distinguish between "needs" and "wants," and may not even be aware of their greatest needs. Moreover, often a gap exists between needs perceived by individuals and needs identified by those responsible for the direction and effectiveness of the entire student affairs operation. An individual residence director, for example, may want to learn more about leadership development, while the institution desperately needs professionals with expertise on

AIDS and the planning and implementation of educational programs on this subject.

Finally, staff development policy should take into account the various components of staff development and, since resources are always limited, provide some guidance on their most efficient use. A high proportion of professional development funds at many institutions is used to support attendance at regional and national conferences. With the exception of seminars or institutes lasting for a week or more or tuition for academic course work (from which, in either case, the professional development "yield" is likely to be substantial), annual conferences of professional associations are likely to be the most expensive form of professional development. Is the value of conference attendance equally high?

Of course, a one-to-one relationship need not exist between cost and benefit, but questions like this, nonetheless, should be asked and, insofar as possible, answered. The all-too-common failure to do so stems from a larger failure at many institutions to identify and assess needs systematically and design comprehensive programs that utilize all five staff development components. Most staff development programs rely too heavily on structured learning opportunities, particularly those that occur off-campus, and fail to take full advantage of the potential "learning power" inherent in the strategies of self-assessment, supervision and evaluation, and peer or mentor relationships—strategies that require a fair amount of time and effort, but practically no financial resources.

This discussion began by noting that no one seems to dispute the basic rationale underlying personal and professional development efforts. This fact, in itself, may account for the more or less ad hoc approach sometimes taken to this critical organizational function. Both individuals and organizations stand to realize far greater benefits from professional development activities when the various components are evaluated in terms of their utility for meeting defined goals and when the larger contexts for student affairs staff development are carefully considered.

REFERENCES

Arnold, K. (1982). Career development for the experienced student affairs professional. *NASPA Journal, 20*, 3-8.

Arseneau, M.M., & Terrell, P.S. (1985). Achieving interdependence through relationships: A student affairs division staff program. *College Student Affairs Journal, 6*, (2), 48-57.

Astin, A. (1982). Why not try some new ways of measuring quality? *Educational Record, 63*, 10-15.

Astin, A. (1987, September-October). Competition or cooperation? Teaching teamwork as a basic skill. *Change*, pp. 12-19.

Astin, A., et al. (1984). *The American freshman: National norms for fall 1984*. Los Angeles: Higher Education Research Institute, Graduate School of Education. University of California.

Baier, J.L. (1985). Recruiting and training competent staff. In M.J. Barr & L.A. Keating (Eds.), *Developing Effective Student Services Programs* (pp. 212-233). San Francisco: Jossey-Bass.

Beeler, K.D. (1976). Professional staff development. *Journal of College Student Personnel, 17*, 253-4.

Beeler, K.D. (1977). Mini-U: A promising model for student affairs staff development. *NASPA Journal, 14*, 38-43.

Beeler, K.D., & Penn, J.R. (1978). *A handbook on staff development in student affairs*. Corvallis, OR: Oregon State University Book Stores.

Bellah, R.N., Madsen, R., Sullivan, W.M., Swidler, A. & Tipton, S.M. (1985). *Habits of the heart: Individualism and commitment in American life*. New York: Harper and Row.

Birch, E.E. (1984). Thoughts on career advancement. In A.F. Kirby & D. Woodard (Eds.), *Career Perspectives in Student Affairs*. NASPA Monograph Series, I. (pp. 43-52). Washington, DC: National Association of Student Personnel Administrators.

Bok, D. (1986). *Higher learning*. Cambridge, MA: Harvard University Press.

Boyer, E.L. (1987). *College: The undergraduate experience in America*. New York: Harper and Row.

Brown, R.D. (1977). Professional development and staff development: The search for a metaphor. In R.P. Wanzek (Ed.), *Staff development* (pp.5-9). DeKalb, IL: Northern Illinois University.

Brown, S.S. (1979). *Student affairs staff development: A systems approach on a shoestring.* Paper presented at National Association of Student Personnel Administrators Conference, Washington, DC.

Brown, S.S. (1988). Approaches to collaboration between academic and student affairs: An overview. *NASPA Journal, 26* (1), 2-7.

Business Week (1978, October). Women finally get mentors of their own (pp. 74-80).

Canon, H.J. (1981). Developing staff potential. In U. Delworth & G.R. Hanson (Eds.), *Student services: A handbook for the profession* (pp. 439-455). San Francisco: Jossey-Bass.

Chickering, A.W., & Associates. (1981). *The modern American college: Responding to the new realities of diverse students and a changing society.* San Francisco: Jossey-Bass.

Collins, E.G.C., & Scott, P. (1978, July-August). Everyone who makes it has a mentor. *Harvard Business Review,* pp. 89-101.

Cox, D.W. (1985). Staff development: A rationale and supporting theory. *College Student Affairs Journal, 6,* (2), 3-11.

Cox, D.W., & Ivy, W.A. (1984). Staff development needs of student affairs professionals. *NASPA Journal, 22,* 26-33.

Creamer, D., & Shelton, M. (1988). Staff development: A literature review of graduate preparation and in-service education of students. *Journal of College Student Development, 29,* 407-414.

Cross, P., & McCarton, A. (1984). *Adult learning: State policies and institutional practices.* ASHE-ERIC Higher Education Report No. 1. Washington D.C.: Association for the Study of Higher Education.

Cross, K.P. (1976). *Accent on learning.* San Francisco: Jossey-Bass.

Cross, K.P. (1987, April). Teaching for learning. *AAHE Bulletin, 39,* 3-7.

Cross, K.P. (1988, June). In search of zippers. *AAHE Bulletin, 40,* 3-7.

Dalton, J.C. (Ed.) (1985). *Promoting values development in college students.* NASPA Monograph Series, 4. Washington, DC: National Association of Student Personnel Administrators.

Davis, M.T., & Schroeder, C.C. (1983). "New students" in liberal arts colleges: Threat or challenge? In J. Watson & R. Stevens (Eds.) *Pioneers and pallbearers: Perspectives on liberal education* (pp. 147-168). Macon, GA: Mercer University Press.

DeCoster, D.A., & Mable, P. (1980). Residence education: Purpose and process. In D.A. DeCoster & P. Mable (Eds.), *Personal education and community development in college residence halls* (pp. 31-55). Washington, DC: American College Personnel Association.

Dewey, J. (1916). *Democracy and education.* New York: Macmillan.

Edgerton, R. (1986, June). Six core convictions. *AAHE Bulletin, 38,* 7-12.

Edgerton, R. (1988, April). All roads lead to teaching. *AAHE Bulletin 40,* 3-9.

Fisher, C.F. (1978). The evaluation and development of college and university administrators. In J.A. Shotgren (Ed.), *Administrative development in higher education* (pp. 1-19). Richmond, VA: Dietz Press.

Forbes, O.Z. (1984). The middle management professional. In A.F. Kirby & D. Woodard (Eds.), *Career Perspectives in Student Affairs.* NASPA Monograph Series, I (pp. 35-42). Washington, DC: National Association of Student Personnel Administrators.

Fowler, D.L. (1982, Spring). Mentoring relationships and the perceived quality of the academic work environment. *Journal of the National Association for Women Deans, Administrators and Counselors,* 27-33.

Fury, K. (1980). Mentor mania. *Savvy,* pp. 42-7.

Gaff, J. (1983). *General education today: A critical analysis of controversies, practices, and reforms.* San Francisco: Jossey-Bass.

Glueck, W.F. (1978). *Personnel: A diagnostic approach.* Dallas: Business Publications.

Green, M.F. (1986). A Washington perspective on women and networking: The power and the pitfalls. In P.A. Farrant (Ed.), *Strategies and attitudes: Women in educational administration* (pp. 65-69). Washington, DC: NAWDAC.

Hall, R.M., & Sandler, B.R. (1983). *Academic mentoring for women students and faculty: A new look at an old way to get ahead.* Project on the Status and Education of Women. Washington, DC: Association of American Colleges.

Harter, C., Moden, G., & Wilson, P. (1982). Women and minority professional staff in student personnel: A census and analysis. *NASPA Journal, 20,* 42-50.

Harvey, V.P., Helzer, T.A., & Young, J.W. (1972). The retreat: Keystone staff development. *NASPA Journal, 9,* 274-8.

Hennig, M., & Jardim, A. (1977). *The managerial women.* New York: Anchor Press.

Holt, M.E. (1986). Strategies for the "ascent of woman" in higher education administration in the 80s. In P.A. Farrant (Ed.), *Strategies and attitudes: Women in educational administration* (pp. 24-27). Washington, DC: NAWDAC.

Kanter, R.M. (1977). *Men and women of the corporation.* New York: Basic Books.

Kennedy, D. (1986, December). Can we help? Public service and the young. *AAHE Bulletin, 39*, 3-7.

Kuh, G.D. (1985). What is extraordinary about ordinary student affairs organizations. *NASPA Journal, 23*, 31-43.

Kuh, G.D., Shedd, J.D., & Whitt, E.J. (1987). Student affairs and liberal education: Unrecognized (and unappreciated) common law partners. *Journal of College Student Personnel, 28*, 252-259.

Kurpius, D.J. (1980). Organization development, systems analysis, and planned change. In C.H. Foxley (Ed.), *Applying management techniques (pp. 11-26)* New directions for student services, No. 9. San Francisco: Jossey-Bass.

Leafgren, F. (1980). Student development through staff development. In D.A. DeCoster & P. Mable (Eds.), *Personal education and community development in college residence halls* (pp. 218-228). Washington, DC: American College Personnel Association.

Levine, A. (1986, April). Hearts and minds: The freshman challenge. *AAHE Bulletin, 38*, 3-6.

Levinson, D.J., Darrow, C.N., Klein, E.B., Levinson, M.H., & McKee, B. (1978). *The seasons of a man's life.* New York: Ballantine Books.

Mable, P., Terry, M.J., & Duvall, W.H. (1980). Student development through community development. In D.A. DeCoster & P. Mable (Eds.), *Personal education and community development in college residence halls* (pp. 103-113). Washington, DC: American College Personnel Association.

Marchese, T.J. (1987, December). An update on assessment: Third down, ten years to go. *AAHE Bulletin, 40*, 3-8.

McDade, S.A. (1987). *Higher education leadership: Enhancing skills through professional development programs.* ASHE-ERIC Education Report No. 5. Washington, DC: Association for the Study of Higher Education.

McIntire, D. (1985). Wellness as an issue for total staff development. *College Student Affairs Journal, 6* (2), 33-38.

McMillan, J.H. (Ed.). (1988). *Assessing students' learning.* New Directions for Teaching and Learning. San Francisco: Jossey-Bass.

McNeer, E.J. (1986). Two opportunities for mentoring: A study of women's career development in higher education administration. In P.A. Farrant (Ed.), *Strategies and attitudes: Women in educational administration* (pp. 70-76). Washington, DC: NAWDAC.

Menges, R.J., & Exum, W.H. (1983). Barriers to the progress of women and minority faculty. *Journal of Higher Education, 54,* 123-143.

Merkle, H.B., & Artman, R.B. (1983). Staff development: A systematic process for student affairs leaders. *NASPA Journal, 21* (1), 55-63.

Meyerson, E. (1974). Mini-university provides staff training for a big university. *College and University Business, 56,* 31-3.

Miller, T.K. (1975). Staff development activities in student affairs programs. *Journal of College Student Personnel, 16,* 258-64.

Miller, T.K. (1980). Professional preparation and development of residence educators. In D.A. DeCoster & P. Mable (Eds.) *Personal education and community development in college residence halls* (pp. 190-205). Washington, DC: American College Personnel Association.

Miller, T.K. (1985). Staff development: Models for making it happen. *College Student Affairs Journal, 6* (2), 58-65.

Moore, K.M. (1980). *What to do until the mentor arrives.* Paper presented at National Association of Women Deans, Administrators, and Counselors Convention, Cincinnati.

Morrill, R.L. (1984, May). Quoted in standards for choice: A roundtable on the role of college in developing character and values. *AAHE Bulletin, 36,* 3-6, 14.

Morse, S.W. (1984). *Employee educational programs: Implications for industry and higher education.* ASHE-ERIC Higher Education Report No. 7. Washington, DC: Association for the Study of Higher Education.

National Center for the Study of the Freshman Year Experience (1988). *The freshman year experience and beyond: Foundations for improving the undergraduate experience* (Announcement of Conference Series). University of South Carolina.

Nejedlo, R.J. (1977). Making staff development happen through organizational renewal. In R.P. Wanzek (Ed.), *Staff development* (pp. 13-17). DeKalb, IL: Northern Illinois University.

O'Connell, B. (1985, November). Citizenship and community service: Maintaining America's voluntary spirit. *AAHE Bulletin, 38,* 3-7.

Perry, S. (1983, April 17). "Networking" gives women in academe new routes to professional growth. *The Chronicle of Higher Education,* pp. 19-20.

Quick, T.L. (1976). *Understanding people at work.* New York: Executive Enterprises Publications.

Reynolds, E.L. (1980). Laboratory education: Methods for personal development and skill building. In D.A. DeCoster & P. Mable (Eds.), *Personal education and community development in college residence halls* (pp. 250-277). Washington, DC: American College Personnel Association.

Rhatigan, J.J., & Crawford, A.E. (1978). Professional development preferences of student affairs administrators. *NASPA Journal, 15* (3), 45-52.

Richardson, R.C. (1975). Staff development: A conceptual framework. *Journal of Higher Education, 46,* 303-11.

Roche, G.R. (1979, January-February). Much ado about mentors. *Harvard Business Review,* pp. 14-28.

Schroeder, C.C. (1976). Adventure training for residence assistants. *Journal of College Student Personnel, 17,* pp. 11-15.

Schroeder, C.C., Di Tiberio, J.K., & Kalsbeek, D.H. (1988). Bridging the gap between faculty and students: Opportunities and obligations for student affairs. *NASPA Journal, 26* (1), 14-20.

Scott, P.B. (1979). Moving up the institutional hierarchy: Some suggestions for young minority and women professionals from the notebook of a novice. *Journal of the National Association for Women Deans, Administrators, and Counselors, 43* (2), 34-9.

Select committee of the Project on Redefining the Meaning and Purpose of Baccalaureate Degrees. (1985). *Integrity in the college curriculum: A report to the academic community.* Washington, DC: Association of American Colleges.

Shaffer, R.H. (1972). Staff development—key to survival. *NASPA Journal, 9,* 261-2.

Shapiro, E.D., Haseltine, F.P., & Rose, M.P. (1978). Moving up: Role models, mentors, and the patron system. *Sloan Management Review, 19* (8), 51-8.

Sheehy, G. (1974). *Passages: Predictable crises of adult life.* New York: E.P. Dutton and Co.

Smith, D.G. (1982). The next step beyond student development—becoming partners within our institutions. *NASPA Journal, 19,* 53-62.

Smith, T.B., & Weith, R.A. (1985). Value-added: The student affairs professional as promoter of intellectual development. *NASPA Journal, 23,* 19-24.

Stamatakos, L.D., & Oliaro, P.M. (1972). In-service development: A function of student personnel. *NASPA Journal, 9,* 269-73.

Study Group on the Conditions of excellence in American Higher Education. (1984). *Involvement in learning: Realizing the potential of American higher education.* Washington, DC: National Institute of Education.

Thomas, R.E. (1985). Applying adult development theory to staff development programming. *College Student Affairs Journal, 6* (2), 39-47.

Tripp, P.A. (1977). Student personnel work—whence it came and wither it may be going. In R.P. Wanzek (Ed.), *Staff development* (pp. 33-37). DeKalb, IL: Northern Illinois University.

Wanzek, R.P., & Canon, H. (1975). Professional growth in student affairs. *Journal of College Student Personnel, 16,* 418-20.

Welty, J.D. (1988). Values education as an opportunity for collaboration: A president's perspective. *NASPA Journal, 26* (1), 21-26.

Wiggers, T.T., Forney, D.S., & Wallace-Schutzman, F. (1982). Burnout is not necessary: Prevention and recovery. *NASPA Journal, 20,* 13-21.

Wilkins, B. (1988, April). Including the rest of the world. *AAHE Bulletin, 40,* 13-14.

Winston, R.B., Herbert, D.A., & McGonigle, R.B. (1985). Professional staff development as management tool. *College Student Affairs Journal, 6* (2), 12-25.

Young, R.B. (1985). Impressions of the development of professional identity: From program to practice. *NASPA Journal, 23,* 50-60.

SUGGESTED READINGS

Baier, J.L. (1985). Recruiting and training competent staff. In M.J. Barr & L.A. Keating (Eds.), *Developing Effective Student Services Programs* (pp. 212-233). San Francisco: Jossey-Bass.

Beeler, K.D., & Penn, J.R. (1978). *A handbook on staff development in student affairs.* Corvallis, OR: Oregon State University Book Store.

Creamer, D., & Shelton M. (1988). Staff Development: A literature review of graduate preparation and in-service education of students. *Journal of College Student Development, 29,* 407-414.

Dalton, J.C. (1989). Enhancing staff knowledge and skills. In U. Delworth, G.R. Harson, & Associates. *Student services: A handbook for the profession* (pp. 533-551). San Francisco: Jossey-Bass.

Leafgren, F. (1980). Student development through staff development. In D.A. DeCoster & P. Mable (Eds.), *Personal education and community development in college residence halls.* Washington, DC: American College Personnel Association.

Richardson, R.C. (1975). Staff development: A conceptual framework. *Journal of Higher Education, 46,* 303-11.

Wanzek, R.P. (1977). *Staff development.* DeKalb, IL: Northern Illinois University.

Dwight O. Douglas, Ed.D., has had experience in residence hall programs and administration at Eastern Illinois University, University of Tennessee, and University of Georgia, where he also been a member of the faculty. At the University of Georgia, he has served as Director of Housing, Associate Dean of Students, Dean of Students, and Vice President for Student Affairs, a position he currently holds. He is involved in youth work and has held regional offices in several community organizations in addition to being active in professional student affairs organizations.

Dr. Douglas holds the B.S. and M.Ed. degrees from Eastern Illinois University, and the Ed.D. from The University of Tennessee.

Chapter 18

FISCAL RESOURCE MANAGEMENT: BACKGROUND AND RELEVANCE FOR STUDENT AFFAIRS

Dwight O. Douglas

The ability to manage programs, allocate resources, and justify increased funding is receiving greater attention than ever before. Staff in student affairs need to be knowledgeable of management applications in order to achieve equitable allocations of increasingly scarce institutional resources. As institutions of higher education continue to grow and reevaluate priorities, the cost effectiveness of student affairs programs may be called into question. Success in fiscal management will determine scope and ultimate success of the total student affairs operation.

While competence in the developmental and programmatic aspects of the field is necessary for the student affairs professional, knowledge of management theory and technical fiscal procedures is also required. Because of specialized technical knowledge and managerial skills required for implementing certain services such as housing and food service, some college presidents have placed these areas under business or fiscal affairs in their organizations. On other campuses where the student affairs professionals have evidenced high levels of management skills, they are viewed by campus fiscal officers as partners in campus management. Acceptance is particularly notable in colleges where student affairs has responsibility for the recruiting and admissions program so essential to the institution's survival.

Student affairs professionals, with their understanding of human dynamics and interest in developmental processes of students, link two critical areas of the institution— academic affairs and business affairs. Nevertheless, some misunderstanding of roles of student affairs professionals often occurs.

Berry (1976) and Crookston (1976) both noted that terminology is still a problem in student affairs. Confusion continues as to specific meanings for terms such as student life, student development, student personnel services, and student affairs, because these terms are often not reflective of actual functions performed. Miller and Prince (1976) reflected a view of student affairs practice that emphasized student development and called for facilitating achievement of higher levels of cultural awareness, personal value systems, self-awareness, interpersonal skills, and community responsibility. Management skills are needed by student affairs administrators to enable them to create environments where student development can flourish. Policy formulation, technical knowledge, and fiscal resource management need to be recognized.

Concerning fiscal resource management, the suggestion has been made that the business office's golden rule is "those who have the gold, rule." From a student affairs perspective, effective leadership must marshal resources to accomplish tasks of enhancing cognitive and personality development in students.

The lack of adequate resources for both personnel and operating expenses has been one of the major problems associated with student affairs administration over the years. Although considerable information is available about funding, most of it concerns managing resources. Minimal information, on the other hand, is available to explain the processes that result in determining funding levels, to outline detailed strategies for justifying increased funding, or to show a need that is greater than other justified needs in the institution. Current practices of fiscal resources management suggest that management involves a combination of resources and activities so as to produce a desired outcome (Harpel, 1976). Today's successful student affairs administrator also must be able to find ways to increase resources by generating additional income, altering institutional budgets, or using a combination of the two.

Although student affairs units may receive proportional increases similar to other institutional units, the actual cost of doing business may be greater for student affairs units such as financial aid, admissions, and registration because of the rate of inflationary increase involved in these activities. For example, because of increasing expenses for recruitment such as postage, printing, and travel, a reasonable budget fund increment only increases the real financial deficit and requires additional cost cutting measures to maintain past levels of activity.

Harpel (1976) noted that student affairs administrators are particularly vulnerable to criticism concerning management skills because student affairs functions historically have been justified more on idealistic and humanistic grounds than on tangible evidence of impact or results. For years the most successful justification for funds, as opposed to the best justification, was based on the role of the institution acting in place of the parent, not on the actual needs of students for developmental programs or services.

Often, the relative lack of importance assigned to student development programming by institutional leaders reflects their limited understanding of this important area and limits the likelihood for larger proportions of institutional resources being invested in student affairs. A greater understanding of student affairs functions is needed by the collegiate community. Student affairs professionals have responsibility to the educational process involved. The successful student affairs administrator is one who has a thorough understanding of the institution's budgeting process, has the capacity to inform others of the importance of student affairs, and utilizes technical management skills to acquire resources essential to accomplish its mission.

BUDGETS AS MANAGEMENT TOOLS

One of the best and most effective management tools is a budget representing the placement of funds in categories designed to achieve goals of the institution. Because of institutional systems, state laws, traditions, and types of educational missions, the budgeting process may vary from institution to institution. Budgeting is to be viewed as a continuous activity of allocating funds to meet changing requirements and priorities.

A common method for budgetary change is the budget amendment. This is an institutional form that, when approved, changes categories or amounts of funds as originally allocated. A misconception regarding permanence of budget cycles hinders far-ranging planning. According to Barber (1974),

> budget considerations really begin every time a planning decision is made, or every time a planning decision is altered to respond to the effects of changing social, economic, and other conditions which cannot be anticipated in the development of the original budget.
>
> A change or alteration of a plan requires a budget action to adjust the allocation of resources. Like sights on a rifle, budgeting serves to direct an aim (planning) . . . if the aimer moves, or if external conditions change (such as a windage change), the sights on a rifle have to be adjusted to provide for the unexpected effects or the original aim will not hit the mark. The same is true of the effects of changing circumstances on original budgetary priorities and cost estimates—hence, the need for amendments to an original budget. (p. 1)

The exact definition of *budget* or *budgeting* depends on whether one conceives the term as specific or general. Budgets are established for various types of projects that require specific treatments. But the word budget itself also is used in an overall generic sense. The National Association of College and University Business Officers (1974) defined a budget as *a statement of proposed expenditures for a fixed period or for a specific project or program and as a proposed means of financing expenditures.*

For the purposes of this chapter such a definition is accurate in terms of the tangible product. However, this definition does not include prior or established funds or the thought processes leading up to or involving these funds. A budget, therefore, is a tool to be used as a yardstick by which activity toward a goal can be measured. In most instances, this measurement is from a previously justified point rather than a reconsideration of what constituted the original justification. The yearly allocation of new resources into specific budgets represents changing priorities of the institution on a continuing basis. Much of this allocation, however, often is based on annualizing expenses, or prorating increases, rather than resulting from decisions regarding pre-established beginning points or establishing new points of departure.

For budgets to be used as planning tools in an optimal sense, one should view the process as having two parts: the formulation of the budget and the continuous analysis of how the desired results are being achieved. For the first purpose, reviewing recent data at the time of budget preparation is desirable. A routine mechanism in the budget preparation cycle allows the current year's budget and expenses to be available for review as well as the expenses of the immediate previous year. This review provides a logical framework from which to plan. However, this approach has at least three disadvantages. First, the approach is based on the assumption that current expenses and programs need annualizing. Second, budget preparation occurs during the current year, and, therefore, any comparison with the current year is incomplete, thus requiring reliance on the previous year. The third disadvantage is that some atypical expense may have affected the base either up or down, thus making application of percentage on the most recent complete year impractical.

The main purpose for budgeting is to provide financial information about a program or rate of achievement toward a goal. Preparation of the budget from a departmental standpoint involves determining what is needed or desired for the coming year. Additional items of expenditure are reviewed through the administrative hierarchy, evaluated, consolidated, and put into an order of priority at each administrative level and then presented at an institution-wide budget conference. When the spectrum of requests has been heard, decisions for allocations or partial allocations can be made. This process allows the adjustment of funds without annualizing the expense level for those areas thought immediately most important. Specific restrictions or modifications peculiar to a particular budget type should be considered in this process.

FINANCIAL STATEMENT AS MANAGEMENT TOOL

A second management tool is the financial statement, which helps monitor how the desired results are being utilized toward a given objective. Too often this part of the program simply is subject to the amount of funds originally allocated or made available at a later time.

Once a budget is approved and the fiscal year (FY) progresses, keeping an exact account of how much money is available, how much has been obligated, and how the spending for the current year compares to a previous year is difficult in most budgetary systems. Statements of income and expense are developed to supply this necessary information.

Statements of income and expense reflect accrued income and expenditures and provide current information with which to update plans continuously. Oversimplified, these documents ordinarily are prepared monthly and compare on both a dollar and a percentage basis the relative amount of income and expenses received and expended for that month and for the year up to the date prepared. These totals can be compared with each month of the previous year or with the previous year-to-date totals to capture an overall perspective of the relative relationships of one month or one year to the previous month or year. Knowledge of the sum of expenses, the amount of income, and the cost of planned expenditures allows goals to be adjusted at any time.

The most frequently used statements appear in monthly reports prepared by the chief business officer, and in public institutions are used as part of a system or legislative report. The major value of these reports is that they express the situation in the simplest terms for external agencies and for general internal use. These reports are not as valuable for specific internal planning, however.

For the purposes of illustration, a residence hall budget and a corresponding financial statement can be analyzed. Figure 18.1 provides a sample of a monthly statement of operations for a residence hall. As the residence hall rents are deposited, the appropriate residence hall account is credited. Thus, the August and September monthly financial reports would show an excess of income over expenditures. For the uninformed reader this operating gain would appear to be a large profit, which might suggest that rates were set too high, funds were available for other purposes, or no rent increase would be necessary the following year. Analysis of the same type of financial report in February also could show that a large profit was realized. Reference to Figure 18.1 shows what might appear to be a 30 % operating gain. Realistically, three income periods—Summer, Fall, and Winter Quarter; or summer, first semester, and second semester— were realized in the income category, but only seven of the twelve monthly expenses were reflected in the expense category. Subsequent monthly statements would show larger increases in expenses than in income until June when income for the year and expenses for the year will even out for a one year budget.

Some institutions compensate for this disparity by holding the income in a single account and crediting the respective residence hall accounts by a predetermined percentage on a monthly basis. This accrual method does have the merit

(Continued on Page 623)

	ACTUAL FY '98	%	YEAR TO DATE BUDGET FY '99	%	ACTUAL FY '99	%
REVENUE						
Student Rentals	2,253,468.81	92.2	2,483,937.00	93.7	2,445,102.60	93.6
Forfeited Deposits	27,883.75	1.1	29,102.00	1.1	22,319.00	.9
Special Groups	70,391.14	2.9	34,800.00	1.3	44,743.77	1.7
Vending Commissions	34,984.79	1.4	47,912.00	1.8	34,062.35	1.3
Laundry Commissions	8,737.84	.4	54,299.00	2.1	5,545.43	.2
Washer/Dryer Revenue	47,636.64	1.9			60,736.10	2.3
Other	1,452.31	.1			1,064.20	
TOTAL REVENUE	2,444,555.28	100.0	2,650,050.00	100.0	2,613,573.45	100.0
OPERATING EXPENSE						
Salaries	260,686.18	10.7	316,356.00	11.9	303,510.70	11.6
Temporary Wages	445,963.43	18.2	337,867.00	12.7	346,640.11	13.2
Employee Meals	14,039.30	.6	9,406.00	.4	2,178.22	.1
Staff Benefits	36,632.35	1.5	36,938.00	1.4	33,050.37	1.3
Supplies & Printing	56,001.46	2.3	62,284.00	2.3	52,630.80	2.0
Laundry	8,690.30	.4	11,792.00	.5	6,527.15	.2
Maintenance & Repairs	184,726.70	7.6	245,366.00	9.3	225,293.17	8.6
Utilities	287,221.65	11.7	321,363.00	12.1	321,164.94	12.3
Equipment	3,430.80	.1	23,839.00	.9	13,412.00	.5
Telephone	107,083.64	4.4	145,868.00	5.5	143,111.49	5.5
Insurance	14,050.83	.6	31,576.00	1.2	28,108.88	1.1
Travel	1,405.05				122.02	
Debt Service	101,095.00	4.1	101,636.00	3.9	100,365.75	
TOTAL EXPENSE	1,521,026.69	62.2	1,644,291.00	62.0	1,576,115.60	60.3
OPERATING GAIN (LOSS)	923,528.59	37.8	1,005,759.00	38.0	1,037,457.85	39.7

Figure 18.1. Monthly operations statement for a residence hall.

of allowing checks of insufficient funds to clear and refunds to be processed, but the income accrued is credited to a holding account rather than the account of the originating agency. The elimination of a holding account results in an income being credited sporadically, but actual activity can be compared between financial statements of different months and of the same months of different years.

A desirable use of an accrual statement is to take the budget amount for the year and allocate both in terms of income and expenses in increments reflecting the actual desired income and spending throughout the budget period. The analysis that then can be made of comparable timeframes in terms of actual income and expenses can be used to determine if optional expenses can be incurred. The comparisons are illustrated in Figure 18.2.

Actual revenue for the month of February was greater than the actual revenue for FY '98 but not as great as had been anticipated for FY '99.

The operating gain for the month was greater than FY '98 but not as great as had been anticipated for the budget of FY '99.

On a year to date basis the revenue was less than anticipated.

On a year to date basis the operating expenses were less than expected.

On a year to date basis the net gain was less than expected.

In Figure 18.3 are indicated the same comparisons at the conclusion of the year. Both the income and the expenses were overstated when the budgeted figures and the actual figures were compared. The net operating gain was not what had been anticipated. Although the figures differ between the budgeted amounts and the actual amounts, comparison

(Continued on Page 628)

			MONTH			
REVENUE	ACTUAL FY '98	%	BUDGET FY '99	%	ACTUAL FY '99	%
Student Rentals	35,945.85	92.8	50,350.00	95.7	45,269.00	93.7
Forfeited Deposits	424.00	1.0			324.00	.8
Special Groups	502.00	1.3			158.50	.3
Vending Commissions	774.42	2.0	1,240.00	2.4	1,031.67	2.1
Laundry Commissions	155.78	.4	1,020.00	1.9	70.95	.1
Washer/Dryer Revenue	953.60	2.5			1,424.90	2.9
Other	19.55				44.90	.1
TOTAL REVENUE	38,775.19	100.0	52,610.00	100.0	48,323.92	100.0
OPERATING EXPENSES						
Salaries	5,365.01	13.8	6,376.00	12.0	6,233.77	12.9
Temporary Wages	6,497.11	16.8	5,048.00	9.6	5,074.66	10.5
Employee Meals	(41.53)	(.1)	100.00	.2		
Staff Benefits	454.18	1.2	545.00	1.0	586.34	1.2
Supplies & Printing	651.63	1.7	1,275.00	2.4	529.68	1.1
Laundry			226.00	.4		
Maintenance & Repairs	2,070.68	5.3	2,826.00	5.4	3,187.85	6.6
Utilities	4,422.90	11.4	5,085.00	9.7	4,636.92	9.6
Equipment						
Telephone	2,533.30	6.5	3,342.00	6.4	3,578.42	7.4
Insurance	298.90	.8	370.00	.7	370.00	.8
Travel						
Miscellaneous						
TOTAL EXPENSES	22,252.18	57.4	25,193.00	47.9	24,197.64	
OPERATING GAIN (LOSS)	16,523.01	42.6	27,417.00	52.1	24,126.28	
Less: Other Expenses						
Administrative Charge	1,600.00	4.1	2,399.00			
Debt Service	2,424.00	6.3	7,574.00			
Sub-Total	4,024.00	10.4				
NET GAIN (LOSS)	12,499.01					

Figure 18.2. Residence hall statement of operations (February FY '99).

Figure 18.2. Continued.

			YEAR-TO-DATE			
FY 2000 BUDGET	ACTUAL FY '98	%	BUDGET FY ''99	%	ACTUAL FY '99	%
369,700.00	184,720.20	85.7	229,350.00	92.3	210,150.00	90.4
4,200.00	4,721.00	2.2	3,150.00	1.3	3,144.00	1.4
5,300.00	15,080.00	7.0	4,600.00	1.9	7,228.50	3.1
10,000.00	5,069.97	2.4	6,200.00	2.5	4,513.10	
8,200.00	712.47	.3	5,090.00	2.0	375.87	
	5,066.10				6,856.25	
	107.91				153.04	.1
397,400.00	215,477.65	100.0	248,390.00	100.0	232,420.76	100.0

63,138.00	34,094.07	15.8
62,931.00	47,608.57	22.1
1,080.00	2,935.34	1.4
6,100.00	3,372.85	
12,750.00	6,193.65	
2,260.00	767.82	
29,880.00	13,821.44	
52,512.00		
3,016.00		
33,420.00		
3,700.00		

REVENUE	ACTUAL FT '98	%	BUDGET FY '99	%	ACTUAL FY '99	%
Student Rentals	6,836.06	44.1	9,320.00	89.2	7,747.00	60.3
Rental Adjustment	7,351.00	47.5			3,138.00	24.4
Forfeited Deposits	166.00	1.0			125.00	1.0
Special Groups	25.00	.2	700.00	6.7	104.00	.8
Vending Commissions	800.49	5.0	240.00	2.3	1,286.90	10.0
Laundry Commissions	(25.04)	(.2)	190.00	1.8	14.35	.1
Washer/Dryer Revenue	393.15	2.4			398.95	3.1
Other	10.01				44.26	.3
TOTAL REVENUE	15,556.67	100.0	10,450.00	100.0	12,858.46	100.0
OPERATING EXPENSES						
Salaries	1,832.90	11.9	5,343.00	51.1	3,286.09	25.6
Temporary Wages	3,980.48	25.8	5,582.00	53.4	4,260.26	33.0
Employee Meals			110.00	1.1	19.67	.1
Staff Benefits	324.33	2.1	508.00	4.9	580.71	4.5
Supplies & Printing	207.10	1.3	1,275.00	12.2	1,241.85	9.7
Laundry	431.37	2.8	226.00	2.2	76.13	.6
Maintenance & Repairs	11,270.13	72.9	2,830.00	27.1	4,203.98	32.7
Utilities	4,421.58	28.6	5,087.00	48.7	4,744.49	36.9
Equipment					910.00	7.1
Telephone	3,437.12	22.3	3,342.00	32.0	3,599.85	28.0
Insurance	298.91	1.9	370.00	3.5	240.63	1.9
Travel						
Miscellaneous	35.00	.2				
TOTAL EXPENSES	26,238.92	169.8	24,673.00	236.1	23,163.66	180.1
OPERATING GAIN (LOSS)	(10,682.25)	(69.8)	(14,223.00)	(136.1)	(10,305.20)	
Less: Other Expenses						
Administrative Charge	1,030.00	6.7	2,399.00	23.0		
Debt Service	2,426.00	15.7	7,573.00			
Sub-Total	3,456.00	22.4	9,972.00			
NET GAIN (LOSS)	(14,138.25)	(92.2)	(24,195.00)	(231.6)		

Figure 18.3. Residential hall Statement of operations (June FY '99).

Figure 18.3. Continued .

			YEAR-TO-DATE			
FY 2000 BUDGET	ACTUAL FY '98	%	BUDGET FY '99	%	ACTUAL FT '99	%
369,700.00	273,688.00	84.5	369,700.00	23.0	329,184.00	89
	7,351.00	2.3			3,138.00	
4,200.00	6,187.00	1.9	4,200.00	1.1	4,619.00	1
5,300.00	19,283.50	6.0	5,300.00	1.3	8,361.00	2
10,000.00	8,321.19	2.6	10,000.00	2.5	8,778.14	
8,200.00	942.73	.3	8,200.00	2.1	516.46	
	7,710.05	2.4			12,026.11	
	154.86				313.82	
397,400.00	323,638.33	100.0	397,400.00	100.0		
63,138.00	51,169.51	15.8	63,138.00	15.9		
62,931.00	68,854.44	21.3	62,931.00	15.8		
1,080.00	3,299.66	1.0				
6,100.00	5,084.18	1.6				
12,750.00	8,554.41	2.6				
2,260.00	1,973.83	.6				
29,880.00						
52,512.00						
3,016.00						
33,420.00						

between the percentages of respective categories reflect the precise differences between categories of income and expenses. For example, it was anticipated that 15.9% of the operating expenses would be for salaries. In actuality 15.4 % was spent for salaries. However, more was spent than had been planned in temporary employee wages.

For the experienced student affairs administrator, much of what has been stated is well understood. Emphasis, then, is placed on refining financial data gathered by the institution into a workable format that can be understood and utilized by all professional staff. The format of financial statements should not take precedent over their use as planning tools. Financial statements are to be designed so that planning can be done with realistic budgetary factors. The first step in this planning is the determination of the fiscal resources.

The fiscal resources used by student affairs units are received on a periodic basis according to a method of allocation. Possibilities for receiving operating resources are numerous and may exist in multiple combinations. The important consideration is the definition or application of the budget as it applies to the institution or program area. Is the budget a commitment toward a direction in an area or for a specific program? Can it be increased or decreased? Is it dependent on external factors? After these questions have been answered, the best budget type can be determined.

TYPES OF BUDGETS

Some budgets are developed on the basis of computation because they derive their identity primarily from a certain cost factor or other mechanisms. Others are formulated according to a base of expenditure (Robins, 1973). A budget is usually labeled as a specific type according to whether a particular fund is referenced from a computational standpoint or from an expenditure standpoint.

Computational Budgets

Line Item Budget. This is a common budget used when overall development of any program or activity initially requires the enumeration of various components. Usually these components are listed by category or sub-category that are represented by respective lines in the calculation. A line can represent a sum of individual expenditures, or individual expenditures may be broken down specifically on additional lines. For example, a line for personal service expenses could be expanded with additional lines listing each position, staff member's name, and source of funds. This approach has the advantage of specifying resources for particular programs, but has a possible disadvantage of limiting flexibility.

Program Budget. When the primary objective is to outline a total program and the cost associated with the various aspects of the program, a program budget could be utilized. This type of budget allows the overall cost associated with various developmental components of a program to be evaluated. Partial allocation might result in accomplishing a predetermined amount or segment of a proposed program. Grant proposals could be considered in this category.

Incremental Budget. Incremental budgets ordinarily take the previous year's total budget or expenses and add some increment or percent increase. The increment may vary from budget to budget based on the perceived value of the program or on the actual cost incurred during the most recent year. This approach works well on budgets that are similar throughout an institution. For instance, if the aggregate of current salaries in a department or larger unit is to be raised by an average amount, this increment may be added to the budget. An extended application of the approach, also based on the previous year's expenditure, may result in a more accurate allocation. If during the previous year an additional allocation was received to meet expenses or designated for a particular project, the sum of this allocation prior to the additional increment would need to be analyzed. In the first case the budget might be adjusted upward before figuring an increment, and in the second case the budget might be restored to the previous level. Unless care is exercised, the one-time allocation as well as the additional increment based on this additional sum of money would appear as a routine part of the budget for the following year.

All categories of expense do not rise at the same rate. An incremental approach across the board may allow expenditures in certain areas to grow at a rapid rate while curtailing efforts in more critically important areas.

Zero Based Budget. This type of budget starts with no assumptions or set priorities according to functions. Although the zero based budget seems ideal in concept, much longitudinal planning can be lost. Flexibility to deal with changing needs is minimized. Zero based budgeting is used to the best advantage in initial planning stages. Zero based budgets also take considerable time and require total institutional commitment if they are to be effective.

Formula Based Budgets. These budgets derive their funding level from a formula that considers predetermined and agreed upon factors (Maw, Richards, & Crosby, 1976). Formula based budgets have the advantage of being flexible. For example, a slight shifting of the formula or formula elements could be made to accommodate a change in appropriations from a state legislature.

Base of Expenditure

Auxiliary Budgets. Auxiliary budgets deal with activities that are self-supporting or largely self-supporting. They are used almost exclusively in public colleges. An auxiliary generates its income by providing sales or services that are different from activities funded from tuition or fees. Auxiliary budgets often include residence halls, food services, bookstores, or many aspects of student centers.

Construction Budgets. Construction budgets are for construction projects. Often these are budgeted separately because of the length of the project or the ability to identify later the cost associated with the project. They may receive resources other than institutional funds such as bonds, grants, and donations. They also may be developed as a category in other budgets.

Student Aid Budgets. These budgets are for very specialized purposes—scholarships, grants, and other student financial aid programs. Funds might come from state and/or federally appropriated monies and are usually augmented by fund drives or contributions. Both public and private institutions also utilize income from endowment funds for student financial assistance.

Education and General Budget. The Education and General budget is for educational programs and general support services. Expenses usually include broad categories such as construction, research, service, and the library.

Lists of budget categories and types of expenditures could be continued. However, the more divisions that are made in the overall expense pattern of an institution, the less the distinction between the budgets. Labels given the budgets outline the type of restrictions that might be present as well as identify some reference point in case a particular item needs review. For example, the overall category of student activity funds might include several types of budget categories. Knowing a student activity fund with generated income was involved would enable budget personnel to determine the precise nature of the account.

LONGITUDINAL FISCAL MANAGEMENT

Once various budgets have been approved, the process of managing and allocating resources according to changing variables begins. Management of functions in umbrella type organizations follows one of two general patterns (1) allocating the total of available funds to the individual departments involved and requiring some percentage of return for a central support, or (2) maintaining funds centrally and allocating basic needs of the departments. Depending on the institution, the relative merits of the major type of budget activity involved is one of refinement, stabilization, or program development. The most common approach is a combination of styles in which funds for operational expenses allow some latitude by the unit head, and some of the allocation is retained in a central account for handling emergencies, changes in priority, or cost overruns. This combination approach to budget allocation eliminates the negative aspect of returning funds to a central administrative agency and provides the positive reinforcement for some degree of decision making at the local budget unit level. Regardless of the planning procedures, monthly financial statements need to be monitored by the chief student affairs officer.

Actualization of plans usually does not occur according to schedule or with the anticipated cost. As a result, considerable deviation may be necessary during the course of the fiscal year. Deviations may occur because of changing priorities, new information, different options, or opportunities that later become available. The staff needs to regard any initial allocation as a reflection of the best thinking at the time the budget is established, rather than identifying it as being permanent or resulting from an unalterable ranking of priorities.

Because change frequently is due to different variables interacting throughout the year, several mechanisms exist for dealing with expenses running above or below estimates. If the general budget plan does not allow for an actual change in the budget during the year, savings realized from projects completed for less than the anticipated amount usually are maintained in a central fund, and additional expenses beyond those budgeted items are not allowed. In cases where over expenditures may be approved, funding is provided from a central pool, or an over expense is reimbursed. The advantage to holding to the original budget is that more accurate initial planning may be accomplished with hard decisions on priorities being decided in the original budget. The disadvantages are that plans must be made well in advance, changes of plans are more difficult to accommodate, and the administrator has to make decisions within established priorities.

Another way of accommodating deviations is through a budget amendment process. This process differs from the earlier example in that the allocation of a certain amount of money is thought of more as representing an allocation to meet a total need rather than the sum of precise needs. During the course of the budget year, money may be moved from one category to another to meet changes in expenses or in priorities. So that an accurate account in terms of types of expenses may be maintained, money is placed originally in categories according to anticipated expense. During the year, a desired addition in one category may be accommodated by a corresponding reduction in another. For example, the equipment category may be reduced and the operating supply category raised. If a staff member resigns in midyear, the remaining salary may be amended to any of several categories. Amendment of major sums may require higher administrative approval to insure that continuing obligations are not incurred, such as using salary savings to purchase a computer with no source of funds for paying future operating expenses.

Regardless of the general budget plan utilized, mechanisms for continued decision making must exist. A requirement to operate within a fixed budget is often mandated. If there have been a large number of staff vacancies, a decrease or increase in expenses, or the receipt of additional money, requests need to be submitted through the administrative structure to have these funds evaluated and considered for other uses.

In institutions where changing budget categories are possible, salary savings from vacant positions is likely. These can be accumulated, marked for priority, and expended at a level higher than the departmental level. In student affairs areas, increased costs have made purchase of major pieces of equipment extremely difficult. Accumulating salary savings can amount to large enough sums to purchase a major piece of equipment. Initial reaction to this approach, where it has not been established previously as an institutional policy, is often neutral at best. It is sometimes viewed as "some other department receiving our savings." For the intermediate term, however, this method is an appropriate way to accelerate services and programs offered students beyond those originally provided in the institutional budget.

The previous example illustrates how savings can be accumulated to make major purchases that small individual departments would be unable to purchase. A corollary to this process is the treatment of areas that have the ability to generate needed funds. Each chief student affairs officer is faced with the problem of how best to handle auxiliary income and personnel. For instance, if the housing department requires 25% of the administrative time of the dean or vice-president, should one-fourth of the officer's salary be charged against the housing budget? Regardless of the answer, should any housing surplus funds be used to underwrite other campus student services? The initial answer to both questions probably is negative, but the principle is the same as that utilized in the general tuition mechanism for students who elect courses in the humanities as opposed to courses in the sciences. In most operations the solution is a matter of custom, tradition, and degree.

This example indicates consideration of utilizing housing or auxiliary generated funds for the good of the general student body. A converse of this situation would be allowing a housing rate to be charged that would accelerate the expansion of programs in the residence life area at a more rapid rate than similar or corresponding student programs receiving appropriated funds.

Recently, longitudinal fiscal management practiced by student affairs administrators has exhibited an increasing emphasis on salary practices. As discussed previously, salary savings from vacant positions are often utilized to purchase items not funded in the original budget. This approach allows for an accelerated ability to develop programs and provide services thought desirable within the student affairs program. However, replacing professional staff that have the necessary training and experience is becoming increasingly more difficult. What is becoming increasingly more necessary, in order to be competitive in salary, is to offer a new staff member a salary close to that earned by current staff. This reduces the savings which have been utilized for the accelerated development of services and programs and, in addition, establishes a salary compression among staff which may not even have the merit of being equitable. Conversely, to not offer a market salary to new colleagues is to repress the value of the student affairs professional in the higher education setting.

A solution to the personnel aspect of this situation is being recognized by several states by providing funds to adjust the salaries of current staff without regard to annual salary increase allocations.

BEYOND THE FORMULA, ALLOCATION, OR BUDGET

Just as the budget represents resources allocated for programs, these programs represent decisions that they are worthy of expenditure. Legislative acts and the tone of society during the past three decades have staunchly supported higher education. Federal programs made resources available for considerable expansion of student financial assistance in higher education. Grant opportunities and other outside income encouraged developing the resource facilities of the institution. Three decades seems like a long period of time, but the change was so gradual that the difference between the beginning and the current complexity of multifaceted institutions was never marked.

For example, 30 years ago the management of residence halls under business officers was a logical arrangement on many campuses. The size of many institutions was such that departments of housing were not necessary. General funds were utilized to cover any deficit, and during periods of financial success profits were used for the good of the institution. This method was logical and worked well. As campuses grew, the scope of the housing and residence life programs on many campuses increased. A decline of the *in loco parentis* concept coupled with the rapid growth in size of institutions accelerated the establishment of separate departments of housing to administer both facilities and programs. The earlier format for administering housing facilities seemed no longer advantageous.

Academic expansion brought about the need to review the best uses for older residence halls. Often located around the perimeter of the old established campus, these buildings were at the core of the emerging campus. At many institutions conversion of housing space to classroom or office space occurred, making newer, cleaner, but also more expensive housing operations. Newer and larger residences often necessitated greater attention to management and business aspects of the operation.

Although departments of housing were established, their authority often was not clear. For example, was the washer and dryer operation a campus auxiliary or a housing operation? If it were an auxiliary operation, should rent be paid to housing for the space utilized? If not, how was the revenue to be replaced? Where was the money from the student housing contracts and the income from vending machines accrued? If institutional income was invested, how was the allocation of interest to be made? The creation of housing departments gave the impression that all of traditional housing functions were incorporated into the new unit. This was not necessarily the case, and these concerns needed attention. In most institutions, no overall plan was adopted. Decisions were made to correct faults brought to the attention of the executive officers of the institution rather than from any studied or long-range plan of action.

The increase in size of many institutions compounded the work load in many areas of campus operations. Many decisions, valid at one time, now needed further review. Using the housing example, does any college area need its own maintenance force? The logical answer would be negative until continued growth resulted in an operation requiring a maintenance staff of a specialized nature. If this concept is considered in terms of duplication of services and applied to the budget process in areas of an instructional nature, the beginning of program conflict is clear. For instance, how many centers for counseling should a campus have? The psychology department, the educational psychology department, the college of education, the mental health unit, the counseling center, and the academic advisement office each might desire to act as the primary counseling service for the campus. In some areas, duplication may be proper; in others, consolidation is better both in terms of quality and economy. Although funds are monitored as expended by an area, monitoring is less effective for funds spent on programs when those programs cross area lines.

For the neophyte in budget management an understanding of the budgeting process in higher education is necessary. Sometimes administrators respond to requests for additional programs by saying no available funds exist. This type of response tends to lead to the theory that if funds can be found, a particular program can be implemented. More realistically, what is meant is that the money that is available has been allocated for something thought to be of a higher priority. Thus no "funds" exist! The question is one of program priority as opposed exclusively to a lack of funds.

In the original budgeting process, legislators have the tendency to take care of particular problems that affect a certain constituency, even though these areas may not be the highest priority of the institution. Funds are allocated, but sometimes not to the area thought most important by the institution. Agreement between all of the parties involved is difficult to achieve, but is extremely necessary.

Allocations and allocation procedures to institutions that are members of a state system of higher education vary. Political processes influence whether allocations are made to a state governing board or an individual institution, whether general allocations are made to a governing body with instructions, or whether allocations are made to an institution for a prescribed purpose.

DETERMINING THE PLANNING BACKGROUND

In preparation for the various levels of budget conferences, student affairs professionals annually review their allocations and program expenditures. Student affairs administrators preparing budgets must have a complete knowledge of financial needs and priorities not only of student affairs but also of other units of the institution. Because of competition for funds, specific knowledge of needs or selling points of the competition will help shape the best arguments for student affairs.

This preparation often takes a three step form: a review of the institution's budgets, a specific review of areas that have received greater than incremental jumps over the past three years, and an analysis of any historical patterns regarding assignment of new functions and new funds. The consolidated budget of most institutions contains data relative to at least the most recent fiscal year so that any comparison does not require the use of a second document.

The first step, a page by page review of various institutional sub-unit budgets set against the knowledge of the increased funds allocated the institution for the second of the two years, will provide the beginning background regarding funding level and the rate of incremental increases. These yearly comparisons need to be reviewed with full knowledge of the number of students, their full-time equivalency (FTE or EFT), and any other factors that might have affected the allocation. This review occasionally will indicate functions, departments, schools, or colleges that received larger increases than what has now been recognized as an incremental jump.

As a second step these areas should be reviewed closely to determine the specific item or program that received the increase. The completed budget review will indicate these areas, and often the type of pattern or prevailing thought that resulted in the allocation of greater than an incremental increase is apparent.

The third step of preparation is an analysis of historical patterns. In some cases, when a new task is assigned within the institution, funds accompany the assignment. In other areas, an assignment is made without the accompaniment of the appropriate additional funds. Too often, student affairs professionals accept additional responsibility without the corresponding remuneration. This may happen because they have a desire to serve students or the educational community and also because they have not been successful historically in the acquisition of additional funds.

Preparation of student affairs statistical and financial data throughout the course of the year plus information received from the review of budgets, the review of the strategy for above average incremental increases, and the analysis of the historical patterns of assignments, and funding of the institution should result in a more successful allocation procedure.

If an unsatisfactory allocation does occur, the next step would be a refinement of the first three steps, plus an institutional review of particular areas for which funds were requested and a corresponding review of those areas in comparable institutions. Although this review might seem to be a first priority, often more questions are raised than answers obtained by comparing institutional programs. The fact that another institution does things differently does not mean one institution is either over managing or under managing, but rather that the policy is more accurate in terms of particular responsibilities.

RECAPITULATION

Effective resource management in student affairs has been examined. In addition, some of the basic fiscal management functions and types of budgets have been outlined. Budgeting and managing are both continuing and cyclical processes needing constant adjustment and evaluation. Therefore, the successful and effective student affairs administrator recognizes the need for money management skills. Effective fiscal management enhances the credibility of student affairs administrators among institutional decision makers and policy planners. This credibility can be used to promote accomplishment of the central mission of student affairs—student development.

REFERENCES

Barber, A. W. (1974). *On the budget.* The University of Georgia Community News, Athens, GA: The University of Georgia.

Berry, M. (1976). The state of student affairs: A review of the literature. *NASPA Journal, 13,* 2-4.

Crookston, B. B. (1976). Student personnel: All hail and farewell. *Personnel and Guidance Journal, 55,* 26-9.

Harpel, R. L. (1976). *Planning, budgeting, and evaluation in student affairs programs: A manual for administrators.* Portland, OR: National Association of Student Personnel Administrators.

Maw, I. I., Richards, N. A., & Crosby, H. J. (1976). *Formula budgeting: An application to student affairs.* Washington, DC: American College Personnel Association.

Miller, T. K., & Prince, J. S. (1976). *The future of student affairs: A guide to student development for tomorrow's higher education.* San Francisco: Jossey-Bass.

National Association of College and University Business Officers (NACUBO). (1974). *College and university business administration.* Washington, DC: Author.

Robins, G. B. (1973). *Understanding the college budget.* Athens, GA: University of Georgia Institute of Higher Education.

SUGGESTED READINGS

Barr, M.J. (1988). Managing money. In M.L. Upcraft, & M.J. Barr (Eds.), *Managing student affairs effectively*, (pp. 21-28). New Directions For Student Affairs (No. 41). San Francisco: Jossey-Boss.

Berg, D.J., & Skogley, C.M. (Eds.). (1985). *Making the budget process work*. New Directions for Higher Education (No. 52). San Francisco: Jossey-Bass.

Chaffee, E.E. (1983). The role of rationality in university budgeting. *Research In Higher Education, 19* (4), 387-406.

Harpel, R. L. (1976). *Planning, budgeting, and evaluation in student programs: A manual for administrators*. Columbus, OH: National Association of Student Personnel Administrators, Division of Research and Program Development.

Hoverland, H.. McInturff, P., & Rohm, E.E.T. (Eds.). (1986). *Crisis management in higher education*. New Directions for Higher Education, No. 55. San Francisco: Jossey-Bass.

Kaludis, G. (Ed.). (1973). *Strategies for budgeting*. New Directions for Higher Education (No. 2). San Francisco: Jossey-Bass.

Maw, I. I., Richards, N. A., & Crosby, H. J. (1976). *Formula budgeting: An application to student affairs*. Washington, DC: American College Personnel Association.

Meyerson, E. (1985). Changing values and priorities in funding student services. *NASPA Journal, 23* (1), 53-58.

Moxley, L.S., & Duke, B.W. (1986). Setting priorities for student affairs programs for budgetary purposes: A case study. *NASPA Journal, 23* (4), 21-28.

Schick, A.G.(1985). University budgeting: Administrative perspective, budget structure, and budget process. *Academy of Management Review, 10* (4), 794-802.

Daniel A. Hallenbeck, Ph.D., is Associate Vice President for Student Affairs at the University of Georgia. Prior to this position, he was Director of University Housing in the same institution for 14 years. Previously he held positions as Assistant Director of Residence at Iowa State University and Director of Housing Facilities at the University of Northern Iowa.

Dr. Hallenbeck hold the Bachelor of Arts degree from the University of Northern Iowa. The Master's degree from Michigan State University and the Ph.D. from Iowa State University. He served as President of the Association of College and University Housing Officers-International in 1988-89. He also has been active in the American College Personnel Association's Commission III and the National Association of Student Personnel Administrators. For nine years he served as advisor to the student organization, the National Association of College and University Residence Hall, Incorporated.

CHAPTER 19

MANAGING PHYSICAL FACILITIES

Daniel A. Hallenbeck

The student affairs administrator is charged with the creation of out-of-class learning environments that support the educational mission of the institution and provide for student growth and development. Three facets of this responsibility are creation of environments, management of physical facilities, and structuring of facilities to provide services to students by promoting staff efficiency and interaction.

CREATION OF ENVIRONMENTS

College campuses are dynamic, ever-changing communities. Individuals who inhabit the campuses are constantly in a state of transition—students are arriving, working, studying, growing, and leaving. Faculty and staff work, administer, teach, conduct research, and leave for other opportunities. Even physical components of the campus—landscape and buildings— are forever changing. As needs for the campus change, landscaped "green spaces" become parking lots or sites for new buildings. New buildings are constructed while older facilities are renovated or demolished.

Collegial environments are shaped by the people who work, study, and live on campus, by the physical facilities, and by the interaction between the two. The architectural influence or physical facilities generally will outlast the influence of any particular individual or group. Gerst and Sweetwood (1973) contended that perceptions of the climate or atmosphere, experienced upon entering any situation, are important variables in determining behavior. Messages conveyed through these first impressions demand congruence in behavior. According to Mehrabian (1976) people's reactions to all environments fall into the categories of either approach or avoidance. Each particular environment causes certain emotional reactions in a person. These reactions then cause the person, to some degree, to be attracted to or repelled by the environment. Consequently, being aware of and sensitive to messages the physical environment conveys to prospective students and their parents are important as well as the emotional reactions caused by the environment. Students, faculty, and staff who live, work, and interact on that campus also experience the impact of the physical environment on their behavior and attitudes.

Numerous components of the physical environment combine to transmit messages throughout the campus. One of these components is the spatial relationship of buildings. For instance, what is the focal point of the campus? Are the academic and nonacademic facilities integrated or separated? What is the relative importance of classroom buildings, residence halls, library, student center, bookstore, football stadium, science laboratories, counseling center, intramural facilities, and health center? Answers to these questions are the content of the messages the physical facilities communicate to those exposed to the campus. As Heyck (1978) pointed out, if the college truly teaches through its buildings that ugliness is an acceptable price for efficiency, and that living is to be separated from learning, then nothing said in the classroom can really counter those messages.

Heilweil (1973) contended that physical surroundings impose absolute limits on human behavior. Furthermore, DeYoung, Moos, VanDort, and Smail (1974) found that the environmental climate exerts a directional influence on behavior. Because the impact of physical surroundings can be either positive or negative, student affairs administrators need to be cognizant of environmental impact and accentuate those components that elicit positive behavior and limit or eliminate those that encourage negative behavior. A goal often espoused in college catalogs and in student affairs philosophy statements is the "creation of a sense of community." Community is only realized through the socialization process of people getting to know one another. If the physical surroundings are arranged or designed in ways that promote socialization by providing opportunities for meaningful interaction among faculty, students, and staff, a sense of community will more likely be realized. For instance, if the library, student center, classrooms, and dining and residence halls are situated so communication and interaction among all those on campus is a normal everyday occurrence, then a sense of campus community will be encouraged. However, on many campuses, the classrooms, libraries, and laboratories are isolated from the student centers, dining rooms, and residence halls, causing isolation and compartmentalization of faculty, students, and staff which effectively inhibits the socialization process. On such campuses, the student affairs administration must create environments in which socialization is promoted if a true sense of community is to be realized.

When a student walks into a campus building, an impression is immediately created. The individual either perceives the climate to be one of warmth, caring, and comfort or one that is cold, impersonal, and institutional. Many times this is not a conscious thought, but the feeling is real. Environments, according to Mehrabian (1976), can cause feelings of anger, fear, boredom, or pleasure in individuals regardless of how they think they should feel in that environment, and those feelings cause individuals to behave in certain ways regardless of how they think they should act. First impressions are influenced by color, lighting, floor covering, cleanliness, furnishings, smell, noise level, and furniture arrangement. Furniture arrangement can, for instance, promote or inhibit conversation and interaction. Conversational groupings where individuals sit at right angles to one another encourage conversation, whereas groupings that place individuals side by side tend to inhibit conversation. Too often, order and ease of cleaning appear to be more important than social interaction in lounges where the furniture is all lined up against the walls. The student affairs administrator must share the knowledge gained from social and environmental psychology when working with students and staff members in determining furniture arrangement as part of creating environments.

For illustrative purposes in this chapter, residence halls are used as examples primarily because (1) more research is available about them, (2) campuses tend to have numerous residence facilities and to view them as "belonging to student affairs," and (3) innovations in facilities management have been numerous in residence halls. However, the basic principles reflected in these examples are applicable to all campus physical facilities.

MANAGEMENT OF PHYSICAL FACILITIES

As early as 1965 Riker identified the relationship between the residential environment and behavior as being significant and important. Gerst and Moos (1972) found that a student's satisfaction with the residential environment influenced self perception and perception of the college experience to the point that pursuit of relationships with others and the degree of involvement in intellectually and emotionally significant activities were affected. Furthermore, Brandt and Chapman (1981) have concluded that student satisfaction, social climate, and perception of the physical environment are highly interrelated. Obviously the physical environment has a strong influence on the level of student satisfaction, the social climate, and the degree of student involvement. To maximize the educational and developmental potential of group living, the student affairs administrator must be an effective facilities manager.

Astin (1984) pointed out that the greater a student's involvement in college, the greater the resulting amount of learning and personal development. His research revealed that living on campus substantially increases the student's chances of persisting and of aspiring to a graduate degree. On campus residents express satisfaction with friendships, student-faculty relations, and social life. These findings substantiate those of Moos (1979) that the residential setting may be one of the most powerful forces influencing students' behavior, and ultimate success during the undergraduate years.

Waldo (1986) found a positive relationship between academic achievement, retention, and the quality of interpersonal relationships among residence hall students. He found that a student's immediate interpersonal environment is at least as important as academic achievement in the student's decision to continue in college.

Through the residential environment, the student affairs administrator can positively influence the socialization process and individual student growth and development by creating an environmental balance between individual privacy and stimulation from a supportive peer group. In fact, Schroeder and Jackson (1987) contend that student development is facilitated by the dynamic balance between challenge and support. One of the challenges facing residence educators, according to Stamatakos (1984), is to find effective ways of encouraging students to come out of the comfortable refuge of their rooms and avail themselves to the stimulation of others which will result in learning and growth (See Chapter 7).

A residence hall social climate, according to Moos and Gerst (1974), generally has three components that influence student behavior; the **relationship component,** the way residents support and help one another; the **personal development component,** the extent to which residents are encouraged to achieve and mature; and the **system maintenance and change component,** the degree of control residents exert over the hall's functioning. The *University Residence Environment Scale* (URES) was developed by Moos and Gerst, (1974) to measure the social-psychological climate of the residential setting. During development of the URES instrument, the authors found that student perceptions of the social climate of their place of residence influenced subjective mood states, such as, depression, alienation, isolation, and also affected satisfaction with the residential environment.

A challenge facing the student affairs administration, according to Pappas (1983), is to provide residential facilities that meet the changing needs of students while costs are increasing and campus resources are limited. At many institutions, residential facilities represent the largest single category of space. Aggregate figures for all institutions in the United States indicate that residential facilities account for more than twice as many assignable square feet of space as the next category (WICHE 1971). Furthermore, on residential campuses, the residence halls are a major source of institutional indebtedness (Williams, 1979). The traditional method of financing living facilities at public higher educational institutions is through the sale of revenue bonds. Retirement of these bonds depends on student rental fees. Obviously a consistently high level of occupancy is desirable for systematic debt retirement. The key to achieving and maintaining a high level of occupancy is an integration of attractive functional physical facilities and an aggressive student-central program which meets the needs of the residents.

Anchors, Schroeder, and Jackson (1978), however, found that most students simply do not feel at home in residence halls. Most residence halls are designed in a highly uniformed, ordered, and regularized fashion. Walls and built-in furniture are designed to be relatively indestructible and resistant to human imprint. Further, they found that students are often treated as visitors or transients. Student complaints about residence hall living include lack of privacy, lack of freedom, and uniformity of rooms and furnishings. According to the report on student housing by the Educational Facilities Laboratory (1972), a double room is used by two people for sleeping, studying, and socializing—all quite different uses for either roommate to truly feel a sense of control over the space or schedule.

Although individual differences exist, students are treated as if they are expected to have much the same needs for space, freedom, and privacy in their living units. Students' inability to control their own space has given rise to the application of the concept of **territoriality** to help understand the need for and recognition of individual differences in the residential setting (Grant 1974; Schroeder 1976, 1980). *Territoriality is the acquisition, demarcation, and defense of a spatial area with corresponding dimensions of implied ownership, personalization, and maximum control.* This concept is a universally recognized vehicle to maintain desired levels of control, organize behavior, and promote freedom of action. Applied to residence halls, territoriality simple means allowing individual students or groups of students to personalize and exert maximum control over their physical environment (Schroeder & Jackson, 1987). The outgrowth of this concept has been realized in room personalization programs in which students have been encouraged to paint the walls and construct lofts, room dividers, or screens as a means of decorating and de-institutionalizing the space. Group personalization programs have resulted in residence hall corridors being painted with graphic and pictorial designs to create a sense of uniqueness and ownership.

Hanson and Altman (1976) found that students who were given the opportunity to personalize and decorate their residence hall rooms were more likely to remain in school than those denied the option. A study by Werring, Winston, and McCaffrey (1981) found that residents who were active participants in their living unit's corridor paint projects had a more positive perception of their environment than either residents who elected not to participate in the project or who lived in units that chose not to paint. Wichman and Healy (1979) reported that students who were able to build lofts in their rooms generally got along better with their roommates. The literature supports the contention that students will be satisfied significantly more in an environment over which they exercise some control and which they helped create. As noted by these studies, a variety of ways exists by which students can gain some control over their environment either through building structures, various forms of decoration such as painting, or the addition or deletion of furniture. Sautter (1988) pointed out that students also personalize their rooms by bringing stereos, small televisions, compact refrigerators, computers, and VCRs.

Furniture is one of those environmental elements over which students definitely desire control. To students, built-in furniture is equated with built-in frustration because it limits room arrangements and defies personalization. Room furniture has the joint property of being one of the single most important and least understood factors in students' immediate environment (Heilweil, 1973). Movable furniture lends itself to the personalization process. As might be expected, the major portion of students' immediate environment consists of the room furniture, and actions in the room are circumscribed by the furniture to a greater degree than by any other element. Because institutional furniture's life expectancy is approximately 20 years, the student affairs administrator must be attuned to the need for selecting residence hall furnishings that will be adaptable, durable, and flexible in meeting student needs through several student generations.

Heilweil (1973) pointed out that the consequences of having no place to call one's own results in alienation, hostility, ruthlessness, and a sense of transience. On the other hand, those factors that give rise to student complaints about uniformity of surroundings such as identical rooms, long, straight corridors, and group bath facilities also reduce architectural and building costs and, therefore, shorten the length of time required to retire the debt. Therefore, the student affairs administrator must weigh and articulate the pros and cons of flexibility verses uniformity in the creation of residential living environments.

Out of class social and physical environments either contribute to or detract from students' social and intellectual development. The interactions between students and their environments shape attitudes, readiness to learn, and the quality of the college experience (Sandeen 1987). Traditionally, residence halls have not been viewed as places for self discovery or experimentation with various lifestyles. Consequently, residence hall staff members must work to overcome the architectural obstacles to personal development. Change can occur through personalization programs, renovation, and refurbishing projects.

STRUCTURING OF FACILITIES

Student affairs administrators must be prepared to play significant roles in planning new and remodeling old facilities. As enrollments fluctuate, the composition of the student body changes, and competition for students continues, maintaining institutional facilities in a manner that attracts students will be seen as increasingly important. As Sautter (1988) pointed out nice-looking, well maintained facilities are a key to attracting students to campuses. Individuals with a firm grounding in student developmental theory and a knowledge of the interrelationships between educational programs (both formal and informal) and the physical environment will be needed to make contributions to campus facilities planning and management. Care in designing and building facilities must be exercised due to the long term impact.

Change has been and will continue to be constant for higher educational institutions. The Carnegie Council (1980) warned of shifts in enrollment patterns and the resulting adjustment of standards. Their report stated that students will be recruited more actively, admitted more readily, and retained more laboriously. Because the pool of traditional 18 to 24 year old students will shrink, the competition to recruit and to retain students will become much more intense. Hodgkinson (1985) predicted a major increase in part-time college students, and a decline in full-time students. By 1992, he predicted that one-half of all college students will be over 25 and 20% will be over 35 years of age.

As this competition for students becomes increasingly acute, a student's impression of the institution upon visiting the campus before enrollment will be even more significant. When a student visits the campus for the first time, an immediate impression is created from the buildings and landscaping. The most influential aspect of the campus choice decision is the overall appearance of the place (Sautter 1988). The first impression is lasting—the institution does not have a second chance to make a first impression.

Institutional facilities and furnishings must reflect institutional goals and priorities. The message conveyed by these facilities to individuals who comprise the college's many publics will determine the institution's survival and success in the coming decades. That the facilities be attractive and adaptable and that they meet student developmental needs are imperative. Because clientele is changing, new and different demands are increasingly being put on facilities. How facilities can be adapted is an important issue facing administrators.

Interaction of students and staff and the variety of activities that can be accommodated in a residence hall depend on the location of staff rooms, apartments, and hall offices as well as study, meeting lounge, and recreational areas. The hall staff must be located in accessible areas that are easily approachable by students. Program and activity spaces must facilitate participation in fulfilling residents' needs and goals.

In the residential setting, Harrie (1968) indicated that a good interior design is flexible and can be converted to meet a variety of needs. The design should be molded to accommodate to the situation at hand instead of molding the student to what is available. Residence hall interiors demand sensitivity to student needs, understanding of and commitment to institutional objectives, and finesse in translating these needs and objectives into furnishings (Walters, 1968). To make residence halls both comfortable and durable is a challenge. The sensitive use of materials is one of the designer's chief tools in creating softer, more inviting spaces (Saylor 1988). Student affairs administrators must be cognizant of student needs, create environments in which these needs are recognized, and provide essential support for maximum student growth and development throughout the campus community.

PRACTICAL ASPECTS OF FACILITY MANAGEMENT

The Council for the Advancement of Standards (CAS, 1986) established minimal standards and guidelines for student services and student developmental programs. In discussing the residential life programs, several goals were outlined that are applicable to this discussion:

1. creating a living-learning environment that enhances student growth and development;

2. providing facilities that ensure well-maintained, safe, and sanitary housing conditions for students; and

3. providing management services that ensure the orderly and effective administration of all aspects of the program.

In specifically addressing residential facilities the CAS Standards recommend a maintenance/renovation program which includes preventive maintenance, a timely efficient repair program, a procedure for renovating and updating facilities, and a systematic replacement program for equipment and furnishing.

The anticipation is that the CAS Standards will be employed by accrediting agencies as a yardstick in evaluating institutional programs and facilities. As student affairs practitioners embark on building new and adapting existing facilities to accommodate programs, activities, and services necessary to serve a changing clientele, attention to these standards and guidelines is advised.

In this section the following areas are discussed from the practitioner's point of view: planning, construction, furnishings, and management.

Planning

The planning process employed to construct new or remodel existing facilities should follow seven basic steps: statement of philosophy, needs assessment, statement of space usage, translation of the philosophy into blueprints, cost estimates, methods of financing, and evaluation.

1. Statement of Philosophy. The initial step in planning is to state concisely the philosophy of the department constructing or remodeling the facility. This statement should be in harmony with the institutional mission and should outline the purpose for which the building is intended. Such a statement provides planners with direction in developing plans. The philosophy is helpful particularly to the architect as plans are developed and decisions are made regarding various spaces within the facility and the overall design. Consideration should be given to the relationship of staff to students, students to students, student development theory, the relationship of the facility to programs and people, as well as the interaction between the users and the environment.

2. Needs Assessment. In developing the needs assessment, one must consider the following: Who will use the facility? How will the facility be used? What programs, activities, and services will be offered within the facility? When will the facility be needed? How many students or other participants will be served by the facility? What are the staffing requirements of the facility? What federal regulations must be met in building or remodeling this particular facility?

By having a planning group answer these questions the building begins to take shape. For example, assume a new residence hall is scheduled for construction. A committee of housing staff members and students have met and reviewed the department's philosophy statement and have drafted a philosophy statement to guide in the planning of this new building. At this point they begin discussing the questions offered in the preceding paragraph. Through their discussion and brainstorming a fairly comprehensive list of "needs" for this residence hall is generated. Some needs are deleted and others expanded as the review process proceeds. Finally, the needs are summarized in a few paragraphs.

This residence hall will house 300 upperclass business majors. The building will be coeducational with the optimum mix being one-half men and one-half women. The living space will be arranged in suites with two double rooms sharing a bathroom. The entire building will be air conditioned, accessible for all, and will meet life safety codes.

Individual student rooms will be equipped with movable wooden furniture. Special requirements in the rooms include wiring for computers, provision for access to the university's mainframe, cable television jacks that access the university's cable system, and telephone jacks.

Other space requirements include two conference/seminar rooms wired for and equipped with audio-visual equipment, study rooms, computer room, exercise room, kitchens, laundries, and a recreation room. In addition space must be allocated for three faculty offices, an apartment and office space for the residence life staff, custodial storage areas, and student storage rooms.

3. Statement of Space Usage. Consideration of the manner in which spaces within the facility are intended to be used also needs to be delineated. This should coincide with programs, activities, and services identified in the needs assessment. For instance, a student center or residence hall lounge could accommodate music listening, conversation, table games, study, formal receptions, group meetings, and parties; however, the same space would not lend itself to all of these activities. Many times when attention is not given to this phase of the planning process, users find the facility and its furnishings inhibit rather than facilitate intended and actual usage. Furthermore, the relationship of one activity to another needs to be considered when making space designations. For example, locating a study room next to a television or recreation room is unwise.

4. Translation of Philosophy into Blueprints. The fourth step calls for an architect to translate the information for the first three steps into drawings. Spending time with the architect reviewing programs, activities, and services that are intended to be accommodated within the facility is important to ensure thorough understanding. The architect can design the facility appropriately only after what is desired and how the facility is intended to be used are understood completely. The architect will enlist the services of other specialities, such as, interior designers, structural, mechanical and electrical engineers and environmental safety personnel as the plans are drawn.

5. Cost Estimates. Two methods are used frequently for arriving at the cost of a project: (a) provide the architect with a dollar figure and instructions to design the facility within that amount, and (2) retain the architect to design the facility with the dollar cost to be determined by the design. Although the first method is most common, the actual construction bids still may be over the specified budget ceiling. If construction estimates or bids are above the budget ceiling, revision of plans to bring the project within the budget or allocation of more money is necessary.

6. Methods of Financing. The actual method of financing various facilities varies across states and among institutions. At state-supported institutions, self-supporting facilities (residential units, student center, intramural facilities) are often financed through the sale of revenue bonds. Other facilities such as classrooms are funded from state appropriated or capital expenditure funds. At private institutions, many facilities are funded from gifts earmarked for specific purposes. As an example, a report from the Research and Information Committee of the Association of College and University Housing Officers-International (ACUHO-I) indicated the following methods for financing construction or renovation of housing facilities were employed by member institutions: (a) surplus and reserve monies, (b) sale of revenue bonds, (c) state appropriations, (d) gifts, and (e) federal grants and loans (Hallenbeck & Ullom, 1980).

7. Evaluation. Before the construction contract is awarded, the final step, an evaluation of the other six planning steps, is in order to ensure that the proposed plans accommodate programs, activities, and services intended for the facility; that enough money is available to complete the project; and that the facility will accomplish the purposes for which it is intended. Assuming everything is satisfactory, the construction phase may begin.

Construction

The construction process is initiated by securing a contractor. At public institutions this commonly is done through a bidding process. Specifications and architectural drawings are provided to interested contractors who submit sealed statements containing their bid to build or remodel the facility. In most instances, the contractor who submits the lowest bid is awarded the contract. Before awarding the contract, however, the institution has the opportunity to evaluate the contractor. Important considerations for this evaluation include the size of the workforce, the probability of meeting the construction deadlines, and the reputation of the firm. The architect's impression of the construction firm and the contractor's willingness to work with the architect are both important. If the low bidder is unsatisfactory, with adequate justification, rejecting the bid is possible. The next lowest bid then can be selected, or plans can be revised and the project rebid.

Once construction has begun, inspection of the project on a regular basis is important. By walking through the project and becoming familiar with the workers, particularly the job foreman and the subcontractors, the institutional representative is able to monitor progress. An additional method of monitoring progress is to attend weekly contractor meetings. Generally the individuals present at these meetings are student affairs administrators, the architect, the contractor, and possible subcontractors. At these meetings the progress of the week is reviewed and discussed. Any problems that have arisen are inspected and decisions made as quickly as possible so the contractor can proceed with the project. These regular meetings are vitally important in monitoring the progress of the project and for ensuring that it will be completed on schedule.

A topic usually discussed at the contractor's meeting is *change orders.* Basically a change order is a deviation from original plans and specifications either to do more work or to do something differently than originally planned. Particularly in remodeling jobs contractors find numerous "surprises" as the work progresses. These unexpected conditions usually require additional work, materials, and money. Frequently in new construction an oversight is discovered that needs to be corrected so that the facility can be constructed properly.

Change orders have the potential of providing the institution with a much better job than would be the case had they not been submitted and approved. However, an institutional representative must evaluate carefully each change order before it is approved or these changes can cause the cost of the project to exceed significantly the budget ceiling. The student affairs administrator should confer with the architect before approving change orders to determine the necessity of the work being suggested.

As the project nears completion, a formal inspection of the complete work should be undertaken by the institutional representative, the architect, and the contractor. During this inspection a **punch list** should be developed that enumerates the items that still need to be completed or corrected by the contractor before the building is accepted by the institution. Final payment should be withheld until all items on the punch list are completed. When the final punch list has been corrected, the building can be accepted and final payment authorized.

Furnishings

Simultaneously with the construction phase, the student affairs administrator begins work with an interior designer to select the furnishings for the building. Furnishings must facilitate programs, activities, and services that are planned for this space. Review of the needs assessment and space usage statement is important in selecting furnishings. The interior designer provides the administrator choices of various color schemes, types of fabric, and pieces and makes of furniture. The interior designer should assist in the specification writing and bidding process required for the purchase of the furniture. In state institutions the low bidder generally is awarded the contract for furnishings. Starting this project during the early stages of construction enables the arrival of furniture when the building is in the completion stage. The furniture should be inspected carefully upon receipt to ensure that it has not been damaged in the shipping process.

Management

A successful facilities management program (Kaiser, 1980) should

- provide healthy and safe facilities environments,

- ensure long life expectancy of facilities,

- ensure economy and efficiency of operation,

- identify priorities for maintenance,

- systematically determine priorities for spending maintenance funds,

- support programs, and

- promote individual student development.

Provide Healthy and Safe Facilities Environments. The student affairs administrator must be concerned with housekeeping, routine maintenance, and repair and replacement programs—in addition to various federal regulations and programs, such as handicapped accessibility and environmental safety. Housekeeping, although many times taken for granted, is vital to providing a safe, healthy environment, as well as ensuring the long life of the facility and reflecting the care that the institution has for the facility and the individuals who inhabit the building.

Housekeeping requirements are reflected in a cleaning schedule that outlines the type and frequency of cleaning required, necessary equipment and supplies, and the number of people needed to implement the program. Keys to an effective housekeeping program are a definite cleaning schedule, thorough training in cleaning methods, equipment and supplies, supervision, and evaluation. Housekeeping, the cornerstone of facility upkeep, is a daily need.

Ensure Long Life Expectancy of Facilities. Scheduled routine maintenance ensures that a facility is available when needed and extends its life expectancy. The institution's motto regarding maintenance should be, "do it now, don't wait!" Deferred maintenance is very costly in time, money, and image. The impression created by deteriorating facilities is always negative and long lasting. With spiraling inflation, the cost of repair work will be higher tomorrow than today. A good preventive maintenance program ensures the longest possible life of the facility.

Ensure Economy and Efficiency of Operation. One of the measures of economy and efficiency in the operation of a facility is to hire, train, supervise, evaluate, and set priorities for housekeeping and maintenance personnel. Having a staff who can respond rapidly to housekeeping and maintenance needs in residence halls, student centers, and health centers is particularly important. Having custodial and maintenance personnel on the student affairs budget is advantageous because it allows for scheduling time and determining the priority in which various tasks and projects are to be completed. The housekeeping and maintenance personnel develop loyalty to and an identification with the facility to which they are assigned, which results in pride of workmanship. Many times loyalty and pride do not develop when the workers come from a centralized campus labor pool with responsibility for the entire campus. For the student affairs administrator to control a particular environment, control of funds and personnel is imperative, particularly as it relates to housekeeping and maintenance. Other arrangements require considerably more negotiation and coordination to gain rapid response to routine maintenance needs.

Identify Priorities for Maintenance. Equipment wears out and becomes obsolete and major repair and renovation projects are necessities. The student affairs administrator needs a planning tool to identify and plan for replacement of equipment and renovation of facilities. One such tool that has proven effective is a five-year repair and replacement program. To establish such a plan, a list is made of all equipment and furnishings, date acquired or date when last maintained, and life expectancy of each item in each facility (Figure 19.1). As an example, in the residential setting mattresses will normally last ten years, desks twenty years, corridor carpet five years, and lounge chairs in public areas five years. Examples of items to be included in the regular repair schedule are painting, roof replacement, and exterior maintenance. From information provided in the equipment and furnishing record (Figure 19.1), a five-year repair and replacement program can be developed (Figure 19.2).

Records such as those illustrated contain information in a concise and sequential outline for the student affairs administrator to gain an overview of replacement and major repair projects for each facility. To be effective, the five-year replacement and renovation schedule should be updated on an annual basis. As unexpected projects surface, they should be added to the plan.

Systematically Determine Priorities for Spending Maintenance Funds. Frequently the student affairs administrator is confronted with replacement and repair items on the five-year plan that exceed funds available. Ranking projects so available resources are spent for the most important or pressing items is necessary. Funds must be allocated or set aside to accomplish those projects that have the highest priority in any particular year. If funds are not available to accomplish all those items on the five-year plan, some projects will need to be moved to another year.

Support Programs. The personalization of student rooms and common areas within residence halls through painting, decorating, and building structures such as lofts or room dividers has become a significant part of housing programs at many colleges. With personalization programs come numerous questions which need to be addressed and answered by each institution in light of its philosophy, operating procedures and guidelines, and the objectives of its personalization program. Examples of these questions follow.

For a student-room-painting program:

Who selects the colors that may be used?

How many times a year can the room be painted?

Who supplies the paint and other equipment, i.e., ladders, brushes, drop cloths, tape, rollers, and brushes?

Are the students charged if they do an unacceptable job?

Is painting designs or graphics on the walls or ceilings of a student room allowable?

Who will inspect the job once it is completed?

Does this program replace the institution's five to seven year paint cycle? If so, what is done about the rooms that students don't elect to paint? If it doesn't, how long will students have to wait before they can paint after the University paints the room?

For introducing lofts or room dividers into student rooms:

Do the structures have to be free-standing or can they be anchored to the walls or floors?

Are additional fire safety precautions necessary, i.e., smoke detectors or flame retardant varnish?

Will the institution remove and store the room furnishings or will the occupants be required to incorporate them into the design of the loft?

Can lofts or dividers be left in the room from one academic year to the next? If allowed to remain, can the institution use the room during the summer to house someone else?

Will the students be charged if they disassemble a loft and leave the wood lying in the corridor?

For corridors or common area paint program:

Who approves the design and the colors?

Who supplies the paint and equipment?

What happens if a project is started but not completed?

How often can a corridor or common area be painted?

What happens when a mural or graphically painted

corridor fades and needs touch up or repainting? How does this fit into the institution's paint cycle? When an entire building is painted, are the student projects painted over or are they left?

As can be seen, the answers to these and other questions are institution-specific. In answering these questions, the student affairs administrator has to weigh the cost of the program against the value derived by students.

Promoting Individual Student Development. Many facilities for which student affairs administrators are responsible are multiuse-multipurpose facilities. During the planning phase, a particular population was targeted, and various programs, activities, and services were identified to be accommodated. Once the facility is functional, student needs, programs, and services may change requiring flexibility and creativity on the part of the student affairs administrator. Establishing policies and procedures governing use of the facility is essential to provide necessary support for student growth and development. Policies and procedures must facilitate use of the facility by the greatest number of people participating in diverse programs, activities, and services. Various factors to be considered in developing these policies and procedures are reservation of space, responsibility for setup-cleanup, damages that result from above normal wear and tear, vandalism, and priority for usage of space.

Staffing a facility with appropriate personnel significantly contributes to individual student development. In a residence hall, for instance, undergraduate staff, commonly called "resident assistants," custodians, maintenance, clerical staff, and professional staff are all necessary. Placement of resident assistant rooms, reception desk, vending and laundry services, and various activity rooms, such as study, recreation and exercise, will either enhance or impede student development.

A variety of functions must be performed in the residence hall if student growth and development are to be facilitated, and various staff members must work together to accomplish

(Continued on Page 666)

| Hall: Douglas | | | Normal Occupancy: 400 | | |
| Year Opened: 1966 | | | Expanded Occupancy: 430 | | |

	Date Acquired	Life Expectancy		Date Maintained	Life Expectancy
Furnishings			**Maintenance**		
Students Rooms:			Painting:		
Mattresses	1982	10 yrs	Student Rooms	1987	7 yrs
Beds	1968	20 yrs	Corridors	1988	5 yrs
Desks	1968	20 yrs			
Desk Chairs	1983	15 yrs	Lounges and Multiuse		
Chest of Drawers	1968	20 yrs	Areas	1985	5 yrs
Draperies	1982	10 yrs			
Floor Covering:					
Carpet	1987	5 yrs	Exterior:		
Multiuse Areas:			Maintenance	1990	2 yrs
Lounge Chairs	1985	5 yrs	Repainting	1981	10 yrs
TV Room Chairs	1986	5 yrs			
Lounge Drapes	1982	10 yrs	Roof:		
Floor Covering:					
Carpet	1987	5 yrs	Replacement	1968	25 yrs

Figure 19.1. Illustration of a facility equipment and furnishings record that contains date acquired or date when last maintained and life expectancy for each item.

1991	1992	1993	1994	1995
Replace Lounge Chairs	Replace TV Room Chairs	Replace Lounge and Corridor Carpet	Paint Corridors	Replace Lounge Chairs
Paint Lounges	Paint Exterior	Replace Carpet in Student Rooms	Replace Mattresses	Paint Lounges
		Replace Draperies in Student rooms and Lounges	Replace Roof	Paint Student Rooms

Figure 19.2. Five-year replacement and renovation program for Douglas Hall.

objectives of the residential community. Programs and services performed by hall staff members must be integrated to facilitate student development. Staff must have the appropriate skills to keep the facility in good working order and to accomplish the purpose for which the building was constructed, while maintaining flexibility to accommodate new programs and services as they are introduced.

SUMMARY

In preparation for the decades ahead, student affairs administrators must be involved actively in the planning of major renovation and new construction projects. Participation by student affairs administrators ensures that facilities both reflect an understanding of student development philosophy and accommodate programs, activities, and services required for a changing clientele. This will necessitate active participation in campus planning and on committees charged with renovation and construction of facilities.

Research has proven that the person-facility interaction is important. As the competition for students continues and the composition of the student body changes, the impression created by institutional facilities will be increasingly important in recruitment and retention. The facilities reflect the institution's philosophy and attitude toward students. The student affairs administrator must be aware of and understand the person-facility interaction to ensure that facilities are staffed and managed to support programs, activities, and services necessary to meet student needs.

Effective facilities management contributes positively to student development by providing space that facilitates student growth and development through interaction. Physical facilities must contribute to, rather than detract from, programming, program development, and student participation. When student affairs administrators have the opportunity to construct or renovate facilities, they must proceed in a systematic manner that includes a planning model consisting of a philosophy statement, needs assessment, program usage, drawings, cost estimates, financing, and evaluation. Furthermore, the student affairs administrator must be sensitive to and aware of the environment that is created by the facilities and the impact that this environment has on student clientele. In the words of Winston Churchill, "we shape our buildings; thereafter they shape us."

REFERENCES

Anchors, S., Schroeder, C.C., & Jackson, S. (1978). *Making yourself at home: A practical guide to restructuring and personalizing your residence hall environment.* Washington, DC: American College Personnel Association.

Astin, A.W. (1984). Student involvement: A developmental theory for higher education. *Journal of College Student Personnel, 25*(4), 297-307.

Brandt, J.A., & Chapman, N.J. (1981). Student alteration of residence hall rooms: Social climate. *Journal of College and University Housing, 11*(1), 37-42.

Carnegie Council on Policy Studies in Higher Education. (1980). *Three thousand futures: The next twenty years for higher education.* San Francisco: Jossey-Bass.

Council for the Advancement of Standards for Student Services/Developmental Programs (CAS). (1986). *CAS standards and guidelines for student services/developmental programs.* Washington, DC: Author.

DeYoung, A.M., Moos, R.H. VanDort, B., & Small, P.M. (1974). Expectations, perceptions and changes in university residence climates: Two case studies. *Journal of College and University Student Housing, 4*(2), 4-11.

Educational Facilities Laboratory. (1972). *Student housing.* New York: Author.

Gerst, M.S., & Moos, R.H. (1972). Social ecology of university student residences. *Journal of Educational Psychology, 63,* 513-25.

Gerst, M.S., & Sweetwood, H. (1973). Correlates of dormitory social climate. *Environment and Behavior, 5,* 440-63.

Grant, W.H. (1974). Humanizing the residence hall environment. In D. DeCoster & P. Mable (Eds.), *Student development and education in college residence halls* (pp. 98-102). Washington, DC: American College Personnel Association.

Hallenbeck, D.A., & Ullom, M. (1980). Survey of new construction, renovation and/or remodeling. *ACUHO News, 19*(4), 18-19.

Hanson, W.B., & Altman, S. (1976). Decorating personal places: A descriptive analysis. *Environment and Behavior, 8,* 491-504.

Harrie, E.F. (1968). The dormitory interior—what the experts think it should be. *American School and University, 41,* 40.

Heilweil, M. (1973). The influence of dormitory architecture on resident behavior. *Environment and Behavior, 5,* 377-412.

Heyck, T.W. (1978). Universities, university housing, and national needs. *Journal of College and University Student Housing, 7*(2), 8-11.

Hodgkinson, H.L. (1985). *All one system: Demographics of education, kindergarten through graduate school.* Washington, DC: Institute for Educational Leadership.

Kaiser, H.H. (1980). Facilities management: A program for the 80's. In H.H. Kaiser (Ed.), *Managing facilities more effectively.* New Directions for Higher Education (No. 30). San Francisco: Jossey-Bass.

Mehrabian, A. (1976). *Public places and private spaces.* New York: Basic Books.

Moos, R.H. (1979). *Evaluating educational environments.* San Francisco: Jossey-Bass.

Moos, R.H., & Gerst, M.S. (1974). *University residence environment scale manual.* Palo Alto, CA: Consulting Psychologists Press.

Pappas, A.T. (1983). Management challenges for the 1980's. *Journal of College and University Student Housing, 13*(1), 3-8.

Riker, H.C. (1965). *College housing as learning centers.* Washington, DC: American College Personnel Association.

Sandeen, A. (Ed.). (1987). *A perspective on student affairs.* Washington, DC: National Association of Student Personnel Administrators.

Sautter, J.A. (1988). All this and cable t.v., too? *American School and University, 60*(1), 43-44.

Saylor, P. (1988). Variety is the challenge. *American School and University, 60*(11), 44c-44f.

Schroeder, C.C. (1976). New stategies for structuring residential environments. *Journal of College Student Personnel, 17,* 386-390.

Schroeder, C.C. (1980). Designing college environments for students. In F.B. Newton & K.L. Ender (Eds.), *Student development practices: Strategies for making a difference* (pp. 52-79). Springfield, IL: Charles C. Thomas Publishers.

Schroeder, C.C., & Jackson, G.S. (1987). Creating conditions for student development in campus living environments. *NASPA Journal, 25*(1), 45-53.

Stamatokos, L.C. (1984). College residence halls: In search of educational leadership. *Journal of College and University Student Housing, 14*(1), 10-17.

Waldo, M. (1986). Academic achievement and retention as related to students' personal and social adjustment in university residence halls. *Journal of College and University Student Housing. 16*(1), 19-23.

Walters, R.R. (1968). The dormitory interior - what the experts think it should be. *American School and University, 41*, 40.

Werring, C.J., Winston, R.B., Jr., & McCaffrey, R.J. (1981). How paint projects affect residents' perceptions of their living environment. *Journal of College and University Student Housing, 11*(2), 3-7.

Western Interstate Commission on Higher Education (WICHE). (1971). *General Support Facilities. Technical Report 17-5.* Denver, CO: Author.

Wichman, H., & Healy, V. (1979). *In their own spaces: Student built lofts in dormitory rooms.* Paper presented at the meeting of the American Psychological Association.

Williams, G.D. (1979). University enrollments and the battle of retiring the bond. *ACUHO News, 18*(5), 5-7.

SUGGESTED READINGS

Anchors, S., Schroeder, C.C., & Jackson, S. (1978). *Making yourself at home: A practical guide to restructuring and personalizing your residence hall environment.* Washington, DC: American College Personnel Association.

Conyne, R.K., & Clack, R.J. (1981). *Environmental assessment and design: A new tool for the applied behavioral scientist.* New York: Praeger.

Frederiksen, C.F. (1980). The future is now. *Journal of College and University Student Housing, 10*(2), 3-5.

Heilweil, M. (1973). The influence of dormitory architecture on resident behavior. *Environment and Behavior, 5,* 377-411.

Heyman, M. (1978). *Places and spaces: Environmental psychology in education.* Bloomington, IN: Phi Delta Kappa Educational Foundation.

Kaiser, H.H. (Ed.). (1980). *Managing facilities more effectively.* New Directions for Higher Education (No. 30). San Francisco: Jossey-Bass.

Mehrabian, A. (1976). *Public places and private spaces.* New York: Basic Books.

Schroeder, C.C. (1981). Student development through environmental management. In G.S. Blimling & J.H. Schuh (Eds.), *Increasing the educational role of residence halls* (pp. 35-49). New Directions for Student Services (No. 13). San Francisco: Jossey-Bass.

Louis C. (Lou) Stamatakos, Ph.D., is Professor of Higher Education at Michigan State University. He holds three degrees from Indiana University, including the doctorate, and served the profession for 17 years as a student affairs administrator in five collegiate institutions prior to assuming full-time professorial responsibilities at Michigan State University in 1967.

As an active member of professional associations, he served as President of the Wisconsin Association of Deans and the Michigan College Personnel Association, as a four term Executive Council Member-at-Large in the American College Personnel Association (ACPA), for six years on the ACPA Monograph Publication Board, for two terms as ACPA Senator, and as the first editor of the ACPA Commissions Publications. He was a recipient of the ACPA Distinguished Service Award and was the first recipient of the NASPA Robert H. Shaffer Award for Academic Excellence as a Faculty Member. In 1989 he was elected as an ACPA Senior Scholar. He has served as consultant for over thirty institutions in the United States, and for institutions and Ministries of Education in Brazil, Mexico, and Greece, and has taught at Cambridge, London, and Oxford in Great Britain.

CHAPTER **20**

STUDENT AFFAIRS
ADMINISTRATORS AS
INSTITUTIONAL
LEADERS

Louis C. Stamatakos

At the time of the writer's entrance into the field of college student affairs in the 1950s, the dean of students (there were no vice presidents of Student Affairs then) was expected to be a person of stature. This institutional leader was well respected throughout the campus community and viewed as possessing wisdom and the required counseling and administrative skills for work with students. Further, this individual was responsible for directing a relatively small division of varied student services and educational support programs. As well, the dean was expected to be an expert in controlling student behavior and in raising or lowering student spirit depending upon the desired direction of the moment (Mueller, 1961; Williamson, 1961; Wrenn, 1951). In jest, deans sometimes referred to themselves as "Directors of Wildlife Management." The National Lampoon movie *Animal House* represents an attempt, though somewhat distorted, to depict the prevailing attitudes and expectations of that era.

Four decades later, professional and external expectations of the Chief Student Affairs Administrator (that is, the Dean of Students or Vice President for Student Affairs) reflect an evolution of American higher education in general—growth in numbers, size, and scope of services; programs; and responsibilities and their attendant interrelationships, complexities, and fiscal constraints in highly competitive and financially burdened collegiate institutions (Commission on National Challenges in Higher Education, 1988; Fiske, 1986; National Institute of Education, 1984). Within this context this chapter is directed for neophyte professionals—to both orient and inform those who aspire to the upper levels of student affairs leadership. Toward this end, the chapter contains a view of student affairs leadership from a broad institutional perspective, and includes discussions about eight Chief Student Affairs Administrator (CSAA) roles including (1) articulator of a philosophy, (2) advocate for student's needs and interests, (3) transmitter of values, (4) interpreter of institutional culture, (5) institutional leader and policy-maker, (6) champion of causes (7) institutional planning, and (8) public relations spokesperson.

ARTICULATOR OF A PHILOSOPHY

The field of student affairs exists within and works in support of a wide variety of postsecondary institutions inclusive of public and private two and four-year colleges and universities as well as proprietary, theological, and technical institutions. Across this broad spectrum of the unique American collegiate system exist, through tradition or practice, various philosophies of education which undergird and give direction to the purposes, structures, processes, and outcomes of instruction, service, and research. These philosophies reflect institutions' *raison d'être* and influence greatly the manner in which student affairs shapes and manifests its philosophy and conducts its services and educational programs.

At the risk of over-generalization, at least four major philosophies can be found to exist in modern American higher education: **Experimentalism, Dualism, Realism,** and **Idealism.**

Experimentalism is best known for its student-centered (progressive) curriculum, while at the other end of the continuum Idealism or (Perennialist) assumes the existence of "great truths" which the student is expected to learn and adapt to changing societal conditions. In institutions which emphasize these philosophies, the role of the faculty is paramount, and the importance of specialized functions such as student affairs tend to be minimized. Between Experimentalism and Idealism, one will find Dualism and Realism. Dualism (also called reconstructionist), views higher education as society-centered, and as society changes so should the institution to better serve the society. Realism (or fields-of-knowledge) tends to be scholar and field-centered and implies or directs that faculty and their specialized disciplines determine what should be taught and how learning should occur (Brubacher, 1969; Johnson, 1975).

Between the two extremes of Experimentalism and Idealism, one will find the most viable and receptive environment for the development of vital and comprehensive student affairs programs. The rationale for making this suggestion is that in institutions that manifest philosophies of Dualism and Realism one usually finds high levels of heterogeneity of curriculum and student body composition. Then, in these institutions one can expect to experience great diversity, which results in an increasing demand for services and programs that student affairs provides.

In an attempt to bring organization, order, common understanding, and philosophical sensibility to the disparate functions of what was then called "student personnel," leaders in the field gathered together in the 1930's and drafted *The Student Personnel Point of View* [SPPV] (American Council on Education, 1937) which was later revised in the years immediately following World War II (1949). The importance of the SPPV can not be overstated for it clearly delimited student affairs functions from "other administrative and instructional functions . . ." (ACE, 1949, p iii), stated basic assumptions and beliefs about students and education, placed its purpose and activities in support of developing the whole student, and proclaimed its allegiance to and support for the basic academic mission of colleges and universities.

In the midst of what is now viewed as a period of American social revolution, the 1960s and 1970s, and recognizing the "dissonance between existing programs and responses of students and youth of the larger society. . ." (Stamatakos & Rogers, 1984, p. 402), the profession initiated the creation of another document, *Student Development Services in Postsecondary Education,* published by the Council on Student Personnel Associations in Higher Education [COSPA] in 1975. The significant contribution of this document to the profession was its provision of human development theories, principles, and beliefs for application in the profession's practice. Subsequently, in 1987, *A Perspective on Student Affairs* was published by the National Association of Student Personnel Administrators [NASPA] to commemorate the 50th anniversary of the *Student Personnel Point of View.* This statement was not a revision of the SPPV. Rather it was intended to reveal "what the higher education community can expect from student affairs . . ." (National Association of Student Personnel Administrators, 1987, p. iv), to stimulate understanding of purpose and function among other higher education executive-level leaders, and to position student affairs as a major component of collegiate institutions.

As revealed above, the profession, its practitioners, and more importantly CSAAs have at least three fundamental documents available guiding professional enculturation and developing professional philosophies. Unfortunately, none of these three statements is adequate to the task of serving as a professional philosophy, although the SPPV comes the closest to fulfilling the task (Stamatakos & Rogers, 1984). Until such time that the profession decides that it can no longer function effectively with the incompleteness and conflicts inherent within and between its major documents, and carries out the task of establishing a comprehensive and acceptable philosophy, CSAAs will have to be content with subscribing to that philosophy which is most compatible with their particular institutions.

Important to the CSAA are four major considerations: (1) the degree to which the CSAA has subscribed to one or more of the profession's documents, (2) the level of professional preparation evident in the student affairs staff, (3) the extent to which a professional philosophy is a functional part of the division's mission and goal statement, and (4) the ability of the CSAA to clearly articulate and communicate the division's philosophy to professional superiors, peers, and subordinates as well as to other faculty and staff members, students, and the public-at-large. A well conceptualized and clearly articulated philosophy serves as both a compass and a rudder in that it provides clear direction for the nature and conduct of the division and keeps it headed in an agreed upon and shared direction.

Simply stated, a national professional or student affairs divisional philosophy should contain at least four components. The first entails basic premises (first principles) about the role and purpose of higher education, the nature of students as human beings, and the dynamic relationships that exist between the two (learning). The second component evolves from the first and expresses the profession's (division's) values— what it values as a preferable state for its first principles. Roles and functions form the third component and involve what has been done, what is being done, and the purposes that guide practice. The fourth component, the profession's identity, clarifies its existence through integration and congruence of what is believed, valued, and done. It identifies and clarifies job definitions, tasks, qualifications, standards of performance, and criteria for evaluation (Stamatakos & Rogers, 1984). In sum, a professional philosophy seeks to respond to and answer the most important question, why?

A CSAA who has developed a solid understanding of professional philosophy will respond to each of the four components as they are reflected in the employing institution. Administrators who can articulate their philosophies simply and effectively are in excellent positions to shape the professional quality of the division through (1) insistence upon staff members being professionally qualified, (2) support of a systematic program of professional staff development (Canon, 1980;

Stamatakos & Oliaro, 1972), (also see Chapter 17), and (3) job enrichment and enlargement opportunities for staff members (Owens, 1981). When a professional philosophy is in place the CSAA has the capacity to effect well considered changes required by shifting institutional missions and goals or internal conflicts. Such change can be implemented through the use of long-range strategic planning initiatives, professional development programming, or the development of divisional administrative policy manuals. Similar activities lend themselves to the creation of a divisional philosophy where one does not exist. Whatever the circumstances, the CSAA's leadership in examining, revising, or creating the division's philosophy dramatizes its importance for providing congruence between the student affairs' and the institution's philosophies. Likewise, it influences the nature, structure, composition, and direction of the entire division and affects the quality of services and educational programs provided for students. As well, through frank and open discussion of important and shared professional beliefs and values, such activities aid immeasurably in the development of professional commitment and high morale.

In general many college administrators and faculty members do not truly understand or appreciate the importance of student affairs and its potential for enhancing the education of students (Appleton, Briggs, & Rhatigan, 1978; Arbuckle, 1953; Williamson, 1961). In consequence, these individuals oftentimes do not materially or psychologically support its work. Where strong commitment and support exist, most often it is a direct result of the CSAA's ability to articulate effectively the division's philosophy to the campus community and to involve faculty members in policy-making and advisory roles in the division's work (Shaffer & Martinson, 1966; Williamson, 1961).

Communicating the division's philosophy is not an easy task. It requires careful planning on the part of the CSAA and staff attendant to at least the following five areas: (1) attention to that which is most important (as contrasted with attempting to reveal everything the division believes and does); (2) spacing communications to inform and not overload; (3) careful attention to consistency of beliefs, assumptions, and assertions; (4) congruence between such statements and the mission of the institution (especially academic affairs); and, most importantly, (5) behavior, performance, service, and the provision of educational programs that are consistent with the division's philosophy. Contributing to the effectiveness of such communication is its consistency as a regular and continuous activity throughout the tenure of individuals and collective staff because staff member turnover is assured in labor-intensive collegiate institutions.

The CSAA's leadership role in communicating the philosophy of the division certainly should not be limited to administrators and faculty. Students, the objects of the profession, the campus community-at-large, and the public (for example, legislators, donors, and alumni) are all a part of the constituency of student affairs and deserve well considered attention. The internal constituencies are most easily and effectively reached through a myriad of publications such as catalogs; handbooks; descriptive services brochures; directories; codes of student conduct; informative series in campus newspapers and alumni magazines; and through new student orientation, convocations, speaker programs, student organization advising, student activities, and sponsored educational programs. What was advocated with regard to communicating the division's philosophy to administrators and faculty applies equally well here, especially clarity and consistency of statements, staff performance, and content of services and programs.

As envisaged, the CSAA, by definition, is the leader of the student affairs division and its chief spokesperson. The extent to which the CSAA has become enculturated into the profession, has accepted its basic assumptions and beliefs, and has made an occupational commitment to it will greatly determine the administrator's effectiveness in transmitting the important mission of student affairs within the division and to its various constituencies.

Of critical importance to this task is the degree to which staff members are involved in developing, promulgating, and modeling the division's philosophy. Those staff members, often the youngest and least experienced, having the most frequent contact with students are in the best position to communicate directly the mission, role, and programs which reflect the division's values and beliefs, as well as alert the CSAA to activities and behaviors which are inimical to it. In this context open and effective lines of communication throughout the division are essential as are frequent conferences and contacts between the CSAA and the young professional staff.

ADVOCATE FOR STUDENTS' NEEDS AND INTERESTS

The optimum development of college students intellectually, emotionally, physically, and spiritually necessitates knowledge, skills, and competencies of human growth and development on the part of CSAAs and other professional staff members in shaping the nature and content of services and educational programs (ACE, 1949; COSPA, 1975). Furthermore, such development requires the effective and efficient transmission of relevant knowledge and its implications for both student affairs and academic affairs areas in ways which will result in program and instructional adjustments and accommodations without sacrificing the quality of the student's educational program or the integrity of the institution.

Acknowledging the diversity of students, the major documents of the profession have charged practitioners with these responsibilities for the purpose of assuring the best student-institution fit to enhance the desired educational experiences. In response to this commitment and its attendant responsibilities, professional preparation programs in student affairs generally have established core programs which require (1) human growth and developmental theory, (2) individual and environmental assessment tools and techniques, (3) counseling and advising skill building, (4) instructional strategies, and (5) consultation skills (Keim & Graham, 1987). In addition, professional associations maintain a long and successful record of commissioning publications and sponsoring professional development workshops and programs to develop and sharpen practitioners' knowledge and skills. Coupled with professional staff recruitment and development, these important activities provide student affairs with its greatest strength: an intimate knowledge of the institution's ethos, culture, environment, and students.

Given the nature of the recruitment and induction process of students into higher education, collegiate institutions have at their fingertips a wealth of information about each student admitted. Additional information is acquired through institutional assessment programs as well as from observations and self-reports of students that reveal similarities and differences among students' interests, preparation, and readiness for college. Such information can be most appropriately utilized if it is accurately interpreted and shared among members of the administration, faculty, and staff who have a need to know, who will maintain confidentiality as appropriate to the information, and who are in positions to affect those changes in curriculum design, instructional expectations, and methodologies mandated by the nature of the information.

Appropriately, the expectation is that through the expertise of student affairs staff members in admissions, orientation, counseling, testing, referral, and developmental programs, important new student information is developed and recommendations for accommodations, adaptation, and change are made (Miller & Prince, 1976; Rodgers & Widick, 1982). For example, significant shifts in test scores and grades of entering students indicate the importance of (1) raising or lowering learning and performance expectations in required courses, (2) changing instructional techniques to accommodate varying student learning styles, (3) changing prerequisites, (4) creating remedial programs to assist students in overcoming deficiencies, (5) establishing developmental programs to help students acquire appropriate learning and study habits, and (6) informing high schools so that curriculum and instructional changes may be considered.

Similarly, and more particular to the student affairs division, information gleaned from entrance interviews, orientation, testing, surveys, self-reports, and staff observations in residence halls and student activities may reveal needs for the institution to accommodate as well as provide facilities and programs for increasing numbers of handicapped, minority, or foreign students. Similarly acquired information may be important to those who develop and administer educational programs dealing with student activities, social skills, wellness, AIDS, and alcohol and substance abuse, to name but a few examples.

No matter how gathered, vital information regarding student needs and interests requires an understanding of (1) its importance to successful adaptation of students to the college experience, (2) the full range of institutional programs and services available to students, and (3) the essential conceptual and organizational skills required for effectively collecting, interpreting, and transmitting such information for pragmatic applications beneficial to students.

Ultimately, the opportunity and responsibility for serving as student advocate are lodged in the office of the CSAA, for this person is by virtue of executive level position, education, professional commitment, and purpose of the division, the one to whom students should feel free to turn when personal needs and interests are unknown or unattended. Such advocacy responsibilities mandate professional knowledge and skills, and require that student affairs staff anticipate as well as accommodate the individual differences of students (ACE, 1949), and through well established professional relationships communicate their knowledge about students to others throughout the campus community.

Fulfilling the advocacy role does not mean that the CSAA or divisional staff members should respond indiscriminately to all identified student interests and needs. The CSAA is, by virtue of position, an educational leader possessing certain experience, knowledge, training, and an orientation particular to the roles, purposes, and limitations of the institution as well as to the nature and developmental needs of its students. Careful and considered judgment is required for the CSAA to determine the legitimacy and appropriateness of responding to expressed needs based upon the limitations inherent in the institution's purpose, nature, traditions, and resources. Although to deny demands for new programs or freedoms often is unpopular, institutional leaders must manifest wisdom on the basis of previous experience and considered judgments. Sometimes to say "no" is important.

As noted earlier, although the CSAA is perceived as being the chief campus advocate for student needs and interests, the timeliness and quality of expressed advocacy will, to a great extent, be contingent upon four variables. These are (1) the thoroughness and quality of staff members' professional preparation and experience, (2) the manner in which he or she executes responsibilities, (3) the sophistication of the individual's information-gathering skills, and (4) his or her ability to accurately interpret and present information in a manner which aids decision-making, policy formulation, resource allocation, and program execution and evaluation. Such crucial responsibilities require careful staff selection as well as continuous professional staff development if advocacy is to be appropriately responsive to student needs and institutional purpose.

TRANSMITTER OF VALUES

One of the most often cited expectations of higher education's traditional missions has been the teaching and development of values (Boyer, 1987). Although the goal of enriching and transmitting the culture is often an implicit one, it is rarely made explicit whose values will be emphasized or what those values will be. Nevertheless, colleges courageously address these expectations in catalogs and recruitment literature. They do so in a manner that conveys an expectation that the most "cherished, traditional, and appropriate" values will be imbued within the behavior of students through classroom and out-of-class experiences and learnings.

Regardless how expressed, one is oftentimes hard-pressed to find clearly defined examples of institutional commitment to the teaching of values. With certainty, faculty members will assert that the cherished values of scholarship, academic honesty, rigor, and integrity are learned as a direct result of becoming involved in the academic enterprise and through their personal examples as scholars. However, students quickly learn that under the protective cloak of objectivity, faculty may be very reluctant to express their own personal values, thus denying students opportunities for selecting and learning from appropriate faculty role models. Ironically, the classroom affords an excellent setting for the critique of traditional values without providing the foundation for a system of thought to replace them (Sanford, 1956).

In co-curricular and residential environments where peer example and pressure prevail, and where all too often younger student affairs staff members are still seeking their own identities and struggling with relative values and conflicts, students are challenged by a sea of social opportunities and new and conflicting values in an environment often so tolerant that it shrinks from expressing value judgments. And, when it does, it often does so as official policy and in direct conflict with antithetical but tolerated behaviors (Stamatakos, 1984). Within the college environment, a setting of extreme tolerance and extremes in behavior, is where students as well as faculty and professional staff attempt to influence, express, be influenced, grow, and seek a balance between absolute intellectual and social freedom and social restraint (Stamatakos & Stamatakos, 1980; Williamson, 1961). And, within this environment is where student affairs professionals have their best opportunities to influence the content of learning experiences essential to student growth and development (Mueller, 1961; Williamson, 1961).

Originating with its traditional control functions, but extending through its educational and support commitments, student affairs has come to serve as the "values educator" in modern higher education largely as a result of faculty default and tradition. Caught between academic freedom, which is essential to the very character of American collegiate institutions, and the expressed need to create conditions which foster student intellectual and social exploration and experimentation with attitudes, values, and behavior, student affairs professionals have a unique opportunity for modeling and promulgating values which are essential to the maintenance of the best in civilized society collegiate traditions. In this effort the CSAA's leadership and the professional staff's involvement are necessary for effecting the following strategies and conditions:

1. **Achieving Consensus** is creating the conditions for reaching consensus within the collegiate community regarding the role and place of values education, and the manner in which all facets of the community will share responsibility for such education. Within this context and process, the CSAA must seek agreement about which values are to be included for study in formal and non-formal educational settings. Agreement also should be sought that intellectual inquiry and example are the desired educational approaches rather than inculcation (Ehrlich, 1987). The natural campus forums of academic and student government and campus convocation series are very appropriate for such discussions and provide excellent opportunities for collaboration among faculty, staff, and students toward important and common ends.

2. **Policy and Program Assessment** is developing all-institutional structures and vehicles that enable a careful examination of desirable and appropriate institutional policies and the degree of consistency in programming and policies appropriate for assuring the necessary congruence between what is said and what is done. Nothing is more disconcerting for young professional staff members than to educate toward appropriate social behavior within an environment that neither reaffirms, rewards, nor substantiates such behavior (Sanford, 1967; Stamatakos, 1984). Academic and student government representative policy advisory boards are examples of the vehicles available for achieving consistency and congruence.

3. **Basic Skills Development** is working closely with the undergraduate teaching faculty to assure provision for reading, writing, and laboratory assignments and experiences designed to stimulate students to examine their values in relation to those of the larger society and those which may be 'best" for a civilized and humane

society. Student activities and residence hall advisors are in crucial positions to advise the faculty about student and campus values issues. As well, such staff members can be especially influential in shaping, coordinating, and directing extra-class educational programming congruent in content with classroom values, activities, and learnings.

4. **Examining Values** is co-sponsoring campus-wide debates, discussions, symposia, convocations, and workshops with academic affairs, which require students to confront and deal directly with personal and social value conflicts. Much benefit will be derived from encouraging students to initiate self-examinations of the value related choices and decisions they are required to make as individuals and as group members. Careful consideration of these activities as they correspond with and complement values education will serve to create a significant campus-wide environmental press on individual students and their learning processes.

5. **Student Conduct** is creating a climate reflective of a "caring confrontation," which necessitates professional student affairs staff to "respond to individuals before the behaviors reach the increasingly remote limits found in current college or university conduct manuals" (Brown & Canon, 1978, p. 428). Such confrontation reaches students in realistic behavioral states and offers unlimited opportunities for values education. Importantly, successful creation of such a climate and provision of basic confrontational skills instruction requires both a total staff commitment and intensive training.

Initiating college-wide dialogue and action oriented programs in support of such fundamental, traditional, and professional responsibilities and desired outcomes is expected and to be commended in a contemporary society where values or lack thereof have been subject to wide spread national concern, discussion, and debate (Bloom, 1987; Boyer, 1987).

INTERPRETER OF
INSTITUTIONAL CULTURE

Because of their established missions, roles, and functions, CSAAs and their staff members are in excellent positions to have more daily contact with students than are members of any other unit within the modern college. This is especially true on residential campuses where such contact is literally around the clock and expected to promulgate, implement, enforce, interpret, and mediate institutional policies and procedures. Of all campus executive officers, the CSAA is the official spokesperson for the institution and principal interpreter of its culture to students (Mueller, 1961; Packwood, 1977; Williamson, 1961).

This responsibility requires an intimate knowledge as well as an acceptance of the institution's history, ethos, policies, and procedures on the part of each student affairs staff member. It also mandates that the CSAA be acutely attuned to and knowledgeable about the expectations and actions of trustees, other administrators, and the faculty because, individually and collectively, these community members and their activities reflect the institution (Corson, 1960; Dressel, 1981; Dressel & Faricy, 1972).

Typically, the CSAA is one of the first campus leaders to welcome students and their parents to the college during "welcome weeks" and "new student orientations." The thoughtful administrator uses these occasions to introduce campus leaders and key staff members; to discuss the institution's cultural heritage, traditions, and values; to describe developmental opportunities; to delineate expectations of student academic and social performance; to communicate the institution's overall culture (Rice, 1965; Upcraft, 1984); and to introduce students and parents to the campus community in general (Dannells & Kuh, 1977). Subsequently, throughout the student's tenure on campus, the CSAA and student affairs staff members will be in constant contact through various student services programs and activities where discussions about and role modeling of the institution's values are natural and appropriate.

The nature of the student affairs functions and educational responsibilities require a reasonable depth of understanding and degree of knowledge about literally every facet of the campus community. Competent student affairs professionals must be able to interpret accurately, advise effectively, and refer appropriately to help students adapt successfully to the institution (Appleton, Briggs, & Rhatigan, 1978; DeCoster & Mable, 1981).

Critically important responsibilities required of the CSAA include assuring that all staff members are knowledgeable about the (1) basic requirements of their positions; (2) relationships and responsibilities they have to other staff and faculty members and their administrative offices and programs; and (3) institution's policies and procedures. Additionally, staff members need to be informed of any contemplated or actual changes in policies, structures, or procedures that would affect their knowledge, understandings, and interpretations. Given the breadth of this requirement, the CSAA must be in constant contact and have developed excellent lines of communications with all significant units of the campus. Campus politics notwithstanding, good public relations skills are necessary if CSAAs and practitioners are to be effective in this role. Equally important are the skills possessed by staff members and CSAAs in helping students to negotiate the system effectively as well as aiding them in their understanding of the institution.

Regularly scheduled weekly meetings with deans, directors, coordinators, and clerical staff members have been found to be effective in promoting staff sophistication. Professional staff development programs specific to such responsibilities also have utility (Appleton, Briggs, & Rhatigan, 1978). Whether regularly scheduled meetings or staff development activities, inviting knowledgeable professionals from other campus programs to serve as resources or speakers serve to achieve this purpose. One CSAA assigned readings and field trips on campus to his staff and had them make presentations and lead discussions about the implications of their readings and findings. Another developed a staff handbook about the campus, its services, policies, traditions, and the like and had her staff make use of it as a desk reference.

Whatever strategy is employed, all student affairs staff members, from the CSAA to the student resident assistant and orientation leader, are interpreters of the institution and its culture to students, and the significance of this responsibility should be included in job descriptions and job evaluations and considered as important to work and job requirements.

INSTITUTIONAL LEADER AND POLICY MAKER

The breadth and complexity of the contemporary American college and university and its growing numbers of services and administrative staff places ever-increasing responsibilities upon the shoulders of its executive officers (McCorkle & Archibald, 1982). Among these responsibilities is the expectation that the CSAA, as the official spokesperson for and expert about students, will speak assertively from an informed institution-wide perspective on behalf of students. Obviously, this expectation mandates a breadth and depth of understanding of the institution's mission, structure, and activities and special knowledge about the composition and character of the student body, student development theory, and the outcomes of interactive relationships between students and their campus environments (DeCoster & Mable, 1981; Mueller, 1961; Williamson, 1961).

Assuming the possession of such understanding and knowledge, the CSAA is in a position to advise, counsel, and propose changes and responses appropriate to the basic characteristics of the institution, its mission, and the manner is which it discharges its responsibilities. From this perspective the informed CSAA possesses legitimacy in sharing and interpreting accurate information and knowledge about student behavior, performance, satisfaction, dissatisfaction, suggestions, and expectations which result from student interaction with the activities of academic affairs, business services, physical plant, external affairs (such as alumni and governmental relations), and even institutional advancement.

On campuses where the CSAA has assiduously worked to develop a viable information base and equally viable working and communication relationships, his or her behavior as a molder and influencer of institutional policy in areas outside traditional student affairs services and programs will not be perceived as unwarranted intrusion or power grabbing. Instead, the CSAA will be viewed as an institutional officer who is working with the best interests of the institution in mind, and will be welcomed as a respected co-equal sharing knowledge, time, and effort to the benefit and dynamism of the college (Dressel, 1981; Shaffer, 1973).

In the best of possible worlds, officers at the executive level are expected to work with and relate to each other in the manner just described (Appleton, Briggs, & Rhatigan, 1978; Dressel, 1981). However, human organizations whether social, commercial, military, or collegiate are administered by all nature of people including those who are unsharing, jealous, tactless, timid, overly-aggressive, or protective of their "turfs." Thus, the campus climate is an important determinant of the degree of diplomacy the CSAA exercises and the extent to which he or she plays the role of leader and molder of institutional policy. In this context the CSAA will have to spend a great deal of time and energy in (1) developing an appropriate knowledge base about students, institutions, and significant others (key players); (2) building appropriate bridges between student affairs and other divisions through cooperative and collaborative sponsorship of mutually beneficial programs and activities; (3) involving highly respected faculty and staff in student affairs policy and advisory groups (Williamson, 1961); (4) becoming involved in and securing student affairs staff representation on important campus advisory, governance, and policy-making committees; (5) offering the skills and services of student affairs staff members to other divisions and units to aid them in achieving program goals; (6) sharpening personal and staff members' understanding and skill in proposal writing for campus-wide consideration and implementation; and (7) following through on tasks and assignments of importance to the total institution. Although not exhaustive, such activities executed diplomatically with altruistic motives should reasonably assure the maintenance or creation of an environment of trust where all executive officers may share their capacities as leaders and molders of institutional policy.

Numerous examples that lend themselves to the achievement of goals implicit in the aforementioned activities can be observed on many campuses and found in the academic content of graduate professional preparation programs of quality. A solid knowledge base about the nature of college students and the dynamics of their development is a basic component of professional preparation, but subject to the unique characteristics of and information collection about each individual campus. Cooperative and collaborative activities between student and academic affairs results from commitment to integrated learning experiences as well as demonstrated understanding of academic purpose and course content. Mutual involvement of the faculty in student affairs and student affairs in the academic arena demands mutual goal-sharing as well as earned respect for the knowledge, skills, and competencies of the student affairs staff members.

Critical to understanding the opportunities and responsibilities inherent in the role of leadership in institutional policy making is acceptance of the belief that the common good of students and institutions preclude self-advantage, and that service that benefits others is its own greatest reward.

CHAMPION OF CAUSES

Surely, one of the most controversial and emotionally charged perennial issues characteristic of the American higher education experience is the nature and extent to which students are free to express their interests. Heated discussions and debates over student academic freedom have seldom been academic (Williamson & Cowan, 1966), nor have they been restricted to academia. Parents, legislators, trustees, taxpayers, faculty, administrators, and even students throughout the past century have been exercised over the conduct of those students who challenge or resist established authority (Hook, 1970; Williamson, 1961). And, during times of campus unrest when some students have challenged the established social order, many students turned to the CSAA and other professional staff members for information, guidance, answers, and support.

The foundations of America's colleges rest upon society's understanding and continued support. As well, their essence as environments of unfettered search for truth requires society's understanding and support of the concept of academic freedom—for faculty and for students (Hook, 1970; Williamson, 1961; Williamson & Cowan, 1966). And, as the acknowledged campus experts on students and student life, it is incumbent upon CSAAs and student affairs staff members to be well versed about and champions of academic freedom for students. This is especially important if the CSAA and the work of the division are to gain respect and merit the support of those they serve—students.

Among the essential elements of college and university mission statements, the purpose of fully developing the individuality of scholars and students alike to the maximum of their potentials is central. For the student affairs professional, this purpose requires that he or she (1) possess fundamental knowledge and a comprehensive understanding of late adolescent and early adult growth and behavior; (2) understand and manifest respect for the basic civil liberties of students and the freedoms and responsibilities accorded them within the framework of the concept of academic freedom; (3) serve as an unwavering advocate in achieving honesty and fairness in institution-student relationships (AAUP, 1968); (4) respect the need for autonomy and privacy as necessary for intellectual, emotional, and social growth; and (5) organize and administer the co-curriculum so that student participation will contribute to intellectual, personal, social, and emotional maturity (Appleton, Briggs, & Rhatigan, 1978; Williamson, 1961).

These advocacies necessitate an understanding of the need for collegiate institutions to be able to conduct affairs in an atmosphere that provides comfort, security, and assurance from unwarranted intrusion and conduct that will disrupt the important business of teaching, research, and service. Simultaneously, this environment should be designed to engender a climate of challenge and support that both stimulates and nurtures debate, discussion, experimentation, and expressions of personal, political, and social concern.

This necessary and ideal balance between freedom and restraint has proven to be extremely troublesome for institutions to achieve and maintain, and all the more difficult to explain convincingly to the college's multiple constituencies (Williamson, 1961). No matter how perplexing and difficult the situation, if student affairs is to own a legitimate stake in the education and growth of students, it must understand both the nature and the forces of adolescent growth and its psychological transitions. Further. it must work to educate students as they progress through the parental and social dependence-independence stages in ways that will help them understand the corollary responsibilities which both accompany and affect the freedoms they seek. Admittedly, this is a monumental task with which colleges have struggled for many decades but, regardless of its complexity, it may be the single most important educational goal of a democratic society. At the very least, it should be a cherished goal that the CSAA must explain and champion with clarity and conviction before the college's many constituencies.

Control is an extremely strong element essential for the accomplishment of effective administration and management and long associated with the attractive concepts of power and authority (Corson, 1960). Yet, the exercise of control in relationship to the constantly evolving growth stages of late adolescents is one which mandates its ever-decreasing exercise so that students striving for maturity achieve "freedom within restraint" (Williamson, 1961, p. 314). In this context, student affairs professionals responsible for implementing the process of educating and developing students toward maturity and freedom must subordinate their personal needs for control in favor of the more effective and acceptable educational strategies of confrontation, encounter dialogue, discussion, and debate (Ivey & Morrill, 1970; Williamson, 1961). This is especially difficult for the young professional whose assignment on the one hand requires him or her to live-in and direct residence life, but on the other requires professional preparation, staff development, and supervised practice to develop the values, attitudes, and skills that will engender students' development toward responsible maturity.

Over the entire tenure of a CSAA's administrative and educational responsibilities, she or he will be called upon by students to champion many causes, some of which are less than fully acceptable to the CSAA's educational sensibilities. Whatever the cause may be, the CSAA will be in a position to serve as "champion of causes" only to the extent that he or she has developed successful programs of educational activities which both enhance students' growth toward freedom, maturity, restraint, and responsibility and project an honest image of the student affairs division as manifesting similar characteristics.

INSTITUTIONAL PLANNING

Long-range planning for a collegiate institution and its major divisions is based upon beliefs of its stewards and supporters that the mission and accomplishments of the college are beneficial to society and worthy of continuance. Relevant planning requires identification of and agreement about the internal and external variables central to the college's mission, and identification and projections of the availability of resources (that is, students, facilities, personnel, and finances) necessary to maintain the institution at a desirable level of operation. An ideally envisaged, long-range strategic planning initiative involves clarity of mission and goals, commitment to the achievement of those goals in accordance with the plan, and the significant involvement of key administrators and critical constituencies in the plan's development and final form (Hopkins & Massey, 1981).

Much has been written during the past two decades about various planning processes (Adamson, 1981; Green & Associates, 1979; Harpel, 1976), and innumerable computer models have been devised to aid college administrators to collect and massage accurate information for arriving at cost figures and contingency options. Whatever the available hardware and software, planning involves organization, leadership, and a plan for planning.

It is both labor-intensive and costly and requires a true commitment to values reflected in its outcomes as being critically important to the future of the institution.

Within the contemporary environment of accelerated costs, extremely unstable enrollments, and dramatically shifting demographics of critical population groups (Commission, 1988), the CSAA and the student affairs division play important roles (Priest, Boer, & Alphenaar, 1980). The recruitment, retention, and educational achievement of students are central to the mission of both the division and the institution and rather naturally become the focus of planning. In this regard, what becomes incumbent upon the CSAA is to (1) become especially knowledgeable about the planning process and its philosophical and operational underpinnings, (2) possess the information required to implement the process, and (3) put in place the appropriate organizational structures and staff members required to facilitate planning the division within the context of the parent institution.

Suggested earlier was a well-developed and congruent philosophy to serve as a compass as well as a rudder for the organization. This advocacy especially evidences its importance in the planning process which, by necessity, requires descriptions of the divisions' and units' roles and missions within the institutional context and the identification of mission and unit goals to be achieved as a consequence of planning.

The CSAA's capability to manifest leadership in the planning process appears to rest largely on the division staff's capacity for acquiring, retrieving, and accurately interpreting critically important information basic to planning. This includes information such as the (1) short and long-range population trends within the elementary and secondary school systems, (2) demographic changes of special sub-population groups within that system, and (3) demographic data on identified groups such as older and returning students (Jones, 1982). Of equal importance is information about (4) graduation rates by major and socioeconomic levels (Noel, 1978); (5) uses of facilities, services, and programs; (6) expressed and projected needs for additional facilities, programs, and services; (7)

demand for and distribution of various financial aid funds as well as repayment performance; (8) knowledge about student values, interests, and developmental changes; and (9) student satisfaction with a variety of collegiate activities, services, and programs within and outside the classroom (Ewell, 1983).

To a great extent the nature, quality, validity, and usefulness of the division's information to the planning process will be contingent upon (1) determination or responsibility for and content of information to be generated or collected, (2) the quality of the information, and (3) the manner in which information can be presented in an honest and useful fashion (Jones, 1982). These contingencies are dependent upon the sophistication of the CSAA's staff in the areas of research, evaluation, and interpretation of information. Foundational to the expression of such sophistication is the extent to which professional preparation programs graduate students with comprehensive research, evaluation, and planning skills, and the CSAA's commitments to hiring well qualified professionals and encouraging the continuing education of professional staff members.

PUBLIC RELATIONS SPOKESPERSON

The CSAA's responsibilities for helping shape and interpret the institution and its student culture extend well beyond the immediate confines of the college campus. External groups that are critically important to the institution include legislators; alumni; public and private school administrators and counselors; donors; foundations; local, state and federal agencies; police; accrediting organizations; and the radio, press and television media, to name a few (Appleton, Briggs, & Rhatigan, 1978). Of the many roles of student affairs addressed by NASPA's "A Perspective on Student Affairs" (NASPA, 1987), six bear directly upon the CSAA's relationships to the public. These are (1) explaining the values, mission, and policies of the institution; (2) providing and interpreting information about students during the development of policies, legislation, and funding of student-related education and out of class life;

(3) explaining and interpreting policies and programs which contribute to campus security and safety; (4) explaining, interpreting, and advancing institutional values and behavioral standards; (5) assuming a leadership role for the institution in its response to student crises; and (6) establishing and maintaining effective working relationships with the local community.

The nature and breadth of these roles require thorough understanding of the institution, its students, and its constituencies in much the same manner as demanded by many of the previously noted CSAA roles. Crucial to the nature of the content of information shared and positions taken with external constituencies will be the (1) level of confidentiality, (2) legal relationships and implications, (3) representativeness of institutional or division-specific perspectives or positions, (4) professional ethics involved, and (5) degree of freedom accorded the student affairs spokesperson by the institution's chief executive officer and governing board (Appleton, Briggs, & Rhatigan 1978). To avoid misunderstandings, confusion, or mixed messages that could ensue, such contingencies will need to be provided through developing specific policies and agreements at the executive levels and through working agreements with organizational units such as Alumni Affairs, Public Relations, Admissions, Campus Security, Residence Life, Student Judiciary, Student Government, Health Services, and the student press (Schuh, 1986).

Given that the basic skills and competencies most closely associated with relating effectively to external constituencies are typically not addressed during most student affairs professionals' academic preparation, the CSAA and division staff members most often rely on their previous experiences, both good and bad in nature, to serve as guides to effective communications. Even at best, this approach often results in unnecessary recalcitrance for dealing with the public or continuance of high-risk behaviors that end in personal and institutional embarrassment. What is suggested as an alternative to that less than reliable approach is the development of working relationships with the on-campus experts in the best positions to advise, counsel, or instruct the CSAA in the understandings, approaches, skills, and techniques best suited for effectively and forthrightly dealing with the many external constituencies under a variety of circumstances. Such experts may often be found in the college's public and governmental relations offices, news bureau, radio/TV stations, communications arts departments, and student press (Schuh, 1986). Upon request, these specialists are usually most willing to provide individual consultations or formal and informal instruction suitable for professional staff development programs.

Although most CSAAs can report from personal experience a horror story to tell colleagues about some unfortunate incident with the media, most would be willing to admit that on the whole, such occasions are rare and the media, by and large, provide excellent opportunities for communicating accurate facts, official positions and policies, and much of the "best" about their students and institutions. More importantly, such opportunities very often provide the CSAA and institution with audiences larger and more difficult to reach effectively than through normal and expensive channels such as press releases and mailings. In this regard, serving as a spokesperson should be viewed as golden opportunities which should be welcomed and dealt with enthusiastically and with honesty and prudence expected of persons representing the institution.

The active and sometimes volatile nature of campus life creates circumstances that often preclude planned and orderly chain-of-command communications leading to the CSAA's serving as the initial contact person with the public media. Thus, a well-informed and prepared professional staff is imperative to assure reasonably that calm, rational, informed, and accurate statements and explanations are made to the press, or as necessary, referrals are made to the CSAA. Additionally, and equally important, well established operational procedures should be in place to assure that, as a CSAA might put it, "I am never going to be surprised." Obviously, those staff members in the "trenches" are vitally important for keeping supervisors and the CSAA apprised about potential or existing problems and activities that are likely to be of importance to the campus community and larger society.

The spokesperson's role demands not only that accurate and appropriately shared information be provided, but includes consideration of the audience, context, content, and likely use to be made of it by recipients. Thus, in the hands of the informed, skilled, and experienced, the opportunity to share information possesses unlimited potential for rendering a fine service for all involved. In the hands of the uninformed, unskilled, and inexperienced however, the converse may all too often be the unintended outcome. To be truly the professional expected of any CSAA requires one to be constantly engaged in the ongoing and challenging enterprise of linking together knowledge, effort, purpose, and reflective thinking; to do otherwise is to abdicate the responsibility of true professionalism and become yet another higher education functionary.

A FINAL NOTE

The contents of this chapter have been structured to provide an overview of a number of basic leadership roles and activities characteristic of the Chief Student Affairs Administrator. Although not exhaustive, these roles reflect the obvious need for professionally educated and experienced student affairs leaders who are not only experts in their own areas of responsibility but who also manifest a solid and comprehensive understanding of the totality of their institution and the critically important relationships that exist among structures, activities, and people.

The ultimate success of a collegiate institution, as well as its student affairs program, is predicated upon the abilities of executive-level officers to develop staff teams who possess the capacities to initiate those critical interrelationships that lead to cooperative and collaborative educational activities of such impact that a rich collegiate experience is assured for all students. Responsibility for the success of student affairs in this endeavor may ultimately rest upon the shoulders of appointed institutional officers, but the task of carrying out its essential activities resides within the dedication, knowledge, skills, and competencies of professional staff members. And, at this level in student affairs is where the degree of competent professionalism distinguishes itself—from the grass roots level of the student resident advisor to the director and dean.

The extent to which professional staff grasp and gain a working understanding of the scope and breadth of the CSAA's leadership role and the division's important mission within the totality of the institution, will directly affect the nature and quality of student affairs' contribution to the overall collegiate experience. As well, such understandings coupled with individual staff contributions and continued growth will be significant determinants of the heights to which student affairs professionals will rise during their careers.

REFERENCES

Association of Colleges and University Professors (AAUP). (1968). *Joint statement on rights and freedoms of students.* Washington, DC: Author.

Adamson, W.D. (1981). *Institutional planning: A systems approach.* Arlington: ERIC Document Reproduction Service, ED 225 045.

American Council on Education. (1937). *The student personnel point of view.* Washington, DC: Author.

American Council on Education. (1949). *The student personnel point of view.* (rev. ed.). Washington, DC: Author.

Appleton, J.R., Briggs, C.M., & Rhatigan, J.J. (1978). *Pieces of eight.* Portland, OR: National Association of Student Personnel Administrators.

Arbuckle, D.S. (1953). *Student personnel services in higher education.* New York: McGraw-Hill.

Bloom, A. (1987). *The closing of the American mind.* New York: Simon and Schuster.

Boyer, E.L. (1987). *College: The undergraduate experience.* New York: Harper and Row.

Brown, R.D., & Canon, H.J. (1978). Intentional moral development as an objective of higher education. *Journal of College Student Personnel, 19,* 425-429.

Brubacher, S. (1969). *Modern philosophies of education.* New York: McGraw-Hill.

Canon, H.J. (1980). Developing staff potential. In H. Delworth & G. Hanson (Eds.), *Student services: A handbook for the profession* (pp. 439-455). San Francisco: Jossey-Bass.

Commission on National Challenges in Higher Education. (1988). *Memorandum to the 41st President of the United States.* Washington, DC: American Council of Education.

Corson, J. (1960). *Governance of colleges and universities.* New York: McGraw-Hill.

Council of Student Personnel Associations in Higher Education (COSPA). (1975). *Student development services in postsecondary education.* Bowling Green, OH: Author.

Dannells, M., & Kuh, G.D. (1977). Orientation. In W.T. Packwood (Ed.), *College student personnel services* (pp. 102-124). Springfield, IL: Thomas.

DeCoster, D.A., & Brown, S. (1983). Staff development: Personal and professional education. In T.K. Miller, R.B. Winston, Jr., & W.R. Mendenhall (Eds.), *Administration and leadership in student affairs: Actualizing student development in higher education* (pp. 341-374). Muncie, IN: Accelerated Development.

DeCoster, D.A., & Mable, P. (1981). *Understanding today's college students.* New Directions for Student Services Series (No. 16). San Francisco: Jossey-Bass.

Dressel, P.L. (1981). *Administrative leadership.* San Francisco: Jossey-Bass.

Dressel, P.L., & Faricy, H. (1972). *Return to responsibility.* San Francisco: Jossey-Bass.

Ehrlich, T. (1987, Oct.). *Education and values* (Inaugural Address). Indiana University, Bloomington, IN: Indiana University Press.

Ewell, P. (1983). *Information on student outcomes: How to get it and how to us it.* Boulder, CO: National Center for Higher Education Management Systems.

Fiske, B. (1986, Sept. 7). At 350, the U.S. university is vast but unfocused. *New York Times,* p. 30.

Green, L. Jr., & Associates. (1979). *Strategic planning and budgeting for higher education.* La Jolla, CA: J.L. Green and Associates.

Harpel, R.L. (1976). *Planning, budgeting and evaluation in student programs: A manual for administrators.* Portland, OR: National Association of Student Personnel Administrators.

Hook, S. (1970, April). *Conflict and change in the academic community.* Paper prepared for National Association of Student Personnel Administrators national conference, Boston.

Hopkins, D.S.P., & Massey, W.F. (1981). *Planning models for colleges and universities.* Stanford, CA: Stanford University Press.

Ivey, A.E., & Morrill, W.H. (1970). Confrontation, communication, and encounter: A conceptual framework for student development. *NASPA Journal,* 7, 226-234.

Johnson, W.F. (1975). *Contemporary philosophies of education in colleges and universities and student personnel—student development point of view.* Unpublished manuscript, Michigan State University, Department of Educational Administration, East Lansing, Michigan.

Jones, D.P. (1982). *Data and information for executive decisions in higher education.* Boulder, CO: National Center for Higher Education Management Systems.

Keim, M., & Graham, W. (Eds.), (1987). *Directory of graduate professional preparation programs in college student personnel.* Alexandria, VA: American College Personnel Association.

McCorkle, C. Jr., & Archibald, S. (1982). *Management and leadership in higher education.* San Francisco: Jossey-Bass.

Miller, T.K., & Prince, J.S. (1976). *The future of student affairs: A guide to student development for tomorrow's higher education.* San Francisco: Jossey-Bass.

Mueller, K.H. (1961). *Student personnel work in higher education.* Boston: Houghton-Mifflin.

National Association of Student Personnel Administrators (NASPA). (1987). *A perspective on student affairs.* Washington, DC: Author.

National Institute on Education (NIE). (1984). *Involvement in learning.* Washington, DC: Author.

Noel, L. (1978). *Reducing the dropout rate.* New Directions for Student Services Series (No. 30). San Francisco: Jossey-Bass.

Owens, G. (1981). *Organizational behavior in education.* (2nd ed.). Englewood Cliffs, NJ: Prentice-Hall.

Packwood, T. (Ed.) (1977). *College student personnel services.* Springfield, IL: Thomas.

Priest, M., Boer, J., & Alphenaar, J. (1980). Long range planning: Implications for the chief student personnel administrator. *NASPA Journal, 18*(1), 2-7.

Rice, J.G. (1965). The campus climate: A reminder. In S. Baskin (Ed.), *Higher education: Some newer developments* (pp. 304-317). New York: McGraw-Hill.

Rodgers, R.F., & Widick, C. (1982). Theory to practice: Uniting concepts, logic and creativity. In H.F. Owens, C.H. Witten, & W.R. Bailey (Eds.), *College student personnel administration* (pp. 100-129). Springfield, IL: Thomas.

Sanford, N. (1956). Personality development during the college years. *Personnel and Guidance Journal, 35,* 74-80.

Sanford, N. (1967). *Where colleges fail.* San Francisco: Jossey-Bass.

Schuh, J.H. (Ed.) (1986). *Enhancing relationships with the student press.* New Directions for Student Service Series (No. 33). San Francisco: Jossey-Bass.

Shaffer, R.H., & Martinson, W.D. (1966). *Student personnel services in higher education.* New York: Center for Applied Research in Education.

Shaffer, R.H. (1973). An emerging role of student personnel-contributing to organizational effectiveness. *Journal of College Student Personnel, 14,* 386-371.

Stamatakos, L..C (1984). College residence halls: In search of educational leadership. *Journal of College and University Housing, 14* (1). 10-17.

Stamatakos, L.C., & Oliaro, P.M. (1972). In-service staff development: A function of student personnel. *NASPA Journal, 10,* 269-273.

Stamatakos, L.C., & Rogers, R. (1984). Student affairs: A profession in need of a philosophy. *Journal of College Student Personnel, 25,* 400-411.

Stamatakos, L.C., & Stamatakos, B.M. (1980). The learning of values through residence education. In D.A. Decoster & P. Mable, (Eds.), *Personal education and community development in college residence halls* (pp. 56-78). University of Cincinnati, Cincinnati, OH: American College Personnel Association.

Upcraft, M.L. (1984). *Orienting students to college.* New Directions for Student Services Series (No. 25). San Francisco: Jossey-Bass.

Williamson, E.G. (1961). *Student personnel services in colleges and universities.* New York: McGraw-Hill.

Williamson, E.G., & Cowan, L. (1966). *The American student's freedom of expression.* Minneapolis: University of Minnesota Press.

Wrenn, C.G. (1951). *Student personnel work in colleges: With emphasis on counseling and group experiences.* New York: Ronald Press.

SUGGESTED READINGS

Alfred, R.L., & Weisman, J. (1987). *Higher education and the public trust: Improving stature in colleges and universities.* ASHE-ERIC Higher Education Report No. 6. Washington: DC: Association for the Study of Higher Education.

Barr, M.J., Keating, L.A., & Associates. (1985). *Developing effective student services programs.* San Francisco: Jossey-Bass.

Floyd, C.E. (1985). *Faculty participation in decision making: Necessity or luxury?* ASHE-ERIC Higher Education Report No. 8. Washington, DC: Association for the Study of Higher Education.

Jacobi, M., Astin, A., & Ayala, F. Jr. (1987). *College student outcomes assessment: A talent development perspective.* ASHE-ERIC Higher Education Report No. 7. Washington, DC: Association for the Study of Higher Education.

Kuh, G.D. (Ed.) (1983). *Understanding student affairs organizations.* New Directions for Student Services Series (No. 23). San Francisco: Jossey-Bass.

Jones, D.P. (1982). *Data and information for executive decisions in higher education.* Boulder, CO: National Center for Higher Education Management Systems.

Moore, L.V., & Young, R.B. (Eds.) (1987). *Expanding opportunities for professional education.* New Directions for Student Services Series (No. 37). San Francisco: Jossey-Bass.

Saddlemire, G.L., & Rentz, A.L. (1986). *Student affairs: A profession's heritage (rev. ed.).* American College Personnel Association Media Publication, No. 40. Washington, DC: American College Personnel Association.

Margaret J. Barr, Ph.D., is Vice Chancellor for Student Affairs at Texas Christian University. She previously served as Vice President for Student Affairs at Northern Illinois University. In addition, she has served in a variety of student affairs positions at the State University of New York at Binghamton, Trenton State College, and the University of Texas at Austin. Her master's degree is from Southern Illinois University-Carbondale, and her Ph.D. was earned at the University of Texas at Austin. She has held a variety of leadership positions in the American College Personnel Association and served as president in 1983-84. A recipient of the Professional Service Award for ACPA and the Contribution to Literature and Research Award from NASPA, she currently serves as a Senior Scholar for ACPA. She is the author of over twenty publications including *Developing Effective Student Services Programs* with L.A. Keating and *Student Services and the Law*. Currently she serves as editor-in-chief of the Jossey-Bass *New Directions for Student Services* monograph series and recently completed service on the NASPA "Plan for a New Century Committee."

Michael J. Cuyjet, Ed.D., is Director of Campus Activities at the University of Maryland—College Park. Prior to his appointment in 1986, he held a number of administrative positions at Northern Illinois University. He holds a bachelor's degree in speech communication from Bradley University and a master's and doctoral degree in counseling from Northern Illinois University. Among his professional activities, he has held several regional and national offices in the National Association for Campus Activities (NACA), including a term on the association's national board of directors. He also has been active among the leadership of the American College Personnel Association (ACPA), having served in a number of roles including chair of the Standing Committee for Multicultural Affairs and several years on the Central Planning Committee for the past two national conferences on Blacks in Higher Education sponsored by the Black Faculty and Staff Association of the University of Maryland.

Chapter **21**

PROGRAM DEVELOPMENT AND IMPLEMENTATION

Margaret J. Barr
Michael J. Cuyjet

Agreement on a clear, precise definition of the term **program** by student affairs professionals is difficult to achieve. Depending on the background of the individual practitioner, the history, mission, and philosophy of the institution and the organizational structure and approach of the student affairs division, a program can mean entirely different things to different people (Barr & Keating, 1985). For purposes of this chapter, **program** is used to encompass three distinct definitions.

First, the term applies to *administrative units organized to deliver specific activities or services that meet either institutional or student needs.* Examples of this first category of programs include admissions, placement services, and new student orientation.

The second definition encompasses *a series of planned interventions to meet a specific goal for a defined target population.* Such programs are characterized by a clear definition of the desired outcomes, a specific time frame for implementation, and an identified target group. Illustrative programs of this definition include leadership development seminars, career exploration courses, fine arts series, and assertiveness training groups.

The third definition covers *programs that are planned as a one-time activity with a planned target and purpose.* Programs that meet this definition include one-time workshops for student leaders; the presentation of a concert, lecture, or film; or an "all nighter" in the student center.

All three definitions are useful and helpful to student affairs professionals as they attempt to plan and implement programs within their institutional settings. No matter what definition is used, however, program development does not "just" happen. It requires a strong theoretical foundation, the skill to translate theory into practice, and a systematic approach to the process. This chapter discusses these issues and presents a strategy for program development of any kind.

THEORY TO PRACTICE
IN PROGRAM DEVELOPMENT

Theory provides one of the most important tools for student affairs professionals engaging in program development. The value of theory is the framework it provides to guide actions (see Chapter 7). Theory helps practitioners both explain what is going on in their environment and predict future actions. Theory also adds stability and consistency to a series of related activities, providing the "common thread" woven into events which comprise a program. "Concepts and theories enable the practitioner to 'make sense' out of the complexities of reality and thus provide for strategic and rational action" (Hoy & Miskal, 1978, p. 23).

Student affairs practitioners can draw upon a wide range of human development and organizational theory as they go about the business of planning and implementing programs. Understanding several alternative theories enhances the ability of the practitioner to develop programs that genuinely meet the needs of students. For example, Kohlberg's (1976) stage theory of moral development can help the practitioner design effective training programs for students involved in campus judicial boards. His work, however, is based only on a male population. William Perry's (1968) approach to intellectual and ethical development accommodated relativistic thinking, a concept absent from Kohlberg's stage theory. In 1980 Murphy and Gilligan "modified Perry's scheme to fit Kohlberg's data" (Gelwick, 1985, p. 31) and developed an approach that clearly differentiated women from men in the arena of moral development. Women used more contextually based relativistic thinking in making moral judgments (Evans, 1985). Thus, a training program for students involved in campus judicial boards should incorporate both theoretical perspectives and help both the men and women involved understand their differences and similarities in making moral and ethical judgments.

Chickering (1969) has been a major force in increasing our understanding of students and their growth and development. His concept of vectors of development in terms of young adults achieving competence, managing emotions, becoming autonomous, establishing identity, forming interpersonal relationships, clarifying purposes, and developing integrity have aided many practitioners in designing appropriate program interventions. While powerful and useful, Chickering's work does not account for different developmental tasks that may be an influence on minority students (Wright, 1987). Thus a residence hall program based only on the Chickering model may *not* be effective in meeting the needs of minority students.

Use of one theoretical base to the exclusion of others may narrow the vision of the program planner and ultimately have a serious negative effect on the program. In earlier chapters of this book, a number of developmental theories were discussed in detail and should be reviewed. Familiarity with the work of Erikson (1963), Maslow (1970), Kohlberg (1976), and Chickering (1969) should be part of the knowledge foundation of an effective program planner. Astin's (1985) involvement theory, in addition, relates these developmental theories to the larger construct of involvement. He posited that "the theory of student involvement is concerned more with the behavioral mechanisms or processes that facilitate student development" (p. 142). Winston and Saunders (1987) provided cogent examples of how the combination of involvement theory and student development theory can help design more effective programs for fraternities and sororities.

Programs also must relate to the broader institutional environment. Barr and Keating (1985) indicated that three equal and critical elements in planning programs: the context, the goal, and the plan. *A Perspective on Student Affairs* (NASPA, 1987) states that the institution is one client of student affairs and also must be accounted for in any program planning process. The context of the institution creates the climate for any successful program and in order to understand the context the astute program planner must understand how organizations work. A foundation in organizational theory is most helpful in that process. Weber's (1947) work on bureaucratic organizations will aid in clarifying decision making structures on campus. The work of Katz and Kahn (1966), Merton (1956), and Bennis, Benne, and Chin (1962) will provide a broad-based understanding of theoretical models of organizations. Finally, the perspective of Argyris and Schon (1974) aids in understanding the translation of such theoretical models into professional interactions and decision making. Their work on defining the dilemmas faced in using theories is particularly valuable to the student affairs practitioner. Argyris and Schon identified five such dilemmas faced in translating theory to practice-those of incongruity, inconsistency, effectiveness, value, and testability (1974, pp. 29-32).(See Chapter 2 for detailed treatment of more theories of organizations.)

The translation of theory into practice is not an easy task. The effort expended will, however, strengthen both the design and implementation processes of student affairs programs. Morrill, Oetting, and Hurst (1974), Moore and Delworth (1976), and Barr and Keating (1985) have provided models of program development that bridge the gap from theory to practice.

The Cube.

Originally designed as a classification system for counselor outreach programs, "The Cube" has evolved into a useful tool for the general student affairs programmer (Morrill, Oetting,

& Hurst, 1974; Morrill & Hurst, 1980). The three dimensions of the cube include defining (1) the target of the intervention, (2) the purpose of the intervention, and (3) the method of the intervention. Because programs by definition are interventions, the use of this model can be helpful in programming. Theory provides the base for the model and practitioners can usefully apply it using "The Cube." A target population can be defined as either an individual or the entire institution. The purpose, or goal of the program, can be determined to be remediation, prevention, or development. Finally, the method of intervention can be chosen as direct, indirect through training and consultation, or using media.

To illustrate, in developing a plan for an administrative program unit to serve handicapped students, the program planner has clear choices. Although these administrative units often concentrate on individual, remedial, direct services, the use of the cube and a knowledge of developmental and organizational theory permits the program planner to become aware of other possibilities. Development of effective indirect interventions is possible by increasing the awareness and sensitivity of non-handicapped students. Training, consultation, and the effective use of media can all be used to accomplish the goal. An institutional intervention can be designed focusing on policy or access questions. A number of possibilities are clarified and choices can be made as the program is planned and implemented.

Moore and Delworth

Through their work with the Western Interstate Commission on Higher Education, Moore and Delworth (1976) developed an extensive model for program development based on the work of Morrill et al. (1974). Their approach to program development is linear, with each step of the model leading to and supporting the work of the following stages. The first stage of the model focuses on the extensive use of a planning team in the analysis of a program idea according to "The Cube" classification system. Only after the target population and the purpose of the program are clearly defined are decisions made about the method of intervention. The model focuses initially on resource and institutional assessment to assure that the original program idea is viable within the context of the institution, is not a duplication of other efforts, and is potentially useful to the target population. Stage two of the model focuses on explicit program goals, training of personnel, evaluation and research decisions, and the need to pilot testing and evaluation of the pilot effort. The fourth stage involves the actual program implementation and additional training needs. In the fifth and last stage, consideration is given to the use of evaluation data to make decisions regarding program maintenance, continuance, and redecision. Throughout the model, primary emphasis is placed on the need to develop a broad-based, highly involved program team and the necessity for constant evaluation and monitoring of the program plan.

Barr and Keating

The work of Barr and Keating (1985) draws both on theory and the models previously described. They define a program as "a theoretically based plan, under which action is taken toward a goal within the context of institutions of higher education" (Barr & Keating, 1985, p. 3). Their model is based on three assumptions. First, that the student affairs practitioner must be able to understand and apply a variety of theories to the task of program development. Second, that there are three equal components in program development: the context, the goal, and the plan or method. Third, all three components must be congruent or the program will fail. (1) They place emphasis on the program planner understanding the institutional context in order to have successful programs. The history of the institution, the commitment of the administration, fiscal constraints, and political realities must all be considered as part of the program planning process. (2) They posited that program success is due in part to determining appropriate goals for programs. Theoretical constructs, assessment data, and needs all combine to establish appropriate goals. (3) The planning and implementation of programs must account for a systematical approach, the skills and competencies of staff, and the short and long range future of the particular program effort. Keating's (1985) diagnostic model of determining errors in program design is particularly helpful. She defines *within errors* as those when a planner lacks adequate knowledge or skill in a specific aspect of the planning process. Examples include an inadequate budget, goals that run counter to developmental theory, and underestimation of the importance of the context (Keating, 1985). *Between errors* occur when a mismatch is between one of the key components: context, goal, and plan. Examples of between errors include a carefully designed program with an appropriate goal that is blocked politically such as a seminar on birth control at an institution affiliated with a church opposed to such practices.

The process for program development previously proposed in this chapter draws on all three of the models previously described. The process is a six-step design using a systematic approach to program development and implementation. A *Program Development Checklist* has been provided at the end of the chapter as a tool to assist program planners. The checklist outlines a series of actions that must be taken to assure program success and is based on the process described in the next section.

A PROGRAM PLANNING PROCESS

A six-step approach to program planning is proposed: assessment, goal setting, planning, implementation, post-assessment (evaluation), and administrative decision.

Step One: Assessment

A detailed assessment of the current institutional environment is part of the first step in the model. Unfortunately, the need for careful assessment of current operations, student characteristics, needs, the environment, and resources is often accomplished quickly; and errors can result. Although the ideal method to carry out such a broad-based assessment is through a planning team, a great deal of data can be gathered by a single professional on an independent basis. A word of caution, however, if necessity dictates independent assessment, the program planner should test his/her conclusions with other knowledgeable persons in the environment. To do less invites program failure.

Current Operations. An essential step in assessment is to find out what activities and programs are already in place on the campus. Often a number of programs concerned with the same topic exist but lack shared information and intentional links between them. For example, at a large state university, a staff member was asked to recommend an institutional direction for health education and wellness efforts. Through careful assessment of current campus efforts over forty distinct programs were discovered, ranging from research projects to individual programs on birth control. None of these efforts were, however, intentionally linked together. In this instance, the recommendation of the staff member wisely recommended that a coordinating function for already established programs be funded and implemented and that a new administrative entity was just not needed.

Student Characteristics. A careful analysis of the demographic characteristics of students can provide useful and valuable information for program planning. Knowledge of the number of students who are in particular age classifications or ethnic groups can assist in understanding whether some programs are actually needed on the campus. Hanson and Yancey (1985) identify both formal and informal sources of such data including existing data bases, previous evaluation data, educational policy analysis data, and ongoing research studies. A sophisticated data base provides a great amount of useful data for program planning. If, however, such a data base is not available, the astute programmer uses all the information that is available including residence hall reservations, admissions data, and the like.

Needs. Unobtrusive measures of student needs provide much of the foundation for program ideas. Observational data can provide important information for program planners. Other student affairs staff members and faculty colleagues can provide a wealth of information about student characteristics through both their formal and informal contacts. For example, can they help determine if common characteristics are among students who fail, students in disciplinary trouble, and students who are involved in alcohol abuse? If they can do this, then a target population for both prevention and remediation efforts can be defined.

In addition, participation counts and utilization data can provide valuable data about student interests and the time, place, and manner that programs should be offered. Questions focused on largest attendance, timing, program length, and who actually comes can provide valuable insight as new programs are contemplated. One often overlooked resource for utilization data is the campus scheduling office where records of all planned events from classes to concerts may be found.

Drum and Figler (1973) cited several other sources of unobtrusive data including conversations with parents, key student leaders, and members of the community. The careful program planner needs to ask questions of others in the environment on a regular basis to gain insight into student needs.

Obtrusive measures of assessment require thought and planning, but they can provide a valuable source of information for program planners. Such "obtrusive measures require the student to provide information" (Hanson & Yancey, 1985) through written questionnaires, telephone interviews, and structured face-to-face interviews. Either method has both positive and negative characteristics. Questionnaires take time to develop, administer, and analyze. In most instances, a random sample should be used rather than the entire population because of time and validity questions. Telephone surveys provide the advantage of immediate follow up to clarify specific responses. Stratified random samples are probably best because of the labor intensity of the effort while structured interviews can provide a richness of detail not available through other methods. The latter, however, have the disadvantage of labor intensity and interviewer bias. A variation on structured interviews which has been successful in a variety of settings is the focus group approach. Small groups of students can be brought together to discuss questions of interest to the programmer, and their responses can be most useful and helpful to the process of program planning. Whatever the method chosen, Hanson and Yancey (1985) caution the program planner to "distinguish between items that measure a 'want' and those that measure a 'need'" (p. 158).

The work of Astin (1968, 1977), Coyne (1975), Feldman (1971), Pace (1969), and Fleming (1984) can provide guidance on methodology for obtrusive measures. In addition, assistance can be sought from faculty members with specialized knowledge in research and evaluation. The key variable is the ability of staff members to sort data and determine which student needs are most dominant in the context of a particular institution's environment.

Institutional Environment. Assessment of the institutional environment can be a more difficult task than that of assessing student needs. Programs that are well-planned and meet student needs may fail because of a mismatch between the program goal and that of the institution (Barr & Keating, 1985).

To succeed, programs must be compatible with the overall goal and mission of the institution. To illustrate, a program focusing on abortion as an alternative to pregnancy may never succeed in an institution with a high identification with conservative religious values. However, a program focusing on the ethical and moral choices associated with sexual behavior may well be both supported and encouraged in such an institution.

Lofty institutional mission statements provide little direct guidance to the student affairs practitioner. The program planner must fill in the data with specific information and use all available resources to understand the institutional environment. Use of historical records is an important first step to increase understanding. Most campus agencies are required to complete an annual or year-end report. Although finding these seldom read documents may prove to be a chore, valuable information on programs which have been previously offered is available from these records. If program planners can understand and appreciate why programs succeeded or failed in the past, they have a firm foundation for current efforts. Talking to individuals who have a span of institutional history is also helpful. One must listen carefully, however, in order to identify the idiosyncratic views of the institution held by those consulted.

Political realities also must be considered in the institutional phase of program development (Barr, 1985). Issues of territoriality, power, and current program responsibilities must be assessed early in the planning process. Questions regarding who supports what must be answered before the development of a program plan. Understanding of campus politics is indeed a critical part of the assessment process.

The use of survey instruments also can provide valuable data on the perceptions of members of the campus community of their environment. Struening and Guttentag's (1975) handbook on evaluation provides a useful reference on approaches. Finally, the assessment process is best served by the adoption of a theoretical basis for analysis of the college environment. Ultimately, however, understanding of the institutional environment rests on the ability of the program planner to synthesize data from many sources and translate them into sound programs.

Resource Assessment. Three resources must be accounted for in the assessment process: staff, money, and physical resources. Each must be evaluated in terms of the ability of the program planner to develop, implement, and sustain the program idea.

Assessment of staff really means getting to know the skills and competencies that are available to support the proposed program. Moore (1987) has developed a model to aid in the process of assessing staff skills and needs that is both useful and helpful. Polling staff members regarding their interests and ideas is an excellent first step. Any successful program requires leadership at a variety of levels and knowledge of the staff's management and administrative skills will identify those who might be involved in the development of the program. If no current staff member has the requisite skills and abilities to carry the program forward, then additional personnel may need to be hired or current staff members retrained. Political realities and fiscal constraints identified in the assessment process will determine if that alternative is feasible.

Another alternative is not to restrict the assessment of staff resources to individuals within the department or agency planning the program. Identifying skills and competencies of others in the institution may uncover new staff resources to aid in the development of new program ideas. Whether polling staff members within the agency or external to it, be certain not to limit the inquiry to job-related interests. An individual's hobby, avocation, or strictly personal pursuit may be an important program resource.

Fiscal resources are also an important part of the assessment process. Failure to identify all the costs associated with a program often cause programs to fail after the initial funding period. No one can be expected to be prepared for every possible eventuality. Yet a careful, comprehensive review of all costs associated with the program is the first step in determining how much money is needed for program implementation. Ask for assistance in this initial assessment phase as it is often easier for someone not directly associated with the program idea to identify hidden costs.

Several sources, in addition to Douglas (Chapter 18), can be of help to the program planner in fiscal planning. Maw, Richards, and Crosby (1976) provided a cogent explanation of fomula budgeting techniques and specifically apply them to student affairs. Pembroke (1985) defined the broad issues of fiscal planning in student affairs including multiple sources of support. Barr (1988) provided practical guidelines for the novice budget manager that should be useful to program planners.

Sources of funds vary from institution to institution; however, the most stable fiscal support is the central or general revenue budget of the institution. Acquiring resources from this source requires both advanced planning and adherence to institutional regulations (Pembroke, 1985).

Other fiscal sources include organizations, fee-allocating bodies, and grants. On-campus clubs or groups that are organized for a purpose related to the intended goal of the program as well as off-campus groups with similar goals can often provide funds. Similarly, some programs might appeal to existing offices and administrative units that would be willing co-sponsors. Every fee collected at the institution should be identified and criteria for the use of those funds determined. Grants from government agencies, foundations, or private enterprise are often overlooked by program developers in student affairs as potential sources of funds. With homework, attention to detail, and adherence to the funding guidelines, success can often follow in getting grant support.

The program itself can be a fiscal resource. If it is a service for which a user fee may be charged, or if it consists of revenue-generating events, the program could be totally or partially self-supported.

Space and potential physical resources also must be considered as a part of the initial assessment. An analysis should be made to determine the kinds of physical resources necessary to assure program success. Physical needs include furnishings, equipment, commodities, and services. Yet, the primary physical resource is the appropriate and adequate configuration of rooms. The proposed space should provide an environment with comfortable temperatures and adequate lighting.

Equipment and supplies are necessary for any program to succeed. Meetings require chairs arranged in a specific manner. Registration areas or clerical functions require a table or desk, a typewriter or computer terminal, and supplies. Ticket takers need stub collection boxes. Ushers need flashlights. Group leaders need chalkboards, chalk, erasers, or flipcharts and marking pens. The important thing to remember to do is to think through all functions of the program in advance and account for them in planning.

Step Two: Goal Setting

Once the assessment phase is completed, the next step involves setting specific, measureable goals for the program. "Goals are important for two reasons. First, program goals provide clear direction for the student services unit and define the accomplishments that should result from any proposed program effort. Second, program goals provide guidance to institutional decision makers by clearly identifying what will *not* be accomplished if the program is *not* supported" (Barr, 1985, p. 159). Successful programs are goal directed and have a clear outcome in mind before the first investment of time, money, and energy is made. Program planners need to determine what specific outcomes should occur for whom and under what conditions. Too often goals for student affairs programs are of the "mom, country, and apple pie" variety. Such goals are certainly difficult to oppose, but they are also difficult to be *for.* More importantly, broad-based goals for any type of program are difficult to evaluate. Thus, time spent determining the differences that program planners believe the program will make is time well spent. As a result, program success or failure is easier to determine, and decisions about program continuance are more systematic.

Specific goals also help determine the actual target population to be served. By focusing on the population early in the planning process, a diffuse program with no measureable impact is less likely to be the result.

At this stage of program development, the program planner also must consider how determination of program success will be made. In other words, will evaluation be possible to determine how effective the program is? If the answer is no, then redefine the objectives before making final program plans.

Step Three: Planning

After a comprehensive assessment is made of student needs, resources, current activities, staff, and the institutional environment and after goals are set, specific planning for the program is ready to begin. The question becomes one of determining the best method for responding to needs within the constraints identified in the assessment process.

Developing a Planning Team. Selecting a planning team is an outcome of the staff resource identification process. Program development activities, at their best, are open to new data, new information, and new ideas throughout the process. Program planning cannot be isolated from the constantly changing larger environment. Development of a broad-based planning team helps assure that this will occur. At a minimum, the planning team should be composed of those individuals who will be directly affected by the program effort. The planning group then can seek consultation from experts such as those in food service or data processing as needs arise. The key to a successful planning team is to establish a small but effective working group. Others can be involved, as needed, in the actual development and implementation of the project.

Selecting an Approach. A wide variety of approaches always exists for a program. The skill of the program planner lies in the ability to choose the best approach for a particular institution at a specific time. Any of the program models previously described can assist with the process. The first question faced by the program planning team revolves around the issue of what theory explains about the target population. For example, how do members of the target population learn? A media intervention might be very appropriate with a traditionally aged student population but relatively ineffective with returning adults. A match must be made between the method used in the program effort and the learning styles of the target population.

Questions should be raised which focus on the *best* way to deliver the program. Technology, including computer support should not be ignored, neither should the alternative of integrating the content of the program with established programs and activities. Every alternative has strengths and weaknesses. None should be rejected out of hand, and all should be evaluated. To illustrate, if the assessment phase indicates that alcohol abuse is increasing on campus, several program responses are possible. Choices might be made between spot announcements on campus radio and television stations, training student staff, an alcohol awareness day, developing and distributing printing materials, making policy changes, in-service training for faculty and staff, offering alternative programs that do not use alcohol, an alcohol hotline, and so forth. Each has validity, and by exploration and evaluation of each alternative, one, or a combination of the best approaches, can be incorporated into the actual program plan. Convergent thinking, on the part of the planning team, limits choices and restricts the planning group to choices solely within their span of control. A divergent approach, on the other hand, opens the possibilities. Where time and resources permit, consider the different learning styles of sub-groups within your target population. For example, a workshop for students on health issues related to AIDS may be approached differently to attract international students, particularly from African countries where the disease is acknowledged as a significant problem, than a program designed for American students who do not see AIDS as relevant to their life experience.

How to Begin. Two questions must be asked by the planning team once an approach is selected. What should be the initial scope of the program and is it necessary to pilot test the agreed upon plan? Three alternatives exist at this phase of planning: moving forward with the total program package, starting at a limited level and adding preplanned components when resources are available, and pilot testing the program. Each choice has strengths and weaknesses, and the final choice should be made in terms of the institutional climate and available resources.

To advocate for only full program implementation may result in a negative response if the assessment phase was not carefully completed. An "all or nothing" approach carries with it a risk that nothing may happen. The advantage of an incremental approach to program implementation is that the program can be initiated on a modest level without major resource allocation. If the program is successful at the initial level, then the way is paved for additional support in the future. A danger, however, is when resources are limited decision makers may be satisfied with the results and no further resources will be forthcoming.

A pilot program provides an opportunity to gain further insight into program alternatives at low risk to students, the agency, and the administrative decision maker. Data gathered through the pilot program can identify strengths and weaknesses of the program design not anticipated during planning. Adjustments can be made quickly and needs identified which may merit further resource allocation. The only negative aspects of pilot programs are the impatience of students and staff *and* the fact that the program may fail. If the program fails, however, resources have not been used on a large scale, and assessment can begin again.

Training. Any new program requires training of staff members charged with responsibility for implementation. A new approach to training paraprofessionals may, for example, require extensive training of staff members operating the program. Such training needs should be considered early in the planning process and be accounted for in the project timeline and resource allocation. Assumptions should not be made regarding the skills, abilities, and knowledge of those charged with program implementation. The assessment phase suggested that an inventory of staff skills and abilities be made. At this step, a match needs to be made between those skills and abilities and the tasks that must be done. If a gap exists, then appropriate training must be provided. A well-trained, competent staff is the single most critical variable in program success (Baier, 1985).

Establishing a Timeline. Successful program implementation is dependent on an accurate estimate of the time needed to complete the project. One useful method for establishing a timeline is to plan backwards from the program implementation date. Working from the target date, the planners can establish a week-by-week activity plan outlining decisions that must be made in order to meet the target date. Problems or unexpected events will inevitably occur, and a realistic timeline allows for such circumstances and helps planners anticipate the unexpected.

Budgeting. A final step in this phase is determining the actual fiscal resources necessary for program completion. The budget should include all costs associated with the program including personnel, materials, space, marketing, postage, food, and equipment. When the program budget is completed, it serves as another checklist at the program implementation step. The information gathered in the assessment step should not be used for final budget preparation.

Step Four: Implementation

Planning should lead to a product—a specific program. If the elements in Steps One, Two, and Three are thoroughly considered, then actual program implementation should be relatively trouble free. A number of issues must be attended to, however, to assure program success.

Defining Responsibilities. Concise directions must be given regarding the expectations of those associated with the program. Accountability lines should be clearly drawn and reporting relationships defined. Everyone should know what his/her specific responsibilities are. The successful program planner should never hear the plaintive cry, "I didn't know I was responsible for that."

Publicity. If the target population is not aware of the program, then poor participation will be the inevitable outcome. The best publicity catches people's attention so they can receive the message being sent. As in other phases of program development, divergent thinking should be employed. People are the best resource for an effective publicity campaign both for ideas and promotion. Determine what effect publicity should have on people and try to focus the entire campaign on that effect. One effective method is to develop a list of free publicity sources on the campus. If the opportunity exists, collaborate with faculty teaching marketing and advertising courses by establishing the promotion campaign as a class project. Even outside the mechanism of a formal class, students are a valuable resource to tap, not only for publicity but for a variety of staffing needs. Students are often very anxious to gain the kind of firsthand experiences that program planning and delivery can provide and in many cases may only require the same orientation and training as staff. Use brainstorming techniques and involve members of your target population in planning the publicity campaign. Remember these two elements of human nature: curiosity and "what's in it for me?" Publicity should make people want to seek more information and should make them feel it is worth their effort to do so.

Location. The physical location of the program, whether it is an administrative agency or a one-time event, can enhance or detract from the effort. Efforts should be made to locate a program unit in an area with high student traffic. Barriers that impede participation by disabled participants should be removed or alternative access provided.

Often the needs of the program limit choices of suitable space. If a location has proven very popular at the institution because of aesthetics or decor, advantage should be taken of this built-in attraction. If participants are likely to drive, consider parking spaces in selecting the location. For an ongoing program, consider a location adjacent to related activities or other established programs that may complement it. For programs consisting of a series of meetings or events, try to hold each session in the same location at a consistent time and day. Visibility is self-fulfilling; the program in a highly visable location serves as its own promoter.

Timing. The timing of the program can have either positive or negative effects. Programs aimed at specific populations must accommodate clients' schedules. A workshop for freshmen on coping with test anxiety after midterms is less effective than one offered just prior to exams. A series of classes on cardio-pulmonary resuscitation (CPR) for residence hall staff members is much more useful in September than in May when the summer intervenes prior to the skill being needed or used. Timing also means coordination with other programs. Starting an AIDS series makes good sense during "health week." A session on resume writing could fit nicely into an all-campus career day program. A comprehensive list of upcoming events, the academic calendar, and holidays is an invaluable tool in scheduling. Probably the most critical aspect of timing is to avoid conflict with and/or build a tie-in with other events. Nothing should be overlooked. Testimony as to the importance of checking sports schedules can be given by anyone who has inadvertently scheduled a workshop on Superbowl Sunday. All factors must be considered in the timing of an effective program.

Evaluation. An evaluation plan and procedure must be considered as an integral part of the planning process. Goals of the program developed in Step Two will define success. The evaluation plan will aid in gathering data needed to make decisions about the future of the program. Too often, however, evaluation procedures are overlooked or are the last elements considered in program planning. This is a mistake.

Two approaches to evaluation need to be taken: process and product. ***Process evaluation*** concentrates on how well all phases of the planning and implementation steps are proceeding. The primary purpose "is to improve the program as it unfolds and to eliminate making the same mistakes the next time around" (Hanson & Yancey, 1985, p. 142). Careful records should be kept and open dialogue maintained during the planning and implementation steps. Such data are also useful beyond the specific program being evaluated. A ***product evaluation*** process, if it is carefully documented, provides valuable guidance for future program endeavors. Hanson and Yancey (1985) urged those engaged in process evaluation to gather data on some relatively simple questions: Who attended?, Were some people there that were unexpected?, Were all the elements of the original plan delivered?, Who dropped out?, Who stayed?, and so forth.

As part of the staffing requirements for the program, someone should be charged with responsibility for evaluation. The additions of an outside evaluator proves the best assurance for objectivity in the process. Often an outside evaluator can be obtained through academic departments seeking projects for students. Whether the responsibility for evaluation rests within or without the planning team, it must be considered both in planning and program implementation.

As part of the staffing requirements for the program, someone should be charged with responsibility for evaluation. The addition of an outside evaluator proves the best assurance for objectivity in the process. Often an outside evaluator can be obtained through academic departments seeking projects for students. Whether the responsibility for evaluation rests within or without the planning team, it must be considered both in planning and program implementation.

Product evaluation permits program planners to assess whether the activity meets the goals defined in Step Two of the planning process. Many product evaluations rely on paper and pencil responses from program participants. Any evaluation procedure must be developed in a manner that does not interfere with the program activity. Therefore, the evaluation scheme must be a joint enterprise between program planners and evaluators.

Other methods of evaluation can and should be explored. The range includes guided group discussion, structured telephone interviews, and face-to-face interviews. One effective technique is to conduct an on-site evaluation at the conclusion of the program followed by structured telephone interviews six to eight weeks after the intervention. The combination of these two approaches reduces the "halo" effect of a positive program and allows planners to see long term influence. In addition, valuable suggestions for change often arise in the follow-up evaluation. For example, a summer orientation program was evaluated by participants at the conclusion of the session. Valuable data were collected helping staff members work with student advisors to improve their performance. The follow-up evaluation, after the first semester of enrollment, uncovered additional information that first semester freshmen wish they had known at the start of the school year. Those suggestions were then incorporated into the program plan for the following summer's program.

The goal of evaluation is to provide accurate, useful data to help decision makers assess the effectiveness of the program. Evaluation as a tool for program planning is a complex but necessary variable in gaining insight into program effectiveness.

Step Five: Post-Assessment

The development and implementation of a program consumes both agency and personal resources. Therefore, when a program has been established for some time, not surprisingly program planners devote less time to the effort. The program can slide off target, resources can be cut back, and interest can wane. Established programs also should be assessed to assure that resources are being effectively used. Each program should be reviewed on a periodic basis to assure that program goals are being met.

Using Evaluation Data. Step Four included evaluation as part of the program planning and implementation process. An evaluation is of no value, however, unless results are used to make decisions about the future of the program. Program planners should relate evaluation data to program goals and then be prepared to make recommendations regarding the program effort. Too often, student affairs programs include elaborate evaluation procedures and produce comprehensive reports that are never read or used by decision makers.

When analyzing evaluation data and preparing reports, analyze who will use it and present different data for different audiences (Hanson & Yancey, 1985). Tell them what they need to know in order to make decisions. Guided questions often help in the analysis of data. But at a minimum, the evaluation report should detail who the participants were, how they reacted, what outcomes were achieved, and an analysis of the cost.

Fiscal Accountability. While the post-assessment phase often focuses on the reactions of people to the program, a concurrent assessment should also focus on costs. Program planners need to be able to document the cost per student for a specific program, the cost per transaction for a particular service, and the cost to the institution for providing support for a program activity if needed. Two uses can be made of such data. First, data can be used to provide a strong sense of support for the program. Second, data can be used as a yardstick to see if alternative methods of delivery that are less expensive are available. Either is legitimate and helpful to the program planners and their administrative superiors. Unfortunately, student affairs practitioners often do not look at these variables in the post-assessment step and are unprepared to defend costly program innovations when resources are scarce.

Program Modification. Post-assessment also has another goal, that of program modification. The best plans can sometimes go awry because of circumstances not under the control of the planning team. Post-assessment that focuses on suggestions for change and modification of the program can assist in adjusting the program to approximate more closely the stated goals and objectives. Small changes such as hours, location, and publicity can all make a difference in the success or failure of the program for the institution and ultimately for students. Unless a structured means is available to gather such suggestions from program participants and staff, they may be lost. A number of methods are helpful including open-ended questionnaires, a suggestion box in the program office, or merely paying attention to the suggestions and concerns of support staff attached to the program.

To illustrate, at a large university, a federally funded tutoring program was established to serve the needs of a group of economically disadvantaged students. Under the guidelines, students seeking tutoring had to meet financial eligibility guidelines for participation. As the program became established and became known to students not in the original target group, many of these students came to the tutoring office to seek assistance. Although the program as funded could not accommodate their needs, the program staff allowed these new students to contact the tutoring staff and pay them for their services. Careful attention was paid to data collection before and after the alternate structure was established. At the end of the fiscal year, data were analyzed by the program staff. Not only did the original program successfully serve the original target population, but the alternate structure provided tutoring services to as many students as the original program. In addition, many students willing to pay for services had to be turned away due to the limited size of the tutoring staff. Not only did a need for tutoring for economically disadvantaged students exist, but a university-wide response for students was needed. After the initial year, the program was redesigned as a university tutoring program serving both economically disadvantaged students and students willing to pay for services. The tutoring pool was expanded and a permanent location was found for the program. Good, sound evaluation data and careful post-assessment by program staff provided an excellent opportunity to expand resources without added cost to the institution.

Institutionalization of student services programs occurs very quickly in student affairs. Once a program is offered, an assumption is often made that it is a permanent part of the enterprise. Unfortunately, some programs fail, resources are limited, or new goals must be met. When that occurs, administrative decision makers must have adequate and useful data to decide on the next step (Thomas, 1979).

Step Six: Administrative Decision

The final step in program planning involves a decision about the future of the program. If the first five steps of the program planning cycle have been carefully followed, then the decision for program continuance is a fairly easy process. Three decisions can be made about any program: continuation, modification, or abandonment. Continuation should be decided for a definite time period with a built-in review process. A careful cyclical review should be made of all student affairs programs to provide needed data to respond to changing institutional and student needs.

Decisions for modification mandate complete reentry into the program planning model. Specific goals and objectives should be established for the modified program and careful attention paid to all phases of planning. Again, modification requires that a redecision be made about the modified program at some future date.

Abandonment of a program is perhaps the most difficult decision of all (Thomas, 1979). Abandonment carries with it overtones of failure. However, "with limited resources and changing needs, it is inevitable that some programs will be discontinued" (Sandeen, 1985, p. 270). The program may have fulfilled its objectives, or the needs of students may not be the same. Fiscal and political realities also change and student affairs administrators must respond to them or risk failure. Finally, the program may be good and may have met its objectives, but is simply not reaching enough people to justify continuation. Whatever the reason for discontinuance, the administrative decision maker must plan carefully at this stage. Issues of staff, student needs, and political pressures all surface when a program is discontinued. The astute administrator plans as carefully for program discontinuance as program implementation.

The decision for program continuance is both a rational and emotional process for program planners. To modify, abandon, or limit the continuation of programs that have taken considerable time and energy to create may indeed be difficult. Program planners must, however, assume the responsibility for making recommendations about the future of the program; otherwise, it will occur without their advice.

SUMMARY AND IMPLICATIONS

In this chapter, a six-step approach for program development that has practical implications in a wide range of institutional settings has been presented. Each of the steps interlocks and guides the practitioner through the process of program development and implementation.

Program planning requires attention to detail as well as broad institutional issues. The assessment step is critical to success in program planning. Failure to assess student needs, human and fiscal resources, and the institutional climate can result in program failure. For both practical and philosophic reasons, careful attention must be paid to a variety of elements in the assessment phase.

Goals for programs also must be clearly defined as they guide the planning and the evaluation process. Vague, unspecified goals do not permit program planners to convince decision makers of what will not happen if the program occurs.

A planning team committed to divergent thinking strengthens the planning effort. The group works cooperation, and goal setting that takes place within such a team transcends the specific program being planned. Careful attention to all the elements of the program by the planning team can assure that both large and small elements are built into the program plan. Evaluation is an integral part of the planning process and must be accounted for in every step of planning.

The post-assessment step has a double application. This procedure serves primarily to evaluate the product and the process of the program. The process itself of conducting a post-assessment can develop a pattern of good, comprehensive recordkeeping. If done properly, post-assessment, even from a program that fails, teaches a lesson about the process of program development and implementation that can be employed in all future programming endeavors.

Finally, programs need to be based on a strong foundation of human development theory. Student affairs practitioners need to apply what they know about how people learn, grow, and develop as they design interventions for students. Campuses should strive to provide not just academic experience, but the comprehensive human development of all students (Brown, 1972). Student development theory advocates not only attention to the developmental needs of students but also providing programs to help them reach their potential. Effective program development and planning skills are essential if the student affairs practitioner is truly going to be successful in translating theory into effective practice.

The Program Development Checklist may be helpful to practitioners as they go about the task of program development and implementation. It is based on the six-step planning process and provides reminders as planners proceed with program development.

PROGRAM DEVELOPMENT CHECKLIST

Step One: Assessment

_____ Identify and analyze the demographic characteristics of the student body

_____ Review what human development theory tells about the population

_____ Develop a clear understanding of the institutional mission and goals

_____ Solicit observations by colleagues of student needs

_____ Analyze obtrusive data regarding student needs

_____ Review the institution's records

_____ Review current and past campus activities

_____ Gain an understanding of the political and decision making structures on campus

_____ Assess staff skills and competencies

_____ Identify sources of fiscal support

_____ Identify potential space and equipment

Step Two: Goal Setting

_____ Define the target population

_____ Determine what the desired outcomes of the program will be

_____ State objectives for the program effort

Step Three: Planning

_____ Select a planning team

_____ Select an approach to developing the program

_____ Identify methods to evaluate all components of the program

_____ Determine whether a pilot program is needed

_____ Determine all resources necessary for the effort

_____ Develop a timeline

_____ Determine training needs

_____ Develop a complete budget

Step Four: Implementation

_____ Assign specific responsibilities to each staff member

_____ Identify and implement publicity program

_____ Select the physical location and equipment needed

_____ Identify necessary physical resources and supplies

_____ Schedule the program in relationship to other events

_____ Collect evaluation data

Step Five: Post-Assessment

_____ Analyze evaluation data in relationship to goals

_____ Identify unanticipated outcomes

_____ Solicit staff reaction

_____ Make recommendations to improve cost-effectiveness

_____ Make recommendations for modification in program process or content

Step Six: Administrative Decision

_____ Decide the future of the program: continuation, modification, or abandonment

REFERENCES

Argyris, C., & Schon, D. (1974). *Theory in practice increasing professional effectiveness.* San Francisco: Jossey-Bass.

Astin, A. W. (1968). *The college environment.* Washington, DC: American Council on Education.

Astin, A. W. (1977). *Four critical years: Effects of college on beliefs, attitudes, and knowledge.* San Franscisco: Jossey-Bass.

Astin, A.W. (1985) *Achieving educational excellence: A critical assessment of priorities and practices in higher education.* San Francisco: Jossey-Bass.

Baier, J.L. (1985). Recruiting and training competent staff. In M.J. Barr & L.A.. Keating (Eds.), *Developing effective student services programs* (212-234). San Francisco: Jossey-Bass.

Barr, M.J. (1985) Internal and external forces influencing programming. In. M. J. Barr & L. A. Keating (Eds.), *Developing effective student services programs* (pp. 62-82). San Francisco: Jossey-Bass.

Barr, M.J. (1988). Managing money. In M.L. Upcraft and M.J. Barr (Eds.), *Managing student affairs effectively* (pp. 21-37). New Directions for Student Service (No. 41). San Francisco: Jossey-Bass.

Barr, M. J., & Keating, L. A. (Eds.). (1985). *Developing effective student services programs.* San Francisco: Jossey-Bass.

Bennis, C., Benne, K. D., & Chin, R. (1962). *The planning of change.* New York: Holt, Rinehart and Winston.

Brown, R. D. (1972). *Student development in tomorrow's higher education: A return to the academy.* Washington, DC: American College Personnel Association.

Chickering, A. W. (1969). *Education and identity.* San Francisco: Jossey-Bass.

Coyne, R. (1975). Environmental assessment: Mapping for counselor action. *Personnel and Guidance Journal, 54,* 150-5.

Drum, D. J., & Figler, H. E. (1973). *Outreach in counseling.* New York: Intext Educational Publishers.

Erikson, E. H. (1963). *Childhood and society (2nd ed.).* New York: Norton

Evans, N.J. (Ed.). (1985). *Facilitating the development of women.* New Directions for Student Services (No. 29). San Franscico: Jossey-Bass.

Feldman, K. A. (1971). Measuring college environments: Some uses for path analysis. *American Education Research Journal, 8,* 51-70.

Fleming, J. (1984). *Blacks in college.* San Francisco: Jossey-Bass.

Gelwick, B. P. (1984). Cognitive development of women. In N. J. Evans (Ed.), *Facilitating the development of women* (pp. 29-44). New directions for student services (No. 29). San Francisco: Jossey-Bass.

Hanson, G. R., & Yancey, B. D. (1985). Gathering information to determine program needs. In M. J. Barr & L. A. Keating (Eds.), *Developing effective student services programs* (pp. 137-158). San Francisco: Jossey-Bass.

Hoy, W. I., & Miskal, C. G. (1978). *Educational administration: Theory, research and practice.* New York: Random House.

Katz, D., & Kahn, R. I. (1966). *The social psychology of organizations.* New York: John Wiley and Sons.

Keating, L. A. (1985). Common pitfalls in program planning. In M. J. Barr, & L. A. Keating (Eds.), *Developing effective student services programs* (pp. 275-298). San Francisco: Jossey-Bass.

Kohlberg, L. (1976). Moral stages and moralization: The cognitive-developmental approach. In. T. Lickona (Ed.), *Moral development and behavior* (pp. 187-321). New York: Holt, Rinehart and Winston.

Maslow, A. H. (1970). *Motivation and personality (2nd ed.).* New York: Harper and Row.

Maw, I., Richards, N. A., & Crosby, H. J. (1976). *Formula budgeting: An application to student affairs.* Washington, DC: American College Personnel Association.

Merton, R. H. (1956). *Social theory and social structures.* New York: Free Press.

Moore, L.V. (1987). Using the model of expanded professional education. In L.V. Moore & R.B. Young (Eds.), *Expanding opportunities for professional education.* New Directions for Student Services (No. 37). (pp. 27-38). San Francisco: Jossey-Bass.

Moore, M., & Delworth, U. (1976). *Training manual for student services program development.* Boulder, CO: Western Interstate Commission for Higher Education.

Morrill, W. H., & Hurst, J. C. (Eds.). (1980). *Dimensions of intervention for student development.* New York: John Wiley and Sons.

Morrill, W. H., Oetting, E. R., & Hurst, J. C. (1974). Dimensions of counselor functioning. *Personnel and Guidance Journal, 52,* 354-9.

National Association of Student Personnel Administrators (NASPA). (1987). *A perspective on student affairs.* Washington, DC: NASPA.

Pace, C. R. (1969). *College and university environment scale technical manual (2nd ed.).* Princeton, NJ: Educational Testing Service.

Pembroke, W. J. (1985). Fiscal constraints on program development. In. M. J. Barr & L. A. Keating (Eds.). *Developing effective student services programs* (pp. 83-107). San Francisco: Jossey-Bass.

Perry, W. (1968). *Forms of intellectual and ethical development in the college years.* New York: Holt, Rinehart and Winston.

Sandeen, A. (1985). Assessing program utility over time. In M. J. Barr & L. A. Keating (Eds.), *Developing effective student services programs* (pp. 252-274). San Francisco: Jossey-Bass.

Struening, E. L., & Guttentag, M. (1975). *Handbook of evaluation research* (2 vols.). Beverly Hills, CA: Sage Publications.

Thomas, W.A. (1979). Exit valor, enter veracity. In M.J. Barr & L.A. Keating (Eds.), *Establishing effective programs.* New Directions for Student Services (No. 7). (pp. 53-67). San Francisco: Jossey-Bass.

Weber, M. (1947). *The theory of social and economic organizations.* New York: Free Press.

Winston, R.B., Jr., & Saunders, S.A. (1987). The Greek experience: Friend or foe of student development? In R.B. Winston, Jr., W.R. Nettles, III, & J.H. Opper, Jr. (Eds.), *Fraternities and sororities on the contemporary college campus.* New Directions for Student Services (No. 40). (pp. 5-20). San Francisco: Jossey-Bass.

Wright, D.J. (1987). *Responding to the needs of today's minority students.* New Directions for Student Services (No. 38). San Francisco: Jossey-Bass.

SUGGESTED READINGS

Barr, M. J., & Keating, L. A. (Eds.). (1985). *Developing effective student services programs.* San Francisco: Jossey-Bass.

Delworth, U., & Hanson, G.R. (Eds.). (1980). *Student services: A handbook for the profession.* San Francisco: Jossey-Bass.

Evans, N. (Ed.). (1985). *Facilitating the development of women.* New Directions for Student Services (No. 29). San Francisco: Jossey-Bass.

Kantor, R. M., & Stein, B. A. (1979). *Life in organizations.* New York: Basic Books.

Miller, T. K., & Prince, J. S. (1976). *The future of student affairs: A guide to student development for tomorrow's higher education.* San Francisco: Jossey-Bass.

Morrill, W. H., & Hurst, J. C. (Eds.). (1980). *Dimensions of intervention for student development.* New York: Wiley.

Saddlemire, G. L., & Rentz, A. L. (Eds.). (1984). *Student affairs: A profession's heritage.* Washington, DC: American College Personnel Association.

Upcraft, M.L., & Barr, M.J. (1988). *Managing student affairs effectively.* New Directions for Student Services (No. 41). San Francisco: Jossey-Bass.

T. Dary Erwin, Ph.D., is director of student assessment and associate professor of psychology at James Madison University. Dr. Erwin completed his B.S. and M.S. from the University of Tennessee-Knoxville and his Ph.D. in student development from the University of Iowa. He is the past recipient of the Annuit Coeptis Award of the American College Personnel Association and Ralph F. Berdie Memorial Research Award of the American Association for Counseling and Development. He is also past chairperson of the Measurement Services Association of the National Council for Measurement in Education. The author of the *Erwin Identity Scale* and the *Scale of Intellectual Development*, Dr. Erwin publishes in the area of assessment of student outcomes in higher education.

Robert L. Scott, Ed.D., is Vice President for Student Affairs at James Madison University. He holds three academic degrees, the B.S. in History, the Ed.M. in Education, and the Ed.D. in Educational Administration, all from the University of Nebraska. Dr. Scott has over 25 years of student affairs experience having been a Financial Aid Advisor and Coordinator of Student Activities at the University of Nebraska, the Dean of Students at University of Wisconsin, Oshkosh, Vice President for Administrative Affairs, Vice President for Student Affairs, and Provost and Vice President for Educational Services at Mansfield University prior to his current tenure at James Madison University which began in 1982.

Alfred J. Menard, Jr., Ed.D., is Associate Vice President for Student Affairs at James Madison University. He holds the B.S. in Mathematics and Psychology and the M.Ed. in Counseling from University of Massachusetts-Amherst and the Ed.D. with specialization in Student Development and Higher Education Administration from The University of Arizona. Prior to his present position he was Associate Dean for Residential Life Services at the University of South Carolina. His current responsibilities include supervision of programs in student activities, minority student affairs, commuter student affairs, Greek life, and the student judicial system.

CHAPTER **22**

STUDENT OUTCOME ASSESSMENT IN STUDENT AFFAIRS

T. Dary Erwin
Robert L. Scott
Alfred J. Menard, Jr.

During the decade of the eighties, representatives from government, accrediting agencies, governing boards, administrators, teachers, parents, some students, and the American public have raised some important, yet troubling questions about the quality of the nation's educational system. Initial attention was centered on public schools, but soon the focus turned to colleges and universities. Best-selling books and critical reports from a variety of credible educational organizations (such as, Study Group on the Conditions of Excellence in American Higher Education, 1984; Association of American Colleges, 1985) reawakened interest in a most basic question—what difference does college make? Certainly, higher education continues to be perceived as a means to an economic end; but doubts persist regarding what is actually being learned and whether it is worth the price. In attempting to answer questions like these in the past, supporters of higher education often turned to indicators of quality of an institution's facilities, faculties, and graduates as a means of marking quality; at times, falsely confusing these input variables with desired outcomes. In the last few years, however, requirements from some accreditation agencies, mandates from a number of legislatures, and strong initiatives within some colleges have been the stimuli for a nation-wide assessment movement. Simply stated, assessment attempts to quantify what students have learned and how they have developed during their college years, particularly from the liberal arts curriculum and from students' major fields of study.

Since its establishment, American higher education has distinguished itself from most other countries' colleges and universities by a commitment to students' total development. Interest and concern for students' non-cognitive or affective development began with the colonial college, withstood a serious challenge in the mid-nineteenth century, and has been at the core of the student affairs profession for more than 50 years (Fenske, 1989). Although defining affective development is considered difficult, distinct ways of identifying how students change psychosocially as a result of their college experience can be ascertained. Intuitively, college graduates recognize that they change in how they perceive the world around them and how they perceive themselves interacting with the world. Student affairs staff members give testimony to these changes, combining their training in student development theory with their practical work experiences. Despite these acknowledgements of affective development's existence and importance, few colleges have embarked on comprehensive and systematic efforts to define or assess student development, to determine institutional characteristics that contribute or detract from this development, and finally to initiate programs to promote students' cognitive and affective development in purposive ways.

In the 1950s, student affairs was principally service oriented. With the human development movement of the 1970s, the profession learned about vectors, developmental tasks, and stages, but with little understanding of how to translate developmental theory into its services and programs.

Today, the challenge for the assessment movement is for the student affairs profession to join with colleagues in academic affairs to define more precisely the common goals of student development, to assess how well students are developing toward these goals, and to strengthen existing programs and services, based on this assessment. Not only can assessment provide guidance in institutional improvement, it can demonstrate the value of student affairs to higher education.

This chapter addresses the issues previously discussed. First, the chapter outlines the process of defining developmental goals for a typical division of student affairs. Second, elementary measurement terminology is discussed. And third, lists of several widely-used developmental instruments are provided.

DEFINING DEVELOPMENTAL PURPOSES AND OBJECTIVES

All colleges should have a clear, realistic, and well-articulated statement of purpose and detailed ways in which that purpose will be pursued prior to the planning for any broad-based assessment or evaluation effort. Parenthetically, it should be noted that the student affairs literature supports the idea that a college's impact on its students' development is increased when that institution's objectives are clear and taken seriously (Chickering, 1969, p. 145). Ideally, the objective-setting process should begin with an institutional mission or purpose statement. At a minimum, statements of purpose should be established for the division of student affairs and for each office or department within the division. These statements should directly and comprehensively specify reasons for the organization's existence. Eminating from the statement of purpose should be a list of continuing objectives that are specific and measurable. The CAS *Standards and Guidelines for Student Services/Development Programs* (1986) can be helpful as a checklist in developing a statement of purpose and a list of continuing objectives (See Chapter 11 and Appendix C). An important point to note however, is that continuing objectives should address not only service goals but affective development as well. In addition, these objectives should describe and delineate activities, programs, and services that are planned for achieving the continuing goals.

The process for arriving at the statement of purpose and objectives should receive almost as much attention as the assessment results or outcomes. Every effort should be made to ensure participation from all levels of the organization and from important constituencies (e.g., alumni) beyond the organization. Initially, the process should be non-evaluative in order to maximize involvement and should conclude with activities that seek group consensus for goals established. This process needs to be facilitated by individuals with consultation skills who are organizationally separated from the office or division. The results of such labors should be widely disseminated and used in a variety of ways including new staff orientation, budget preparation, and any other assessment or evaluation initiatives.

Formulating a Developmental Purpose
For the Division of Student Affairs

The Chief Student Affairs Administrator (CSAA) must take the lead in formulating an institutional statement of purpose for student development. This process of developing a mission statement, goals, and objectives assumes that each participant has a basic understanding of developmental theory. The excerpts that follow are examples of how one division of student affairs (Erwin, Menard, & Scott, 1988, p. i) incorporated student development into its mission statement and goals.

> The mission of the division of student affairs is to advance the educational purpose of the University by promoting the various goals of the University and by providing a supportive yet challenging environment so that affective and cognitive development are attained. This mission is accomplished by providing consultation, instruction, and a stimulating environment for students and by assisting faculty, staff, and members of the community at large in understanding the needs of students.

> **Goals:** To enhance students' development through departmental programs and services in the following dimensions:

> a) Moving toward a more flexible, tolerant and altruistic style of thinking and behaving, that acknowledges varying perspectives to a question or problem, ultimately resulting in commitments to action or belief;

b) Moving toward greater independence and then interdependence in one's values, attitudes, and interactions with other people;

c) Developing a deeper understanding of one's self and a strengthening of relationships with others through greater openness, respect, and trust;

d) Developing confidence in one's capabilities within the potential of one's skills, talents, competencies, and experiences;

e) Developing purpose and direction in one's life through increased responsibility to oneself, to other people and to the broader community; and,

f) Developing acceptance of individual differences due to diversities in values, religion, ethnicity, sexuality, race, physical disabilities, and intellectual capabilities.

The division of student affairs bridges the academic and non-academic areas of the student experience by providing experiential learning opportunities, personal growth experiences, and developmental programs. The professional staff members of the division of student affairs function as educators in the development of the student as a whole person, permitting students the freedom to identify options and make choices within defined boundaries of behavior.

Formulating Developmental Objectives
For the Departments of Student Affairs

In his or her work with the divisional directors, the chief student affairs officer strives to raise the level of comfort the directors have in discussing developmental theory and its relationship to their work.

This can be accomplished through a series of informal meetings with all of the directors in which a college's developmental constructs are discussed and related to the specific work performed in each office. Directors are encouraged to discuss their programs, services, and activities and to identify the developmental constructs they believe they are impacting.

When this process is continued over several meetings, it allows each director the opportunity to relate developmental theory to student affairs practice. Furthermore, the process of setting objectives breaks down the barriers that practicing professionals, who are not developmentally conversant, often feel in trying to relate their everyday work to developmental theory.

Listed in Figure 22.1 are specific examples of how departments in one division of student affairs (Erwin, Menard, Scott, 1988, pp. 1-7) related selected programs, services, and activities to particular areas of student development.

MEASUREMENT CONCEPTS

The previous section described the process of defining what developmental outcomes might be assessed and listed examples of purposes and objectives. This section discusses several measurement concepts as background knowledge for evaluating and using assessment methods. Whereas **assessment** includes the entire process of defining objectives and of collecting and using information, **measurement** is essentially the assignment of numerals to student observations and behavior in a systematic way (Allen & Yen, 1979). Stated another way, measurement is the quantification of the degree of students' development. Within measurement, two primary concepts are necessary to consider whether one selects or designs methods to measure students' development. These concepts are **reliability** and **validity.**

Reliability

Reliability is the consistency or precision with which a construct or concept is measured. Several sources of problems or measurement error exist that can reduce the reliability of an assessment instrument. First, a problem may be with the way a student responds to a survey and/or a rater on a particular day. If a student is not responding in a typical manner, reliability or precision may be reduced. For example,

(Continued on Page 752)

Programs, Services, Activities	Areas of Development

Office of Associate Vice President for Student Affairs

Orientation social activities such as sharing a room, going to a dance, meeting and eating with many new and different people.	Changing existing values, developing tolerance, assisting in the estabishment of an identity, strengthening the quality of interpersonal relationships and increasing positive self-perceptions.
Orientation academic activities such as receiving placement scores, meeting with an advisor, deciding on courses or registering.	Increasing positive self-perceptions and developing a sense or purpose.

Financial Aid Office

Responsibility is placed upon the student to complete all necessary applications for financial assistance. The Financial Aid Office encourages students to apply for programs that are self-help in nature. Through student employment and loans, it is deemed desirable by the Financial Aid Office that students help finance their education. Through these means student perceptions are affected by . . .	The development of an awareness for the value of money, a precious commodity that is not easy to earn and must be spent wisely.
	The awareness that one must save his/her earnings to gain the most from his/her education.
	Taking an active role in decision making and developing independence from his/her parents.

Figure 22.1. Example of how departments in one division of student affairs related selected programs, services, and activities to particular areas of student development. From Erwin, Menard, and Scott, 1988.

Figure 22.1. Continued.

Programs, Services, Activities	Areas of Development
Health Centers	
Decision to seek information regarding birth control	Moral Development
Discuss with health/wellness staff options/opportunities for health care/prevention	Develop confidence/positive self-perceptions
Counseling and Student Development Center	
Personal counseling (group and individual)	Moral Development: ego-centered community
Outreach programs	
Pre- and paraprofessional training	
Consultation	
Personal Counseling (group and individual)	Development of Confidence
Outreach programs	
Educational skills	
Career development	
Pre- and paraprofessional training	

Figure 22.1. Continued.

Programs, Services, Activities	Areas of Development
Office of Admissions	
College night programs	The student develops autonomy from family and peers
Group conferences	
Individual contacts	
Special prospective student events	

Comment: The Admissions staff emphasizes with students the importance of focusing on their own interests, goals, and needs in selecting a college.

Selection Process in the Office of Admissions

Comment: One of the goals in the selection process is to develop a diverse student body with the belief that diversity will foster a stimulating and challenging educational environment both inside and outside of the classroom.

The student develops tolerance for differing opinions and recognizes alternative perspectives.

Career Planning and Placement

Career counseling

Job search workshops

Career days

Classes

Career library

Figure 22.1. Continued.

Programs, Services, Activities	Areas of Development

**Career Planning
and Placement (Continued)**

On campus recruiting

Experimental education
(internships, externships,
part-time, and summer work)

Job search workshops

**Office of the Dean
of Students**

Leadership development

Cultural programming

Town and campus outreach

Workshops addressing:
  study skills
  test anxiety
  time management
  experience affecting career
    choice

Office of Residence Life

Student involvement in
decision making through hall
councils, residence hall
association, SGA Housing
Advisory Committee. Pro-
gramming centered on cul-
tural, social, ethnic, and
sexual diversity.

Self-Confidence
Increased self-confidence

Positive self-perceptions

Move students to more
complex structures for
organizing and viewing the
world (i.e., from dualism to
commitment).

How students change their
way of thinking from a
dualistic, right/wrong perspective to a way of thinking
that recognizes alternative
perspectives to a view that
we never have all the answers
but commitments need to be
made.

Figure 22.1. Continued.

Programs, Services, Activities	Areas of Development
Office of Residence Life (Continued)	
Holding students responsible for their actions, feelings, emotions, living environments, alcohol education (peer counseling).	How a student develops autonomy from family and peers.
Office of Student Activities	
Development of these dimensions continually takes place with at least two of the primary audiences involved with programming. Student programmers are developed to identify, create, and present programming for the diverse needs of the campus community. In its simplest form, this activity broadens the group to think in terms of a wider constituency than the individual or the immediate group. Additionally, the presentation of programs helps to develop citizenship and involvement in the democratic process for recipients of the programs, facilitating on-going dialogue and development.	How a student's moral development changes from a perspective that moral decisions are based on what is good for me, to what is good for the people around me, to what is just for the larger community.

How a student develops tolerance for differing opinions. |

if a student is ill and is forced to participate, student responses may be affected. A second major source of error is with the instrument itself. If students do not interpret the wording or coding of an instrument in a uniform or similar way, inconsistencies among their responses occur. For example, how would the following statement be interpreted, "rate your leadership ability." What does leadership mean? To one person, leadership may mean independence or autonomy. To another person, leadership may mean public speaking ability; others may claim leadership is the ability to lead small group discussions. Many other definitions of leadership could be listed. In an assessment instrument, however, multiple interpretations of test stimuli (the test items) reduce consistency or reliability. A third major source of measurement error lies in the scoring of the student's responses. "Objectively scored" instruments do not produce the inconsistencies that "subjectively" obtained ratings do. Different raters may interpret or rate the same student's response in different ways, producing low inter-rater reliability. The goal is to eliminate as much rater disagreement as possible. Other sources of unreliability abound. Overall, the goal in measurement is to be clear and well-defined in what one is trying to measure. Most problems with reliability occur when the developmental construct has not been clearly defined.

As one reviews test manuals and test design, studies focus first on reliability estimates of the developmental constructs, then review validity studies. Reliability coefficients range from 0 (not reliable) to 1.0 (perfect consistency). If the instrument is to be used for program or group summary purposes, a reliability of .60 or higher is considered acceptable. If the assessment device is to be used for individual student feedback and use, reliability estimates should be higher, preferably .80 or higher. Information with reliability levels below .60 is essentially worthless for most decision making purposes.

For norm referenced instruments, reliability is operationalized in generally three ways: stability, equivalence, or homogeneity. **Stability** is commonly computed as a test-retest comparison where the instrument is given to the same people twice with a short interval in between (usually 2 to

4 weeks). This method presumes that the instrument is stable if the correlation between the two test administrations is high. The **equivalence** method correlates the two scores from two different forms or split halves of the same instrument. This approach is infrequently applied in developmental assessment. The last method, **homogeneity,** is the internal consistency or interrelatedness of the items measuring a single construct. It can be calculated using Cronbach's (1951) alpha coefficient of internal consistency. Statistical Package for the Social Sciences Version X (1986) contains a procedure for its calculation as do several others.

For criterion referenced instruments, consider the use of **generalizability theory** for a framework (Brennan, 1983) for calculating reliability. Generalizability theory also can be used to calculate inter-rater reliability and reliability given a particular cutoff score or level. Overall, designing and using criterion referenced instruments requires greater statistical sophistication.

Validity

Validity is the degree to which one has evidence that the instrument is measuring what is intended to be measured. This explanation centers around construct validity in student development, but readers should consult other sources for other types of validity (Brown, 1976). Construct validity is the degree to which the instrument is measuring the intended psychological or developmental construct. In contrast to reliability, validity unfortunately cannot be simplified to a single number. Validity is an accumulation of evidence or studies with the instrument. Specifically, has the instrument been used successfully in a prior setting similar to the intended use? Construct validity studies are often reported as correlations with more established but similarly defined instruments or as average score differences among student groups that support the theoretical construct. For example, the *Identity Scale* differentiated between a group of high school students who had made a decision about college attendance (either yes or no) versus those who had not made a decision (undecided) (Erwin, 1983).

Norm and Criterion Referenced

Several statistical issues are mentioned here for the beginning student affairs practitioner. The terms of norm and criterion referenced instruments have already been mentioned. *Norm referenced instruments* are appropriate because of their accompanying percentiles which allow for comparisons of a developmental score with the scores in a defined reference group or for producing student differences in scores.

Criterion referenced instruments are associated with a mastery level or cutoff level denoting competency. For instance, interview methods that type students into "stages" may be conceived in some situations as criterion referenced instruments. Students placed in a certain stage have mastered or progressed to a particular developmental level.

Most instruments used to measure development fall into the norm referenced category where percentiles are available for comparisons to designated reference groups. Such groups may be based on gender, race or ethnic background, educational level, or another logically appropriate group. Some test developers also suggest using a certain percentile for describing a competency level similar to criterion referenced instruments.

Sampling

Sampling issues are mentioned only briefly here because other sources (e.g., Mendenhall, Ott, & Scheaffer, 1971) exist for in-depth reviews. The main point is to draw a random sample from the group from which one wishes to generalize. For example, to generalize about the sophomore class, select a sample from that sophomore class. Do not draw a random sample from the student body as a whole and later generalize about sophomores.

Cross-sectional and Longitudinal Designs

Cross-sectional and longitudinal designs are two other important sampling concepts. A cross-sectional design is the sampling of students from several groups at a single time. Longitudinal designs involve retesting a single group or cohort of students on more than one occasion. When one desires a quick profile of freshmen, sophomores, juniors, and seniors, a cross-sectional design may be appropriate. When one desires a more powerful and in-depth analysis of a single class, employ a longitudinal design, following a single class over the undergraduate years. Developmental studies generally call for longitudinal studies following students, for example, from new student orientation to mid-point sophomores to graduating senior.

One caution about longitudinal designs should be noted. Guard against the indiscriminate use of change scores, posttest minus pretest, over time. Linn and Slinde (1977) discussed this subject in depth statistically; however, the popular notion of "value-added" analyses (Astin, 1982), or use of change scores is fraught with problems of unreliability. For instance, institutions might assess entering freshmen with the *Student Developmental Task and Lifestyle Inventory* (SDTLI) (Winston, Miller, & Prince, 1987), later re-administer the SDTLI to the same students, who are now seniors. To simply subtract the freshmen scores from the seniors scores and attribute any differences due to educational impact is erroneous. Just as reliability estimates can be calculated on any set of test scores, reliability estimates can be calculated on change or difference scores. In practice, pretest scores are highly correlated with posttest scores, and the change or difference scores produce very low reliability coefficients, such as .10 or .20, making their value essentially meaningless for use.

Consult Hanson and Lenning (1979) and Oetting and Cole (1978) for more detailed explanations of the statistical design issues mentioned here.

INSTRUMENTS

This section identifies several well recognized instruments that are commonly used in measuring development with college students. This list is by no means comprehensive; in fact, much opportunity exists for new instruments and methods not covered here. Consult Mines (1982) for good reviews about interview methods, Robinson and Shaver (1973) for attitudinal scales descriptions, Moore (1988) for cognitive instruments, and Miller and Winston (1990) for psychosocial developmental scales.

Student Developmental Task and Lifestyle Inventory (SDTLI), Copyright 1987 by Student Development Associates, Inc., 110 Crestwood Drive, Athens GA 30605. Developmental Tasks and Scales are Establishing and Clarifying Purpose, Developing Mature Interpersonal Relationships, Academic Autonomy, Intimacy, and Salubrious Lifestyle. Earlier versions of this instrument were designed to measure three of Chickering's (1969) vectors.

The Iowa Student Development Inventories (Hood, 1986). HITECH PRESS, P.O. Box 2341, Iowa City, IA 52244. Six of Chickering's (1969) vectors of development are previewed and listed. The instruments are as follows: (1) **Iowa Developing Competency Inventory,** Copyright 1983 by Lorraine M. Jackson and Albert B. Hood. Sub-scales are Competency in Mathematics, Competency in Writing, and Self-Confidence. (2) **Iowa Managing Emotions Inventory** by Albert B. Hood and Lorraine M. Jackson. Sub-scales are Depression, Anger, Frustration, Happiness, and Attraction. (3) **Iowa Developing Autonomy Inventory,** Copyright 1985 by Lorraine M. Jackson and Albert B. Hood. Sub-scales are Mobility, Time Management, Money Management, Interdependence, Emotional Independence Regarding Peers, and Emotional Independence Regarding Parents. (4) **Mines-Jensen Interpersonal Relationship Inventory** by Robert A. Mines. Sub-scales are Tolerance, and Quality of Relationships. (5) **Developing Purposes Inventory** by William R. Barratt. Sub-scales are Avocational-recreational, Vocational Purpose, and Style of Life. (6) **Parker Cognitive Development Inventory,** Copyright 1983 by John C. Parker. Sub-scales are Dualism-Education, Dualism-Career, Dualism-Religion,

Relativism-Education, Relativism-Career, Relativism-Religion, Commitment in Relativism-Education, Commitment in Relativism-Career, and Commitment in Relativism-Religion.

Erwin Identity Scale, Copyright 1977 by T. Dary Erwin; Developmental Analytics, P.O. Box 855, Harrisonburg, VA 22801. Sub-scales are Confidence, Sexual Identity, and Conceptions about Body and Appearance. Designed to measure Chickering's (1969) vector of identity.

Scale of Intellectual Development, Copyright 1981, by T. Dary Erwin; Developmental analytics, P.O. Box 855, Harrisonburg, VA 22801. Sub-scales are Dualism, Relativism, Commitment, and Empathy. Originally based on Perry's (1970) scheme.

Defining Issues Test, Copyright 1979 by James Rest; Center for the Study of Ethical Development, University of Minnesota, 141 Burton Hall, 178 Pillsbury Drive S.E., Minneapolis, MN 55455. Based on Kohlburg's theory, the DIT is a multiple-choice instrument designed to measure moral judgment development.

Omnibus Personality Inventory, Copyright 1968 by the Psychological Corporation, P.O. Box 9954, San Antonio, TX 78204. Sub-scales are Thinking Introversion, Theoretical Orientation, Aestheticism, Complexity, Autonomy, Religious Orientation, Social Extroversion, Impulse Expression, Personal Integration, Anxiety Level, Altruism, Practical Outlook, and Masculinity-Femininity.

These instruments were selected because of their use to measure the developmental objectives listed in the first section. However, many other reliable instruments exist to measure developmental constructs. To find a standardized instrument that will assess all the developmental objectives that might be stated at a particular institution is very unlikely. Designing one's own reliable and valid instruments might be necessary. Such a design process can be valuable because it is an effective way to involve many people and to increase understanding of the desired developmental construct. Be sure to remember to base the selected assessment method upon the intended developmental objective and under the measurement standards previously discussed.

A popular and often convenient approach for student affairs professionals is to use qualitative research methods in their approach to assessment. Qualitative methods do not preclude quantitative measures, but emphasize a more unstructured approach to information collection that can be helpful in the initial stages of an assessment project. Howard (1985) described several qualitative data gathering strategies including interviewing techniques, participant observations, personal accounts, life histories, and unobtrusive measures.

Interviews can be structured or unstructured. *Participant observations* allows the inquiries to become a part of the activity under observation. *Personal accounts* include not only face-to-face interactions with inquirer and student but also written accounts of autobiographies, diaries, and letters. More extensive autobiographies involve life histories, which can be analyzed for understanding life span activities. *Unobtrusive measures* do not involve direct contact with students, but study the traces of their behavior. Such measures might include records in the counseling center, placement office, and judicial system where patterns of development of students as a group may be discerned. Other unobtrusive measures on the environmental side could be observed from use of physical facilities: worn carpets, library and computing lab use, roommate changes, and attendance at various student activities.

Qualitative information collection is commonly used at the very beginning or ending of an assessment project. At the beginning, qualitative information helps the inquirers to frame questions, build hypotheses, and formulate theories. At the end, qualitative information can supplement quantitative information for deeper understanding and explanation of quantitative results. For greater reliance of qualitative information for reporting to outside constituents, apply the same rules of reliability and validity for the accuracy and worth of the qualitative information. Lastly, if one's assessment program is tailored toward outside sources such as state agencies, qualitative information is often not acceptable in lieu of quantitative information.

IMPLEMENTING AN ASSESSMENT PROGRAM

As divisions of student affairs and individual offices within student affairs increase their commitment to developmental goals, attention needs to be focused on broadening both professional development activities and staff evaluation criteria. Clearly, if a division or office decides to pursue student development goals, administrative staff must not only understand student development theory but also must be able to apply this body of knowledge to new programming efforts. Professional development activities that realistically and concretely address the accompanying staff challenges and anxieties should be encouraged. If a chief student affairs officer or a director wishes to communicate genuine support for student development assessment, division or office employees should be evaluated in part on their success in establishing and achieving these goals. For staff members in divisions or offices that have been primarily service oriented, this change in emphasis might be met, at a minimum, with some initial hesitancy.

In the design of an assessment program in a student affairs division, an individual must be identified to serve as an assessment consultant to work with the CSAA and the directors. The consultant should possess a background and understanding of student development as well as extensive knowledge in educational measurement. If it is organizationally feasible, the individual also should be part of institution-wide assessment efforts.

Working closely with the CSAA, the assessment consultant would assist the program directors in identifying, defining, and articulating developmental goals and objectives for the division and for their individual offices. A major component of the consultant's work is to assist the CSAA and the directors in constructing programmatic goals and objectives that are developmentally based and capable of evaluation.

The student development instruments selected should reflect the needs of the total college program, as well as the objectives of the student affairs division. The administration of instruments must be coordinated with the institutional testing schedule in order to reduce confusion and excessive testing demands on students and faculty. A typical schedule for administering developmental instruments might include samples taken prior to students' entering their freshman year at orientation; at the end of their sophomore year, at the end of their senior year, and five to ten years after leaving the institution. In conjunction with the CSAA and directors, the assessment consultant also should coordinate the collection of the assessment information and the assimilation and analysis of results.

An essential part of the process of establishing an assessment program is the decision of what will be done with the results. On most campuses, this is a sensitive question that must be dealt with early. In most cases, the information gathered through institutional assessment is primarily for the internal use of the institution and its departments unless otherwise dictated by state higher education councils or legislatures.

Care must be taken to convey to the academic community that the division of student affairs is involved in the longitudinal study of student development and the impact the institution and its programs are having on students. The establishment and assessment of programmatic developmental objectives must be viewed as a long-term commitment of the institution and the division of student affairs. Do not expect too much too soon. In the absence of a long term commitment, the chief student affairs administrator must seriously consider the prospect of what could be accomplished before implementing any divisional assessment initiatives. On the other hand, the failure to respond to outcries for accountability can cause other kinds of problems.

SUMMARY

External pressure from state legislatures, regional accrediting agencies, and the public have prompted institutions of higher learning to address the need for assessment.

While the emphasis has been placed on the assessment of subject matter achievement in the classroom, plans should be made to include broader aspects of students' development in the institutional assessment process. The chief student affairs administrator must work closely with the chief academic affairs officer to insure the inclusion of both cognitive and affective development in the institution's assessment plan.

The institution, through its mission statement and goals, has the ability to demonstrate its commitment to the comprehensive assessment of students. Through mission statements and continuing goals, divisions of student affairs can increasingly articulate the role of cognitive and affective development in the education of students.

Although mounting pressures from outside higher education may dictate assessment, the process of assessment has many advantages for the student affairs profession. The use of assessment results causes practitioners to focus on what they are doing, why they are doing it, and how well they are doing it. Such benefits not only increase credibility outside the profession, but also can produce a broader type of informational feedback to students. This more comprehensive feedback to students could be the most valuable benefit of all.

REFERENCES

Allen, M.J., & Yen, W.M. (1979). *Introduction to measurement theory*. Monterey, CA: Brooks/Cole Publishing.

Association of American Colleges. (1985). *Integrity in the classroom*. Washington, DC: Author.

Astin, A.W. (1982). Why not try some new ways of measuring quality? *Educational Record, 63,* 10-15.

Brennan, R.L. (1983). *Elements of generalizability theory.* Iowa City, IA: American College Testing Program.

Brown, F.G. (1976). *Principles of educational and psychological testing.* New York: Holt, Rinehart & Winston.

Chickering, A.W. (1969). *Education and identity.* San Francisco: Jossey-Bass.

Council for the Advancement of Standards for Student Services/Development Programs (CAS). (1986). *CAS standards and guidelines for student services/development programs.* Washington, DC: Author.

Cronbach, T.J. (1951). Coefficient alpha and the internal structure of tests. *Psychometrika, 16,* 297-334.

Erwin, T.D. (1983). College plans and the development of identity. *School Counselor, 30,* 217-222.

Erwin, T.D., Menard, A.J., & Scott, R.L. (1988). *Student development outcome assessment: A model for beginning.* Paper presented at the meetings of the American College Personnel Association, Miami, FL.

Fenske, R.H. (1989). Historical foundations of student services. In U. Delworth, G.R. Hanson, & Associates, *Student services: A handbook for the profession (rev. 2nd ed.),* (pp. 5-24). San Francisco: Jossey-Bass.

Hanson, G.R., & Lenning, O.T. (1979). Evaluation of student development programs. In G.D. Kuh (Ed.), *Evaluation in student affairs* (pp. 163-182). Cincinnati: American College Personnel Association.

Hood, A.B. (Ed.). (1986). *The Iowa student development inventories.* Iowa City, IA: Hitech Press.

Howard, G.S. (1985). *Research methods in the social sciences.* Glenview, IL: Scott, Foresman.

Linn, R.L., & Slinde, J.A. (1977). The determination of the significance of change between pre- and posttesting periods. *Review of Educational Research, 47,* 121-150.

Mendenhall, W., Ott, L., & Scheaffer, R.L. (1971). *Elementary survey sampling.* Belmont, CA: Wadsworth Publishing.

Miller, T.K., & Winston, R.B., Jr., (1990). Assessing students' psychosocial development. In D.G. Creamer & Associates, *College student development: Theory and practice for 1990's.* (pp. 99-126). Alexandria, VA: American College Personnel Association .

Mines, R.A. (1982). Student development assessment techniques. In G.R. Hanson (Ed.), *Measuring student development.* New Directions for Student Services (No. 20). (pp. 65-92). San Francisco: Jossey-Bass.

Moore, W.S. (1988). Current issues in the assessment of cognitive development. *Georgia Journal of College Student Affairs, 3,* 11-14.

Oetting, E.R., & Cole, C.W. (1978). Method, design, and implementation in evaluation. In G.R. Hanson (Ed.), *Evaluating program effectiveness.* New Direction for Student Services (No. 1). (pp. 35-55). San Francisco: Jossey-Bass.

Perry, W.G., Jr. (1970). *Forms of intellectual and ethical development in college years.* New York: Holt, Rinehart & Winston.

Robinson, J.P., & Shaver, P.R. (1973). *Measures of social psychological attitudes.* Ann Arbor, MI: Institute for Social Research.

Statistical Package for the Social Sciences Inc. (1986). *SPSSX, User's Guide* (2nd ed.). New York: McGraw-Hill.

Study Group on the Conditions of Excellence in American Higher Education. (1984). *Involvement in learning: Realizing the potential of American higher education.* Washington, DC: National Institute of Education.

Winston, R.B., Jr., Miller, T.K., & Prince, J.S. (1987). *Student developmental task and lifestyle inventory.* Athens, GA: Student Development Associates.

SUGGESTED READING

Creamer, D.G., & Associates, (Ed.). (1990). *College student development: Theory and practice for the 1990s.* Alexandria, VA: American College Personnel Association Media.

Erwin, T.D. (1989). New opportunities: How student affairs can contribute to outcomes assessment. In U. Delworth & G.R. Hanson & Associates, *Student Services: A handbook for the profession* (pp. 584-603). San Francisco: Jossey-Bass.

Ewell, P.T. (1984). *The self-regarding institution: Information for excellence.* Boulder, CO: National Center for Higher Education Management Systems.

Ewell, P.T., & Lisensky, R.P. (1988). *Assessing institutional effectiveness: Redirecting the self study process.* Washington, DC: Consortium for the Advancement of Private Higher Education.

Light, R.J., Singer, J.D., & Willett, J.B. (1990). *By design: Planning research on higher education.* Cambridge, MA: Harvard University Press.

William S. Moore, Ph.D., was Acting Assistant Professor in the Department of Counseling and Human Development Services at the University of Georgia in Athens when this chapter was written. He has since taken a position as Director of Student Outcomes Assessment, Washington State Board for Community College Education, Olympia, Washington. He spent five years working as a Student Development Educator at Longwood College in Virginia with primary responsibility for comprehensive coordinating of a comprehensive developmental student assessment and intervention program called the Longwood Involvement Project. Dr. Moore's B.A. degree is from the University of Texas, where he majored in Plan II, an interdisciplinary honors program. He has a master's degree in counseling psychology from the University of Texas, and his Ph.D. in College Student Personnel Administration is from the University of Maryland, with a concentration in college student development.

Dr. Moore's primary areas of research interest and expertise are student outcomes assessment, cognitive-developmental assessment, teaching-learning issues, and developmental interventions. In particular, he has wide-ranging experience with the Perry scheme of intellectual and ethical development. Since 1982 he has also operated the Center for the Study of Intellectual Development, designed to facilitate research on the Perry scheme, and in 1988 assumed responsibility for the Perry Network, the national organization for researchers and practitioners interested in Perry's model.

CHAPTER **23**

ISSUES FACING STUDENT AFFAIRS PROFESSIONALS

William S. Moore, Ph.D.

Those associated with American higher education are frequently reminded by reports and scholarly works, such as those by AAC (1985), Bloom (1987), Boyer (1987), and the report of the NIE Study Group on the Conditions of Excellence in American Higher Education (1984), that a pervasive crisis exists. On the whole, most student affairs practitioners would have difficulty arguing to the contrary, what with the continuing concerns about the academic preparation of today's students, regular mailings from private consulting firms doing big business offering to share their "secrets" of recruitment and retention magic, and growing questions about accountability and the nature of the education provided. When, as Cross (1985) indicated, only one-third of all organized learning for adults takes place within traditional higher education institutions, there appears to be increasing competition with the corporate world. Consequently, with students more consumer-oriented and shopping for the "best deals" available, many institutions may understandably feel a bit under siege.

For student affairs, this growing crisis may be translated into a concern for the viability of professional practice on a given campus, for in times of belt-tightening, back-to-basics, and excellence in education, student affairs and the "co-curriculum" may be viewed by some as a luxury no longer affordable. The crisis, to the extent that it actually exists, is for student affairs not so much the threat of extinction, but rather a subtle, more serious threat of being *discounted,* ignored, and shunted aside at a time when the perspectives and expertise that student affairs professionals can bring to bear on the higher education agenda as a whole are more crucial than ever. The purpose of this book has been to focus the collective wisdom of professional practitioners upon the integration of administrative and leadership applications in student affairs. Some would contend that this is an extremely important objective as we enter the final decade of the 20th Century, for it can be readily argued that while both areas are important, there has been far too much administration and far too little leadership. Therefore, student affairs professionals, chief student affairs administrators (CSAAs), and entry-level practitioners alike need at this time to take a more active leadership in addressing the major issues faced by higher education today. By bringing to bear its expertise in the principles of management and leadership in the service of the developmental goals of higher education, student affairs professionals can articulate a much-needed, broad-based developmental vision to the entire academic community.

PURPOSE OF HIGHER EDUCATION

In large measure, the current crisis in higher education and the range of responses to it come down to the fundamental question: *What is the primary business of higher education?* A basic premise of this book was to answer this question in much the same way as did Sanford (1966) when he asserted that higher education's purpose is to facilitate mature personality development or, as stated more broadly by Cross (1985), the facilitation of human development. For both theorists, such a mission reflects a reaffirmation of the classical notions of a liberal education (Gamson & Associates, 1984; Heath, 1968; Hutchins, 1969; Jaspers, 1959; Kuh, Shedd, & Whitt, 1987), including a central focus on intellectual development— or as Cleveland (1985) suggested, education for integrative thinking. The critical issue is that neither Sanford nor Cross believed higher education should limit itself to the intellect alone. This broadened position, however, may contribute to the difficulties faced by student affairs practitioners who are all employed in an academic setting (Kuh et al, 1987). Nevertheless, as Lynton (1982) argued, higher education needs to move beyond purely cognitive rationality; a need exists to understand both the significance of reason and intellect and their limits as well (Perry, 1970). The excellent work of Klemp and his colleagues (1980) provides empirical support for a connection between career success and both cognitive and noncognitive skill dimensions. Despite this work, and other compelling research evidence (Winter, McClelland, & Stewart, 1981), the focus of today's higher education is almost entirely on the acquisition of knowledge, largely ignoring the competencies involved in using that knowledge, much less the noncognitive skills associated with career success. Given the enormous complexity of the problems faced by today's society, McDaniel's (1975, p. 21) comments to the American College Personnel Association are as applicable now as they were then: "perhaps our last hope is in our ability to create a society where not capital development, not technological development, but human development is the keystone to our existence."

This vision for higher education, that its mission lies in the business of developing people, offers a response to the current crisis by calling for a reexamination and renewal of the stated missions of most colleges and universities, as well as the traditional aims of a liberal education, in terms of the education of the "whole person." It is a vision that sounds as if created by student affairs professionals, but in one form or another it has been a part of higher education since long before the field of student affairs was established, and it continues to be promoted by respected observers of higher education (Astin, 1985; Boyer, 1987) outside of student affairs.

However, given the nature of contemporary higher education, the complexity of the student population and the variety of issues confronting most campuses, the fact remains that student affairs professionals must play a central role if institutions are to take this vision seriously and pursue it. As Blake (1979) observed a decade ago, student affairs is the one segment of the higher education campus community with the best opportunity to take a generalist perspective of the "big picture" within a given institution. Knefelkamp (1984) described this unique role as "living in the in-between." In other words, student affairs is the organizational unit in the academic community that creates connections between the co-curricular and the curricular, the world of education and the world of work, the cognitive and the affective realms, knowledge and action, and freedom and self-control. In the broadest sense, living in this complex world of the "in-between" is what accepting human development as the mission of higher education demands of all educators no matter what their official title may be. By the very definition of much of student affairs work, however, professionals in the field have for years struggled with those issues. More specifically, then, what does this vision of higher education call upon student affairs professionals to do?

ROLE OF STUDENT AFFAIRS PROFESSIONALS

As a foundation, student affairs practitioners need a sophisticated grasp of an interdisciplinary knowledge base, drawing on strands from psychology, sociology, education, and organizational development among others. This interdisciplinary approach often automatically raises questions about the legitimacy of the endeavor in the minds of those faculty members who view such synthesis as "fuzzy" and less rigorous than the confines of a single discipline. This interdisciplinary conflict, however, appears to be inherent in the nature of the challenges facing student affairs and higher education. Quality scholarship in these interdisciplinary realms is crucial both to understand better the complex world of students in higher education and to provide more solid academic credibility among faculty colleagues.

Quality scholarship for student affairs professionals *does not* mean that everyone in the field must do research or publish regularly in high quality journals; it *does* mean, however, that practitioners need to make a concerted effort to stay abreast of the cutting-edge issues and research being done. More than anything, as Knefelkamp, Widick, and Parker (1978) argued over a decade ago, student affairs professionals need a firm grasp of a knowledge base that includes

- a conceptualization of the mature personality,

- specific understanding of how development occurs, and an analysis of the significant environmental influences on development,

- an in-depth perspective on the student "voice" (e.g., who they are, what they believe, what their issues/ concerns are), and

- clear notions of the ends toward which development in college should be directed.

As Strange pointed out in Chapter 6, considerable progress has been made on some aspects of this agenda since Knefelkamp et al. defined it, but much more remains to be done.

With this scholarship and knowledge base as a foundation, student affairs professionals can address the crisis of higher education by deliberately designing or reshaping the higher education environment, broadly defined, to facilitate development—or as Perry (1970) has said, find ways to encourage students in their developmental journeys. Higher education has the potential to offer learning opportunities across the whole spectrum of development, among others: (1) *intellectual,* through integration, synthesis, and a focus on quality of thinking displayed rather than quantity of information retained; (2) *interpersonal* particularly group work and confrontation skills; (3) *personal,* focusing on a sense of both community and individual responsibility and a desire for lifelong learning; and (4) *career,* including both transferable and specific skills relevant to success and a more complex view of careers and the world of work.

While other domains (physical and spiritual development for example) are also important, particularly for certain specialized institutions, these four are the primary areas addressed by most colleges and universities. The environments existing within an institution, both inside and outside the classroom learning experience, offer enormous potential for learning and growth in these areas, much of it untapped. A major role for student affairs professionals, then, in the pursuit of the "business" of human development, or "talent development," to use Astin's (1985) phrase, is to clarify these learning opportunities and redesign the environments we create to better tap this potential. Projects of this nature are in process at two different institutions in Virginia—Longwood College (Gorski, Moore, Strohm, & Taylor, 1985; Moore, 1987) and James Madison University (see Chapter 22)—and the results to date are promising.

One of the joys and frustrations of being in the business of human development is that the work is inevitably interactive; the people for whom these environments are designed play a significant role in both the process and the outcomes. Indeed, Astin (1984, 1985), Pace (1987) and others (NIE Study Group, 1984) remind us clearly that fostering this personal involvement in learning is crucial to the success of the enterprise, that the investment students make in their educational experience consistently pays off for them in terms of persistence in higher education, satisfaction with their educations, and individual growth and achievement. Thus, student affairs professionals not only need to intentionally design developmental environments, they need to promote goal-directed student involvement, and help students understand their own learning and development in the process. This effort might mean, for example that professionals in student affairs design and utilize feedback tools for results of outcomes assessment efforts (Moore, 1987, 1988; Winston & Miller, 1987) that translate the information into student language and day-to-day student experiences. More indirectly, major student affairs systems, for example, room sign-up in residence halls, hall programming and governments, and judicial processes, can be revamped to provide greater student involvement and personal responsibility. Throughout the student affairs realm, students need to be encouraged to be *active*, not passive. To shake many students from their complacency and narrow notions of what their education should be may be difficult, but students can be crucial allies in reshaping higher education. An emphasis on the significance of *involvement* is the key to helping students understand the developmental aims of education.

In a similar fashion, but with different approaches, student affairs professionals need to communicate the urgency of the developmental mission of higher education to the entire academic community, particularly faculty colleagues. This urgency can be shared in a variety of ways, including the provision of information about students' college experiences, how they learn, and how a developmental framework for understanding students can be useful in the context of teaching and advising. Certainly many faculty members are neither open to nor interested in receiving such information, causing many student affairs practitioners to be overly cautious about sharing what they know in these areas. On the other hand, many faculty members who teach undergraduate students across the country are willing to listen because they are concerned about their students' learning and are often in pain (Knefelkamp, 1980) about the difficulties they face in teaching the heterogeneous student population most encounter.

Given the gaps in the training and background of most faculty members with respect to students and learning, opportunities for student affairs professionals to share their expertise clearly exist if they are but willing to act. However, the likelihood that formal invitations will be extended for this role is very minimal. In effect, student affairs professionals will be required to go more than halfway in reaching out to faculty colleagues with this information about students and development. Much of this effort's success may hinge on the credibility and involvement of the CSAA in forging roles for student affairs practitioners to play throughout the campus community, such as making presentations to faculty groups or participating in campus-wide committees on issues like retention or assessment. Still, individual student affairs professionals, even those in entry-level positions, can pursue this goal by establishing personal credibility through contacts with faculty members, both professionally and personally. For example, more attention could be given in student activities programs to relationships with faculty organization advisors, or joint projects with academic departments with shared interests, like art, music, and theatre. On a personal level, student affairs professionals might make the effort to participate in faculty-oriented campus events, possible sit in on a class in an area of interest, and create social situations in which faculty and student affairs professionals can mingle informally. To contribute significantly to the institution's educational vision is difficult indeed without first earning a reasonable degree of personal and professional credibility from those most involved, that is, the faculty.

Finally, and implicit in the foregoing discussion of critical roles, is the notion that student affairs professionals are perhaps above all required by this vision of higher education to be effective agents for change (see Chapter 5)—or to use Kanter's (1983) term, *change masters.* This construct makes many student affairs professionals uncomfortable and, as Shafer (1973) and Blake (1979) have noted, tends to contradict the traditional orientation of student affairs toward preserving order, institutional stability, and the status quo. This perspective, however, does not imply the pursuit of change purely for the sake of change, or suggest that change is inherently better than the status quo. Rather, accepting this role as primary acknowledges, as Kanter noted in terms of the corporate community, that rarely are organizations perfect, thus making constant change of one kind or another essential to continued health and favor. Further, the most successful organizations are those that actively promote *innovation* (Kanter, 1983; Peters & Waterman, 1982). And, as argued earlier, accepting even part of the notion that higher education is in crisis demands this focus on change and innovation in the pursuit of a new, or renewed, vision of its purpose. Change is needed in the nature of the classroom and nonclassroom environments, and change is needed in the way systems encourage or inhibit student involvement and the taking of personal responsibility. If student affairs professionals do not take the leadership in such change, who will?

The irony in this change master role, noted by Blake (1979) among others, is that administrators, including student affairs professionals, generally are paid to maintain the status quo, not to innovate or promote institutional change. Blake argued on the other hand that faculty members by the very nature of academic scholarship, are constantly seeking change, new knowledge, and alternative ways of doing things. Day-to-day experience in higher education would suggest that this contrast is not so sharly drawn in reality, and that for many faculty, what innovation they pursue is confined to the narrow band of their discipline and work. Still, the image exists, and does create an obstacle for student affairs professionals in pursuing this role. Other, more substantive obstacles, can be characterized as being either external or internal.

EXTERNAL OBSTACLES TO CHANGE

Professional Obstacles
to the Change Agent Role

The long term debate about whether student affairs is a profession (see Chapter 8) reflects a continuing identity crisis. Whether based in reality or not, this unanswered question *does* provide a major obstacle to the assumption that student affairs plays a significant role in the higher education enterprise. The resulting uncertainty tends to produce two opposite, but equally damaging responses: (1) a withdrawal into the day-to-day work of administering student affairs operations, avoiding explicit connections to or interactions with faculty (and by extension, scholarship), and (2) an effort to create legitimacy for the field by discussing its major concepts with as much academic esoterica as possible. The former creates distance by exacerbating the natural ignorance many faculty have concerning the nature of student affairs work, the latter by obscuring fundamental notions about students with unnecessary jargon and undermining efforts to translate these concepts to the very audiences who most need to hear the message. As a result, too often student affairs professionals spend much of their time talking to each other, and are perceived as being isolated from the "real world" of student affairs work in higher education (Bloland, 1986). Echoing Schroeder's (1988) assertion, the student affairs profession needs to move beyond this perspective by simply pursuing an active competent role within the higher education community.

A corollary problem to this professional identity crisis is the apparent backlash reaction to the growing developmental knowledge base for student affairs (Bloland, 1986; Hughey, 1986), some of which no doubt relates to the "common-sense" school of student affairs (see Chapter 7), which holds that the profession simply has no need for such complex notions about students and their development in order to provide its basic functions. Bloland's argument that it is dangerous to accept uncritically any orthodoxy, developmental or otherwise, certainly has merit. Nevertheless, other aspects of this backlash seem to reveal an underlying strain of anti-intellectualism that may reflect either an active rejection of the values of academe or a reflection of the fundamental pragmatism of many of the people in the field of student affairs. As noted earlier, the knowledge base of student affairs administration is varied and interdisciplinary, perhaps making it difficult to be defined as precisely as some would like. In particular, the significant developmental dimensions often referred to as "affective" (see Chapter 22), because they tend to be denigrated by many academic discipline oriented faculty members, require more deftly defined, quality scholarship. Even within the profession, a recent monograph was published that allegedly defined the "student personnel point of view" from the perspective of the 1980s yet included not one reference to a developmental perspective (National Association of Student Personnel Administrators, 1987). Others (Stamatakos & Rogers, 1984) have argued that developmental goals are clearly secondary to the fundamental mission of the educational enterprise. And, as Kuh, Bean, Bradley, and Coomes (1986) observed, even the literature in professional student affairs journals tends to focus less on personal growth issue than on academic achievement. If student affairs professionals cannot agree among themselves about the foundations of the field, or choose to back away from the tenets of development, how can they hope to articulate a clear educational vision of human development?

What appears to be anti-intellectualism may in fact simply be a function of another major professional obstacle for student affairs: the continuing, perhaps widening, gap between theory and practice, or more precisely, the significant difficulties that seem to prevent student affairs professionals from effectively integrating theoretical perspectives or research findings into daily practice. As Winston (1990) argued, these problems stem largely from an adequate view of the nature and role of theory; a superficial and uncritical understanding of the major theories of human development; and a failure to distinguish adequately among philosophy, theory, and process models and their respective roles. Developmental theories do not define a philosophy or mission because they do not directly answer the question, development for what? Nor do they define explicitly a framework for interventions such as the structure provided by **process models** (see Chapter 7 for one example, the grounded-formal-theory model). Lack of clarity among these concepts tends to undermine practitioners' efforts to link theory and practice.

The understanding of the fundamental nature and role of theory is also a major concern. Developmental theories help explain and predict behavior in specified contexts, but they do not, and cannot, reflect completely the complexity of human behavior. Perry (1985, p.7), one of the major developmental theorists, expressed his personal concern about this issue when he wrote "When we are in the act of deriving concepts from the complexities of persons, we are still aware of the complexities of the persons before us, our abstraction helps enlighten only an aspect of that complexity." Practitioners need to be reminded that developmental theories deal with probabilities and tendencies of human behavior. Given the complexity of the phenomena involved, one cannot approach these theories with the same degree of certainty one might apply to a physical science model of theory (Winston, 1989). Despite what some have suggested (Hughey, 1986), this uncertainty does not mean that theories are useless for practice.

Parker (1977) aptly characterized the central paradox involved in the theory-practice link. "The nature of theory is such that it does not lead directly to practice, and the nature of practice is such that it does not proceed without theory" (p. 420). To resolve this paradox, Parker drew a distinction between *formal* and *informal* theories. The former referred to the explicit hypotheses and conceptual frameworks about given phenomena, while the latter reflected the "common knowledge" (p. 421) upon which individuals act in their day-to-day practice. Both kinds of theories have utility and limitations. Generally, however, if the focus is on an individual student, informal theories and constructs are more useful while if the focus is on a specific environment or an overall system such as a college or university, formal theories are more useful. Because of their failure to understand this distinction, and thus the precise nature of theory, many graduate students and entry-level practitioners are frustrated in their efforts to apply formal theories to work with individual students.

Rodgers (Chapter 7) outlined a four-step continuum for understanding a given theory or model, characterized roughly by a progression from simplistic to complex and contextual. Strange (1983) observed that few professionals in student affairs are very far along that continuum with respect to the major theories of the field. This failure to appreciate and utilize theoretical frameworks adequately further undermines the credibility necessary for student affairs professionals to operate effectively with faculty, and without this credibility it is difficult to be taken seriously when attempting to define the educational agenda for an institution.

INTERNAL OBSTACLES TO CHANGE

Beyond the external, professional obstacles to student affairs practitioners taking on the much-needed role of change master, also two parallel sets of obstacles exist to innovation *internal* to a given institution: one from an *individual* perspective and another from an *institutional* perspective (see Chapter 5). Even if student affairs as a profession was accepted as a significant agent for change and voice for an educational agenda, these factors would mitigate against movement toward innovation at the campus level.

Individual Obstacles
To the Change Agent Role

Discrepancies Between Academic Training and Job Expectations. As several authors in this volume (Creamer, Kuh, Stamatakos) have observed, being an effective agent for change is an enormously complex undertaking even in the best of circumstances because most faculty and staff members have not been educated to implement such complex interventions. In particular, entry-level student affairs professionals frequently suffer from a failure to understand organizational dynamics and campus politics, two elements essential to the change master role. This failure is especially crucial in traditional, status quo oriented student affairs operations. In such situations, entry-level practitioners may be eager to assume the change agent role but are constantly thwarted by their lack of position power and their inability to "work the system."

Lack of Ownership in the Agenda. Generally speaking, people tend to react negatively to changes that affect them but in which they had no voice; this situation is not uncommon in higher education institutions when change is imposed from the top (Gorski et al., 1985), especially given the unique nature of such institutions' organizational environments (see Chapter 2).

Lack of Consensus on the Process Involved. Ideally, to encourage ownership on the part of as many people as possible, the process of change involves a collaborative team that works to promote change by and through consensus. Because consensus is extremely difficult to achieve in highly fractious higher education environments, what Cohen and March (1974) aptly referred to as *organized anarchies,* slow progress, false starts, and sidetracks are inevitable, even though the eventual results may be strengthened by the overall process.

Paralysis Through Politics. In some ways the reverse of the previously noted consensus-seeking process, where some individuals pursue positive political agendas within an institution (e.g., building liaisons, keeping everyone informed, not offending anyone) so diligently that the entire innovation grinds to a halt. Because to satisfy everyone's agenda in a given college or university is virtually impossible; a delicate balance exists between judicious political skills and paralysis.

Perfectionism. In some instances the potential success of an institutional change process (Gorski et al., 1985) can be partially undermined by insisting that a "product" be perfected before sharing it with the academic community as a whole. This perfectionist attitude can delay visible results from being shared with others in the institution, and thus the credibility of the innovators and innovation can be lost because faculty and staff members were not informed about what was going on.

Institutional Obstacles
to the Change Agent Role

Lack of Resources. Just because some very valuable innovations do not require great amounts of money, comprehensive institutional change is not free of the need for additional funding. Unfortunately, many institutions of higher education have most of their budget allocations tied up by relatively inflexible costs, such as personnel, operations, and maintenance, and often have little left over to support expenditures to implement projects and innovations. Even if an overall commitment to change existed limitations are present as to what the institution can afford.

Competing Obligations and Priorities. Even with a commitment to change and the available resources, colleges and universities, as much as any other relatively complex bureaucracies, experience constant battles over how to allocate the resources available; many different priorities, all with advocates and many with solid arguments, compete every year for a budgetary pie that rarely grows much larger.

Rigid and Overly Formal Definitions of Roles and Responsibilities. The existing hierarchical bureaucracies in most educational institutions can often lead to a range of problems (see Kuh & Whitt, Chapter 2; Kuh, Whitt, & Shedd, 1987), not the least of which is a tendency toward rigid definitions of appropriate territory, and woe to unsuspecting change agents who cross the borders into someone else's "turf." The result, as Kanter (1983) noted, is that innovation is stifled because of a failure to share resources, information, and support across these formal lines.

Lack of Clarity about Who's in Charge. The obverse of the rigid hierarchy coin is a change process without a clearly identified leader (see Chapter 4) or champion (Chapter 5), which tends to produce a muddled and often directionless innovation, undermining the likelihood of its implementation. Even though a core team of people may be involved in the change process, a clearly-defined leader and a champion are usually necessary for effective functioning within the bureaucracy.

External Pressure to Produce Quick Results and Solutions. Just as individual pressure may exist to perfect the proposed innovation before implementing anything, often an institutional pressure exists for just the opposite: a "quick fix," something to show various constituencies, from faculty to external boards or legislators, that action is being taken. A balance needs to be struck between these two pressures, offering interim reports or results while continuing the work on improving the eventual product, whatever it may be.

OVERCOMING OBSTACLES TO CHANGE

Despite the array of formidable obstacles to change and implementation of the change master role, whether in the professional, individual, or institutional context, crucial to the accomplishment of higher education's mission is that student affairs professionals take active leadership in the change processes demanded. Much provocative wisdom is in the chapters of this book that can provide institutional leaders with possible solutions. Examples include the cogent arguments of Kuh and Whitt in Chapter 2 who suggested that student affairs practitioners need to see the "big picture" from multiple perspectives, innovate without being bound by formal organizational structures, and remember that "leadership is everybody's business;" Strange's thorough overview of college environment issues in chapter 6; and Stamatakos' articulation of the significant roles of the Chief Student Affairs Administrator in Chapter 20.

In addition to these examples and other thoughtful perspectives found in this book, several other suggestions are worthy of consideration.

Understand the Important Levels
of Developmental Influence

Saying that student affairs administrators are in the business of human development should not be interpreted as meaning that their only, or even their primary task, is to develop and implement explicit developmental programs designed to educate students or provide challenging experiences that will guide them toward some grand developmental end. Such programs may be appropriate and useful at times, but more fundamental ways exist to define developmental environments; for example, focusing on basic student-centered approaches to systems, services, and functions, and examining to what extent programs and services are based in legitimate student needs (Strohm, 1983). Winston (1990) offers a relevant reminder that while developmental theories and process models are powerful and useful for many educational aspects of student affairs work, they are not necessary for all aspects, nor should they be; the point here is that work that is not based in a specified development model can still be developmental in its fundamental aims and outcomes. Many aspects of daily administrative and management practice, including most systems, policies, and procedures that affect students' lives, can be construed as interventions with a developmental influence, positive or negative. This broadened, and more complex, understanding of developmental interventions can be particularly useful to entry-level professionals in tradition-bound, service oriented student affairs operations. The task, pursued in a nonthreatening way, is to take a student centered approach to services and administrative functions whenever possible and to be able to understand this approach as being fundamentally developmental in nature.

Build Relationships with Faculty Members

Comprehensive and significant educational change in higher education must involve faculty members, large numbers of whom tend to maintain institutional connections for longer periods than do their student affairs counterparts. Likewise, they often tend to be skeptical or even ignorant of the work accomplished by student affairs professionals as well. Unfortunately, in most institutions significant work or social opportunities rarely exist for faculty and student affairs professionals to interact in meaningful ways. Crucial to the change processes defined is the necessity that such opportunities be found or created.

Move Slowly in the Change Process, and Establish Credibility

Assuming that any significant change agentry inevitably will include multiple constituencies in the institution, especially faculty members, a crucial point is that the change process move slowly and that an important initial emphasis be placed on finding ways for student affairs practitioners to establish credibility within the academic community as individuals who exhibit expertise, scholarship, and a strong commitment to the institution. This kind of credibility-building may well require longer periods of time to be established than is available during the typical two or three year tenures of many entry- and mid-level student affairs professionals, but a change agent will very unlikely have a significant impact without it.

Get Involved with Broad, Institutional Issues
Beyond the Confines of Student Affairs

One of the best ways to establish the necessary credibility with faculty members is to become active in significant institutional issues and concerns that cut across structural lines, for example, outcomes assessment, retention, advising, or freshman year experience. These issues, and the opportunities for inclusion, will obviously vary depending on the nature and political climate of an individual campus, but they are excellent ways to demonstrate to faculty members and institutional administrators the competence and expertise available within student affairs.

Help Create a Developmental Environment
for Faculty and Staff

In some ways, this final suggestion may seem like the Impossible Dream, as most institutions have more than enough problems simply considering the complexity of a developmental environment for students. At the same time, how can educators be expected to be positive developmental influences on students if the campus work environment stifles their own growth? If anything has been learned from the developmental research over the past two decades, it is that an individual's development does not end with college graduation—indeed, in many ways, it has barely begun by that time. As DeCoster and Brown (Chapter 17) suggested, the time is now to focus on both professional *and* personal education in staff development activities. Focusing on a more developmental environment for staff and faculty will at the very least foster their ability to engender such environments for their students as well.

SUMMARY

A crisis exists in higher education, and as much as anything the crisis is of vision and purpose. This crisis, and the needs of students and society at large, calls for a new and renewed commitment to a mission of higher education that focuses increased attention on the broad spectrum of human development. Such a commitment will require an active and effective change agent role from within the academy, and no segment of the higher education community is potentially better suited to carry forward such a role than that of student affairs. The crisis for higher education thus presents for the 1990s a tremendous opportunity for student affairs professionals, especially entry-level practitioners and current graduate students seeking a niche in the higher education community and a more active voice in the educational enterprise. Particularly as the turnover in the professorate increases through the coming decade, young student affairs professionals have an excellent opportunity for a fresh beginning with new faculty colleagues. Taking advantage of this opportunity will require a sophisticated understanding of higher education, organizational politics, human development, and the appropriate uses of developmental models, all of which should be available through professional preparation programs and staff development efforts. If not, CSAAs and the student affairs establishment need to be held accountable for the obvious shortcomings that would exist.

In the 1990s, as before, creative and constructive administration and leadership will be needed from the student affairs profession. The crucial difference, and the reason the field desperately needs leadership even more than administration, is the difference between *managing* the crisis, that is, putting out the fire, and *leading* the institution, and higher education as a whole, out of the crisis toward a more productive vision of the enterprise of higher education. As Cross (1985) observed, the focus on the development of human potential can be higher education's unique contribution to education for the next century, and student affairs professionals are essential to achieving that goal.

REFERENCES

American Association of Colleges (AAC) (1985). *Integrity in the college curriculum: A report to the academic community.* Washington, DC: AAC Project on Redefining the Meaning and Scope of Baccalaureate Degrees.

Astin, A.W. (1984). Student involvement: A developmental theory for higher education. *Journal of College Student Personnel, 25,* 297-308.

Astin, A.W. (1985). *Achieving educational excellence.* San Francisco: Jossey-Bass.

Blake, E. (1979). Classroom and context: An educational dialectic. *Academe, Bulletin of the AAUP, 65,* 280-292.

Bloland, P. (1986). Student development: The new orthodoxy? Part II. *ACPA Developments, 13*(4), 1.

Bloom, A. (1987). *The closing of the American mind.* New York: Simon and Schuster.

Boyer, E.L. (1987). *College: The undergraduate experience.* New York: Harper & Row.

Cleveland, H. (1985, July/August). Educating for the information society. *Change,* 13-21.

Cohen, M., & March, J.G. (1974). *Leadership and ambiguity: The American college presidency.* New York: McGraw/Hill.

Cross, K.P. (1985). *Education for the 21st century.* Paper presented at the National Association of Student Personnel Administrators annual conference, Portland, OR.

Gamson, Z.F., & Associates. (1984). *Liberating education.* San Francisco: Jossey-Bass.

Gorski, B., Moore, W.S., Strohm, M., & Taylor, K. (1985, June). Student development: The Longwood experience. *ACU-I Bulletin, 53*(3), 21-25.

Heath, D. (1968). *Growing up in college.* San Francisco: Jossey-Bass.

Hughey, A. (1986). Response to Bloland. *ACPA Developments. 13*(4), 2.

Hutchins, R.M. (1969). *The learning society.* New York: Mentor.

Jaspers, K. (1959). *The idea of the university.* Boston: Beacon Press.

Kanter, R.M. (1983). *The change masters: How people and companies succeed through innovation in the new corporate era.* New York: Simon and Schuster.

Klemp, G.O., Jr. (1980). *The assessment of occupational competence: The definition and measurement of competence in higher education.* Boston: McBer & Company. (ERIC No. ED 192 168)

Knefelkamp, L.L. (1980). *Faculty and student development in the 80's: Renewing the community of scholars.* Washington, DC: American Association for Higher Education.

Knefelkamp, L.L. (1984). *A workbook for the practice-to-theory-to-practice model.* Alexandria, VA: American College Personnel Association.

Knefelkamp, L.L., Widick, C., & Parker, C.A. (1978). *Applying new developmental findings.* New Directions for Student Services (No. 4). San Francisco: Jossey-Bass.

Kuh, G.D., Bean, J.P., Bradley, R.K., & Coomes, M.D. (1986). Contributions of student affairs journals to the college student research. *Journal of College Student Personnel, 27,* 292-304.

Kuh, G.D., Whitt, E.J., & Shedd, J.D. (1987). *Student affairs work, 2001: A paradigmatic odyssey.* Alexandria, VA: American College Personnel Association.

Kuh, G.D., Shedd, J.D., & Whitt, E.J. (1987). Student affairs and liberal education: Unrecognized (and unappreciated) common law partners. *Journal of College Student Personnel, 28,* 252-360.

Lynton, E.A. (1982, October). *Universities today: A crisis of purpose.* Address presented at the University of Illinois at Urbana.

McDaniel, R.R. (1975, March). *Goal setting for student development.* Paper presented at the American College Personnel Association annual convention, Atlanta, GA.

Moore, W.S. (1987). Assessing student development: The Longwood College experience. *VASPA Interchange, 16*(2), 1-4.

Moore, W.S. (1988). *Understanding your results on the learning environment preferences: Classroom learning strategies.* Athens, GA: Center for the Study of Intellectual Development.

National Association of Student Personnel Administrators. (1987). *A perspective on student affairs: A statement issued on the 50th anniversary of the student personnel point of view.* Washington, DC: Author.

NIE Study Group on the Conditions of Excellence in American Higher Education. (1984). *Involvement in learning: Realizing the potential of American higher education.* Washington, DC: National Institute of Education.

Pace, R. (1987). *Manual for the college student experiences questionnaire.* Los Angeles: Center for the Study of Evaluation.

Parker, C.A. (1977). On modeling reality. *Journal of College Student Personnel, 18,* 419-425.

Perry, W.G. (1970). *Forms of intellectual and ethical development in the college years.* New York: Holt, Rinehart & Winston.

Perry, W.G. (1985, June). *Perry's perplex: Issues unresolved and irresolvable.* Unpublished paper. Presentation at the Project Match Conference, Davidson College.

Peters, T., & Waterman, R. (1982). *In search of excellence: Lessons from America's best run companies.* New York: Harper & Row.

Sanford, N. (1966). *Self and society: Social change and individual development.* New York: Atherton press.

Schroeder, C. (1988). Student affairs-academic affairs: Opportunities for bridging the gap. *ACPA Developments, 15*(4), 1.

Shafer, R.H. (1973). An emerging role of student personnel—contributing to organizational effectiveness. *Journal of College Student personnel, 14,* 386-391.

Stamatakos, L.C., & Rogers, R. (1984). Student Affairs: A profession in need of a philosophy. *Journal of College Student Personnel, 25,* 400-411.

Strange, C. (1983). Human development theory and administrative practice in student affairs: Ships passing in the daylight. *NASPA Journal, 21*(1), 2-8.

Strohm, M. (1983). *Planned change strategies appropriate to student development goals.* Unpublished paper. College Park, MD: University of Maryland.

Winston, R.B., Jr. (1990). Using theory and research findings in everyday practice. In D.D. Coleman & J.E. Johnson (Eds.), *The new professional: A resource guide for new student affairs professionals and their supervisors.* (pp. 30-55). Washington, DC: National Association of Student Personnel Administrators.

Winston, R.B., Jr., & Miller, T.K. (1987). *Understanding and using the SDTLI: A guide for students.* Athens, GA: Student Development Associates.

Winter, D.G., McClelland, D.C., & Stewart, A.J. (1981). *A new case for the liberal arts.* San Francisco: Jossey-Bass.

SUGGESTED READINGS

Educational Testing Service. (1987). *Assessing the outcomes of higher education: Proceedings of the 1986 invitational conference.* Princeton, NJ: Author.

Gamson, Z.F., & Associates. (1984). *Liberating education.* San Francisco: Jossey-Bass.

Grant, G., Elbow, P., Ewens, T., Gamson, Z., Kohli, W., Nuemann, W., Olesen, V., & Riesman, D. (1979). *On competence: a critical analysis of competence-based reforms in higher education.* San Francisco: Jossey-Bass.

Halpern, D.F. (Ed.). (1987). *Student outcomes assessment: What institutions stand to gain.* New Directions for Higher Education (No. 59). San Francisco: Jossey-Bass.

Kanter, R.M. (1983). *The change masters: How people and companies succeed through innovation in the new corporate era.* New York: Simon and Schuster.

Knefelkamp, L.L., Widick, C., & Parker, C.A. (1978). *Applying new developmental findings.* New Directions for Student Services (No. 4). San Francisco: Jossey-Bass.

Kuh, G.D., Whitt, E.J., & Shedd, J.D. (1987). *Student affairs work, 2001: A paradigmatic odyssey.* Alexandria, VA: American College Personnel Association.

Winter, D.G., McClelland, D.C., & Stewart, A.J. (1981). *A new case for the liberal arts.* San Francisco: Jossey-Bass.

APPENDICES

Appendix A

ACPA STATEMENT OF ETHICAL PRINCIPLES AND STANDARDS

American College Personnel Association. (1989). *ACPA Statement of Ethical Principles and Standards.* Alexandria, VA: Author. Reprinted by permission.

Statement of Ethical Principles and Standards

American College Personnel Association

PREAMBLE

The American College Personnel Association (ACPA), a Division of the American Association for Counseling and Development (AACD), is an association whose members are dedicated to enhancing the worth, dignity, potential, and uniqueness of each individual within post-secondary educational institutions and thus to the service of society. ACPA members are committed to contributing to the comprehensive education of the student, protecting human rights, advancing knowledge of student growth and development, and promoting the effectiveness of institutional programs, services, and organizational units. As a means of supporting these commitments, members of ACPA subscribe to the following principles and standards of ethical conduct. Acceptance of membership in ACPA signifies that the member agrees to adhere to the provisions of this statement.

This statement is designed to complement the AACD *Ethical Standards* (1988) by addressing issues particularly relevant to college student affairs practice. Persons charged with duties in various functional areas of higher education are also encouraged to consult ethical standards specific to their professional responsibilities.

USE OF THIS STATEMENT

The principle purpose of this statement is to assist student affairs professionals in regulating their own behavior by sensitizing them to potential ethical problems and by providing standards useful in daily practice. Observance of ethical behavior also benefits fellow professionals and students due to the effects of modeling. Self-regulation is the most effective and preferrred means of assuring ethical behavior. If, however, a professional observes conduct by a fellow professional that seems contrary to the provisions of this document, several courses of action are available.

Initiate a Private Conference

Because unethical conduct often is due to a lack of awareness or understanding of ethical standards, a private conference with the professional(s) about the conduct in question is an important initial line of action. This conference, if pursued in a spirit of collegiality and sincerity, often may resolve the ethical concern and promote future ethical conduct.

Pursue Institutional Remedies

If private consultation does not produce the desired results, insti-tutional channels for resolving alleged ethical improprieties may be pursued. All student affairs divisions should have a widely-publicized process for addressing allegations of ethical misconduct.

Contact ACPA
Ethics Committee

If the ACPA member is unsure about whether a particular activity or practice falls under the provisions of this statement, the Ethics Committee may be contacted in writing. The member should describe in reasonable detail (omitting data that would identify the person(s) as much as possible) the potentially unethical conduct or practices and the circumstances surrounding the situation. Members of the Committee or others in the Association will provide the member with a summary of opinions regarding the ethical appropriateness of the conduct or practice in question. Because these opinions are based on limited information, no specific situation or action will be judged "unethical." The responses rendered by the Committee are advisory only and are not an official statement on behalf of ACPA.

Request Consultation From
ACPA Ethics Committee

If the institution wants further assistance in resolving the controversy, an institutional representative may request on-campus consultation. Provided all parties to the controversy agree, a team of consultants selected by the Ethics Committee will visit the campus at the institutions' expense to hear the allegations and to review the facts and circumstances. The team will advise institutional leadership on possible actions consistent with both the content and spirit of the *ACPA Statement of Ethical Principles and Standards*. Compliance with recommendations is voluntary. No sanctions will be imposed by ACPA. Institutional leaders remain responsible for assuring ethical conduct and practice. The consultation team will maintain confidentiality surrounding the process to the extent possible.

Submit Complaint to
AACD Ethics Committee

If the alleged misconduct may be a violation of the *AACD Ethical Standards*, the person charged is a member of AACD, and the institutional process is unavailable or produces unsatisfactory results, then proceedings against the individual(s) may be brought to the AACD Ethics Committee for review. Details regarding the procedures may be obtained by contacting AACD headquarters.

ETHICAL PRINCIPLES

No statement of ethical standards can anticipate all situations that have ethical implications. When student affairs professionals are presented with dilemmas that are not explicitly addressed herein, five ethical principles may be used in conjunction with the four enumerated standards (Professional Responsibility and Competence, Student Learning and Development, Responsibility to the Institution, and Responsibility to Society) to assist in making decisions and in determining appropriate courses of action.

Ethical principles should guide the behaviors of professionals in everyday practice. Principles, however, are not just guidelines for reaction when something goes wrong or when a complaint is raised. Adhering to ethical principles also calls for action. These principles include the following.

Act to Benefit Others

Service to humanity is the basic tenet underlying student affairs practice. Hence, student affairs professionals exist to (a) promote healthy social, physical, academic, moral, cognitive, career, and personality development of students; (b) bring a developmental perspective to the institution's total educational process and learning environment; (c) contribute to the effective functioning of the institution; and (d) provide programs and services consistent with this principle.

Promote Justice

Student affairs professionals are committed to assuring fundamental fairness for all individuals within the academic community. In pursuit of this goal, the principles of impartiality, equity, and reciprocity (treating others as one would desire to be treated) are basic. When there are greater needs than resources available or when the interests of constituencies conflict, justice requires honest consideration of all claims and requests and equitable (not necessarily equal) distribution of goods and services. A crucial aspect of promoting justice is demonstrating an appreciation for human differences and opposing intolerance and bigotry concerning these differences. Important human differences include, but are not limited to, characteristics such as age, culture, ethnicity, gender, disabling condition, race, religion, or sexual/affectional orientation.

Respect Autonomy

Student affairs professionals respect and promote individual autonomy and privacy. Students' freedom of choice and action are not restricted unless their actions significantly interfere with the welfare of others or the accomplishment of the institution's mission.

Be Faithful

Student affairs professionals are truthful, honor agreements, and are trustworthy in the performance of their duties.

Do No Harm

Student affairs professionals do not engage in activities that cause either physical or psychological damage to others. In addition to their personal actions, student affairs professionals are especially vigilant to assure that the institutional policies do not: (a) hinder students' opportunities to benefit from the learning experiences available in the environment; (b) threaten individuals' self-worth, dignity, or safety; or (c) discriminate unjustly or illegally.

ETHICAL STANDARDS

Four ethical standards related to primary constituencies with whom student affairs professionals work—fellow professionals, students, educational institutions, and society—are specified.

1. *Professional Responsibility and Competence.* Student affairs professionals are responsible for promoting students' learning and development, enhancing the understanding of student life, and advancing the

profession and its ideals. They possess the knowledge, skills, emotional stability, and maturity to discharge responsibilities as administrators, advisors, consultants, counselors, programmers, researchers, and teachers. High levels of professional competence are expected in the performance of their duties and responsibilities. They ultimately are responsible for the consequences of their actions or inaction.

As ACPA members, student affairs professionals will:

1.1 Adopt a professional lifestyle characterized by use of sound theoretical principles and a personal value system congruent with the basic tenets of the profession.

1.2. Contribute to the development of the profession (e.g., recruiting students to the profession, serving professional organizations, educating new professionals, improving professional practices, and conducting and reporting research).

1.3. Maintain and enhance professional effectiveness by improving skills and acquiring new knowledge.

1.4. Monitor their personal and professional functioning and effectiveness and seek assistance from appropriate professionals as needed.

1.5. Represent their professional credentials, competencies, and limitations accurately and correct any misrepresentations of these qualifications by others.

1.6. Establish fees for professional services after consideration of the ability of the recipient to pay. They will provide some services, including professional development activities for colleagues, for little or no remuneration.

1.7. Refrain from attitudes or actions that impinge on colleagues' dignity, moral code, privacy, worth, professional functioning, and/or personal growth.

1.8. Abstain from sexual harassment.

1.9. Abstain from sexual intimacies with colleagues or with staff for whom they have supervisory, evaluative, or instructional responsibility.

1.10. Refrain from using their positions to seek unjustified personal gains, sexual favors, unfair advantages, or unearned goods and services not normally accorded those in such positions.

1.11. Inform students of the nature and/or limits of confidentiality. They will share information about the students only in accordance with institutional policies and applicable laws, when given their permission, or when required to prevent personal harm to themselves or others.

1.12. Use records and electronically stored information only to accomplish legitimate, institutional purposes and to benefit students.

1.13. Define job responsibilities, decision-making procedures, mutual expectations, accountability procedures, and evaluation criteria with subordinates and supervisors.

1.14. Acknowledge contributions by others to program development, program implementation, evaluations, and reports.

1.15. Assure that participation by staff in planned activities that emphasize self-disclosure or other relatively intimate or personal involvement is voluntary and that the leader(s) of such activities does (do) not have administrative, supervisory, or evaluative authority over participants.

1.16. Adhere to professional practices in securing positions: (a) represent education and experiences accurately; (b) respond to offers promptly; (c) accept only those positions they intend to assume; (d) advise current employer and all institutions at which applications are pending immediately when they sign a contract; and (e) inform their employers at least thirty days before leaving a position.

1.17. Gain approval of research plans involving human subjects from the institutional committee with oversight responsibility prior to initiation of the study. In the absence of such a committee, they will seek to create

procedures to protect the rights and assure the safety of research participants.

1.18. Conduct and report research studies accurately. They will not engage in fraudulent research nor will they distort or misrepresent their data or deliberately bias their results.

1.19. Cite previous works on a topic when writing or when speaking to professional audiences.

1.20. Acknowledge major contributions to research projects and professional writings through joint authorships with the principal contributor listed first. They will acknowledge minor technical or professional contributions in notes or introductory statements.

1.21. Not demand co-authorship of publications when their involvement was ancillary or unduly pressure others for joint authorship.

1.22. Share original research data with qualified others upon request.

1.23. Communicate the results of any research judged to be of value to other professionals and not withhold results reflecting unfavorably on specific institutions, programs, services, or prevailing opinion.

1.24. Submit manuscripts for consideration to only one journal at a time. They will not seek to publish previously published or accepted-for-publication materials in other media or publications without first informing all editors and/or publishers concerned. They will make appropriate references in the text and receive permission to use if copyrights are involved.

1.25. Support professional preparation program efforts by providing assistantships, practica, field placements, and consultation to students and faculty.

As ACPA members, preparation program faculty will:

1.26. Inform prospective graduate students of program expectations, predominant theoretical orientations, skills needed for successful completion, and employment of recent graduates.

1.27. Assure that required experiences involving self-disclosure are communicated to prospective graduate students. When the program offers experiences that emphasize self-disclosure or other relatively intimate or personal involvement (e.g., group or individual counseling or growth groups), professionals must not have current or anticipated administrative, supervisory, or evaluative authority over participants.

1.28. Provide graduate students with a broad knowledge base consisting of theory, research, and practice.

1.29. Inform graduate students of the ethical responsibilities and standards of the profession.

1.30. Assess all relevant competencies and interpersonal functioning of students throughout the program, communicate these assessments to students, and take appropriate corrective actions, including dismissal when warranted.

1.31. Assure that field supervisors are qualified to provide supervision to graduate students and are informed of their ethical responsibilities in this role.

2. **Student Learning and Development.**

Student development is an essential purpose of higher education, and the pursuit of this aim is a major responsibility of student affairs. Development is complex and includes cognitive, physical, moral, social, career, spiritual, personality, and educational dimensions. Professionals must be sensitive to the variety of backgrounds, cultures, and personal characteristics evident in the student population and use appropriate theoretical perspectives to identify learning opportunities and to reduce barriers that inhibit development.

As ACPA members, student affairs professionals will:

2.1. Treat students as individuals who possess dignity, worth, and the ability to be self-directed.

2.2. Avoid dual relationships with students (e.g., counselor/employer, supervisor/best friend, or faculty/sexual partner) that may involve incompatible roles and conflicting responsibilities.

2.3. Abstain from sexual harassment.

2.4. Abstain from sexual intimacies with clients or with students for whom they have supervisory, evaluative, or instructional responsibility.

2.5. Inform students of the conditions under which they may receive assistance and the limits of confidentiality when the counseling relationship is initiated.

2.6. Avoid entering or continuing helping relationships if benefits to students are unlikely. They will refer students to appropriate specialists and recognize that if the referral is declined, they are not obligated to continue the relationship.

2.7. Inform students about the purpose of assessment and make explicit the planned use of results prior to assessment.

2.8. Provide appropriate information to students prior to and following the use of any assessment procedure to place results in proper perspective with other relevant factors (e.g., socioeconomic, ethnic, cultural, and gender-related experiences).

2.9. Confront students regarding issues, attitudes, and behaviors that have ethical implications.

3. Responsibility to the Institution. Institutions of higher education provide the context for student affairs practice. Institutional mission, policies, organizational structure, and culture, combined with individual judgment and professional standards, define and delimit the nature and extent of practice. Student affairs professionals share responsibility with other members of the academic community for fulfilling the institutional mission. Responsibility to promote the development of individual students and to support the institution's policies and interests require that professionals balance competing demands.

As ACPA members, student affairs professionals will:

3.1. Contribute to their institution by supporting its mission, goals, and policies.

3.2. Seek resolution when they and their institution encounter substantial disagreements concerning professional or personal values. Resolution may require sustained efforts to modify institutional policies and practices or result in voluntary termination of employment.

3.3. Recognize that conflicts among students, colleagues, or the institution should be resolved without diminishing appropriate obligations to any party involved.

3.4. Assure that information provided about the institution is factual and accurate.

3.5. Inform appropriate officials of conditions that may be disruptive or damaging to their institution.

3.6. Inform supervisors of conditions or practices that may restrict institutional or professional effectiveness.

3.7. Recognize their fiduciary responsibility to the institution. They will assure that funds for which they have oversight are expended following established procedures and in ways that optimize value, are accounted for properly, and contribute to the accomplishment of the institution's mission. They also will assure that equipment, facilities, personnel, and other resources are used to promote the welfare of the institution and students.

3.8. Restrict their private interests, obligations, and transactions in ways to minimize conflicts of interest or the appearance of conflicts of interest. They will identify their personal views and actions as private citizens from those expressed or undertaken as institutional representatives.

3.9. Collaborate and share professional expertise with members of the academic community.

3.10. Evaluate programs, services, and organizational structures regularly and systematically to assure conformity to published standards and guidelines. Evaluations should be conducted using rigorous evaluation methods and principles, and the results should be made available to appropriate institutional personnel.

3.11. Evaluate job performance of subordinates regularly and recommend appropriate actions to enhance professional development and improve performance.

3.12. Provide fair and honest assessments of colleagues' job performance.

3.13. Seek evaluations of their job performance and/or services they provide.

3.14. Provide training to student affairs search and screening committee members who are unfamiliar with the profession.

3.15. Disseminate information that accurately describes the responsibilities of position vacancies, required qualifications, and the institution.

3.16. Follow a published interview and selection process that periodically notifies applicants of their status.

4. Responsibility to Society.
Student affairs professionals, both as citizens and practitioners, have a responsibility to contribute to the improvement of the communities in which they live and work. They respect individuality and recognize that worth is not diminished by characteristics such as age, culture, ethnicity, gender, disabling condition, race, religion, or sexual/affectional orientation. Student affairs professionals work to protect human rights and promote an appreciation of human diversity in higher education.

As ACPA members, student affairs professionals will:

4.1. Assist students in becoming productive and responsible citizens.

4.2. Demonstrate concern for the welfare of all students and work for constructive change on behalf of students.

4.3. Not discriminate on the basis of age, culture, ethnicity, gender, disabling condition, race, religion, or sexual/affectional orientation. They will work to modify discriminatory practices.

4.4. Demonstrate regard for social codes and moral expectations of the communities in which they live and work. They will recognize that violations of accepted moral and legal standards may involve their clients, students, or colleagues in damaging personal conflicts and may impugn the integrity of the profession, their own reputations, and that of the employing institution.

4.5. Report to the appropriate authority any condition that is likely to harm their clients and/or others.

REFERENCE

American Association for Counseling and Development. (1988). *Ethical standards.* Alexandria, VA: Author.

Appendix B

AN INTRODUCTION
TO LEGAL RESEARCH

Donald D. Gehring

AN INTRODUCTION TO
LEGAL RESEARCH

Donald D. Gehring

HOW TO BEGIN LEGAL STUDY

Reading Chapters 12 and 13 in this book is a good place to begin legal study of higher education but it is only a beginning. Entire books have been published that lay good foundation for practitioners interested in the legal aspects of college administration. There are also some excellent subscription services that can be used to keep informed. Many of these books and services are written for the lay reader. All student affairs professionals should have at least one basic text and an updating service as part of their library.

Reading texts and subscription services is an excellent way to develop a basic understanding and keep abreast of current case law. Sometimes, however, more in-depth knowledge is required, and the administrator may want to read the entire case referred to by an author or examine a specific statute or regulation. One need not be an attorney to read the law.

RESOURCES AND
HOW TO FIND THE LAW

The law affecting student affairs administration can generally be found in three sources: federal and state statutes, federal regulations, and case law.

Statutes

All federal statutes (laws passed by the Congress) are codified in the *United States Code (U.S.C.)*. Commercial printers also publish versions of the Code that contain useful cross indexes and annotations. Many volumes make up the Code, and each volume contains laws related to a specific topic. In some instances several volumes may be devoted to one topic. Each topic is referred to as an Arabic numeral title. For example, Title 42 refers to public health and welfare laws while Title 20 contains the laws related to education. References to Arabic numeral titles should not be confused with references to Roman numeral titles such as Title VI. Title VI, which prohibits discrimination on the basis of race in federally assisted programs, is a part of the Civil Rights Act of 1964. Once that Act was passed by the Congress and signed by the President it became a law and was codified as a specific section of Title 42 (which contains all the federal civil rights laws). Citations to federal statutes will be written with the title number first, the name of the publication (*U.S.C.*, *U.S.C.A.* or *U.S.C.S.*) and the section. For example, 42 U.S.C. 2000d refers to Title 42 of the United States Code, Section 2000d. The symbol § is sometimes used and simply means "section." More popular sections such as section 1983 of the Civil Rights Law of 1871 may be referred to simply as § 1983. Each of the published codes will also have index volumes filed at the end of volumes containing the statutes.

State statutes are also codified in several volumes. There are usually one or more index volumes filed at the end of the state code. State statutes are generally cited with an Arabic number representing the chapter or section of the code following an abbreviation for the name of the state statutes. For example *KRS 164.891* refers to Kentucky Revised Statutes Chapter 164 (Colleges and Universities), Section 891 (defines "agents" for purposes of malpractice insurance at the University of Louisville). Administrators who wish to become familiar with their state laws may want to peruse the index volumes for such topics as "Colleges and Universities," "Students," "Education," "Alcoholic Beverages," "Open Public Records Law," or other topics of interest.

The reference room of most college and university libraries will have copies of the *United States Code* and state statutes. These basic references can also be found in most county court houses, attorney's offices, and public libraries.

Regulations

Often when a federal law is enacted, it will call for executive agencies (i.e., Department of Education) to issue rules to effectuate the law. For example, when Title IX of the Higher Education Amendment of 1972 was made law, it required federal agencies to make rules to implement the law. Those rules or regulations have significant impact on the daily administration of programs in postsecondary education.

Proposed regulations are first published in the *Federal Register (F.R.)*, and the public is encouraged to comment on them. Once the comment period has ended, the regulations are again published in the *F.R.* in their final form and then incorporated in the *Code of Federal Regulations (C.F.R.)*. Both the *F.R.* and *C.F.R.* usually may be found in the federal documents section or reference room of most college or university libraries. They also will be in the library of a U.S. Attorney or Federal Court House.

References to federal regulations normally will cite the *C.F.R.* Like the *U.S. Code*, the *C.F.R.* is codified by title with each title covering a specific topic and designated by an Arabic numeral. For example, Title 34 refers to education while Title 29 contains regulations pertaining to labor. The title number appears first followed by *C.F.R.* (designating the publication) and the specific part to which referred. Thus, 34 *C.F.R.* 99 refers to Title 34 (education topic) of the *Code of Federal Regulations*, part 99 (The Buckley Amendment or Family Educational Rights and Privacy Act).

Case Law

Another primary source of law affecting the administration of student affairs programs is case law. Statutes are enacted by the legislative branch of government; regulations are one of the ways the executive branch of government effectuates the law, and when a controversy is settled in court, a judicial interpretation attaches to the constitution, statute, or regulation. The latter is referred to as case law.

Case law becomes very important. For instance, Title VI (part of the Civil Rights Act of 1964 passed by Congress) in essence prohibits discrimination on the basis of race in programs receiving federal financial assistance. However, the case law related to that title has held that an institution may under certain circumstances use race as one of several factors in evaluating candidates for admission without violating Title VI. However, courts also have held that the institution may not operate a quota system in which a specific number of places in an entering class are reserved for members of a particular race. Such a quota system in admissions programs would violate the intent of Title VI.

Cases decided by state courts appear in reports as indicated by the following:

N.E. 2d.   Northeastern Reporter, Second Series. Cases decided in the state courts of Massachusetts, Rhode Island, Ohio, Indiana, and Illinois.

A. 2d.   Atlantic Reporter, Second Series. Cases decided in the state courts of Maine, New Hampshire, Vermont, Connecticut, New Jersey, Pennsylvania, Delaware, and Maryland.

So. 2d.   Southern Reporter, Second Series. Cases decided in state courts of Florida, Alabama, Mississippi, and Louisiana.

S.E. 2d.   Southeastern Reporter, Second Series. Cases decided in the state courts of Virginia, West Virginia, North Carolina, South Carolina, and Georgia.

S.W. 2d.   Southwestern Reporter, Second Series. Cases decided in the state courts of Kentucky, Tennessee, Missouri, Arkansas, and Texas.

P. 2d.   Pacific Reporter, Second Series. Cases decided in the state courts of Montana, Wyoming, Idaho, Kansas, Colorado, Oklahoma, New Mexico, Utah, Arizona, Nevada, Washington, Oregon, and California.

N.W. 2d.   Northwestern Reporter, Second Series. Cases decided in the state courts of Michigan, Wisconsin, Iowa, Minnesota, North Dakota, South Dakota, and Nebraska.

N.Y.S. 2d. New York Supplement, Second Series. Cases decided in certain New York state courts. Some of these cases also may be reported in N.E. 2d.

Cal. Rptr. California Reporter. Cases decided in the state courts of California. Some of these cases also will appear in P. 2d. The California Reporter was started in 1960 and California cases decided prior to 1960 can be found in P. 2d.

The 2d appearing after the names of the publication simply means second series.

Cases decided by United States District Courts are primarily reported in the *Federal Supplement (F.Supp.)* although some are also reported in the *Federal Rules Decisions (F.R.D.)*. There are many District Courts, and they exercise jurisdiction over a geographic area (e.g., Western District of Michigan).

Only 12 Federal United States Courts of Appeals exist and they have jurisdiction over geographic areas as listed in the following:

CIRCUIT	GEOGRAPHIC AREA COVERED
First	Rhode Island, Massachusetts, New Hampshire, Maine, Puerto Rico
Second	Vermont, Connecticut, New York
Third	Pennsylvania, New Jersey, Delaware, Virgin Islands

Fourth	Maryland, Virginia, West Virginia, North Carolina, South Carolina
Fifth	Mississippi, Louisiana, Texas, Canal Zone
Sixth	Ohio, Michigan, Kentucky, Tennessee
Seventh	Indiana, Illinois, Wisconsin
Eighth	Minnesota, North Dakota, South Dakota, Iowa, Nebraska, Missouri, Arkansas
Ninth	California, Oregon, Nevada, Washington, Idaho, Montana, Hawaii, Alaska, Arizona, Guam
Tenth	Colorado, Wyoming, Utah, Kansas, Oklahoma, New Mexico
Eleventh	Alabama, Florida, Georgia

The District of Columbia is a separate judicial circuit.

Appeals Court decisions are currently reported in the second series of the Federal Reporter (*F.* 2d.)

The United State Supreme Court is the highest court in the land and its opinions are of great significance. Thus, U.S. Supreme Court opinions are reported in several sources. The government publishes decisions of the Supreme Court in *United States Reports (U.S.)*. Several commercial companies also publish the Court's opinions—*Supreme Court Reporter (S.Ct.); Lawyers Edition 2d (L.Ed.2d);* and *United States Law Week (L.W.).*

How to Read a Citation

All published opinions are cited in a similar fashion. The first name generally refers to the person initiating the suit or action, the plaintiff. The second name is the individual defending against the action, the defendant. Next there will be a series of numerals preceding and following the abbreviation for the reporter in which the case appears. The first numbers refer to the volume of the reporter while the following numbers refer to the page on which the case may be found. Finally the court (if necessary) and the year of the decision are given.

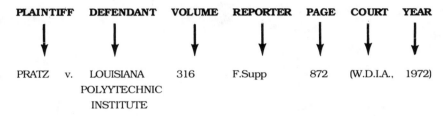

PLAINTIFF	DEFENDANT	VOLUME	REPORTER	PAGE	COURT	YEAR
PRATZ v.	LOUISIANA POLYYTECHNIC INSTITUTE	316	F.Supp	872	(W.D.I.A.,	1972)

Thus, in this citation Pratz brought an action against Louisiana Polytechnic Institute. The opinion in that case was given by the United States District Court (only U.S. district court cases are reported in F. Supp.) for the Western District of Louisiana (W.D.LA.) in 1972. The opinion of the court may be found in volume 316 of the *Federal Supplement* on page 872.

Citations in U.S., S. Ct. or L. Ed., list only the year in parentheses since the United States Supreme Court is assumed as court.

Nyquist v. Mauchlet, 97 S. Ct. 2120 (1977)

Citations of Regional Reporters for State Supreme Courts list only the name of the state and the year in parentheses.

Melton v. Bow 274 S.E. 2d 100 (GA., 1978)

State reporters can be found in attorneys' offices, county court houses and law school libraries. Federal reporters will generally be maintained by U.S. Attorneys, U.S. Court House libraries, and law school libraries. They will normally not be kept by local attorneys or, except possibly for Supreme Court cases, by college or university libraries.

Appendix C

CAS STANDARDS for STUDENT SERVICES/ DEVELOPMENT PROGRAMS

General—Division Level

CAS SELF ASSESSMENT GUIDE

CAS developed the Self Assessment Guide to be used in conjunction with the 1986 and 1987 *CAS Standards and Guidelines.* A separate Self Assessment Guide has been prepared for each of the nineteen CAS Functional Area Standards and Guidelines. Each Guide reprints, in an integrated format in the appendix, the CAS General Standards and the CAS functional area standards and guidelines with which it is to be used. The guide is designed to aid interpretation and evaluation of the CAS Standards during a self-study process.

Copies of the CAS Self Assessment Guides can be obtained from: CAS, Office of Student Affairs, 2108 North Administration Building, University of Maryland, College Park, MD 20742-5221

This document is a product of the Council for the Advancement of Standards. Those primarily responsible for its development and editing are:

Theodore K. Miller, CAS President
University of Georgia

William L. Thomas, CAS Secretary
University of Maryland

Sara C. Looney, CAS Treasurer
George Mason University

Jean Yerian, CAS Board of Directors
Virginia Commonwealth University

CAS Member Associations

American Association for Counseling and Development (AACD)

American College Personnel Association (ACPA)

Association of College and University Housing Officers-International (ACUHO-I)

Association of College Unions-International (ACU-I)

Association for Counselor Education and Supervision (ACES)

Association of Fraternity Advisors (AFA)

Association on Handicapped Student Services Programs in Postsecondary Education (AHSSPPE)

Association for School, College and University Staffing (ASCUS)

College Placement Council (CPC)

National Academic Advising Association (NACADA)

National Association of Campus Activities (NACA)

National Association of College Admission Counselors (NACAC)

National Association of Student Personnel Administrators (NASPA)

National Association for Women Deans, Administrators and Counselors (NAWDAC)

National Clearinghouse for Commuter Programs (NCCP)

National Council on Student Development (NCSD) [A Council of AACJC]

National Intramural-Recreational Sports Association (NIRSA)

National Orientation Directors Association [NODA]

Southern Association of College Student Affairs (SACSA)

This document produced and disseminated for CAS under the auspices of ACT: American College Testing Program, 2201 North Dodge Street, Iowa City, Iowa 52243

Word processing and design by Kimberly K. M. Wentworth, Graphics Associates, Athens, GA

© Copyright 1988 Council for the Advancement of Standards for Student Services/Development Programs [CAS]

CAS General/Division Standards

Part 1: MISSION

The institution and each functional area must develop, review, and disseminate regularly its own specific goals for student services/development, which must be consistent with the nature and goals of the institution and with the standards in this document.

Part 2: PROGRAM

The overall student services/development program must be (a) purposeful, (b) coherent, (c) based on or related to theories and knowledge of human development and learning characteristics, and (d) reflective of the demographic and developmental profiles of the student body.

Student services/development programs must promote student development by encouraging such things as positive and realistic self-appraisal, intellectual development, appropriate personal and occupational choices, clarification of values, physical fitness, the ability to relate meaningfully with others, the capacity to engage in a personally satisfying and effective style of living, the capacity to appreciate cultural and esthetic differences, and the capacity to work independently and interdependently.

Student services/development programs must assist students in overcoming specific personal, physical, or educational problems or skill deficiencies.

Student services/development programs must identify environmental conditions that may negatively influence welfare and propose interventions that may neutralize such conditions or improve the environment.

The educational experience of students consists of both academic efforts in the classroom and developmental opportunities through student services and development programs. Institutions must define the relative importance of these processes.

Part 3: LEADERSHIP AND MANAGEMENT

The institution must appoint a chief student service/development officer or designate an individual to fulfill that role. This leader must be positioned in the organization so that the needs of the students and the functional areas are well represented at the highest administrative level of the institution. This leader must be an experienced and effective manager, must have substantial work experience in one or more of the student services/development functional areas, and either be an acknowledged leader on the campus or have the obvious background and experience to command such respect. The specific title and reporting relationship of this individual may vary among institutions. The individual must be selected on the basis of personal characteristics and formal training.

The appointed officer must create an effective system to manage the services and programs. The officer must plan, organize, staff, lead, and assess programs on a continuing basis. The result must be an integrated system of student services and development activities for the institution, funded and otherwise supported at a level that permits the effective delivery of these programs.

The appointed officer must be able to develop, to advocate, and to use a statement of mission, goals, and objectives for student services/development on the campus. The officer must attract and select qualified staff who make effective decisions about policies, procedures, personnel, budgets, facilities, and equipment. The officer must assume responsibilities for program and personnel development, assessment, and improvement of the services and development activities of the organization.

Part 4: ORGANIZATION AND ADMINISTRATION

Each functional area must develop its own set of policies and procedures that include a detailed description of the administrative process and an organizational chart showing the job functions and reporting relationships within and beyond the program.

Part 5: HUMAN RESOURCES

Each functional area must have adequate and qualified professional staff to fulfill the mission of that service and to implement all aspects of the program. To be qualified, professional staff members must have a graduate degree in a field of study relevant to the particular job in question or must have an appropriate combination of education and experience. In any functional area in which there is a full-time director, that director must possess levels of education and/or professional experience beyond that of the staff to be supervised.

Preprofessional or support staff members employed in each functional area must be qualified by relevant education and experience. Degree requirements, including both degree levels and subject matter, must be germane to the particular job responsibilities. Such staff members must be trained appropriately and supervised adequately by professional staff.

Paraprofessionals must be carefully selected, trained with respect to helping skills and institutional services and procedures, closely supervised, and evaluated regularly. Their compensation must be fair and any voluntary services must be recognized adequately. Paraprofessionals must recognize the limitations of their knowledge and skills and must refer students to appropriate professionals when the problems encountered warrant.

To ensure that professional staff members devote adequate time to professional duties, each functional area must have sufficient clerical and technical support staff. Such support must be of sufficient quantity and quality to accomplish the following kinds of activities: typing, filing, telephone and other receptionist duties, bookkeeping, maintaining student records, organizing resource materials, receiving students and making appointments, and handling routine correspondence.

Salary level and fringe benefits for staff must be commensurate with those for similar professional, preprofessional, and clerical positions at the institution and in the geographic area.

To ensure the existence of suitable and readily identifiable role models within the campus teaching and administrative ranks, staff employment profiles must reflect representation of categories of persons who comprise the student population. However, where student bodies are predominantly nondisabled, of one race, sex, or religion, a diverse staffing pattern will enrich the teaching/administrative ranks and will demonstrate institutional commitment to fair employment practices.

All functional areas must have a regular system of staff selection and evaluation, and must provide continuing professional development opportunities for staff including inservice training programs, participation in professional conferences, workshops, and other continuing education activities.

Part 6: FUNDING

Each functional area must have funding sufficient to carry out its mission and to support the following, where applicable: staff salaries; purchase and maintenance of office furnishing, supplies, materials, and equipment, including current technology; phone and postage costs; printing and media costs; institutional memberships in appropriate professional organizations; relevant subscriptions and necessary library resources; attendance at professional association meetings, conferences, and workshops; and other professional development activities. In addition to institutional funding commitment through general funds, other funding sources may be considered, including: state appropriations, student fees, user fees, donations and contributions, fines, concession and store sales, rentals, and dues.

Part 7: FACILITIES

The functional area must be provided adequate facilities to fulfill its mission. As applicable, the facilities for each functional area must include, or the function must have access to, the following: private offices or private spaces for counseling, interviewing, or other meetings of a confidential nature; office, reception, and storage space sufficient to accommodate assigned staff, supplies, equipment, library resources, and machinery; and conference room or meeting space. All facilities must be accessible to disabled persons and must be in compliance with relevant federal, state, and local health and safety requirements.

Part 8: LEGAL RESPONSIBILITIES

Staff members must be knowledgeable about and responsive to relevant civil and criminal laws and must be responsible for ensuring that the institution fulfills its legal obligations. Staff members in all functional areas must be well versed in those obligations and limitations imposed on the operation of the institution, particularly in their functional area, by local, state, and federal constitutional, statutory, regulatory, and common law, and by institutional policy. They must utilize appropriate policies and practices to limit the liability exposure of the institution, its officers, employees, and agents. The institution must provide access to legal advice to professional staff as needed to carry out assigned responsibilities.

Part 9: EQUAL OPPORTUNITY, ACCESS, AND AFFIRMATIVE ACTION

Each functional area must adhere to the spirit and intent of equal opportunity laws in all activities. Each area must ensure that its services and facilities are accessible to and provide hours of operation that respond to the needs of special student populations, including traditionally underrepresented, evening, part-time, and commuter students.

Personnel policies shall not discriminate on the basis of race, sex, color, religion, age, national origin and/or handicap. In hiring and promotion policies, student services professionals must take affirmative action that strives to remedy significant staffing imbalance, particularly when resulting from

past discriminatory prac-
tices. Each functional area
must seek to identify, prevent and/or remedy other
discriminatory practices.

Part 10: CAMPUS AND
COMMUNITY RELATIONS

Each functional area must
maintain good relations with
relevant campus offices and
external agencies, which
necessarily requires regular
identification of the offices
with whom such relation-
ships are critical.

Part 11: MULTI-CULTURAL
PROGRAMS AND
SERVICES

The institution must provide
to members of its majority
and minority cultures' educational efforts that focus
on awareness of cultural
differences, self-assessment
of possible prejudices, and
desirable behavioral changes.

The institution must provide
educational programs that
help minority students identify their unique needs,
prioritize those needs, and
meet them to the degree that
numbers of students facilities, and resources permit.

The institution must orient
minority students to the
culture of the institution and
promote and deepen their
understanding of their own
culture and heritage.

Part 12: ETHICS

All persons involved in the
provision of services to
students must maintain the
highest standards of ethical
behavior. Staff members of
each functional area must
develop and adopt standards
of ethical practice addressing
the unique problems that
face personnel in that area.
The standards must be
published and reviewed by
all concerned. In the formulation of those standards,
ethical standards statements
previously adopted by the
profession at large or relevant professional associations may be of assistance
and must be considered.

Certain ethical obligations
apply to all individuals
employed in student ser-
vices/development programs,
for example: All staff members must ensure that
confidentiality is maintained
with respect to all communications and records con-
sidered confidential. Unless
written permission is given

by the student, information disclosed in individual counseling sessions must remain confidential. In addition, all requirements of the Family Educational Rights and Privacy Act (Buckley Amendment) must be complied with and information contained in students' educational records must not be disclosed to third parties without appropriate consent, unless one of the relevant statutory exceptions applies. A similar dedication to privacy and confidentiality must be applied to research data concerning individuals.

All staff members must be aware of and comply with the provisions contained in the institution's human subjects policy and in any other institutional policy addressing ethical practice.

All staff members must ensure that students are provided access to services on a fair and equitable basis. All staff members must avoid any personal conflict of interest so they can deal objectively and impartially with persons within and outside the institution. In many instances, the appearance of a conflict of interest can be as damaging as an actual conflict. Whenever handling funds, all staff must ensure that such funds are handled in accordance with established and responsible accounting procedures.

Staff members must not participate in any form of sexual harassment. Sexual harassment is defined to include sexual advances, requests for sexual favors, as well as other verbal or physical conduct of a sexual nature if "(1) submission to such conduct is made either explicitly or implicitly a term or condition of an individual's employment, academic progress, or any other outcome of an official nature, (2) . . . is used as the basis for such decisions or outcomes . . . , (3) . . . has the purpose or effect of unreasonably interfering with an individual's work performance or creating an intimidating, hostile, or offensive working environment."

[29 Code of Federal Regulations, C.F.R., Section 1604.11 (a).]

All staff members must recognize the limits of their training, expertise, and competence and must refer students in need of further expertise to persons possessing appropriate qualifications.

Part 13: EVALUATION

There must be systematic and regular research on and evaluation of the overall institutional student services/development program and each functional area to determine whether the educational goals and the needs of students are being met. Although methods of evaluation may vary, they must utilize both quantitative and qualitative measures. Data collected must include responses from students and other significant constituencies. Results of these regular evaluations must be used in revising and improving the program goals and implementation.

INDEX

INDEX

A

Ansonia Board of Education v. Philbrook 427, 443
Appeal process
in evaluation 513
Appenzeller, H. 413
Appenzeller, T. 413
Appleton, J.R. 23, 25, 31, 254, 256, 274, 279, 319, 320, 351, 678, 688, 690, 692, 696, 697, 701
Appointment 419-23
Appraisers
trained 512
Approach, sociotechnical 85
Arbuckle, D.S. 678, 701
Archibald, S. 689, 703
Ard, B. 344
Argyris, C. 32, 43, 44, 51, 57, 66, 79, 83, 88, 104, 138, 142, 154, 206, 243, 244, 710, 736
Arkin, M. 543, 558 Arndt, R.T. 294, 304
Arnold, K. 565, 603, 607
Arseneau, M.M. 567, 607
Artifacts 55
Artman, R.B. 567, 611
Asian-American
students 292-3
Aslanian, C.B. 286, 287, 304
Assembly of Institutuional Accrediting Bodies (AIAB) 353
Assembly of Specialized Accrediting Bodies (ASAB) 353
Assembly rights
demonstrations 387-8
Assessment 746
current operations 714
function 19
implementing program 759-60
in student affairs 741-63
institutinal environment 716-7
needs for program planning 714-6
outcomes 595-6
policy and program 685
program planning 713-19, 733
resource 717-9
student characteristics 714
Association of American Colleges 353, 741, 761
Association of American Universities 353

Association of College and University Housing Officers 310
Association of College Unions-International 310
Association of Governing Boards 353
Assumptions 57-8
comparison of conventional and non-orthodox, *Table* 61
Astin, A.W. 29, 31, 94, 102, 104, 165, 155, 175, 195, 304, 377, 359, 375, 595, 599, 600, 607, 646, 668, 705, 709, 716, 736, 755, 762, 767, 770, 783, 784
Astin, R.W. 217, 244
Astuto, T.A. 52, 67
Aulepp, L. 17, 31, 191, 195, 217, 225, 244, 450, 490, 533, 559
Authority
delagation 417
Avila, J. 268, 274
Axelrod, J. 13, 34
Ayala, F., Jr. 377, 705
Ayers, A.R. 10, 31

B

Baca, M.C. 345, 352, 422, 423, 444
Baier, J.L. 567, 60, 613, 723, 736
Baier, K. 326, 341
Baird, L.L. 217, 248
Baird, L.S. 531
Baldridge, J.V. 42, 46, 47, 52, 63, 67, 460, 490
Ballou v. Sigma Nu General Fraternity 405, 407
Baltes, P.B. 217, 244
Bandura, A. 127, 130
Banet, A.G. 228, 229, 247
Banning, J. 102, 104, 108
Banning, J.H. 14, 31, 222, 244
Banta, T.W. 377
Barber, A.W. 618, 640
Barbie, M. 205, 244
Barclay, J. 323, 341
Barker, R.G. 175, 195, 217, 244
Barkhaus, R. 502, 528
Barley, S.R. 55, 70
Barnard, C. 45, 67, 138, 154
Barnes v. Converse College 399, 407

Dickerson, B.A. 537, 560
Dickson, W.J. 138, 156
Dictionary of Occupational Titles 462
Dilemma of Bill Brown 332-3
Dilemma of Jane Smith 330-1
Dilemma of Pat Martin 333-5
Dimensions
    system maintenance and system
      change 180
Dimensions, *Tables* 181-2, 187
    personal growth and development
      180
    relationship 180
Disabilities
    students 295-6, *Table* 303
Distinction
    public-private 416
Diversity
    dealing with 598-9
Division of Eligibility and Agency
    Evaluation (DEAE) 352
Dixon v. Alabama State Board of
    Education 381, 390, 391-2
Doctrines
    emergency 389
    plain view 389
Donnelly, J.H., Jr. 523, 528
Doromal, Q.S., Jr. 345
Douglas, D.O. xviii, 614, 615, 718
Douglas, L.H. 119, 131
Downs, A. 142, 154
Drane, J.F. 324, 342
Dressel, P.L. 687, 690, 702
Drucker, P. 139, 140, 141, 154
Drum, D. 205, 216, 225
Drum, D.J. 17, 32, 35, 715, 736
Dualism 674-5
Duarte v. State 402, 408
Due process 390-3
Duke, A. 268, 276
Duke, B.W. 641
Dunnette, M.D. 228, 250
Duran, R.P. 291, 304
Durland, W.R. 342
DuVall, W.H. 537, 559, 566, 610

E

Eble, K.E. 452, 490

Ecker, G.P. 42, 67
Edgerton, R. 593, 594, 597, 609
Education Amendments 1972, 318-9, 398
Education Commission of the States 63, 67
Educational Facilities Laboratory 648, 668
Educational Rights and Privacy Act of 1974, 400
Educational Testing Service 787
Edwards, P. 340
Efficiency 173
Efrid, F.D. 268, 276
Ehrlich, T. 685, 702
Eisele v. Ayers 396, 408
Eiseman, J.W. 228, 229, 246
Eisen v. Regents 386, 408
El-Khawas, E. 319, 342
Elbow, P. 787
Elman, S. 508, 529
Emery, F. 76, 106
Emotions
    managing 211-4
Employer expectations
    appointment 419-23
    entry-level professionals' skills 457-9
    issues 418-35
    layoffs 435
    retention of staff 419-23
    selection 419-23
Employment practices
    legal issues 415-45
    student affairs 415-45
Encounter groups 85
Ender K.L. xviii, 34, 35, 163, 196, 250, 537, 559, 560, 669
Ender, S.C. 320, 342, 532, 533, 535, 536, 537, 538, 541, 542, 543, 550, 555, 559 560, 561
Environment
    congruence 169
Environment, college
    student development 188-94
Environment, distinguishing
    consistency 167
    differentiation 167

Furhmann, B. 217, 246
Furnco Construction Company v. Waters 426, 443
Furnishings
facilities 658
Furniture
residence halls 650
Fury, K. 582, 609

G

Gaff, J. 594, 609
Gamson, Z.F. 766, 787, 784
Garaudy, R. 209, 210, 246
Gardenhire v. Chalmers 392, 408
Gardner, J.W. 55, 65, 67
Garni, K. 375
Gay and Lesbian Student Association 387, 408
Gehring, D.D. xvii, 378, 379, 413, 445, 803, 805
Gelwick, B.P. 375, 709, 737
Generalizability theory 753
Generalizations
management theory 137, 140-3
George, C. 136, 154
Georgiou, P. 51, 68
German, S.C. 542, 559
Gerst, M. 189, 197
Gerst, M.S. 644, 646, 647, 668, 669
Getz, H.G. 536, 560
Getzels, J.W. 45, 68
Gibb, J. 84, 105
Gibson, J.L. 523, 528
Gilbreth, F. 138, 155
Gilbreth, L. 138, 155
Gilligan, C. 174, 196, 209, 217, 246, 288, 305, 307
Girardier v. Webster College 400, 409
Girrell, K. 297, 305
Givhan v. Western Line Consolidated School District 424, 443
Gleick, J. 50, 68, 111, 131
Glidewell, J.C. 228, 250
Glueck, W.F. 577, 609
General Order on Judicial Standards of Procedure & Substance in Re-

view of Student Discipline 390, 409
Goal setting 18-9
program planning 720, 733
Goals 744-5
formulate for an intervention 234-5
Goals and expectations
paraprofessinals 537-8
Goldberger, N.R. 217, 245, 251, 288, 304
Goldenberg, J. 163, 198
Golightly, C.L. 312, 343
Good v. Associated Students 386, 409
Gorman v. University of Rhode Island 392, 409
Gorski, B. 770, 777, 778, 784
Goslin, D.P. 33
Gott v. Berea College 254
Gould, R. 217, 246
Graham, W. 680, 703
Grant, G. 787
Grant, W.H. 268, 275, 649, 668
Grasha, S. 217, 246
Greeley, A. 94, 104
Green, L. Jr. 694, 702
Green, M.F. 584, 609
Greene, E. 292, 305
Greenleaf, R.K. 65, 68
Greenwood, E. 317, 343
Grid
academic administrator 117, *Figure* 118
Griggs v. Duke Power Company 426
Grossner v. Trustees of Columbia University 382, 409
Group
encounter 85
target 86
Group Environment Scale (GES) 184, *Figures* 185, 187
Group-task 85
Grove City College v. Bell 397, 409
Guba, E. 79, 105
Guba, E.G. 45, 68
Guidelines
accreditation 349
definition 349
interpreting 367
student affairs administrators 441-2

I

Interview form, *Figure* 473-4
Interview questions, *Figure* 475-9
Iowa Developing Autonomy Inventory 756
Iowa Developing Competency Inventory 756
Iowa Managing Emotions Inventory 756
Iowa Student Development Inventories, The 756
Issues
    employment 418-35
    ethics 323-29
    facing student affairs professionals 765-87
    in higher education 593
    legal 379-413, 415-45
    why study 379-80
Ithaca College v. Yale Daily News Publishing Co 403, 409
Ivancevich, J.M. 523, 528
Ivey, A.E. 693, 702
Ivy, W.A. 567, 602, 608

J

Jackson, G.S. 647, 649, 669
Jackson, L.M. 756
Jackson, S. 163, 195, 648, 668, 671
Jacobi, M. xvii, 377, 705
Jacoby, B. 280, 281, 297, 305, 307
James Madison University 770
Jantsch, E. 122, 132
Jardim, A. 582, 609
Jaspers, K. 766, 784
Jenkins, H.M. 307
Job specifications 465
Joenig, K.E. 248
Johnson v. Transportation Agency 435, 443
Johnson, C.S. 454, 491
Johnson, E. 139, 155
Johnson, G. 67
Johnson, J.E. 251, 492, 786
Johnson, M.M. 537, 558
Johnson, W.F. 675, 702
Johnston, J.A. 537, 560
Joint Commission on Accreditation of Health Care Organizations 354

Joint Statement on Principles of Good Practice in College Admissions and Recruitment 310
Jones v. Illinois Dept of Rehab Svc 399, 409
Jones v. Vassar 396, 409
Jones, D.P. 695, 696, 702, 705
Jones, J. 84, 87, 89, 90, 104, 106, 107, 228, 229, 247, 249, 250, 251
Josselson, R. 217, 247
Judging-Perception (JP) 169

K

Kagan, J. 111, 132
Kahn, R. 74, 76, 106, 108
Kahn, R.I. 710, 737
Kaiser, H.H. 659, 669, 671
Kalsbeek, D. 223, 247
Kalsbeek, D.H. 603, 612
Kaludis, G. 641
Kammeyer, K.C.W. 59, 67
Kane, N. 163, 196
Kanter, R. 86, 106
Kanter, R.M. 511, 529, 582, 610, 739, 772, 779, 784, 787
Kaplin, W. 413
Kaplowitz, R.A. 480, 491
Kast, F. 74, 106
Katz, D. 74, 76, 94, 104, 106, 108, 710, 737
Kauffman, J. 94, 104
Kavanagh, M. 79, 80, 81, 106
Kaye, B.L. 496, 529
Kearney, R.C. 530
Keating, L.A. 460, 490, 607, 613, 705, 707, 710, 712, 713, 716, 736, 737, 738, 739
Keene v. Rodgers 388, 409
Kegan, R. 217, 247, 251
Keim, M. 680, 703
Keirsey, D. 217, 247
Keller, G. 119, 132, 135, 155, 157
Kells, H.R. 377
Kelly, J.P. 269, 275
Kelly, K.E. 503, 529
Kelly, L.P. 537, 560
Keniston, K. 217, 247
Kennedy, A.A. 38, 60, 67

Libel 403
Licensure 350, 351
Lickona, T. 737
Life
early collegiate way 5-7
Light, R.J. 763
Likens, J. 101, 107
Likert, R. 139, 155
Likins, J.M. 283, 305
Limitations
paraprofessionals 538-40
Lincoln, Y.S. 60, 67, 68, 70, 71
Lindquist, J. 147, 155
Linn, R.L. 755, 762
Lippitt, G.L. 4, 10, 33
Lippitt, R. 79, 81, 102, 107, 108, 109, 114, 133, 147, 155
Lipsetz, A. 205, 248
Lipsitt, L.P. 217, 244
Lisensky, R.P. 377, 763
Lloyd-Jones, E. 255, 276
Local 28 of Sheet Metal Workers' International Association v. EEOC 435, 443
Loevinger, J. 217, 248, 565
Longwood College 770
Looney, S.C. 361, 376, 815
Lorentz, E. 98, 107
Lorsch, J. 74,76, 84, 107, 109
Love, P. 51, 68
Lowell, C. 413
Lowenthal, M.F. 288, 305, 565
Luarent, A. 79, 106
Lucian, J. 537, 560
Lumbard v. Fireman's Fund 402, 409
Lurent, A. 108
Lynton, E. 508, 529
Lynton, E.A. 767, 785

M

Mable, P. xvii, 153, 196, 245, 341, 346, 347, 454, 564, 566, 609, 610, 611, 612, 613, 668, 689, 702, 704
Maccoby, M. 496, 429
Madsen, R. 600, 607
Mahar, L. 115, 131
Mahavongsana v. Hall 396, 409

Maher v. Gagne 440, 443
Maine v. Thiboutot 440, 444
Malkas, M. 69
Maloney, G. 537, 559
Management
facilities 659-66
human relations 43-4
of residence halls 635-6
physical facilities 643-71, 646-50
scientific 39-40
Management by Objectives (MBO) 521
Management process
perspectives of management 136-7, Figure 139
Management theory 135-56
See theory management tools
budgets 618-20
financial statement 620-8
Management, fiscal
longitudinal 631-5
Management, perspectives
See perspectives on management
Manese, J.E. 294, 305
March, J.G. 51, 52, 63, 67, 777, 784
Marchese, T.J. 595, 610
Marshall, D. 223, 247
Marston v. Gainesville Sun 392, 400, 409
Martin, Pat, dilemma 333-5
Martinson, W.D. 678, 704
Martorana, S. 94, 107
Martorana, S.V. 147, 154
Maryland Public Interest Research Group v. Elkins 386, 409
Masland, A.T. 56, 69, 71
Maslow, A. 139, 155
Maslow, A.H. 116, 132, 498, 529, 694, 702, 709, 737
Matkin, J.L. 61
Maton, K. 98, 107
Mauclet v. Nyquist 394, 409
Mausner, B. 498, 528
Maverick, L.A. 10, 33
Maw, I. 718, 737
Maw, I.I. 630, 640, 641
Mayo, E. 138, 155
Mazart v. State 403, 410

N

National Association of College and University Business Officers 619, 640
National Association of Campus Activities 310
National Association of Deans and Advisors of Men 256
National Association of Secondary School Principals 310-1, 341
National Association of State Universities and Land-Grant Colleges 353
National Association of Student Personnel Administrators (NASPA) 57, 69, 309-10, 343, 676, 696, 703, 710, 738, 774, 785
National Association of Women Deans 256
National Association of Foreign Student Advisors 310
National Board of Certified Counselors 351
National Center for the Study of the Freshman Year Experience 598, 611
National Commission on Accrediting (NCA) 352-3
National Institute on Education (NSE) 674, 703
National Movement v. Regents 389, 410
National Strike Information Center v. Brandeis 386, 410
Needs
    assessment 654-5
    comprehensive approach 296-7
    responses 281-307
    students 281-307
Neeman, R. 163, 198
Negligence 401-3, 437
Nejedlo, R.J. 566, 611
Neo-orthodox theory 45, 49
Nettles, W.R. III, 738
Neuberger, C.G. 533, 538, 541, 543, 555, 559
New Jersey v. T.L.O. 389, 410
Newcomb, T. 67
Newcomb, T.M. 217, 248, 534, 559
Newgarten, B.L. 217, 248

Newton, F.B. xvii, 34, 35, 110, 111, 250, 537, 559, 560, 669
Nicholls, G. 223, 247
Nicholls, G.E. 59, 69
Nicolis, G. 121, 132
NIE Study Group on the Conditions of Excellence in American Higher Education 765, 770, 785
Nielson, K. 326, 340
Noe, R.M. III, 510, 512, 522, 528
Noel, L. 102, 108, 109, 695, 703
Nolan, T.W. 537, 560
Nomenclature 348-51
Non-orthodox
    assumptions 50-60
    perspectives 49-60
Nondiscrimination statutes
    legal implications 425-33
Norm referenced instruments 754
Norms 317
Notice 391
Nucci, L. 217, 248
Nuemann, W. 787
Nuss, E. 391, 409
Nygreen, G.T. 257, 276, 279
Nystrom, P. 51, 68
Nzuve v. Castleton State College 393, 410

O

O'Connel, B. 600, 611
O'Connor v. Ortega 439, 444
Oberlin College in Ohio 8
Objections
    defining developmental 743-6
    formulate for an intervention 234-5
    ideological 207
Observations
    participant 758
Obstacles
    external to change 773-6
    individual 777-8
    institutional 778-9
    internal to change 776-9
    overcoming 779-82
Odiorne, G. 139, 155, 157

Odiorne, G.S. 504, 506, 515, 521, 522, 524, 429
Oetting, E. 180, 197
Oetting, E.R. 710, 737, 755, 763
Offices
    definition xvi
Ogi, A.Y. 292, 304
Ogilvy, J. 60, 69
Ohio State University (The) 114, 220, 227-8
Olesen, V. 787
Oliaro, P.M. 567, 587, 612, 678, 704
Omnibus Perosnality Inventory 757
Open-system
    framework for OD 74-7
Opper, J.H., Jr. 738
Organization-environment interfact 84-5
Organization
    behavior 44-5
    theory 37-71
Organization development (OD) 73-109
    definition 73-4, *Table* 75
Organizations
    conventional views 38-49
    student 385-7
Ostroth, D.D. 268, 276, 541, 542, 560
Ott, L. 754, 762
Ouchi, W. 139, 141, 156
Outcomes
    evaluate 239
Output 74
Owen, H. 139, 155
Owens, G. 678, 703
Owens, R.G. 39, 40, 41, 43, 44, 69

P

Pace, C.R. 14, 34, 17, 176, 197, 716, 738
Pace, R. 770, 785
Packwood, T. 687, 703
Packwood, W.T. 3, 4, 701
Papish v. Board of Curators of University of Missouri 384, 410
Pappas, A.T. 648, 669

Parameters
    constitutional 382-95
Paraprofessionals 452
    budget restrictions 535-6
    developing job descriptions 541
    developing staff commitment 556
    effectiveness 536-7
    enhancing skill of professionals 536
    establishing selection criteria 541
    focus and direction 540
    goals and expectatons 537-8
    impact of the peer group 534-5
    impact on student 535
    implementing programs 540-5
    involvement in program coordinaton 552-3
    involvement in program development 553-4
    legal liabilities 556-7
    limitations 538-40
    program evaluation 549-52
    ratio to professional 555
    ratio to student 555
    rationale for using 534-7
    recruitment procedures 541-2
    reward system 544-5
    roles 537
    selection procedures 542
    special issues 554-7
    staff qualifications for training 555-6
    students as 533-61
    study skills counselors 545-9
    three phase model 545-9
    training program 543-4
    tutors 545-9
Parker Cognitive Development Inventory 756
Parker, C. 175, 198
Parker, C.A. 25, 34, 35, 163, 188, 189, 197, 206, 222, 225, 229, 249, 251 769, 776, 785, 787
Parker, J.C. 756
Pascarella, E. 102, 107
Patchoque-Medford Congress of Teachers v. Board of Education of Patchoque-Medford Union Free School District 440, 444

Risch, T.J. 467, 491
Rituals 55
Rivers, C. 217, 244
Robins, G.B. 628, 640
Robinson v. Davis 382, 411
Robinson v. Eastern Kentucky University 398, 411
Robinson, D.C. 288, 306
Robinson, J.P. 756, 763
Roche, G.R. 582, 612
Rockford College 8
Rodgers, R.F. xvii, 17, 25, 34, 189, 197, 202, 203, 205, 207, 214, 216, 223, 225, 226, 238, 247, 249, 250, 455, 491, 681, 703, 776
Rodgers, R.R. 238, 250
Roemer v. Board of Public Works 383, 411
Roethlisberger, R. J. 138, 156
Rogers, R. 676, 677, 704, 774, 786
Rogers, R.E. 140, 141, 142, 156
Rohm, E.T. 641
Role
    of student affairs professionals 768-73
    personnel office in staffing 488
Role definition
    staff position 463-4
Roles
    paraprofessionals 537
Rose, M.P. 580, 581, 582, 612
Rosenbaum, M. 342
Rosenberg, S.D. 217, 246
Rosenzweig, J. 74, 106
Rosenzweig, M. 104, 108
Ross, W.D. 326, 343
Roth, G. 70
Rovai, E. 62, 70
Rowe v. Chandler 382, 411
Rubin, L. 217, 250
Rudolph, F. 6, 7, 8, 34, 254, 277, 347, 376
Rudy, W. 3, 5, 6, 7, 8, 31, 35
Rue, P. 97, 108, 282, 283, 306
Ruhnke, H.O. 466, 490
Ruscio, K.P. 46, 69
Russel, J.H. 10, 31

S

Saddlemire, G.L. 260, 277, 319, 320, 343, 705, 739
Saint Francis College v. Al-Khazroji 427, 444
Salovey, P. 543, 558
Sampling 754
    cross-sectional 754-5
    longitudinal designs 754-5
Sandeen, A. 454, 491, 650, 669, 731, 738
Sandler, B.R. 288, 289, 305, 307, 583, 609
Sanford, N. 13, 15, 34, 179, 197, 216, 217, 218, 250, 360, 376, 684, 685, 703, 766, 786
Sarason, C. 98, 107
Sashkin, M. 79, 80, 81, 106, 133
Satisfying 44
Saunders, S.A. xvii, 308, 309, 709, 738
Sautter, J.A. 649, 651, 669
Saxton, M. 109
Saxton, M.J. 59, 68
Saylor, P. 652, 669
Scale of Intellectual Development 757
Scales, W.R. 296, 305
Scheaffer, R.L. 754, 76
Schein, E. 84, 91, 92, 107, 109
Schein, E.H. 55, 56, 57, 69, 261, 277
Schick, A.G. 641
Schmidt, M.R. 295, 306, 307
Schmidt, W.H. 4, 10, 33, 115, 132
Schmit, J. 51, 68
Schneider, L.D. 9, 34
Schneier, C.E. 531
Schoenberg, B.M. 375
Schollar, B. 543, 558
Schon, D. 710, 736
Schon, D.A. 51, 57, 66, 206, 243, 244
School Board of Nassau County Florida v. Arline 400, 411, 433, 444
Schools of management
    theory 136-7
Schornstein v. New Jersey Division of Vocational Rehabilitational Services 399, 411

Solid Rock Foundation v. Ohio State University 384, 411
Southeastern Community College v. Davis 400, 411
Southern Association of Colleges and Schools 349, 357, 376
Space useage
    statement of 655
SPAR
    model 297-304, *Tables* 302, 303
Speech and Expression 384-5
Sprandel, D. 102, 108, 109
Sprandel, H.Z. 295, 306, 307
Sprunger, B.E. 462, 463, 465, 472, 473, 491, 493
Stability
    in measurement 752-3
Staff
    allied professionals 450-1
    commitment to paraprofessionals 556
    evaluation 422-3
    filling position vacancies 466-88
    filling support positions 481, 484-8
    forecasting 460-2
    horizontal 467-81
    interview process 472, 480-1, *Figures* 473-4, 475-9
    job specifications 465-6
    needs and values 501-2
    paraprofessionals 452
    personnel office role in filling positions 488
    personnel planning 460-2
    position analysis 462-4
    position description 465-6
    professional search check list, *Figure* 482-3
    professionals 450
    recruiting and selecting 467-81
    role definition 453-4
    selection 449-93
    separation 423-4
    student affairs division 459-66
    student affairs 450-3
    student volunteers 452-3
    support 451-2
    vertical 466-7

Staff development
    components of 569-92
    contexts for 592-606
    individual motivation 569-575
    institutional commitment and resources 604-6
    mentoring relationships 580-5
    organization development 566-7
    personal and professional circumstances 603-4
    personal and professional education 563-613
    philosophical foundation 563-9
    professional contributions 591-2
    professional participation 590-2
    self-assessment 569-575, *Figure* 572
    structured learning opportunities 585-9
    student affairs 567-9
Stage
    additive 267
    application 266
    generative 267-9
Stages, *Figure* 264-5
    formative 263-6
Stamatakos, B.M. xvii, 684, 704
Stamatakos, L. 206, 250
Stamatakos, L.C. 258, 277, 309, 343, 357-8, 376, 567, 587, 612, 647, 669, 672, 673, 676, 677, 678, 684, 685, 704, 774, 777, 780, 786
Standard operating procedures (SOPs) 64
Standards
    accreditation 349
    implications 358-61
    importance 356-8
    interpreting 367
    meaning 356-8
    practicality 356-66
    preparation 455-9
    professional practice 347-77
    purpose 356-66
    use 361-3
Stanton, E.S. 467, 484, 486, 491

Z

ABOUT
THE
AUTHORS

THEODORE [TED] K. MILLER, Ed.D.

Theodore K. Miller is Professor of Counseling and Human Development Services at the University of Georgia in Athens, Georgia in the Division of Counseling, Educational Psychology, and Educational Technology in the College of Education. He is currently the Director of the University of Georgia's Southern Association of Colleges and Schools (SACS) Accreditation Reaffirmation Self-Study and is Chairman of the Self-Study Steering Committee.

Miller was awarded the B.S. degree in Business and English and the M.A. degree in Counseling and Guidance by Ball State University. He received the Ed.D. degree in Counseling and Student Personnel Services from the University of Florida. His higher education work experience includes employment as a Counselor to Men and Counseling Psychologist. He has been a professor at the University of Georgia since 1967.

Miller has authored or edited six professional books: *The Future of Student Affairs* (with Judith Prince in 1976), *Students Helping Students* (with Steve Ender and Sue Sanders in 1979), *Developmental Approaches to Academic Advising* (with Roger Winston and Steve Ender in 1982), *Developmental Academic Advising* (with Roger Winston, Steve Ender, and Tom Grites in 1984), *Administration and Leadership in Student Affairs* (with Roger Winston and Bill Mendenhall in 1983), and *Promoting Student Development Through Intentionally Structured Groups* (with Roger Winston, Warren Bonney, and John C. Dagley in 1988). He has published widely in professional journals and has been a contributing chapter author in numerous edited books and mongraphs. He has served on the editorial boards of the *NASPA Journal, Journal of College Student Affairs*, and the *Georgia Journal of College Student Affairs*. He is also co-author of the *Student Developmental Task Inventory* (1974 and revised in 1979) and *The Student Developmental Task and Lifestyle Inventory* (1987 with Roger Winston and Judith Prince). In addition, Miller was coeditor of the *CAS Standards and Guidelines for Student Services/Development Programs* (1986 with William Thomas and Sara Looney) and the *CAS Standards Self Assessment Guides* (1988 with William Thomas, Sara Looney, and Jean Yerian), a set of 18 student development service program evaluation workbooks. He also edited, with Jean Yerian, *Putting the CAS Standards to Work: A Training Manual for the CAS Self Assessment Guides* (1989).

Ted K. Miller has been active in professional associations and was the first president of the Georgia College Personnel Association (1969) and president of the American College Personnel Association in 1975-76. He was President of the Council for the Advancement of Standards for Student Services/ Development Programs (CAS), a consortium of 20 professional associations from its inception in 1980 to 1989.

ROGER B. WINSTON, JR., PH.D.

Roger B. Winston, Jr., is Professor in the Student Personnel in Higher Education Program, College of Education, at The University of Georgia. He was awarded the A.B. in history and philosophy from Auburn University and the M.A. in philosophy and Ph.D. in counseling and student personnel services from The University of Georgia. Prior to joining the faculty at The University of Georgia in 1978, he was Dean of Men and Associate Dean of Students at Georgia Southwestern College.

Winston is co-author or co-editor of the following books: *Developmental Approaches to Academic Advising* (with S.C. Ender and T.K. Miller, 1982), *Developmental Academic Advising: Addressing Students' Educational, Career, and Personal Needs* (with T.K. Miller, S.C. Ender, and T.J. Grites, 1984), *Students as Paraprofessional Staff* (with S.C. Ender, 1984), *Fraternities and Sororities on the Contemporary College Campus* (with

W.R. Nettles and J.H. Opper), and *Promoting Student Development through Intentially Structured Groups: Principles, Techniques, and Applications* (with W.C. Bonney, T.K. Miller, and J.C. Dagley, 1988). He is also co-author of the *Student Developmental Task and Lifestyle Inventory* (with T.K. Miller and J.S. Prince, 1987) and the *Academic Advising Inventory* (with J.A. Sandor, 1984).

Professionally, Dr. Winston has been particularly active in the American College Personnel Association (ACPA), serving as the first editor of *ACPA Developments*, an Executive Council member, member of the Ethical and Professional Conduct Committee, and a member of the Directorate of Commissions XII and IX. He chaired the task force that drafted the first ethical standards statement for ACPA (1979-81) and also served on the committee that recently revised it (1988-1989). He has served on the Editorial Boards of the *Southern College Personnel Association Journal* and the *Journal of College Student Personnel*. He was associate editor of the *College Student Affairs Journal* for four years. Currently, he is the associate editor of the *Journal of College Student Development* and serves on the Editorial Board of the *Georgia Journal of College Student Affairs*. Winston has served on the Boards of Directors of the National Academic Advising Association, the Council for the Advancement of Standards for Student Services/Development Programs (CAS), and the Georgia College Personnel Association.

His professional and scholarly contributions have been recognized by the National Academic Advising Association, which acknowledged his outstanding contributions to research on advising in 1984; by the American College Personnel Association, which named him a senior professional for the Annuit Coeptis dinner (1987) selected him a Senior Scholar (1989) and extended him recognition for his "Outstanding Contribution to Knowledge" (1990); and by the Southern Association for College Student Affairs, which presented him the Melvene D. Hardee Award for outstanding contribution to the student affairs field in 1989.